You Are All Free

The abolitions of slavery in the French Caribbean colony of Saint-Domingue in 1793 and in revolutionary France in 1794 were the first dramatic blows against an institution that had shaped the Atlantic world for three centuries and affected the lives of millions of people. Based on extensive archival research, *You Are All Free* provides the first complete account of the dramatic events that led to these epochal decrees, as well as to the destruction of Cap Français, the richest city in the French Caribbean, and to the first refugee crisis in the United States. Taking issue with accounts that claim that Saint-Domingue's slaves simply freed themselves, or that French revolutionaries abolished slavery as part of a general campaign for universal human rights, the book shows that abolition was the result of complex and often paradoxical political struggles on both sides of the Atlantic that have frequently been misunderstood by earlier scholars.

Jeremy D. Popkin, T. Marshall Hahn, Jr., Professor of History at the University of Kentucky, has written numerous books on the French and Haitian revolutions and on the subject of autobiographical literature, including *Revolutionary News: The Press in France, 1789–1799* (1990), *History, Historians and Autobiography* (2005), and *Facing Racial Revolution: Eyewitness Accounts of the Haitian Revolution* (2007). He has been a visiting professor at the Collège de France (2009) and Brown University (2005) and held numerous fellowships, including awards from the J. S. Guggenheim Foundation, the National Humanities Center, the Fulbright Program, the National Endowment for the Humanities, the Institute for Advanced Study, and the Newberry Library.

You Are All Free

The Haitian Revolution and the Abolition of Slavery

JEREMY D. POPKIN

University of Kentucky

CAMBRIDGE
UNIVERSITY PRESS

CAMBRIDGE
UNIVERSITY PRESS

University Printing House, Cambridge CB2 8BS, United Kingdom

One Liberty Plaza, 20th Floor, New York, NY 10006, USA

477 Williamstown Road, Port Melbourne, VIC 3207, Australia

314-321, 3rd Floor, Plot 3, Splendor Forum, Jasola District Centre, New Delhi - 110025, India

79 Anson Road, #06-04/06, Singapore 079906

Cambridge University Press is part of the University of Cambridge.

It furthers the University's mission by disseminating knowledge in the pursuit of
education, learning and research at the highest international levels of excellence.

www.cambridge.org
Information on this title: www.cambridge.org/9780521731942

© Jeremy D. Popkin 2010

First published 2010

A catalogue record for this publication is available from the British Library

Library of Congress Cataloging in Publication data
Popkin, Jeremy D., 1948–
You are all free : the Haitian revolution and the abolition of slavery / Jeremy D. Popkin.
p. cm.
Includes bibliographical references and index.
ISBN 978-0-521-51722-5 (hardback)
1. Haiti – History – Revolution, 1791–1804. 2. Slavery – Haiti – History. I. Title.
F1923.P67 2010
972.94′03–dc22   2010023058

ISBN 978-0-521-51722-5 Hardback
ISBN 978-0-521-73194-2 Paperback

Contents

Figures

Preface

The inspiration for this book can be traced to two very different sources: a Sunday morning walk in one of Lexington, Kentucky's, local parks and the experience of the presidency of George W. Bush. In mid-2006, I had recently finished the manuscript of an earlier book on the Haitian Revolution, *Facing Racial Revolution: Eyewitness Accounts of the Haitian Revolution*, a project that had drawn on my interests in autobiographical writing. In my commentaries on the various selections included in that volume, I had taken pains to put readers on their guard against the partiality of the texts I included and of their many omissions. I had, so to speak, kept the literary analyst's hat that I had acquired in the course of nearly a decade of writing about autobiography firmly on my head and put the constructed and subjective nature of these narratives in the middle of my interpretation of them. In the course of my walk – in a park that, like much of central Kentucky, occupies what was once farmland originally cleared with the help of slave labor in the years around 1800, even as slavery was being so spectacularly dismantled in Haiti – I was pondering what to do for my next research project. It occurred to me to wonder how the events described in the eyewitness documents I had collected, and especially the most spectacular episode of the Haitian Revolution – the burning of the main city of the French colony of Saint-Domingue and the simultaneous issuance of the first emancipation proclamation in the French empire in June 1793 – would look if I switched headgear and wrote from the perspective of my original discipline of history. I already knew where most of the relevant archival sources were located, and I calculated, optimistically, that an upcoming two-month stay in Paris would allow me to go through most of them. Refreshed from my walk, I went home and began to work out a research plan.

My decision to revert to working as a "pure" historian also responded, however, to some reflections about the way in which President Bush had launched the United States into the bloody adventure in Iraq, the outcome of which remains, as I write this in the spring of 2010, deeply uncertain. From the start of my graduate training in history in the early 1970s, I had imbibed the lesson that the great events of history were to be explained in terms of large impersonal forces – social structures, cultural paradigms, intellectual discourses – and that "traditional" political history, with its emphasis on individuals, short time frames, and contingent events, was inevitably superficial. Yet, here the United States was, in the fall of 2006, bogged down in the third year of a war that seemed less the product of long-term and inevitable processes than of decisions taken by a handful of political leaders. Whatever its ultimate results, the Iraq war will undoubtedly be remembered as a historical event of considerable proportions. It occurred to me that it might be fruitful to take a fresh look at the political circumstances in which the first total abolition of slavery came about in 1793 with this perspective in mind and to ask whether it was wholly explainable in terms of structural factors such as the cruelty of the plantation system, the enormous numerical advantage of the black population over its white oppressors, and the power of the moral arguments put forward by the abolitionists of the day.

In attempting to write, for the first time in my professional career, a "simple" narrative political history, I soon discovered that this venerable genre of scholarship is not simple at all. In contrast to the sources employed in social or cultural history, the official papers, letters, and published documents on which political history relies may seem to speak for themselves, but in fact they require careful analysis and interpretation. The motives for human action can be as artfully concealed behind a flood of words as they can be in quantitative data or enigmatic forms of behavior. The reconstruction of events offered here depends on certain assumptions about human psychology and on the dynamics of political conflict; although I have tried to document my claims about the events that took place in Saint-Domingue (today's Republic of Haiti), France, and the United States as carefully as possible, I am under no illusion that I have produced a completely objective account, or that other scholars cannot interpret the evidence differently.

I also originally thought of this project as a "small" piece of historical research, because I intended to limit it to a period of no more than a year and a half, from the arrival in the colony of Saint-Domingue of the French civil commissioners Léger-Félicité Sonthonax and Etienne Polverel in September 1792 to the passage of the National Convention's decree abolishing slavery in February 1794. As it has developed, however, I have realized that although the scope of this study may be narrow, its implications are broad. The episode described here was a crucial one in the struggle that led, almost a century later, to the final abolition of Negro slavery in the Americas. It raises important questions about the relative weight of moral and political ideas and of conscious human intentions in bringing about the most radical act of abolition in that entire century of struggle. I do not intend to deny the importance of the abolitionist critique of slavery in undermining the institution, or to minimize the determination with which the black insurgents in Saint-Domingue fought to escape their chains. I do argue, however, that circumstances played a much greater role in determining the outcome of events in Saint-Domingue than previous historians have been willing to concede. Certainly the eventual abolition of slavery was not the result of a series of accidents. Nevertheless, the history of that abolition would have looked very different if the events surrounding the violent journée of June 20, 1793, had not taken place or had had a different outcome, two eventualities that could easily have occurred, just as our contemporary world would look very different if George W. Bush had not decided to embark on his "war of choice" in the Middle East in 2003.

Although this book has taken on a very different form, and its conclusions have come to seem to me to have much greater significance than I realized when I embarked on it, I was correct about one thing: the sources for the study of the events covered here are rich and fascinating. In recent decades, it has been fashionable to decry the "fetishism of the archives" associated with older approaches to historical research. In this case, however, the documentary sources available to the historian are so varied and so vivid that it has been hard to resist the temptation to exploit them to the fullest. There is an additional justification for doing so: the history of the Haitian Revolution, when it has not been neglected altogether, has all too often been written on the basis of only a handful of sources, many of them cited by authors who never looked at the original papers and relied instead on sometimes inaccurate or incomplete versions of key documents found in published books. Now that the events in the French colony of Saint-Domingue are assuming their rightful place in the history of modern struggles for freedom, it certainly behooves scholars who have the opportunity to do so to use the original sources that are available.

Like all historians who work on the early years of the Haitian Revolution, I have relied heavily on the documents in series D XXV of the Archives nationales in Paris. These papers, collected by the French parliamentary commission set up in 1795 to determine the responsibility for the "disasters" in Saint-Domingue between 1789 and 1794, form the basis for all serious scholarly research on the first years of the Haitian Revolution. Unlike the more standardized contents of many of the other document series in the Archives nationales, series D XXV contains an extraordinary hodgepodge of materials: official letters, orders, proclamations, private correspondence, ships' logs, police interrogations, captured documents from the black insurgents, and many other items. I was able to exploit this gold mine as extensively as I did thanks to fortunate timing. For several years around the turn of the millenium, the Archives nationales was crippled by a crisis resulting from the discovery of asbestos contaminating the CARAN, the modern research building opened in the 1980s. From the late 1990s to 2006, scholars were forced to work under difficult conditions in various temporary reading rooms. Committing oneself to a project that relied heavily on access to documents in the Archives nationales became something of a gamble. Fortunately for me, I embarked on this project just when the Archives's main reading room finally reopened. From 2006 to 2009, I enjoyed the benefit of its excellent working environment and of a helpful staff who seemed genuinely pleased to be able to offer readers the services that they had not been able to provide during the "time of troubles." The Archives nationales has also been at the forefront of the revolution that has allowed researchers to use digital cameras to photograph documents, which can then be read at leisure on the computer screen. As I write this, however, plans are under way for the construction of an entirely new archival center in the northeast suburbs of Paris, currently scheduled to open in 2011. One can only hope that the period of transition from the Archives's historic home in the atmospheric quarter of the Marais to their new location will not be too prolonged or disruptive. In any event, I will always have fond memories of crossing the Seine in the early morning, en route to the Archives, enjoying the sights of the city and anticipating the surprises to be found in yet another promising carton from the D XXV series.

In addition to the Archives nationales, this project has drawn on materials from many other libraries and archives whose assistance I would like to acknowledge. These include the Bibliothèque nationale de France, the Centre des Archives d'Outre-Mer in Aix-en-Provence, the Centre des Archives Diplomatiques de Nantes, the Service historique de l'armée de terre, the Service historique de la marine, the Newberry Library, the John Carter Brown Library, the Library Company of Philadelphia, the Van Pelt Library at the University of Pennsylvania, the Library of Congress, the New York Public Library, the New York Historical Society, and the University of Kentucky Library. I have been a relatively late comer to the international community of scholars interested in the history of the revolutionary era in the Caribbean and the struggle for the abolition of slavery. Colleagues in this field have been exceptionally generous in providing encouragement, bibliographical tips, and often copies of their own research notes. I would especially like to thank Anja Bandau, Madison Smartt Bell, Yves Bénot, Jean-Charles Benzaken, Elizabeth Colwill, Myriam Cottias, John Davies, Daniel Desormeaux, Marcel Dorigny, Seymour Drescher, Laurent Dubois, Carolyn Fick, Andrée-Luce Fourcand, Julia Gaffield, John Garrigus, David Geggus, Malick Ghachem, Jean Hébrard, Laënnec Hurbon, Erica Johnson, Martha Jones, Darrell Meadows, Joanne Melish, Claire Payton, Knox Peden, Anne Perotin-Dumon, Jennifer Pierce, Dwayn Pruitt, Dominique Rogers, Alyssa Sepinwall, Miranda Spieler, Aletha Stahl, Jeffery Stanley, and Ashli White for their advice and assistance. Invitations to lecture at the Ecole des Hautes Etudes en Sciences Sociales, the Institut d'Histoire de la Révolution Française, and the Collège de France provided valuable occasions to extend my research. I am grateful to Christophe Prochasson, Jean-François Revel, Jean-Clément Martin, Pierre Serna, Daniel Roche, and Roger Chartier for these opportunities. Audiences at the Consortium on the Revolutionary Era, the Society for French Historical Studies, the American Society for Eighteenth-Century Studies, the Haitian Studies Association, and at colloquia on "The French Atlantic" at Florida State University, "Paris Croisé" at the Freie Universität Berlin in 2007, "Républiques en miroir" at the Institut de l'histoire de la Révolution française in 2008, and "Affranchis et descendants d'affranchis dans le monde atlantique (Europe, Afrique et Amériques) du XVe au XIXe siècle," in Bordeaux in 2009 offered helpful criticism of my work, as did those who attended my presentations at the University of California, Riverside, Reed College, the McNeil Center for Atlantic History at the University of Pennsylvania, the University of Virginia, the Early American History Seminar of the Kentucky Historical Society, and the Rocky Mountain Early American History Seminar. Elizabeth Colwill, Seymour Drescher, David Geggus, Lynn Hunt, and Joanne Melish read the manuscript, in whole or in part, in its later stages and provided help-ful suggestions for improvement. At Cambridge University Press, Eric Crahan shared my excitement about this project. Appointment as the T. Marshall Hahn, Jr., Professor of History at the University of Kentucky provided welcome funding for my research. Although I am grateful to all the individuals and institutions named here for their assistance, it goes without saying that the opinions expressed in this book are my own responsibility. Unless otherwise indicated, translations from sources in other languages are also my own.

In November 2008, thanks to the Haitian Studies Association and particularly to Aletha Stahl, I was able to make a short trip to Haiti and, in particular, to visit the city of Cap Haitien, where the crucial events of June 1793 described in this book took place. Together with our wonderful guide, Harry Nicholas, Aletha Stahl, Elizabeth Colwill, and I used the 1795 street map reproduced in this book to find the location where the future Convention deputy Jean-Baptiste Belley led the defense of the civil commissioners Sonthonax and Polverel, and the spot on the quays where their opponent, General Galbaud, made the plunge into the harbor that marked the end of white domination in the colony. Short as it was, this trip gave me a glimpse, not only of the difficulties facing present-day Haitians as they try to build a functioning democratic soci-ety, but of the obstacles facing Haitian scholars and teachers of history who would like to study and transmit the story of their country's past. Even before the devastating earthquake that struck much of the coun-try on January 12, 2010, severely damaging most of Haiti's documen-tary repositories and its institutions of higher education, it was the rare Haitian historian who could hope to enjoy the possibilities that I, as a well-funded faculty member from an American research university, have benefitted from. One can only hope that the reconstruction efforts now under way will include programs that will give our colleagues from the country where these vitally important events took place the opportunity to study them.

This book is dedicated to my mother, Juliet Greenstone Popkin, who has encouraged my love of reading and writing ever since I was a small child. It was her patience and hard work that made it possible for our family to accompany my father, Richard H. Popkin, to Paris in 1952–53, a trip that was my introduction to French culture. In 2008, it fell to me to help my mother prepare to move out of the Los Angeles apartment in which she and my father had spent many happy years before his death in 2005. My father, a prominent historian of philosophy, published numerous books, but it was only as I sorted through the piles of paper in my mother's apartment that I discovered how much writing she herself had done over the years. I was especially moved by several insightful autobiographical essays she had written about her own childhood and about some of the foreign trips she had made with my father. The time and effort she put into raising her three children and supporting my father's career held my mother back from becoming a published author in her own right. Unlike my father and me, my mother has always been happier talking to people than sitting at a desk taking notes. Late in life, when my father retired, my mother finally realized her lifelong dream of entering the publishing business by setting up a small literary agency. None of the books she helped shepherd to publication made her rich, but she loved talking to authors and editors, and she took pleasure in facilitating the appearance of a number of books she truly admired, some of which, like Margaret McCord's *The Calling of Katie Makanya*, the life story of a black woman from South Africa, won literary awards. Helping me put together a prospectus for *You Are All Free* was one of the last tasks my mother took on before she had to wind up the Julie Popkin Literary Agency. It was an act of faith in her son, but also an act of faith in the importance of books. I hope the final result will justify my mother's confidence, both in her offspring and in the importance of the printed word.

Introduction

The Journée of June 20, 1793 in Cap Français and the Abolition of Slavery

On the afternoon of June 20, 1793, a white resident hurrying home in the Caribbean trading port of Cap Français witnessed an extraordinary scene. Groups of dark-skinned men were running through the streets, crying loudly to the city's thousands of black slaves, "You are all free! The commissioners say you are all free, all whites are now equal to us, this whole country belongs to us."[1] The men spreading this message were not the black slave insurgents whose revolt, begun almost two years earlier on the night of August 22–23, 1791, had shaken revolutionary France's valuable colony of Saint-Domingue – today's Haiti – and the entire Atlantic world. They were members of the colony's population of free people of color, a group that had been granted citizenship rights and equality with the whites by the French government in April 1792 in the hope of creating a common front to fight the slave insurrection. Now that strategy had failed. The general sent from France to command the forces fighting the slaves and the sailors from the ships in Cap Français's busy harbor were in revolt against the two revolutionary national civil commissioners sent from France in 1792 to save the colony, and against the free men of color who supported them. Outnumbered, the commissioners and their free colored allies took the drastic step of appealing to the slaves, the overwhelming majority of the city's population. For the first time in the 300-year history of colonial settlement in the Americas, the representatives of a European government set themselves on a path that would lead to the abolition of slavery, which the French National

---

[1] *Extrait d'une lettre, sur les malheurs de Saint-Domingue en général, et principalement sur l'incendie de la ville du Cap Français* (Paris: Pain, An II [1793]), 13.

Convention decreed of February 4, 1794 as a direct result of the events in Cap Français a half year earlier. What this anonymous chronicler witnessed in Cap Français on June 20, 1793 was a true historical turning point.

When he recorded his experience in October 1793, however, this witness did not see it as an inspiring moment of liberation. For him, and for virtually all of the whites who lived through the event, the date of June 20, 1793 would be forever associated not with the end of slavery, but with the violent destruction of a major city, a proud symbol of European civilization in the tropics. The fighting that broke out in the city of Cap Français on that hot Caribbean morning set off, over the next three days, a conflagration that cost thousands of lives and reduced the wealthiest port in the French colonies to ashes. The destruction of Cap Français was bloodier than any of the episodes of urban violence in revolutionary Paris, claiming at least twice as many victims as the journée of August 10, 1792 or the September massacres of that year in Paris, and the death toll – somewhere between 3,000 and 10,000 – makes it the most murderous instance of urban conflict in the entire history of the Americas. The flames that consumed Cap Français had a devastating impact on the overseas trade that had fueled France's prosperity since the beginning of the eighteenth century. No single event in the history of France's second overseas empire, not even the Algerian war of 1954–62, delivered such a sudden and massive jolt to the metropole's prosperity as the destruction of Cap Français in 1793.

In Saint-Domingue itself, the destruction of Cap Français and the proclamation offering freedom to any slaves who would put themselves under the orders of the French revolutionary commissioners transformed the struggle that had begun with the slave uprising of August 1791 and the simultaneous but separate revolt of the colony's free people of color. Appalled by the commissioners' decision, the whites in Saint-Domingue who did not flee the island called on France's enemies, Britain and Spain, to come to their aid. Invasions were launched from the nearby colonies of Jamaica and Santo Domingo, turning the colony into a major front in the war of Europe's monarchies against the revolutionary movement. For Saint-Domingue's free people of color, the crisis of June 20, 1793 represented both a victory and an unprecedented threat. In the fighting for Cap Français, they had been the French republican commissioners' most loyal supporters, but in order to defeat their opponents, the commissioners and the free people of color had had to call on the more numerous slave population. These new "citizens of 20 June" threatened the privileged political position the free men of color had hoped to occupy thanks to their alliance with the French authorities.

When they made their offer of freedom to the blacks on June 20, 1793, the French commissioners certainly expected that it would be welcomed by the black insurgents whose uprising in August 1791 had struck the first blow against slavery. Eventually, the reversal of French policy carried out on June 20, 1793 did provide the "opening" through which the most capable of the insurgent leaders, a certain Toussaint of Bréda, moved to join the French forces under the new name he adopted just after that event: Toussaint Louverture. Initially, however, Toussaint and the other insurrectionary leaders saw the proclamation of June 20, 1793 as a desperate gamble by a defeated faction. Still embittered by the war that the French authorities had conducted against them since the start of the uprising, and distrustful of the agents of a government that had proclaimed in 1789 that "men are born and remain free and equal in rights" but that had sent thousands of troops to defend slavery in its colonies, the black insurgents cast their lot with France's enemies. It would take nearly a year before Toussaint would break with the other black insurgents and ally himself with the French to create a "colony of citizens" whose population would eventually win their independence in a war against a Napoleonic France that had abandoned its own republican ideals.[2] Without the events of June 20, 1793, the black insurrection might still have prevailed, but the fusion of that movement and the French republican tradition that took place in 1794 would not have occurred, and the significance of an eventual black victory would have been quite different.

The effects of the destruction of Cap Français were not confined to France and Saint-Domingue. France's most valuable colony was a vital part of the vast network of trade and commerce that defined the Atlantic world of the eighteenth century. The events of June 20, 1793 drove thousands of survivors – whites, blacks, and free people of color – to the shores of the new republic of the United States, producing the country's first refugee crisis. The horrifying stories the white colonists brought with them changed the American debate about slavery, convincing

---

[2] The phrase "colony of citizens" comes from the title of Laurent Dubois's book on French revolutionary colonial policy: *A Colony of Citizens: Revolution and Slave Emancipation in the French Caribbean, 1787–1804* (Chapel Hill, NC: University of North Carolina Press, 2004).

southerners that their "peculiar institution" needed to be defended in the most intransigent terms.[3] The refugees of color, many of whom settled permanently in cities such as Philadelphia and New York, had their own versions of events in Saint-Domingue and brought a new spirit of self-assertion to the growing African-American communities there. Fear of the effect that their testimonies might have on slaves in the United States led to the first American panic about foreign subversion; legislators in states such as South Carolina tried to expel any persons of African descent coming from the French islands. The embattled French minister Edmond Genet, remembered in history primarily for having alienated American political leaders by his clumsy attempts to draw the United States into France's conflict with Britain, actually spent more of his time dealing with the consequences of the events of June 20, 1793 in Saint-Domingue than with any other problem. His decision to favor the antislavery faction among the white refugees over their more numerous opponents was critical in making the French National Convention's vote for abolition possible.

Although the crisis, or the journée, to use a French revolutionary term, of June 20, 1793 in Cap Français had profound effects on the history of Saint-Domingue, France, and the United States, it has never been the focus of a thorough historical study. Dramatic and important as it was, the burning of Cap Français soon receded from public memory, crowded out by other events. In debates about slavery, the flames that consumed the "Paris of the Antilles" in June 1793 merged with images of the fiery destruction of Saint-Domingue plantations at the beginning of the slave insurrection in August 1791 to create one generalized memory of violence. Later, memories of the journée of June 1793 were overlaid by reports of the horrors that followed Napoleon's effort to reimpose white rule in the colony in 1802 and 1803, which led, among other things, to a second burning of the city. After the final defeat of the French in November 1803 and the proclamation of Haitian independence, Saint-Domingue became a taboo topic, mentioned only by a few unhappy former colonists who still dreamed of recovering their lost properties. In the United States, the events in Cap Français were soon overshadowed by reports of the yellow fever epidemic that devastated the East Coast in 1793 and that was often said to have been brought by the refugees from Saint-Domingue.

---

[3] For an overview of American reactions to the upheavals in Saint-Domingue in the 1790s, see Winthrop D. Jordan, *White Over Black: American Attitudes Toward the Negro, 1550–1812* (Baltimore, Md.: Pelican Books, 1969 (orig. 1968)), 375–86.

As modern historians have sought to reconstruct the story of what we now call the Haitian Revolution, they have rarely given much attention to the episode of June 20, 1793. The most extensive recent account of the journée – the one that first attracted my attention to the event – is the concluding chapter of the American novelist Madison Smartt Bell's powerful novel, *All Souls' Rising*, which ends with the protagonist and his mixed-race mistress making a narrow escape from the burning city into the surrounding hills.[4] It is no surprise that the story of June 20 would attract a writer of fiction. From the time of Homer's *Iliad* and Virgil's *Aeneid*, whose lines came spontaneously to the minds of many of those who experienced the burning of Cap Français, the vision of a rich city invaded and engulfed in flames has had a horrid but irresistible fascination. Like the siege of Troy, the destruction of Cap Français was the occasion for memorable human dramas. Madison Smartt Bell wove historically accurate accounts of some of them into the tale of his fictional characters, but as I have delved into the archival documents about the event, I have realized that, in this case, it is fair to say that what really happened was more extraordinary than what a novelist could imagine.

If historians have not paid much attention to the details of the journée of June 20, 1793, it is not because sources are lacking. The amount of information available about this episode is eloquent testimony to the accuracy of David Geggus's assertion that historians have only begun to exploit the documents available for the study of the Haitian Revolution.[5] Although the revolutionary politicians in Paris took months to grasp the significance of what had taken place, the French National Convention eventually ordered an exhaustive inquiry. Its investigating committee gathered thousands of documents, all still preserved in the Archives nationales in Paris: hastily scrawled orders given by the republican officials in the city, logs kept by the captains of the ships in the Cap Français harbor, correspondence written by Toussaint Louverture and other insurgent leaders, testimonies and depositions by individuals of all sorts who were present. American newspapers from the summer of 1793 are filled with the stories told by the refugees, as are the papers of the minister Genet and of the French consuls in Norfolk, Baltimore, Philadelphia, Charleston, and New York. Many of those who survived

4 Madison Smartt Bell, *All Souls' Rising* (New York: Penguin, 1995), 477–500.
5 David P. Geggus, "Underexploited Sources," in David Geggus, *Haitian Revolutionary Studies* (Bloomington, IN: Indiana University Press, 2002), 43–54.

the catastrophe later wrote memoirs.[6] The events leading up to the journée can be reconstructed from the official correspondence of the republican commissioners and military commanders who scrupulously observed the French government's rules about record keeping, as well as from the papers of their opponents and from the gazettes published in Saint-Domingue. It is true that the vast majority of these documents tell stories seen through the eyes of white participants and witnesses, whereas we have only scanty testimony from free people of color and blacks. This imbalance is regrettable but inevitable: the white participants belonged to a culture of records and the written word, whereas most of the black population was illiterate. Indeed, the whites' virtual monopoly over the generation of paper records was one of the means by which a small minority of European colonists had dominated a much larger slave population. As we shall see, however, the documents written by whites at the time of June 20, 1793 enable us to say a good deal about the behavior of free colored and black participants in these events, and the fact that these documents come from individuals with widely varying perspectives means that the historian is not the prisoner of a single "white" point of view.

Since the documentation about the journée of June 20, 1793 is so abundant, why has this event received so little attention in historical accounts of the Haitian uprising? In part, it is because the details of the journée do not fit the overall frameworks into which the story of the Haitian Revolution and the struggle against slavery in France and in the wider Atlantic world are now usually set, particularly the two "ready-made but deceptive approaches to emancipation" that Robin Blackburn already challenged twenty years ago in his magisterial work on *The Overthrow of Colonial Slavery*. "One of these concentrates all attention on respectable metropolitan abolitionism," he wrote, while "the other nourishes a romantic regard for the pristine virtues of rebellion."[7] These two contrasting narratives of the abolition of slavery share the common assumption that this outcome was the result of the conscious intentions and actions of those involved. In fact, both the rebellious slaves in Saint-Domingue and the French abolitionists frequently put other priorities, such as struggles for power among the insurrection's leaders and the

[6] For excerpts from some of these accounts, see Jeremy D. Popkin, *Facing Racial Revolution: Eyewitness Accounts of the Haitian Revolution* (Chicago: University of Chicago Press, 2007), 180–232.

[7] Robin Blackburn, *The Overthrow of Colonial Slavery, 1776–1848* (London: Verso, 1988), 530.

defense of French national interests among the abolitionists, ahead of their concern about slavery. Furthermore, the events that led to emancipation in Saint-Domingue and in France often resulted from interventions of groups and individuals for whom slavery was not a major concern.

Although it was the moment when the immediate abolition of slavery suddenly emerged as a practical possibility, the journée of June 20, 1793 was not directly provoked by the black insurgents who had been fighting the whites since August 1791. The journée began as a conflict between rival white groups, both of them led by outsiders to the colony. The city's free men of color were also involved in the struggle from the outset, but armed black insurgents only entered the fray after its outcome had already been determined, and the main leaders of the black struggle, including Toussaint Louverture, not only played no part in the journée, but also rejected the appeal for help made by the beleaguered republican commissioners. Recent research has underlined the important role of the black population in pushing the commissioners to broaden their emancipation offer after June 20, 1793, but the blacks who pressured the commissioners in the summer of 1793 were not the veteran insurgents who had taken up arms in 1791.[8] Only Toussaint Louverture's belated conversion in May 1794 enabled him to claim a place in the coalition supporting the Republic and, eventually, to emerge as its leader.

Even those historians who have understood that the conflict on June 20, 1793 began as a fight among whites have often relied on the highly partisan version of events endorsed by the French National Convention when it passed its abolition decree of February 4, 1794 and have thus mischaracterized the parties involved. C. L. R. James, who devoted only a page of his classic *Black Jacobins* to the event, summarily dismissed the opponents of the commissioners as "counterrevolutionaries," and, in his recent *A Colony of Citizens*, Laurent Dubois perpetuates a common myth when he describes General François-Thomas Galbaud, leader of the attack on the commissioners, as a "royalist."[9] The role of the black

[8] Elizabeth Colwill shows the importance of the demands put forward by the population in Le Cap after June 20, 1793 in her article, "'Fêtes de l'Hymen, Fêtes de la liberté': Marriage, Manhood, and Emancipation in Revolutionary Saint Domingue," in David Geggus and Norman Fiering, eds., *The World of the Haitian Revolution* (Bloomington, IN: Indiana University Press, 2009), 125–55.

[9] C. L. R. James, *The Black Jacobins* (New York: Vintage Books, 1963 (orig. 1938)), 126–7; Laurent Dubois, *A Colony of Citizens*, 155. In his more detailed history of the Haitian Revolution, *Avengers of the New World: The Story of the Haitian Revolution* (Cambridge,

population has also frequently been misunderstood. In *The Making of Haiti*, Carolyn Fick writes that "over ten thousand slaves in Le Cap were now in open revolt" at the moment when the republican commissioners issued their emancipation decree, although in fact, blacks played little role in the first day of violence in the city, and those who subsequently entered the fray were fighting to uphold the authority of the representatives of the French government, not rising against them.[10] The mid-twentieth-century Haitian historian Gérard Laurent, author of a four-volume study of the commissioner Léger-Félicité Sonthonax, is one of the few to have recognized that the whites on both sides sincerely believed they were fighting for the cause of patriotism and the Revolution: "They fought each other in the name of the same country, for the same goal."[11]

The fact that much of the literature about the Haitian Revolution and the abolition of slavery in Saint-Domingue has focused on two specific figures, Toussaint Louverture and the French emancipator Sonthonax, has also worked against a recognition of the nature and significance of the crisis of June 20, 1793. Debate continues about how involved Toussaint was in the outbreak of the slave uprising in August 1791, but there is no argument about his absence from the drama in Cap Français. Not only was he not present at the event, but for many months afterward, he refused to concede that its outcome had any significance for the cause for which he was fighting. Whether they admire Toussaint or take a critical view of him, scholars who make his actions the center of their narratives accord only minimal attention to the journée of June 20, 1793.[12] Gérard Laurent and Robert Louis Stein, Sonthonax's American biographer, have written the best-documented and most accurate recent accounts of the events leading up to June 20, 1793, but the fact that both their books focus

---

MA: Harvard University Press, 2004), Dubois gives a more accurate characterization of Galbaud and a more substantial account of the journée of June 20, 1793 (pp. 154–9).

[10] Carolyn E. Fick, *The Making of Haiti: The Saint Domingue Revolution from Below* (Knoxville, TN: University of Tennessee Press, 1991), 159.

[11] Gérard Laurent, *Le Commissaire Sonthonax à Saint-Domingue. I: Le Lutteur* (Port-au-Prince: La Phalange, 1965), 159. One of the better accounts of the details of the fighting on June 20 is the Haitian historian Pauléus Sannon's *Histoire de Toussaint-Louverture*, 3 vs. (Port-au-Prince: n.p., 1920–23), I: 120–5.

[12] Pierre Pluchon, whose critical biography of Toussaint Louverture is the best documented life of the black leader, dispatches the events of June 20, 1793 in three sentences (Pierre Pluchon, *Toussaint Louverture* (Paris: Fayard, 1989), 81). The novelist Madison Smartt Bell's biography, more admiring of its subject, gives the drama of Cap Français two pages (Madison Smartt Bell, *Toussaint Louverture: A Biography* (New York: Pantheon, 2007), 52–3).

heavily on Sonthonax means that they give only passing mention to many crucial aspects of the crisis, such as the central role of French sailors in the assault on the commissioners and the importance of the French consuls and the minister Genet in determining its outcome.[13] The biographic approach also tends to make abolition in Saint-Domingue appear to be primarily a consequence of one man's pre-existing convictions. A more careful examination of the circumstances leading to the crisis of June 20, 1793 highlights both the complexities and ambivalences of Sonthonax's actions and the important roles played by many less well-known figures surrounding him and his colleague, Etienne Polverel. These include not only the black insurrectionists, but also the free colored leader Charles Guillaume Castaing, the white plantation owner Louis Dufay – whose speech led to the French National Convention's vote to abolish slavery in 1794 – and, above all, the republican general François-Thomas Galbaud, whose name has remained attached to the crisis in Haitian memory, where it is known as "*l'affaire Galbaud.*"

In the past decade, as the Haitian Revolution has moved from the margins of history to occupy a central place in our understanding of the revolutionary era, it has been presented primarily as a rare and heroic example of successful self-liberation by an oppressed subaltern group. The story of the secret meeting of insurrectionary leaders at Bois Caïman that launched the uprising in August 1791 has become, for the people of Haiti, what the tale of the Minutemen at Lexington and Concord is for Americans and the storming of the Bastille for the French: one of the epic moments in the modern struggle for freedom.[14] Despite the troubled history of modern Haiti, the country's declaration of independence on January 1, 1804 is another milestone in that history. For the first time, a colonized population of people of color overthrew white domination and asserted its right to govern itself. It is tempting to assume that this victory was in some sense the inevitable result of the courage and determination shown by the authors of the original insurrection, and that the outcome of the insurrection was inscribed in its origins. To suggest that the connection between 1791 and 1804 was instead highly contingent, that it depended on the outcome of a crisis that was not directly

[13] Robert Louis Stein, *Léger Félicité Sonthonax: The Lost Sentinel of the Republic* (Rutherford, NJ: Fairleigh Dickinson University Press, 1985).

[14] Marc A. Christophe, "The Ceremony of Bois Caïman," in Cécile Accilien, Jessica Adams, and Elmide Méléance, eds., *Revolutionary Freedoms: A History of Survival, Strength and Imagination in Haiti* (Coconut Creek, FL: Caribbean Studies Press, 2006), 97–100.

produced by the insurrection and that might have had very different results, is to challenge deeply held beliefs about the power of libertarian ideals and of human agency.

To look at the Haitian Revolution in this light – as a sequence of events whose outcome was by no means inevitable – is not to question the courage of the insurgents who rose up against slavery in 1791. The uprising begun in August 1791 was indeed significant: it was the largest slave revolt in modern history, and the only one that ultimately had a successful outcome. As we will see, however, there are important questions about whether the insurgents, prior to the journée of June 20, 1793, had expressed an "unequivocal and unwavering commitment to universal emancipation based upon natural human rights," as a recent essay by Nick Nesbitt claims,[15] and they had certainly not begun to think of demanding independence. It is also far from clear that the insurgency was on the verge of success at the time of the events in Cap Français. Contrary to the image conveyed in many publications about the subject, the slave insurrection did not resemble an avalanche, steadily gaining force as it proceeded. As a structured movement, it was confined to the North Province, one of the three divisions of the colony, and even there, many districts remained unaffected until after the destruction of Cap Français and the proclamation of general liberty in the summer of 1793. Nor was the insurrection's progress a story of unbroken success. The insurgent leaders spent much time quarreling with each other, and in early 1793, their forces suffered such severe defeats that the republican commissioners were able to leave the North Province and turn their attention to suppressing white dissidence in the rest of the colony. On June 20, 1793, the man who would in the end supply the black population with real leadership was not yet aware of his destiny, and he had not yet adopted the name – Toussaint Louverture – under which he would become famous. It was only after the journée of June 20, 1793 that it became clear that the French revolutionary government would not be able to defeat the slave insurrection. It was in the aftermath of this unexpected and far from inevitable event that it became apparent for the first time that victory for the insurgents might be achieved in alliance with the French, rather than by struggle against them.

In addition to challenging overly determinist narratives of the Haitian Revolution, a close examination of the events of June 20, 1793 raises

[15] Nick Nesbitt, *Universal Emancipation: The Haitian Revolution and the Radical Enlightenment* (Charlottesville, VA: University of Virginia Press, 2008), 145.

questions about explanations of the Haitian uprising that put their emphasis exclusively on the dynamics of plantation slavery. The insurrection certainly began as a movement by the slaves of the rural plantations on which the great majority of the colony's population worked; "Fire in the Cane," the title of the chapter of Laurent Dubois's *Avengers of the New World* devoted to the outbreak of the insurrection, evokes the image of plantation work gangs setting the fields alight with their torches. The blacks were able to drive the whites out of many of the island's rural areas, but the movement did not spread to the cities, even though the majority of their population also consisted of black slaves. As long as the whites were able to retain control of the colony's ports, they could balance the insurgents' forces with resources drawn from the outside world: troops from France and supplies from the United States. It took the spectacular breakdown of an urban order that had survived nearly two years of insurrection to break the stalemate between the French authorities and the blacks. This points to the importance of understanding the specific nature of the urban community of Cap Français and what made it fall apart on June 20, 1793. In posing the problem this way, this study follows in the footsteps of other scholars whose work has pointed to the importance of the role of colonial cities in understanding how the Atlantic economy and the system of Caribbean slavery functioned, and to the important differences between urban and rural slavery.[16] The way in which the complex urban community of Cap Français shattered on June 20, 1793 sheds important light on the dynamics of colonial cities and the reasons why they remained largely immune to slave insurrection in normal times.

In addition to forcing us to revise widely accepted notions about the development of the slave insurrection, an examination of the events of June 20, 1793 underlines the importance of Saint-Domingue's free people of color in shaping the events of the Haitian Revolution. Wherever whites had imported black slaves to the Americas, populations of free people had developed, both as a result of white progenitors' concern for their mixed-race descendants and because even the most oppressive slave

[16] See the essays in Franklin W. Knight and Peggy K. Liss, eds., *Atlantic Port Cities: Economy, Culture, and Society in the Atlantic World, 1650–1850* (Knoxville, TN: University of Tennessee Press, 1991), the monograph of Anne Pérotin-Dumon, *La ville aux îles, la ville dans l'île. Basse-Terre et Pointe-à-Pitre, Guadeloupe, 1650–1820* (Paris: Karthala, 2000), and Dominique Rogers, "Les Libres de couleur dans les capitales de Saint-Domingue: Fortune, Mentalités et intégration à la fin de l'ancien régime (1776–1789)" (Thèse de doctorat, Université de Bordeaux III, 1999).

codes always left open some possibility for manumission or the purchase of freedom. In most of the Americas, these free people were relatively few in number and constituted at most an anomaly in the social structure. In Saint-Domingue, however, free people of color had come, by 1791, to be almost as numerous as the whites and to own substantial amounts of property, including slaves. The French Revolution of 1789 offered them an opportunity to put forward claims for political rights and even to imagine the possibility of displacing the whites as the colony's dominant group. In historical retrospect, the conflict between the whites and the slaves appears as the fundamental issue in the Haitian Revolution, but until June 20, 1793, it was the question of equality for the free people of color that dominated politics in Saint-Domingue and debates about the colony in France.

From the white point of view, the slave uprising was akin to the earthquakes and hurricanes that periodically devastated the island: a disaster, but one that would eventually be overcome. The notion that black "savages" or "children of nature" could overthrow white rule and establish their own society was simply unthinkable. Until June 20, 1793, there was no conflict on this point between the white colonists of Saint-Domingue and the French revolutionary government: both agreed that the insurrection had to be suppressed and the plantation system restored. The issue of the free people of color was very different. They were not a "natural" category whose place in the colonial order appeared essentially fixed: instead, as all parties realized, their status was a political matter subject to alteration. Furthermore, the issue of the free people of color divided the white colonists and the metropole. From 1789 onward, many leading revolutionaries outspokenly supported the demands of the free people of color. The group's self-appointed lobbyist, Julien Raimond, had the ear of important figures in the Jacobin movement and the revolutionary assemblies. As we will see, the conflict over the position of the free people of color played a much greater role in setting off the conflagration of June 20, 1793 than did the slave uprising.

If the story of June 20, 1793 upsets accepted historical wisdom about the nature and logic of events in Saint-Domingue itself, it also disturbs standard historical narratives about the French Revolution's policy toward slavery. Just as there is a temptation to conclude that the successful outcome of the black insurrection in Saint-Domingue was inscribed in its dramatic beginning in August 1791, there is a temptation to argue that the French National Convention's decree of February 4, 1794 abolishing slavery was an inevitable consequence of the arguments raised against slavery by members of the *Société des amis des noirs*, the reformist group founded by Jacques-Pierre Brissot in February 1788, and of the principles laid down in the Declaration of the Rights of Man in 1789. How could revolutionary France, the "country of the rights of man," not have intended from the outset to end the scandal of slavery? Recent historical scholarship has made it clear that the original revolutionary legislature, the Constituent Assembly of 1789–91, whose members overwhelmingly endorsed the Declaration of Rights, nevertheless consistently refused even to discuss the issue of slavery, voting to leave the matter to the discretion of assemblies to be elected by the whites in the colonies themselves. Like the American revolutionaries of 1776, the French legislators of 1789 managed to reconcile positions that seem incompatible to our twenty-first century minds. Just as the United States, despite its constitutional commitment to liberty and equality, continued to allow slavery until 1863, revolutionary France initially constituted itself as a polity half slave and half free.[17]

Historians who recognize that the Constituent Assembly of 1789–91 never confronted the issue of slavery nevertheless sometimes argue that abolition of slavery must have been an integral part of the program of the radical and democratic Jacobin movement of 1793–94, since Robespierre and his supporters constantly emphasized their principled commitment to natural human rights, and since the French assembly had granted political rights to the free people of color in 1792.[18] Unlike

---

[17] Important recent discussions of the National Assembly's debates about slavery include Yves Bénot, *La Révolution française et la fin des colonies* (Paris: La Découverte, 1987), David Geggus, "Racial Equality, Slavery, and Colonial Secession during the Constituent Assembly," in Geggus, *Haitian Revolutionary Studies* (Bloomington, IN: Indiana University Press, 2002), 157–70, Jean-Daniel Piquet, *L'Emancipation des Noirs dans la Révolution française* (Paris: Karthala, 2002), Florence Gauthier, *L'Aristocratie de l'épiderme: Le combat de la Société des Citoyens de Couleur 1789–1791* (Paris: CNRS Editions, 2007), and Jeremy D. Popkin, "The French Revolution's Other Island," in Geggus and Fiering, eds., *World of the Haitian Revolution*, 199–222.

[18] The claim that the essence of the French Revolution was a universalist conception of natural rights, and that only those who held such a position can really be considered supporters of the Revolution, has been articulated most clearly in the works of Florence Gauthier, particularly in her book *Triomphe et mort du droit naturel en Révolution 1789–1795–1802* (Paris: Presses Universitaires de Paris, 1992). Jean-Daniel Piquet, in *L'Emancipation des Noirs dans la Révolution française (1789–1795)* (Paris: Karthala, 2002) has extended Gauthier's argument by trying to show that the radical Montagnard movement of 1793–94 was committed to the abolition of slavery, and that the revolutionary government's failure to act on the issue until February 4, 1794 reflected only a brief "dérapage," or deviation, from its principles. As will become apparent in Chapter 10 of this book, I am not in agreement with Gauthier's and Piquet's reading of much of the evidence concerning the radical revolutionaries' actions regarding slavery in 1793,

the 1789 Declaration of Rights, the list of basic principles included in the constitution approved by the Jacobin-dominated National Convention on June 24, 1793 – ironically, at the very moment when Cap Français was going up in flames, although the news would not reach France for another two months – explicitly condemned slavery. As we will see, however, even this argument is not convincing. The 1793 constitution was never put into effect, and no one suggested that it implied the immediate end of slavery in the colonies, which were not even mentioned in the document. The passage of the constitution was a consequence of the radical Montagnard group's victory over its enemies, the Girondins, in the journée of May 31–June 2, 1793, but the expulsion of the Girondins meant the removal from the Convention of the revolutionary politicians most identified with opposition to slavery and with the policy of granting rights to the free people of color. Among the charges brought against the Girondins was the accusation that they had destroyed France's colonies, "under the veil of philanthropy," by raising the issue of abolition.[19] As a result, any French politician who spoke against slavery in the second half of 1793 risked being tarred with the Girondin brush. A pro-slavery colonial lobby worked feverishly to silence potential abolitionists.

Between June 2, 1793, when the Girondins were defeated, and February 4, 1794, the Convention's most significant decision regarding race and slavery was its decree of July 16, 1793, ordering the recall and indictment of the two republican commissioners, Léger-Félicité Sonthonax and Etienne Polverel, who had issued the decree of June 20, 1793 in Cap Français. Only the unexpected arrival in Paris in February 1794 of pro-abolition deputies from Saint-Domingue, bringing an official report about the journée of June 20, 1793 that contradicted the version of events the revolutionary government had previously accepted, led the Convention to reverse itself and endorse the commissioners' emancipation decrees. The Convention took this action without any encouragement from the famous Committee of Public Safety, none of whose members were even present at the debate on February 4, 1794. The committee members who were in Paris were, in fact, meeting privately with the representatives of the pro-slavery white colonists to discuss the danger of hasty action regarding Saint-Domingue when they learned what

and in particular with their attempt to make Robespierre a key figure in the story of abolition.

[19] Report of André Amar, on behalf of the committees of Public Safety and General Security, cited in Piquet, *L'Emancipation des Noirs*, 282.

their colleagues in the Convention had done.[20] There was thus nothing inevitable or ideologically predetermined about the Convention's abolition decree: it took the shock wave emanating from Cap Français to bring it about.

Recognizing that there was no inevitability to the abolition of slavery, either in Saint-Domingue in 1793 or in France in 1794, highlights the importance of understanding the circumstances under which the decisive steps toward emancipation were taken. There is no doubt that the journée of June 20, 1793 was the event that set the emancipation process in motion, first in Saint-Domingue, where the commissioners Sonthonax and Polverel quickly found themselves compelled to expand their initial offer of freedom to blacks who would join their forces to a general grant of freedom to the entire slave population of the colony, and then in France. This is not to suggest that the ultimate abolition of slavery in the western world was the result of a chance event in Cap Français in June 1793. The movement for abolition had important "structural foundations ... on both sides of the Atlantic," as Seymour Drescher has shown.[21] Black resistance to enslavement was endemic throughout the Atlantic world; the Saint-Domingue revolt, although it was on a larger scale than any other, was part of a long series, some of which, such as the rebellions in Jamaica and Surinam, had resulted in treaties recognizing the establishment of autonomous maroon communities. On both sides of the Atlantic, an abolitionist movement had gathered strength in the 1780s. During that decade, most of the northern states of the new American republic passed legislation or took other measures meant to lead to the eventual emancipation of their slaves,[22] and in 1789, the British Parliament held a lengthy debate about abolishing the slave trade, the first of many discussions that would finally lead to the law to that effect in 1807.[23] Nevertheless, groups with an economic stake in the continuation of slavery were powerful on both sides of the Atlantic. As of 1793, slavery had been successfully challenged only in a few of America's "societies with slaves," regions where the institution had not been central

---

[20] Register of the colonial commissioners Page and Brulley, in Archives nationales D XXV 76, entry for 16 plu. II.

[21] Seymour Drescher, *Abolition: A History of Slavery and Antislavery* (Cambridge and New York: Cambridge University Press, 2009), 113.

[22] On the abolition laws in the New England states, see Joanne Pope Melish, *Disowning Slavery: Gradual Emancipation and 'Race' in New England, 1780–1860* (Ithaca, NY: Cornell University Press, 1998), 50–79.

[23] This story has been vividly retold in Adam Hochschild, *Bury the Chains: Prophets and Rebels in the Fight to Free an Empire's Slaves* (Boston, MA: Mariner Books, 2005).

to the economy and where blacks were a small minority of the population. Whether the movement for abolition would ever spread to the New World's "slave societies," those in which slavery was the basis of the whole economy and in which the slave population rivaled or exceeded the number of whites, remained unclear.

In Saint-Domingue in 1793, slavery was abolished in a territory in which blacks were the overwhelming majority of the population and in which servile labor had been the defining institution of an entire society. In France in 1794, the national government of a major slave-holding and slave-trading empire declared that slavery was an inherently inadmissible violation of human rights. Unlike the earlier emancipation acts in most of the northern American states or the abolition of slavery in the British colonies after 1833, the emancipation decrees of 1793 and 1794 took effect immediately, and they provided no compensation for the former slave owners. These decrees made the freed slaves full citizens of France: the Convention's decree of February 4, 1794 was accompanied by the seating of the former black slave (and leading participant in the events of June 20, 1793 in Cap Français), Jean-Baptiste Belley, as a voting member of the French legislature. Until the decrees of 1793 and 1794, the prospect of a world without slavery or racial discrimination was a utopian hypothesis; after 1794, it could no longer be dismissed as something outside the realm of possibility. Whether the French experiment with radical emancipation accelerated or retarded the movement for abolition elsewhere, there is no doubt that it had profound influence on debates in the rest of the western world.[24] Understanding the circumstances in which emancipation occurred in the French empire in 1793–94 is thus vital to understanding why the larger story of the abolition of slavery followed the course that it did.

The detailed examination of the events of 1793 and their sequel, the Convention's decree of February 4, 1794, also helps us understand some complexities concealed in the question of emancipation. There are understandable reasons why many contemporary scholars, reacting against two centuries of historiography that has emphasized the ideas of white thinkers and the actions of white politicians, administrators,

---

[24] For a recent argument minimizing the impact of the Haitian Revolution on the abolition of slavery in the rest of the Americas, see João Pedro Marques, "Slave Revolts and the Abolition of Slavery: An Overinterpretation," trans. Richard Wall, in Seymour Drescher and Pieter C. Emmer, eds., *Who Abolished Slavery? Slave Revolts and Abolitionism. A Debate with João Pedro Marques* (New York: Berghahn, 2010), 1–89.

and soldiers in explaining the end of with slavery, have insisted that the blacks of Saint-Domingue, unlike slaves in any other American society, demonstrated their human agency by freeing themselves through armed struggle. The insurgent slaves of Saint-Domingue themselves, however, realized from the start of their movement that success would require some kind of acknowledgment from their former masters and from the French government. The uprising that began in August 1791 was too large and had inflicted too much damage on colonial society to be seen as a large-scale episode of *marronage*, an effort by a limited number of slaves to escape to some remote area where they could live in isolation. In any event, even the most important collective escapes from slavery in New World societies had always ended with agreements between the *marrons* and the whites, agreements that usually recognized the escaped slaves' freedom in exchange for their promise not to encourage other slaves to join them.[25]

In the case of Saint-Domingue, the black insurgents destroyed the richest and most valuable plantations in France's largest and most important colony. The whites whose lands they overran were powerful and influential people, and the rebelling slaves anticipated from the start that France's metropolitan government would intervene with all its forces to regain control of the lost territory. Their intent was to achieve some kind of negotiated settlement with the white world that would improve their situation, not to try to isolate themselves and the island altogether. Indeed, when the slaves asserted that they had risen up to gain the three free days a week that a pervasive rumor claimed the king of France had granted them, they were, in effect, appealing for royal intervention, hoping that Louis XVI would impose reform on their recalcitrant masters. Even the one manifesto from the period of the insurrection preceding the events of June 20, 1793 that explicitly calls for the granting of human rights to Saint-Domingue's black population – a controversial document whose authenticity has been challenged by some scholars – concludes by proposing that if the whites would recognize the blacks' freedom and grant amnesty to those who had participated in the insurrection, the insurgents, for their part, would return to their plantations and resume their work, in exchange for a fixed salary.[26]

---

[25] Fick, *Making of Haiti*, 55; Yvan Debbasch, "Le Marronnage. Essai sur la désertion de l'esclave antillais," *Année sociologique*, ser. 3 (1962), 188–9.

[26] The most accessible version of this letter is Nathalie Piquionne, "Lettre de Jean-François, Biassou et Belair, juillet 1792," *Chemins critiques*, 3 (1997), 206–10. For

The full realization of the blacks' freedom required not just a de facto victory in Saint-Domingue itself, but also recognition of the former slaves' new status by their former masters and by the French government. The black insurrection begun in 1791 might eventually have forced the French out of Saint-Domingue, but the victors would still have been, in the eyes of the French and the larger western world, nothing more than escaped slaves. In fact, as the rulers of Haiti discovered after their military victory in 1804, the freedom of their country and of its citizens remained precarious as long as France continued to regard the colony as a rebellious territory to be reoccupied when circumstances permitted, a situation that continued until president Jean-Paul Boyer accepted the harsh French terms (including compensation to the former plantation owners) imposed in 1825.[27] The world-historical impact of the emancipations of 1793–94 stemmed from the fact that they entailed not just a revolt against slavery on the part of the slaves,

---

an abridged English translation, see Nick Nesbitt, ed., *Toussaint L'Ouverture: The Haitian Revolution* (London: Verso, 2008), 5–8. (Nesbitt's claim that the third signatory of the document, Belair, was actually representing Toussaint Louverture is unsubstantiated.) The document was originally published in Paris in 1793, first in the royalist colonel Cambefort's defense of his conduct in Saint-Domingue, and then by the antislavery journalist Milscent's *Créole patriote*. There is no reference to it in any known document emanating from Saint-Domingue in 1792–93, and none of the manuscript letters written by the black insurgent leaders in this period mention the Declaration of the Rights of Man. This document and a highly dramatized episode in the memoirs of an as-yet-unidentified colonist from the period constitute the only documentary sources for the claim, made by Nesbitt and others, that the black insurgents were directly inspired by the French Declaration of Rights of 1789 (Nesbitt, *Universal Emancipation*, 62, 144–5). The story of the black insurgent found to have in his pockets "pamphlets printed in France, filled with commonplaces about the Right of Man," is most often cited on the basis of a partial and not entirely accurate English translation of an anonymous colonist's memoir, Althéa de Puech Parham, ed. and trans., *My Odyssey* (Baton Rouge, LA: Louisiana State University Press, 1959). The full French manuscript of "Mon Odyssée" has not been published, as it richly deserves to be. It is certainly the most imaginative work of literature to have been inspired by the Haitian Revolution, and its author, a young scion of a slave-owning family who enjoyed fine cuisine, fighting, and occasional cross-dressing, is an engaging personality. Although I have drawn on his account of the events of June 20, 1793 in several places in this book, I would nevertheless hesitate to put too much weight on his assertion that the insurgents had access to printed revolutionary propaganda, a claim which is not confirmed by any of the voluminous archival evidence about the insurrection. For a translation of the passage in question that corrects some important errors in the Puech Parham version, see Popkin, *Facing Racial Revolution*, 79, and for my own analysis of the passage's significance, see 63–4.

[27] On the Haitian struggle for international recognition, see Jean-François Brière, *Haïti et la France 1804–1848. Le rêve brisé* (Paris: Karthala, 2008).

but also a legitimation of that revolt on the part of the French government. The story of the first radical emancipation in the Atlantic world is thus truly a trans-Atlantic story, one that took place on both sides of the ocean and that required the actions of people of both African and European descent.

Understanding the role of the violence in Cap Français on June 20, 1793 in precipitating the emancipation decrees of 1793 and 1794 has special relevance for thinking about the process of emancipation in that other republic created in the late eighteenth century, the United States. Once we recognize that the French revolutionary abolition of slavery was not, as French historians and politicians sometimes like to imply, a simple and logical consequence of the Declaration of the Rights of Man and Citizen, but rather the outcome of a civil war among Saint-Domingue's free population, we can also recognize the curious parallel between the histories of the two countries. The two republics most identified with notions of individual liberty were also the two major slave-holding societies in which emancipation came about from a clash of arms, not from debate and gradual reform shaped by humanitarian principles or from foreign pressure. It may seem incongruous to compare the four days of disorganized streetfighting in Cap Français in 1793 with the four long years of large-scale combat in the American Civil War, but it can be argued that a similar dynamic was at work in both cases. (It is also worth pointing out that the four days of fighting in Cap Français were the culmination of struggles over the colony's relationship to the metropole that had begun with the outbreak of the French Revolution in 1789, so that one can speak of a civil war whose duration was more comparable to the American one.) The events in Cap Français on June 20, 1793, like those at Fort Sumter on April 12, 1861, involved an armed assault on the representatives of a national government by whites claiming to be republicans who distrusted the government's commitment to defend slavery. In both cases, the resulting conflict brought about a far more sudden and radical abolition of slavery than national leaders had foreseen. These conflicts resulted from the impossibility of reconciling constitutional guarantees protecting slaveholders' property rights with assertions of slaves' natural rights. We are left to contemplate the possibility that constitutions based on explicit recognitions of rights, rather than accelerating the process of abolition, may actually have created situations where only violence could break the deadlock over the rival rights claims generated by the institution of slavery.

The reconstruction of the events of June 20, 1793 in Cap Français is thus more than an antiquarian exercise. Giving this episode the place it deserves in the story of the Haitian Revolution, in the analysis of the French Revolution's debates about human rights, and in the wider narrative of the struggle against slavery in the Atlantic world, will require changes in our perspectives on all three of these fundamental events. Not only were the dramatic events of June 20, 1793 in Cap Français a turning point in the Haitian Revolution, but that crisis very nearly failed to happen and could easily have had a completely different outcome. As we will see, it took a unique and unforeseeable set of circumstances to bring about the explosion that destroyed Cap Français and led to the sudden emancipation of its slaves. The individuals who set the events of June 20, 1793 in motion were not black insurgents fighting for freedom, or white colonists defending their privileged positions, but white sailors from outside the island and a white general who thought he was defending the interests of revolutionary France. On the other side, those who fought against them were not the city's oppressed slaves; instead, the main combatants were free men of color, who saw the political equality they had just gained in danger of disappearing. The historic emancipation proclamations of 1793 in Saint-Domingue and the French National Convention's decree of 1794 came about, not through the systematic efforts of slave insurgents in Saint-Domingue, nor in response to an organized campaign for abolition in revolutionary France, but as a result of a crisis that had little to do with slavery.

Not only did slave emancipation in the French empire result from an unexpected clash between groups that had no intention of bringing about such a result, but the two organized groups that might have been expected to welcome the proclamation of slave emancipation – the insurgent slaves in Saint-Domingue and the radical revolutionary legislators in France – both initially rejected the measures taken by the commissioners Sonthonax and Polverel in the summer of 1793. From the point of view of the black insurgents, the commissioners' offer of emancipation appeared as a concession granted under duress and in circumstances that made its value seem questionable. As we will see, many of the blacks thought their interests would be better served by an alliance with revolutionary France's enemy, the Spanish monarchy. In France, where the news of the crisis of June 20, 1793 and its aftermath arrived as the embattled revolutionary government was facing foreign invasion, domestic uprisings, and economic collapse, slave emancipation was initially regarded as a traitorous blow against the national interest, carried out by agents of the Girondin faction, whose members were also blamed for many of the country's domestic woes. The success of Sonthonax's and Polverel's emergency decrees depended not only on the eventual "volte-face," or turnabout, of Toussaint Louverture, whose causes David Geggus has analyzed in a justly celebrated article,[28] but also on an equally startling reversal of policy by the Montagnard National Convention.

Furthermore, a detailed reconstruction of the events of June 20, 1793 shows that the sailors and the general very nearly succeeded in their attack on Sonthonax and Polverel and their supporters. A single musket ball on June 20, 1793 and a moment of panic the following day turned the tide of battle, not just once, but twice. Without those historical accidents, it is doubtful that there would have been any emancipation proclamation in Saint-Domingue, and without that proclamation, there would have been no decree from the National Convention abolishing slavery and no mass arrival of refugees in the United States. The ex-slave Toussaint de Bréda could well have ended his career as an officer in the Spanish royal army, as several of the other leaders of the black insurrection did, and the entire history of the struggle against slavery would have taken a different course. Given the significance attributed to the Saint-Domingue uprising and the National Convention's decree of 16 pluviôse II in all general histories of that struggle, it is bound to be disturbing to have to recognize the profound element of contingency in the sequence of events that led up to them.

Today, slavery is universally recognized as a crime against humanity, and it requires a considerable leap of historical imagination to understand a world in which it was accepted as a normal social arrangement. In retracing the complicated series of events that led to the emancipations of 1793 and 1794, and in showing that they were not simply the straightforward consequences of slaves' desires for freedom or of French revolutionaries' devotion to the rights of man, I am certainly not attempting to offer an apology for a cruel and oppressive institution, or for those who benefited from it. Slavery in the Atlantic world was an inhuman system, but it was a human creation. If we want to understand how it functioned and why it was so hard to destroy, we have to look at the human beings involved in it – slaves, slave owners, and would-be reformers – in all their complexity. Only thus can we understand how

---

[28] David Geggus, "The 'Volte-Face' of Toussaint Louverture," in Geggus, *Haitian Revolutionary Studies*, 119–36.

difficult it was to break out of the system of beliefs that made slavery seem tolerable or inevitable, and to define what we now regard as the obvious principles of human freedom. The purpose of this book is to bring to life one of the crucial episodes in that process, and to show the many obstacles that had to be overcome before the epoch-making steps taken on the two sides of the Atlantic in 1793 and 1794 could be taken. It is a story full of heroism, but also of human folly, of misunderstandings and unintended consequences. In short, it is a story of real people, of all races, with their limitations and contradictions, who found themselves in extraordinary circumstances. If its lessons are sometimes less clear-cut than some readers would like, that is, perhaps, a reminder that history is not a simple morality play.

I

A Colony in Revolution

The news spread rapidly through the city of Cap Français, the principal port of the French Caribbean colony of Saint-Domingue: a messenger boat dispatched by the island's new rulers had arrived. The date was September 13, 1792, some three years since the first news of the revolution in France had reached the island and more than a year since the slaves in the colony's North Province surrounding Cap Français had risen up in insurrection. After seemingly endless delays, the government in revolutionary France had finally taken measures meant to secure its control of its most valuable overseas colony and to end the slave uprising. Approaching the island was a fleet led by the 74-gun warship *America* with three National Civil Commissioners and a newly appointed Governor General on board; accompanying them were 6,000 fresh troops from the metropole, an expeditionary force larger than the army France had sent to aid the Americans in their war for independence. Throughout the colony, everyone knew that the situation in Saint-Domingue was about to change dramatically.

Although the local newspaper announced that the news of the fleet's imminent arrival had generated universal enthusiasm, the civil commissioners – three little-known Frenchmen, only one of whom had any prior acquaintance with the colonies – were well aware that they were about to take charge of a society in crisis. If they had any doubts on this score, the first letter dispatched to them after their messenger reached the city dispelled them. It was from the outgoing governor of the island, a royal appointee with the aristocratic name of Philibert-François Rouxel de Blanchelande, and it warned them that they would need to take extreme measures to control "a people who, for three years, has been accustomed to live in the most absolute anarchy." Strange as it now seems, Blanchelande was not referring to the insurgent slaves: the anarchy he proceeded to describe had been fomented by the colony's whites. To be sure, Blanchelande told the new commissioners when they first landed, "you will be perfectly welcomed and received; you are awaited like protecting deities." But this was only because each faction in the colony hoped to win the commissioners over to its own side and use them to defeat its enemies. In consequence, Blanchelande's advice to the men coming to replace him was that when their ship anchored in Cap Français's harbor, they should "prevent any delegation, of whatever sort, from coming on board": they risked being seen as the allies of whatever group managed to get their ear first. Ironically, Blanchelande, a loyal servant of the monarchy and a man universally blamed for his chronic indecisiveness, went on to suggest to the commissioners a truly revolutionary program. They should, he urged, immediately suspend all the organs of local government – the colonial assembly elected by the whites of the whole island in 1791, the North Province's local assembly, and the Cap Français city council – and ban the printing of all newspapers and pamphlets. "You will forestall the dangerous agitation that your arrival might cause in the city of Le Cap," he told them. If they encountered resistance, they should not hesitate to use the threat of force to compel obedience.[1]

Governor Blanchelande knew only too well how chaotic conditions had become in Saint-Domingue since the outbreak of the revolution in France: for nearly two years, he had struggled without success to impose his authority on the colony's free population and to defeat the slave insurrection. His problems reflected the breakdown of legitimacy in France itself and in the colony. Although Blanchelande had been appointed to his post over a year after the start of the Revolution in France, supporters of that movement on both sides of the Atlantic were deeply suspicious of him: was he not a nobleman who had devoted his life to the service of the king? In 1789, even before the news of the storming of the Bastille had reached Saint-Domingue, the whites there had followed the example of their fellow citizens in the metropole and begun demanding the right to govern themselves. By October 1790, when Blanchelande arrived in the colony, the appointment of a military governor in any part of European France would have been unimaginable. To the colonists, the

---

[1] Blanchelande to civil commissioners, September 15, 1792, in Archives nationales (hereafter AN) D XXV 11, d. 103.

continuation of this practice inherited from the old monarchy was proof of a conspiracy against their freedom. On March 4, 1791, white "patriots" in Port-au-Prince, supported by newly arrived French troops who had turned against their own officers, lynched Colonel Thomas-Antoine Mauduit, the commander of the royal troops in the colony, demonstrating the depth of distrust of the king's government that pervaded the colony.[2]

By September 1792, Governor Blanchelande was a broken man, reviled by every group in the colony. Since August 1791, he had been struggling with little success to contain a massive insurrection among the colony's slave population. In August 1792, a month before the arrival of the commissioners, he had lost much of his army in an unsuccessful attack on a rebel stronghold at Platons, in the south of the colony.[3] He had been equally unsuccessful in winning the support of the colony's free population, which accused him of incompetence or even treason. In France itself, where the Revolution was threatened by foreign invaders whose defeat at Valmy on September 20, 1792 – almost the same moment when the commissioners reached Saint-Domingue – would not be known in the colony until the end of the year, no one had any sympathy for a royal appointee who had so singularly failed to defend the nation's interests. As he wrote his long letter of advice to the men sent to replace him, recommending a policy of firm action that he himself had never been able to carry out, Blanchelande must have wondered whether they would have any better luck than he had in dealing with the seemingly insoluble challenge of bringing the colony back under control. He probably suspected that he would end up being blamed for the disasters afflicting the colony, and indeed, one of the commissioners' first actions after they landed was to order him to return to France to face accusations that he had engaged in a deliberate policy of sabotage, accusations that would make him the first prominent victim of the Revolutionary Tribunal created in April 1793.[4] Blanchelande's fate, already predictable when the commissioners arrived in Cap Français, was a warning of what his successors themselves could expect if they could not do better than he had at mastering the problems of Saint-Domingue.

[2] J.-P. Garran-Coulon, *Rapport sur les troubles de Saint-Domingue, fait au nom de la Commission des Colonies, des Comités de Salut Public, de Législation, et de Marine, réunis*, 4 vs. (Paris: Imprimerie nationale, An V (1797–98)), 1: 335.

[3] Garran-Coulon, *Rapport*, 2: 572–609.

[4] AN, D XXV 47, d. 444 and d. 444bis; for Blanchelande's trial, see the *Bulletin du Tribunal criminel révolutionnaire*, no. 10 (April 1793).

Much of the white colonists' distrust of Blanchelande and the government he represented reflected not just a dislike of arbitrary government, but also the fundamental reality of life in Saint-Domingue: the island, like all of France's Caribbean possessions, was a society based on slavery and racial hierarchy, institutions whose principles were largely alien to the metropole. Indeed, Saint-Domingue in 1789 was the most extreme example of the slave-based society that Europeans had created throughout the Americas. Nowhere else in the world did so few whites exploit the labor of so many black slaves with such ruthless efficiency. At a time when the slave population of the thirteen American states was just 700,000, Saint-Domingue – a territory about the size of New Jersey – had a slave population of nearly 500,000, outnumbering the 30,000 to 40,000 whites by more than ten to one. (If one counts the slaves in France's other major Caribbean colonies, Martinique and Guadeloupe, each of which had close to 100,000 slaves in 1789, and the smaller islands of the Lesser Antilles, the French possessions may have had a larger slave population in 1789 than the United States.)[5] Thanks to the labor of their slaves, Saint-Domingue's whites could legitimately boast that the colony was the motor of France's economy and the most valuable of the country's provinces. By 1789, Saint-Domingue was producing almost half of the world's supply of sugar and coffee, two commodities that had become essential to western notions of civilization. Particularly in the quarter-century since the end of the Seven Years' War in 1763, a period during which the island's slave population more than doubled, Saint-Domingue was France's El Dorado, a land of opportunity where fortunes could be made on a scale almost unimaginable in the metropole or in the American slave states. Itemizing his losses in the Haitian Revolution, one man listed a sugar plantation with 342 slaves, a coffee plantation with 46 slaves, a stud farm with 48 mares and 148 mules, and a lime-making establishment employing 25 slaves; he was by no means the wealthiest of Saint-Domingue planters.[6] (Figure 1.1)

It is not surprising that men who had accumulated so much wealth chafed at being ruled by military governors and civil intendants appointed by ministers on the other side of the Atlantic, and that they saw the developments in France in 1789 as an opportunity to assert themselves. It is also not surprising that they were determined to defend the system of slavery on which their wealth was based. Prosperous and successful

---

[5] Blackburn, *Overthrow*, 163.
[6] AN, 5 mi 1434, deposition of Mirande, n.d.

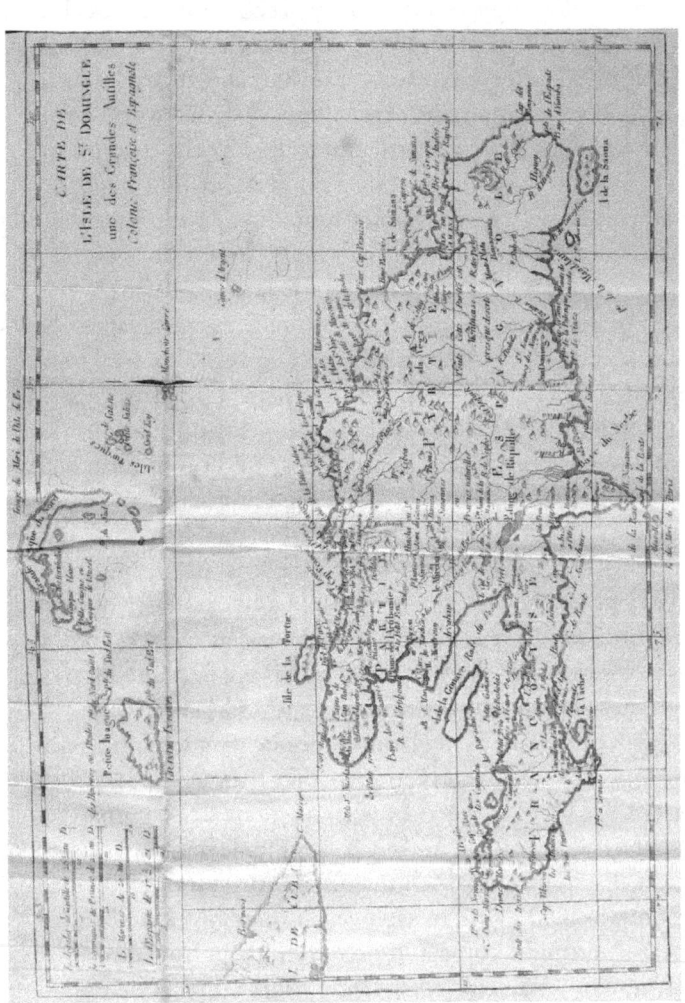

FIGURE 1.1. Map of Saint-Domingue (1795).

This crudely drawn map was included in the proslavery colonist François Laplace's *Histoire des désastres de Saint-Domingue*, the first detailed account of the political events there that culminated in the burning of Cap Français and the emancipation proclamations of 1793 to be published in France during the revolutionary era. Cap Français is on the island's north coast; Port-au-Prince, the colony's official capital and second-largest city, is at the angle where the long southern peninsula juts out from the coastline of the West Province.

Source: Rare Book Collection, University of Pennsylvania Library.

as many of them were, the slave owners of Saint-Domingue were nevertheless deeply insecure. They saw enemies everywhere: among the slaves
on whom their fortunes depended, among the growing population of
free people of color in the colony, whose existence reflected the contradictions of the white slave owners' own behavior, and in the metropole
that enjoyed the benefits flowing from the colony's economic success but
objected to the methods used to generate them. The violent dissensions
among the white colonists, reflected in Governor Blanchelande's letter to
the newly appointed commissioners in September 1792, were the result
of these fears, all of which had been greatly intensified by the revolutionary movement in France in 1789 and its effects in the Caribbean.

Try as they might to convince metropolitan public opinion that their
slaves were well treated and content with their lot, colonial slave owners
knew that the slave population was inherently hostile to them. When
they could, slaves ran away and became "maroons," escaping into the
mountains and sometimes succeeding in establishing veritable free communities. Disappointed by the low birth rate on their plantations, owners accused slave women of aborting their pregnancies or even killing
their babies to avoid seeing them grow up as slaves.[7] Whites lived in fear
of being poisoned by their slave servants or, more commonly, of seeing
their livestock decimated by deliberate sabotage. Marronage, infanticide,
and poisoning were forms of individual resistance to slavery, but there
was always the fear of a collective revolt. Even thirty years later, whites
in Saint-Domingue still remembered the panic caused by the Makandal
conspiracy in 1758, when a slave was accused of having fomented a plot
to poison white plantation wners throughout the island.[8]

To keep their slaves obedient, Saint-Domingue slave owners throughout the eighteenth century consistently argued that they needed to have
unlimited authority over them. If need be, defenders of slavery insisted,
slave owners had to be free to torture and even execute slaves who resisted
them; otherwise, the discipline on which the plantation system depended
would be fatally undermined. This insistence on their unlimited rights
over their "property" brought the slave owners into periodic conflict
with the royal administration. The 1685 *Code noir*, Louis XIV's edict
regulating slavery in the Caribbean colonies, legitimized the institution

---

[7] Arlette Gautier, *Les soeurs de solitude. La condition féminine dans l'esclaveage aux
   Antilles du XVIIe au XIXe siècle* (Paris: Editions caribbéennes, 1985), 222–3.
[8] Pierre Pluchon, *Vaudou, sorciers, empoisonneurs. De Saint-Domingue à Haïti* (Paris:
   Karthala, 1987), 165–82.

but also laid down some rules meant to protect the slaves: owners were responsible for feeding and clothing their slaves, they were supposed to see to their religious instruction, and, in certain circumstances, the *Code* allowed slaves to appeal to the authorities if their masters disregarded its provisions. Throughout the history of the French colonies, the provisions of the *Code noir* that favored the slaves were routinely ignored, but to the slave owners they constituted a warning: as long as they had to acknowledge metropolitan authority, they always faced a potential threat to their most vital interests.

Even as Saint-Domingue's economy boomed in the 1770s and 1780s, the threats menacing the slavery system seemed to be growing. The greatest danger came not from the slaves themselves – after the Makandal episode in 1758, there were no large-scale slave conspiracies in Saint-Domingue until after the start of the French Revolution – but from the metropole. In the seventeenth century, when slavery was established in the colonies, French society accepted the notion that all human beings needed to submit to their superiors. Children were to obey their parents, apprentices their masters, peasants their seigneurs, and women their fathers or husbands. Beggars, vagabonds, the insane, and the ill were forcibly institutionalized, soldiers were subject to stringent discipline, and whites who indentured themselves to work in the colonies had virtually no rights during the term of their contract. In these circumstances, the slavery imposed on captured Africans seemed of a piece with the condition of the king's other subjects. By the middle of the eighteenth century, however, the authoritarianism of the age of Louis XIV had largely disappeared. Jansenist insistence on the rights of individual religious conscience, the Enlightenment's defense of individual reason, economic growth that encouraged pursuit of individual opportunities – all contributed to the development of a spirit of criticism of existing institutions.[9]

The year 1770 saw the publication of the first edition of the *Histoire philosophique des Deux Indes*, a history and critique of European colonialism that became one of the period's great bestsellers. The work, attributed to the abbé Guillaume-Thomas-François Raynal but actually the product of many hands, including that of the radical *philosophe* Denis Diderot, reflected contradictory attitudes toward slavery – attitudes that

---

[9] For a recent survey of eighteenth-century French attitudes toward slavery, see Jean Ehrard, *Lumières et esclavage. L'esclavage colonial et l'opinion publique en France au XVIIIe siècle* (Brussels: André Versaille, 2008).

seemed to change over the course of its successive editions – but some of its pages, nevertheless, provided a thoroughgoing denunciation of the institution. In the 1780 edition, Diderot prophesied the coming of an avenger who would overthrow the slave system, "this great man that Nature owes to its vexed, oppressed tormented children … He will show himself and will raise the sacred banner of liberty … Then the *Code Noir* will disappear, and the *Code Blanc* will be terrible if the victors consult only the law of revenge!"[10] The *Histoire philosophique des Deux Indes* was officially banned, in France and in the colonies, but in fact it circulated with little hindrance: as many colonists knew, its ostensible author, Raynal, had close ties with the officials of the Ministry of the Navy, which was responsible for the administration of the colonies, and much of the book's content reflected the thinking of enlightened bureau-crats who were open to suggestions for the reform of slavery, with an eye to its eventual replacement by some more humane system of plantation agriculture.[11]

In the mid-1780s, the menace posed by the royal administration took on concrete form. Two edicts drawn up by the marquis de Castries, Louis XVI's minister for the colonies, reiterated the principles of the *Code noir* and, among other things, restricted the physical punishments owners could inflict on their slaves.[12] The ministry attempted to limit the use of hired managers, blamed for their indifference to the fate of the slaves, and gave the latter greater opportunities to bring complaints about their treatment. The whites in the colonies responded with fury. "We sit here on top of a barrel of gunpowder, which can be set off by the slightest error in administration, and that is what will happen if the court does not change its policy. In substance, this edict violates the sacred rights of property, and puts a dagger in the hands of the slaves, by giving con-trol over their discipline and their regime to someone other than their masters," one of them wrote.[13] They actively resisted the implementation of the Castries edicts, and in 1788, the colony's high court dismissed a

---

[10] Cited in Laurent Dubois and John D. Garrigus, *Slave Revolution in the Caribbean 1789–1804* (New York: Bedford/St. Martin's, 2006), 56.

[11] Michèle Duchet, *Anthropologie et histoire au siècle des Lumières* (Paris: Albin Michel, 1995 (orig. 1971)), 129–36.

[12] Jean Tarrade, "L'esclavage est-il réformable? Les projets des administrateurs coloniaux à la fin de l'ancien régime," in Marcel Dorigny, dir., *Les abolitions de l'esclavage. De L. F. Sonthonax à V. Schoelcher* (Paris: Editions UNESCO, 1995), 133–41.

[13] Letter of Pierre Céloron de Blainville, May 8, 1785, cited in Gabriel Debien, *Les Esclaves aux Antilles Françaises (XVIIe-XVIIIe siècles)* (Basse-Terre and Fort-de-France: Sociétés d'histoire de la Guadeloupe et de la Martinique, 1974), 486.

case against a slaveowner who had admitted torturing two of his slaves to death.[14] Even this victory did not reassure the slave owners, however, and when the revolutionary movement against arbitrary government developed in 1788, many of them eagerly joined it, hoping for a new constitution that would allow Saint-Domingue, like France's other provinces, a large measure of self-government.

That the movement for radical reform in France would pose its own dangers to the slave system was clear to the white colonists from the start. In the rhetoric of the pamphlets inundating France in 1788, "slavery" was the worst of evils, although the servitude that these "patriot" authors stigmatized was that imposed on the metropolitan population by the system of absolute monarchy, not the condition of Africans in the colonies. In April 1788, a group of Saint-Domingue colonists drew up a long memorandum addressed to the king, demanding the revocation of several recent changes in the island's government; they included a long and very explicit justification of the necessity to keep the slaves convinced of their masters' unlimited power over them.[15] Significantly, when the colonists' supporters in France revised this document to present it to the king, they removed this defense of slavery and limited themselves instead to arguing for the colony's economic importance to the kingdom and its' white inhabitants' right to be protected from arbitrary ministerial actions; evidently, they realized that it would be inadvisable to remind the metropolitan public that the right the colonists were most concerned with was their right to punish their slaves.[16]

Despite the doubts of some colonists about the wisdom of demanding seats in the Estates General or the National Assembly into which it soon transformed itself, since their participation would legitimate those bodies' pretentions to intervene in colonial affairs, a group of self-proclaimed

---

[14] Malick Ghachem, "Sovereignty and Slavery in the Age of Revolution: Haitian Variations on a Metropolitan Theme," Ph. D. diss., Stanford University, 2001, Ch. 5, "The Lejeune Affair."

[15] "Mémoire au roi," in *Journal historique du Comité colonial de St. Domingue* (1788), Library of Congress, ms. MMC 2671, dated April 20, 1788. This manuscript is the register of deliberations of the Comité colonial de St. Domingue, established in France in July 1788 to advocate representation of Saint-Domingue in the upcoming meeting of the Estates General. On this campaign, see Jeremy D. Popkin, "Saint-Domingue, Slavery and the Origins of the French Revolution," in Thomas Kaiser and Dale Van Kley, eds., *From Deficit to Deluge* (Stanford, CA: Stanford University Press, forthcoming 2011).

[16] "Lettre adressée au Roi par les Propriétaires planteurs &c. de la colonie de St. Domingue," dated May 31, 1788, in AN, B III 135.

representatives from Saint-Domingue successfully lobbied for admission and won their case on July 4, 1789.[17] The lengthy debate that preceded this decision, however, showed that many metropolitan deputies had misgivings about the institution of slavery. For the next two years, the colonists would wage an unremitting struggle to convince the Assembly that it had no right to make any decisions regarding the internal affairs of the colonies, and particularly what the deputies euphemistically labeled "the status of persons" in France's overseas possessions.[18] The danger facing the colonial slave owners because of their connection with France was exemplified by the passage of the Declaration of the Rights of Man and Citizen on August 26, 1789, the first article of which proclaimed that "men are born and remain free and equal in rights." The revolutionary spokesman, Honoré Gabriel de Riqueti, better known as Count Mirabeau, one of the slaveholders' most vocal enemies, immediately insisted that the clear sense of the Declaration amounted to a condemnation of slavery. "What [the Assembly] will say to the blacks, what it will say to the planters, what it will tell the whole of Europe, is that there are not and cannot be, either in France or in any territory subject to French laws, any men other than *free men*, other than *men equal to each other*, and that any man who keeps another in involuntary servitude acts against the law," he thundered.[19] The Assembly refused to see things this way, however; instead, it decided that the question of whether the Declaration applied to the colonies would be settled at a later date.

Meanwhile, the white colonists on the island vigorously imitated their metropolitan cousins by creating local revolutionary assemblies to take over the powers of the royal administration. The last royal intendant, François Barbé-Marbois, had to flee the colony when the revolution began, and the self-proclaimed assemblies that replaced him banned the circulation of the Declaration of Rights in the colony.[20] In May 1790, a colonial assembly chosen exclusively by white property owners passed a colonial constitution that amounted to a virtual declaration

---

[17] Popkin, "Saint-Domingue, Slavery and the Origins of the French Revolution," in Kaiser and Van Kley, eds., *From Deficit to Deluge*.

[18] On these debates, see David Geggus, "Racial Equality, Slavery, and Colonial Secession during the Constituent Assembly," in Geggus, *Haitian Revolutionary Studies*, 157–70, and Yves Benot, *La Révolution française et la fin des colonies 1789–1794* (Paris: La Découverte, 1987). An older source still worth consulting is H. D. Bradby, *The Life of Barnave*, 2 vs. (Oxford: Clarendon Press, 1915).

[19] *Courier de Provence*, no. 30, August 20–21, 1789.

[20] Garran-Coulon, *Rapport*, 1: 75–7, 85.

of independence. The move highlighted divisions among the colonists themselves – the North Province's local assembly raised troops to oppose it – and the French assembly reacted angrily to the colonists' pretensions. In a stormy debate in October 1790, they were reminded in strong terms that no part of the French empire had the right to legislate for itself, but at the same time, the metropolitan deputies reaffirmed their commitment to take no decisions about "the status of persons" in the colonies.[21] Within Saint-Domingue itself, the whites were also deeply divided. A "pompon blanc" faction looked to the king as its best protection against the excesses of the metropolitan revolutionaries, while a rival "pompon rouge" group adopted revolutionary rhetoric and denounced the remaining royal officials in the island.

While the colony's whites fought the representatives of the national government and each other, they also had to confront another group: the free people of color. Throughout the Americas, the possibility of manumission – of purchasing freedom or obtaining it as a gift – was one of the mechanisms that helped persuade slaves to conform to their masters' commands. Together with the chronic shortage of white women, which led white men to take black concubines and father mixed-race children whom they sometimes freed, the result was the creation of a free population that was wholly or partly of African descent. In the early days of French colonial settlement, when there were hardly any white women in the islands, white men had routinely formed households with black women. The offspring of these unions had been accepted as free, and white men often freed their black concubines as well. It was not unusual for mixed-race children to inherit their father's property. By the last decades of the eighteenth century, Saint-Domingue had become home to the largest and most influential free population of color in the Caribbean islands.[22] The 28,000 members of this group were scattered throughout the colony, and in some regions, particularly in rural parts of the West and South provinces, they outnumbered the whites. The 1685 Code noir had specified that free people of color were to have the same rights as whites, although it also insisted that they "retain a particular respect for their former masters."[23]

---

[21] Bradby, *Barnave*, 1: 342–6.
[22] On the history of the free population of color in eighteenth-century Saint-Domingue, see John D. Garrigus, *Before Haiti: Race and Citizenship in French Saint-Domingue* (New York: Palgrave MacMillan, 2006) and Yvan Debbasch, *Couleur et liberté. Le jeu du critère ethnique dans un ordre juridique esclavagiste. T. 1: L'affranchi dans les possessions françaises de la Caraïbe (1635–1833)* (Paris: Dalloz, 1967).
[23] Cited in Dubois and Garrigus, *Slave Revolution*, 53.

The wealthiest free colored families in Saint-Domingue owned large plantations and slaves; poorer members of the group were artisans, shop-keepers, and domestic servants. It was common for free colored women to manage the households and business affairs of whites, whether or not they also served as their sexual companions; these free colored *menag-ères* often accumulated solid fortunes of their own and created family dynasties.[24] Like the children of white families, the sons and daughters of prosperous free colored families were sent to France for their educa-tion, where some of them settled and married. The free colored popula-tion played an essential role in maintaining order in the colony: free men of color made up most of the police force that hunted down runaway slaves. The last decades before the Revolution saw contradictory trends in the relations between the whites and the free population of color. On the one hand, as the white population swelled with new immigrants from France after the end of the Seven Years' War in 1763, laws meant to enforce the distinction between the two racial groups multiplied. Notaries were forbidden to put honorific titles in front of the names of free people of color in legal documents, free people of color could not use the family names of their white ancestors, and they were barred from occupying administrative posts or entering the clergy. At the same time, however, social relations between whites and free people of color remained frequent, and many of the discriminatory laws were more or less ignored in practice. The French government, although its officials were responsible for these laws, sometimes saw the free people of color as the most loyal and dependable element in the population. Unlike the whites, they were rooted in the colony and were often said to have a greater inter-est in its long-term prosperity. In 1783, the intendant, Guillaume Léonard de Bellecombe, encouraged Julien Raimond, a wealthy *quarteron* (a man with three white grandparents), to go to France to lobby the government for better treatment for the group. Raimond was received politely at Versailles and allowed to present four lengthy memoranda urging reforms on their behalf, although no actual changes in policy were made.[25] From

---

[24] On the economic importance of the free colored population, see Stewart R. King, *Blue Coat or Powdered Wig: Free People of Color in Pre-Revolutionary Saint Domingue* (Athens, GA: University of Georgia Press, 2001), and Dominique Rogers. "Les Libres de couleur dans les capitales de Saint-Domingue."

[25] On Raimond and his mission to France in the 1780s, see John D. Garrigus, "Opportunist or Patriot? Julien Raimond (1744–1801) and the Haitian Revolution," *Slavery and Abolition* 28 (2007), 1–21, and Gabriel Debien, *Gens de couleur libres et colons de Saint-Domingue devant la Constituante (1789-mars 1790)* (Montréal: Revue d'histoire de l'Amérique française, 1951).

the point of view of the white colonists, however, the encouragement given to Raimond was another sign of the danger of metropolitan interference in colonial affairs.

Just as the early stages of the revolution in France revived antagonisms between nobles and commoners that had declined in the later decades of the old regime, the revolution also upset the delicate balance between whites and free people of color in Saint-Domingue. However willing many whites may have been to associate socially with free people of color, they were determined to maintain the color line when it came to the exercise of political power in the colony. For the free people of color like Raimond, the prospect of a colonial government monopolized by whites and determined to end the influence of the metropolitan government in the island's affairs was an unattractive one. Seeing how effectively the white colonists were organizing to promote their interests in Paris, free people of color formed their own lobbying group, determined to claim the equal rights that the National Assembly's declaration seemed to promise them. Their first initiative was to approach the Club Massiac, formed at the end of August 1789 by white colonists to represent their interests.[26] Both Julien Raimond and a more radical group calling itself the Société des colons américains met with the white planters in early September, only to be told firmly that the whites would not make any concessions to them.[27] Raimond then made contact with the *Société des amis des noirs*, the reform group founded by Brissot in February 1788, and persuaded them to support his campaign for parliamentary representation for the free colored population in the colonies.

From the fall of 1789 to the spring of 1791, Raimond and his supporters experienced repeated frustration in their efforts to overcome the power of the white colonial lobby. In December 1789, the Club Massiac and its supporters managed to block a proposal to grant the free men of color in Saint-Domingue two deputies in the National Assembly, and in March 1790, the legislature legitimized the all-white colonial assemblies that had been formed in the colony. Exasperated by the whites' intransigence, Vincent Ogé, another free man of color who had been part of the lobbying group in Paris, returned to Saint-Domingue in October 1790 and started a small rebellion in the mountains of the

[26] On the Club Massiac, see Gabriel Debien, *Les Colons de Saint-Domingue et la Révolution. Essai sur le Club Massiac (août 1789-août 1792)* (Paris: Armand Colin, 1951).

[27] *Extrait du procès-verbal de l'Assemblée des citoyens-libres et propriétaires de couleur des Isles et Colonies Françoises, constituée sous le titre de Colons américains* (N. p., 1789), 9–10.

North Province. Ogé, a wealthy property owner with extensive hold-ings in Cap Français, was careful not to raise the issue of abolishing slavery: he insisted that he was seeking only to create a situation in which the two classes of free people in the colony could work together on the basis of equality to preserve a system that benefitted them both. The whites responded violently, quashing Ogé's movement by force. Ogé fled across the border into Spanish Santo Domingo, but the authorities there turned him over to his enemies, and he was tortured to death in Le Cap in February 1791.[28]

Short-lived and unsuccessful as it was, Ogé's rebellion transformed the political situation on both sides of the ocean. In Saint-Domingue itself, his movement constituted the first armed revolt against the colo-nial system of racial hierarchy. Although Ogé did not try to raise the slaves against their masters, he had been prepared to at least threaten to do so in his efforts to persuade the whites to accede to his demands.[29] The intransigence of the whites and the brutality of Ogé's execution worsened relations between them and the free colored population in the island, preparing the way for the insurrection that broke out in the West Province, where the two groups were almost equal in size, in August 1791. In France, the news of the treatment inflicted on Ogé made revo-lutionary proponents of equality more determined than before to force the white colonists to accept, if not the abolition of slavery, at least the necessity of granting rights to a group that was legally free, owned prop-erty and met all the other qualifications for citizenship.[30]

The result was the stormiest of the National Assembly's heated debates about colonial issues, a four-day confrontation on May 12–15, 1791. The occasion was a proposal from the Assembly's colonial committee con-cerning the powers of colonial assemblies to regulate their own affairs, including the issue of the "status of persons." Deputies sympathetic to the free people of color, including Henri Grégoire, Maximilien Robespierre, Antoine Destutt de Tracy, and several others, objected that the commit-tee's proposal, like the arrangements approved in March 1790, permit-ted the continuing exclusion of the members of that group, in violation

[28] Dubois, *Avengers*, 87–8.
[29] See the testimony of the white planter, L.-F.-R. Verneuil, taken prisoner by Ogé, in Popkin, *Facing Racial Revolution*, 47.
[30] Petitions in favor of the free men of color were drafted by a number of provincial Jacobin clubs in the early spring of 1791: *Lettres des diverses sociétés des Amis de la Constitution, qui réclament les droits de citoyen actif en faveur des hommes de couleur des colonies* (Paris: Imprimerie du *Patriote françois*, 1791).

of their natural rights. Members of the colonial lobby responded with their familiar argument that if the Assembly could force them to grant rights to the free people of color, it could also go further and demand the emancipation of the slaves. Finally, the colonial deputy Médéric Louis Élie Moreau de Saint-Méry made a direct challenge to the radicals: he proposed an amendment stating explicitly that "no law concerning the status of slaves in the American colonies … would be made unless the colonial assemblies made a spontaneous and explicit request in that regard." His proposal set off a furor. "Monsieur Robespierre objected strongly to the word *slaves*," one newspaper account reported, "saying that it was an attempt to consecrate slavery … and that the colonies should be left to perish, if they were going to force us to renounce our principles!"[31] The best Robespierre and his allies could achieve, however, was to force the substitution of the word "non-libres" for "esclaves" in Moreau de Saint-Méry's amendment; despite the radicals' objections, the French constitution would give the slave owners the assurance they had demanded.

Before the Assembly could turn its attention to other issues, however, the deputy Jean-François Rewbell offered another amendment: he proposed to decree that while the colonists would retain authority over their internal affairs, they would have to grant political rights to free people of color whose parents had been free. The motive behind Rewbell's amendment remains obscure. Raimond and the other defenders of the free-colored cause had consistently argued that all members of their group deserved the same rights, so Rewbell was certainly not speaking for them. To defenders of white privilege like Moreau de Saint-Méry, Rewbell's proposal was as flagrant an interference with their promised power to determine "the status of persons" as a blanket grant of rights to the entire free colored population would have been, and they opposed it bitterly, walking out of the Assembly when it was approved. Rewbell probably was seeking a compromise that would allow the Assembly's radicals the satisfaction of having made it clear that race was not an absolute barrier to full citizenship, while at the same time ensuring – since only a small number of the free people of color would meet the requirements – that whites would retain a safe majority. The exhausted legislators finally accepted the proposal as "something everyone could rally around," as one journalist put it.[32] Rather than smoothing over

---

[31] *Gazette universelle*, May 14, 1791 (Assemblée nationale, May 13).
[32] *Gazette universelle*, May 16, 1791 (Assemblée nationale, May 15).

conflicts in Saint-Domingue, however, the decree of May 15, 1791 intensified them.

Although whites in several of France's other colonies were prepared
to accept the National Assembly's measure, in Saint-Domingue, the
reaction against it was ferocious. Governor Blanchelande was forced to
inform Paris that he would be unable to put it into effect.[33] A newly
elected Colonial Assembly, convened in early August 1791 and still composed exclusively of whites, prepared to resist this metropolitan pressure. Hoping to persuade the recalcitrant white colonists to compromise
on the issue, the National Assembly dispatched three commissioners –
Frédéric Mirbeck, Philippe Roume, and Edmond de Saint-Léger – to the
island. Some revolutionary groups in France had offered to sail for the
colony to help impose the movement's egalitarian principles, but this
First Commission was sent without any accompanying military forces.[34]
As the commissioners were making the two-month trip across the ocean,
events on both sides of the Atlantic took courses that they had not anticipated and that rendered their mission impossible. In France, the white
colonists' allies launched a furious campaign to overturn the Rewbell
proposal. On September 24, 1791, the National Assembly reversed its
vote of May 15 and once again left any decision concerning the rights of
nonwhites to the discretion of the white-controlled colonial assembly.[35]
By the time this news reached Saint-Domingue, however, both the colonists and the members of the Commission found themselves confronting
entirely new and far more serious problems: violent revolts of the slaves
in the North Province and of the free population of color in the West.

Although they broke out almost simultaneously, the slave insurrection and the free-colored movement were not directly connected. The
geography of Saint-Domingue separated the colony into isolated regions
with little communication between them. The North Province, where
the slave revolt began, was the richest, dominated by the large sugar
plantations that covered the flat expanse of the plain that spread out
south of Cap Français, the first major port reached by ships coming from

---

[33] Garran-Coulon, *Rapport*, 2: 106.
[34] In Bordeaux, members of the departmental National Guard unit offered to go to the
colonies to enforce the edict. *Extrait du registre des délibérations de la Chambre du
Commerce de la ville de Bordeaux, et adresses du Directoire du département de la
Gironde à l'Assemblée nationale; de la Société des Amis de la Constitution; du Club
du café national de la ville de Bordeaux, à l'Assemblée nationale: relatifs au décret
rendu par Elle le 14 Mai 1791, au sujet des colonies* (Paris, Imprimerie nationale, 24
May 1791).
[35] *Gazette universelle*, September 25, 1791.

France. The boom after 1763 had led to the establishment of coffee plantations on the slopes of the mountains surrounding the plain. Rugged mountains separated the region from the West Province, where sugar production was concentrated in the smaller plains around the colony's second-largest city, Port-au-Prince, and in the regions of the Artibonite valley and the plain of Cul-de-Sac. More centrally located than Cap Français, Port-au-Prince was the colony's administrative capital, but it was less accessible to shipping coming from France and lacked the urban amenities of its wealthier rival.

The island's highest mountains divided the West Province from the South Province, which extended along the southern coast to the tip of a long peninsula almost touching the British colony of Jamaica. Less populated than the other two provinces, and cut off from the trade routes to Europe and from the rest of the colony, the South Province was a notorious hotbed of smuggling and illegal trade with its British neighbor, with the Dutch islands off the coast of South America, and with the Spanish on the mainland. In both the West and the South, free people of color had benefitted from the fact that land was more available than in the North. Many of them had established small plantations growing coffee or indigo, crops that did not require as much investment as sugar.

Slaves of African origin greatly outnumbered the other population groups throughout the island. Purchased in West Africa and, in the last years before the Revolution, from areas as distant as the coast of Mozambique, those slaves who survived the horrors of the Middle Passage found themselves in a world very different from anything they had known in their homelands. Although slavery existed in Africa, it did not resemble the highly organized plantation system that Europeans had developed in the Americas. Driven to maximize their profits, Saint-Domingue planters worked their slaves intensively; the average life expectancy of a black brought from Africa was only seven to ten years after arrival in the colony, and the island needed a constant influx of new slaves to maintain their numbers. In 1789, roughly half of the slaves in the colony were *creoles*, born in the Americas; the other half, the *bossales*, had been shipped from Africa. Taken from widely separated regions of that continent and thrown together on the plantations, blacks developed a common language – Creole – and a set of religious beliefs – *vodou* – that incorporated rituals from their homelands with elements of European Christianity. Although all slaves were at the bottom of the colonial hierarchy, the slave population had its own internal status divisions. Some slaves, such as the *commandeurs*, or drivers who supervised

the plantation work gangs, or *atteliers*, and the skilled workmen who
directed the complicated operations involved in extracting the juice from
harvested sugar cane and boiling it to make sugar, occupied positions of
considerable authority and often enjoyed a good deal of de facto freedom. Most ordinary field work was actually performed by slave women,
who had fewer opportunities to acquire specialized skills. Female slaves
were also more exposed to sexual exploitation than men, but some of
them were able to obtain privileges through these liaisons with plantation owners and managers. Another important division was the one
separating rural and urban slaves. In the cities, slaves were more likely
to share the same households as their masters and to acquire specialized
skills that often enabled them to earn some income of their own and, if
they were fortunate, to eventually purchase their freedom.[36]

By 1791, slaves throughout the island had certainly become aware of
the ferment affecting their masters. Despite the ban on the circulation of
newspapers from France in the colony, whites and free people of color
publicly discussed the revolution on the other side of the Atlantic. Among
the slaves, the news of the revolution was translated into a persistent and
widespread rumor that the king of France had granted them three days a
week to work for their own benefit instead of their masters', but that the
whites in the colony were refusing to implement this reform.[37] The notion
that the king was concerned about the slaves made a certain amount of
sense: as we have seen, even before the Revolution, royal officials had
indeed attempted to make some reforms in the slavery system, and the
colonial whites' violent denunciations of the royal administration after
1789 could well have persuaded many slaves that the government was
on their side. Whether the ideas contained in the French revolutionaries' Declaration of Rights also inspired the slaves is less certain. By the
summer of 1791, those slaves who might have overheard their masters
discussing the news from France or come into contact with sailors and
other visitors from Europe could have been forgiven for concluding that
the revolutionaries had no intention of extending liberty and equality

---

[36] On slave life in pre-revolutionary Saint-Domingue, see Debien, *Esclaves*; Jean
Fouchard, *The Haitian Maroons: Liberty or Death*, trans. A. Faulkner Watts (New
York: Edward W. Blyden, 1981 (orig. 1972)); Gautier, *Soeurs de Solitude*; Bernard
Moitt, *Women and Slavery in the French Antilles, 1635–1848* (Bloomington,
IN: Indiana University Press, 2001); and Frédéric Régent, *La France et ses esclaves.
De la colonisation aux abolitions* (Paris: Grasset, 2007).

[37] Yves Bénot, "La chaîne des insurrections des esclaves dans les Caraïbes de 1789 à
1791," in Marcel Dorigny, dir., *Les abolitions de l'esclavage*, 179–86.

to any of the nonwhites in Saint-Domingue. With the exception of the decree of May 15, 1791, the implementation of which the white colonists had blocked, the National Assembly had consistently reaffirmed the power of the island's white slaveholders. Although the slaves may not have had a very clear notion of what was happening in France, they could certainly see that the revolution had divided the colony's free population and created a unique opportunity to challenge their oppressors.

The slave uprising that began in the North Province on the night of August 22–23, 1791 was, therefore, not an extension or an imitation of the revolutionary movement in France, but rather an autonomous initiative reflecting the blacks' own situation. The movement started on the large sugar plantations in the parishes close to Cap Français, where members of the slave elite – *commandeurs*, or drivers who led the work gangs, and occupants of other specialized positions, such as coachmen – had been able to form a network and hold at least one large organizational meeting to make their plans.[38] On one plantation after another, slave insurgents set fire to the highly flammable cane fields and attacked the masters' houses; within days, over 200 sugar plantations and hundreds of coffee plantations had been destroyed. The smoke from the fires could be clearly seen in Cap Français. The appeals for help drafted by the Colonial Assembly meeting in the city insisted that the blacks were also murdering as many whites as they could. A number of plantation owners and managers were indeed killed in the early days of the uprising, but the extent of the carnage was exaggerated. Women and children were generally spared, and rival black leaders executed the most violent of their own generals, Jeannot Bullet, in October 1791.[39] In a report written at the end of December, the members of the First Civil Commission, who had found themselves unexpectedly forced to deal with the uprising, estimated the number of whites killed in the first four months of the uprising at 400, a considerable toll but hardly enough to be considered as a campaign of extermination.[40] (See Figure 1.2.)

[38] Evidence concerning the outbreak of the insurrection has been painstakingly analyzed in David Geggus's classic article, "The Bois Caïman Ceremony," in Geggus, *Haitian Revolutionary Studies*, 81–92. Saint-Domingue's Colonial Assembly published a first account of the start of the uprising in a pamphlet, *Discours fait à l'assemblée nationale, le 3 novembre 1791, par MM. les Commissaires de l'Assemblée générale de la partie Françoise de Saint-Domingue* (Paris: Imprimerie nationale, 1791).

[39] For eyewitness accounts of the opening phase of the insurrection, see "The First Days of the Slave Insurrection" and "Inside the Insurgency: Gros's *Historick Recital*," in Popkin, *Facing Racial Revolution*, 49–58, 105–55.

[40] AN, D XXV 1, d. 4, report of December 23, 1791.

FIGURE I.2. The Slave Uprising of August 1791.

One of the rare images of the slave uprising in Saint-Domingue from the revolutionary era, this engraving, part of a series devoted to major events of the French Revolution, emphasizes the violence that was the main theme of proslavery propaganda and the burning of the plantations. The original caption blames the revolt on "the contradictory decrees of the National Assembly about the freedom of the blacks," although in fact, the legislators had never discussed abolishing slavery.

Source: Bibliothèque nationale de France.

Even though the slave uprising remained confined to the North Province, it clearly posed a serious threat to the entire colony. The crisis facing the whites was intensified by the simultaneous outbreak of an insurrection among the free colored population in several parts of the West Province, near Port-au-Prince. The goals of the two movements were not the same: the free colored insurgents, like Ogé a year earlier, were demanding equality for themselves, not freedom for the slaves. Their challenge to the whites, however, made it impossible for the West Province to send forces to help fight the slaves in the North. The royalist "pompons blancs" in the West, led by an aristocratic landowner named Hanus de Jumécourt, were willing to accept the demands of the free colored leaders in order to form a common front against the slaves; the two groups signed an agreement, called a concordat, promising full equality between the races.[41] The concordat was violently opposed, however, by the radical "pompons rouges," who had especially strong support from the poorer whites in Port-au-Prince and who claimed to be the strongest supporters of the French revolutionary movement. Several successive attempts to put the terms of the concordat into effect broke down, leading to renewed fighting and culminating in a confrontation that led to the burning down of much of Port-au-Prince in November 1791.[42] The partial destruction of the colony's second-largest city did not have the same apocalyptic quality as the burning of Cap Français a year and a half later, but it foreshadowed the journée of June 20, 1793: Port-au-Prince was not put to the torch by its slave population, but by the breakdown of trust between its white and free colored inhabitants.

Governor Blanchelande, who had been unable to control the rival white factions before the start of the insurrections, was even less successful in defeating the two rebellions that now confronted him. The demands on the colony's small garrison were overwhelming. When Blanchelande ordered troops to march from Cap Français to the districts most affected by the first wave of attacks, the city's white population cried that he was leaving them defenseless. Rural districts that had not yet come under assault also clamored for protection, forcing him to disperse his soldiers. He succeeded in setting up a line of guard posts to block the routes from the North Province to the West, known as the Cordon de l'Ouest, but he was unable to stop the insurgents from destroying the plantations in the area east of the northern plain. As the devastation spread, so did the white colonists' distrust of Blanchelande and the other commanders of the army. Unable to admit that the blacks might have organized a successful movement on their own, the panicked colonists insisted that the only explanation for the revolt's success was a conspiracy on the part of the colony's royal officials, whom they accused of deliberately planning

---

[41] *Concordat passé entre les citoyens du Port-au-Prince & les citoyens de couleur de la même partie de Saint-Domingue* (N. p., September 11, 1791).

[42] These events are retraced in Garran-Coulon, *Rapport*, 2: 138–71.

to destroy the colony as a means of discrediting the revolutionary movement in France. When the governor endorsed the concordats with the free people of color in the West, many whites accused him of rewarding a movement that had resorted to violence.[43]

When news of the slave uprising reached France at the end of October 1791, an equally divisive debate broke out in the newly elected Legislative Assembly that had replaced the original revolutionary legislature at the beginning of that month. The first reports from Saint-Domingue arrived at a critical moment. In the newly elected assembly, Jacobin radicals like Jacques-Pierre Brissot, the founder of the Société des amis des noirs, were pushing for a preventive war against the foreign powers who were sheltering noble émigrés and threatening, in the Pillnitz declaration issued in August 1791, to take action on behalf of Louis XVI, whose unsuccessful attempt to flee from France in June 1791 had confirmed his deep-rooted hostility to the Revolution. Suddenly, from the other side of the Atlantic, there arrived reports that confirmed the radicals' worst fears: an outbreak of violence that the royally appointed local authorities, all of them nobles, seemed suspiciously unable to control and that provided an opening for foreign powers to involve themselves in French affairs, since the Colonial Assembly in Saint-Domingue had appealed to Jamaica and the Spanish for aid before notifying Paris. Furthermore, the revolt threatened to force a diversion of French troops to the Caribbean at a moment when the Jacobin war hawks wanted them deployed on the Rhine. Brissot immediately voiced a suspicion that would poison French politics for years to come: "Don't we have here one branch of a great plan ...?"[44]

Fears of conspiracy had pervaded revolutionary politics since the movement's inception, but aside from the king's abortive flight to Varennes, the Saint-Domingue uprising was the most impressive piece of evidence of their reality. In a December 1791 speech, Brissot pointed out that the black revolt had started on August 22, 1791: "This date is full of meaning: they had just learned of the king's flight. Was it an accident that favored this rapprochement so favorable to the factious, of that flight so advantageous for them, of that so opportune revolt; or rather, didn't the news of the flight accelerate the revolt?"[45] Consequently, Brissot and his

[43] For the white "patriot" colonists' denunciations of Blanchelande, see AN, D XXV 46, d. 438.

[44] Jacques-Pierre Brissot, *Discours sur un projet de décret relatif à la révolte des Noirs, prononcé à l'Assemblée nationale, le 30 octobre 1791, par J. P. Brissot, député* (Paris: Imprimerie nationale, 1791), 8, 12.

[45] Jacques-Pierre Brissot, *Discours de J. P. Brissot, député, sur les causes des troubles de Saint-Domingue, prononcé à la séance du premier décembre 1791*, 48, 49, 67, 70.

supporters refused to endorse the sending of troops to the colony unless measures were taken to guarantee that the principles of the Revolution were going to be applied there. Above all, the Jacobins insisted that the colonial whites be forced to yield on the issue of equality for the free men of color. "The cause of the men of color is the cause of the patriots," Brissot proclaimed.[46] The white colonists, who had expected that the news of the slave uprising would silence their critics in France, were surprised by the hostility they encountered. When an official delegation appointed by the Colonial Assembly in Saint-Domingue addressed the Legislative Assembly in January 1792, "murmurs and catcalls greeted us," according to a report sent back to the colony; they were reduced to urging the Colonial Assembly to make concessions to the free people of color themselves, before the metropolitan legislature took the initiative on the matter.[47]

On March 24, 1792, five months after the news of the slave uprising in Saint-Domingue reached Paris, the Legislative Assembly finally made a response to the crisis. The measure it passed, approved by the king on April 4, 1792 and usually referred to as the law of that date, reflected the views of the Brissot party, whose members had taken control of the ministry just as the Assembly was debating the colonial problem.[48] Louis XVI had decided to accept their demand for an aggressive policy aimed at provoking war with Austria, a war the king secretly hoped would lead to the defeat of the Revolution and the restoration of his powers. The king also acquiesced in the Brissot group's policy in Saint-Domingue. The free men of color were granted complete equality with the white population; all the colonial political assemblies elected since the start of the Revolution were to be dissolved and replaced with new ones in which the free colored population would be represented alongside the whites. The avowed purpose of this measure was to reaffirm the metropole's control over the colony and to unify the free population there so as to form a solid bloc against the slaves. To carry out this policy, a new three-member Civil Commission was to be appointed, replacing the First Commission whose members had already abandoned their mission. The new commissioners, unlike their predecessors, were to be accompanied

[46] Brissot, *Discours ... du premier décembre 1791*, 6.
[47] Register of correspondence of the commissaires de l'Assemblée générale de la Partie française de St. Domingue près la Métropole, AN D XXV 76, letter of January 20, 1792.
[48] The announcement of the appointment of the Brissotin ministers interrupted a speech by the procolonial deputy Vaublanc. *Annales patriotiques*, March 25, 1792 (Legislative Assembly, March 24).

by a substantial military force, to overawe the colonists and to end the slave uprising.

The law of April 4, 1792 represented a sharp reversal of the Revolution's colonial policy. Instead of conceding extensive autonomy to the white colonial population, the metropolitan government now intervened aggressively on the sensitive subject of the "status of persons." The debates of the previous five months left little doubt that the Jacobins were determined, not just to see a token number of free people of color allowed to participate in a white-dominated colonial government, but to give the newly minted "citizens of 4 April," whom they regarded as the only loyal element in the Saint-Domingue population, a decisive voice in colonial affairs. Like so many of Brissot's policies, the law of April 4, 1792 was a mixture of high principles and political delusions, the most dangerous of which was that it would both facilitate victory over the slave insurrection and pave the way for the eventual abolition of slavery. In his main speech on the subject, Brissot made no secret of his conviction that slavery was inherently unjust and fated eventually to disappear, a conviction he had expressed many times since the founding of the Société des amis des noirs in February 1788. At the same time, however, he had insisted that it was necessary to grant rights to the free people of color because a slave society needed "numerous and faithful guardians to prevent [slave] revolts, and the men of color are, in the nature of things, the only defenders against revolts."[49] Just as he recklessly steered France into war against Austria, confident that revolutionary zeal would guarantee an easy victory, he also confidently assumed that the measures included in the law of April 4, 1792 would quickly bring the troubles in Saint-Domingue to an end. Events were soon to prove otherwise: the attempt to enforce the law would indeed shatter the system of white domination in the colony, but in the process it would set off a string of events that would prove Brissot's contradictory policy impossible and would ultimately help cost him his own head.

While the debates leading up to the law of April 4, 1792 dragged on in France, the uprising begun on August 22–23 had experienced its own problems. The conspirators had apparently hoped for a rapid and complete triumph over the whites. A plantation manager taken captive on the first night of the insurrection was told by his captors that their plan "consisted of nothing less than the destruction of all the whites except some who didn't own property, some priests, some surgeons, and some

[49] Brissot, *Discours ... du premier décembre 1791*, 59.

women, and of setting fire to all the plantations and making themselves masters of the country."[50] The free men of color in the North Province's rural areas, a relatively small minority, initially sided with the slaves, although their support was less than wholehearted: many of them had seen their own plantations destroyed. Their initial momentum enabled the insurgents to sweep through the Northern Plain and then, in October, to destroy the plantations in the northeast section of the province, but they were unable to storm the cities of Cap Français and Fort Dauphin or to stand up to the white military units sent to attack them.

By mid-November 1791, the high hopes with which the movement had begun were fading. The insurgents' principal leader, Boukman Dutty, was killed in battle, and armed free men of color began defecting to the whites. An "Evaluation of the number of Negroes in Revolt in the Ten Parishes in Insurrection," published in Cap Français in the fall of 1791, was meant to help sustain white morale by refuting exaggerated claims about the size of the revolt, but its author's calculations probably had some basis in fact. By his estimate, some two-thirds of the 68,664 slaves in the affected area were unable to fight because they were women and children or else too elderly or infirm to take up arms. The author estimated that only half of the actual insurgents had any weapons at all, and that only a fifth had firearms. The heavy casualties inflicted by the whites in the early stages of the revolt had reduced the insurgents' numbers, and a considerable number of blacks had surrendered to the white forces. Furthermore, as this author noted, the shortage of food supplies prevented the insurgents from assembling large numbers of men in a single place; instead, they were compelled to establish a number of small camps in dispersed locations.[51] By late 1791, the black leaders themselves were anticipating the imminent arrival of military forces from France, a fear inculcated in their minds by some of their white captives; they could calculate that if news had been sent to France in late August, a response might be expected by the end of the year. Jean-François Papillon and Georges Biassou, the two commanders who had emerged as the primary leaders of the black movement,

---

[50] "La Révolution de Saint-Domingue," cited in Popkin, *Facing Racial Revolution*, 53. In his reconstruction of the insurgents' original plans, David Geggus surmises that they hoped to capture Cap Français as well as attacking the plantations. Geggus, "Bois Caïman Ceremony," in Geggus, *Haitian Revolution Studies*, 88.

[51] Lefèvre, "Evaluation de la quantité des nègres révoltés dans les dix paroisses en insurrection" (Cap : Imprimerie de l'Assemblée prov. du Nord, n.d.), in AN, D XXV 113, d. 987.

consequently made peace overtures to the colonial assembly, an initiative in which the future Toussaint Louverture appeared for the first time as an active participant in Saint-Domingue's history. According to a group of free people of color who acted as mediators, the black leaders were prepared to end the uprising in exchange for four concessions: (1) amnesty and personal liberty for all the leaders of the revolt; (2) a general amnesty for all the blacks who had taken part in the revolt; (3) a guarantee that the black leaders could leave for a foreign country of their choice, if they chose to do so; and (4) the right of those leaders to keep whatever property they had in their possession, provided that they assisted in "making the slaves return to their duty."[52] Toussaint reportedly persuaded Jean-François and Biassou to reduce the number of emancipations they sought from 300 to 50.[53]

The black leaders themselves expressed some doubt about their ability to compel their own followers to accept these terms, which would have given the rank-and-file nothing but the promise of forgiveness, but they were never put to the test: the white colonists refused any concessions and insisted on an unconditional end to the revolt. The black leaders warned them that they were demanding "something both impossible and dangerous. A hundred thousand men are in arms ... and you will realize from that that we are entirely dependent on the general will, and what a will! That of a multitude of negroes from the Coast [of Africa] who barely know two words of French but who, however, in their country were accustomed to making war ... " The author of this letter went on to say that the difficulty of getting these fighters to put down their arms was increased because of the "false principles" that had taken root among them, principally the belief that "the king has given the slaves three days [to work for themselves] a week." Nine days later, another letter from the black generals urged the whites to recognize the necessity of preventing white masters' abuse of their slaves: "Improve the condition of this class of men so necessary to the colony, and we dare to assure you that they will take up their work once again and will return to order."[54] Nevertheless, one can see that their aspirations had been

---

[52] "Adresse à l'Assemblée générale de la partie française de St. Domingue, par MM. les citoyens de couleur, de la Grande Rivière, Ste. Suzanne et autres quartiers malheureusement enveloppés dans le funeste événement du 23 aoust dernier," n.d., in AN, D XXV 1, d. 4.

[53] Gros, "Historick Recital," in Popkin, *Facing Racial Revolution*, 147.

[54] AN, D XXV 1, d. 4; Dubois and Garrigus, *Slave Revolution in the Caribbean*, 102.

greatly reduced: they no longer hoped to gain control of the colony, or to eliminate the whites, or even to abolish the system of slavery.

Despite the opposition of the white diehards in the Colonial Assembly, the members of the First Commission, who had arrived in the colony to find the slave revolt spreading through the North Province, managed to negotiate the release of a number of white prisoners, but they were unable to work out an arrangement under which the insurgents might have put down their arms. The situation settled into a stalemate: the blacks controlled most of the inland parts of the North Province, but the whites held the cities along the coast, and the Cordon de l'Ouest kept the insurgents from making contact with slaves in the rest of the colony. Preoccupied with problems in the west and the south, Blanchelande made no effort to dislodge Jean-François and Biassou from their positions. The two warlords divided up the territory they had overrun, with Biassou establishing his headquarters near Dondon, in the mountains south of the northern plain, and Jean-François basing himself further to the east. Both sides were awaiting the arrival of more troops from France and trying to anticipate what the next development in the metropole's colonial policy would mean for them.

Between the failure of the peace negotiations in December 1791 and the arrival of the Second Commission in September 1792, little actual fighting took place in the North Province. The violence that had characterized the start of the insurrection subsided; whites who found themselves in insurgent-controlled territory were watched over to keep them from leaving but not otherwise molested.[55] Near Cap Français, the plantation owner François Carteaux, was able to continue working his estate with the help of his slaves, even though, as he noted, they could easily have joined the rebellion at any time. One reason they didn't, he suspected, was that they drew their own conclusions about living conditions among the insurgents from the fact that the latter regularly visited the plantation during the night to forage for food that was evidently in short supply in their camps.[56] To obtain munitions, Jean-François and Biassou, the two principal insurgent leaders, resorted to selling other blacks, particularly women and children who could not serve as fighters, to the Spanish in Santo Domingo, in exchange for muskets and gunpowder.[57]

---

[55] See the accounts of Marie Jeanne Jouette, the abbé de la Haye, and the doctor Thibal, in Popkin, *Facing Racial Revolution*, 156–68.

[56] Carteaux, cited in Popkin, *Facing Racial Revolution*, 176–7.

[57] [Alexis] Beaubrun Ardouin, *Etudes sur l'histoire d'Haïti, suivies de la vie du général J.-M. Borgella* (Port-au-Prince: Dr. François Dalencour, 1958 (orig. 1853)), 1: 64.

Finding themselves forced to continue the insurrection after the failure of the negotiations at the end of 1791, the black leaders also had
to reformulate their objectives. A "lettre de Jean-François, Biassou et
Belair," supposedly addressed to the new commissioners on their way
from France and dated July 1792, is the major piece of evidence about
their thinking in this period.[58] The authenticity of this document has
been disputed: David Geggus, the most scrupulous student of the archival sources about the Haitian Revolution, objects that "the language of
the text has a suspiciously inauthentic look. Its combination of sophisticated vocabulary and rhetoric with simplistic errors of spelling and
grammar makes it unlike any other surviving text from this milieu." In
his view, the text, known only through two versions published in France
in 1793, was probably concocted by a royalist colonist in an effort to put
the blame for the insurrection on the French revolutionaries.[59] Geggus's
opinions always deserve to be taken seriously, but in this case, his arguments are not entirely convincing. The spelling and grammar in the
"lettre" are similar to those found in many of the letters from Jean-
François and Biassou, which are presumed to have been dictated to their
white or free colored secretaries. The free colored population in particular was certainly familiar with the language used by the revolutionaries in France, and the combination of a religious argument – that all
men are made in God's image – with a reference to natural right might
suggest the influence of one of the white priests with whom the black
leaders were in contact during this period. Furthermore, the program
suggested in the letter is not unrelated to the demands the black leaders
had put forward in the 1791 negotiations. Unlike any other documents
discussed here, this letter does make explicit reference to the principles
of the French Revolution.

Although the "lettre" is written in ungrammatical French with many
spelling mistakes, its meaning is unmistakable: "Placed on earth like
you, being all children of one father created in the same image we are

---

[58] Nathalie Piquionne, "Lettre de Jean-François, Biassou et Belair, juillet 1792,"
Chemins critiques, 3 (1997), 206–10. The letter was originally published in two places
in France in 1793: as part of the royalist colonel Cambefort's defense of his conduct in
Saint-Domingue, *Quatrième partie du Mémoire justificatif, de Joseph-Paul-Augustin
Cambefort, colonel du régiment du Cap* (Paris, 1793), pp. 4–11, and in the antislavery
journalist Claude Milscent's *Créole patriote*, February 9, 1793.

[59] David Geggus, "Print Culture and the Haitian Revolution: The Written and the
Spoken Word," in *Liberty! Egalité! ¡Independencia!: Print Culture, Enlightenment,
and Revolution in the Americas, 1776–1838* (American Antiquarian Society, 2007),
89, 91.

therefore your equals according to natural right and if it has pleased nature to diversify the colors of the human species it is no crime to be black or any advantage to be white." The document refers explicitly to the Declaration of the Rights of Man and insists that it is incompatible with slavery; it further blames the whites for proposing to grant liberty to the black leaders in exchange for their help in maintaining the rest of the black population in slavery. Despite this radical language, the letter ends with some less extreme proposals: if the whites would recognize the blacks' freedom, grant amnesty to those who had participated in the insurrection, and have the Spanish government guarantee the terms of the agreement, the insurgents, for their part, would return to their plantations and resume their work, in exchange for a fixed salary.

The call for "general liberty" for the slaves is, of course, much more radical than the demands of 1791, but the request for amnesty repeats a point from those negotiations, and the suggestion that the agreement be guaranteed by the Spanish reflects the fact that the insurgents had found them willing to exercise a neutrality favorable to their cause. The black leaders' promise to put down their arms and lead the former slaves back to their plantations paralleled their offers in late 1791, although the demand that work now be salaried went beyond what had been sought earlier. Finally, the document is consistent with the black leaders' frequently proclaimed loyalty to the king: its proposals were to be submitted to both the king and the National Assembly for their approval. The program is thus more moderate than the one outlined by Boukman's followers at the start of the insurrection but more extensive than what the black leaders had been willing to settle for in December 1791, when, under the influence of one of their white captives, they feared the imminent arrival of French forces. By July 1792, they might well have concluded that they had been misled, since few French troops had arrived, and they could well have decided that the situation warranted a more expansive bargaining position.

While the black insurgents waited to see how events were going to develop, the island's whites were also being driven to reconsider their position. The intransigent attitude with which they had reacted to both the National Assembly's decree of May 15, 1791 and the outbreak of the slave insurrection in August 1791 could no longer be maintained. News of the law of April 4, 1792 granting full equality to the free people of color demonstrated that the metropolitan government would not brook further defiance on this issue, and the whites' inability to subdue the slave revolt made it clear that they were dependent on metropolitan assistance to regain their properties. In the West Province, armed free men of color and their "pompon blanc" allies created an assembly of their own, the Council of Peace and Union, that challenged the all-white Colonial Assembly located in Cap Français. In June 1792, Blanchelande arrived in Port-au-Prince, where the armed free people of color had been keeping their white antagonists under siege, and brokered a shaky reconciliation between the two groups on the basis of acceptance of the April 4, 1792 decree. He also gave his imprimatur to the Council of Peace and Union.[60] It was his last major success before his ill-fated assault on the black "republic" at Platons. Across the colony, whites, blacks, and free people of color waited anxiously to learn what the arrival of the new commissioners from France would mean for the violent conflicts that had torn the colony apart for the previous three years. Nowhere was anxiety about the future greater than in the colony's principal city, the northern port of Cap Français. The slave insurrection had begun in the sugar-growing plains outside Le Cap, but its ultimate impact on the colony would be decided in the city itself.

[60] *Relation du séjour de M. de Blanchelande, lieutenant pour le roi au gouvernement général de Saint-Domingue, au Port-au-Prince. Par un Créole* (Port-au-Prince: Chaidron, 1792); *Moniteur général de la partie française de Saint-Domingue,* (hereafter *Moniteur général*) July 17, 1792 (Blanchelande proclamation of July 3, 1792).

2

Municipal Revolution in a Colonial City

Although the insurrections that began in Saint-Domingue in 1791 started in rural areas, it is no accident that the crucial confrontation that determined their outcome took place in the colony's main city. Saint-Domingue's main commercial port was the crossroads where the colonial world and the system of slavery met the urban civilization of the Enlightenment and the radical challenge of the French Revolution. The city's layout and architecture reflected European influences, but the brown and black faces of the majority of the city's inhabitants revealed their African heritage, and the Creole language spoken in its streets was a symbol of the new "American" culture created by the interaction of Europeans and Africans in the New World. Just as the unique nature of politics and social conflict in Paris made the revolution there different from the movement in the rest of France, the special characteristics of Cap Français – its geography, its social and racial structure, and the local political struggles that developed after 1789 – helped account for the events that took place there in June 1793. The destruction of the city during those events marked the end of an experiment in which members of different racial groups had lived together, on unequal terms, to be sure, but in relationships that were not based solely on force and violence, and under conditions that offered members of the nonwhite population some real opportunities to make a better life for themselves.

Thanks to the more than 200 pages devoted to the city in Médéric Louis Élie Moreau de Saint-Méry's *Description topographique, physique, civile, politique et historique de la partie française de l'isle Saint-Domingue*, we know more about Cap Français on the eve of the Revolution than about any other colonial urban community of

the time.[1] Nowhere are the contradictions inherent in the confrontation between colonial realities and the transatlantic urban culture of
the Enlightenment era more apparent than in Moreau de Saint-Méry's
life and writings. Indefatigable defender of slavery and racial hierarchy,
Moreau de Saint-Méry was also deeply committed to scientific inquiry
and the propagation of knowledge.[2] A Freemason and one of the founders
of Cap Français's learned society, the Cercle des Philadelphes, Moreau
promoted every initiative to expand cultured sociability in the city: the
publication of newspapers, the creation of reading rooms, the support of
the local theater. Most importantly, he made himself the major colonial
representative of the encyclopedist movement, devoting himself to the
collection of information about Saint-Domingue, and particularly of the
institutions of Cap Français. Even as he was writing this description of
an urban society based on slave labor in 1789, however, Moreau was
also taking a central role in the revolutionary movement for liberty in
France. So at home was he in the metropolitan community of Paris that
he found himself, on July 14, 1789, presiding over the assembly of elec-
tors of the capital's Third Estate and helping to establish the emergency
city government that took over power there after the storming of the
Bastille. At that crucial moment, he was "the arbiter of our destinies,"
one eyewitness wrote.[3]

Thoroughly engaged in promoting the Revolution in France, Moreau
de Saint-Méry nevertheless remained a man of the colonial world. Elected
to represent his birthplace, Martinique, in the National Assembly, he
defended slavery, white racial privilege, and colonial autonomy. It was
his motion to explicitly legitimize the institution of slavery in the French
constitution in May 1791 that provoked Robespierre's cry, "Perish
the colonies rather than a principle!" Well as he knew the colonies,
however, Moreau failed to anticipate the troubles about to break out
there. In Paris in 1791, he published a collection of elegant engravings

[1] Médéric Louis Elié Moreau de Saint-Méry, *Description topographique, physique, civile,
politique et historique de la partie française de l'isle Saint-Domingue*, nouv. ed. by Blanche
Maurel and Etienne Taillemite, 3 vs. (Paris: Société de l'histoire des colonies françaises,
1958), 1: 294–531.

[2] On Moreau de Saint-Méry, see Anthony Louis Elicona, *Un colonial sous la Révolution en
France et en Amérique : Moreau de Saint-Méry* (Paris: Jouve, 1934) ; James E. McClellan,
Colonialism and Science: Saint-Domingue in the Old Regime (Baltimore, MD: John
Hopkins University Press, 1992); and Dominique Taffin, ed., *Moreau de Saint-Méry ou
les ambiguïtés d'un créole des Lumières* (Martinique: Société des amis des archives et de
la recherche sur le patrimoine culturel des Antilles, 2006).

[3] J. B. Dusaulx, *L'Oeuvre de sept jours* (Paris, 1790), 44.

of Saint-Domingue's cities, which appeared just as the orderly white-dominated society they depicted began to disintegrate.[4] By the time his monumental *Description* appeared in print in 1798, the slave colony it recorded no longer existed, and Moreau himself, forced to flee from both France and Saint-Domingue, was living in Philadelphia, the birthplace of the American abolitionist movement.[5]

Moreau de Saint-Méry compiled his description of Cap Français in 1788, just as his French contemporary Louis-Sébastien Mercier was completing his celebrated *Tableau de Paris*. Mercier's enormous project – in its original form, it ran to twelve volumes – depicted the French metropolis as a gigantic organism that defied rational analysis or control. Its origins lost in the mist of time, Paris was an accumulation of buildings, institutions, and customs built up over the centuries, without any plan. Fascinated by the city's variety and energy, and full of piecemeal ideas for its improvement, Mercier nevertheless despaired of making sense of it for his readers. All he could do was describe for them the inextricable contradictions that defined it: wealth and poverty, magnificence and squalor, cosmopolitanism and provinciality.[6] The colonial city described by Moreau was quite different. He was able to document virtually every step of Le Cap's development, from the first settlement in the late 1600s to the latest improvements in the 1780s. Cap Français's streets, "drawn with surveyor's chains and crossing each other at right angles," were nothing like the crooked medieval alleyways of Paris.[7] Moreau understood that the biggest difference between the European and the colonial city was the dominance of the black slave population in the latter. The new arrival from France could not help but remark that "one sees four or five black or dark faces for every white one," he wrote.[8] Although he commented occasionally on the difficulty of keeping the slave population properly disciplined, Moreau did not see their presence as an obstacle to the creation of a rational, modern city. If anything, the

4 [Ponce], *Recueil des vues des lieux principaux de la colonie française de Saint-Domingue, gravées par les soins de M. Ponce* (Paris: Moreau de Saint-Méry, 1791).

5 Moreau recorded his struggle to publish the work and his impressions of Philadelphia in a journal, published as *Moreau de Saint-Méry's American Journey 1793–1798*, trans. and ed. Kenneth Roberts and Anna M. Roberts (Garden City, NY: Doubleday, 1947).

6 Jeremy D. Popkin, "Editor's Preface: A City in Words: Louis-Sébastien Mercier's *Tableau de Paris*," in Louis-Sébastien Mercier, *Panorama of Paris*, trans. Helen Simpson and Jeremy D. Popkin, ed. Jeremy D. Popkin (University Park, PA: Penn State University Press, 1999), 1–19.

7 Moreau de Saint-Méry, *Description ... de la partie française*, 1: 299.

8 Moreau de Saint-Méry, *Description ... de la partie française*, 1: 296.

fact that most of the city's inhabitants were slaves offered its administrators the opportunity to impose regulations without having to take the opinions of the population into account, as their Parisian equivalents were obliged to do.

Cap Français, as Moreau explained to his readers, owed its location to its harbor, the most accessible arrival point for ships arriving in Hispaniola from Europe. Trade winds made it easy to reach the island's north coast – Columbus's first landing took place there in 1492 – but a line of reefs threatened oceangoing vessels trying to reach the shore. Near Le Cap, however, an opening in this barrier allowed shipping to reach its harbor, easily spotted from a distance because of the towering Morne du Cap peak above the town.[9] Once ashore, voyagers discovered a city built in the natural basin at the foot of the mountain. The terrain sloped uphill from the harbor in the east to the base of the *morne* that surrounded the city on its western and northern sides, but not steeply enough to disrupt the rectangular grid of streets laid out early in the eighteenth century. Two roads ran south from Le Cap, connecting it to the rich plantations of the colony's northern plain. The first went through the hamlet of Haut du Cap and continued to the southwest; the second, reached by taking a ferry across a stream running through the marshy terrain along the shore, led to the parish of Petite Anse and to the coastal plain southeast of the city. (See Figure 2.1.)

Unlike any of Saint-Domingue's other urban settlements, Le Cap was a city built of stone, much of it carried across the Atlantic from quarries in France. Many of its houses were sizable two-story constructions, and it could boast of no fewer than 79 public buildings, a half dozen public squares, a theater seating 1,500 spectators, up-to-date hospitals for both men and women, and a large barracks complex for its military garrison. Many of the city's most impressive features were quite new: paving of the streets had begun only in 1776, new public baths had been opened on the waterfront in 1788, and a system of aqueducts to supply the major public institutions was completed in the same year. "Le Cap has tripled [in size] in fifty years," Moreau boasted; he certainly did not imagine that this upward curve of progress was about to stop.[10]

Le Cap's architecture followed European patterns, but its climate was distinctly tropical. From April to October, the heat was unbearable for those accustomed to the weather in France. "In general, the nights are as

---

[9] Moreau de Saint-Méry, *Description ... de la partie française*, 1: 295–6, 461.
[10] Moreau de Saint-Méry, *Description ... de la partie française*, 1 :479.

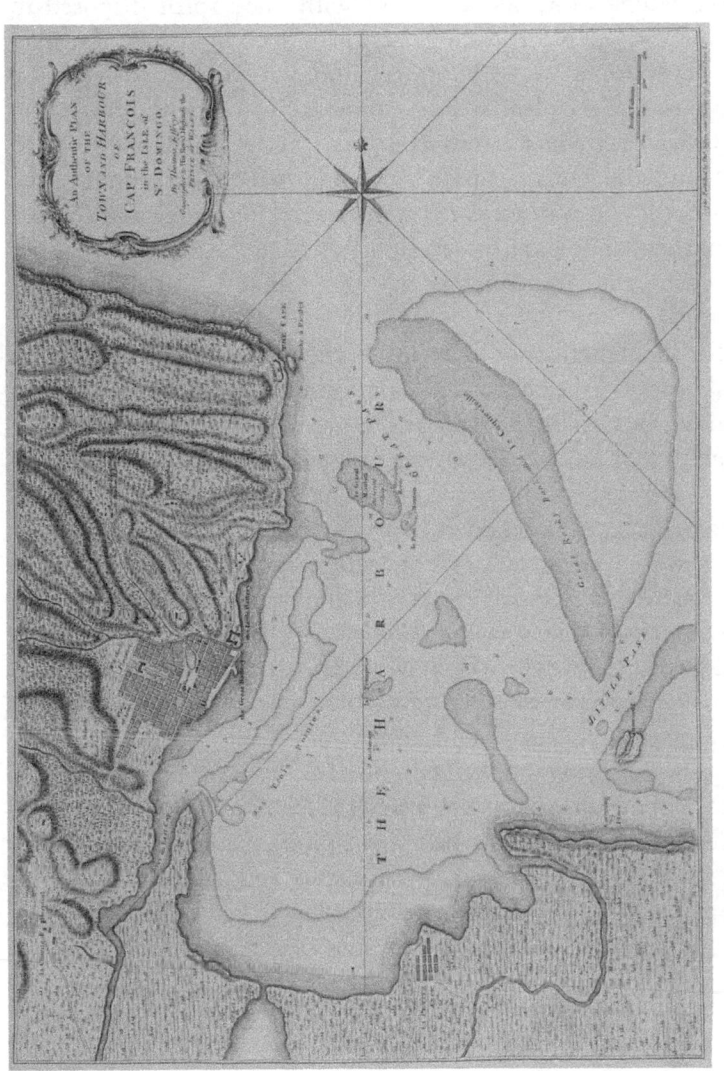

FIGURE 2.1. Le Cap, its harbor and hinterlands.

A British map from 1769 shows the city of Le Cap surrounded by the steep *mornes* to its north and west. The passages between the coastal reefs that made the city's harbor accessible are clearly marked. Ships picking up sugar and coffee from the plantations on the northern plain often anchored off the landing at la Petite Anse, which was more convenient than the city itself.

Source: Leeds University Library.

hot as the days," Moreau wrote, "and sleep is more a matter of exhaustion than a state of rest and recuperation of vital forces." During the winters, winds from the north brought some relief; the cooler nights made sleep more refreshing, "and if this sensation is mixed with the sound of the falling rain, one dozes off with one's spirit disposed to dream of even sweeter pleasures," he recalled. Such moments of respite were rare, however, and, in addition to its normal weather patterns, Le Cap was exposed to "violent storms, inundations of rain, devastating droughts, windstorms, hurricanes and those movements that seem to shake the foundations of the earth." The high *morne* surrounding the town on the west and north created a microclimate wetter and foggier than most of the island, and its steep slopes "add to the noise of thunder, whose claps echo and vibrate before the sound finally escapes from this enclosure."[11]

Amid this combination of rational European town planning and exotic Caribbean weather lived a population that Moreau estimated at 18,500, making Le Cap in 1788 about the size of Boston; modern scholarship suggests that he may have exaggerated the figures slightly.[12] Of these, 10,000 were black slaves, as compared to 3,500 whites, 1,500 free people of color, and 3,500 outsiders from Europe: at least 1,000 soldiers in the garrison and 2,500 sailors from ships in the harbor that could hold up to 600 vessels. The slaves were the majority of the city's inhabitants, but the ratio of slaves to free people was considerably lower than in the rural districts; by comparison, Moreau gave the population of the coffee-growing parish of Valière as 160 whites, 160 free people of color, and 2,000 slaves.[13] In Le Cap, members of different racial groups lived in close proximity. As Moreau described, most houses were built to occupy one-quarter of one of the city's square blocks, with an elegant façade facing the street and a rectangular courtyard behind. A white family might occupy the rooms at the front of the building, while slaves and other tenants lived in smaller spaces around the courtyard.[14] Although the city's free colored population was relatively small, members of the group – a

---

[11] Moreau de Saint-Méry, *Description ... de la partie française*, 1: 509, 511.
[12] Moreau de Saint-Méry, *Description ... de la partie française*, 1: 479–80; for a critical examination of his figures, see David Geggus, "The Major Port Towns of Saint Domingue in the Later Eighteenth Century," in Franklin W. Knight and Peggy K. Liss, eds., *Atlantic Port Cities: Economy, Culture, and Society in the Atlantic World, 1650–1850* (Knoxville, TN: University of Tennessee Press, 1991), 102–8.
[13] Moreau de Saint-Méry, *Description ... de la partie française*, 1: 161.
[14] Moreau de Saint-Méry, *Description ... de la partie française*, 1: 300.

majority of whom where women – owned property throughout the city; there was no pattern of residential segregation.[15] What the French scholar Anne Pérotin-Dumon has written about other major colonial cities in the French Caribbean applies to Cap Français: "The town brings people together in a limited space and this makes it hard to avoid interaction among members of different groups, whose numerical disequilibrium is also less marked."[16]

Like most colonial cities, Cap Français existed to support its rural hinterland by providing governmental services and organizing the exchange of colonial products for European goods. Counting the military garrison, one-third of the city's whites were employed by the colonial administration.[17] Although the smaller city of Port-au-Prince in the West Province was the colony's official capital, Cap Français was too important to be left without official institutions. It had courts, prisons, hospitals, and administrative offices connected with the port, the regulation of commerce, and a host of other activities. The buildings housing most of these institutions occupied the northwest quadrant of the town, with the steep slopes of the *morne* rising above them. A ravine that served as an open sewer emptying into the sea ran just north of the government complex, marking the town boundary. From this "upper town," and particularly from the impressive Government House, taken over from the Jesuits when the order was expelled in 1763, "the view extends over the sea and the plain … One sees the masts that mark the harbor, one grasps the great size of the city," as Moreau wrote.[18] On June 20, 1793, the republican commissioners would be able to watch the sailors coming to attack them from the Government House windows. A formal garden in front of the Government House was the city's most popular promenade; on June 20, the commissioners' defenders would take up positions behind the iron fence surrounding it. Between the Government House and the *morne* stood the *casernes*, the barracks for the garrison. The large open plaza north of the barracks, known as the Champ de Mars, was the site of several explosive confrontations in the months leading up to the journée of June 20, 1793.

The part of the city nearest the harbor and its quays, the bustling "lower town," was the merchants and seamen's quarter, separated from the more elevated upper town by the Place Montarcher. "I was surprised

---

[15] Rogers, "Libres de couleur," 434.
[16] Anne Pérotin-Dumon, *La ville aux îles, la ville dans l'île*, 465.
[17] Geggus, "Major Port Towns," 109.
[18] Moreau de Saint-Méry, *Description … de la partie française*, 1: 384.

at the activity everywhere," one visitor wrote in 1791. "The stores bordering the wharf were immense, and filled with precious merchandise. A large population of all countries and colors passed in the streets. On all sides, workmen were ardently busy with all kinds of labor that is essential to a seaport. Some were lowering aboard hogsheads of sugar or kegs of indigo; others were baling cotton or filling sacks of coconuts. Here were spread out still-wet coffee beans; there were piles of wood pulp with which to make dye, or men laboriously rolling numerous logs of mahogany. While many carts departed for rural centers filled with wares from Europe, others were coming to discharge the rich products of this country upon the docks, whence they were carried to waiting vessels."[19] (See Figure 2.2.)

The ships anchored offshore formed a floating extension of the city. In making his estimate of the number of seamen to be counted as part of the population, Moreau de Saint-Méry calculated that on an ordinary day, there would be some 80 French ships, 30 smaller American vessels – in 1784, France's navigation act, the *exclusif*, had been modified to allow trade with the new republic, universally referred to in Saint-Domingue as "New England" – and perhaps an additional 10 foreign ships in the harbor, along with several dozen small vessels serving local needs.[20] Merchant ships often stayed in the harbor for weeks or months while their captains sold their cargoes and bargained for goods to carry on their return voyage. Slave traders were warned that the city's buyers were finicky: "At Cap Français, they care a lot about the appearance of the male blacks as well as the women."[21] While they were in port, the ships' crews were very much a part of the city's life. Duty parties rowed ashore at dawn every day to pick up fresh water and food. Ships' captains set up shop near the waterfront to trade their wares for the coveted colonial goods they would take back to France or to New England. On Sunday mornings, sailors swarmed to the city's *marché aux blancs*, supplementing their wages by selling small items they had brought from abroad for

---

[19] [Anon.], *My Odyssey*, cited in Popkin, *Facing Racial Revolution*, 68–9.
[20] Moreau de Saint-Méry, *Description ... de la partie française*, 1: 480. A French slave trader who visited the city in 1777 counted more than 150 ships in the harbor. Manuscript of Jacques Proa, in Régis Antoine, "Aventures d'un jeune négrier français d'après un manuscrit inédit du XVIIIe siècle," *Notes africaines* no. 142 (April 1974), 53.
[21] "Journal des routes faites par Pascal Marie Urbain Cauvin, lieutenant à bord du brigantin *Le Raphael*," (1789), cited in Evelyne Camara, Isabelle Dion and Jacques Dion, *Esclaves. Regards de Blancs 1672–1913* (Marseille: Archives nationales d'outre-mer, 2008), 52.

FIGURE 2.2. Le Cap viewed from the ocean side.

One of the engravings from Moreau de Saint-Méry's portfolio of views of Saint-Domingue, published in Paris in 1791, shows the city of Cap Français as seen from the landing at la Petite Anse. Merchants' warehouses line the quays, and ships crowd the harbor. Populated by figures in European dress, the picture provides no hint of the importance of slavery to the city's daily life.

Source: The Library Company of Philadelphia.

their personal account. Ailing seamen were sent ashore for care; those in better health landed in the afternoons and evenings to drink and to look for entertainment. "I went every evening, either to the promenade, or to visit some white ladies, or to see some very pretty and very rich mulatresses, and sometimes to the theater," one French merchant recalled.[22] (Figure 2.3)

Prior to the Revolution, the white residents were Le Cap's dominant class. The wealth of the island's *grands blancs* came from their plantations, but many planters kept a second residence in the city. Merchants involved in the colonial trade made up another segment of the city's elite. Many were part of what American scholar Darrell Meadows has called transatlantic families, with one branch in the colony and another in one of France's major port cities.[23] Moreau de Saint-Méry did not have to explain that whites monopolized the city's educated professions and held all the prestigious administrative posts: free people of color were excluded from all these positions. To be sure, not all whites were wealthy: descriptions from the period invariably mention the "petits blancs," those who did not own property, particularly recent immigrants who had come from Europe hoping to make their fortune. A list of refugees from Le Cap who landed in Norfolk, Virginia, in 1793 included six clerks, four innkeepers, three bakers, three furniture makers, two carpenters, several other skilled artisans, and one "ouvrier" or worker; however, these "petits blancs" were considerably outnumbered by plantation owners and merchants.[24] In contrast to Port-au-Prince, where the "petits blancs," militantly hostile to the free people of color, helped maintain an atmosphere of political extremism during the Revolution, in Cap Français, this element of the white population seems to have had relatively little influence in local affairs.

The number of poor whites in Cap Français was small because almost all of the city's manual labor was done by members of the free population of color or by slaves. The wealthiest male members of the free colored population were either plantation owners or owners of urban real estate; it was not uncommon for whites to rent property from a free colored

---

[22] Antoine, "Aventures d'un jeune négrier français," 54.

[23] R. Darrell Meadows, "The Planters of Saint-Domingue, 1750–1804: Migration and Exile in the French Revolutionary Atlantic," unpub. ms., 2008, cited with permission of the author.

[24] "Notes sur les malheureux venus de St. Domingue à Norfolk en Virginie et dans les autres lieux du continent américain," in Moreau de Saint-Méry papers, CAOM F 3 198.

VUE DU CAP FRANÇOIS.

Isle St Domingue.

FIGURE 2.3. Cap Français from the land side.

This view of Cap Français shows the city as seen from the foot of the *morne* on its north side. The broad street toward the right of the picture is the rue Espagnol, which ran through the city from south to north; in the right background, the Government House and the barracks (*casernes*), sites of key confrontations during the events of June 20, 1793, are clearly visible.

Source: The Library Company of Philadelphia.

63

owner. Other free men of color worked in the construction trades, as fishermen, or in the service sector, where they dominated professions such as wigmaking and hairdressing.[25] An armed unit of free men of color, housed in barracks in the center of the city, played a key role in keeping the slave population under control. Whereas white men heavily outnumbered white women in the city, among the free colored population, there were about twice as many women as men.[26] Unlike the white women, most of the free women of color were employed. Some worked as *menagères*, managing the households and sometimes the businesses of white employers; others were shopkeepers or domestic servants.

Indispensable elements of the city's economy and its police force, the city's free colored population, both men and women, had extensive contacts with the whites and shared much of their style of life. As Dominique Rogers's study of the free population of color in the colony's two major cities has documented, in Cap Français, both groups showed considerably less devotion to religion than their peers in Port-au-Prince; white and free colored women had a similar penchant for finery. "The mulatto and black women, of whom many serve as household managers for the whites of the country, are richly dressed and covered with jewelry," a visiting Frenchman wrote.[27] Rogers concludes that, far from seeing themselves as close to the city's slaves, the free colored population, somewhat like the upper strata of the Third Estate in France, saw itself as an integral part of colonial society and enjoyed most of the same civil rights as the whites: "They could marry, dispose of and inherit property, and go where they pleased, in spite of official restrictions. They had full economic freedom: they could acquire, buy, sell, rent, work, and associate with whomever they pleased. Finally, they could appeal to and obtain justice from the courts to protect their goods and their persons."[28] (Figure 2.4)

The freedoms enjoyed by the *libres de couleur* distinguished them from the far larger number of slaves in the city. Making up more than half of the population, slaves did almost all the manual labor necessary to keep Cap Français running. Over a thousand of them worked as longshoremen and wagoneers, moving goods to and from the quays.[29] "The blacks during the working days enlivened the scene by their rough but

---

[25] Rogers, "Libres de couleur," 177.
[26] Geggus, "Major Port Towns," 103.
[27] Antoine, "Aventures d'un jeune négrier français," 53.
[28] Rogers, "Libres de couleur," 398.
[29] A proposal for reconstructing the Cap Français wharves, published in the *Moniteur général de la partie française de Saint-Domingue* on April 6, 1793, said that

COSTUMES
DES AFFRANCHIES ET DES ESCLAVES
des Colonies.

FIGURE 2.4. "Costumes des affranchies et des esclaves."
For white men, the free women of color in Cap Français were one of the colony's main attractions. The free women of color in Saint-Domingue's cities were noted for their elaborate clothing and headdresses, often made from madras scarves imported from India; white women sometimes tried to imitate their fashions. A more simply dressed slave woman sits in the doorway to the right, and in the background a male slave can be glimpsed working in the street.
Source: The Library Company of Philadelphia.

cheering songs as they pursued their labor, with constant explosions of loud laughter at the absurdity of their own roundelays," the American merchant Samuel Perkins recalled.[30] Advertisements in the city's newspapers in 1792 and 1793 show that other slaves were employed in an impressive range of skilled jobs. Male slaves for sale were described as sailors, cooks, masons, carpenters, cigarmakers, barrelmakers, bakers,

transporting goods to and from the quays required 1,500 to 2,000 mules and "almost as many blacks."
[30] Perkins, "Sketches of St. Domingo from January, 1785, to December, 1794. Written by a Resident Merchant at the Request of a Friend, December 1835," in *Proceedings of the Massachusetts Historical Society*, 2nd. ser. 2 (1886), 363.

sawyers, wigmakers, tailors, fishermen, boatmen, blacksmiths, and metalworkers. Among the women were laundresses, housekeepers, skilled needleworkers, wetnurses, shopkeepers, a surgeon's assistant, maids, bakers, and a midwife.[31] A slave trained for such specialized tasks represented a significant investment for his or her owner.

Urban slavery was certainly an oppressive system – slaves were subject to arbitrary arrest, physical punishment, and the threat of being sold as plantation laborers – but slave life in the city was different from that on the island's plantations. Slaves in the city rarely belonged to hierarchically organized work teams, or *atteliers*, like those in the countryside, which meant, among other things, that there were no urban equivalents to the slave foremen, or *commandeurs*, who furnished much of the leadership of the August 1791 insurrection. More typical of slave life in Cap Français was the relationship between the white shop owner Rodrigue and the two teenaged slave boys he had trained in the skills of design and embroidery, so that they could work in his shop on the Place d'Armes in the middle of the busy merchant district.[32] It is hardly likely that their owner stood over them with a whip while they worked. Surrounded by luxurious textiles, ribbons, and buttons imported from Europe, and dealing on a daily basis with customers, some white and some dark-skinned like themselves but legally free, these slaves must have been conscious of possessing a rare talent, but a talent whose value depended on the continued existence of colonial society. To be sure, we know of these young men only because their owner put them up for sale in 1792, listing them along with the inventory of his shop. Nevertheless, their outlook on the world surely differed from that of the mass of the rural slave population.

Unlike plantation slaves, those in the city were often hired out by their owners and had opportunities to accumulate savings of their own, a *pécule* that might eventually allow them to purchase their freedom. A Saint-Domingue slaveowner who admitted that plantation slaves were often chronically undernourished because of their masters' indifference to their welfare claimed that conditions in Cap Français were very different: "As long as a slave in the town is industrious, the resources that surround him mean that he will never know any kind of need." Whereas rural slaves were often sickly and in poor physical condition, those in the city were "strong and muscular; their limbs acquire an admirable

---

[31] Advertisements in the *Moniteur général de la partie française de Saint-Domingue*, August 1792 – June 1793.
[32] Advertisement by Rodrigue, in *Moniteur général*, September 2, 1792.

vigor and proportion," this observer wrote.[33] As Anne Pérotin-Dumon has shown, "the development of an urban slavery, different from that on the plantations, [created] mechanisms by which some slaves integrated themselves into the market economy and earned wages, acquired greater control over their own time, their movements, and their place of residence. The town turned the relationship between master and slave into a monetary one, and the average of three or four slaves per master made that relationship more individual." Perhaps the most striking sign of the difference between plantation and urban slavery was the contrast in the predominant form of slave resistance. For plantation slaves, *marronage* meant escape into the mountains, away from the whites; for urban slaves, it meant staying in the city but passing as free and integrating themselves into the mixed society around them. [34]

Moreau de Saint-Méry was only too aware of the relative autonomy that slaves could enjoy in Cap Français. On market days, as many as 15,000 blacks came together in the Place Clugny, site of the *marché aux noirs*, as plantation slaves exchanged products from the private plots on which they grew their own food for products from the town; the police force available to supervise them amounted to fewer than two dozen, and even white residents were dependent on the market for their own supplies. Moreau complained that blacks condemned to the chain gang for crimes were in fact allowed to roam the city freely. "As far as the slaves are concerned, it seems that the police pay no attention to them," he grumbled. "The blacks go about armed with heavy sticks; they rent rooms, they gamble, they form assemblies, in short, they violate all the regulations, and the police are simple spectators of their misbehavior." One reason for this laxity, as Moreau knew, was that slaveowners made it a point of honor to insist that only they, and not the police, could discipline their own slaves.[35] The loose surveillance of the city's black population made it a magnet for maroons, slaves who had run away from their masters. Mingling with the city's own slaves and free blacks, they easily found casual employment and lodging. In 1786, the municipal

---

[33] François Laplace, *Histoire des désastres de Saint-Domingue* (Paris: Garnéry, 1795), 112. The authorship of this work, the most detailed account of events in Saint-Domingue to be published by an eyewitness during the revolutionary era, has recently been determined by Jean-Charles Benzaken: "Who was the author of *l'Histoire des désastres de Saint-Domingue*, published in Paris in the Year III?" *French History* (2009), 262–7. Laplace, a *procureur* or lawyer in Le Cap before the Revolution, owned a plantation near Plaisance, in the North Province of Saint-Domingue.

[34] Pérotin-Dumon, *Ville aux îles*, 465.

[35] Moreau de Saint-Méry, *Description ... de la partie française*, 1: 433, 391–2, 475, 476.

authorities punished a free black man "for having rented rooms and
closets in the house of one Larose, a free black, to several slaves and
for being suspected of having had knowledge of the mischief committed by these renters."[36] Public hangings of blacks convicted of theft and
other crimes, like the well-attended public executions in European cities,
seem to have had little effect on the population. On Sundays, slaves and
other blacks enjoying their day off filled the streets and public squares.
"Groups of dancers took the place of laborers, and the drum and the
pipe, and the laugh and the song, made the air ring with gayety and
frolic," Samuel Perkins wrote.[37]

The urban society of Cap Français was thus a good deal more complicated than the world of the plantations. Whereas slaves in the countryside had little reason to interest themselves in the success of their
masters' enterprises, those in the town had a stake in the welfare of
the community around them. Plantation slaves might dream of ridding
themselves of the whites, dividing the land, and becoming self-sufficient
peasants; those in the city wished instead to enjoy the luxuries they saw
around them, and they understood that this required maintaining the
connections with the larger world of which Le Cap was a part. As evidence of the possibility of such integration, the slaves in Cap Français
had only to observe the free population of color, whose very real success
within the structures of colonial society showed that the system of racial
hierarchy was less inflexible than the laws suggested. Until 1793, both
the free population of color and the slaves dreamed more of improving
their status within the city than of destroying it.

The French Revolution unleashed forces that would ultimately tear
apart the fragile bonds that had made colonial Cap Français a functioning urban community. At first, the Revolution's impact was felt primarily by the whites. Cap Français had been a center of the movement to
obtain seats in the Estates General for the colony, and the news of the
storming of the Bastille caused great enthusiasm. Le Cap enacted its
own version of the municipal revolutions that swept metropolitan cities, replacing officials named by the king's ministers with locally elected
administrators. In the spring of 1790, a local journalist wrote that "the
revolution in the northern part of Saint-Domingue began with assemblies, cries, menaces, unfounded fears, hasty measures, many ridiculous
things and a few useful ones." Compared to Paris, however, "the reign of

[36] Municipal proclamation of 14 June 1786, cited in Fouchard, *Haitian Maroons*, 272.
[37] Perkins, "Sketches" 363.

passions and of force wasn't bloody ... everyone soon felt the necessity of returning to a legal order." The city was divided into electoral districts and chose representatives to a provincial assembly; the revolutionaries overturned the government's unpopular decision of 1787 that had abolished the *Conseil supérieur,* the appeals court that had been a symbol of Le Cap's political importance.[38]

In April 1790, the new local government was installed at a great patriotic ceremony. The entire panoply of white notables turned out for a parade celebrating its achievement of local self-rule: a local newspaper listed delegations of "court employees, surgeons, master pharmacists, notaries, solicitors, doctors, barristers, administrators of the charity hospital, surveyors, the captains of the merchant ships, the Chamber of Commerce, the Royal Society of Sciences and Arts, the Chamber of Agriculture, the admiralty, the local judges, the administrative officials, the royal navy and the engineering corps, the commanders of the garrison, the commandant of the province, the council, the harbor commissioners and the provincial assembly." Militia units made up of free men of color, under white command, also took part; their presence was a reassuring reminder of the city's resources for keeping its slaves under control. The newly elected mayor summed up the transformation that had taken place, telling the citizens that they were now going to enjoy "the degree of liberty that man in society can hope to have under the rule of law, and that this city, so rich thanks to its commerce ... will now be governed only by administrators chosen by the free vote of its citizens." In harmony with the prevailing sentiments in the metropole in early 1790, he reminded his audience not to confuse "civil liberty with that license so close to anarchy" and not to "confound social equality ... with the complete abolition of ranks and distinctions."[39] There was not a hint of a suggestion that the revolution that had occurred, in France and in Cap Français, would have any implications for slavery.

The mayor's words were meant to persuade his audience that the revolution begun in 1789 was now effectively over. Not everyone agreed, however. The same issue of the local newspaper that recounted this municipal ritual also reported that there had been a mutiny among the cannoneers of the local garrison, quashed only by the execution of several ringleaders. The following week's issue brought more disquieting news. A free man of color had been arrested; his crime was "to have

[38] *Courrier politique et littéraire du Cap Français,* March 5, 1790.
[39] *Courrier politique,* April 22, 1790.

tried to stir up a revolt of the people of color against the white citizens."[40] Even more disturbing for the local white elite than these signs of discontent within the city in 1790, however, was the growth of a movement for virtual autonomy among whites in other parts of the colony. To replace the old royal administration, the colonists had elected deputies to a Colonial Assembly, which began meeting in the western port city of Saint-Marc on April 22, 1790. Its dominant faction was determined to assert the colony's right to govern itself in the strongest possible terms. At stake was not only the question of slavery and the "status of persons," on which there was no dissent, but also the issue of abolishing the much-resented restrictions of the *exclusif*, which forced the colonists to sell their produce only to French merchants and to buy their supplies only from the metropole.

Cap Français, with its powerful merchant community and its close ties to France, was considerably less enthusiastic about this challenge to the metropole than the other sections of the colony. The North Province's own assembly took a strong stand against the Colonial Assembly's autonomist pretentions, to the point of sending a detachment of its National Guard to support the royal governor when he confronted the Saint-Marc assembly. Separate from the provincial assembly, however, the city's municipal council actually sided with the Colonial Assembly, and the political temperature in the city rose to a fever pitch. Rival journalists backed different factions, and supporters of the Provincial Assembly formed a club from whose meetings they "exited inflamed with a divine fire."[41] The Revolution also had repercussions for the equilibrium between the different racial groups in the population. Whites may have been willing, as Dominque Rogers's research shows, to do business with free people of color, attend their weddings, and treat them fairly in court cases, but they insisted on maintaining their monopoly on political power. A local newspaper loyal to the North Province assembly condemned the lynching of a free black man by local whites but felt obliged to warn the free people of color against exaggerated pretentions inspired by the political news coming from France. "Remind yourselves that in the most glorious periods of Roman freedom, social institutions traced a boundary between the freedmen and their patrons that was carefully maintained," the paper told them. "Enjoy among yourselves the pleasures that no one can deny you, those of fathers, husbands, and friends; but don't let

---

[40] *Courrier politique*, April 29, 1790.
[41] *Courrier politique*, June 24, 1790.

yourselves develop crazy hopes that imaginary forces can overturn the political system which reason and experience have constructed."[42]

The immediate crisis facing the city and the colony calmed somewhat at the beginning of August 1790, when the more radical deputies of the Colonial Assembly fled to France aboard a French warship, the *Léopard*, whose crew had mutinied against their captain when he tried to carry out orders from the colony's royal governor to break up the assembly.[43] The behavior of the *Léopard*'s crewmen, who sympathized with the radical white deputies' denunciation of the metropolitan government's interference in local affairs, foreshadowed the intervention of French sailors in the journée of June 20, 1793, but the departure of the *Léopardins* silenced advocates of colonial autonomy. Shortly afterward, however, Cap Français was shaken by the insurrection among the free population of color led by Vincent Ogé at the end of October 1790.

Before leaving for France at the beginning of the Revolution, Ogé was one of the wealthiest free men of color in Cap Français. He made his fortune as a merchant and by managing property for absentee owners, as well as by purchasing real estate on his own account.[44] In 1789 and early 1790, Ogé took a leading role in the campaign to get the National Assembly to grant political rights to those free people of color who met the necessary financial qualifications. On 28 March 1790, the French Assembly passed an ambiguous decree whose language stated that all "persons" meeting those qualifications were entitled to vote in colonial elections. Antoine Barnave, head of the Assembly's colonial committee, warded off efforts by supporters of the free people of color to specify explicitly that they were included in the decree's provisions, but he apparently gave oral assurances that this was the case. In the colony, however, the decree was interpreted as authorizing the whites to maintain their exclusionist policy. In June 1790, Ogé left France, determined to return to Saint-Domingue and demand that the free people of color be given the rights he contended the National Assembly had granted them. After his arrival in Saint-Domingue in October 1790, he avoided Le Cap and instead gathered a small force in the mountains south of the northern plain. From Le Cap, the wife of one of the deputies in the *Léopardin* group wrote to her husband about the consternation caused by the rebellion. "The mulattoes … fired on our army on the first day, after which

---

[42] *Courrier politique*, May 27, 1790.
[43] Garran-Coulon, *Rapport*, 1: 252–5, 269.
[44] King, *Blue Coat or Powdered Wig*, 208–9.

they retreated to a high crest," she reported.[45] Ogé stopped short of trying to stir up the slave population, but, as he pointedly reminded his
white opponents, he might easily have done so.[46] His movement was
quickly defeated, and he fled to the neighboring Spanish colony. The
authorities there handed him over to the French, who gave him and his
supporters a show trial in Cap Français and sentenced him and one associate to be broken on the wheel, while another twenty-one participants
were hanged. The free people of color in the city made no overt attempt
to support Ogé's insurrection; few of them would have qualified to vote
under the provisions of the French constitution that he was seeking to
extend to Saint-Domingue.[47] One can imagine their horror, however, at
witnessing one of the most successful and respected members of their
group tortured to death in one of Le Cap's public squares.

Shock at the news of Ogé's execution spurred the metropolitan campaign to grant rights to at least some portion of the free population
of color in the colonies. The resulting decree of May 15, 1791 intensified white opposition to metropolitan policy. When the news reached
Cap Français, "the agitation was extreme, and the representatives of
the province thought they needed to meet; the gallery, the gardens and
the space behind the city building were filled with citizens," one local
journalist wrote. "One heard cries and violent propositions." When they
learned that the municipality of Bordeaux, the French port most closely
connected with Cap Français, had passed a resolution congratulating
the National Assembly for its action and offering to send its National
Guard to implement the decree, the whites in Le Cap threatened to cut
off all dealings with the Bordelais.[48] Governor Blanchelande's refusal to
enforce the decree gave the whites confidence that their views would prevail. In the meantime, elections for a new all-white colonial assembly, to
replace the dissolved Saint-Marc group, had gone forward. The deputies
assembled first in Léogane, south of Port-au-Prince, but in early August,
they voted to move to Cap Français, where they would be in easier communication with France.

As the deputies were making their way to Le Cap, some of them
paused to investigate a curious incident: on August 16, 1791, a building

---

[45] Mme. Larchevesque-Thibaud to husband, November 5, 1790, in AN, D XXV 38,
d. 385.
[46] Testimony of Verneuil, in *Débats entre les accusateurs et les accusés, dans l'affaire des
colonies* (Paris: Imprimerie nationale, 1795), 1: 252–5.
[47] Rogers, "Libres de couleur," 388.
[48] *Courrier politique*, July 7, 1791.

on the Chabaud plantation in the parish of Limbé was set on fire. A slave from the plantation was arrested for arson and told his interrogators that "all the *commandeurs*, coachmen, house servants and the most trusted slaves on the neighboring plantations and those in the adjacent districts had formed a plot to set fire to the plantations and to murder all the whites."[49] Other slaves denied any knowledge of a plot, however, so the deputies continued on their way to Le Cap; the Provincial Assembly there, notified of the incident, decided that the whites in Limbé were imagining nonexistent dangers.[50] The insurrection that began on the night of August 22–23, 1791 thus took the residents of Cap Français by surprise.

As reports of the attacks on nearby plantations – the first ones struck were less than ten miles distant from Le Cap – began to arrive in the city, panic broke out. A hastily assembled unit of volunteers tried to go to the rescue of the nearby plantations on the afternoon of the 23rd but was driven back by armed blacks.[51] Fortifications were quickly thrown up around the town, which had only been prepared to meet attacks by sea, and all ships were forbidden to leave the harbor in case they were needed as refuges for white women and children.[52] Inside the city, whites turned on members of the other racial groups with whom they had previously lived more or less peacefully. Convinced that mere slaves could not have organized such a massive conspiracy, some of the whites blamed the free people of color and took "a terrible vengeance, in massacring seven or eight of them, no doubt the least guilty."[53] The municipal authorities had to issue a stern edict to prevent such outbreaks. On August 25, the free men of color, hoping to ward off further attacks, went in a group to promise to help defend the town, offering their wives and children as hostages for their good behavior; after some debate, the whites accepted their proposition.[54] In exchange, the Colonial Assembly agreed

---

[49] *Discours fait à l'assemblée nationale, le 3 novembre 1791*, 2.
[50] "La Révolution de Saint-Domingue," p. 202, in CAOM, Moreau de Saint-Méry papers, F 3 141.
[51] "La Révolution de Saint-Domingue," p. 220.
[52] Blanchelande to minister of the navy, September 2, 1791, in AN, D XXV 46, d. 431.
[53] [Antoine] Dalmas, *Histoire de la Révolution de Saint-Domingue*, 2 vs. (Paris : Mame, 1814), 127.
[54] *Procès-verbaux de l'Assemblée générale de la partie française de Saint Domingue* (Cap Français : Dufour de Rians, 1791), August 25, 1791, in AN, D XXV 112, d. 889; letter from Le Cap, September 27, 1791, in *Patriote françois*, November 21, 1791; Paul de Cadusch, speech to Colonial Assembly, March 22, 1792, in *Moniteur général*, 24 March 1792.

to abandon its opposition to the decree of May 15, 1791, a concession to the free men of color that was rendered moot when the colony learned that the French National Assembly had repealed that law on September 24, 1791.[55]

Initially, the whites' fear of the city's slaves was even greater than their fear of the free men of color. One chronicler wrote that "since the Negroes of the town seemed dangerous, guard posts were set up at all the entry points; the citizens spent the night in front of their gates to prevent any fires and only went out armed. Some individuals, to control their Negroes, had them shut up at night in the cathedral or put them on board ships in the harbor. Others had them taken to the jail or the drydock of Grammont, a small island half a league off the coast. Then there were those who kept only the women and children as servants. The adult black men could only go out of the houses with passes from their masters."[56] The whites were ready to massacre all the blacks in the city, "if the security of the people and the supreme law require it," the captain of a ship in the harbor wrote.[57] On August 25, the third day of the uprising, a group of black prisoners brought into the city were hacked to death at the Champ de Mars before they could be turned over to the provost's court set up to judge them.[58] Suspicion spread even to those blacks the city's whites knew best. A Le Cap merchant told a French correspondent, "I had Aza and Zamor put in the jail, both out of suspicion and to protect them from the fury of our troops; I nearly did the same with Françoise, who permitted herself some insolence; the epidemic has spread to all those folks, and it is clear that they are all criminals."[59] While the city's residents were eyeing their own slaves with suspicion, plantation owners fleeing from the countryside were trying to bring their work gangs into the city with them. Fearing that the swollen population would exhaust food supplies, the Colonial Assembly ordered these slaves returned to their plantations.[60]

The violent agitation of the first few days of the insurrection receded as it became clear that the city was not in immediate danger, although

[55] Debbasch, *Couleur et liberté*, 201.
[56] "La Révolution de Saint-Domingue," 229–30.
[57] Letter from Le Cap, September 27 1791, in *Patriote françois*, November 21 1791.
[58] "La Révolution de Saint-Domingue," 232.
[59] *Nouvelles arrivées de Saint-Domingue, depuis celles officielles venues par l'ambassadeur d'Angleterre* (Paris: Didot, 1791), in CAOM, F 3 197, Moreau de Saint-Méry papers.
[60] *Procès-verbaux de l'Assemblée*, August 26, 1791.

mass executions of captured insurgents continued on an almost daily basis for several weeks. Most victims were plantation slaves, although the city's own black population remained suspect. Two of them, a man and a woman, were hanged in the Place d'Armes, in the center of the city, because "he had said that soon the blacks would put the whites in their place and the other, that soon she would have the pleasure of being waited on by white women," one observer recorded.[61] Hundreds of refugees from the countryside crowded into the town, bringing their tales of horror with them. The thick columns of smoke rising from the burning sugarcane fields in the northern plain were clearly visible from the city. "Everything seemed to combine to offer the colonist nothing but lugubrious images of destruction, misery, and death," another resident later wrote.[62] Commerce ground to a halt. "All the warehouses are closed; no one sells or buys anything," a ship captain reported three weeks after the start of the insurrection.[63] The presence in the city of three rival authorities, the governor general, the provincial assembly, and the colonial assembly, produced endless confusion about what to do. When Blanchelande tried to mount an armed expedition against the blacks, the two assemblies "expressed to me the greatest fear about the town, which contains 8,000 to 10,000 black males," he wrote to the navy minister on September 2, 1791.[64]

Gradually, Cap Français settled into the routine of a city under siege. White residents took turns guarding their blocks at night; buckets of water were kept ready to put out fires, and extra lamps were lit to facilitate surveillance. "We have bread and wine for six months, although we lack everything else," one of Moreau de Saint-Méry's correspondents wrote to him. "We don't lack munitions. The town is surrounded by a palisade ... The blacks cannot circulate in the town without a pass from their masters." The whites attempted to ban the circulation of newspapers from France that might inform the free people of color about the debates concerning their rights being conducted there, but copies were smuggled to them, concealed in barrels of fish.[65] Outside the city, insurgent bands controlled the countryside; only heavily armed patrols could

---

[61] "La Révolution de Saint-Domingue," 250.
[62] Dalmas, *Révolution de Saint-Domingue*, 130.
[63] Letter from Le Cap, September 27, 1791, in *Patriote français*, November 21, 1791.
[64] Blanchelande to minister of the navy, September 2, 1791, in AN, D XXV 46, d. 431.
[65] "Notes de quelques evenemens particuliers arrivés dans l'insurrection des noirs à St. Domingue en 1791," January 14, 1792, in CAOM, F 3 197, Moreau de Saint-Méry papers.

safely use the roads. Once ships were allowed to enter and leave the harbor again, sea traffic enabled the city to remain in touch with other points in the colony and with the outside world.

There was little debate in Cap Français about the necessity of combating the slave uprising; there was much more controversy about the treatment of the free population of color. Given the seriousness of the crisis, some members of the Colonial Assembly were willing to advocate concessions in order to ensure their loyalty. Several free men of color who had been held in prison on suspicion of involvement in Ogé's movement were released when they offered to fight against the slaves, and in early October, the assembly voted to create an armed unit of free colored volunteers.[66] At the same time, however, the assembly was infuriated by the outbreak of insurrectionary movements among the free men in parts of the West Province, which led the whites in some parishes to sign treaties, or *concordats*, granting them rights. On September 13, 1791, a deputy called on the free men of color to "end their horrible excesses, to lay down their arms, under pain of being pursued as incendiaries and assassins and punished accordingly."[67] The fact that white royalists in the West were willing to make agreements with the free men of color convinced the white "patriots" in Le Cap that maintaining the color line was an essential part of the struggle against the counterrevolution.

In early November, the news of the French National Assembly's decision, on September 24, 1791, to revoke its decree of May 15, 1791 scuttled any possibility that the whites would grant concessions to the free men of color: if the metropole was not going to insist on a softening of the color bar, the colonists were not about to do so on their own. Apprehensive about the consequences of the French Assembly's decision, the city's free men of color sent two spokesmen, Charles Guillaume Castaing and La Forest, to assure the Colonial Assembly that they had no intention of "brandishing flaming torches against the heads of our fathers, our brothers, and our birthplaces." Although the two men claimed that their group was pleased to hear that France had given the local whites the power to decide on their status, they nevertheless insisted that "you owe us a political existence ... Reason, justice, nature, always eloquent, unite in our favor to claim it from you."[68] The appearance of Castaing and La

---

[66] *Procès-verbaux de l'Assemblée*, September 27, 1791, September 28, 1791, October 4, 1791, October 12, 1791.

[67] *Procès-verbaux de l'Assemblée*, September 13, 1791.

[68] Castaing and La Forest, *Procès-verbaux de l'Assemblée*, 4 Nov. 1791 (address of November 2, 1791).

Forest indicated that Le Cap's free men of color had established some kind of political organization, but their cautious language showed that they knew their position was weaker than in the West Province, where the free population of color often outnumbered the whites.

Castaing's and La Forest's plea fell on deaf ears. On November 5, 1791, the Colonial Assembly decreed that no change in the status of the free people of color would be considered until the slave revolt was ended. Two days later, the assembly, thinking primarily of the conflicts in the West Province, issued a stern address to the free population of color, warning them to "fear the terrible and just vengeance of an entire people, all of whose interests have been so cruelly violated."[69] Le Cap's free men of color understood the message: many of them worried that the whites meant "to disarm them and then massacre them."[70] Meanwhile, the city faced a threat of violence from a different direction: on November 17, 1791, sailors from three warships in the harbor rioted in the city. Their anger was directed mainly at their own officers, whom they accused of counterrevolutionary inclinations, but they also threatened the free men of color, who "took refuge in their barracks and armed themselves," according to the Colonial Assembly's report.[71] Governor Blanchelande managed to defuse the crisis, but it foreshadowed the violence that would break out on June 20, 1793. Sailors from the *Eole*, one of the warships involved in this incident, would play an important role in the later *journée,* and hostility between the seamen and the free men of color would again be central to the events.

The arrival in Le Cap at the end of November 1791 of the members of the First Civil Commission, sent from France to persuade the colonists to accept the decree of May 15, 1791, added to the political tensions in Le Cap. Learning that the insurgents had actually proposed negotiations to end the uprising, the commissioners tried to get the colonial assembly to go along with the idea of an amnesty for all slaves willing to lay down their arms. The white colonists, however, dug in their heels; the president of the colonial assembly, Paul de Cadusch, rejected the extension of this principle to insurgent slaves who had committed what he called "crimes of *lèse-humanité.*"[72] Throughout the winter and spring of 1792, the colonial assembly continued to meet in Cap Français and

[69] *Procès-verbaux de l'Assemblée,* November 5, 7, 1791.
[70] *Procès-verbaux de l'Assemblée,* November 11, 1791.
[71] *Procès-verbaux de l'Assemblée,* November 17, 1791.
[72] *Moniteur général de la partie française de Saint-Domingue,* January 16, 1792 (session of January 14).

to reject any proposal to grant concessions either to the slaves or to the free population of color. The town's free men of color regularly had to listen to local officials, such as the city attorney, Jean-Baptiste Gabriel Larchevesque-Thibaud, denouncing their supposed schemes to destroy the city. "If, when political rights did not amount to much," wrote one Colonial Assembly deputy, "prudence dictated denying them to the caste of freedmen, how much more reason is there to exclude them, now that these rights embrace all parts of the organization of the colony, seeing that the projects of this caste have been revealed in the most atrocious manner, seeing that the fires they set show that the first use they want to make of these rights is to make the colony exclusively theirs?"[73]

Despite living in a virtual state of siege, in the midst of a slave population that outnumbered them, and alongside the restless free men of color, the whites of Cap Français developed a local political culture similar to that of their metropolitan cousins. The debates in the colonial and provincial assemblies provided ample fodder for public discussions; in April 1792, the colonial assembly officially closed its visitors' gallery to try to reduce the partisan animosities generated in its sessions. The white citizenry participated actively in these debates. In August 1792, when the colonial assembly considered the right of petition, one deputy remarked that it was already well established: "He had always seen petitions being carried from door to door to gather signatures, some demanding the dissolution of the assembly, others trying to force it to enact laws against the local needs of this country, others to require the executive power to keep all the armed forces in the northern part."[74] The revolution also led to a proliferation of militia forces in the city. Under the Old Regime, whites had strongly resisted military service, but after 1789, white male citizens were supposed to serve in the National Guard. After the outbreak of the slave insurrection, the Colonial Assembly created a new "paid guard," which attracted poorer members of the population.[75] Whites wealthy enough to furnish their own mounts joined the "volontaires à cheval," a unit often suspected of royalist sympathies. In November 1791, as part of its campaign to intimidate the free men of color, the Colonial Assembly called on the various white volunteer and

[73] *Extrait des minutes de la municipalité du Cap*, April 29, 1792 (speech by Larchevesque-Thibaud); De Pons, *La Question politique des affranchis et descendans des affranchis* (Cap Français : Batilliot, 1792), 11 ; both in AN, D XXV 113, d. 897.
[74] *Moniteur général*, August 31, 1792.
[75] *Extrait des registres de l'assemblée générale de la partie française de Saint-Domingue*, August 27, 1791 (in AN, D XXV 113, d. 892).

National Guard units to endorse its refusal to consider any modification of the colony's racial order.[76]

As in France, newspapers communicated the assemblies' actions to the public in the city and throughout the island. A number of new publications had appeared in Le Cap since the start of the Revolution, competing with the local edition of the *Affiches américaines*, the only authorized pre-revolutionary periodical. From November 1791 onward, the city's dominant paper was the daily *Moniteur général de la partie française de Saint-Domingue*, edited by a certain H. D. de Saint-Maurice and printed in the Batilliot shop on the Place d'Armes. Batilliot was a successful entrepreneur who also sold books and stationary; his printing shop employed twelve people.[77] Between them, the editor and the printer offered Le Cap's readers a well-printed publication on the level of the most professional provincial newspapers in France itself or of the periodicals published in the United States. Saint-Maurice gave readers few details about himself; he did once mention that he had lived for six years in Turkey, where, he said, he had seen "white slaves with black masters," and he claimed to be convinced that "the man who looks at everything with a little philosophy, pays no attention to skin color, which is nothing but a caprice of nature," but he was careful not to say anything critical about slavery in Saint-Domingue.[78] He took a certain role in local politics and occasionally found himself at odds with some of those he covered in his columns, but in general the paper tried to stay on the side of whichever faction seemed to hold power in the town. Until October 1792, the city also had a second daily, the *Journal politique de Saint-Domingue*. Few provincial cities in metropolitan France, and certainly none as small as Cap Français, supported two daily newspapers in this period.

As debates about the Saint-Domingue crisis dragged on in Paris with no decision and no dispatch of troops to the island, the besieged city of Le Cap became a claustrophobic snake pit of political hatreds. Self-proclaimed "patriots" denounced conspirators whom they accused of seeking to destroy the colony in order to provoke a metropolitan reaction against the Revolution, "by reducing to famine and despair the quarter of the French population that has made its living up to now thanks to maritime commerce."[79] In the absence of a visible royalist movement,

[76] *Procès-verbaux de l'Assemblée*, November 12, 1791.
[77] Letter of Robin, March 12, 1794, in AN, D XXV 81, d. 790.
[78] *Moniteur général*, September 26, 1792.
[79] Daugy, in *Moniteur général*, January 19, 1792.

such as the one that existed in the Port-au-Prince region, the patriots
directed their accusations against the governor general, Blanchelande,
and the commanding officers of the city's garrison, the *regiment du Cap*.
The proof of their treasonous intentions, according to these denunciations, was their failure to bring the slave uprising under control. When
Blanchelande sent an expedition to drive the insurgents out of the Limbé
district that they had devastated at the beginning of the uprising, one
participant from Le Cap complained that "the government [was] always
faithful to the principles from which it never wavered, namely, of abandoning to themselves the districts that were still intact and of reconquer-
ing ashes."[80]

In July 1792, a Cap Français printer published the first edition of an
account by Gros, a white man who had been held prisoner by the blacks
from October to December 1791. Gros's *Récit historique*, by far the
most widely circulated eyewitness description of the insurgency during
the revolutionary era – it was republished in both France and the United
States in 1793 – claimed that the blacks thought they were fighting to
defend the rights of the king of France. "I heard an uniform language
among the Negroes, by which they believed in the imprisonment of the
king, that he had issued them orders to arm themselves, and to restore
him liberty," Gros wrote. He was sure that this idea had been implanted
in the blacks' heads by white conspirators. Governor Blanchelande's failure to send troops to protect rural districts clamoring for aid struck
Gros as suspicious, as did the fact that Colonel Joseph Cambefort of the
Cap regiment "was idolized by these unhappy wretches;" the insurgents
claimed that "he always spared them, whenever he was necessitated to
come to close quarters with them."[81] One can imagine the effect of such
accusations in the closed community of a city under siege and dependent
on these same military commanders for its protection.

On May 28, 1792, after several days of tumultuous debates and an
invasion of its meeting hall by a white mob, the Colonial Assembly
formally voted to bar any concessions whatever to the free people of
color or the blacks until "they laid down their arms."[82] Just as it took

[80] Leclerc, "Campagne du Limbé, et détail de quelques événements qui ont eu lieu dans
ce quartier (ou commune) jusqu'au 20 juin 1793," CAOM, CC 9 A 8, cited in Popkin,
Facing Racial Revolution, 94.
[81] Gros, *Historick Recital, of the Different Occurrences in the Camps of Grand-Reviere
[sic], Dondon, Sainte-Suzanne and others* (Baltimore, MD: Samuel and John Adams,
1793), cited in Popkin, *Facing Racial Revolution*, 132, 123, 149.
[82] On the invasion of the Assembly on May 23, 1792, see *Moniteur général*, May 25, 1792.

this decision, however, the Assembly learned of the text of the French Legislative Assembly's decree of April 4, 1792, granting political rights to all free men of color. A year earlier, the whites in Saint-Domingue had not hesitated to defy the National Assembly's much more limited decree of May 15, 1791, but circumstances had changed: the Colonial Assembly immediately nullified its own resolution and promised to conform to the national government's decision as soon as it was officially communicated to them.[83] The Provincial Assembly, also still holding sessions, tried to profit from the French government's decision by sending a copy of it to the leaders of the black insurgents, presumably to show them that they now faced a united front of whites and free people of color and should therefore abandon their struggle.[84] Free men of color were invited to take part in the city's official celebration of July 14, and in return, the members of the Colonial Assembly and other public officials accepted an invitation to a banquet hosted by the men of color, an event the *Moniteur général* noted in an article entitled "Prejudices Overcome."[85] Ostensibly, the white population of Cap Français was now committed to accepting the free people of color as its legal equals.

Anticipation of the landing of the new Civil Commission and the fresh forces accompanying it raised hopes in the city. "The impending arrival of a convoy with troops, which ... must have left France about the end of June, will soon give us the rest we need so badly. Some difficulties will probably be encountered in reducing the rebels in the mountains, but if we can get the chiefs in our power, or destroy them, the rest will not hold out long. The plantation owners will then return to their homes and there will be an active demand for commodities of every kind," one merchant wrote.[86] Within the city, however, racial relations remained tense. The *Moniteur général* complained about illegal gambling rooms catering to slaves: "The Negroes steal from their masters, lose interest in work, pick up the germ of all the vices, because of the lack of surveillance to prevent these gatherings which in any case are dangerous from every point of view." Everyone agreed that more police were needed to keep an eye on the more than 600 cabarets in the city, in which, according to a

---

[83] *Moniteur général*, May 29, 1792 (Colonial Assembly, May 28); May 30, 1792.

[84] *Moniteur général*, June 10, 1792 (letter from Biassou and Jean-François, acknowledging receipt of the law).

[85] *Moniteur général*, July 21, 1792. Thanks to Jeffery Stanley for this reference.

[86] Aubert to Stephen Girard, cited in John Bach McMaster, *The Life and Times of Stephen Girard, Mariner and Merchant*, 2 vs. (Philadelphia: J. B. Lippincott, 1918), 1: 159.

deputy to the colonial assembly, "abuses are committed every day ... one often sees whites compromising themselves with slaves."[87] Members of the free population of color complained about the paper itself, which had to deny a charge that it refused to sell them subscriptions. Jealous of their newly granted equality with the whites, the free people of color resented any slights, while the whites continued to regard them with mistrust, as an incident in the summer of 1792 demonstrated. A party of men of color on horseback wanted to pass through one of the city's guarded gates into the countryside; the white sentinel demanded to see a permit authorizing them to leave. The men objected that whites were not required to show such a document. "The sentinel gave them an answer that admitted of no reply, that there were no white slaves, but that there were indeed many of their color, and he could only be sure of their status by checking their papers," a chronicler wrote. "In spite of that, they insisted on being let through ... As they rode off, they covered the guard with a thousand insults."[88]

In mid-August, a more serious racially charged incident led to open fighting between whites and free men of color, threatening the city with "a total subversion," as one author put it.[89] The journée of August 13–14, 1792 was the first time that internal racial conflict seriously threatened to tear Cap Français apart. The episode began on the evening of August 13, when a white man named Sourbes charged out of the front door of his house and used his saber to break up a street fight between a slave man and a slave woman. Waving his weapon wildly, he struck and seriously injured a free black man, appropriately named Hasard. Although two surgeons hastened to treat the victim and although the authorities promptly arrested Sourbes, an armed crowd of free people of color gathered in the streets to protest the incident. They were successfully dispersed that evening, but in the morning, when a white woman who lived in Sourbes's house emerged and went to the *marché aux noirs* at the Place Clugny to do her shopping, she was mobbed by "men of color and free blacks" and had to be rescued by a policeman.

News of the incident led to the arrival of angry whites, and a street fight broke out between them and the group of free men of color in which one of the latter, Desmangles, was killed. "His companions ran

[87] *Moniteur général*, August 24, 1792 (Colonial Assembly, August 21).
[88] "La Révolution de Saint-Domingue," in CAOM, F 3 141 (Moreau de Saint-Méry papers), 406–7.
[89] "La Révolution de Saint-Domingue," in CAOM, F 3 141 (Moreau de Saint-Méry papers), 406.

through the town, crying, 'To arms, to your barracks, citizens of color,'"
according to the official report published in the *Moniteur général* several days later. Traditionally part of the white-controlled forces of order,
the militia unit had now become a potential source of opposition to the
white authorities. Not all the free men of color were eager for a confrontation with the whites, but a small group of them headed for the rue
Espagnole, the main north-south street cutting through the city, where
they encountered some white National Guards and opened fire on them,
killing two and wounding three others. (One of the victims was listed
as an "Anglo-American," testimony to active part that American merchants and seamen took in the city's affairs.) These killings raised the
fear of white reprisals. "Some whites, indignant over the excesses of the
men of color, threatened to launch an attack on their barracks," according to the official report.[90] The city government called on Cambefort and
his troops. "I separated them, and I prevented the whites from heading
for the barracks of the men of color, whom they had sworn to massacre,"
the colonel later wrote.[91]

The violence found the local authorities badly disorganized.
Blanchelande, the governor, had been gone for nearly two months, dealing with problems in other parts of the colony. Unwilling to act on his
own authority, Cambefort, the commander of the garrison, asked the
Colonial Assembly to declare martial law. No doubt reluctant to entrust
such broad powers to someone many of them accused of collusion with
the slave insurgents, the three elected bodies in the city – the Colonial
Assembly, the Provincial Assembly and the municipal council – put aside
their own quarrels for once and worked together to calm the situation
down. To protect them from a white pogrom, the free men of color were
persuaded to take refuge in their barracks, where they found themselves
under a sort of house arrest: once they were inside, Cambefort refused
to let them leave. The conjoined assemblies sent a delegation to negotiate
with the men of color, eventually agreeing that the latter would single
out any dangerous hotheads in their own ranks, and that the others
would be allowed to return to their homes, escorted by members of the

---

[90] *Moniteur général*, August 19, 1792.
[91] Joseph-Paul-Augustin Cambefort, *Mémoire justificatif de Joseph-Paul-Augustin Cambefort, Colonel du Régiment du Cap; Commun à Anne-Louis Tousard, Lieutenant-Colonel, à tous les officiers, sous-officiers & soldats du même regi-ment, déportés de Saint-Domingue, par ordre des commissaires civils, délégués par le Pouvoir-Exécutif aux Isles Françaises de l'Amérique-sous-le-vent* (Paris: Frères Chaigneau, 1793), pt. 3, 16.

assemblies. White hardliners in the Colonial Assembly objected to any special protections for the men of color, claiming that such measures indicated an unwarranted suspicion of the whites' intentions, but in the end a majority of the deputies accepted the wisdom of not trying to oust the free colored militia unit from its barracks by force.[92]

The deputies of the three assemblies were well aware of the danger the city had run as a result of this incident. In a joint appeal, they warned the population, "Citizens, a moment of excitement and error almost annihilated the precious remains of the colony. For a few instants, you were in the grip of the horrors of a civil war. Can you contemplate without trembling the immense abyss that opened at your feet?"[93] A massacre of free men of color at a time when civil commissioners and troops from France were about to arrive in the colony to enforce the law granting their group equal rights would have amounted to an open revolt against the metropole. On their side, the free people of color, aware that commissioners and troops were on their way from France to enforce the decree of April 4, 1792, clearly sensed that they now held some real power in the city. When the slave uprising had broken out in August 1791, they had had to beg for protection against the white mob; now they were able to meet force with force. After the events of August 13 and 14, 1792, the three local assemblies, anxious to improve relations with the soon-to-be citizens of color in the wake of the violence, invited them to send nonvoting observers to their sessions.[94] Instead of rushing to accept this concession, the free men of color held a formal meeting, presided over by elected officers, and decided not to take up the offer until they had a chance to consult their "brothers from the South and West provinces," the formidable armed movements who had repeatedly imposed their demands on the whites in those areas.[95] The journée of August 13–14, 1792 was a clear warning that the new commissioners were about to arrive in a city racked by explosive tensions. Nevertheless, the events of August 13–14, 1792 also showed that the slaves of Cap Français were not yet ready to involve themselves in the quarrels dividing the free population. As long as they remained passive, the city could survive even armed conflict between whites and free people of color.

[92] *Moniteur général*, August 13–14, August 15, August 16, August 19, 1792.
[93] *Moniteur général*, August 19, 1792.
[94] *Procès-verbaux de l'Assemblée*, August 19, 1792.
[95] *Moniteur général*, August 26, 1792 (meeting of August 24, 1792).

3

French Jacobins and Saint-Domingue Colonists

Complicated as the conflicts between colonial whites, insurrectionary slaves, free people of color, and French government representatives had become by the summer of 1792, politics in Saint-Domingue as a whole and in the city of Cap Français in particular were about to become even more explosive with the arrival from France of the members of the new National Civil Commission appointed to enforce the law of April 4, 1792. From 1789 to the fall of 1792, rival groups in the colony had fought among themselves, with little intervention from the metropole. Between September 1792, when they arrived in the island, and June 20, 1793, National Civil Commissioners Sonthonax and Polverel would change that situation drastically. Encouraged by the wording of the instructions they received from Paris, they would assert essentially dictatorial powers to defend what they saw as French national interests in the colony. Imbued with the conviction that the spirit of the French Revolution required the end of discrimination against the free people of color, they would ally themselves with that group and use force to establish their rights. And when the crisis of June 20, 1793 threatened to overwhelm them, they would take it upon themselves to emancipate the slaves, in the absence of any explicit encouragement for such a step from the revolutionary government in France and in spite of their own very real doubts that such a drastic policy could succeed.

The road from the appointment of the Second Civil Commission in June 1792 to the first emancipation decree of June 21, 1793 was a long one, with many twists and turns that no one, including Sonthonax and Polverel, could have imagined when they were selected to go to Saint-Domingue. The law of April 4, 1792 was, as we have seen, the culmination of a long struggle in the Legislative Assembly over the question of how to react to the slave uprising in the colony. Accepted by Louis XVI as part of the unnatural alliance he made with the Girondins in March 1792 to prepare the way for the declaration of war against Austria a month later, the law ordered the appointment of three new Civil Commissioners to replace the members of the First Commission sent in 1791, two of whom had already returned from Saint-Domingue.

Accompanied by 6,000 fresh troops and a new military governor to replace Blanchelande, who had requested his own recall, the Commissioners were assigned three main tasks. In the first place, they were to proclaim the complete equality of the free people of color with the whites. French legislators who voted for the law hoped that this measure would end the violent disputes that had set off the insurrections in the West and South provinces and left the colony vulnerable to a slave uprising. The Commission was then supposed to dissolve the colonial assembly, the assemblies of the three provinces, and the municipal councils in the island's cities, and supervise new elections in which free men of color who met the necessary qualifications would be allowed to vote and to be elected to office. Finally, the Commission was to end the slave uprising. According to the optimistic calculations of armchair strategists in Paris, the troops sent from Europe – a larger number than the French had sent to support the American rebels in 1781 – together with the forces already in the island would more than suffice to defeat an insurrection of untrained and undisciplined blacks.

There was considerable disagreement in Paris about the choice of the commissioners. In the first flush of their success in gaining control of the royal ministry and in defeating the colonial lobby's opposition to the granting of rights to the free people of color, Brissot and his supporters had wanted to make an emphatic statement by naming the most prominent member of that group in France, Julien Raimond, as a member of the commission. The colonists' supporters in the Legislative Assembly had blocked his appointment by inserting a clause in the law barring anyone who owned property in the colonies from serving as a commissioner.[1] The newly appointed navy minister, Jean de Lacoste, had once been an official representative of Saint-Domingue's merchants and was

[1] AN, D XXV 76, "Copies des lettres de MM Millet, Cougnacq-Mion, Chesneau de la Mesgrière, Lebugnet, La Gourgue, de Sainte James, commissaires de l'Assemblée générale de la Partie française de St. Domingue près la Metropole. commencé le 17 8bre 1791," letter of April 1, 1792; Raimond, letter of June 18, 1792, in AN, D XXV 13, d. 127.

sympathetic to the colonists,[2] but in the end he was outmaneuvered by Brissot and his supporters. Two of the men selected – Sonthonax and Polverel – were known to be opponents of slavery and advocates of rights for the free people of color. Although he was disappointed at being excluded from the commission, Raimond gave Sonthonax and Polverel his enthusiastic endorsement.[3]

Léger-Félicité Sonthonax and Étienne Polverel were in many ways typical members of the new political class that had come to power in France by 1792. Both were lawyers from provincial backgrounds. Both had settled in Paris before the Revolution and actively supported that movement, which opened new possibilities for members of the Third Estate like themselves.[4] Both had joined the Jacobin club, where they came in contact with more prominent figures such as Brissot, although neither had made much of a name for himself in the group. Neither had ever visited the colonies. Sonthonax, just twenty-nine years old in 1792 when he was appointed as Civil Commissioner, was the younger and more energetic of the two.[5] Insiders like Raimond knew that Sonthonax was the author of an unsigned article that had appeared in the weekly *Révolutions de Paris* in September 1790, which prophesied that "As for the slave trade and Negro slavery, the governments of Europe will have a fine time resisting the cries of philosophy and the principles of universal liberty which are germinating and spreading among the nations ... Yes, we dare to predict with confidence that the day will come – and the day is not too far off – when you will see a curly-haired African, relying only on his virtue and good sense, coming to participate in the legislative process in the midst of our national assemblies."[6] Although he rarely spoke at the Jacobins, Sonthonax had served on its correspondence committee at a time when Brissot was also a member, and the two men had probably had a chance to discuss the slavery issue.[7]

---

[2] AN, D XXV 76, "Copies des lettres," letter of March 20, 1792.

[3] Raimond, letter of June 18, 1792, in AN, D XXV 13, d. 127.

[4] During the pre-revolutionary crisis, Polverel had published a *Tableau de la constitution de la royaume de Navarre* in an effort to guide the movement in his native province. AN, AA 55, d. 1511, settlement of legal case between Polverel and Marie Victoire Michaux.

[5] Sonthonax and Polverel were notified of their selection on April 29, 1792, although they did not receive their official letters of appointment until early June. AN, D XXV 13, d. 120 (letter of April 29, 1792) and D XXV 11, d. 102 (official letters, dated June 2, 1792).

[6] *Révolutions de Paris*, September 18–25, 1790, cited in Stein, *Sonthonax*, 21.

[7] Stein, *Sonthonax*, 22–4 ; Marcel Dorigny, "Sonthonax et Brissot : le cheminement d'une filiation politique assumée," in Marcel Dorigny, dir., *Léger-Félicité Sonthonax. La première*

Polverel had also been a member of the Jacobin correspondence committee. He was twenty-five years older than Sonthonax and had a more
legalistic approach to things; coming from the region of Bordeaux, he
had also had, as he later said, "more than thirty years of relations with
shippers trading with the colonies and with colonists."[8] Like Sonthonax,
he had written articles against slavery in the revolutionary press, and
he had voted for the expulsion from the Jacobins of members who supported the repeal of the May 15, 1791 law granting rights to some free
men of color.[9] Both Sonthonax and Polverel had the advantage, from
Brissot's point of view, of having expressed firm opposition to racial discrimination without having become publicly known as abolitionists; neither had been a member of the Société des Amis des Noirs, which would
have been a red flag to the colonial lobby. The third commissioner, Jean-
Antoine Ailhaud, was added to the group as a replacement for another
nominee who backed out.[10] Having spent ten years as an administrator
in the Ile de France, one of France's Indian Ocean slave colonies, he was
the only one of the three with any experience in the colonial world.[11]
Despite this background, Ailhaud lacked the forceful personality of his
two colleagues. Overwhelmed by the situation in Saint-Domingue, he
deserted the colony and fled back to France as soon as he could.[12]

Since Sonthonax and Polverel ended up proclaiming the abolition of
slavery in Saint-Domingue, contemporaries and historians have speculated endlessly about whether they arrived in the colony with the intention of bringing about this result, and whether they may have had secret
instructions from Brissot to do so. There is no doubt that, in the abstract,
both men, and Brissot as well, considered slavery as a violation of natural
rights and hoped for its abolition. Brissot's Société des Amis des Noirs
deserves credit for making the legitimacy of slavery a matter of debate
from the outset of the Revolution and for clearly demonstrating that the

---

abolition de l'esclavage. *La Révolution française et la Révolution de Saint-Domingue*
(Paris: Association pour l'étude de la colonisation française, 2005 (orig. 1987)), 29–41.

[8] Polverel, in *Débats entre les accusateurs et les accusés dans l'affaire des colonies*, 9 vs.
(Paris: Imprimerie nationale, 1795) 2: 349.

[9] Stein, *Sonthonax*, 42; Jean-Daniel Piquet, *L'émancipation des Noirs*, 185–6; Jacques
Cauna, "Polverel ou la révolution tranquille," in Michel Hector, ed., *La Révolution fran-
çaise et Haïti: Filiations, Ruptures, Nouvelles Dimensions*, 2 vs. (Port-au-Prince: Société
Haïtienne d'histoire et de géographie et Editions Henri Deschamps, 1995), 1: 384–99.

[10] Lacoste to Polverel, May 8, 1792, in AN, D XXV 13, d. 120.

[11] Ailhaud, speech to citizens of Cap Français, in AN, D XXV 112, d. 890.

[12] Ailhaud to Convention nationale, January 22, 1793, in AN, D XXV 12, d. 112; Stein,
Sonthonax, 54–5.

institution violated basic human rights. As scholarship concerning the French abolitionist movement has shown over and over again, however, it was a long way from condemning slavery in theory to being prepared to decree its immediate destruction.[13] From its inception, Brissot's Société des Amis des Noirs had always insisted that it was seeking only "sure and gradual means to allow the freeing of the slaves without upheavals dangerous to their owners," as the group's very first manifesto had said.[14] The French abolitionists believed as firmly as their opponents that France's national interest required the maintenance of its colonial empire. Slavery needed to be phased out, but only under conditions that would protect that interest. Simply surrendering Saint-Domingue to its slaves, in the name of natural rights, was inconceivable to anyone in France. The conduct of Sonthonax and Polverel would demonstrate that they fully subscribed to these views.

If Sonthonax and Polverel had had secret discussions with anyone in Paris, they presumably would have discussed these issues with Brissot and Raimond.[15] Although little documentation of any exchanges Brissot may have had with Sonthonax or Polverel at the time of their nomination to the Commission has been found, he probably took part in the meetings with them described by his close political ally Raimond. Brissot did draft a letter to representatives of the free people of color in the colony, to be sent with the same ship that was taking the commissioners to Saint-Domingue, which makes it clear that he was still looking for a consensual way of abolishing slavery, as he had since the formation of the Société des Amis des Noirs in 1788. "It is up to you," he told these correspondents, "to embarrass the whites first by improving the situation of the blacks. It is with this hope that the friends of liberty have supported your cause here. It will be simple, once you reflect on the matter, to reconcile the interests of the owners with what humanity requires of you. The patriots of the National Assembly await from you and from

---

[13] See, for example, the discussion of Condorcet's views in Dubois, *Colony of Citizens*, 177–83.

[14] *Journal de Paris*, February 25, 1788. The publication, in 1998, of the minutes of the Société des Amis des Noirs' meetings has rendered much of the earlier scholarship on the group out of date. See Marcel Dorigny and Bernard Gainot, eds. *La Société des Amis des Noirs 1788–1799. Contribution à l'histoire de l'abolition de l'esclavage* (Paris: Editions UNESCO, 1998) and Popkin, "Saint-Domingue, Slavery and the Origins of the French Revolution," in Kaiser and Van Kley, eds., *From Deficit to Deluge*.

[15] On the evidence concerning Sonthonax's relations with Brissot, see Dorigny, "Sonthonax et Brissot," in Dorigny, dir., *Léger-Félicité Sonthonax*, 35–7.

the future Colonial Assembly a good plan on this important subject."[16]
Brissot's letter indicates that his thinking at the moment of the commissioners' departure was still confined to the gradualist framework that
had always characterized the Amis des Noirs group: he spoke only of an
unspecified improvement in the condition of the slaves, rather than an
immediate end to slavery. Furthermore, he hoped that the initiative on
the matter would be taken by representatives of the colonies themselves,
rather than being imposed on them by the metropole. Brissot's optimistic conviction that it would be simple to achieve meaningful reform of
slavery reflected his characteristic lack of political realism.

While Brissot thus seems unlikely to have given the commissioners
secret encouragement to make the abolition of slavery an immediate
goal, Raimond was explicitly opposed to the idea. Like Brissot, he took
advantage of the commissioners' departure to write a letter to the free
men of color in Saint-Domingue. In the first place, he wanted to dispel
rumors circulating among the free colored activists in Saint-Domingue
insinuating that he favored the abolition of slavery. "The lie was a crude
one, as you will see, since one can hardly imagine that I would want to
suddenly ruin my whole family, which owns between 7 and 8 millions
in property in Saint-Domingue," Raimond wrote. He had participated
in several discussions with the commissioners about their mission, he
continued, and especially about

the method to use to get the insurgent slaves to return [to the plantations] and
what one could offer them to improve their situation without doing too much
damage to the interests of the owners and of the whole society. Different opinions were put forward on this subject but there seemed to be agreement on
the idea of giving them a day to work for themselves, in addition to Sunday.
I observed that this plan could be dangerous, especially as they would just be
coming out of a state of insurrection; it would be possible and even probable
that they would use this day to get together in groups and conspire instead of
using it for work whose profits would enable them to improve their condition.
Also, they might conclude from this kind of capitulation that since they had
obtained one full day by staging an insurrection, they could obtain another by
using the same method.

Raimond proposed instead establishing regulations that would encourage slaves to work harder in order to be able to purchase their individual
freedom. He went on to summarize the advice the group had given the
commissioners on strategy for ending the insurrection. They should issue

[16] Brissot, draft letter, June 19, 1792, in AN, 446 AP 13.

a proclamation "promising pardon and their freedom to the leaders of the rebels if they make the slaves return. This proclamation would promise a reform in the condition of the slaves that would be worked out as soon as they return. Speak to them in this proclamation about the power of the nation which will punish them if they don't obey; on the contrary, if they do, [the nation] will do something to improve their condition."[17] Whereas Brissot at least looked to the abolition of slavery as a long-range goal, Raimond limited himself to vague ideas about its reform; one can see that he was certainly not urging Sonthonax and Polverel to consider doing away with the system. On the other hand, unlike Brissot, he foresaw that change in the colony would have to be brought about through the use of "the power of the nation," but the main target of this power, in his mind, was to be the rebellious slaves, not their owners.

A third figure who may have had some influence on the future commissioners' views at the time they left France was the journalist Claude Milscent, a former Saint-Domingue planter who had been driven out of the island by pro-slavery whites because of his reformist views and who had established a newspaper, the *Créole patriote*, which opposed the colonial lobby in Paris. Sonthonax would write to him in February 1793, to express his view that some reform of the slave system was necessary.[18] Milscent, however, was also not an advocate of immediate abolition. He had consistently argued that the granting of rights to the free men of color was essential if slavery was to be maintained, but he minimized the significance of the August 1791 slave uprising, putting it in the context of the long history of slave resistance, which, he argued, had never really jeopardized the system.[19] In a letter published in Brissot's *Patriote françois* in March 1792, Milscent called slavery "the most revolting violation of all natural rights," but insisted that since French laws had authorized it, the colonists needed to be reimbursed for the value of their property.[20] Thus he, too, is unlikely to have encouraged Sonthonax to think of the abolition of slavery as an immediate goal.

A final, if ambiguous, piece of evidence about the intentions of Sonthonax and Polverel comes from their interactions with another outspoken advocate of rights for the blacks, Pierre Chaumette. Like Sonthonax, Chaumette was a contributor to the *Révolutions de Paris*

---

[17] Raimond, letter of June 18, 1792, in AN, D XXV 13, d. 127.
[18] Sonthonax to Milscent, February 11, 1793, in AN, AA 55, d. 1511.
[19] [Claude Milscent], *Sur les Troubles de Saint-Domingue* (Paris: Imprimerie du *Patriote français*, 1791).
[20] Milscent, letter of February 25, 1792, in *Patriote françois*, March 13, 1792.

and may have written some of the paper's articles about colonial issues.
At Brissot's trial, he testified that Sonthonax had offered him the position of secretary to the commission. After some discussion, Chaumette
claimed, he had turned the position down because he realized "that the
opinion that he was taking to the colony was not the same as mine; I had
always been for the liberty of the blacks."[21] Articles in the *Révolutions
de Paris* at the time of the commissioners' appointment had indeed
denounced slavery and the slave trade, but the one article in the paper
that directly discussed the civil commission gave a gloomy assessment of
its chances for success. To bring peace to the colony, the journal wrote,
would require humbling "the barbarous pride of the whites" and over-
coming the "wild and suspicious" character of the "mulattoes;" as for
the black man in the colonies, the revolt had made him "an unchained
tiger who needs to be tamed and rendered incapable of causing harm." If
Chaumette was, in fact, the author of this article – Julien Raimond also
claimed to have provided the journal with articles about the colonies
in this period – it is not clear whether he declined the invitation to join
Sonthonax because he thought the latter was too moderate or whether
he simply despaired of the mission's chances for success.[22]

If they did not set sail from France with clear intentions to do away
with slavery, Polverel and Sonthonax did bring with them the political
convictions they shared with their Jacobin milieu. Like all supporters of
the revolutionary movement, they believed unswervingly in the principle
of national authority. "I will defend to my last breath the principles and
the rights of the nation, and I will perish before I will allow any infringe-
ment on its sovereignty," Polverel proudly declared in February 1793.[23]

---

[21] *Bulletin du tribunel criminal révolutionnaire*, no. 41. On June 19, 1792, the mayor of
Paris, Jérôme Pétion, a long-time ally of Brissot in the campaign against slavery, wrote
a letter of recommendation for Chaumette. AN, D XXV 13, d. 120.

[22] *Révolutions de Paris*, April 7–14, 1792, "Motion faite dans l'Assemblée nationale
pour la suppression de la traite des noirs" ibid., "Envoi d'une nouvelle commission à
Saint-Domingue," June 9–16, 1792. Jean-Daniel Piquet cites a passage of this latter
article to argue that Chaumette wanted the Commission to enter into direct contact
with the black insurgents, but in fact, the passage suggests that if the commissioners
could hear the blacks, they would realize that no compromise with them was possible.
Piquet, *Émancipation des noirs*, 187–8. On Raimond's relations with the editor of
the *Révolutions de Paris*, see his letter to the leaders of the free men of color in Saint-
Domingue, April 15, 1792, in Raimond, *Lettres de J. Raimond, à ses frères les hommes de couleur*, 69–70.

[23] Polverel, letter to General La Salle, February 2, 1793, in A. Corre, ed., *Papiers du
général A. N. de La Salle (Saint-Domingue, 1792–1793)* (Quimper: Cotonnec, 1897),
122.

Only the nation as a whole, embodied in its national legislature, could make laws, and those laws applied to the entire national territory, including its overseas extensions. Any opposition to the will of the nation, as expressed in the laws, was, in this view, illegitimate and needed to be opposed in the firmest manner. The Jacobins were acutely conscious, of course, that not everyone in France accepted the authority of the laws passed by the revolutionary assemblies. Measures such as the controversial restructuring of the Catholic Church had caused widespread protest. To the Jacobins, such resistance was inherently suspect: opponents of laws passed by the national legislature were defending particular interests in conflict with that of the nation as a whole. Revolutionary ideology refused to recognize the notion of legitimate opposition; anyone who resisted duly passed laws was a counterrevolutionary, and any organized effort to prevent the enforcement of revolutionary decrees was a conspiracy. Furthermore, the revolutionaries' tendency to divide the population into supporters and opponents of the movement implied that all of the latter were, in reality, members of a single conspiracy. Whatever specific issue they might be identified with, the revolutionaries saw them as "royalists" or "aristocrats," bent on re-establishing a society based on arbitrary authority and social inequality.

From the Jacobin point of view, Saint-Domingue in 1792 was a hotbed of counterrevolutionary resistance to the national will that needed to be brought back to obedience. Distrust of the white colonists had become an article of faith among the Jacobins: they denounced the colonial whites either for being nostalgic supporters of the monarchy that had maintained the slave system, or else "independentists" bent on separating the colonies from the mother country; in any case, they were "aristocrats of the skin," determined to deny the free people of color their natural rights. In a three-hour speech to the Legislative Assembly on December 1, 1791, Brissot insisted that the slave rebellion was a consequence of "the system of independence put forward by the white colonists since the start of the Revolution" and of their "aristocratic tyranny" toward the free population of color. The white planters wanted to avoid paying their metropolitan creditors, and the *petits blancs* were "adventurers, men without principles and nearly all of them without morality."[24]

As for the slaves, although Jacobin ideology regarded their servitude as unjust, only a few extremists such as the journalist Jean-Paul Marat were prepared to endorse their violent attempt to liberate themselves.

---

[24] Brissot, *Discours ... du premier décembre 1791*, 61–5, 4, 7.

The fact that the insurgent leaders claimed to be fighting to restore the king to his throne provided powerful fuel for the belief that they were being manipulated by the all-encompassing royalist and aristocratic conspiracy that Jacobins were sure lay behind all of the revolution's troubles. Upon their arrival in the colony, Sonthonax and Polverel concluded that the reports of the slaves' royalist beliefs circulating in France had, if anything, understated the situation. The slaves "only speak of liberty as something almost inconsequential in making them take up arms," they wrote to Gaspard Monge, the new minister of the navy, after their first month in Le Cap. "They say they want to avenge their good king Louis XVI, they want to put him back on the throne. Woe to anyone who falls into their hands wearing the tricolor symbol of liberty, he is pitilessly attacked, the only safety is in the white cockade or scarf."[25] Even in the face of this discouraging reality, however, the commissioners maintained the conviction that they had brought from France: if the slaves could only be disabused of their misguided loyalty to the throne, they would understand that their proper course of action was to return to work on their plantations and wait for the nation's representatives to enact that simple program of reforms promised by Brissot and his supporters that would grant the slaves their natural rights without damaging the interests of their owners or those of the nation.

Classifying the white colonists as inveterate counterrevolutionaries and the black slaves as unwitting dupes of the counterrevolution, the Jacobins were led to put their trust in the only remaining group of the Saint-Domingue population: the free people of color. Ignoring inconvenient contradictory evidence, such as the coalition between the wealthy white landowners in the West Province and the free colored proprietors there, and oblivious to the fact that the majority of the *libres de couleur* were women and hence unable to play the political role assigned to them, the Jacobins convinced themselves that this group's interests necessarily made them loyal supporters of the revolutionary cause. Jacobin rhetoric attributed to them all the virtues: not only were they the only genuine patriots in the island, but they were also hardworking, whereas the whites preferred pampered idleness and the slaves shirked labor whenever they could. In view of their other virtues, the free people of color, it was assumed, would also be eternally grateful to the French nation for ensuring them the enjoyment of their natural rights through the law of April 4, 1792. Julien Raimond, a member of the group, knew that the

[25] Commissioners to minister of the navy, October 26, 1792, in AN, CC 9 A 7.

situation was not so simple; much of the letter he wrote to the free men of color in June 1792 was devoted to refuting arguments popular among the free colored landowners of the West that their rights would be better protected by a strong royal government than by one based on revolutionary principles.[26] But Sonthonax and Polverel sailed for Saint-Domingue with the conviction that they would find in the free population of color the firmest support for their mission of enforcing the national will in the colony. Once he left Cap Français for the western part of the colony in late October, Polverel realized that the situation was different from what the metropolitan revolutionaries had assumed. "In general, we can count on the enlightened men among the citizens of color," he wrote to the Convention, "but the mass of them don't think for themselves, and gratitude keeps them dependent on the [white] counter-revolutionaries who protected them earlier."[27] In Cap Français, however, Sonthonax found firm support from the local free men of color, eager for his backing in their struggle with the more numerous whites.

While Sonthonax and Polverel had certainly been exposed to the impassioned Jacobin rhetoric against the whites in the colonies, their official instructions, prepared by the navy minister Lacoste, had quite a different tone. Rather than laying all the blame for the problems of the colony on the whites, Lacoste emphasized the mutually destructive behavior of the whites and the free men of color on the island. The commissioners were to remind the free men of color of "the greatness of the deed that restores their exercise of all their rights of liberty and equality," but also of their duty to help restore order and of the "respect which they must never lose toward those who elevated them from the state of servitude," a rephrasing of a clause from the 1685 *Code noir* that implied that, even when free, individuals of African descent still needed to show deference to the whites. As for the whites, they were to be reminded that their rational self-interest dictated acceptance of equality with the free men of color. The commissioners, who were told to inspire specified sentiments of gratitude and respect in the free people of color, were not given equivalent instructions regarding the whites. Finally, the commissioners themselves were warned to treat all parties with "the consideration that one owes to our brothers, even in punishing them for the interest and the security of the country."[28] Officials in

[26] Raimond, letter of June 18, 1792, in AN, D XXV 13, d. 127.
[27] Polverel to Convention, December 3, 1792, in AN, D XXV 56, d. 557.
[28] "Mémoire du roi," June 17, 1792, in AN, D XXV 13, d. 123.

Lacoste's ministry met regularly with representatives of the white colonists and were attentive to their concerns. Just before the ships sailed, for instance, the colonists were assured that the troops had been ordered to change the motto on their flags from "Live free or die" to "The Nation, the Law, and the King," to make sure that they did not spread dangerous ideas in the island.[29]

Along with the conflicting advice they received from their Jacobin associates and the government, the commissioners were given very little guidance on how they were to carry out their mission. Both Brissot and Lacoste, who agreed on very little else, expressed the pious hope that the commissioners would succeed in installing a new colonial assembly, representing a racially mixed electorate, that would then work out a plan for the reform of slavery. Lacoste reminded them that once the assembly had been elected, their powers were limited to "exhortation." As for the rebellious slaves, some highly optimistic arithmetic allowed the minister to conclude that the commissioners would have 13,000 or more soldiers at their disposal. In addition to the 6,000 men being sent with the commissioners, he counted the permanent garrison, the reinforcements dispatched in December 1791, after the arrival of the first reports of the uprising, and even the sailors on the warships sent to the colony, and he made no allowance for the staggering losses from disease that befell every unit of European soldiers sent to the Antilles, which had actually reduced the number of combat-ready soldiers to about 2,000 at the time of the commissioners' arrival. He therefore concluded that the commissioners would have no trouble imposing their authority.[30]

In metropolitan France itself, the Revolution was about to improvise a procedure for dealing with the kind of situation Sonthonax and Polverel were to find themselves in once they landed in Saint-Domingue: the appointment of deputies on mission, members of the national legislature dispatched to a particular region as direct representatives of the sovereign

---

[29] "Registre des délibérations du bureau de la Commission de l'Assemblée coloniale de la partie française de Saint-Domingue," AN, D XXV 76, July 20, 1792. On the carrying out of this order, see General La Salle's report to Desparbès, July 11, 1792, in Corre, ed., *La Salle*, 27.

[30] "Mémoire du roi," June 17, 1792, in AN, D XXV 13, d. 123. A more detailed summary of the forces supposedly available in the colony listed 1,941 troops there as of November 1, 1791, 5,734 more sent in late 1791, and an additional 1,876 regular soldiers and 4,344 National Guards being sent with the commissioners, for a total of 13,895 men. "Tableau de l'expédition à St. Domingue au 5 juin 1792," in AN, D XXV 68, d. 690. For the actual number of men available in September 1792, see Blanchelande's report to the commissioners, n.d., in AN, D XXV 4, d. 32.

nation, with authority to commandeer local resources, to supersede or replace local officials, and to take all necessary measures to guarantee the nation's security. These deputies on mission, several hundred of whom would be named at various times during the period while Sonthonax and Polverel were in Saint-Domingue, were the architects of what came to be known as "revolutionary government." They enforced the emergency measures of the Terror and could claim responsibility for ensuring the victory of the Revolution during the critical years of 1793 and 1794.[31] Although Sonthonax and Polverel would, in the end, carry out changes in Saint-Domingue more radical than anything any of the deputies on mission in France could have dreamed of, the colonial commissioners were not copying the techniques developed in the metropole. For one thing, they were not deputies; they had had no direct role in making the laws they were attempting to enforce, and they were always acutely conscious that the legislators might not uphold their actions. Equally significantly, they sailed from France before the fall of the monarchy on August 10, 1792 and the creation of the system of deputies on mission. Only dimly aware of what other Jacobins were doing across the ocean in late 1792 and the first half of 1793, Sonthonax and Polverel were forced to improvise their own version of revolutionary government.

The two men's achievement in creating a colonial version of revolutionary government was all the more remarkable in that, unlike the deputies on mission in France, they soon found themselves at the far end of a highly uncertain chain of authority. Appointed by orders of the king in June 1792, they sailed from France a few weeks before the journée of August 10, 1792, which toppled the monarchy and the entire constitutional system created with so much effort in 1791. They would not learn about these events until October 2, 1792, several weeks after they landed in the colony.[32] Before handing over powers to the National Convention, the rump Legislative Assembly did confirm the commissioners' powers, but at the time of the June 20, 1793 crisis, supporters of General Galbaud would not hesitate to remind the commissioners that they had been appointed by the fallen king, whereas the general owed his office to the Republic. With the fall of the monarchy, the commissioners found themselves corresponding with new ministers – first Gaspard

[31] On the deputies on mission, see the pathbreaking work of Michel Biard, *Missionnaires de la République. Les représentants du peuple en mission (1793–1795)* (Paris: Comité des Travaux Historiques et Scientifiques, 2002).
[32] *Moniteur général*, October 3, 1792 (Colonial Assembly, October 2).

Monge, then Jean Dalbarade – whom they had never met and who had had nothing to do with their appointment. "Corresponding" is something of a euphemism: the two-month delay for letters crossing the ocean meant that conditions had often changed beyond recognition before the commissioners got any response to their messages. Monge was able to send the commissioners only a handful of missives before they found themselves facing a new crisis that had not been anticipated when they were appointed: the outbreak of war with Britain and Spain. In addition to the other points on their agenda, the commissioners, both of them civilians, now had to oversee military operations on both land and sea.

As Sonthonax and Polverel were attempting to manage these multiple problems, the Convention was changing its mind about colonial policy. On July 16, 1793, even before it received word of the disaster on June 20, 1793, it would officially vote to recall and indict Sonthonax and Polverel. They were not officially notified of this decision until June 1794, but Sonthonax learned the news from unofficial sources by September 1793,[33] shortly after he issued his edict of general emancipation on August 29, 1793, and before Polverel made his own emancipation proclamations. Less determined men might well have abandoned their posts or at least their radical policies in these circumstances. Even with the very real possibility of a death sentence for abusing their authority hanging over their heads, however, Sonthonax and Polverel pursued their experiment in revolutionary government until an official from France finally arrived to deliver the decree recalling them.

The lengths to which the two commissioners would find themselves going in their attempt to carry out their mission could not have been foreseen as they set out to cross the ocean in the summer of 1792, although they knew from the start that they would encounter difficulties. In addition to their colleague Ailhaud's evident lack of enthusiasm for the mission – he only arrived in the port of Rochefort two weeks after Sonthonax and Polverel – they soon realized they were going to have problems with the man appointed to replace Blanchelande as governor general and military commander in Saint-Domingue, Jean-Jacques-Pierre Desparbès. Why this elderly aristocrat had been appointed to such a critical post has never been explained.[34] "When one is 72 years old, with 57 years of service and the gout, one should not come to Saint-Domingue in troubled

---

[33] Stein, *Sonthonax*, 104.

[34] His appointment was noted, without any special enthusiasm, by the representatives of the white colonists in Paris on June 9, 1792. AN, D XXV 76.

times," another officer in the colony wrote.[35] Desparbès certainly did not share the commissioners' enthusiasm for the Revolution. During the two-month voyage across the Atlantic, Desparbès dined with the ship's captain, emphasizing his superior social status, while Sonthonax and Polverel were seated at a less prestigious table with the ship's other officers.[36] By the time the party arrived in Saint-Domingue, the commissioners had developed a thorough distrust of the man who was supposed to ensure the military support they would need to execute their mission.

They had fewer worries about the troops themselves. Three-quarters of the soldiers accompanying the expedition were members of the National Guard, the new citizen army created in the wake of the storming of the Bastille. Many of them shared the Jacobin commitment to racial equality. The members of the 1st battalion from the Aube department had petitioned to be included in the expedition so that they could support "our brothers, called the men of color," according to one of their officers.[37] Defying the military chain of command, a captain in the 41st regiment wrote directly to the commissioners before they sailed, announcing that "Since my arrival, I have observed that the troops are well disposed to support your mission, the National Guard is animated by an excellent spirit, all the battalions are ready to rise to the demands of the circumstances." Even if his unit was ordered back to France, the captain insisted, "I would stay to defend the just cause of our oppressed brothers, the men of color, who, in courage and in virtue, are worth a hundred times more than their oppressors, these unworthy whites, these colonial princes, who bear the blame for all the misfortunes of Saint-Domingue."[38] A particularly important role in the events leading up to the journée of June 20, 1793 would be played by the men of one of the older "line" units sent with the expedition, the 16th dragoons, known as the "dragoons of Orléans," and especially by one of that unit's officers, a 42-year-old lieutenant-colonel named Étienne Laveaux. Recommending him for a decoration just before he sailed, the unit's commanding officer noted that Laveaux, "going beyond the call of duty, sought and obtained permission to sail with the 200 men from this regiment bound for the colonies."[39] Next to Sonthonax and Polverel, no other white would do

---

[35] Rochefontaine to La Salle, October 20, 1792, in Corre, ed., *La Salle*, 44.

[36] AN, D XXV 13, d. 120.

[37] "Mémoire" from Pierre Mazingant, lieutenant-colonel, in AN, D XXV 80, d. 787.

[38] AN, D XXV 13, d. 120.

[39] Letter of April 27, 1792, in Service historique de l'armée de terre (SHAT) 7 Yd. 137 (Laveaux). Despite its name, the unit, only part of which was sent to the colony, had

more to further the triumph of freedom and racial equality in the colony than Laveaux.

Encouraged by the enthusiasm of the troops, the commissioners do not seem to have paid as much attention to the attitudes of the sailors. In July 1792, France was not yet at war with its great naval rival, Britain, and the commissioners probably did not realize how important the navy was going to become in their operations. The ordinary sailors had more in common with the slaves than any other group of whites: the seamen were largely illiterate and subject to harsh discipline on their ships.[40] By 1792, France's sailors had already proved themselves to be a major element of revolutionary unrest, and in fact, both the crew of the ship on which the commissioners crossed the ocean, the *America*, and that of the *Jupiter*, the flagship of the Saint-Domingue squadron, had participated in the series of mutinies that rocked the navy's main Atlantic port of Brest in the fall of 1790.[41] The men on the ships in the Saint-Domingue *station*, or squadron, professed revolutionary sentiments, but many of them were anxious to return home after long stays in the Caribbean. The *Eole*, one of the three ships of the line in the colony, had been on duty there since 1790, and its sister ship, the *Jupiter*, since early 1791. Noting the newly appointed squadron commander Joseph Cambis's concern about the crews' homesickness in early 1793, a naval official remarked that "reason will be on the side of the men."[42]

In addition to their desire to return to France, the sailors posed a threat to the commissioners' mission because they refused to accept the new values of racial equality embodied in the law of April 4, 1792. "Prejudice has always led the sailors sent to the islands to share the sentiment of white superiority over the men of color," one French official commented.[43] The commissioners may have succeeded in establishing a bond with the *America*'s sailors during their crossing: that vessel would

been stationed in Rennes since the outbreak of the Revolution, where it had earned a reputation for its "sustained patriotism," according to a testimonial from the city's municipality in May 1792 included in Laveaux's dossier.

[40] A measure of the sailors' low level of literacy is provided by a document drawn up by the men of the *America* on July 23, 1793. The vast majority of the 290 men who signed this declaration made an "x" rather than writing their own names. AN, D XXV 54, d. 523.

[41] William S. Cormack, *Revolution and Political Conflict in the French Navy 1789–1794* (Cambridge: Cambridge University Press, 1995), 104–5, 107.

[42] Report of February 16, 1793, in Service historique de la marine (SHM), BB 4 24; report from Ports et Arsenaux department, February 14, 1793, in AN, CC 9 A.

[43] "Réflexions sur l'affaire du Cap françois," in Library of Congress (hereafter LC), Genet papers, reel 6.

be the only major warship in the colony whose men did not join the uprising against them on June 20, 1793. As the events of that day would show, however, Sonthonax and Polverel failed to understand the attitudes of most of the sailors or to anticipate the effect their disaffection might have on the political situation in Saint-Domingue.

Confident of the loyalty of the troops, if not of their ostensible commander, Desparbès, the commissioners were more concerned with the reception awaiting them in Cap Français, their intended point of arrival. Even their official instructions from Lacoste discussed the possibility that opposition might make it impossible for them to land there. Via Julien Raimond, the men of color in the colony tried to persuade the commissioners to avoid Le Cap altogether and put ashore in Saint-Marc, where the free men of color and the wealthy white plantation owners had established the "Council of Peace and Union" to challenge the all-white Colonial Assembly in Cap Français.[44] The commissioners decided to test reactions to their mission in Cap Français before making a decision about their destination. When the *America* was still almost a month out of port, they dispatched their secretary, Olivier Delpech, on an *aviso*, a fast messenger boat, to carry copies of the law specifying their powers to Le Cap and to bring back a report on the political situation in the city.[45] When the *aviso* arrived on September 12, Delpech found a situation different from what the commissioners had been led to expect. Chastened by Blanchelande's catastrophic defeat at Les Platons in early August and by the near-disaster that had taken place in Cap Français on August 13–14, the white authorities were ready to do whatever was necessary to convince the commissioners that they accepted the law of April 4, 1792; they wanted at all costs to facilitate the arrival of the troops who, they hoped, would finally put an end to the slave uprising.[46]

Rather than threatening to obstruct the commissioners' arrival, the whites in Le Cap immediately announced an elaborate welcoming ceremony for them. The Colonial Assembly, the Provincial Assembly and the Municipality all sent delegations to meet the commissioners before

---

[44] Letter of June 29, 1792, unsigned but probably by Julien Raimond, in AN, D XXV 13, d. 120. On the Council of Peace and Union, see Yvan Debbasch, *Couleur et liberté*, 215, 221. Another letter sent to the commissioners while they were waiting to sail, from a former printer in Cap Français, warned them that if they went to Saint-Marc, they would not have access to a printing press to issue their proclamations. Mozard to commissioners, June 18, 1792, in AN, D XXV 13, d. 120.

[45] Instruction to captain Cambis, August 23, 1792, from Sonthonax, Polverel, Ailhaud, and Desparbès, in AN, D XXV 13, d. 120.

[46] *Moniteur général*, September 14 and 15, 1792.

they landed. The city authorities decreed that when the commissioners arrived, all businesses would close for the day. The local National Guard would line the quays. The three local political assemblies would send deputations to greet the new arrivals and lead them to the city's church, where the members of the assemblies would await them.[47] Everything would be done to convince the commissioners that they were in the midst of a loyal and patriotic citizenry, ready to obey the national will.

The commissioners understood that in order to maintain this apparent harmony, they needed to give the colonists the assurance that they had not arrived with hidden intentions. They were strongly urged in this direction by the veteran white agitator, Larchevesque-Thibaud, who would later become one of their leading enemies. In April 1792, Larchevesque-Thibaud had publicly denounced the free men of color, but he now managed to persuade the commissioners that he favored the law of April 4, 1792.[48] Representatives of the white colonists in Paris had warned their colleagues in Saint-Domingue that Sonthonax, in particular, was a dangerous abolitionist. Sonthonax and Polverel, therefore, both spoke to the crowd in the church on the day of their arrival and unequivocally promised to maintain slavery. "We declare that only the colonial assemblies, once they are constitutionally formed, have the right to pronounce on the condition of the slaves. We declare that slavery is necessary for the agriculture and the prosperity of the colonies," Sonthonax announced.[49] "It was not the moment to go into my private opinion about the emancipation of the blacks," he said in 1795, explaining why he had been willing to make such a statement. "It is true that, in some political writings, I had expressed opinions favorable to the emancipation of the slaves, but ... the opinion of a private person is one thing, the conduct of a public official responsible for carrying out the law is something else."[50]

Having pledged to uphold the slave system, the Jacobin commissioners found themselves plunged into the alien political world of the colonists. P. J. Raboteau, president of the Colonial Assembly, delivered a long harangue repeating the colonists' catechism on the subject of slavery: the blacks were better off on the plantations than they had been in Africa, the maintenance of the system required that the masters have unrestricted authority over their slaves, and the French constitution explicitly

---

[47] *Moniteur général*, September 15, 1792.
[48] Larchevesque-Thibaud to Leborgne, September 17, 1792, in AN, D XXV 80, d. 784.
[49] *Moniteur général*, September 21, 1792.
[50] *Débats entre les accusateurs et les accusés dans l'affaire des colonies*, 6: 372.

left all regulations concerning slavery to the discretion of the colonists. He referred openly to the rumors that the commissioners intended to free the slaves, saying that if that was the case, then "you cannot do less, without combining the most striking injustice with a ferocious and homicidal barbarism, than to send these slaves back to the place where your European brothers got them." The president of the provincial assembly followed Raboteau's speech with a grim description of the destruction caused by the slave insurrection. Nevertheless, he assured the commissioners, "You will soon recognize that our unfortunate slaves, seduced, armed, made to revolt against masters they cherish, are only the blind instruments that the enemies of the Revolution and of France manipulate as they please."[51] The commissioners made no protest against these diatribes, which were both published immediately in the *Moniteur général*. If he had said anything critical, "an insurrection would have broken out then and there," Sonthonax testified at the hearings into the mission that the Convention ordered in 1795.[52] Charles Guillaume Castaing, who had emerged as one of the leaders of the free men of color in the fall of 1791 and who had played an important role at the time of the troubles in August 1792, also spoke at the ceremony, expressing his group's hope that the commissioners would implement the law of April 4, 1792; a plantation owner himself, he said nothing about slavery.[53]

The arrival of the troops and the commissioners' unequivocal endorsement of the status quo regarding slavery raised hopes among the whites. On September 25, 1792, the manager of the marquis de Gallifet's properties near Le Cap wrote to his employer asking for funds so that he could begin putting their plantations back in operation.[54] The Commission had been in Saint-Domingue for less than two weeks when news arrived from France that the monarchy and the Constitution of 1791 had been overthrown. Although the metropolitan Jacobins had often denounced the whites in the colony for their supposed royalist sentiments, many of the colonists were as rabidly suspicious of the "executive power" as any metropolitan revolutionary, and the change of regime in France did not alter the situation in Cap Français. The commissioners were quick to publicize the fact that the French legislature had confirmed their powers

[51] *Moniteur général*, September 22, 1792.
[52] *Débats entre les accusateurs et les accusés dans l'affaire des colonies*, 6: 372.
[53] *Moniteur général*, September 24, 1792. In addition to Castaing and the presidents of the two assemblies, the mayor of Cap Français and the town's curé also gave short speeches.
[54] Mossut to Gallifet, September 25, 1792, in AN, 107 AP 128 (Gallifet papers).

and, indeed, extended them (although, unbeknownst to them, the new navy minister, Monge, had also assured the white colonists in France that "the National Assembly had no intention of extending to the unfree Negroes the edict concerning liberty and equality.")[55] According to the announcement read to the Colonial Assembly by the Commission's secretary, Delpech, "the national assembly has converted the civil commissioners' power to give orders into a dictatorial power, which it has no doubt decided was needed for the regeneration of the colony."[56] While the events of August 10, 1792 in France and the subsequent proclamation of the Republic in September 1792 did not alter the opinions of the white population in Le Cap, they had a powerful impact on the black insurgents in the nearby mountains. If their white enemies were going to turn against their king, the black leaders saw an opportunity to gain the ruler's favor. Biassou, one of the two main black leaders, reaffirmed his loyalty to the deposed monarch, "Louis XVI, king of France, our superior," and even assumed the title of viceroy, saying that he was "waiting for the orders of the king, our master, and I hope with the aid of the Lord to uphold his rights."[57]

The commissioners' first attempt to use their powers decisively failed, however. Knowing that the strength of their army would quickly diminish once the soldiers began to contract the diseases that invariably attacked Europeans arriving in the country, the Commission tried to launch an immediate offensive against the black insurgents. Their military resources were unexpectedly augmented at the end of September when an additional 3,000 troops commanded by general D. M. J. Vimeur de Rochambeau arrived in Saint-Domingue. Rochambeau's force had been destined to reinforce metropolitan control of the colony of Martinique, but royalist opposition there had kept them from landing. On October 5, 1792, the *Moniteur général* printed an appeal for volunteers for the imminent "general assault": "There is no more reason not to attack. The government has been renewed; the officials who we suspected are no longer in command. The town will be guarded by patriotic and regular troops, by public officials and by the older men, and everyone understands that we need to conquer our homes!" Instead,

---

[55] AN, D XXV 76, entry for August 25, 1792. Three days later, the white colonists met with Danton, who "showed the greatest interest in the misfortunes of Saint-Domingue."

[56] *Moniteur général*, October 3, 1792 (Colonial Assembly, October 2). Gaspard Monge, appointed as navy minister after August 10, 1792, wrote to the commissioners to confirm their appointments on August 25, 1792. AN, D XXV 11, d. 103.

[57] Biassou, letters of August 24, 1792 and December 18, 1792, in AN, D XXV 5, d. 48.

nothing happened: the commissioners and General Desparbès, who was supposed to command the campaign, accused each other of being unwilling to take the responsibility for setting the troops in motion.[58] Four weeks after he had written optimistically about his plans for putting the Gallifet plantations back in operation, the manager Mossut was in despair. The newly arrived soldiers "fall sick by the hundreds and even die ... these new troops will disappear from the soil of the colony without having been of any use. For the shame of the human species, we are occupied with nothing except vengeances and personal hatreds."[59] Rather than taking the war to the insurgents, the commissioners found themselves preoccupied with political conflicts in Cap Français itself.

The arrival of the commissioners and the troops gave the white political leaders in Cap Français the opportunity to win their struggle against their local enemies, the remaining royal colonial officials and, above all, the commanding officers of the permanent garrison. The day after they set foot on shore, the Colonial Assembly presented the commissioners with its accusations against Blanchelande, their principal *bête noire*.[60] Blanchelande had, in any case, submitted his resignation; the commissioners interrogated him and decided that there was no conclusive evidence of his counterrevolutionary intentions, but decided that "the general cry raised against him forces us to regard the prolongation of his stay in Le Cap as very dangerous for public order."[61] They ordered him to take ship for France and turn himself over to the National Assembly. Once the commissioners had accepted their demand for the ouster of Blanchelande, the local white "patriots" stepped up their campaign against the rest of their enemies. "You cannot bring about the triumph of the party of the revolution except by expelling, by putting under the avenging blade of the laws the chiefs of the opposing party," Larchevesque-Thibaud wrote to them.[62]

---

[58] Commissioners to Desparbès and Desparbès to commissioners, September 27, 1792, both in AN, D XXV 4, d. 32; Stein, *Sonthonax*, 50; draft report of commissioners, n.d., in AN, D XXV 13, d. 125, and final version, October 22, 1792, in AN, D XXV 5, d. 35.

[59] Letter of October 22, 1792, in AN, 107 AP 128.

[60] AN, D XXV 47, d. 444. After submitting an initial list of charges on September 21, the Assembly forwarded a voluminous "Mémoire" attacking Blanchelande on September 25, 1792. Suspicious as they were of Blanchelande, the commissioners nevertheless concluded that the colonists had not come up with any actual evidence that "is both sufficiently serious and sufficiently proved to allow one to conclude with certainty that he deliberately stirred up the troubles that have agitated and continue to agitate the colony." AN, D XXV 47, d. 444bis, letter of September 30, 1792.

[61] AN, D XXV 47, d. 444bis.

[62] Larchevesque-Thibaud to commissioners, September 30, 1792, in AN, D XXV 73, d. 731.

   In early October, the commissioners, following their instructions, dissolved the all-white Colonial Assembly and replaced it with a twelve-
member Interim Commission, composed of six white members selected
by the former Colonial Assembly and six free men of color chosen by the
civil commissioners themselves. This procedure had been foreseen in the
commissioners' instructions; they justified it as "the only way to reconcile the necessity of having a representative body for the colony with the
interests of a people which, at war with its slaves, has no time to waste on
political discussions."[63] The free colored members were established leaders of that group, including Pierre Pinchinat, Castaing, who had emerged
as a spokesman for the men of color in Le Cap in November 1791, Louis
Boisrond, whose nephew, Boisrond-Tonnerre, is usually credited with
drafting the Haitian constitution of 1804, and Julien Raimond's brother,
François.[64] In 1793, the white colonists would make the commissioners' "arbitrary" choice of members to the Interim Commission one of
their major accusations against Sonthonax and Polverel, but at the time,
there were few protests about the matter. The white members included
Raboteau, who had harangued the commissioners about the need to
defend slavery at the ceremonies welcoming them, and several other
prominent "patriot" fire eaters from the Colonial Assembly; the decision
to create a governing body with representatives of the free men of color
had the approval of white leaders such as Larchevesque-Thibaud, who
worked closely with the commissioners during the first weeks of their
mission.[65] The white colonists' attention was still focused on following
up on their success in using the commissioners to avenge themselves
against Blanchelande by demanding a broader purge of their enemies.
   Facing the loss of their institutional stronghold, the Colonial Assembly,
which was dissolved on October 12, 1792, the self-proclaimed patriots
followed the model of municipal revolutions in metropolitan France and
of the Paris uprising of August 10, 1792 by organizing a club, the Société
des Amis de la Convention nationale, which held its first open meeting
on October 15, 1792. The club announced that it would "work to shape

[63] Proclamation of October 12, 1792, Le Cap, in CAOM, F 197, Moreau de Saint-Méry
    papers.
[64] A letter published in the *Patriote françois* listed them as Pinchinat, Castaing, Latortue
    (a free black), François Raimond (a brother of Julien Raimond) and Boisrond-Daquin.
    Letter from Cap Français, November 5, 1792, in *Patriote françois*, January 9, 1793.
[65] *Extrait des registres de l'Assemblée coloniale*, October 13, 1792, in AN, D XXV 112,
    d. 892; Larchevesque-Thibaud to the civil commissioners, October 12, 1792, in AN,
    D XXV 73, d. 728.

the public spirit in the colony, and to purge it of this aristocratic madness, innate in Saint-Domingue ... " and that it would "keep a close eye on all the perfidious plots that may still be aimed at the happiness of the colony."[66] Participants in the club included not only leading members of the colonial "patriot" movement, but also some of the ardently revolutionary soldiers from France, to whom it must have looked like the revolutionary clubs they were familiar with from the metropole, and sailors from the warships in the harbor. As the newly arrived French soldiers began to succumb to tropical diseases, they were particularly receptive to club propaganda accusing counterrevolutionary conspirators of poisoning their food and drink.[67] In the pages of the *Journal politique*, a local newspaper hostile to the club, Colonel Cambefort complained publicly about the "patriot" agitators' efforts to influence the newly arrived troops.[68]

Lieutenant-colonel Laveaux from the 16th dragoons spoke at the club's inaugural meeting on October 15, and soldiers from his unit provoked a crisis the next day when they publicly accused officers from the regiment du Cap, the city's permanent garrison troops, of having insulted the new republican constitution. Sonthonax had to rush to the scene to keep the confrontation between the two units from escalating into open violence; he succeeded in getting soldiers from both units to stage a public reconciliation at the club.[69] In a scenario familiar from French revolutionary politics, the club rapidly became a virtual countergovernment. In defiance of the commissioners, the club circulated a printed list of "names of traitors to the country" and demanded their arrest and deportation to France. The list included Desparbès, Cambefort, and over a hundred other suspected counterrevolutionaries.[70]

The club's session of October 17, 1792 turned into a mass meeting, highlighted by the appearance of a battalion of free men of color commanded by Cairou, one of the leaders of the group at the time of the August events, who announced their support for the protest against Cambefort. Sonthonax pleaded with the group to give the commissioners

---

[66] *Moniteur général*, October 16, 1792.

[67] *Mémoire de la Société des amis de la Convention nationale* (Cap Français: Parent, 1792), in AN, D XXV 112, d. 892.

[68] Cambefort to civil commissioners, in *Journal politique*, October 9, 1792.

[69] *Moniteur général*, October 17, 1792; "Suite du supplément, 16 oct. 1792," in CAOM, F 3 197, Moreau de Saint-Méry papers.

[70] "Avis aux citoyens patriotes," printed by Baillio, in CAOM, F 3 197, Moreau de Saint-Méry papers.

time to consider their demands, but the *Moniteur général* reported that on the October 18, club members had nearly taken matters into their own hands, renouncing their intention to seize Cambefort and his colleagues only because the night was too dark for them to see. "All night, the Place d'Armes echoed with shouts," Moreau de Saint-Méry's correspondent reported.[71] On the morning of October 19, the general alarm was sounded throughout the city, and a large crowd, made up not only of whites but also of some of the town's armed free men of color, assembled at the Place d'Armes. As they would on June 20, 1793, "the sailors from the harbor came ashore and offered their services to their endangered brothers," the club's official account claimed.[72] General Desparbès refused the crowd's demand that he hand over Cambefort, but the 3rd battalion of the Aisne, one of the units from the Martinique expedition, disobeyed Desparbès and joined the crowd, along with the 16th dragoons. The civil commissioners decided that they needed to yield to the demand for the deportation of Cambefort in order to avoid further violence. They sent orders to the governor general, Desparbès, to prepare an escort to enforce the deportation order, and to Cambefort, insisting that he report to them so that they could put him under their protection.[73] Desparbès refused to obey them, and Cambefort took refuge in his unit's barracks, protected by loyal soldiers. The furious crowd seized several cannon from the city arsenal and prepared to attack the barracks. At this point, the mounted National Guards, wearing their yellow coats, tried to drive the crowd out of the Place Montarcher in front of the Government House. Yellow was the color of the prince of Condé, the leader of the counterrevolutionary émigré army in Germany, and the angry crowd reacted by massacring the unit's commander and several of his men.[74]

With great effort, Sonthonax, Laveaux, and soldiers from some of the other units managed to defuse the crisis, although there were several casualties.[75] Cambefort and the officers loyal to him finally agreed to let themselves be put onto a ship that would carry them back to France. The

[71] *Moniteur général*, October 20, 1792; "Suite du supplément, 16 oct. 1792," in CAOM, F 3 197, Moreau de Saint-Méry papers.

[72] *Mémoire de la société des amis de la Convention nationale*, in AN, D XXV 112, d. 892.

[73] Draft report of commissioners, n.d., in AN, D XXV 13, d. 125.

[74] *Moniteur universel* (Paris), December 19, 1792 (letter from Le Cap, October 21, 1792).

[75] The marquis de Gallifet's correspondent Mossut claimed seven people were killed. Mossut to Gallifet, October 22, 1792, in AN, 107 AP 128.

Moniteur général, which had enthusiastically supported the club movement, crowed over the spectacle of the royalist officers marching to the
port, surrounded by a crowd singing the *ça ira*, the French revolutionary anthem. Cambefort remembered the "atrocious" scene bitterly: "the
harbor, the waterfront, the battery were filled with armed men; the cries,
the shouts, the insults the threats, the muskets pointed at the officers'
chests, the demand that they surrender their arms, the cannon that had
been brought along, finally seven or eight thousand men to take away
forty." At the following day's club meeting, its president congratulated
the members on "a triumph that assures you the quick defeat of the
slaves in rebellion, since you have taken away their guides, their protectors, their suppliers."[76] The commissioners were not far from sharing the
club radicals' point of view. In a draft of a letter to the minister of the
navy describing the events, they asserted that "the connivance between
the government officials and the rebellious slaves was obvious" and
claimed that without the measures taken on the October 19, "the friends
and correspondents of Coblentz and Martinique were going to raise the
white standard," the symbol of the royalist movement. "The journée of
19 October was for the colony what the journée of 10 August was for the
metropole," they wrote.[77] They were aware that they had practically lost
control of the city to the club, but they claimed to have persuaded the
members to end their meetings, since "these outbursts of liberty could be
dangerous in a country with slavery."[78]

The events of October 19, 1792 also allowed the commissioners to
rid themselves of Desparbès, whom they blamed for refusing to take the
offensive against the slave insurgents and for disobeying their orders
to deport Cambefort. The elderly general agreed to resign his post and
return to France; the Commission appointed Rochambeau, the commander of the troops meant for Martinique, in his place. Ten years
later, the same Rochambeau would take command of the forces sent by
Napoleon to reinstate slavery in the colony and would become notorious
for his cruelty in fighting the blacks. In 1792, however, he was regarded
as a staunch supporter of the new republican regime, who even claimed
to have abolitionist sympathies. "I foresaw that France would one day
emancipate the slaves she was then fighting against, and that she would
repent for having given legal cover in the New World to massacres of

---

[76] *Moniteur général*, October 20, 21, 1792; Cambefort, *Mémoire justificatif*, 36.
[77] Draft report of commissioners, n.d., in AN, D XXV 13, d. 125.
[78] Civil Commissioners to Minister of the Navy, October 26, 1792, in AN, CC 9 A, 7.

those who claimed the benefit of the principles that had made the French take up arms in Europe," he wrote.[79] The commissioners, relieved to have an energetic republican officer they could count on, assured the minister in France that "his first successes ... against the rebellious slaves will show you that if he is supported by the good will of the citizens, the war won't last long."[80]

The news of the commissioners' first accomplishments in Saint-Domingue impressed their principal supporter in France, Julien Raimond, who congratulated Sonthonax on "the miracles that you have carried out in Le Cap. What! you have gotten Larchevesque Thibaud to dine between two black men and he didn't eat them up; if that it not a miracle, I don't know how to describe one." Even the white colonists in Paris were "singing the praises" of the commissioners for deporting the hated royalist officials. The appointment of the racially mixed Interim Commission fulfilled Raimond's dreams; as he wrote, "it is a natural thing to see animals of the same species live together even though they are of different colors, but the problem was to open the eyes and the minds of the colonists, and that it what you have done." As far as Raimond could see, there was only more task to carry out: "All we still need to do is to get the slaves to return to order. How can it be that no one has had the idea of a proclamation that I think would have a great and salutary effect? One does much more harm in granting freedom to armed men, than if one would promise them that they could gain it by work and the practice of virtues."[81]

With the crisis in Cap Français seemingly resolved and with the military situation in the North Province apparently in good hands, the three commissioners decided that the time had come to pay attention to the rest of the colony. Their instructions had given them permission to separate if they felt the need to do so, and on October 29, 1792, Polverel and Ailhaud departed to extend the Commission's authority to the West and South Provinces.[82] Sonthonax was left alone to face the club movement and to deal with the North Province's other pressing problems. Their

---

[79] D. M. J. Vimeur de Rochambeau, "Sur les Antilles," ms. Ruggles 410, Newberry Library. This manuscript is undated but seems to have been written in the mid-1790s, after the emancipation decree of 1794, when Rochambeau was sent on a second mission to the Caribbean.

[80] Draft report of commissioners, n.d., in AN, D XXV 13, d. 125.

[81] Raimond to Sonthonax, December 21, 1792, in AN, D XXV 16, d. 158, responding to Sonthonax's letter of November 8, 1792.

[82] Sonthonax, report to Convention, n.d., in AN, D XXV 4, d. 41.

success on October 19, 1792 had only whetted the club leaders' appetite for power. "Should you allow a small number of ambitious men, without jobs, driven by the desire for appointments, or blinded by hatred and vengeance, to designate victims and mislead the people?" Sonthonax asked the members in an open letter on October 31, 1792, but his appeal was ignored.[83] "Every crazy thing the human spirit in delirium could imagine, every atrocity that fanaticism could inspire, that was the awful spectacle that the city of Le Cap offered" under the domination of the club, one colonist later wrote.[84]

Tension remained high in the city; on November 11, a delegation from the crew of the *Eole* visited the club to complain that their patriotism had been impugned by civilians, and there were rumors that the warship might open fire on the town.[85] Violence broke out again on November 14, when whites attacked a group of prisoners sent back to the city by Rochambeau after the capture of the town of Ouanaminthe, at the eastern tip of the North Province. The dead included two white deserters, and the *Moniteur général* came close to excusing the massacre, editorializing that "soldiers, furious no doubt at the thought that men who had marched under the same flag with them had been barbarous enough to join slave brigands, and to stain their hands with the blood of their brothers, could not restrain themselves," but Sonthonax and Rochambeau reacted sharply. The incident undermined Rochambeau's attempt to assure the slaves that they would not be punished if they surrendered, and it renewed Sonthonax's fear that the white mob, egged on by the club, was gaining control of the city.[86] Meanwhile, Sonthonax had become embroiled in a dispute with his colleague Polverel because of his effort to impose an emergency tax to meet the government's desperate need for money. The measure had actually been proposed by the Colonial Assembly before its dissolution and then endorsed by the Interim Commission,[87] but Polverel questioned both the Commission's authority to take such action and the wisdom of trying to compel contributions. He preferred to try to raise money in his region by appealing

---

[83] *Moniteur général*, November 1, 1792.
[84] Dalmas, *Révolution de Saint-Domingue*, 64–5.
[85] *Moniteur général*, November 14, 1792.
[86] *Moniteur général*, November 15, 1792 (report of killings), November 16 (proclamation of Sonthonax), November 17 (proclamation of Rochambeau).
[87] Pouget, letter to commissioners, September 13, 1792, in AN, D XXV 4, d. 41; *Extrait des registres de la Commission intermédiaire de la partie française de Saint-Domingue*, no. 3 (November 7, 1792), in AN, D XXV 63, d. 639.

for voluntary donations. Sonthonax responded irritably, "In the present state of things, one can't take the time to debate principles, we must act, we must save the colony, and this is the only means left to us."[88] The argument between the two men, which soon became public, was a major distraction for Sonthonax and undermined his effort to impose his authority.

At the end of November, Sonthonax and Rochambeau came into direct confrontation with the Amis de la Convention Nationale. The apparent harmony between white "patriots" and the free men of color that had prevailed in October had now dissolved. The free men of color pressed Sonthonax to show that the law of April 4, 1792 had real meaning by appointing some of them as officers in predominantly white units. "Since their lack of education and deep knowledge naturally excluded the citizens of color from civil positions, it was just to let them have military jobs for which they are well suited," the free colored leaders wrote in their account of events in the fall of 1792.[89] Despite their ostensible acceptance of the law of April 4, 1792, many of the city's whites rejected these demands. The prominent Philadelphia merchant Stephen Girard's brother wrote to him complaining that "the criminal, execrable and low class of the m's [mulattoes] occupies a position on the level with, or above my class, which represents its benefactors."[90] Within the Le Cap club, there were angry charges that Sonthonax and Rochambeau were favoring the men of color and their own supporters for appointments to military and government posts. Étienne Laveaux, the commander of the 16th dragoons, came under attack for his defense of the law of April 4 and his public promise that the next vacant officer's position in his unit would go to a man of color.[91] Sonthonax, for his part, charged that white opponents of the law were stirring up trouble by showing the soldiers copies of a forged Convention decree that supposedly forbade the appointment of free colored men as officers in white units and encouraging them to resist the integration of the officer corps.[92]

---

[88] Sonthonax to Polverel and Ailhaud, November 21, 1792, in AN, D XXV 12, d. 110.

[89] "Les citoyens de couleur et nègres libres de la partie française de Saint-Domingue, à la Convention nationale," February 20, 1793, in AN, D XXV 110, p. 18.

[90] Jean Girard to Stephen Girard, November 1792, cited in Ashli White, "'A Flood of Impure Lava': Saint-Dominguan Refugees in the United States, 1791–1820," (Ph. D. diss., Columbia University, 2003), 31.

[91] Letter of Gervais, January 29, 1793, in AN, D XXV 80, d. 782.

[92] Copies of Sonthonax's "Rélation officielle des événemens arrivés au Cap les 1.er, 2, 3, 4, 5, 6, 7, et 8. X.bre 1792" are in AN, D XXV 5, d. 43, and D XXV 12, d. 111. I have used the version in D XXV 5.

On December 1, 1792, Sonthonax decided the moment had come for a showdown. He banned a communal assembly announced for that day and forbade any further meetings of the Amis de la Convention Nationale. On December 2, 1792, the régiment du Cap, whose men had said that they would not accept the appointment of an officer of mixed race, were ordered to assemble on the Champ de Mars to take an oath to obey the law of April 4, 1792. The unit's "resistance had the support of many," a white chronicler recalled, while "the mulattoes showed the most violent resentment" against the recalcitrant soldiers.[93] To guard against any disturbances, Sonthonax also summoned both white and free colored National Guards to the Champ de Mars. The white National Guards never responded, leaving several hundred armed men of color from the Sixth Battalion confronting the soldiers from the Cap regiment, who continued to defy Sonthonax's commands.[94]

News of the standoff on the Champ de Mars set off agitation throughout the city. Rumors exaggerated the number of free men of color involved. One witness saw Louis Verneuil, one of Sonthonax's opponents from the club, in the streets telling people "that if all the citizens were like him, the civil commissioner would soon be on board a ship, that this was the only way to restore calm, adding that he was a Jacobite [sic], a philanthropist, that if he hadn't been paid off by the men of color, he wouldn't be so keen on enforcing the so-called law."[95] At 2 P.M., as the white crowd neared the Champ de Mars, a bizarre incident shattered the tense standoff between the troops there. A man carrying a large sack entered the square and approached the free colored National Guards. Stopped by several whites, he said that he was just bringing the soldiers some bread; they had been standing in formation since early morning. The whites claimed, however, that under the biscuits in his sack were cartridges, proof that the free colored troops were preparing to fire on the unarmed soldiers from the Cap regiment.[96]

News of the incident spread rapidly, and white activists immediately sounded the call to arms throughout the town. Verneuil was seen leading a crowd of whites to the arsenal, crying "I'm going to get weapons for you, and we're going to march against the mulattoes and the

[93] Laplace, *Histoire des desastres de Saint-Domingue*, 249.
[94] "Rapport fait au comité des colonies, par Guadet," 11 fri. III, in AN, D XVI 3, pp. 49ff.
[95] Deposition of Antoine Balley, December 8, 1792, in AN, D XXV 14, d. 127.
[96] Sonthonax, "Relation officielle," in AN, D XXV 5, d. 43.

civil commissioner."[97] The whites took rifles and several cannon and headed toward the barracks behind the Government House. While the leadership in the movement seems to have come from figures like Verneuil, a planter and member of the Colonial Assembly, *petits blancs* also joined the assault. Several witnesses testified that they had heard a merchant's clerk named Perier utter "the most incendiary things against the national civil commissioner, saying loudly that his only idea was to bring on the general emancipation of the slaves, and trying to whip up the white citizens' hatred and rage against the representative of the nation and against the citizens of color, adding that if all the whites would do as he did, the entire caste of mulattoes would soon be wiped out."[98] The long-feared race war inside the city had finally broken out.

As the white crowd approached, the Champ de Mars exploded into chaos. "We saw a column of furious men, led by a man on horseback, and bringing up a cannon. We were indignant and saddened to learn that the brave Laveaux, commander of the province ... had been attacked, outraged, mistreated, and had been exposed to the greatest dangers," Sonthonax wrote. Soldiers from the Cap regiment joined the attackers, while the free colored National Guards of the Sixth Battalion prepared their weapons. Sonthonax appealed to them not to open fire, but at that moment, shots rang out, followed by a round from a cannon. The men of the Sixth Battalion surrounded the Civil Commissioner to protect him. "I escaped by a miracle from two cannonballs and some sustained musket fire," Sonthonax told his colleagues.[99] There were a half dozen fatalities in the square, and other killings elsewhere in the town, with most of the deaths, according to Sonthonax's report, occurring on the white side; other witnesses gave higher estimates.[100] Outnumbered, the men of the Sixth Battalion retreated through the southern part of the city to the village of Haut du Cap, which guarded the main road into the town from the black insurgents. From that position, they could easily make contact with "the plain that leads to the principal camps of the

---

[97] Deposition of Pierre Gignoux, December 7, 1792, in AN, D XXV 14, d. 127.
[98] Deposition of Jacques Contois, François Renaud, Benjamin Courroy, Cathérine Chateau-Briant and Généviève Voyart, December 11, 1792, in AN, D XXV 14, d. 127.
[99] Sonthonax to Polverel and Ailhaud, December 8, 1792, in AN, D XXV 12, d. 111.
[100] Sonthonax, "Relation officielle," in AN, D XXV 5, d. 43; Mossut to Gallifet, December 13, 1792, in AN, 107 AP 128 (12 white deaths and 12 men of color); François Raimond, letter of December 18, 1792, in *Patriote françois*, February 10, 1793 (6 men of color and more than 30 whites).

brigands," as one account of the events noted: if they chose, they could let the black insurgents invade Le Cap.[101]

"This encampment and the action of the whites threw the city into a state of war that spread fear among the citizens," Sonthonax wrote in his report. Some of the white citizens blamed him for the crisis; others hastened to get their wives and children to safety on ships in the harbor. Agitators demanded an all-out assault on the Sixth Battalion: "They continued to excite the troops, they did everything to keep them in a state of revolt, they even recruited some sailors, everything breathed fury and war."[102] Sonthonax himself was at a loss: Three admittedly hostile accounts claim that he even offered to resign his post and let the local authorities handle the situation.[103] Sonthonax reported that throughout the crisis, General Rochambeau was too ill to provide any leadership, although Rochambeau himself asserted that "I succeeded by force of determination, strong lungs, and effort" in calming things down. A drenching rainstorm that lasted for the next day and a half prevented further fighting.[104]

The key figure in resolving the crisis was Pierre Pinchinat, one of the leaders of the free men of color from the West Province and of the Council of Peace and Union in Saint-Marc, whom Sonthonax had named to the Interim Commission. Detested by many of the whites – one of them accused him of being "the soul of the conspiracy" that had caused the crisis – but recognized even by his opponents as "the guide and the oracle of his caste" and as possessing "intelligence, education, even the talent to speak and write with skill," Pinchinat headed a delegation sent by the Interim Commission and the municipality to try to talk the men of the Sixth Battalion into giving up their fortified position and returning to the town.[105] He had difficulty calming the men down: Many of

---

[101] Letter from Cap Français, March 6, 1793, in *Indicateur politique, mercantile et littéraire, par le Citoyen Petit*, no. 1, May 11, 1793, in CAOM, Moreau de Saint-Méry papers, F 3 197.

[102] Sonthonax, "Relation officielle," in AN, D XXV 5, d. 43.

[103] Letter of Gervais, January 29, 1793, in AN, D XXV 80, d. 782; Guillaume Thomas Dufresne, "Considérations politiques sur la Révolution des colonies françaises mais particulièrement sur celle de Saint-Domingue," Bibliothèque nationale de France, Ms. n.a.f. 4372, 181; Laplace, *Histoire des desastres de Saint-Domingue*, 250.

[104] Sonthonax, "Relation officielle," in AN, D XXV 5, d. 43; Rochambeau, "Sur les Antilles," in Newberry Library, Ms. Ruggles 410, p. 64; letter from Cap Français, March 6, 1793, in *Indicateur*, no. 1, May 11, 1793, in CAOM, Moreau de Saint-Méry papers, F 3 197; Mossut to Gallifet, December 13, 1792, in AN, 107 AP 128; Guadet, "Rapport," in AN, D XVI 3.

[105] G. F. Mahé [de] Corméré, "Précis des faits relatifs à la malheureuse colonie de Ste. Domingue, jusqu'à l'epoque du 1er avril 1793. Et historique fidèle des evenemens de

them were determined to exact revenge for what they saw as the whites' unjustified attack on them and their persistent refusal to acknowledge their legal rights. After two days of talks, Pinchinat finally worked out an agreement, but when the men of the unit began to return to the city on the morning of December 5, 1792, they were met by some of their "brothers" from the town who warned them that the whites were still plotting to massacre them. They "immediately went back up to Haut du Cap, determined to fortify themselves there more strongly than ever and cursing this barbarous town from which one cannot expect either humanity, or good faith, or justice," Sonthonax wrote.[106]

Sonthonax, for his part, was making frantic efforts to pacify the white population. He attempted to establish a local version of the *levée en masse* that the National Convention would impose in France in 1793, announcing that all males between the ages of sixteen and fifty-five would be summoned to help defend the town. Recognizing that part of the explosive atmosphere in the city reflected an economic crisis caused by the loss of revenue from the plantations, he proclaimed a moratorium on unpaid rents. In order to "put to rest ... the uneasiness that was being spread about our principles," he and Rochambeau repeated the unequivocal pledges they had made earlier to defend slavery; Sonthonax's statement was printed and posted on walls around the city. According to one white colonist, he also initially threatened to declare the free colored soldiers who had left the city "traitors to the country" if they did not return to their posts.[107] The deadlock was finally broken on the night of December 5, 1792. After dithering for several days and then seeking to placate the whites, Sonthonax decided on a decisive stroke: he ordered the arrest of four men – Verneuil, Jean Baillio, Claude Fournier, and Charles Gervais – whom he had identified as the leading white troublemakers. They were seized by some of the loyal troops in the middle of the night and hustled aboard a ship in the harbor whose captain was given orders to set sail as quickly as possible for France.

On the same night, the black insurgents tested the resolve of the Sixth Battalion at Haut du Cap, "imagining," as Sonthonax wrote, "that they

---

sa perte & ruine absolue, depuis le 1er avril jusqu'au 29 juillet 1793," in AN, D XXV 14, d. 127; Dalmas, *Révolution de Saint-Domingue*, 2: 4–5.

[106] Sonthonax, "Relation officielle," in AN, D XXV 5, d. 43.

[107] Proclamation of December 4, 1792, in AN, D XXV 5, d. 44; C.-D Duny, letter of 18 May 1793, in Georges Bruley, ed., *Les Antilles pendant la Révolution française, d'après la correspondance inédite de César-Dominique Duny, consul de France à Curaçao, né à Tours le 22 juillet 1758* (Paris: Editions Caraibéennes, 1989 (orig. 1890)), 41.

would not meet any resistance from men to whom they offered an opportunity to be revenged on their enemies. They even used several women to try to win them over. The *régénérés* rejected these propositions with horror, and, forgetting their grievances, they protected those who had assaulted them and vigorously resisted the brigands' attacks." The sound of firing caused panic in the town, but "when they learned who had saved the city, and that these men were as generous as they were brave and had shown that they deserved their rights and justified the law of 4 April," the whites finally accepted the agreement worked out by Pinchinat.[108] "The citizens of color saw only the general welfare and the conservation of the rest of the colony ...," Julien Raimond's brother François wrote, "which earned them the thanks of the colonial commission and of all the constituted authorities."[109] The armed men of color marched back into the town and were greeted by Sonthonax and other officials. Sonthonax rejected petitions from the municipality and the Interim Commission to pardon the four men arrested the previous day, and he was now able to purge the Cap regiment of its most intransigent soldiers as well.

The journée of December 2, 1792, the third major crisis in Cap Français in just four months, was in many ways a dress rehearsal for the catastrophe of June 20, 1793. It revealed the depth of the hatred that had developed between the city's whites and the free men of color since the start of the Revolution, and the willingness of both groups to resort to violence to defend themselves. The clashes on August 13 and 14, 1792 had already made this clear, but the fighting on December 2 was much more serious, involving organized military units and the use of cannon. By occupying the strategic position at Haut du Cap, the free men of color showed that they were prepared to threaten to open the city's gates to the black insurgents, thus raising the stakes in the conflict to their limit. The outcome of the crisis showed, however, that their goal was not to destroy the city or to turn it over to the insurgents, but rather to secure their own rights within it. At the same time, the journée of December 2, 1792 demonstrated that the city's white civilian population was capable of staging a violent riot, but not capable of defeating the free men of color in a showdown. The free men of color were trained soldiers; the town's whites were not. Furthermore, the whites were distracted by fears about their families and their property, and many were ready to flee the

---

[108] Sonthonax, "Relation officielle," in AN, D XXV 5, d. 43.
[109] François Raimond, letter of December 18, 1792, in *Patriote françois*, February 10, 1793.

colony,[110] whereas the free population of color had nowhere else to go. Some white soldiers from the Cap regiment had joined the riot, but none of the other military units in the town had revolted against their commanders, and the effort to rouse the sailors had little success. A group of them did drag a cannon to the Champ de Mars during the fighting on December 2, 1792, but most remained on their ships; Admiral Cambis wrote that "the harbor was calm; the crews stayed at their posts."[111]

Even by his own account, Sonthonax did not exactly distinguish himself in dealing with the December crisis. Although he was well aware of the agitation building up in the days preceding the outbreak, he provoked a public confrontation with the soldiers of the régiment du Cap without making preparations to prevent trouble in the town. It took three full days before he took any firm action to bring things under control. It was fortunate for him, and for the city, that Pinchinat was able to step in and prevent the hotheads in his group from escalating the crisis. Pinchinat and other leaders of the free men of color, eager to consolidate their alliance with Sonthonax, collaborated in a campaign to exalt Sonthonax's courage in the December events; they gave a more heroic account of his conduct than the commissioner himself did.[112] In June 1793, however, Pinchinat would be at the other end of the colony, overseeing a campaign against the whites in the South Province, and there would be no equivalent figure among the free men of color to take his place in Cap Français. Sonthonax also benefitted from the fact that there was no rival on the scene who could claim to represent the national government. Whatever his actual role in the crisis, Rochambeau did not contest his authority.

The most striking difference between the journée of December 2, 1792 and that of June 20, 1793, however, was the absence of any involvement on the part of the slaves of Cap Français. Neither the whites nor the free people of color made any attempt to rouse them. In June 1793, Sonthonax would offer the slaves their freedom in exchange for military support, but in December 1792, he instead repeated his oath to defend slavery. During their retreat to Haut du Cap, the men of the Sixth Battalion had to pass through the *Petite Guinée* neighborhood of the city, with

[110] Mossut to Gallifet, December 13, 1792, in AN, 107 AP 128.
[111] For the role of the sailors at the Champ de Mars, see the deposition of the National Guard commander Lachaise, December 7, 1792, in AN, D XXV 4, d. 38; for the state of the harbor, Cambis, ship's journal, in AN, D XXV 54, d. 521.
[112] François Raimond, letter of December 18, 1792, and Pinchin[at], letter of December 18, 1792, in *Patriote françois*, February 10, 1793.

its dense black population, but there is no mention of their making any appeal for support. The whites certainly feared the slaves – Mossut, the marquis de Gallifet's correspondent, told him that the white women in the town were terrified of "perishing at the hands of their slaves who for sixteen months have seen their fellows in a condition that they think is very happy"[113] – but on this occasion, their fears were unfounded. In the numerous accounts of these events preserved in the French archives, I have found only one reference to involvement by a slave: one witness claimed that when a few sailors agreed to try to rally their comrades to join the fighting, they had a black beat out the general alarm on a drum.[114] The inertia of the city's slave population on December 2, 1792 demonstrated that they were not, contrary to the fear often expressed by the whites, waiting impatiently for the first opportunity to turn against their masters; it also indicates that they were no more eager than the free population of color to see the city destroyed. Only when they were offered the hope of a tangible benefit – their freedom – would the slaves intervene in the struggle between the two groups of free people in Cap Français.

Although he had nearly been overwhelmed by the whites' wild assault on December 2, 1792, Sonthonax emerged from the crisis with a new political strategy. Already after the journée of October 19, he had written to Monge that "it is a strange error that prevails in Europe to believe that there is a single white in the colony who is sincerely the friend of the free citizens of color."[115] In the wake of the December events, he let his fury at the whites explode. They might use the rhetoric of the metropolitan revolution, he wrote to Paris, but they were complete hypocrites. "A few intriguers, consumed with ambition, have carried out a revolution in Saint-Domingue to put themselves in power ... They have talked people and constitution, they have formed assemblies, they have gotten an ignorant multitude to follow them, they claim to be patriots ... At the same time, they have broken with France, they have fought against her, they have fought to the last ditch against the rights of free men, they have covered the earth with human blood in the interest of their pride and to maintain the most absurd of aristocracies ... "[116] Forwarding a copy of this report to Brissot, Sonthonax added that the only way of restoring

---

[113] Mossut to Gallifet, December 13, 1792, in AN, 107 AP 128.
[114] Deposition of Jacques Contois, in AN, D XXV 14, d. 127.
[115] Letter of October 26, 1792, in AN, CC 9 A 7.
[116] Sonthonax, "Relation officielle," in AN, D XXV 5, d. 43.

peace to the colony was "a good law that will ameliorate the fate of the slaves." It was no use sending more white troops, he insisted, since they were so vulnerable to tropical diseases, but "united with the men of color, French principles will triumph."[117] Sonthonax could express himself so openly because the December events had also shown him the weakness of the white "patriot" movement in Cap Français. Despite their bluster, the whites had shrunk from an all-out confrontation with the free men of color, knowing that it would leave them defenseless in the face of the slave insurrection, and they had limited themselves to toothless protests against Sonthonax's arrest of their leaders.

From the December events, Sonthonax drew the lesson that the colonial whites, although they were incorrigibly hostile to the Republic, could safely be treated as a negligible factor in local politics. His subsequent policy toward them would be one of harsh confrontation, meant to show them their powerlessness to oppose him. For support, he counted on the French troops – after the purge of the Cap regiment, he was convinced that none of them would defy the lawful representative of the national government – and, above all, on the free men of color. Just as Raimond and Brissot had promised before the commissioners left, the free men of color had proved to be the only reliable supporters of French policy. Sonthonax was convinced that they had saved his life on December 2, and their willingness to accept the compromise worked out by Pinchinat and to defend the city against an insurgent attack demonstrated, in his eyes, that they sincerely wanted his mission to succeed, whereas the whites were trying to sabotage it. He was now committed to an unswerving alliance with the "citizens of 4 April."

[117] Sonthonax to Brissot, January 4, 1793, in Dorigny, ed., *Léger-Félicité Sonthonax*, 195.

4

Creating Revolutionary Government
in the Tropics

The crisis of December 2, 1792 foreshadowed the journée of June 20, 1793 in many respects, but for the moment, it ended the period of intense agitation in Cap Français that had begun in the summer of 1792. Sonthonax now realized that he did not need to worry about opposition from the white population of Cap Français, or about an uprising by the city's slaves. Despite Sonthonax's blanket condemnation of the whites in his report to the Convention, he had seen that they were, in fact, divided. Some of them, such as Guillaume Henry Vergniaud, the city's *sénéschal* and cousin of the prominent Girondin deputy Pierre Vergniaud,[1] actually sided with him and provided essential support for his actions. Others, even if they distrusted Sonthonax, also opposed the demagogic agitation that had led to the violence on December 2. The Gallifet plantation manager, Mossut, an avowed royalist, denounced the club firebrands for antagonizing the free men of color, "whose situation makes them indispensable and whose interests are the same [as ours]." According to Mossut, many whites simply wanted to get away from the colony as quickly as possible, and those who could not leave were prepared to accept any government that could restore order and protect their properties.[2]

By late February, when he decided to leave Cap Français to deal with problems in the West Province,[3] Sonthonax had built a base of supporters in the city whom he trusted to keep him informed about the

[1] Letter from Le Cap, November 5, 1792, in *Patriote françois*, January 9, 1793.
[2] Mossut to Gallifet, December 13, 1792, in AN, 107 AP 128.
[3] *Moniteur général*, February 27, 1793.

situation there. The most important of these allies were the political and
military leaders of the free men of color. Sonthonax's respect for Pierre
Pinchinat was evident in the report he sent to the National Convention
about the crisis in December. Even before Sonthonax's arrival, Pinchinat
had established himself as the main figure among the free men of color
throughout the colony; although he was willing to work with the civil
commissioner, he had his own ideas about policy, and he was more concerned with affairs in the West and South Provinces, where the free men
of color had created their own autonomous movements, than with Cap
Français. In early February, Pinchinat departed for a tour of the free
colored strongholds in the West Province; he would not return to Le Cap
before its destruction.[4]

Sonthonax was closer personally to Charles Guillaume Castaing,
referred to by a well-informed white colonist as the commissioner's
"ame damnée," his most trusted advisor.[5] In November 1790, Castaing,
who owned a substantial plantation in the Sainte-Rose parish near
Grande Rivière, had been compelled to make a humiliating public condemnation of Ogé's rebellion in front of the whites of his parish.[6] He
nevertheless managed to avoid being accused of complicity in Ogé's
plot, even though Ogé had visited Castaing's mother's house in Le Cap
when he returned from France.[7] Castaing was recognized as one of
the leaders of the city's free men of color by November 1791, when he
addressed the Colonial Assembly on behalf of his group, this time in
less obsequious terms; he spoke for them again at the ceremonies welcoming the commissioners in September 1792. The letters that he wrote
to Sonthonax after the latter set out for the West Province in early 1793
give a sense of the relationship that had developed between Castaing
and Sonthonax. In one of them, Castaing exclaimed, "I love you; I think
I do more than that, I adore you like a lover who idolizes his mistress."
In a subsequent letter, he told the rabidly anticlerical Sonthonax that
"my mother has had masses said for your health and your triumphs;"

---

[4] *Moniteur général*, February 9, 1793.
[5] Laplace, *Histoire des désastres de Saint-Domingue*, 296n. On Castaing, see Jean-Charles
   Benzaken, "Documents inédits sur la famille Castaing de Saint-Domingue," *Bulletin de la
   Société Archéologique de Tarn-et-Garonne* 129 (2004), 81–86, and Eric Noel, "Le Sang
   Noir des Castaing, ou l'insolite ascension d'une famille des isles (milieu XVIIIe-fin XIXe
   siècles)," *Bulletin du Centre d'histoire des espaces atlantiques* 7 (1995), 171–82.
[6] Castaing, speech of November 2, 1790, cited in Benzaken, "Documents inédits," 83.
[7] Ogé, interrogation, January 20, 1791, in AN, D XXV 58, d. 574. According to Ogé,
   Castaing was the uncle of his collaborator, Chavannes. I would like to thank John
   Garrigus for sharing with me his transcript of the Ogé interrogation.

he also passed along greetings from Sonthonax's mixed-race mistress Eugénie.[8]

Whereas Castaing and the other leaders of the free men of color in Le Cap were solidly established figures with strong roots in the colony, the whites who became part of Sonthonax's inner circle tended to occupy more marginal positions in its society. Louis Dufay, who would deliver the speech that would persuade the French National Convention to pass its decree abolishing slavery on February 4, 1794, was born in Paris and came to the colony after serving in the French forces during the American war of independence. He had reportedly passed himself off as an aristocrat and made a favorable marriage, thanks to which he acquired property in Grande Rivière, where he may have known Castaing. When he arrived in France in 1794, white colonists denounced him for having scandalously abused both his wife and his mistress in the years before the Revolution; his parish had supposedly refused to accept him as its military commander because of his immoral behavior.[9] Vergniaud, who, like Dufay, would play a crucial role in the events leading up to the crisis of June 20, 1793, had "vegetated at Le Cap without a position and without resources," according to the civil commissioners' secretary Jean-Baptiste Picquenard. He may have attracted Sonthonax's attention because his family name was the same as that of Brissot's Girondin colleague. Appointed as the city's *seneschal* in the fall of 1792, "his patriotism consisted in making a quick fortune for himself. He was soon living in a richly furnished apartment, with numerous domestics and a sumptuous table," according to Picquenard, who was himself another of the marginal figures who attached himself to the commissioners.[10]

Other whites who became part of Sonthonax's entourage were *mésalliés* married to women of color; two of them, the future Saint-Domingue Convention deputy, Pierre Nicolas Garnot and the army captain,

[8] Castaing to Sonthonax, letters of March 7 and May 4, 1793, in AN, D XXV 16, d. 158. The "Eugénie" mentioned in this letter is probably Marie Eugénie Bléigeat, the free colored widow of a white colonist who had been killed in the 1791 uprising, and whom Sonthonax married in 1796. Stein, *Sonthonax*, 129.

[9] Interrogation of Dufay, 10 plu. II, and testimony of Barré St. Venant, in AN, F 7 4685, d. Dufay, and *Histoire des désastres de Saint-Domingue*, 233n.

[10] Letter of Picquenard to Prieur de la Marne, 13 mess. II, in AN, D XXV 81, d. 794. Arrested after his return to France in 1794, Vergniaud would try to insist that he was not related to the famous Girondin orator. Letter of Vergniaud, n.d., in AN, D XXV 78, d. 766. On Picquenard, see Chris Bongie, "Introduction," in Jean-Baptiste Picquenard, *Adonis suivi de Zoflora et de documents inédits*, Chris Bongie, ed. (Paris: L'Harmattan, 2006), ix-xiii.

Pierre Charles Robquin, were married to sisters of Castaing.[11] While Sonthonax's white supporters were clearly willing to accept the equality of whites and free men of color, there is no indication that any of them had supported the abolition of slavery prior to 1793. They had tied their fortunes to those of Sonthonax for personal, rather than ideological, reasons. Given the hostility he encountered among the more established members of the white population, Sonthonax had little choice but to rely on the few allies he could trust, but his closeness to men who despised most of the other white colonists and were despised by them in return accentuated his tendency to regard all the other whites as enemies.

Keeping Cap Français under control had been Sonthonax's main pre-occupation since his arrival in Saint-Domingue in September 1792; until his departure in late February 1793, he had hardly left the city. Now, confident that his allies would keep order there, he set off to join Polverel in the West. Although Le Cap was not at the center of the civil com-missioners' preoccupations during the next three-and-a-half months, it is essential to understand their actions in this period in order to grasp the origins of the crisis that exploded in the city on June 20, which led them to make their historic appeal to the slaves. It was during this period that Sonthonax and Polverel first confronted the issue of slavery and the black population, which they had initially put aside while they dealt with the conflicts arising from their efforts to implement the law of April 4, 1792. Faced with a new crisis in the form of impending war with Britain and Spain, the two men were also driven to establish their own ver-sion of what the republicans in France would soon label "revolutionary government." Abandoning any idea of creating functioning institutions chosen by local citizens, the commissioners created a dictatorship in the name of the French nation and did not hesitate to use military force, recruited largely from the free men of color, to impose their authority. By May 1793, they had disarmed any potential opposition among the white population in most regions and taken measures that they thought would prevent any further spread of the slave insurrection; they then expected to be able to turn their full attention to preparing the colony to defend itself against threats from the British in Jamaica and the Spanish in Santo Domingo. Just as the commissioners were completing their preparations for war, however, they found their plans jeopardized by an unexpected intervention on the part of the metropole. The arrival of a new military governor for the colony, sent to strengthen republican authority, instead

---

[11] Noel, "Le sang noir des Castaing," 173.

revealed how unstable the situation Sonthonax had left behind in Cap
Français really was.

Once the events of December 2, 1792 had shown him the weakness of
the white agitators in Le Cap, Sonthonax moved decisively to consolidate
his control of the city. On December 16, 1792, he issued a proclamation
denouncing the reluctance of the whites to take up arms to defend the colony. Ignoring white protests that the law of April 4, 1792 had outlawed
the creation of institutions limited to members of a single racial group, he
decreed the creation of military "free companies," to be composed exclusively of free men of color, thus creating an armed force on whose loyalty
he could depend.[12] Polverel protested against Sonthonax's increasingly
high-handed measures, but Sonthonax replied that they were in line with
the policies being followed in France itself, and argued that it was better
"to make a horde of white brigands take flight, rather than to expose the
colony to a civil war between the two colors, which would sooner or later
end with the annihilation of ours."[13] Although his dispute with Polverel
about the tax he had announced in November was still dragging on,
Sonthonax was convinced that the situation justified whatever emergency
measures he decided were necessary. On December 22, he announced that
the levy would be collected in the North Province, regardless of whether
the other commissioners agreed.[14] By this time, news of the proclamation of the Republic in France on September 22, 1792 had reached Saint-
Domingue, encouraging Sonthonax to take an even more militant tone.
On December 30, 1792, he announced that "the throne is overturned, the
people is free, France is now a Republic, One and Indivisible, all the institutionalized authorities are provisionally maintained, the colonies are a
part of the French empire."[15] As in France, all soldiers and officials were
required to take an oath to the new regime.

At the beginning of January 1793, Sonthonax ordered the arrest
and deportation of several more prominent white "patriots," including
Raboteau and Daugy, both of whom had been presidents of the Colonial
Assembly before its dissolution, and Larchevesque-Thibaud, the former

[12] Sonthonax, proclamation of December 16, 1792, in *Moniteur général*, December 17, 1792.
[13] Sonthonax to Polverel, December 23, 1792, in AN, D XXV 12, d. 111.
[14] Sonthonax, proclamation of December 22, 1792, in *Moniteur général*, December 22, 1792. Sonthonax justified his action in a letter to Delpech, January 8, 1793, in AN, D XXV 5, d. 46.
[15] Sonthonax, proclamation of December 31, 1792, in *Moniteur général*, December 31, 1792.

deputy to the National Assembly, whom the commissioners had at first regarded as a political ally. His measure had the desired effect of intimidating the other whites. "The nocturnal embarkments continue, the zealous patriots are torn from their beds, and many are afraid to sleep in their own homes," one of them wrote. Meanwhile, Louis Boisrond, one of the free men of color on the Interim Commission, proudly reported to Julien Raimond that "it was the free companies [the free colored militia that Sonthonax had created] who carried out the arrests." A month earlier, Sonthonax's attempt to appoint a few free men of color as army officers had set off a bloody riot; now, when he sent armed men of color to arrest leading white political figures, there was no resistance. The leaders of the free colored movement were ecstatic at this evidence of the backing they now enjoyed from the French government's representative. Indulging in a degree of hyperbole rare even in a period awash in overstatement, Boisrond wrote that "Sonthonax behaved like a god."[16]

Well known on both sides of the Atlantic, Larchevesque-Thibaud was the most prominent target of Sonthonax's purges, even though he was often distrusted by his own fellow colonists because of his frequent changes of political position. Sonthonax, who had earlier appointed him to several local political positions, now denounced him at length as an advocate of "revolt and of independence from the mother country" and claimed that "he constantly surrounded himself with a horde of assassins, the executors and accomplices of his vengeances."[17] On arrival in France, Larchevesque-Thibaud was able to show that he had supported the appointment of the mixed-race Interim Commission and to complain that he had been betrayed by a man he "truly loved." His presence in Paris would galvanize the campaign against Sonthonax and Polverel in the capital, where he presented himself as a patriot who had "been chosen seven times by the vote of his fellow citizens ... one of the firmest supporters of the Revolution in a country where it has encountered obstacles greater perhaps than in France,"[18] but his deportation simplified the commissioner's problems in Saint-Domingue considerably.

[16] Letter of C.-D. Duny, in Bruley, ed., *Les Antilles pendant la Révolution*, 38; Louis Boiron [sic-Boisrond], letter to Raimond, January 9, 1793, in *Patriote françois*, February 25, 1793.

[17] Proclamation of January 18, 1793, in AN, D XXV 5, d. 45. For Sonthonax's earlier attempt to use Larchevesque-Thibault as a political ally and to appoint him as the civilian overseer of the navy installations, see Sonthonax to Ailhaud, November 4, 1792, in AN, D XXV 12, d. 110.

[18] Larchevesque-Thibault to "Citoyen ministre," from Rochefort, February 14, 1793, in AN, CC 9 A 8.

No longer concerned about another crisis in the city, Sonthonax now turned his attention to dealing with the black insurrection. For almost a year and a half, the former slaves had kept Cap Français under siege. After November 1791, Governor Blanchelande had decided that any effort to drive them out of the northern plain would have to wait until there was a substantial infusion of troops from France. As a result, the black rebels had been able to build up fortified camps and create an embryonic society of their own. Jean-François and Biassou, the two principal leaders who had emerged in the fall of 1791 after the death of Boukman, the original chief of the insurrection, had divided the black-held territory between them, with Jean-François, based at the eastern end of the province in the town of Ouanaminthe, assuming the title of Vice Admiral or Grand Admiral, while Biassou, whose headquarters was in the valley of the Grande Rivière south of the northern plain, called himself Governor General. The two leaders did not trust each other – in late August 1792, Jean-François wrote to the Spanish complaining about Biassou's intrigues against him – but in general, they avoided open conflict.[19] Loosely subordinate to them were lesser leaders who commanded particular towns or regions; among them was Toussaint de Bréda, the future black leader, nominally under the orders of Biassou. Biassou and Jean-François corresponded with their subordinates on a regular basis, issued passes – one document given out by Biassou still has the remnants of an official wax seal in the corner[20] – and held occasional councils to discuss policy. Neither Jean-François nor Biassou, both of whom had been slaves until the start of the insurrection, seem to have been able to write, but they were able to call on secretaries with some degree of literacy, even if the phonetic spelling and ragged syntax in many of their letters contrasts sharply with the greater fluency and clearer handwriting in letters dictated by Toussaint, who had been a free man before 1789 and who was able to read his scribes' handiwork.

The violence that had characterized the first months of the insurrection subsided as conditions stabilized. Whites who had survived the killings in the early stage of the insurrection and who remained in black-held territory were assigned to plantations where they could be kept

---

[19] Jean-François, letter of August 26, 1792, cited in Antonio del Monte y Tejada, *Historia de Santo Domingo*, 4 vs. (Santo Domingo: Imprenta de Garcia Hermanos, 1890–92), 3: xii–xiii.

[20] Passport headed "De par le roy," [By the king], November 9, 1792, signed Biassou, in AN, D XXV 20, d. 198.

under surveillance, but their lives were usually not in danger.[21] With no
military operations to carry out, the black population dispersed itself, as
former slaves took over plantation lands to grow crops for themselves.
This rudimentary economy did not produce enough resources to supply a
large army concentrated in one place for any length of time; in September
1792, Blanchelande told the commissioners that 60,000 blacks in the
North Province – about a third of the total population – were in areas
controlled by the insurgents, but that no more than 3,000 of them were
camped in any one location.[22] The insurgent movement may have initially supported itself by plundering the plantations it overran, but by
1792, a more organized economy was functioning again. Documents
now in the French archives include an order to Jean-François's "commissioner of war" to pay for cattle delivered to his troops and instructions for some 250 milliers of coffee – the produce of several good-sized
plantations – to be credited to his account.[23] Obtaining munitions was a
major concern for the insurgents. The weapons they had seized as they
overran the plantations could not have been sufficient to arm most of
them, and their only source of powder and ammunition was trade with
the Spanish in Santo Domingo. The main resource Jean-François and
Biassou could offer in payment for these supplies were other blacks, sold
as slaves. A letter from Jean-François to the Spanish justified his policy,
explaining that the individuals concerned were "very bad people, and
not having the heart to destroy them we appeal to your good heart to
ask you to take them out of the country. We would rather sell them for
the benefit of the king and use the same sums to buy useful things for
the army ..."[24] In selling their captives, the black leaders were of course
behaving like the black rulers in Africa who kept the slave trade supplied
with victims.

   Much ink has been spilled over the question of whether the slaves who
joined the insurrection were inspired by the ideas and rhetoric of the
French Revolution. As we have seen, the only document attributed to the
insurrectionary leaders that explicitly cites the Declaration of the Rights
of Man, the supposed "letter of Jean-François, Biassou and Belair" from

[21] See, for example, the testimonies of three whites who had lived in the black-held territories until January 1793 – the abbé de la Haye, Marie Jeanne Jouette, and Dr. Thibal,
in Popkin, *Facing Racial Revolution*, 156–68.
[22] Blanchelande to commissioners, n.d., in AN, D XXV 4, d. 32.
[23] Note of July 12, 1792 and "Compte du café livré à M. Titus," both in AN, D XXV 20,
d. 198.
[24] Letter signed by Jean-François and Binjamin, n.d., in AN, D XXV 20, d. 198.

the summer of 1792, is of dubious authenticity. Those documents that unquestionably emanate from the leaders of the insurrection suggest, however, that they had their own reasons, both ideological and pragmatic, for putting themselves forward as proponents of religion and royalty rather than adopting the language of natural rights proclaimed by the French. As their willingness to barter other blacks to the Spanish in exchange for supplies indicates, the insurrectionary leaders did not take a consistent position against slavery.

The insurgent leaders' letters and proclamations speak much more about religion and royalty than about slavery. That the black population of Saint-Domingue did not share the antireligious sentiments of the French Jacobins should hardly be a surprise. Both in Africa and in the French colonies prior to the Revolution, the blacks lived in worlds structured by belief in supernatural powers. *Vodou*, the syncretic mixture of African and Catholic beliefs and rituals that the slaves had created for themselves in the colony, was central to black culture and played a key role in uniting the insurgents.[25] Not only did the blacks remain loyal to religion, but, to a certain extent, the church remained loyal to them. Most of the priests in the North Province had stayed in their parishes despite the insurrection. The insurrectionary leaders had close contacts with a number of these clergy. "Among the black insurgents," the historian of the Haitian Church Alphonse Cabon wrote, "priests were not only tolerated but they had great influence."[26] In 1793, the public prosecutor in Le Cap claimed that he had seen receipts for payments for the celebration of masses requested by Jean-François, Biassou, and Toussaint in the records of one priest suspected of sympathy for the uprising.[27] Biassou relied on the abbé de la Haye, the curé of Dondon, a town close to his headquarters, to perform religious services and even asked him to serve

[25] On vodou during the revolutionary era, see Pierre Pluchon, *Vaudou, Sorciers, Empoissonneurs. De Saint-Domingue à Haïti* (Paris: Karthala, 1987), 54–139, and Sidney Mintz and Michel-Rolph Trouillot, "The Social History of Haitian Vodou," in Donald J. Cosentino, ed., *Sacred Arts of Haitian Vodou* (Los Angeles: UCLA Fowler Museum of Cultural History, 1995), 123–52.

[26] Alphonse Cabon, *Notes sur l'histoire religieuse d'Haïti. De la Révolution au Concordat (1789–1860)* (Port-au-Prince: Petit Séminaire Collège Saint-Martial, 1933), 41. See also Laennec Hurbon, "Le clergé catholique et l'insurrection de Saint-Domingue," in Laënnec Hurbon, dir., *L'Insurrection des esclaves de Saint-Domingue (22–23 août 1791). Actes de la table ronde internationale de Port-au-Prince (8 au 10 décembre 1997)* (Paris: Karthala, 2000), 29–39.

[27] Leclerc, "Notes de Monsieur Le Clerc sur le Précis historique de M. Gros," ms. in CAOM, bound in Recueil colonies, 2e série, 36, Bibliothèque de Moreau de Saint-Méry.

as his speechwriter when he declared himself viceroy for the imprisoned Louis XVI in December 1792; around the same time, another black general wrote to the same priest asking him to use his influence to persuade the black women in the camp that they needed to continue doing their customary work.[28] The blacks were aware of the Revolution's hostility toward the Church, and there is little reason to doubt the sincerity of their conviction that in opposing the whites, they were upholding the cause of religion.

In addition to defending the Church, the black insurgents were proud to call themselves "the king's men." In August 1792, Jean-François wrote that "I have always stood up for our God and the king."[29] Like belief in a higher power, acknowledgment of the legitimacy of kingship was a value that had been shared, until 1789, by Africans and by the whites who brought them to the Americas. The story that the future Toussaint Louverture was the son of an Arada chief or prince is not true, but it is not unlikely that the young Toussaint grew up listening to stories about the African kingdoms from which his father and other slaves had been taken.[30] As the African historian John Thornton has shown, blacks from West Africa, the source of most of Saint-Domingue's slaves, were not simply superstitious worshipers of arbitrary authority. They judged their rulers according to their respect for justice and their success in maintaining order and defeating their enemies – criteria similar to those applied by European populations.[31] Starting in 1789, if not before, the blacks in Saint-Domingue undoubtedly began to overhear their masters denouncing their own monarch as a "despot." One of the signs of that despotism, according to the colonial whites, was that the king and his ministers wanted to limit slave owners' arbitrary authority over their slaves. White colonial "patriots" thus helped implant in the blacks' minds the notion that the king of France was on their side, a belief crystallized in the widespread rumor that he had granted the slaves three days a week to work on their own behalf.

The slaves' belief in Louis XVI's sympathy for them had little basis in fact. When news of the slave revolt reached France in October 1791, the king was quoted as having consoled one of his courtiers whose properties

---

[28] Biassou to abbé de la Haye, December 18, 1792, and Fayette to abbé de la Haye, December 13, 1792, in AN, D XXV 5, d. 48.
[29] Cited in Monte y Tejada, *Historia*, 3: xii.
[30] Pierre Pluchon, *Toussaint Louverture* (Paris: Fayard, 1989), 56.
[31] John Thornton, "'I am the Subject of the King of Kongo': African Ideology and the Haitian Revolution," *Journal of World History* 4 (1993), 181–214.

in Saint-Domingue had been devastated by saying, "That is the result of the preachings of the abbé Grégoire and the other so-called friends of the blacks."[32] But as far as the blacks in the colonies could see, the revolutionary assemblies had even less concern for them. The National Assembly had seated deputies representing the white plantation owners and explicitly promised that no changes would be made to the slave system unless they were proposed by the slave owners themselves. Confronted with news of the slave uprising, the Legislative Assembly, by the fall of 1792, had sent some 12,000 troops to Saint-Domingue to put it down. "If the Negroes wore the colors of the counterrevolution, if they invoked a power that no longer exists, it is because the civil and military authorities who were fighting them wore the patriotic colors," Colonel Cambefort asserted.[33] The Legislative Assembly's law of April 4, 1792 had been a major concession to the colony's free men of color, but, as the slaves knew only too well, they had a large stake in the maintenance of slavery, and the declared purpose of the law was to strengthen the forces opposing the insurrection. The insurrection's leaders had undoubtedly heard that there were some French revolutionaries who were opposed to slavery, and they may well have had some hopes for the Second Commission; when Biassou summoned Jean-François and other leaders to a conclave on September 20, 1792, he may have been responding to news of the group's arrival in Cap Français.[34] If the black leaders understood that Sonthonax and Polverel were regarded as abolitionists, however, they must have been disappointed when they learned that the two men had taken public oaths to uphold the slave system and suppress the uprising. When he proclaimed himself viceroy in December 1792, Biassou was both reaffirming his commitment to principles of religious and political legitimacy and also following the adage that the enemy of his enemies – the white colonists and the French revolutionaries – must logically be his friend.[35]

The Second Commission made no effort to communicate with the leaders of the black insurrection during its first months in the colony. At the same time, however, as we have seen, the French troops were not sent into the field against the blacks, as Jean-François and Biassou had feared when they first landed.[36] The insurgents must have been baffled: the whites continued to proclaim the indispensability of

[32] *Gazette universelle*, October 24, 1791.
[33] Cambefort, *Mémoire justificatif*, pt. 3, 9.
[34] Letter from Biassou, September 20, 1792, in AN, D XXV 20, d. 198.
[35] Letter from Biassou to abbé de la Haye, in AN, D XXV 5, d. 48.
[36] Spanish memorandum of September 30, 1792, in Monte y Tejada, *Historia*, 3: xv.

defeating the insurrection and of maintaining slavery, but took no military action; at the same time, they showed no signs of wanting to make peace. Biassou, more active than Jean-François, responded by trying to consolidate his own government. Rather than appropriating the language of liberty used by his enemies, however, he appealed to the principles of religion and monarchy. Having learned of the overthrow of Louis XVI in France, Biassou had his followers proclaim him viceroy, with Toussaint, the future Louverture, as his second-in-command, and he turned to the abbé Guillaume Silvestre de la Haye, a white priest who had remained in his parish during the insurrection, for advice. "I beg you to shape my words for me so that I can address the people and thank them for the confidence that they have shown in me, to be read after a solemn grand mass to be held for this purpose. After this has been received, I beg you also to give us a law, by which I mean a form of government that will maintain order while awaiting instructions from the king our master, whose rights I hope to support, with the help of the Lord, until it pleases him to send us his own established laws," he wrote.[37]

The black insurgents' sense that the white republicans were more hostile to them than the king could only have been confirmed by the major offensive that Sonthonax finally ordered in January 1793. The Cap Français newspaper cheered the troops on with a *"Marseillaise coloniale"*: *"Allons enfans de l'Amérique, / le jour de gloire est arrivé; / De cette horde frenetique / poursuivez le reste égaré."*[38] Rochambeau had overseen preparations for the campaign, but he left Saint-Domingue just before the operation began in order to finally assume his post in Martinique. Elevated to the command of the troops in the North Province in his place, Étienne Laveaux, the leader of the 16th dragoons, took charge of the campaign and conducted it brilliantly. "The camps of La Tannerie, Grande-Rivière, Grand-Pré and Dondon have been taken, with sword in hand, by the brave young men of Le Cap, united with our troops from Europe," Sonthonax wrote to Polverel on January 22, 1793. "We have captured 18 cannon, with their equipment ... We're on the heels of Biassou and he probably will not escape. In a word, the

---

[37] Biassou to abbé de la Haye, in AN, D XXV 5, d. 48.

[38] "Arise, children of the fatherland, the day of glory has arrived. Pursue the remnant of this frenzied horde." *Moniteur général*, January 15, 1793. Another version of the "Marseillaise," printed a day earlier, warned the slaves that "You have worn out the clemency / Of your masters, your benefactors, / You have left only one sentiment / In their hearts: Vengeance!"

operations of General Laveaux are almost a miracle."[39] The expedition had united soldiers from France, white volunteers from Le Cap, and units made up of free men of color, such as the 6th battalion of the National Guard, whose men published a letter in the *Moniteur général* appealing for support and praising Laveaux, who had "sworn not to return to town until he has seen every plantation-owner restored to his home, and exterminated this horde of brigands who cause all our misfortunes."[40] At almost the same time, Polverel reported that the insurgents in the South Province, who had defeated Blanchelande's troops in August 1792, had been routed.[41] "Last Sunday, we overran all the camps of the slave rebels at Platons. Three hundred of these brigands were killed; the others took flight and are dispersed. Some returned to their work teams, others are wandering in the woods like savage beasts," Polverel wrote to General Adrien de La Salle, adding, "One must admit that these patriots [the French soldiers] have done me a bad turn, if it were true that my plan was to grant the slaves liberty."[42] With the slaves at Platons defeated, Polverel's only concern, as he wrote to Monge, was the distrust among the whites who continued to believe that the commissioners were preparing to abolish slavery.[43]

For the black insurgents, the French offensive was a stinging humiliation that strengthened their hostility toward the commissioners. Biassou and Jean-François – weakened, according to Spanish reports, by their quarrels with each other – were both chased out of the camps they had occupied since the fall of 1791 and forced to flee into the mountains along the Spanish border.[44] At La Tannerie, the "royal palace" that Biassou had built for himself went up in flames; when Laveaux's forces attacked his position, "Jean-François was lucky to escape, but he lost his war-horse," a white participant in the campaign reported.[45] In August 1793, at the moment when Sonthonax was about to issue his proclamation of general emancipation, Toussaint Louverture was still smoldering about the January campaign. "You had us pursued like ferocious beasts," he wrote to the commissioner.[46] Both commissioners had clearly signaled

[39] Sonthonax to Polverel, January 22, 1793, in AN, D XXV 12, d. 113.
[40] *Moniteur général*, January 28, 1793.
[41] Polverel to Sonthonax, January 15, 1793, in AN, D XXV 12, d. 113.
[42] Polverel to La Salle, January 17, 1793, in Corre, *Papiers de La Salle*, 108.
[43] Polverel to Monge, January 22, 1793, in AN, D XXV 11, d. 101.
[44] Cabrera to Casasola, January 28, 1793, in Monte y Tejada, *Historia*, 4: 11–2.
[45] Laplace, *Histoire des desastres de Saint-Domingue*, 260, 264.
[46] Toussaint Louverture, letter of August 27, 1793, in AN, AA 55, d. 1511.

that they took their assignment to defeat the armed insurgents seriously; if they decided to make any concessions to the slaves, they would do so from a position of force. The participation of the 6th battalion of the Cap Français National Guard showed that the free men of color supported this policy. Morale among the whites in Le Cap soared in the wake of these victories. Large numbers of slaves – 14,000 in Grande-Rivière alone, according to one white chronicler – submitted to the commissioners. Mossut, the Gallifet manager, was able to visit two of his employer's plantations, where he found the buildings intact; Sonthonax had set up a camp to take in slaves who surrendered, where they were "well fed and put to light work."[47]

Buoyed by his success at Platons, Polverel urged a broadened campaign. "Let's defeat or exterminate the insurgent slaves in the three provinces," he told General La Salle, who had been elevated to interim governor general of the colony after Rochambeau's departure.[48] Sonthonax soon became less optimistic, however. White troops simply could not stand up to the rigors of a prolonged campaign in the country-side. "It was decided, on account of the number of the sick, the malcontents and the deserters, to retire without having subdued the brigands, although they were already almost reduced to the last extremity," Jean Girard, a participant in the fighting, wrote to his brother Stephen in Philadelphia.[49] In a long letter to the National Convention, Sonthonax explained that although Laveaux's troops had indeed reclaimed the entire northern plain, they had been unable to destroy the insurgent army before their own losses and a shortage of supplies had brought the offensive to a halt. The blacks' "method is to harass our camps with night attacks; they charge vigorously, rarely try to hold a position after a first round of firing and, when they are pursued, they usually retreat into the mountains or the woods where it is almost impossible to follow them," he reported.[50]

Captured documents and interviews with prisoners, including the abbé de la Haye, Biassou's advisor, gave Sonthonax his first direct picture of the black movement. "There seems to be a considerable mass who are resolved to die rather than surrender," he wrote, but this was not

---

[47] Laplace, *Histoire des desastres de Saint-Domingue*, 264 ; Mossut to Gallifet, March 4, 1793, in AN, 107 AP 128.
[48] Polverel to La Salle, February 2, 1793, in Corre, *Papiers de La Salle*, 123.
[49] Jean Girard, letter of February 14, 1793, in APS, Girard papers, roll 9.
[50] Sonthonax to National Convention, February 18, 1793, in AN, D XXV 5, d. 48.

because they had become imbued with French-style notions of liberty and natural rights:

Unthinking agents of the fury of a bloody cause, the unfortunate Negroes fight only for their religion and for their king, whom they believe they are destined to restore to the throne. Their passions stirred up, their vanity tickled by titles, decorations, the iron rod wrested from their masters and put in their own hands, the lures of pillage and of idleness, these are the odious means that the barbaric emissaries of despotism have used to mislead these simple men and incite them to crime. Liberty is not in their minds, if you set aside the chiefs who dream less of being free than of ruling over slaves. It is not this noble sentiment that inspires them; they speak of it only as a secondary matter, like a benefit that they might ask for, but that they desire as little as they understand it.[51]

The National Convention, Sonthonax argued, needed to take some action that would show the mass of the black population that its true interests lay with the Republic, not with its counterrevolutionary enemies. "I don't pretend to tell the Convention when to undertake a complete reform of the colonial regime," he wrote, "but if it is not promptly modified, if no improvement is made in the condition of the slaves, it is impossible to see how the misfortunes of Saint Domingue can be brought to an end. The salutary decree that will be issued on this subject will be the natural sequel to the law of April 4, 1792; it will assure the National Convention of respect and authority in the colonies." Above all, a proper reform would cement the loyalty of "the class that is the most concerned with the welfare of the colony, the citizens of 4 April."[52] Sonthonax laid out his thoughts even more clearly in a letter to the abolitionist journalist, Milscent, written a few days prior to his memorandum to the Convention. After saying that he did not want any more troops from France, although he desperately needed money to pay the wages and medical expenses of those who were already in the colony, he continued, "Get the Convention to do something for the slaves; it's the only way to make them appreciate it. These poor men fight for a king whom they would detest, if the representatives of the nation dared to remind themselves that the slaves in the New World are fighting for the same cause as the French armies."[53] Sonthonax warned Milscent not to publish his letter: He knew that the idea of abandoning the fight against the slaves and abolishing slavery would set off a firestorm of opposition on

---

[51] Sonthonax to National Convention, February 18, 1793, in AN, D XXV 5, d. 48.
[52] Sonthonax to National Convention, February 18, 1793, in AN, D XXV 5, d. 48.
[53] Sonthonax to Milscent, February 11, 1793, in AN, AA 55, d. 1511.

both sides of the Atlantic. His public letter to the Convention was more diplomatic, speaking only of "improvement" in the slaves' situation and stressing the need to maintain the support of the free men of color, who, as Sonthonax well knew, were by no means in favor of abolition. Unlike Polverel, however, Sonthonax had clearly abandoned any idea of defeating the black insurrection by force.

A genuine detestation of slavery was one motive for Sonthonax's change of heart; another was the looming danger of war with Britain and Spain. Although the official proclamation of hostilities did not reach Saint-Domingue until late February, rumors were already swirling in Le Cap by the middle of the month, driving up prices and causing unease.[54] Sonthonax reacted quickly, long before he received the letters that the navy minister Monge had written him at various dates in February 1793 announcing the dispatch of a naval squadron to protect merchant shipping, urging the commissioners to "deploy all the energy of which you are capable," informing them of the appointment of a new military governor, a certain General Galbaud, and even encouraging them to "consider whether it would not be possible to make use of the insurgent slaves against the Spanish. Consult those who you think can give you useful advice on this subject; consult the circumstances, the state of public spirit, let them be your guides."[55] Sonthonax had already decided that he and his fellow commissioner Polverel needed to confer about the measures necessary to prepare the colony's defense. Before leaving Le Cap, he took steps to ensure that the hundreds of black prisoners taken during Laveaux's offensive would not be summarily executed in his absence. His insistence that they needed to be given some kind of trial kept them alive and showed that he wanted to preserve the possibility of some kind of accommodation with the rebels.[56] On February 26, he boarded the warship *America*, accompanied by a number of men from the 16th dragoons, and set sail for the West Province, leaving Le Cap in the hands of General Laveaux and the Interim Commission.[57] Before departing, Sonthonax forbade the local government from taking any political decisions in his absence. "The dictator wants to keep us in the same condition, and there is no longer

[54] *Moniteur général*, February 17, 1793.
[55] Monge to Sonthonax, February 2 and 15, 1793, in AN, D XXV 11, d. 103; Monge to Sonthonax, February 26, 1793, in AN, D XXV 11, d. 102.
[56] *Moniteur général*, February 10, 1793; letter of Bernard Barthélemi Leclerc, 2nd décade of ventôse, An II, in AN, D XXV 81, d. 789, denouncing Sonthonax's policy.
[57] *Moniteur général*, February 27, 1793.

any talk of undertaking a new campaign to finish off the rebels," one of his white critics complained.[58]

At the moment of Sonthonax's arrival in the West Province, that region was in much greater disorder than the North. The desertion of his colleague Ailhaud had forced Polverel to take on the task of managing the South Province as well as the West. Unlike Sonthonax, who had been able to concentrate on problems in one small area, Polverel had to deal with a bewildering mosaic of local conflicts. In some of them, rival white factions opposed each other; in others, whites were fighting the free men of color, who outnumbered them in many rural districts. As the two men's disagreement about Sonthonax's tax levy had shown, Polverel was temperamentally inclined to avoid confrontation when he could. In December 1792, at almost the same moment when Sonthonax had risked provoking violence to force the regiment du Cap to accept the appointment of free colored officers, his colleague had abandoned his effort to integrate the National Guard in the southern city of Jacmel rather than test the whites' resolve to resist him.[59] In January 1793, while Polverel was overseeing the campaign against the slave insurgents at Platons, a major slave revolt broke out in the plain of Cul-de-Sac, part of the parish of Croix-des-Bouquets near Port-au-Prince. Control of that city itself fell into the hands of a white faction headed by Auguste Borel, a violent hothead who had led resistance to any agreement with the free men of color in 1792 and participated in the troubles in Cap Français on December 2, 1792 before returning to the West. Under Borel's command, the main military force in the region, the Port-au-Prince National Guard, persistently refused to obey orders from General La Salle, the province's military commander. Supporters of the commissioners in the city were menaced and even imprisoned.[60] By the end of January, La Salle was a virtual hostage in Port-au-Prince, unable either to gain command of the troops he needed to put down the spreading slave insurrection or to escape from the city. All through the month of February, La Salle wrote desperate letters begging Polverel and Sonthonax to send troops and a naval force to rescue him.[61]

While the whites in Port-au-Prince were rejecting the authority of the republican commissioners, Pierre Pinchinat, the free colored leader

---

[58] Anon., letter of March 9, 1793, in AN, D XXV 80, d. 782.
[59] Procès-verbal of Polverel's trip to Jacmel, December 8, 1792, in AN, D XXV 15, d. 146.
[60] Declaration of Catineau, in AN, D XXV 82, d. 804.
[61] Corre, ed., *Papiers de La Salle*, 114–18, 145–9.

Sonthonax had learned to trust during the crisis in Le Cap in December
1792, was working to win his group over to the republican cause. In
early February, he had left Cap Français for the northern part of the
West Province, where many of the free colored plantation owners had
been happy to ally themselves with white royalists in the Council of
Peace and Union, as Polverel had complained when he had arrived in that
region the previous fall.[62] Pinchinat made a tour of the region, explaining to the men of color why he now regarded the republican Sonthonax
as their firmest ally and getting them to sign a lengthy memorandum to
the National Convention excusing their earlier support for the royalists
and pledging their loyalty to the new French regime.[63] At the same time,
Pinchinat wrote to Sonthonax to underline the seriousness of the new
slave revolt in Cul-de-Sac and the necessity of bringing the whites who
continued to resist the national government's representatives to heel.
"The moment has come when the mandatories of the Republic should
use all the powers they have been granted for the reestablishment of
order and public tranquility to silence the dissidents who want to govern
the colony," he insisted. "If those with bad intentions continue to ignore
the national authority, we are lost without resource."[64]

Sonthonax landed at Saint-Marc on March 5, 1793 and began assembling forces for an expedition against Port-au-Prince. Coming from the
south, Polverel bypassed Port-au-Prince and joined his colleague; General
La Salle also finally succeeded in extricating himself from the rebellious
city and making his way to the commissioners' headquarters. Together,
they planned a full-scale assault on Borel and his supporters. On March
21, 1793, Sonthonax issued a proclamation warning the "audacious
criminals" in the city to submit themselves to the lawful authorities or
face severe punishment.[65] To bolster their forces, the commissioners
called on the free men of color in the districts around Saint-Marc to furnish volunteers for the campaign, thus tightening the alliance Sonthonax
had forged in Cap Français. "Let us rally around the representatives
of the law and let our bodies fall a thousand times under the blows
of our wretched enemies rather than to let the laws of the republic be

[62] Polverel to National Convention, December 3, 1792, in AN, D XXV 56, d. 557.
[63] "Les Citoyens de couleur et nègres libres de la partie française de Saint-Domingue, à la
Convention nationale," February 20, 1793, in AN, D XXV 110, 18. Between February
20 and March 7, 1793, the document was signed by large numbers of free men of color
in Saint-Marc, Saint-Louis de Mirebalais, Verettes, and Petite-Rivière.
[64] Pinchinat to Sonthonax, February 20, 1793, in AN, D XXV 5, d. 46.
[65] Sonthonax, proclamation, March 21, 1793, in AN, D XXV 5, d. 50.

treated with contempt," an appeal from the free men of color in Saint-Marc announced.[66] Under Borel's influence, the municipal government in Port-au-Prince prepared to resist, ordering all citizens to send their slaves to help build fortifications, and protested to the other parishes of the province that "a frightening proclamation has been extorted from the nation's representative; he is deceived about our intentions." The commissioners were implacable, however. Polverel sternly replied to the municipality, "It is indispensable, it is urgent to reestablish order and respect for the national authority that has been treated outrageously for too long. It is precisely because we are on the eve of a foreign war, that we need to deal promptly with the criminals who have sworn to see that the colony is lost."[67]

On April 5, 1793, the commissioners arrived off Port-au-Prince on board the *America*, blockading the harbor. In a last attempt to forestall an assault, the city's merchants appealed to the commissioners to consider the effect the destruction of the city would have on French commerce. "Can you be sure that, at the moment when you order an attack on the city, the merchants' warehouses will be spared, and don't you think you will be held responsible for the losses commerce will suffer from their looting, or their burning?" they wrote. "You will ruin the colony instead of saving it, and under the pretext of avenging insults that France has not suffered, you will plunge her into mourning, misery, and consternation."[68] The commissioners ignored them, demanding unconditional submission to their orders, and the Borel faction was equally uncompromising. It took the commissioners' 1,200 troops, commanded by General La Salle, another week to arrive by land, but on April 12, after the city government had refused a summons to surrender, Sonthonax and Polverel ordered an attack. The seventy-four-gun *America* and a smaller frigate bombarded the town for eight hours, preparing the way for an assault on the city's hastily erected defenses. "Fortunately the houses are made of wood, so there wasn't too much damage," one inhabitant reported, but he counted at least fifty civilian casualties. "You will appreciate what I had to suffer during the siege," a woman resident wrote, "hearing at every moment the whistling of the

[66] AN, D XXV 48, d. 461 (n. d.).

[67] *Affiches américaines* (Port-au-Prince edition), March 28, 31, April 7, 1793.

[68] *Adresse des Négocians de la ville du Port-au-Prince, aux citoyens commissaires Nationaux-Civils, à bord de l'Amérique en rade du Port-au-Prince* (Port-au-Prince: F. Chaidron & Cie, April 8, 1793), in AN, D XXV 5, d. 46. The address was signed by forty of the city's merchants.

balls that menaced our lowered heads, and knowing that my husband was exposed to the most immediate dangers."[69] Finally realizing the lengths to which the commissioners were prepared to go, the more moderate elements in the white population turned against Borel and forced him and his supporters to flee the city, which was then occupied by the commissioners' forces. "Four hundred citizens are in prison, and threatened with embarcation [for France]," one resident wrote to a correspondent in Marseille. "About two hundred fled with the Captain General [Borel], and two hundred are in hiding to avoid arrest."[70] Most of the arrested whites were put aboard ships that were ordered to sail to Cap Français, where, in accordance with instructions received from France, a large convoy was assembling in the harbor, waiting for a naval escort to help it evade British privateers and the enemy blockade that had been set up along the Atlantic coast when the war was formally declared.[71]

Their assault on Port-au-Prince showed that the two civil commissioners had developed their own version of what had come to be known in metropolitan France as "revolutionary government." Driven by the same imperatives as the "deputies on mission" in France, Sonthonax and Polverel were now ready to demand unquestioning compliance with their orders, to use the military against their foes, and to risk causing the destruction of a city in order to put down a rebellion. Whereas the arrests and deportations Sonthonax had carried out in Cap Français after the affair of December 2, 1792 had been narrowly targeted, in Port-au-Prince, the commissioners' dragnet swept up hundreds of suspects, even though everyone recognized that the guiltiest parties – Borel and his diehard supporters – had fled the city. The commissioners' victory had been achieved by forging an alliance with the region's free men of color. Their leader, Pinchinat, had played a key role in convincing Sonthonax and Polverel to adopt a confrontational strategy, and the bulk of their army consisted of free colored troops.

Confident of the strength of these forces, the commissioners also felt free to treat the acting governor general La Salle as a mere subordinate. His failure to stand up to the Borel movement before the crisis and his dilatory conduct during the campaign had disappointed them. During

[69] Rey la Rousse, née Vaudez, April 19, 1793, in AN, D XXV 81, d. 790.

[70] Letter of Lestuges, April 23, 1793, letter signed "Ton frère," April 24, 1793, and letter of April 24, 1793 to David Maystre in Marseille, in AN, D XXV 80, d. 783.

[71] Sonthonax had embargoed departures for Europe and ordered Admiral Cambis to begin organizing a convoy on February 14, 1793 (*Moniteur général*, February 14, 1793). This was a standard procedure, used in earlier trans-Atlantic wars.

the fighting, Sonthonax and Polverel suddenly gave one of La Salle's free colored subordinates an independent command, and once they landed in the city, they unceremoniously took over for themselves the house he had been occupying. When La Salle complained about their interference with his authority, they brusquely informed him that "the first action on your part that violates the relations that the decrees of the National Convention and the instructions of Executive Council have established between you and us will be the signal of your destitution, and you will be sent to answer to the National Convention."[72] Even before their fateful encounter with General Galbaud, Sonthonax and Polverel had made it clear that, in their view, even the highest-ranking military official in the colony owed them total obedience. La Salle restricted himself to writing a letter to the minister Monge, asking him "to trace for me the boundary line between the authority of the civil commissioners and myself;" Galbaud would not be so submissive.[73]

The Port-au-Prince campaign and the subsequent occupation of Jacmel, which had defied Polverel's authority during his earlier stay in the south, left only the whites in the Grande Anse, at the western end of the South Province's long peninsula, in open rebellion against the commissioners' authority. Sonthonax and Polverel now had a free hand to deal with the issue of the slave population. After the occupation of Port-au-Prince, the main area affected by an active slave rebellion was the plain of Cul-de-Sac near that city, where the insurrection that had broken out just as the commissioners were inflicting defeats on the insurgencies in the northern plain and at Platons continued. A letter from a plantation manager in the region described the exhaustion of the forces confronting the slaves after three months of fighting: "We are continually in the camps, sleeping on the ground and fed as badly as possible. One has to mount up and go on patrol all the time ... The blacks come to attack the camps with unbelievable audacity. Most of them are very badly armed, some have lances and some who don't have any weapons come at us as if they were armed. You can imagine how we drive them back and how many we are forced to kill." In the wake of the commissioners' occupation of Port-au-Prince, however, the insurrection's leader, Hyacinthe, offered to negotiate an end to the revolt.[74] "Hope revives in our hearts," a letter from Port-au-Prince reported at the beginning of

[72] Corre, *Papiers de La Salle*, letters of April 13, April 16, April 27, 197, 204, 206.
[73] La Salle to Monge, n.d., in Corre, *Papiers de La Salle*, 207.
[74] Lestuges to "Monseigneur," April 23, 1793, in AN, D XXV 80, d. 783.

May. "The Cul-de-Sac plain is finally beginning to return to order. Some fifteen *atteliers* have returned to their respective plantations ..."[75]

The commissioners boasted that they had persuaded the slaves of Cul-de-Sac to return to work at the price of minimal concessions. "It cost the republic only two grants of liberty," they told the French minister in the United States, Edmond Genet, "and a promise from us to see that the Code Noir was strictly executed."[76] On April 23, they issued a proclamation prohibiting slave owners from punishing slaves who returned to their plantations.[77] On May 5, 1793, they went further and extended their effort at pacification to the entire colony. Their procedure was a remarkable one: four months after the execution of Louis XVI, the representatives of the French Republic reissued Louis XIV's edict of 1685, the legal charter of slavery in the French empire, along with the royal ordinance of December 1784, which attempted to limit slave owners' abuses of their powers.

The decree of May 5, 1793 was the commissioners' last major initiative with respect to slavery prior to the events of June 20, 1793, and understanding its significance is crucial to evaluating their intentions before they were confronted with that crisis. Obviously, the provisions of the Code Noir were not a program for the abolition of slavery. Instead, the commissioners' action reaffirmed that the Revolution had left the previous laws concerning slavery in effect. The defenders of slavery understood the commissioners' actions in a very different sense, however. Major provisions of the Code noir, particularly those meant to provide the slaves with some protection from their masters, had never been enforced, and defenders of slavery had insisted that their application would fatally undermine the institution. The pro-slavery journalist, Claude-Corentin Tanguy-Laboissière, responded to the commissioners' initiative by reiterating this position:

It has always been judged so absurd that its execution has never been attempted. It is completely contrary to the spirit of slavery that any authority should be interposed between the master and the slave. Obviously this undermines the respect and obedience that the one owes to the other. See, in this respect, what Montesquieu wrote in his great work, *The Spirit of the Laws*, on the nature and the principle of despotic government.[78]

---

[75] *Affiches américaines* (Cap Français edition), May 10, 1793 (letter from Port-au-Prince, May 2).
[76] Sonthonax and Polverel to Genet, July 8, 1793, in AN, D XXV 5, d. 46.
[77] *Moniteur général*, May 5, 1793.
[78] Tanguy-Boissière to General Galbaud, May 17, 1793, in AN, D XXV 47, d. 453.

The most radical feature of Sonthonax and Polverel's proclamation, however, was not its content but the form in which it was published. In addition to reprinting the French text of the Code noir, the commissioners had it translated into Creole, the language of the colony's black population, with instructions that it be posted on all plantations and read aloud to the slaves. They thus clearly signaled their intention to bring the blacks under the protection of the law and to enable them to take advantage of its provisions. In contrast to some modern scholars of slavery, who have argued that the essence of slavery consisted in the "social death" of the slave who "had no social existence outside of his master" and was denied any enforceable claim to rights, Sonthonax and Polverel attempted to institute a situation in which the slaves of Saint-Domingue, while still obligated to work for their masters, would have had a certain minimum of guaranteed rights and protection from the government.[79] Their pro-slavery opponents understood what was at stake. "Have you read the proclamation translated into Creole?" the agitator Thomas Millet wrote. "There we see that the civil commissioners, after having spread a spirit of dizziness among all the colored colonists, are now doing the same among the slaves, by accustoming them to thinking of them ... as the only arbiters of their destiny."[80]

The proclamation of May 5, 1793 was thus a challenge to the bases of slavery as the white colonists understood them. The commissioners certainly intended it as a gesture to the black population. The preamble to the Creole version stated that they were issuing their decree to protect the blacks from mistreatment, and the commissioners added that they did not hold the slaves responsible for the insurrection: "It is not among the Negro slaves that one needs to look to find the cause of the your uprising, they are not the leaders of it ..., it is others who misled you."[81] The decree of May 5, 1793 was meant as an "improvement" of slavery, along the lines that Sonthonax had recommended to the Convention in February 1793. At the same time, however, the commissioners continued to insist that they were not aiming at the immediate abolition of the institution. In Port-au-Prince, Polverel's secretary, Picquenard, the editor of a journal devoted to the commissioners' party, denounced rumors spread by the whites that the Convention was moving toward such a step. "It knows, better than you yourselves, that this class of men is not

---

[79] Orlando Patterson, *Slavery and Social Death: A Comparative Study* (Cambridge, MA: Harvard University Press, 1982), 38.
[80] Thomas Millet to Galbaud, May 28, 1793, in AN, D XXV 47, d. 453.
[81] Proclamation of May 5, 1793, Creole version, in *Moniteur général*, May 26, 1793.

ready for freedom ... It knows that the first use a slave makes of his freedom is to murder the man who kept him in chains with the irons that he has broken, and that freedom granted to *these* would be as dangerous as a dagger in the hands of a child."[82]

The most important argument the commissioners made in defense of their decree was that it offered a chance of success, whereas experience had shown that military measures were insufficient. In a letter to General Galbaud, Sonthonax and Polverel argued that force had failed as a method for bringing the slave rebellion to an end. Continuing military operations against the insurgents would cost too many soldiers' lives, leaving the colony defenseless against foreign enemies. Their proclamation offered an alternative solution to the problem: "If one could end the war against the slaves in the North and the South by peaceful means, wouldn't you prefer that ... to any hostile measure?"[83] To the Convention, they reported the success of their measures in the West Province in glowing terms: "In eight days, all the Negroes returned to their *atteliers*. All it cost the owners was two emancipations, and from us the promise to compel the whites to obey the Code noir, which, as execrable as it is, would nevertheless constitute a softening of the condition of the Africans in Saint-Domingue. It is impossible to communicate to you, citizens," Sonthonax and Polverel continued, "the delicious sensations we experienced when we came together with them. Happiness and trust were painted on their faces. They cried 'Long live the Republic, long live the civil commissioners. Our fathers won't allow anyone to cut off our ears or to bury us alive or to throw us in ovens for having displeased our masters,' they said."[84]

On the eve of the crisis of June 20, 1793, Sonthonax and Polverel thus believed that they had found a solution to the slave uprising that was consistent with their mandate. By reasserting that slavery was subject to legal regulation, they left the door open to further modifications by the national legislature, but they did not presume to act in the Convention's place. They could truthfully say that all they had done was reiterate the existing laws on the subject. They had nevertheless done so in a way that they hoped would communicate to the black population the Republic's genuine concern for their welfare. The success of their policy

---

[82] *Ami de l'égalité* (Port-au-Prince), May 9, 1793. On Picquenard's authorship of the *Ami de l'égalité*, see his letter of 6 ther. II in AN, D XXV 81, d. 798.
[83] Sonthonax and Polverel to Galbaud, May 22, 1793, in AN, D XXV 47, d. 450.
[84] Sonthonax and Polverel, report to Convention, June 18, 1793, in AN, D XXV 5, d. 51.

in terminating the uprising in the plain of Cul-de-Sac had convinced them that no more radical measure was necessary for the time being. Their policy also avoided any confrontation with the free men of color, the main base of their support; many members of that group were themselves slave owners with no desire to see the immediate abolition of the institution, and some of the free men of color who had joined the commissioners' forces had even brought their own slaves along as servants.[85] The civil commissioners hoped that they could now turn their attention to their most pressing problem, preparing Saint-Domingue to defend itself against attacks from the British and the Spanish, as well as other issues that they tried to resolve in a string of proclamations issued after the occupation of Port-au-Prince: the financial crisis facing the colony, the fate of plantations whose owners had abandoned them, the allocation of military rations.[86]

Meanwhile, the situation in Cap Français was rapidly deteriorating. The main threat to order in the city did not come from the slave population: a complaint from the commander of one of the outposts defending the approaches to the city that he had found slaves "outside the boundaries and exchanging food with the brigands" was one of the rare indications of concern about their behavior.[87] The city's two newspapers – at the beginning of April, the Cap Français edition of the *Affiches américaines*, which had been suspended for some time, resumed publication – continued to carry routine advertisements of slaves for sale and notices about runaways until the morning of June 20, 1793. The main danger to the city's stability came instead, as it had since the start of the Revolution, from elements of the white population. Sonthonax's absence emboldened his opponents to raise their heads again. Just days after he left for Saint-Marc, the municipal council challenged the authority of the Interim Commission, proposing to hold elections for a new colonial assembly. Sonthonax had to write a stern letter forbidding any such action.[88]

At the end of March, Claude-Corentin Tanguy-Laboissière, a white from the South Province who had been appointed to the Interim Commission in January to replace one of the members deported by Sonthonax, resigned and denounced the commissioners' decree of March 21 against the Borel party in Port-au-Prince. "Your proclamation ... has

[85] Captain Nully to civil commissioners, June 12, 1793, in AN, D XXV 20, d. 208.
[86] *Moniteur général*, April 28, 30, May 4, 1793.
[87] Dubuisson, commander at Morne Rouge, in *Moniteur général*, April 7, 1793.
[88] *Moniteur général*, March 10, 25, 1793.

spread fear and consternation in Cap," he wrote. "It has chilled all hearts and dismayed the spirits of honest friends of domestic peace."[89] Tanguy-Laboissière then created his own newspaper, in which he published, among other things, the text of Sonthonax's official report on the events of December 2, 1792, copied from a Paris newspaper. His readers could see for themselves what the journalist called "the libelous statements against a large number of citizens of this city that it contains; many will see themselves treated as violent men, brigands, and designated by the citizen commissioner as enemies of France," as well as the evidence of what he stigmatized as Sonthonax's "exclusive predilection in favor of our new brothers," which, he claimed, "is reviving distinctions between them and us, that eternal seedbed of divisions and hatred, which the law of 4 April was supposed to eliminate."[90] Tanguy-Laboissière was quickly confined on board a ship in the harbor, pending deportation to France, but he had supporters in the city. The editor of the city's main newspaper, the *Moniteur général*, was also briefly arrested for publishing parts of Sonthonax's report.[91]

Political agitation was not the only danger facing Le Cap. With war looming on the horizon, the alarming state of the army was another critical problem. By early April, General Laveaux was complaining to the Interim Commission on an almost daily basis about the lack of funds to pay the troops and the shortage of supplies. "The camps lack everything, the soldier complains about his situation," he warned.[92] The publisher of the *Moniteur général* launched a campaign to collect private donations to aid soldiers confined to the hospital; from his shipboard prison, Tanguy-Laboissière seized the opportunity to win favorable publicity by pledging 33 livres.[93] With British privateers threatening shipping in the area, the Interim Commission was also preoccupied with finding supplies for the civilian population. On April 17, 1793, its members received a report warning them that "the public warehouse is out of every kind of necessity, and cannot do anything about it, since its resources are exhausted."[94]

---

[89] *Adresse de Tanguy-Laboissière à la Commission Nationale-Civile de Saint-Domingue* (Cap Français, March 29, 1793), in CAOM, F 3 198 (Moreau de Saint-Méry papers).
[90] *Journal des Révolutions de la Partie Française de Saint-Domingue*, April 1, 1793. Sonthonax's report had appeared in the Paris journal *Courrier de l'Egalité* on January 13, 1793.
[91] *Moniteur général*, April 1, 1793.
[92] Laveaux to Interim Commission, April 10, 1793, in *Moniteur général*, April 13.
[93] Batilliot, in *Moniteur général*, April 12, 1793; Tanguy, in *Moniteur général*, April 14, 1793.
[94] *Moniteur général*, April 19, 1793.

The morale of the city's white population, briefly raised by Laveaux's victories in January, plunged again when it became clear that the campaign would not bring a quick end to the slave insurrection. The confirmation of hostilities with Britain, which threatened to cut Saint-Domingue off from the metropole for an indefinite period, led large numbers of whites to try to make arrangements to return to France or to take refuge in the United States. "As soon as I arise from my bed I begin to cudgel my brains for some means of getting away safely and without loss from St. Domingo which I regard as a doomed land," Jean Girard wrote to his brother in Philadelphia.[95] The local newspapers carried increasing numbers of advertisements offering properties, including slaves, for sale and notifying creditors to file claims before the individuals concerned departed. Because of the embargo, however, no ships actually sailed from Cap Français; those who had made the decision to escape the colony found themselves in limbo, not knowing when they would be able to leave. The population of the city in the spring of 1793 undoubtedly presented a different picture from that sketched by Moreau de Saint-Méry in 1789, although precise statistics are hard to come by. Many whites who normally resided on their plantations had taken refuge in the city because of the slave uprising. Some had brought their slaves with them – one white man would arrive in Norfolk, Virginia, with ninety-nine slaves during the mass exodus following the events of June 20, 1793 – but other city slaves may have slipped away to join the insurrection or to escape the massacres perpetuated by the whites at its outset. An unknown number of whites had already managed to leave the city before the imposition of the shipping embargo. The free women of color who made up the majority of that group before 1791 probably remained in the city; the number of free men of color may have risen as plantation owners fled the turmoil in the rural districts.

The population of soldiers and sailors in the city was certainly more than it had been when Moreau de Saint-Méry made his calculations in 1789. Even though many of the thousands of troops sent to the island in 1792 had died, mostly of disease, and others had been dispersed to posts throughout the colony, the number in the city was still larger than the normal peacetime garrison. As more and more ships gathered waiting for the departure of the convoy, the floating population of sailors also grew, particularly because of the presence of the warships with their large crews. Whereas Moreau de Saint-Méry estimated the crew

95 Jean Girard to Stephen Girard, March 31, 1793, in APS, Girard papers, roll 10.

of a typical French merchant vessel at 25 men, the full complement of a
74-gun warship was over 700. The commissioners themselves had augmented the white population in the harbor by dispatching hundreds of
prisoners from Saint-Marc and Port-au-Prince. Over all, the total number of whites – including civilians, soldiers, sailors, and political prisoners – was almost certainly higher than the total of 7,200 Moreau de
Saint-Méry had estimated four years earlier. The number of slaves may
have shrunk somewhat, and the population of *libres de couleur* had
probably increased modestly.

Statistics gathered when the refugees from Cap Français arrived in
Norfolk in July 1793 give some idea of the composition of the city's
white population at the moment of its destruction. A register of "Notes
about the unfortunates arriving in Norfolk," which eventually came
into the hands of Moreau de Saint-Méry (who was not personally in the
colony in June 1793) lists 635 individuals. Of the 562 who were identified by sex, 57 percent were men and 43 percent women – a less lopsided
ratio than that traditionally estimated for the colonial population, which
may reflect a greater tendency for women than men to take shelter in the
city after the start of the uprising. Forty percent of the refugees identified by age were children or adolescents under the age of twenty. Of
the 106 men identified by occupation, close to one-half – 46 percent –
were either plantation owners or managers, and thus presumably refugees stranded in the city because of the slave insurrection. Twenty-seven
percent were engaged in commerce, either as *négociants* – wholesale
traders – or *marchands*, selling to local customers, or clerks. Artisans
made up 14 percent of the group, while the remaining 13 percent were
in service occupations, the professions, or the military.[96] (Most of the
sailors and soldiers on the warships coming from Cap Français were
not allowed to come ashore in Norfolk.) The chaotic conditions under
which refugees got on ships in Cap Français in June 1793 give us reason
to believe that this list is probably representative of the white population at that moment, since almost all whites made an effort to leave,
but it gives minimal information about the other racial groups, who did
not participate as much in the mass exodus. Fifteen individuals, all of
them women, were identified as "mulattoes," and sixteen were listed as
blacks, but notes in the document suggest that many black slaves who
arrived with their masters were not recorded, including the ninety-nine
blacks accompanying Monsieur Bouthillier.

[96] "Notes sur les malheureux venus de St. Domingue à Norfolk en Virginie," in CAOM,
F 3 198 (Moreau de Saint-Méry papers).

By the end of April 1793, the mood among the white population, nearly half of them driven from their homes by the insurrection and another quarter tied to the flow of commerce that had almost ceased because of the uprising and the embargo on shipping, was certainly at a low point. An article in the *Courrier maritime du Havre*, summarizing several letters written around that time, warned that "the situation of this city is becoming more and more precarious." Fear of British privateers had stopped the flow of supplies from the United States, and food supplies were running short.[97] The whites feared that the slaves in the city were conspiring with the insurgents. "There is no doubt that the rebels have lots of reliable informers who warn them before any attack and send them munitions of all sorts," a letter written at the beginning of May reported. "All these difficulties, coming together, drive the good citizens to despair, and give them no hope of an end to their sufferings. Indeed, it seems as though all possible misfortunes are united to extinguish the white race."[98] Whites also complained that free men of color, particularly those in uniform, behaved insolently to them in the streets.[99]

The soldiers serving in the colony were as dispirited and discouraged as the white civilians. At the end of April, Laveaux tried to drive away the bands of black insurgents who had remained in the hills immediately surrounding the city despite the January offensive. Men in several units threatened to refuse to fight because they had not been paid; to get them to march at all, Laveaux had to promise them that they would only spend one day outside the city before returning. Very few of the white citizens volunteered to aid the soldiers, and the city government issued an exasperated condemnation of shopkeepers who had stayed home and kept their stores open, thus gaining an advantage over their colleagues who agreed to join the troops. Some even "hid their blacks rather than sending them to serve as laborers in the army." The lack of civilian support caused resentment among the soldiers. Furious at the unsupportive white population, Laveaux demanded a census of the population to identify all those capable of fighting.[100]

[97] *Indicateur politique, mercantile, et littéraire*, July 8, 1793, in F 3 198, Moreau de Saint-Méry papers.

[98] Letter from Le Cap, May 5, 1793, in *Gazette française*, September 6, 1793. By the time this long-delayed letter reached France, news of the destruction of Cap Français had already appeared in some of the other Paris papers.

[99] See the reports of street incidents on May 8 and 10, 1793, in AN, D XXV 47, d. 451.

[100] Laplace, *Histoire des desastres de Saint-Domingue*, 279 ; *Moniteur général*, May 1, 1793 (Interim Commission, April 29); May 5, 1793 (Interim Commission, May 3).

The sailors on the French warships and the immobilized merchant ships in the harbor were as unhappy as the soldiers. By late 1792, conditions on board the warships in the Saint-Domingue *station*, or squadron, that had been in the Caribbean for nearly two years were alarming, as Joseph Cambis, the new naval commander appointed at the beginning of 1793, tried to explain to Sonthonax and Polverel. The ships lacked supplies, "sickness and death have done great damage," and the *Jupiter*, his flagship, was down to only 250 men, a third of its normal complement, with most of those "hav[ing] shown the desire to return to France," he warned them. Two months later, he had to report an instance of flagrant disobedience on one of the vessels.[101] A dutiful professional sailor who had been in the colony since 1791, Cambis continued to do his best to carry out the orders, but he became increasingly frustrated at his inability to make Sonthonax and Polverel understand the "great difficulties that prevent the naval service here from performing as it should for the honor of the French name."[102] According to orders sent to Cambis in February 1793, on the eve of the declaration of war with Britain, the ships of the Saint-Domingue *station* were supposed to form the escort for a convoy that would conduct the merchant vessels safely to the United States and France. The convoy's departure was to coincide with the arrival of replacements for the squadron from France, but, unbeknownst to the admiral and to the civil commissioners, naval officials in France had concluded that they could not spare major warships for service in the Caribbean.[103]

By early May, 1793, Cambis had decided that the situation in the harbor had become completely untenable. The Executive Council could not have imagined how desperate the shortages of supplies and naval munitions were in the colony when it issued its order for the entire convoy to sail as one group, he wrote. "In addition, the commercial ships count on a rapid departure. Some have had a full cargo for a long time; others have made sacrifices to get loaded quickly. All insist that their interests have preference. Finally, isn't it a risk to have in harbor of Le Cap an assembly of men whose interests have been frustrated,

[101] Cambis to civil commissioners, December 24, 1792 and February 12, 1793, in AN, D XXV 51, d. 489.
[102] Cambis to commissioners, January 1793, in AN, D XXV 51, d. 489. On Cambis's length of service, see SHM, BB 4 24, letter of February 16, 1793.
[103] Ministry of Navy to Cambis, February 13, 1793, in AN, D XXV 51, d. 489, cahier 2; memorandum, memorandum from bureau of ports and arsenals, February 14, 1793, in AN, CC 9 A8.

A good contemporary model of the French 74-gun Eole, whose commander, Captain Bertrand Keranguen, was killed at the First of June

FIGURE 4.1. Model of a French 74-gun warship.

A contemporary model of the *Eole*, one of the 74-gun warships that formed part of the Saint-Domingue *station*, or squadron, in 1793. Constructed to standardized plans, these ships of the line carried crews of over 700 men and supplies sufficient for voyages of up to six months. The crews of the *Eole* and its companion ship, the *Jupiter*, played major roles in the events of June 20, 1793 in Cap Français and their prolongation in the United States later that year.

Source: Musée de la Marine, Paris.

and wouldn't it be easier to prevent the spread of discontent that the enemies of public order know how to incite?" He proposed that half of the merchant ships be allowed to depart, with an escort comprising a part of the naval squadron.[104] Even though a spy had reported that the British naval squadron in Jamaica was too small to mount an attack on Saint-Domingue, Sonthonax and Polverel stuck to the letter of their instructions from Paris and refused to authorize any of the ships to leave.[105] (See Figure 4.1)

Trapped in the sweltering heat in Cap Français harbor, the sailors were only too ready to take out their anger on the commissioners' main supporters, the free men of color. An incident on the *Jupiter* in early May demonstrated the intensity of the sailors' attitudes. The vessel had just returned to Le Cap after a short patrol to chase away British privateers, and new troops were being sent from the shore to replace the military garrison that was stationed on board to maintain order. Among the soldiers sent for this duty were some of the free men of color from the

[104] Cambis, memorandum of May 11, 1793, in AN, D XXV 19, d. 186.
[105] "Précis historique du journal du citoyen Voisin," May 13, 1793, summarizing his visit to Jamaica on February 26–March 1, 1793, in AN, AA 55, d. 1511. Voisin had determined that the British naval force in Jamaica was only half the size of the Saint-Domingue squadron. Sonthonax and Polverel to Galbaud, May 22, 1793 and May 31, 1793, in AN, D XXV 47, d. 449.

compagnies franches organized by Sonthonax. "The crew appeared very upset that they were being sent on board," according to the ship's log, "and they muttered seditiously. A *contremaître* came forward and asked the duty officer why they were sending 'faces of night' to guard white men. The officer, seeing that the man was drunk, told him to go sleep it off. At this, the crew began a riot and one sailor, speaking for all of them, said that neither blacks nor mulattoes could stay on the ship. The whole crew cried out, 'No, no, no faces of night.'" Only with great difficulty did Cambis succeed in restoring discipline and forcing the sailors to accept the garrison.[106]

The commissioners' response to Cambis's warnings about the mood of the crews and the condition of the ships was to accuse him of a lack of patriotism. "Do our generals in Europe think they have done their duty to the fatherland by complaining to the National Convention because our ministers leave our soldiers without shoes and uniforms?" the commissioners demanded. "No, they use the means they have at hand and the French armies have triumphed over the leading powers of the world. In Saint-Domingue, the enemy dares to defy the guns along our coast, he seizes commercial vessels in our very ports, and the warships of the Republic commanded by rear admiral Cambis stay anchored in the harbors. Go figure out what you need to do."[107] By this time, Cambis had become thoroughly disaffected with the commissioners and their policies. In a letter that he drafted to the French minister in the United States, Genet, but which was probably not sent, he wrote, "It is my duty to tell France of the deluge of misfortunes that has fallen on the white citizens, the natural effect of which could not fail to be an indestructible hatred for the caste that is now in power [the free men of color]."[108] Faithful to his duty, Cambis continued to carry out the commissioners' orders as best he could until June 20, 1793, but he obviously had little enthusiasm for their policies.

Sonthonax's allies among the free men of color in Le Cap were also increasingly unhappy with the commissioner's absence. "There was

---

[106] Log of *Jupiter*, May 9, 1793, in AN, D XXV 54. On the prevalence of racial prejudice among the sailors, see "Réflexions sur l'affaire du Cap françois," n.d., in LC, Genet papers, reel 6.

[107] Sonthonax and Polverel to Cambis, April 29, 1793, in AN, D XXV 51, d. 489.

[108] Cambis to Genet, April 26, 1793, in AN, D XXV 51, d. 489. This draft is heavily overwritten with corrections, as though Cambis never completely decided what he wanted to say, and no version of it appears in Genet's collection of correspondence received from Saint-Domingue.

nothing to compare to their suspicion and their active surveillance of everything the whites did," a white colonist later recalled.[109] Acutely aware of the mood among the whites, Castaing wrote to the commissioner in early March to warn him that "when the cat is away, the rats dance" and urged him to return as soon as possible. In early April, Boisrond forwarded copies of Tanguy's newspaper and reported that Laveaux's appeals for money and supplies for his soldiers were causing alarm. "All this comes from the aristocrats," he claimed; "the commander Laveaux is completely duped by them, he falls completely into their trap, he is surrounded by a crowd who don't love the revolution, he tells everybody what he thinks with the frankness that you will recognize." In contrast, Boisrond told the commissioners, "the free companies and all the other mulattoes remain faithfully attached to good order as you left them[;] they do not cry out for money." Observing the agitation in the city, however, these loyal supporters awaited the commissioners' return "with the greatest impatience."[110]

The contrast between the optimism of Sonthonax and Polverel, inspired by their success in squelching white opposition in the West and South provinces and in pacifying the slave insurrection in Cul-de-Sac, and the glum mood of both the white population in Cap Français, resentful of the commissioners' alliance with the free men of color and suffering from an economic crisis, as well as that of the free men of color, fearful that the absence of their protectors would undermine the privileged position they had achieved, created a situation fraught with danger. The unhappiness of the troops and, even more so, of the sailors added to the tension. So long as the disparate coalition of white grumblers in Le Cap lacked leadership, though, there was little chance of an open revolt against the commissioners' authority. The free men of color, a significant force in the city, supported them, and their representatives on the Interim Commission made sure that the local government did not become a focus of opposition, as happened in many of the French cities that rebelled against the Convention in the spring and summer of 1793. The loyalties of the naval commander, Admiral Cambis, may have been doubtful, but his army counterpart, General Laveaux, was solidly on the side of the commissioners. On May 7, 1793, however, a frigate carrying General François-Thomas Galbaud, the newly appointed governor general of the colony, arrived in the Cap François harbor. A republican war

[109] Laplace, *Histoire des desastres de Saint-Domingue*, 269.
[110] Boisrond to Sonthonax and Polverel, April 11, 1793, in AN, D XXV 115.

hero with family roots in Saint-Domingue, he brought with him a *brevet*, or letter of appointment, approved by the National Convention, giving him powers limited only by those of the Civil Commissioners. Coming ashore, Galbaud instantly filled the vacuum created by Sonthonax's absence. No one contested his authority. Throughout Cap Français, everyone waited anxiously to see how Galbaud would respond to the crisis confronting the beleaguered city.

5

A Model Republican General

Short stature was one of the few qualities General François-Thomas Galbaud shared with Napoleon Bonaparte. Barely five feet tall, Galbaud was an even less imposing figure than the "Little Corporal." Like Napoleon, he was described as having lively eyes, but no one would have mistaken him for his Corsican contemporary: he had blond eyebrows, a reddish face, and wore a wig.[1] Unlike his fellow artillery officer, Galbaud was fated to vanish from historical memory, mentioned only briefly in accounts of the revolution in the French colonies. And yet, like Napoleon, he changed history's course. In just six weeks after he landed in Cap Français on May 7, 1793, this fifty-year-old military officer would bring about both the reversal of revolutionary France's policy toward the insurgent slaves of Saint-Domingue and the destruction of the colony's richest and most important city. Whereas Napoleon made his mark because he mastered events and bent them to his will, Galbaud had the unhappy knack of provoking results that were the opposite of what he intended. Nevertheless, the story of the French Revolution's confrontation with slavery would have been very different without his intervention.

François-Thomas Galbaud was born in Nantes on November 28, 1743. His father had the title of "*conseiller du roy maître ordinaire des comptes de Bretagne*," but spent most of Galbaud's childhood managing the family's plantations in Saint-Domingue, while his mother ran the family in Nantes.[2] Following the example of many of his relatives,

---

[1] Edmond Genet to Governor Clinton, August 30, 1793, in LC, Genet Papers microfilms, reel 6.
[2] Gabriel Debien, *Esclaves aux Antilles*, 110.

Galbaud entered the army: in 1761, he was admitted to the royal artillery corps as a cadet. During the Revolution, Napoleon Bonaparte would rise from lieutenant to general in four years, but old regime careers progressed more slowly. Too young to have served in the Seven Years' War, Galbaud became a first lieutenant in 1765 and reached the rank of captain in 1772. In 1775, he married Marie-Alexis Tobin, the daughter of a Nantes merchant; according to one source, she was a Creole from a family with extensive property in Saint-Domingue.[3] They had three sons, all of whom would eventually pursue military careers of their own. Galbaud fought in the war of American Independence and then vegetated in the garrison town of Strasbourg until the Revolution. In 1788, he was recommended for the *croix de Saint-Louis*, strictly on the basis of his long years of service; it was the only decoration he ever received.[4] It is not clear whether Galbaud had ever seen his family's two Saint-Domingue plantations; aside from his service overseas with the French forces supporting the American struggle for independence, he had spent his adult life in France.[5]

Galbaud was one of the minority of aristocratic officers who embraced the French Revolution. Like Sonthonax and Polverel, he joined the Jacobin movement: certificates in his dossier show that he was among the founding members of the club established in Strasbourg in January 1790, and he later participated in the club in Metz.[6] Passed over for promotion in the spring of 1791, he complained that he was being discriminated against because of his revolutionary sentiments.[7] Like many army officers of his generation, he was as at home with words as he was with weapons.[8] He spoke frequently in club meetings and left behind a copious paper trail, a habit he would maintain during his mission in the New World. Speeches such as the one he read in January 1792 to the Metz Jacobin club warning against partisan divisions showed that he had mastered the rhetoric of the period: "Citizens! Do we want to

[3] Laplace, *Histoire des desastres de Saint-Domingue*, 283.
[4] Service historique de l'armée de la terre (SHAT), 4 Yd. 3912 (Galbaud).
[5] The Galbaud du Fort plantation, located in Saint-Domingue's West Province, is the subject of one of the many monographs compiled by Gabriel Debien, the specialist on the history of the French Antilles: *Une Plantation de Saint-Domingue. La Sucrerie Galbaud du Fort* (Cairo: Institut français du Caire, 1941).
[6] Membership certificates in AN, D XXV 49, d. 475.
[7] Letter of June 1, 1791, in SHAT, 4 Yd. 3912 (Galbaud).
[8] On the importance of writing in pre-revolutionary officers' culture, see David A. Bell, *The First Total War: Napoleon's Europe and the Birth of Warfare as We Know It* (Boston, MA: Houghton Mifflin, 2007), 26–7.

remain free? Let us form ranks around the constitution. Don't let us be weakened by internal dissensions."[9] When war broke out in April 1792, Galbaud was assigned to the staff of General Charles-François Dumouriez, commander of the forces facing the Austro-Prussian invasion. Ordered to lead 1,500 troops to reinforce the garrison in Verdun, Galbaud was unable to reach the fortress before it surrendered, but he held off the enemy in an engagement at the ridge of Biesme, and was present at the victory of Valmy on September 20, 1792.[10]

A few weeks later, fate gave Galbaud his chance for republican glory. Dispatched to negotiate a local armistice with the Prussians, who were preparing to withdraw from Verdun, he found himself parlaying with no less a personage than the Duke of Brunswick, the generalissimo of the enemy forces and author of the notorious "Brunswick manifesto" that threatened to punish the population of Paris if they harmed Louis XVI. Brunswick politely congratulated Galbaud on the skill with which he had deployed his artillery in the Biesme affair, and then complained about the violent language being used in France to denounce his manifesto. Drawing himself up to his full five feet, Galbaud retorted, "It is somewhat astonishing that the duke of Brunswick had the insane presumption (permit me this expression) to try to dictate laws to a people who the whole of Europe could not conquer even if all the despots united against them." Galbaud himself wrote up this encounter for the press and sent a copy to the *Moniteur général de la partie françoise de Saint-Domingue*. It may well have been this incident that brought him to the attention of the new republican government in Paris and resulted in his appointment as governor general of Saint-Domingue.[11]

After the disaster of June 20, 1793, accusations that there had been a conspiracy behind Galbaud's appointment to Saint-Domingue found a wide audience, particularly in view of the fact that his superior in the 1792 campaign, Dumouriez, had so spectacularly betrayed the revolutionary government at the beginning of April 1793, when he ordered his troops

---

[9] AN, D XXV 49, d. 470.
[10] Galbaud, "Demande en traitement de général de brigade réformé," n.d., in SHAT, 4 Yd. 3912 (Galbaud). There are some documents concerning Galbaud's role in the 1792 campaign in AN, AA 61.
[11] "Conference tenue entre les citoyens La Barolliere et Galbaud, maréchaux de camp des armées de la Republique d'une part, Le Duc de Brunswick, Generalissime des armées confedérés prussiennes, autrichiennes et hessoise, la General Kalkreuth commandant l'arrière garde de l'armée prussienne ...," in AN, D XXV 49, d. 473; *Moniteur général*, January 22, 1793.

to march on Paris and then went over to the Austrians after his men defied him. In November 1792, when Galbaud was originally chosen for a mission in the colonies, neither Dumouriez nor anyone else could have imagined the chain of events that would lead him to try to overthrow the government five months later, and Galbaud's nomination seems to have been more or less accidental. In November 1792, the navy minister Monge needed a general to serve as governor of Martinique, since Rochambeau, originally destined for that post, had ended up in Saint-Domingue instead. Monge originally selected another of Dumouriez's subordinates, but Dumouriez refused to release him, and so Galbaud was picked as a second choice.[12] The appointment also had the approval of Jean-Nicolas Pache, the radical war minister.[13] Galbaud spent several months preparing for this mission, only to have it cancelled when news of Rochambeau's successful landing in Martinique in January 1793 reached France.[14] Monge then decided that since Rochambeau's departure had left Saint-Domingue without a military governor, Galbaud might as well be sent there.[15]

Unlike the appointments of Sonthonax and Polverel nine months earlier, Galbaud's nomination did not cause much controversy. The Paris representatives of the white Saint-Domingue colonists were, not surprisingly, pleased with his selection. "Finally, Saint-Domingue will have a leader who, taking a real interest in its welfare, and having the capacity and the will to do so, will soon reestablish the order and peace that are as much desired as needed," they wrote to him.[16] But the representative of the free men of color, Julien Raimond, was equally enthusiastic, telling his correspondents in the colony that "a general, a compatriot of yours who has covered himself with glory, is sent to you: you can count on his attachment to the fatherland and his civic loyalty, of which he has given many proofs," and assuring Sonthonax that Galbaud was "absolutely in line with the Revolution."[17] In reality, no one in Paris knew

---

[12] Monge to "Mon cher ami," November 26, 1792, in SHAT, 4 Yd. 3912 (Galbaud).

[13] Pache to Galbaud, November 27, 1792, in AN, D XXV 47, d. 446.

[14] On Rochambeau's activities in Martinique in 1793, see his account in the volume headed "Sur les Antilles" in Rochambeau papers, Newberry Library, Ms. Ruggles 410.

[15] Galbaud to Monge, February 20, 1793, in AN, CC 9A 8. Galbaud wrote that he had been informed on February 6, 1793 that he would be going to Saint-Domingue rather than Martinique.

[16] AN, D XXV 64, entry for February 11, 1793.

[17] Raimond, letter of March 21, 1793, in Raimond, *Lettres de J. Raimond, à ses frères les hommes de couleur,* 108; Raimond to Sonthonax, February 10, 1793, in AN, D XXV 16, d. 158.

Galbaud very well; he had spent hardly any time there since the outbreak of the Revolution.

For his own personal reasons, Galbaud was pleased with his assignment to Saint-Domingue. Just as he was learning about his appointment, his mother, the legal owner of the family's property there, had died. Although the revolutionaries had passed legislation requiring inheritances to be shared equally among heirs, they had maintained an old-regime provision that exempted colonial plantations from being parceled out, on the grounds that these properties were economic units that needed to be kept intact.[18] As the oldest child in the family, Galbaud consequently stood to take over the family holdings, which were still untouched by the insurrection; in December 1792, Galbaud's mother had written to one of her managers instructing him to tell the slaves that she was pleased with their loyalty.[19] A clause inserted into the law of April 4, 1792 in order to prevent Julien Raimond from being named as civil commissioner, barred owners of colonial property from being appointed to positions there. Galbaud dutifully notified Monge about this potential impediment, writing that "my frankness would not let me leave you ignorant of my situation," but the minister, overburdened with other concerns, never responded to him. The general therefore assumed that he was to go ahead with his assignment.[20]

From the outset, Galbaud's voyage to the Antilles was very much a family affair. In December 1792, when he still thought he was headed for Martinique, he had sought and obtained Monge's approval to have his younger brother César appointed as his adjutant and to take his wife and his three children with him.[21] His desire to have the company of family members was not unique – Polverel had brought his son François to Saint-Domingue as his secretary – but Galbaud's relatives would considerably complicate his life. César Galbaud, eight years younger than his brother and recommended by the republican navy minister Monge as "an excellent fellow," made no secret of the fact that the chance to be closer to the family's plantations was an opportunity to consolidate his financial situation. "My entire fortune depended on my stay in the island," he wrote.[22] Upon arrival in the colony, the Galbaud brothers

[18] Meadows, "Planters of Saint-Domingue," 56.
[19] Veuve Dufort to Berouet, December 28, 1792, in AN, D XXV 49, d. 476.
[20] Galbaud to Monge, February 25, 1793, in AN, CC 9A 8.
[21] Monge to Galbaud, December 29, 1792, in AN, D XXV 47, d. 446; Pache to Galbaud, November 27, 1792, in AN, D XXV 47, d. 446.
[22] Monge, letter of November 26, 1792, in SHAT, 4 Yd. 3912; César Galbaud, memorandum of January 1, 1795, in AN, D XXV 48, d. 463.

immediately contacted the managers of their mother's two plantations, one near Léogane in the West Province and the other at Abricots in the South. Both assured them that production was prospering, and one even suggested purchasing some new slaves.[23] Unlike Sonthonax and Polverel, who had agreed to uphold slavery even though they personally favored its abolition, the Galbauds clearly hoped for the institution's continuation. Except for promising to carry out his assignment to defeat the slave insurrection, General Galbaud was careful never to state his views on the subject, but his brother was more outspoken. In a long statement written more than a year after the Convention's decree abolishing slavery in the French colonies, he still defended its legitimacy. "It is not a question of deciding whether this form of property is in conformity or in contradiction with the law of nature, but simply whether the nation has recognized it as ... a true form of property," he wrote, adding that, as far as he was concerned, what really mattered was whether the slave system benefited France. "For myself, I confess that I prefer my fellow citizens to Negro slaves and all other men," he concluded.[24]

Galbaud's decision to bring his wife and young children with him showed how little he understood the situation of the colony. Like his brother, Galbaud's wife was an outspoken personality, highly articulate both verbally and in writing, and she did not hesitate to intervene in her husband's business. On public matters as well as family affairs, Madame Galbaud considered it her job to stiffen her husband's spine. Before they left France in March 1793, she had congratulated him for standing up to his siblings about the division of his mother's property, while reminding him that he had not supported her in a similar dispute about her own inheritance.[25] Her opinions were not counterrevolutionary – in August 1792, she had written a letter to her brother, a military officer who had emigrated, arguing in favor of the revolution[26] – but they were always forcefully expressed. On the ship bringing them from France, Madame Galbaud attracted attention when she overruled her husband and talked the ship's captain and crew out of pursuing a British vessel they had sighted. "'Citizen,' she told [the captain], 'you are responsible for an important mission: you have on your ship the general, his adjutant and his family ... Not only should these considerations stop you, but an

---

[23] Berouet to Galbauds, June 2, 1793, and Inginac to Galbauds, June 4, 1793, in AN, D XXV 49, d. 476.

[24] César Galbaud, letter of March 30, 1795, in AN, D XXV 48, d. 465.

[25] Mme Galbaud to Galbaud, March 6, 1793, in AN, D XXV 49, d. 476.

[26] [Mme Galbaud] to "Jémi," August 7, 1792, in AN, D XXV 49, d. 476.

even more important one obliges you to stick to your course. Have you thought of all the gold your frigate is carrying? If by bad luck we were taken, what a loss for the Republic!'"[27] Throughout the events leading up to and following the events of June 20, 1793, Madame Galbaud was always at her husband's elbow, offering her views and sometimes taking a direct role in affairs. Unfortunately, her judgment was no match for her outspokenness, and her interventions often served to exacerbate the crises facing the general.

The Galbaud party – in addition to his family, he was accompanied by a young aide-de-camp, André Conscience, who would become the faithful chronicler of the general's misadventures in the New World,[28] and by several other newly appointed officials, of whom the most important was Jean-Pierre Masse, the colony's new "ordonnateur" or chief financial officer – arrived in Cap Français harbor on 6 May 1793.[29] Galbaud found the city's demoralized white population more than ready to welcome him. For more than two months, Sonthonax's absence had left the city without real leadership; General Laveaux, the local military commander, had just abandoned his effort to drive the black insurgents out of the nearby hills, and the Interim Commission was under orders from the civil commissioners not to take any action in their absence. Boucher, the Interim Commission's president, would later claim that Galbaud had intimidated the group into recognizing his authority, but in reality they had been as eager as the rest of the free population to see him take charge of the situation. According to the *Moniteur général*, Boucher had publicly told Galbaud that, with his arrival, "the most beautiful day succeeds the darkest night." Boucher added that Galbaud's "presence among us, together with his respectable family that now becomes ours, ought to revive the courage of our fellow citizens, since his well known zeal and courage will be strengthened by his strong interest in reestablishing his properties, without which he would have nothing to leave his children except the glorious heritage of his republican virtues."[30]

At public ceremonies extending over several days, Galbaud was hailed by spokesmen for several other groups. The head of the local clergy

---

[27] Pouzols to Sonthonax, August 18, 1793, in AN, D XXV 14, d. 130bis.
[28] According to one of his letters, Conscience had served with Galbaud in the Ardennes campaign in 1792. He also claimed that he had helped arrest Louis XVI at Varennes in 1791. Conscience, letter of 17 prair. II, in AN, D XXV 81, d. 793.
[29] *Moniteur général*, May 7, 1793.
[30] *Moniteur général*, May 9, 1793 (Interim Commission, May 7); Boucher, "Galbaudiana," in BN, Ms. n.a.f. 6846.

expressed the certainty that "soon ... the Negroes in revolt will return
to their duties, the murderous steel will fall from their hands, which are
stained and still wet with the blood of their masters" and that "calm
and tranquility will be reestablished, all hearts united, all party spirit
completely annihilated."[31] The city's main newspaper editorialized that
"the citizen governor general inspires the unfortunate inhabitants of the
North Province with the greatest confidence, and we have every reason to believe that his reputation has planted the same sentiment in the
hearts of all the colonists."[32] The representatives of the city's free men of
color were less effusive in their endorsement of Galbaud. When the general and his brother took their oaths of office in front of the assembled
troops in the city, Cairou, the commander of the free colored soldiers,
saluted him on their behalf. Galbaud assured them that "my principles
are known, I am a republican, I count heavily on you and your love
for the country," but he did remark that "prejudices are the children of
centuries and of pride; their total destruction cannot be brought about
over night."[33] A few days later, a delegation from the Sixth Battalion of
the National Guard, the unit composed exclusively of free men of color,
called on the general and on Masse, the new *ordonnateur*. They were
cautious in addressing Galbaud, telling him that "the visit we have the
honor of paying you is that of a regenerated people who have suffered,
for many years, the weight of the most arbitrary despotism ... We will
continue to march, as we have up to now, under the protection of the
law, of which you are the representative." Speaking to Masse, however,
they were more forthright, complaining about "those with bad intentions, who, one cannot doubt, will not stop seeking ways of attacking
these rights."[34]

As he went through these rounds of public welcoming ceremonies,
Galbaud was also bombarded from all sides with private appeals and
advice. Some of those who wrote to him were simply seeking assistance,
such as Madame Laporte, the "poor mother of a family with five children" who had been "burned out and all the Negroes killed," and a
group of soldiers who claimed that their term of enlistment had expired
and that they had not been paid, but others had more political concerns. The numerous prisoners arrested by Sonthonax and Polverel in

---

[31] *Affiches américaines* (Cap Français), May 13, 1793 (ceremony of May 8).
[32] *Moniteur général*, May 11, 1793.
[33] *Moniteur général*, May 10, 1793.
[34] *Affiches américaines* (Cap Français), May 15, 1793.

Saint-Marc and Port-au-Prince who were being held on board ships in
the Cap Français harbor seized the opportunity to lobby Galbaud on
their own behalf and to denounce the commissioners. "Tyranny has
never been exercised with more skill and imposture," one of them wrote,
accusing Sonthonax and Polverel of "having used the pretext of conspiracies to foment discord and division among the two classes" of free citizens.[35] An anonymous letter writer warned Galbaud that "the reunion
of the free men [of color] with the whites is only simulated, they remain
assassins, thieves, arsonists, the civil commissioners are vampires who
feed off our blood," while another claimed that the general's children
were in danger.[36] Cambis, the naval commander, although careful not to
criticize Sonthonax and Polverel openly, advised Galbaud that "precautions and formalities are necessary to stay out of trouble with the Civil
Commissioners."[37] Two prominent white colonial agitators held on the
ships, the journalist Tanguy-Laboissière and his friend Thomas Millet,
waged an especially vigorous epistolary campaign to win the general
over. In a joint letter, the two told him, "Citizen! This is the moment: You
hold the fate of the national economy in your hand. Surround yourself
with true friends of the republic, and Saint-Domingue is saved."[38] Both
men continued to send him regular letters denouncing the commissioners, although Galbaud initially paid them no special attention.

As he sorted through his correspondence and prepared to live up to
his notion of what a colonial governor should be – the Galbaud household ran up a grocery bill of 8,766 livres in a month, a sum amounting
to more than 10 per cent of the general's annual salary, with two-
thirds of it going for wine alone, and the general ordered himself new
clothes[39] – Galbaud also worked on a proclamation setting out his "true
sentiments, and the principles that will guide my conduct." Addressing
himself first to "property-owning colonists," he assured them that
"I share your sufferings: My greatest concern will be to reduce them."
He called on them to abandon their prejudices against the "citizens of
color" and accept them as "brothers," and to abandon any thought of
a return to "the old order of things." Turning next to the "citizens of

---

[35] Letters from femme Laporte, May 9, 1793, from several soldiers, May 7, 1793, and
from Jolliot, May 8, 1793, in AN, D XXV 47, d. 450.
[36] Anonymous letters, May 14, 1793 and n.d., in AN, D XXV 48, d. 462.
[37] Cambis to Galbaud, May 10, 1793, in AN, D XXV 51, d. 489.
[38] Tanguy-Laboissière and Thomas Millet, letter to Galbaud, May 10, 1793, in AN,
D XXV 47, d. 450.
[39] AN, D XXV 49, d. 468.

color," Galbaud acknowledged that "an absurd prejudice had deprived you of the right of all free men to participate in the formation [of the law]." Now, however, the French legislature and the white population had "seen their error," and the duty of all citizens was to support the government. "I declare to you that I can only see an enemy in the man who, disdaining the protection of the law, acts on his own to demand justice," Galbaud warned; "I will use all the forces at my disposal to punish him." Galbaud then assured the city's merchants that "I know all the problems that you are experiencing" and promised to consult them about the best ways to revive commerce. He called on all public officials to support him and appealed to the troops to show "the same zeal you have always displayed on the continent." Aware that the soldiers had not been paid for several months, he promised to find money for them, but insisted on their duty of obedience. Galbaud ended his declaration by swearing to maintain, "with rigor, the distance that exists between the free man and the slave: It is this boundary that I will never allow anyone to violate."[40]

Galbaud's proclamation was fully in line with the policies the French government had adopted at the time of his appointment, and which had been explained to him at length in the written instructions provided to him by the ministers Etienne Clavière and Monge.[41] He carefully balanced promises to the white colonists and the "citizens of 4 April" with warnings against opposition to the law from either group, and emphasized the need for unity to defeat the slave insurrection. Unimpeachably republican in tone, Galbaud's proclamation nevertheless showed that he viewed the situation in Saint-Domingue very differently from the way Sonthonax and Polverel had come to see things after seven tumultuous months in the colony. While Galbaud, at least rhetorically, was still committed to the notion that whites and free people of color could be brought to cooperate to save the colony, the commissioners had concluded that only the latter group actually supported French policy. And while Galbaud relied on the effects of persuasion and reason, their experiences had driven the civil commissioners to adopt a peremptory tone, emphasizing their authority as representatives of the national will and insisting on the population's duty to obey their orders.

[40] Galbaud, *Proclamation*, (Cap Français: Imprimerie de la commission civile de la république, May 12, 1793) in AN, D XXV 19, d. 186.
[41] "Mémoire en forme d'instructions données par le Conseil exécutif provisioire au maréchal de camp Galbaud Gouverneur de la partie française de St. Domingue," in AN, D XXV 47, d. 448.

The most striking aspect of Galbaud's proclamation, however, was an omission. Even though his official instructions reminded him "that he is in all circumstances obliged by the law to fulfill the demands of the commissioners," he made no mention of them.[42] Boucher, the president of the Interim Commission and a distinctly hostile witness, claimed that he had urged Galbaud to acknowledge the commissioners' authority, but that the general had replied, "I know that there are civil commissioners here, but I don't know what their powers are or their authority over me ... If they are willing, I will get along with them, but in my position I know neither equals nor superiors." Galbaud also supposedly expressed doubt about the commissioners' republican orthodoxy, pointing out to Boucher that they had not done anything to rename the rue de Bourbon or other streets in Cap Français that still commemorated the monarchy.[43] Whether or not he actually expressed himself as openly as Boucher claimed, Galbaud certainly acted as though he had the power to take whatever measures he thought were necessary to deal with the situation confronting him in Cap Français. The commissioners' enemies took note of Galbaud's tone. From Port-au Prince, their secretary, Picquenard, left behind when Sonthonax and Polverel set off for Jacmel, wrote to his colleague Delpech, "Rumor spread that Galbaud came with higher powers, that the commissioners were in flight, that the time of oppression was over."[44]

Although his failure to acknowledge the commissioners in his proclamation sent a strong message, Galbaud's first communications with them were friendly. "It would have been very useful to have the benefit of your ideas and your patriotism at the outset," he wrote to them the day after he landed. "It was that hope that calmed me, when I thought about the difficulties of all sorts that were going to confront me." He urged them to return to Cap Français as quickly as possible. Four days later, he wrote again, saying that he hesitated to take any important decisions before consulting them, since "the crowd of people who surround me don't inspire me with enough confidence to allow me to choose a direction." He was, however, eager to seize the opportunity created by the warmth with which he had been welcomed. "Citizen commissioners, it

---

[42] "Mémoire en forme d'instructions données par le Conseil exécutif provisioire au maréchal de camp Galbaud Gouverneur de la partie française de St. Domingue," in AN, D XXV 47, d. 448.

[43] Boucher, "Galbaudiana," in BN, Ms. n.a.f. 6846.

[44] Picquenard to Delpech, May 26, 1793, in AN, D XXV 12, d. 115, cited in Bongie, *Adonis*, 247.

seems to me that one cannot act too quickly to annihilate the brigands who have caused all the sufferings of this unfortunate colony," he wrote. "At the moment, the public has an enthusiasm in my favor that every day of delay necessarily diminishes; let us profit from this situation if we can, so hurry back here ..."[45]

The commissioners' first letters to Galbaud also expressed confidence that they would be able to cooperate effectively. "It is with the greatest pleasure that we have learned of your arrival in this colony," they wrote from Port-au-Prince on May 12. "Your patriotism is known, you know our principles; it is impossible that we should not, together, bring about the triumph of the cause of the Republic." Nevertheless, they informed him that they intended to complete their campaign against the recalcitrant whites of Jacmel before returning to the north. When they did so, however, they promised that "we will join you in finishing the slave war, and in starting the war of the Republic against the tyrants." Without knowing anything specific about Galbaud's intentions, the commissioners were nevertheless clearly concerned that he might upset the delicate equilibrium Sonthonax had established before leaving Cap Français. "We urge you ... to hold off on any sort of decisive measure until we arrive," they wrote. "We have the highest regard for your intentions and your talents, but perils surround you, and it would be dangerous to let yourself be influenced by men who disguise themselves in the national colors but who are the most violent enemies of French principles." They told Galbaud to be guided by the advice of Laveaux and "not to name any officers until we arrive." A day later, they announced that they were sending Louis Dufay, one of their white loyalists, to meet with him: "We urge you to greet him as a good Jacobin and a true republican." Undoubtedly Sonthonax and Polverel counted on Dufay to report to them his impressions of Galbaud's real motives. [46]

The commissioners' biggest concern at this point was that Galbaud might torpedo their efforts to persuade the slaves to return to the plantations. On May 18, they sent the general a packet of copies of their proclamation of May 5, 1793 restating the principles of the Code noir, with orders to distribute them in Cap Français.[47] Four days later, Sonthonax and Polverel sent Galbaud a long letter, setting out in detail their strategy

---

[45] Galbaud, letters of May 8 and 12, 1793, in AN, D XXV 48, d. 460.
[46] Sonthonax and Polverel to Galbaud, May 12 and 13, 1793, in AN, D XXV 47, d. 449.
[47] Picquenard to Galbaud, May 18, 1793, in AN, D XXV 47, d. 449.

for dealing with the slave rebellion, a document that provides the clearest statement of their intentions prior to the crisis of June 20, 1793. "The eagerness you show to speed up the annihilation of the rebellious slaves does not surprise us," they wrote. "To defeat them, but not to exterminate them, is also our wish, and it should be that of all the friends of the colony. But is it so simple to achieve this goal?" Retracing the process by which they had come to believe that concessions to the slaves were necessary, they reminded the general that

when we arrived from Europe, our forces were more than twice what they are today. The plantation-owners would not listen to talk about peaceful methods; they only wanted to exterminate. The general cry forced us to agree, we made war on the slaves; what was the result? Many slaves have been killed, camps have been overrun, but this has merely forced them to move their outposts; the armies of the brigands still exist, and every day they can find new recruits at the expense of the colonists. Meanwhile the climate, fatigue and combat have reduced our armies to almost nothing, and, unlike the brigands, we have no way to add recruits. One, four, ten victories against the slaves, and we will neither have defeated them nor exterminated them, and we will have made ourselves unable to resist an attack from our external enemies.[48]

Rather than continuing futile assaults against the insurgent forces, Sonthonax and Polverel touted the strategy they had used in their campaign against Port-au-Prince. "We revealed a great truth in our proclamation of the 5th of this month," they told Galbaud, "when we said, 'One must strike the heads of some free men, if one wants to bring the slave insurrections to an end.' As soon as we defeated the white rebels of Port-au-Prince, we were able to get the rebel slaves of Cul-de-Sac to return to their work gangs and disarm them without violence. If one could use the same gentle methods to end the slave war in the North and the South, wouldn't you prefer that, Citizen, to any hostile measure?"[49] Less than a month before the crisis that would force them to open the door to emancipation, the commissioners were still convinced, firstly, that the slave uprising only persisted because of secret encouragement from white counterrevolutionaries, and secondly, that it could be ended with reforms that stopped well short of actual abolition. Galbaud was certainly not converted; even after the catastrophic failure of his assault on the commissioners on June 21, 1793, he would be overheard claiming that he had been on the point of "seiz[ing] the *mornes* in order to put a

---

[48] Sonthonax and Polverel to Galbaud, May 22, 1793, in AN, D XXV 47, d. 449.
[49] Ibid.

quick end to this war."⁵⁰ Nevertheless, by the time he received the com-missioners' letter, he had become too preoccupied with other matters to undertake military operations against the insurgents.

Instead of waiting patiently for Sonthonax and Polverel to return to Cap Français, Galbaud immediately set about trying to tackle all the problems in the city. Not since the first days of the slave insurrec-tion in August 1791 had the citizens seen such energetic local leader-ship. Whereas Sonthonax and Polverel, upon their arrival, had treated the local white population with suspicion, Galbaud proceeded on the assumption that they would cooperate with him if he took their views into account. As he sized up the problems of finding supplies for the army and the civilian population, obtaining money to pay the soldiers the wages they had not received for several months, preventing the political prisoners in the harbor from causing unrest in the city, and satisfying the demands of the ship captains blocked in the port by the commissioners' embargo, Galbaud began to envisage a comprehensive plan. He would bring all parties together to work out a solution to the supply crisis and an arrangement that would let at least part of the fleet depart. On May 18, he convened a special assembly with representatives of the various groups concerned. Galbaud began with a ringing appeal to the popula-tion's patriotism, after which the *ordonnateur* Masse laid out the extent of the economic crisis. The government warehouses, the source of sup-plies for the army and the numerous refugees in the city, were short of every kind of necessity: "flour, salt meat, wine, vegetables, butter, oil, candles, and other goods. Clothing, shoes, a list that is scary to read." The merchant ships were able to furnish much of what was needed, but they were holding out for payment in cash, which was unavailable. Meanwhile, merchants on shore were hoarding their stockpiles of sugar and coffee, also hoping to be able to sell them for cash. With Galbaud's backing, Masse proposed to requisition this produce and exchange it for needed supplies, compensating the colonial merchants with bills on the French treasury and the American ship captains with bills to be paid out of their own government's debt to France.⁵¹

This initial proposal broke down because of complaints from the American ship captains, who feared that their government would not release funds to honor the bills of exchange they were promised; the Cap

⁵⁰ "Récit historique du malheureux événement qui a réduit en cendres la ville du Cap français," cited in Popkin, *Facing Racial Revolution*, 197.
⁵¹ Procès-verbal of assembly, May 18, 1793, in AN, D XXV 48, d. 461.

Français merchants also refused to give up their goods voluntarily. The Americans offered instead to accept payment in coffee and sugar, arguing that requisitioning goods from the city merchants "may seem hard, but if it is necessary to make a sacrifice, who ought to make it? An American individual, who has no other interest in this colony, than his good wishes for his allies, or the Colonist, who, by this momentary sacrifice (we presume, he will be ultimately paid) avoids the greatest misfortunes."[52] At a second meeting, on May 24, 1793, Galbaud and Masse presented a revised version of their plan, offering the ship captains payment in goods; city residents would be compensated with bills to be redeemed by future tax collections, which Masse promised would be sufficient to reimburse them. The one demand Galbaud could not satisfy was a fixed date for the departure of the convoy; as he reminded the participants, only the commissioners could authorize its sailing, and in any event, the naval vessels destined to escort it were not yet prepared for the voyage.[53] There was still some grumbling about the sacrifices demanded from the residents of Cap Français, but the *Moniteur général* proclaimed the outcome a triumph for Galbaud: "In this meeting, which will always be remembered in the colony, and especially in the unhappy North Province, the citizen governor general showed that the choice the republic made of him to direct the government of Saint-Domingue was truly based on merit and ability. He spoke with this sentimental flow of words that charms, carries along and persuades even the coldest egoists. He used the occasion adroitly to remind the Americans of the crises they experienced when, like us, they tried to throw off the yoke of despotism in order to acquire the enjoyment of their rights and he made on them and the whole assembly an impression that was as useful as it was agreeable."[54]

Galbaud was equally pleased with himself. In a long review of the situation sent to Sonthonax and Polverel on May 26, 1793, he expressed his satisfaction with the way he had succeeded in uniting the various factions in the city. He noted in particular that he had had to overcome the tensions between the whites and the free men of color. The former still resented having to treat the latter as equals; the free men of color, for their part, wanted to "take too much advantage of the benefits of the law, and to persecute those who, once powerful enemies, are now [brought low] by misfortune." Having, as he thought, successfully resolved the

[52] Letter from 43 American ship captains, May 22, 1793, in AN, D XXV 47, d. 450.
[53] Minutes of assembly, May 24, 1793, in AN, D XXV 48, d. 461.
[54] *Moniteur général*, May 25, 1793.

problems in the city, he was now anxious to turn his attention to preparations for warding off the looming British and Spanish attacks. His
brother César had made an inspection tour of the province's military
outposts and found them in disastrous condition. Galbaud demanded
that the commissioners send troops from the South and West, and above
all that they help him come up with money to pay the soldiers' wages
and buy necessary supplies. "Once more, citizen commissioners," he
concluded, "come back here quickly. Every moment of delay does considerable damage to the Republic."[55] By the time they received this letter,
Sonthonax and Polverel were already on their way back from the South
Province. They replied to Galbaud from Port-au-Prince on May 31, reiterating their order that no ships from the convoy were to be allowed to
depart before their return to Cap Français; four days later, they wrote
from Saint-Marc, sending some money to cover urgent bills.[56]

Not everyone in Cap Français was pleased with the measures Galbaud
had ordered. Boucher, the president of the Interim Commission, wrote
to Sonthonax and Polverel to justify the decisions taken on May 24 to
"maintain peace and harmony in minds and stomachs," but without
mentioning Galbaud at all.[57] Some of the merchants objected that the
prices set for their goods were too low; they "persuaded themselves
that the despotism of the commissioners was preferable to the government of M. Galbaud," one colonist wrote, and they cheated as much as
they could in valuing their goods.[58] On June 4, 1793, Galbaud publicly
denounced "the fatal and stupid egoism" of city residents who were trying to conceal their merchandise, and authorized the seizure of all the
goods found in their warehouses.[59] In addition to alienating the merchants, the general irked the whole of the white population by reinstating the requirement that they take turns guarding the streets at night,
an emergency measure imposed in August 1791 that had long since been
allowed to lapse.[60] Tension in the city was further heightened on May 25,

---

[55] Galbaud to Sonthonax and Polverel, May 26, 1793, in AN, D XXV 47, d. 449.
[56] Sonthonax and Polverel to Galbaud, letters of May 31 and June 4, 1793, in AN,
    D XXV 47, d. 449.
[57] Boucher to Sonthonax and Polverel, May 26, 1793, in AN, D XXV 64, d. 648.
[58] Dalmas, *Révolution de Saint-Domingue*, 2: 156 ; "Conduitte et exposé vrai des faits à
    la connoissance du Citoyen Gd. Sautet, captaine de Port du Cap Isle St. Dominque qui
    ont eu lieu dans le trop malheureux evenement du Cap dans les journées du 20 au 24
    juin 1793," in AN, D XXV 81, d. 798.
[59] Copy in CAOM, F 3 198 (Moreau de Saint-Méry papers). See also Laplace, *Histoire
    des desastres de Saint-Domingue*, 284–5.
[60] Declaration of Garnier, 17 bru. III, in AN, D XXV 82, d. 799.

1793, when Cap Français was hit by an earthquake. "Almost all the houses, especially those with an upper story, were damaged," one journalist wrote. "The women, half dressed and out of their minds, thought it was the end of the world," a young colonist recalled. "The children and the slaves joined their cries to the barking of the dogs and the neighing of the horses. Three shocks, coming one after the other, redoubled the fear, the disorder and the tumult, and no one dared to go back into his house, for fear of being crushed under the ruins."[61]

More serious than the disaffection of some of the whites was the general's failure to win over the free population of color. As a group, they played little role in his negotiations to resolve the city's economic crisis. In his official proclamations, Galbaud had been careful to insist that he would enforce the egalitarian law of April 4, 1792, and he had appointed a free man of color as one of his adjutants and another as a secretary.[62] Boucher, president of the Interim Commission, maintained, however, that Galbaud had constantly expressed his distaste for those whom he referred to as "mulattoes." When Boucher cautioned him about his language, Galbaud supposedly replied, "I was pressured to have two mulattoes with me … I wasn't good enough to be thrown to the dogs if I didn't. The commissioners would hold it against me if I didn't have a good escort. It needed to be done, so I did it."[63]

As they made their way overland toward Cap Français, Sonthonax and Polverel were receiving increasingly alarming reports about the atmosphere in the city and about Galbaud. Castaing, who had emerged since November 1791 as the main spokesman for the free men of color, warned them that counterrevolutionaries were speaking openly about surrendering the city to the British, and that Galbaud was doing nothing to stop them. Was the general himself a patriot, Castaing asked? "He seems to be, he says he is, but I am not convinced."[64] More devastating were the letters the commissioners received from Dufay, their agent and the man whose speech on February 4, 1794 would convince the National

---

[61] *Affiches américaines* (Cap Français edition), May 27, 1793; *"Mon Odyssée,"* Historic New Orleans Collection, ms. 85–117-L, 1: 127.

[62] Deposition of Mme. Galbaud, in AN, D XXV 56; "André Conscience à la Convention nationale, sur les derniers évènemens de Saint-Domingue," in CAOM, F 3 193 (Moreau de Saint-Méry papers). Poissat or Poizat, Galbaud's free colored aide-de-camp, was an adversary of Julien Raimond, who had denounced him in one of his letters to Sonthonax (Raimond to Sonthonax, February 16, 1793, in AN, D XXV 16, d. 158).

[63] Boucher, "Galbaudiana," in BN, Ms. n.a.f. 6846.

[64] Castaing to commissioners, June 1, 1793, in AN, D XXV 16, d. 158.

Convention to decree the abolition of slavery. Dispatched to size up the situation in Le Cap, Dufay sent back a chilling assessment. "Revolt, internal and external war, the mutiny of the troops who are influenced in every direction, an empty treasury, a shortage of everything, the most atrocious acts of perfidy, the treason of the aristocrats ... assail us from every side, and are ready to destroy us if you do not promptly come to our rescue," he wrote on May 25, 1793. Bleak as the situation was, in this first letter, Dufay described Galbaud favorably, writing that "he seems to be a man of character, and worthy of being associated with your work."[65]

Within a week, however, Dufay had completely reversed his opinion about Galbaud. What changed his mind, he claimed, was overhearing a lengthy conversation between the general's brother César and another of the commissioners' white supporters, Vergniaud. According to Dufay, César Galbaud had complained about the commissioners' insistence that no actions should be taken in Cap François until they returned. He had expressed sympathy for the whites of Port-au-Prince and swore that he would not obey the commissioners' orders, even though he assumed his brother would. To be sure, Dufay wrote, General Galbaud was different from his brother. "He has all the appearance of a supporter of the laws, and even of a republican. Maybe he is one." Nevertheless, Dufay asked, why did the general tolerate his brother's reckless talk? And "why, instead of underlining and supporting with all his power and all his influence the authority of the commissioners, does he not say a word about them in his proclamations or his public discourses?" Although he could not cite anything overtly counterrevolutionary that Galbaud had done, Dufay ended by writing, "I say that as long as the military commanders in Saint-Domingue are either nobles or plantation-owners, which is all the same as far as their views are concerned, there can hardly be any hope for this unfortunate colony."[66]

Dufay's denunciations of the Galbauds undoubtedly reflected real differences of principles, although he also had a personal motive for wanting to discredit César Galbaud. General Galbaud had sent his brother on a mission to inspect the North Province's border defenses, which César had found to be in a "truly appalling" condition.[67] Dufay's official position was that of "inspector of the frontiers," so César Galbaud's report

[65] Dufay to commissioners, May 25, 1793, in AN, D XXV 16, d. 158.
[66] Dufay to commissioners, June 2, 1793, in AN, D XXV 16, d. 158.
[67] General Galbaud to commissioners, May 26, 1793, in AN, D XXV 47, d. 449.

was a direct reflection on him. Dufay's letters may have stemmed from a personal quarrel with the Galbauds, but they were also part of a coordinated campaign to turn the commissioners against them. Dufay's allegations were echoed, sometimes in almost identical language, in letters from the free colored leader Castaing and from Pierre Charles Robquin, a white army officer married to one of Castaing's sisters.[68] Later, after they had already dismissed Galbaud and ordered him to return to France, Sonthonax and Polverel took depositions from Dufay, Robquin, and Vergniaud, who all repeated the same accusations.[69] There is little doubt that César Galbaud was a rash and impulsive character, and it was probably not difficult to draw him into making careless statements. Accusations against Galbaud himself were much vaguer: that he had not disavowed his brother, that he had tolerated expressions of discontent among the white colonists, and that he had failed to acknowledge his subordination to the civil commissioners. In the paranoid atmosphere of the spring of 1793, however, such charges were enough to raise grave suspicions.

While the commissioners' white and free colored supporters were undermining Galbaud, Sonthonax's enemies in Le Cap were making a similar effort to sow distrust in the general's mind. The imprisoned journalist Tanguy-Laboissière summed up all the evidence he could find to convince Galbaud that Sonthonax and Polverel wanted to free the blacks. He claimed that the army deployed against Port-au-Prince had included armed slaves, that the commissioners had spared the lives of even the worst criminals among those captured during the January campaign in the north, and that they had illegally deprived slave owners of their property by enrolling slaves armed by the whites in the south in their own forces. "The pen refuses to set down all the destabilizing horrors of Saint-Domingue," he concluded. Together with his friend Thomas Millet, Tanguy drew Galbaud's attention to several articles published in the *Ami de l'égalité*, a Port-au-Prince newspaper edited by the

---

[68] On the Castaing-Robquin family, see Eric Noel, "Le sang noir des Castaing, ou l'insolite ascension d'une famille des isles (milieu XVIIIe – fin XIXe siècles)," *Bulletin du Centre d'histoire des espaces atlantiques* 7 (1995), 171–82. Castaing went to France with Dufay and Robquin in 1794; after the death of his first wife in 1797, he married into the family of Napoleon's wife Josephine's first husband, the Beauharnais.

[69] Castaing to commissioners, June 1, 1793, and Robquin to commissioners, June 2, 1793, in AN D XXV 16, d. 158; depositions of Robquin (June 15, 1793), Dufay (June 15, 1793), and Vergniaud (June 18, 1793), in AN, D XXV 5, d. 51. On Robquin's marriage to Laure Castaing, see his letter to his father, December 8, 1793, in AN, D XXV 80, d. 786.

commissioners' secretary, Jean-Baptiste Picquenard, which had pointed out Galbaud's close connection to the traitor Dumouriez.[70] "You can decide now, General, toward what conclusion the public spirit is being directed, and why someone has printed that you were the second-in-command of Dumouriez, on whose head there is said to be a price," Millet wrote.[71] As the commissioners neared Cap Français, both they and Galbaud must have been increasingly uneasy about the meeting that was about to take place.

Whatever Galbaud's true sentiments may have been, he decided to welcome Sonthonax and Polverel with appropriate ceremony. He ordered Admiral Pierre-César-Charles de Sercey to have the warships fire a salute,[72] and he accompanied the large crowd that went to greet the commissioners as they entered the city. Galbaud's faithful Boswell, the aide-de-camp André Conscience, recorded that the general found them surrounded by "a crowd of armed citizens of color, and dragoons from the 16th regiment. He descended from his horse, congratulated them on their return, and invited them to call on him at home. They said nothing, except that it was very hot, and that they could not accept his invitation, since they had promised to go with the citizens who had come out to meet them (Castaing and Vergniaud)."[73] The crowd escorted them back to the Government House, where they had decided to establish their residence. As on the occasions of the commissioners' arrival in September 1792 and Galbaud's landing a month earlier, a formal ceremony was held to demonstrate the unity of the population and of the government leaders, but Sonthonax and Polverel were barely willing to play the game. Polverel set the tone, announcing that he and his colleague meant to bring peace, equality, and happiness to the colony, and that "no consideration will stop us from carrying out this great work." The only groups in the population he addressed directly were "the friends of the law of 4 April, and the class of the people who were formerly oppressed;" the white colonists were passed over in silence, and there was no promise to defeat the rebellious slaves. "We will make Saint-Domingue happy, regardless of the price," he concluded, "even if we must sacrifice ourselves."[74] The

[70] *Ami de l'égalité*, May 19 and 23, 1793.
[71] Tanguy to Galbaud, May 26, 1793, and Thomas Millet to Galbaud, May 28, 1793, in AN, D XXV 47, d. 453.
[72] Galbaud to Sercey, June 10, 1793, in AN, D XXV 48, d. 461.
[73] André Conscience, ms. in AN, D XXV 14, d. 130.
[74] *Moniteur générale*, June 11, 1793.

ordonnateur Masse tried to give a less confrontational tone to the occasion, announcing that he saw in the crowd "the happy mixture of colors, all the different shades, it's the harmony of nature."[75] Galbaud's speech never appeared in the *Moniteur général*; by the time the paper could have set it in type, he was no longer the colony's governor.

As the commissioners went off to celebrate their return with their supporters – the same men who had been plying them with letters denouncing Galbaud – the general read the handwriting on the wall. "We won't have much time to get to know each other," he reportedly told his staff, "because from all appearances, I will be leaving in a few days to report to the Convention on the condition of the colony ... It seems that here a governor general is no more than a phantom, a passive agent of two men who rule by themselves and before whom everyone must bow." The scenario was familiar: it was exactly what had happened to Galbaud's predecessor, Desparbès. Boucher, president of the Interim Commission, claimed that Galbaud had already anticipated this outcome before Sonthonax and Polverel had returned. Unlike Desparbès, however, he expected the confrontation to end in his favor. Once he got back to Paris, he told Boucher, "the French know my name and my record; my word will be believed, and after having spent just the time necessary to unmask them and obtain troops, I will return to fight them."[76] Galbaud's calculation was not far from the mark: had he kept to his resolution, he would have reached France just when the Convention, egged on by the exiled Saint-Domingue colonists, ordered the recall and arrest of Sonthonax and Polverel.

On the morning of June 11, 1793, Galbaud went to meet the commissioners, leaving behind instructions for a banquet to which he had invited them, with "the table flanked by four tricolor hangings."[77] By the time he returned, without the commissioners, his breach with them was complete. According to André Conscience's detailed account, the commissioners began the meeting by asking about the political situation in Paris at the time of Galbaud's departure; as Conscience realized, they wanted to know "the political position of certain individuals whose credit or disfavor was the thermometer that guided them," namely Brissot and his allies and the white Saint-Domingue colonists whom Sonthonax had deported. They were dissatisfied with the general's reply that he paid no

[75] *Moniteur générale*, June 13, 1793.
[76] Boucher, "Galbaudiana," in BN, Ms. n.a.f. 6846.
[77] Boucher, "Galbaudiana," in BN, Ms. n.a.f. 6846.

attention to politics, and alarmed to learn that the Convention had dismissed the charges against the deportees.[78] The conversation then turned to the general's brother. Sonthonax and Polverel announced that reliable sources had told them that "he professes the most anticivic principles" and demanded that Galbaud persuade him to agree to resign his post and return to France.[79] In their subsequent report to the Convention, the commissioners alleged that César Galbaud had made "constant declamations against the Republic, the Convention and the virtuous ministers who make up the executive council," and that he had delivered "repeated panegyrics about Dumouriez and all the traitors who the perilous circumstances in which France finds itself are unmasking every day."[80] When Galbaud defended his brother's intentions, the conversation grew more heated. Conscience's account, hostile to the commissioners, claims that "they did not blush to repeat the infamous phrase that Dufay had uttered more than once in Galbaud's presence, that it was necessary to entirely destroy the white race in the colony."[81] According to another account of the meeting, the commissioners were irritated when Galbaud complained that the free men of color were provoking the whites.[82] One can hardly doubt that Sonthonax and Polverel insisted in one way or another that the free men of color were the only reliable patriots in Saint-Domingue.

When Galbaud continued to disagree with the commissioners, "they spoke of obedience to their orders." Galbaud told them that he "owed obedience to their specific requests, provided that they were not contrary to the laws. 'Here,' the commissioners responded, 'the civil commissioners are everything; they have full powers in every respect.'" Galbaud refused to concede the point: it would amount, he claimed, to allowing himself to be reduced to "the lieutenant of the civil commission." Finally, Sonthonax and Polverel raised the question of Galbaud's eligibility for his position, citing the provision of the law of April 4, 1792 that excluded colonial property owners from holding government positions.

---

[78] Anon., "Précis historique de l'événement du Cap des 20, 21, 22 & 23 juin 1793," in AN, D XXV 14, d. 130. On June 15, the commissioners ordered the journalist, Saint-Maurice, to turn over to them the information about the denunciation of them that the colonist, Verneuil, had made in Paris in March. AN, D XXV 40.

[79] Conscience, ms. in AN, D XXV 14, d. 130.

[80] Sonthonax and Polverel, report to National Convention, July 10, 1793, in AN, D XXV 5, d. 52.

[81] Conscience, ms. in AN, D XXV 14, d. 130.

[82] Anon., "Précis historique de l'événement du Cap des 20, 21, 22 & 23 juin 1793," in AN, D XXV 14, d. 130.

Galbaud told them that he had informed Monge about his situation, but, when pressed, he had to admit that Monge had never specifically authorized an exception to the law in his favor. At this point, the general had had enough. "Send me back to France," he told the commissioners, "let me serve my country on the frontiers. And why? Because I will not promise to blindly obey the will of men, especially when they put themselves above the laws."[83]

The conflict between Galbaud and the commissioners certainly had something to do with their differing views about race and slavery. In a set of notes for a response to the commissioners, written after he had gone aboard the ship meant to return him to France, Galbaud warned that "the sudden abolition of slavery would completely destroy the colony without any benefit to those affected," and he added that "it is true that I strongly criticized your negrophile system." But this was not the issue that led to his dismissal. As he noted, and as the commissioners well knew, the Convention had taken no position regarding slavery, and so "each of us can state his opinion without fear of violating the law."[84] He also did not share the commissioners' favorable view of the free people of color; his enemy, Boucher, alleged that Galbaud had said that one of his offenses in the eyes of Sonthonax and Polverel was that "he had never consented to make his wife receive all the concubines in the city as part of her society."[85] Nevertheless, he had adhered to the letter of the law of April 4, 1792, just as the commissioners, despite their abhorrence of slavery, had maintained the laws authorizing it. There is no evidence to suggest that Galbaud had any royalist inclinations. He had thrown in his lot with the Revolution and the Jacobins at a time when few veteran officers had been willing to do so. Insofar as he had any public reputation before the disaster of June 20, 1793, it was for his flamboyant defiance of the Duke of Brunswick. When he came ashore on June 20, 1793 to lead the attack on the commissioners, he would do so singing the "Marseillaise," the anthem of the republican military.

Although, as we have seen, Galbaud may have calculated that returning to France would allow him to take revenge on the commissioners, abandoning his appointment in Saint-Domingue cannot have been easy for him. Up to this moment, the French Revolution had brought

---

[83] Conscience, ms. in AN, D XXV 14, d. 130; the substance of Conscience's account is confirmed in the commissioners' report of July 10, 1793 to the Convention, in AN, D XXV 5, d. 52.

[84] Galbaud, "Observations," n.d., in AN, D XXV 48, d. 460.

[85] Boucher, "Galbaudiana," in BN, Ms. n.a.f. 6846.

him opportunities of which he could never have dreamed during his slow-moving career under the Old Regime. In a matter of months, he had risen from obscurity to become a republican hero, defeating the Prussians on the battlefield and standing up to the Duke of Brunswick at the conference table. Entrusted with the mission of saving France's most valuable colony, he had, in his own eyes at least, proven his abilities by resolving the crisis he had found on his arrival in Cap Français. He was no Desparbès, too old and feeble to oppose the two civilians now confronting him. His sense of his status as a military officer and as a representative of the Republic, together with an unwillingness to betray his brother, made it impossible for him to accept the subordinate status Sonthonax and Polverel intended to impose on him. In his notes, Galbaud strongly denounced the commissioners' claim that his authority as governor was limited to giving orders to the troops. "The place of the governor in the colony is that of the executive power," Galbaud maintained, "although of course under the authority of the executive power of the metropole. Now you know that in France the executive power has other functions to fill besides that of military command."[86]

Sonthonax and Polverel naturally saw things differently. Anticipating by some months the Convention's own recognition that the Republic required a revolutionary form of government with a single center of authority, they sternly informed Galbaud that "you revealed the limits of your patriotism when you formally declared that you would never be the *passive instrument* of our orders. We are not establishing a new doctrine, in demanding from you the obedience due to the delegates of the Republic. We are simply recalling you to the observance of the constitutional principles that imperatively establish the submission of the military to the civil authority."[87] Galbaud had not actually disobeyed any of their instructions, but the independent initiatives he had taken during their absence showed, in their view, that he had a dangerously broad notion of his powers. Although he had respected the law of April 4, 1792, Galbaud's unhappiness about the privileged position the commissioners had accorded to the free men of color was palpable, and he clearly opposed the conciliatory policy Sonthonax and Polverel had decided to adopt with regard to the slave population. Whether he intended to act as a party leader or not, Galbaud obviously represented a potential rallying point for white opposition to the commissioners. The

---

[86] Galbaud, "Observations," n.d., in AN, D XXV 48, d. 460.
[87] Sonthonax and Polverel to Galbaud, June 13, 1793, in AN, D XXV 47, d. 449.

authority over the colony that they had worked so hard to establish was too precarious for the commissioners to tolerate the risk of public disagreement with their policies on the part of an official who could claim to have been appointed directly by the metropolitan government. The removal of Galbaud would leave General Lasalle as the titular governor general of the colony: after his humiliation in Port-au-Prince, he was totally under the commissioners' thumb.[88] Command of the troops in the North Province would fall to Etienne Laveaux, on whom Sonthonax and Polverel knew they could count.

Galbaud returned from his confrontation with the commissioners in a state of high dudgeon. If he had any doubts about what to do, Madame Galbaud must have resolved them. Boucher, who had been waiting for the banquet to begin, heard her, "with tears in her eyes and rage in her soul," telling the general, "'Let us flee this land of blood, the air is contagious, breathing it will turn my children into monsters. Let these mulattoes rule under the command of their despots. Go, my son, a word from you to the National Convention will unmask them. You will be believed, and it will be a happy day for you when you return here to punish them and avenge the whites for the atrocities that those people have inflicted on them.'"[89] Galbaud was more diplomatic. As was his wont, he expressed himself in writing: on June 12, 1793, he composed two long letters in which he tried to oblige the commissioners to take the responsibility for ordering him to depart. He was willing to return to France, as was his brother, but, he explained, neither of them would voluntarily resign his post. "The law forbids me to do so, and certainly it would not be the one who is willing to sacrifice himself to uphold it who would permit himself to violate it," he wrote. Nevertheless, if the commissioners would issue formal orders, both Galbauds would obey them, and indeed, Galbaud claimed, that was all he wanted. "Send me back to my country, where I can join my comrades-in-arms in fighting the enemies of liberty ... I am no good for anything in a place where calumny venomously misrepresents even my thoughts," he told them.[90] The commissioners obliged him, and on June 13, 1793, both Galbauds were escorted on board the *Normande*, leaving Madame Galbaud to negotiate with Sonthonax and Polverel about arrangements for herself, her

[88] The commissioners notified Lasalle that he would replace Galbaud on June 12, 1793. Corre, *La Salle*, 216.
[89] Boucher, "Galbaudiana," in BN, ms. n.a.f. 6846.
[90] Galbaud to Sonthonax and Polverel, two letters of June 12, 1793, in AN, AA 54, d. 1509, and AA 55, d. 1511.

FIGURE 5.1. Model of the *Normande.*
After his dismissal by the civil commissioners Sonthonax and Polverel on June
13, 1793, General Galbaud joined other political prisoners, including his brother
César, on the corvette *La Normande.* The sailors from the ship were among the
instigators of the assault on Cap Français on June 20, 1793.
Source: Musée de la Marine, Paris.

children, their governess, and her two female companions, all of whom
were also to return to France.[91] (See Figure 5.1.)
    Having decided to dismiss Galbaud, the commissioners had to manu-
facture a case against him. On June 13, 1793, they issued a public proclamation denouncing him for his "formal declaration that he would not

[91] Galbaud to commissioners, June 13, 1793, in AN, D XXV 48, d. 462; Mme Galbaud
    to Sonthonax, June 13, 1793, in AN, D XXV 19, d. 186.

carry out our decrees" and his "perfidious maneuvers to create himself a party in the North," and explaining that his nomination violated the April 4 law's prohibition against the appointment of colonial landowners.[92] Two days later, they issued a second proclamation lambasting the "absurd and illegal measures" agreed to at the public meetings Galbaud had organized on May 18 and May 24, 1793 to deal with what Sonthonax and Polverel called "an imaginary evil." The colony, they claimed, was not short of supplies, and no one except them had the right to convene such assemblies.[93] Recognizing, however, that it would ruin Saint-Domingue's trade with the United States if the promises made to the American merchant ship captains were not honored, they ordered the Le Cap merchants who had been personally present at the meeting to pay the whole sum involved, accusing those merchants of having offered to pay the Americans with goods from their warehouses that actually belonged to others, and they provided an itemized list of how much each of the trading houses concerned owed.[94] This drastic measure must have enraged the merchants on the list, although it may have won the commissioners some support from traders who had been fortunate enough to avoid committing themselves to Galbaud's plan. In addition to denouncing Galbaud's economic measures, Sonthonax and Polverel undertook to gather evidence of his nefarious political intentions. They took depositions from the group of their supporters who had written them letters denouncing the Galbaud brothers during their absence from the city, and from other witnesses who claimed that the general had talked of organizing resistance to the commissioners after his brother's arrest.[95] Presumably, they intended to dispatch these documents, which they were still assembling when the crisis of June 20, 1793 exploded, to France to justify their deportation of the general.

The destitution of Galbaud signaled to the discontented whites in the city that they no longer had a potential protector. Meanwhile, Sonthonax and Polverel moved to reassure their supporters among the free population of color. Under Galbaud, they had been compelled to

[92] Printed proclamation in AN, D XXV 5, d. 51.
[93] Printed proclamation in AN, D XXV 5, d. 51.
[94] *Moniteur général*, June 17, 1793; declaration of Cordeil, July 8, 1793, in LC, Genet papers, reel 5.
[95] Depositions of Robquin, Dufay, Vergniaud and Armand, in AN, D XXV 5, d. 51; depositions of Suire and Mancomble, in AN, D XXV 48, d. 461.

watch their step, knowing that the general had no great love for their group. It is not surprising that they greeted his disgrace with enthusiasm. When the news of Galbaud's pending deportation spread on June 14, the general's aide-de-camp, Conscience, reported that the free men of color "filled the streets, insulting, mistreating, even injuring the whites who had the bad luck to encounter them. It was no use protesting to the commissioners, they greeted the complaints they received from all sides with mocking smiles." The commissioners, who had so firmly snubbed Galbaud's invitations to dine at his home before his dismissal, made a point of entertaining the leading members of the free colored community at their own residence, and they announced a theater performance of a well-known comedy, "The Servant Turned Mistress," whose theme of the reversal of social hierarchies seemed clearly to reflect their policy in Cap Français. [96]

Sonthonax and Polverel, who both had mistresses of mixed race – Sonthonax would later marry a free woman of color from Saint-Domingue[97] – particularly outraged the whites by admitting women whom the colonists regarded as no better than courtesans to their gatherings. "You cannot imagine these orgies, called patriotic fêtes, at which the women of color, proud of having become the idols of the day, were given the leading place. You have to have seen the air of false modesty and the vulgar self-confidence of all these young mulatresses, have heard their jargon, sometimes affected and sentimental, more often equivocal and erotic, have observed the clumsy efforts they made to cover vice with the mask of virtue and disguise under a façade of innocence the habitudes of debauchery," the white colonist Dalmas wrote.[98] While the women of color were being admitted to the commissioners' entertainments, the men of the group were trying to break up the relationships that many of them maintained with whites. Captain Tzechouart, commander of the frigate *La Surveillante*, reported that they harassed mixed-race women who lived with white men.[99]

As in the period between the journée of December 2, 1792 and Sonthonax's departure at the end of February, there was little the city's

---

[96] Conscience, ms. in AN, D XXV 14, d. 130; Dalmas, *Révolution de Saint-Domingue*, 2: 183.

[97] For the mistresses, see Mahé de Cormeré, in AN, D XXV 14, d. 127. On Sonthonax's marriage in 1796, see Stein, *Sonthonax*, 129.

[98] Dalmas, *Révolution de Saint-Domingue*, 2: 184.

[99] "Compte rendu par le citoyen Tzechouart, commandant la frégate la Surveillante," in AN, CC 9 A 8.

whites could do to resist the alliance between the commissioners and the free people of color. Sonthonax's deportations in December and January had removed the agitators who might have played the role that Borel had assumed in Port-au-Prince. Although the commissioners accused Galbaud of trying to organize support among the white population, he had done little to recruit a party of loyalists. "The merchants and the inhabitants of Le Cap, offended by both parties, restricted themselves to observing them in silence," a white colonist wrote.[100] Galbaud's repeated declarations of devotion to the Republic and his hesitation to confront the commissioners exasperated the royalist Mahé de Corméré, a municipal official who was part of a group that tried to dissuade the general from voluntarily leaving the colony. Galbaud said that he would only change his mind if the city council passed a resolution recognizing his authority, in effect leaving it up to the councilors to take the risk of making the first move against the commissioners. Corméré's group decided that there was no point in having any further contact with him.[101] The deportation of the Galbauds "was talked about for two days," the journalist Saint-Maurice recalled, "after which the indescribable inhabitants of Le Cap had almost forgotten these two men, who had put in only a passing appearance."[102] Judging from the steadily increasing number of advertisements of planned departures in the city's newspapers, most of the city's white civilians simply wanted to escape from the colony as rapidly as possible.

Once on board the *Normande*, one of the smaller vessels, Galbaud was subjected to an intensive lobbying campaign by the commissioners' white opponents. An anonymous note, probably addressed to the journalist Tanguy-Laboissière, reported that Galbaud had been given copies of Gros's memoir and other documents, and that he was "occupied with reading the work of the courageous Millet; he is very pleased with it."[103] The general, however, persisted in his plan of returning to France to denounce Sonthonax and Polverel to the Convention. From the *Eole*, on which he was being held, Millet himself wrote to Galbaud to discuss arrangements to meet him after they both arrived in France, indicating that even the most violent opponents of the commissioners had abandoned hopes of confronting them in the colony.[104] On shore, there

[100] Laplace, *Histoire des desastres de Saint-Domingue*, 287.
[101] Mahé de Corméré, in AN, D XXV 14, d. 127.
[102] "Récit historique," in Popkin, *Facing Racial Revolution*, 187.
[103] Anonymous note, n.d., in AN, D XXV 48, d. 461.
[104] Millet to Galbaud, June 15, 1793, in AN, D XXV 54, d. 523.

were no white forces left to counter the free colored militia units that constituted the basis of the commissioners' support in the city. Under Laveaux's watchful eye, the surviving soldiers from France did not intervene in the city's politics.

Only one group of whites was still willing to confront the commissioners and their supporters: the sailors from the ships in the harbor. Because of the embargo, no merchant ships had been allowed to leave Cap Français since March 24, 1793. On May 10, Admiral Sercey had brought a convoy of forty-five merchant vessels from the ports on the colony's west coast to Cap Français,[105] raising the number of ships in the harbor to more than a hundred. In addition to the restless sailors, some of the ships held the political prisoners from Port-au-Prince and Saint-Marc, whose hatred for the commissioners knew no bounds. On June 11, 1793, the *Jupiter*, Admiral Cambis's flagship, returned to Cap Français after a short sortie meant to intimidate potential British privateers. A month earlier, the *Jupiter*'s men had distinguished themselves by staging a near-mutiny to protest the assignment of free men of color as part of the military garrison on their ship. Cambis had succeeded in quashing their protest, but he knew that his sailors harbored a strong dislike for those they stigmatized as "faces of night." Tempers were further frayed when the free colored soldiers on the *Jupiter* defied Cambis's orders and joined their comrades ashore on June 14, 1793. The admiral assumed that they were going to complain to the commissioners about their treatment on the ship. Some of them were set upon by sailors in the city.[106] The commissioners were alarmed by these incidents; on the June 15, 1793, they directed Laveaux to have the streets patrolled by units "of citizens of all colors ... particularly around the place Clugny [the bustling "marché aux noirs"] and close to the seafront. Order these patrols to break up any groups that form, either in the streets and squares, or in the cabarets and other public establishments."[107]

Despite these precautions, things became worse on the following day, June 16, 1793, a Sunday, when large numbers of sailors went ashore. Admiral Cambis noted with alarm that there had been numerous fights between the seamen and members of the free colored population. "Aside from events due to wine," he wrote in the ship's log, "it seemed there

[105] Sercey, report of August 2, 1793, in Service historique de la marine (SHM), BB 4 24.
[106] Deposition of Pierre Robert and Pierre Bertole, June 14, 1793, in AN, D XXV 14, d. 130.
[107] Commissioners to Laveaux, June 15, 1793, in AN, D XXV 43, d. 414.

was a plan to insult and provoke the sailors."[108] The commissioners wrote Cambis a stern letter, complaining about the sailors' behavior.[109] The next day, Sonthonax and Polverel issued an order forbidding sailors and their officers from staying on shore after 7 P.M. in the evening. "This order excited strong protests from the sailors on the merchant ships and the warships," Cambis noted; the crew on one ship threatened to mutiny.[110] Dissatisfaction spread from the men to the naval officers. A delegation of officers made a joint complaint to the commissioners, who warned them that "your words smell of revolt," according to one account; they nevertheless modified their order somewhat, but the agitation among the crews and the clashes with free men of color in the city continued.[111] Matters came to a head on Wednesday, June 19. Sailors in the city complained of several incidents in which whites were menaced by men of color. In one of them, an armed man of color supposedly attacked a white, Dupond, who was standing in the doorway of his own house, cleaning a rifle; in another incident, a group of free men of color linked arms to block several naval officers walking in the street.[112] Again a delegation of naval officers went ashore to protest to the commissioners but got no satisfaction; their complaints were waved aside and, according to some reports, they themselves were insulted and menaced as they returned to the harbor. Later, an unarmed group of sailors waiting on the quay for longboats to take them back to their ships were jeered and harassed by men of color.[113] Two ensigns from the *Favorite*, who had been involved in some of the incidents on shore, attempted to rouse their comrades to make an immediate attack on the men of color. On board the *Normande*, the ship where Galbaud was housed, angry sailors and political prisoners were ready to go ashore; David Maistral, the ship's captain, struggled to control them and finally summoned Admiral Cambis to remind them of their duty.[114]

[108] Cambis, "Journal de bord," in AN, D XXV 54, entries for June 15 and 16, 1793.
[109] Commissioners to Cambis, June 16, 1793, in AN, D XXV 43, d. 414.
[110] Cambis, "Journal de bord," in AN, D XXV 54, entry for June 18, 1793.
[111] Anon., "Détail des événements qui se sont passés au Cap dans les journées des 20, 21, 22 et 23 juin 1793," in AN, D XXV 14, d. 130.
[112] Manuscript copy of letter from Norfolk, Va., July 13, 1793, published in *Feuille maritime du Havre*, September 10, 1793, in AN, D XXV 80, d. 785; testimony of Jean Baptiste Auguste Paris, in AN, D XXV 81, d. 796.
[113] Testimony of Delage, in AN, D XXV 80, d. 787; Conscience, ms. in AN, D XXV 14, d. 130; Cambis, ship's log of *Jupiter*, in AN, D XXV 54.
[114] Deposition of Joseph Avril, in AN, D XXV 80, d. 784; depositions of Obet and Le Breton in AN, D XXV 81, ds. 795 and 796.

After rebuking the sailors, Cambis went ashore to meet personally with Sonthonax and Polverel. He found them at a large fête with their free colored and white supporters. Both the commissioners and the free men of color had much to celebrate: Sonthonax and Polverel had fulfilled their mission to implement the law of April 4, 1792 and to eliminate all white "counter-revolutionaries," and the free men of color had now achieved a dominant political position throughout the colony. Armed free men of color who had accompanied the commissioners on their campaign in the west and the south had helped break the resistance of the whites there; they were clearly convinced that they were now entitled to a reward. "Their physical and moral force, even their courage, had been shown to be superior to that of their enemies," an author favorable to them wrote. "They consequently sought and obtained civil and military positions in the country where they lived, which they cultivated and which they have always defended on behalf of their ungrateful oppressors."[115] The party to which Sonthonax and Polverel had invited some eighty of their supporters on June 19, 1793 was no ordinary social occasion: it was the ultimate consecration of the equality between the races promised by the law of April 4, 1792.[116] A day earlier, the *Moniteur général* had published a lengthy list of individuals, mostly women, who had just been granted their freedom, together with the names of their sponsors, primarily free colored figures such as Castaing. There can be little doubt that most of these *affranchissements* were granted in order to make the women eligible to attend the commissioners' gala. With their rights now so fully recognized, the free men of color were in no mood to tolerate slights from the sailors.

When Cambis confronted Sonthonax at the party, the commissioner, surrounded by armed free men of color, told him that one man of color who had provoked some of the sailors had been arrested, but, according to Cambis, he then broke into a tirade "against all those who weren't children of the law of 4 April [1792], his sole support, all those who could be classified as property-owners ... He insisted on the backing of the commission, and that he could in an instant, thanks to his power (that was his expression) create four hundred thousand soldiers for the Republic, and joining to that the abolition of slavery, the aristocracy of the skin, and the independence of all the colonies of the European nations." Cambis contested Sonthonax's interpretation of his powers

---

[115] "Relation de ce que c'est passé au Cap François," in LC, Genet papers, reel 5.
[116] See the testimonies of two invitees, Duverger and Jean Nicolas Martin Isnard, in AN, D XXV 81, ds. 795 and 796.

and appealed to Polverel, who agreed with the admiral that "the Civil Commission is not the National Convention," but nevertheless insisted that its orders had to be obeyed. "How could one hope for a sure and prolonged calming according to these misleading principles?" Cambis asked. He nevertheless succeeded in getting the remaining sailors back on board their vessels before the 7 P.M. curfew. He visited several of the warships to remind the sailors of the law and only ended his efforts when he was convinced that there would be no further trouble that night.[117]

Unhappy with Cambis's refusal to confront the commissioners more forcefully, some of the sailors, naval officers and political prisoners turned to General Galbaud. Because he had been appointed by the metropolitan government, Galbaud was the only official in the colony whose authority was comparable to that of the civil commissioners. "He was strongly urged to reclaim his position, to deliver the colony from these two monsters who had ignored his authority in order to carry out their plan to destroy the colonial system," one chronicler reported.[118] Galbaud's brother César joined in the effort to persuade the general. "Any opportunity to avenge myself and resist oppression seemed legitimate to me," he later wrote. Nevertheless, Galbaud continued to hesitate. An anonymous denunciation, dated 19 June 1793, claimed that the general's aide-de-camp had been overheard telling another conspirator that Galbaud wanted assurances of support from the whites in the city and information about the attitudes of admirals Cambis and Sercey.[119] But by 7 P.M., Galbaud had apparently made up his mind. At that moment a longboat filled with crewmen from the Concorde approached the warship America to announce that "General Galbaud was going to put himself at their head, as well as at the head of the crews from all the other ships... to exterminate all the men of color who had supposedly insulted them."[120] A dispute between a republican general and the two republican commissioners, joined to the quarrel between the sailors, who had no stake in slavery, and the free men of color, who were at best ambivalent about its abolition, was about to determine the fate of slavery in the French colonies.

As Galbaud and the sailors were making their plans on the evening of June 19, 1793, the typesetters and printers of the Moniteur général were

[117] Cambis, ship's log of Jupiter, entry for June 19, 1793, in AN, D XXV 54, d. 521.
[118] "Précis historique de l'événement," in AN, D XXV 14, d. 130.
[119] César Galbaud, letter of 25 August 1793, in AN, D XXV 82, d. 804 ; anonymous letter, 19 June 1793, with postscript dated "Cap, 1 Aug. 1793," and signature "Christophe," in AN, D XXV 80, d. 784, also in AN, CC 9 A 8.
[120] "Journal du vaisseau l'America," in AN, D XXV 54, d. 523, entry for 19-20 June 1793.

preparing the next day's edition. As usual, the paper's last page contained legal announcements from residents planning to leave for France
on the convoy, one of them offering "four splendid Negro sailors" for
a bargain price. From the point of view of the paper, firmly under the
authority of Sonthonax and Polverel since the dismissal of Galbaud,
the main news of the day had been the dinner and concert held by the
commissioners. "The mixture of colors and different classes of citizens
made a happy combination, presided over by harmony and equality," the
paper reported. "May this little civic festival be a sample of the general
sentiment! The hymn of the Marseillais was sung several times, and the
voice of the women in the choirs did much to give to the singers this
sentimental tone, without which this hymn would not produce the effect
that the author sought and that the subject inspires." The *Moniteur* concluded its account of the festivities by mentioning a "private quarrel, in
the town, which produced a little fermentation while people were eating,
but the fraternal interventions of the leaders and the quick and prudent
measures that were taken, provided a remedy as quick as it was salutary,
and public tranquility wasn't affected."[121] This oblique reference to the
clashes between the sailors and the men of color was the last item of
local news that the paper would ever publish.

[121] *Moniteur général*, June 20, 1793.

6

The Powder Keg Explodes

By the evening of June 19, 1793, General Galbaud had finally made up his mind. Instead of crossing the Atlantic to persuade the National Convention to recall Sonthonax and Polverel, he would put himself at the head of the angry sailors, transforming what might have remained a racial brawl between them and the free men of color into an assault on the French republic's official representatives in the colony. He and the sailors would land in the city, overwhelm the commissioners' out-numbered defenders, arrest the two men, and send *them* back to France to defend their actions. With Sonthonax and Polverel out of the way, Galbaud would be the symbol of French authority in Saint-Domingue. Converted to the idea of taking up arms against the civil commissioners only at the last minute, Galbaud does not seem to have had given much thought to what he would do if he succeeded, beyond sending Sonthonax and Polverel back to France. Perhaps he thought that the removal of the commissioners would be enough to intimidate the free colored popula-tion into submission, and that his military skills would enable him to defeat the slave insurrection. How he would have dealt with the threat of British and Spanish invasions is completely unclear. On the morning of June 20, 1793, the only thing that mattered was to settle scores with the two men who had dismissed him so brusquely a week earlier.

Although Galbaud hoped for support from the city's white popu-lation, some of whom were unquestionably hostile to the Revolution, the clash that was about to occur was not the result of a counterrevo-lutionary conspiracy or of British intrigue, as the commissioners and their supporters in France would assert and as many historians have continued to assume. There were indeed counterrevolutionary plotters among the colonists: in February 1793, pro-monarchist representatives of Saint-Domingue's white landowners signed an agreement with the British government, under which the latter promised to occupy the territory and protect slave owners until France's revolutionary regime was overthrown. In September 1793, colonists in the island would turn the southern city of Jérémie and the naval base of Môle Saint-Nicolas over to the British, but in June 1793, the latter were not yet prepared to act, and there is no evidence of any foreign encouragement for Galbaud's movement.[1] Like the Federalist revolts that were occurring in several French provincial cities at precisely the same time – unbeknownst to anyone in the colony, of course – the battle for control of Cap Français on June 20, 1793 was a fight between rival groups of French republicans.[2]

The morning of June 20, 1793 dawned bright and sunny in Cap Français.[3] By 6 A.M., small boats began crisscrossing the harbor, as sailors from the *Normande* set out to enlist the support of those on the other ships. The conspirators' plan had been worked out hastily, but it proved effective. They made no attempt to win over the warships' commanding officers, who could be expected to hesitate before joining an attack on the French government's duly appointed representatives. Instead, they appealed directly to the rank-and-file sailors, who had less concern for legal niceties or the possible effects on their careers, and urged them to act "without even informing our superiors," as two cannoneers from the *Normande* later testified.[4] Toussaint Chesnu, who helped row Galbaud to some of the other ships, reported that the sailors did not need much urging. "We all went along : we all cried, 'Ashore ! Ashore !'"[5] The plotters' rallying cry, "Long live the Republic! Long live Galbaud!" reassured those who did not want to be caught up in a counterrevolutionary movement: it portrayed joining the general as a patriotic act. At 9 A.M. Galbaud himself, accompanied by his brother César and sailors from the *Normande*, descended into a longboat and headed for Admiral Cambis's flagship, the seventy-four-gun *Jupiter*. According to several witnesses, Madame Galbaud was among those cheering

[1] On the contacts between the colonists and the British, and the latter's policy toward Saint-Domingue in 1793, see David Patrick Geggus, *Slavery, War, and Revolution: The British Occupation of Saint-Domingue 1791–1798* (Oxford: Clarendon Press, 1982), 58–64.

[2] On the republican character of the Federalist uprisings, see Paul Hanson, *The Jacobin Republic under Fire* (University Park, PA: Penn State University Press, 2003).

[3] "Journal du vaisseau l'*America*," in AN, D XXV 54, d. 523, entry for June 20–21, 1793.

[4] Testimony of Pillois and Jean-Marie, cannoneers on the *Normande*, in AN, CC 9 A 8.

[5] Interrogation of Toussaint Chesnu, in AN, D XXV 81, d. 795.

him on.[6] As Galbaud's longboat neared the *Jupiter*, Cambis loudly forbade him to come on board, but his own crew overruled him and helped the general onto the deck. Surrounded by the sailors, "Galbaud called for silence, explained his reasons, his complaints, his rights, asserted that he was still the Governor General, spoke to the crew, who heard him favorably," according to the ships' officers. Galbaud's brother César gave a more inflammatory speech, accusing the commissioners of protecting the sailors' enemies, the men of color. Cambis, the only person in the fleet whose rank equaled Galbaud's, tried to argue with him but was shouted down by the sailors. Cambis and the ship's officers went below to their council chamber and decided that the circumstances left them no way to oppose Galbaud's takeover of the vessel except to draw up a signed statement disavowing any responsibility for the situation.[7] Soon afterward, armed sailors imprisoned Cambis in his cabin and posted guards at the door to prevent anyone from communicating with him. The *Jupiter* was now Galbaud's headquarters.

Having gained control of the fleet's flagship, the Galbaud party rowed themselves to most of the other warships, with the same results; their commanders were either imprisoned like Cambis or simply ignored by their crews.[8] On the frigate *Fine*, Captain Augustin Truguet fought a losing battle to keep his men from joining the movement. "It seemed to me that fear of the big warships and of being blamed by their comrades for not going along influenced them the most," he recalled.[9] The only naval vessel Galbaud bypassed was the *America*, whose participation in the commissioners' attack on Port-au-Prince seemed to indicate that its crew did not share the other sailors' hostility to Sonthonax and Polverel.[10] Once the rebellious crews had taken over the warships, Galbaud gave his orders. At his first signal, the larger naval vessels were to form a line of battle and position themselves broadside to the town, with their gunports open, ready to fire. The merchant ships and small warships were to move

---

[6] Interrogation of Etienne Le Tellier, first pilot of the *Normande*, in AN, D XXV 81, d. 798.

[7] Statement of the officers of the *Jupiter*, June 20, 1793, AN D XXV 48, d. 461; Dalmas, *Révolution de Saint-Domingue*, 190.

[8] Deposition of Groignard, AN DXXV 80, d. 784; deposition of Emeriau, D XXV 80, d. 784; "Détail des événements qui se sont passés au Cap dans les journées des 20, 21, 22 et 21 juin 1793," AN D XXV 14, d. 130; journal of Cambis, D XXV 51, d. 489.

[9] "Evenements du 20 juin, l'an 1er de la République, à bord de la frégate *La Fine*," in AN, D XXV 47, d. 446.

[10] "Journal du vaisseau l'*America*," in AN, D XXV 54, d. 523, entry for June 20–21, 1793.

to the back of the harbor, where they would not be in the way if Galbaud
called for a bombardment of the city. When he gave a second signal, by
hoisting a blue flag and firing another cannon shot from the *Jupiter*, the
sailors from all the ships were to get into their longboats and row toward
the harbor, so that they would all come ashore together. In addition to
the sailors, Galbaud called on the numerous political prisoners held on
some of the ships, particularly the several hundred white opponents of
Sonthonax and Polverel from Port-au-Prince, who had been confined on
the *Saint-Honoré*, to join the assault. His force also included some of
the soldiers carried on the ships to be deployed when naval operations
required fighting on shore; they were the only men he had with any real
training for this kind of operation.

   While the sailors prepared themselves for the attack on the town,
Galbaud composed an appeal to the population, which showed how
completely he had endorsed the white colonists' point of view. Sonthonax
and Polverel, he wrote, "have dared to put their criminal hands on the
Governor-General of this colony, named by the Provisional Executive
Council of the Republic ... they gave arms to your slaves, they wanted
either to massacre or to deport you ... they would not limit themselves
to the role of organs of the law, they blasphemously proclaimed, 'We are
the law.'" In consequence, Galbaud continued, "We declare Sonthonax
and Polverel *traitors to the country.*" He ordered all good citizens to
refuse to recognize their orders and to "pursue them and bring them to
us, so that they can be sent to the bar of the National Convention."[11] In
contrast to his earlier proclamations, Galbaud dropped any pretense of
making an appeal to the free people of color, whom he assumed would
stand by the commissioners. By promising to protect citizens' "properties," he committed himself to defending slavery and continuing the fight
against the black insurrection. He insisted, however, on his loyalty to the
Republic, and painted his action as an emergency measure against two
renegade officials, rather than a revolt against the regime. "He thought
it useful to his cause to emphasize his Jacobinism, and necessary for the
success of his plan to include a lot of insults to kings," a disgruntled
white colonist complained; "this was not the way to succeed." His supporters persuaded him to remove these overtly antiroyalist statements,
but his insistence on his republican principles discouraged many of the
whites in the city.[12]

---

[11]   Galbaud, draft proclamation, June 20, 1793, on board *Jupiter*, AN D XXV 80, d. 784.
[12]   Dalmas, *Révolution de Saint-Domingue*, 189.

While Galbaud was writing his manifesto and the ships were taking up their positions in the harbor, unease gripped the town. "All was bustle and agitation. The balconies were filled with persons armed with spyglasses, looking attentively at the ships of war, and asking each other in loud tones what all this meant," the American Samuel Perkins wrote.[13] Merchants closed their stores and ran home, to find their families and grab their weapons. "Between ten and twelve o'clock," Lefebvre, a worker in one of the town's printing shops, testified, "I saw a big movement in the town. All the shops closed; I asked what was the reason for this alarm? They told me that the sailors were going to land, and that it was going to be quite a show, that they wanted to kill all the mulattoes and send the commissioners to the National Convention." Lefebvre went down to the harbor, where he saw for himself that the warships were poised to open fire. A few hours later, he went back and observed the sailors lowering themselves into the small boats that would carry them ashore.[14] Everyone knew how much damage a naval bombardment could do to a city. Just two months earlier, Sonthonax and Polverel had demonstrated the point when they used the guns of the *America* against the recalcitrant white population of Port-au-Prince. But now the navy's cannon were being aimed at the commissioners themselves.

Across the town, in the Government House on the west side of the city, the two republican commissioners quickly realized that trouble was brewing. To some extent, they had expected it: two days earlier, rumors of a plot had led them to order the captain of the *Normande* to prevent anyone from communicating with Galbaud or his family.[15] The notion that any opposition to their policies had to be inspired by former "aristocrats" like Galbaud fit with the Jacobin convictions Sonthonax and Polverel had brought to Saint-Domingue with them, but it misled them as to the nature of the danger they faced; they certainly underestimated the danger posed by the sailors' anger at the free men of color. At 8:30 a.m., before Galbaud took over the *Jupiter*, Admiral Cambis, alerted by a message from sailors on the *America*, sent them a warning. No friend of Sonthonax and Polverel, the cautious Cambis nevertheless refused to join Galbaud's risky enterprise; he settled for telling the commissioners that they were responsible for their own problems because of their partiality toward the free people of color.[16] His tone only served to convince

---

[13] Samuel Perkins, "Narrative," 337.
[14] Declaration of Lefebvre, Brest, 26 mess. II, AN D XXV 14, d. 130.
[15] Commissioners to captain of *Normande*, June 18, 1793, in AN, D XXV 5, d. 51.
[16] Cambis to Sonthonax and Polverel, 8 am, June 20, 1793, AN D XXV 47, d 449.

the two men that the admiral was also part of the plot against them. Nevertheless, the threat of attack was obvious. By mid-morning, an officer stationed at the harbor reported, "the maneuvers of the Republic's warships have me more and more convinced that if they have not yet positioned themselves broadside, they intend to do so before the offshore wind gives way to the one from the land. The *Jupiter* just fired a signal shot and raised a signal flag."[17]

Even as the sailors were preparing to come ashore, Sonthonax and Polverel still refused to accept that so many supposedly patriotic Frenchmen were ready to turn against the official representatives of their own government. "They had seen all the movements taking place in the harbor, but they weren't yet ready to believe that the sailors would follow Galbaud's orders so blindly," Polverel's son recalled.[18] Sonthonax's experience on December 2, 1792 should have made him more aware of the dangers of a white response to provocative gestures in favor of the men of color; instead, that experience seems to have made him overconfident. In December, the sailors had stayed out of the fighting, and the free men of color had succeeded in facing down their white opponents. On that occasion, an experienced free colored leader, Pierre Pinchinat, had been on hand to moderate the pretentions of his group; on June 20, 1793, he and the most capable free colored military commander, André Rigaud, were at the other end of the colony, leading the campaign against the white stronghold of Jérémie. A number of free colored leaders, including Jean-Louis Villatte, Jean-Baptiste Belley, Antoine Chanlatte, and Henri Christophe,[19] fought valiantly on behalf of the commissioners in the June crisis, but none of them had the political skills of Pinchinat.

As they had so many times in the past nine months, the two commissioners first resorted to the printing press. The shop of the printer Batilliot, publisher of the city's daily newspaper, was on the Place d'Armes, a few blocks from their headquarters, the Government House; they had him rush out a printed proclamation addressed to the "citizen sailors, artillerymen and soldiers on the warships of the Republic." "Generals Galbaud, Cambis and Sercey have misled you ... Turn them over to the

[17] Sautet to Sonthonax and Polverel, June 20, 1793, AN D XXV 48, d. 462.
[18] François Polverel, *Coup d'oeil impartial sur Saint-Domingue, ou Notions sur les événements qui ont eu lieu dans cette isle, depuis le commencement de la Révolution, jusqu'à la proclamation de la liberté générale* (Paris: Marchands de nouveautés, An III (1795)), 49.
[19] Christophe and Villatte are specifically mentioned in orders issued by the commissioners on June 20 and 23, 1793, in AN, D XXV 7, file for 6–26 June 1793.

representatives of France, to the delegates of the National Convention, and you will be pardoned," they announced.[20] But Sonthonax and Polverel knew that words alone were not going to be enough to protect them. They summoned the military commander, Etienne Laveaux, and whatever reliable troops they could find.[21] There were not many of them. The commissioners could count on a few hundred members of the armed *compagnies franches*, the militia companies made up of free men of color, and on a few units of the regular army that had shown their loyalty on earlier occasions. The scarcity of references to army units in the accounts of the day's fighting suggests that Sonthonax and Polverel did not trust most of the soldiers to be willing to fire on fellow white Frenchmen. In theory, the commissioners could also call on the whites enrolled in the citizen militia, the National Guard, but their sentiments were more than doubtful. The only other men of military age in the city were black: the thousands of slaves who lived in the city, and the approximately 700 captive black insurgents in the city's prisons. To appeal to them would mean overturning the colony's racial hierarchy and abandoning the struggle to maintain the slavery system. As they waited for Galbaud and the sailors to land, the commissioners were not yet ready to take such a monumental step.

While Galbaud, on the *Jupiter*, and the commissioners, in the Government House, prepared themselves for the coming battle, the rest of the town's population waited fearfully to see what would happen. "As we were well convinced that serious consequences would ensue, and perhaps the town be battered down," the American merchant Samuel Perkins recalled, "we sent off our books and valuable papers, together with such specie as we had on hand, on board a brig which was consigned to the house ..."[22] Other whites took refuge in their houses, hoping to be able to protect their families and their valuables. Many of the free colored men in the town took up arms to defend the commissioners, but the rest of their group had as much reason to worry as the whites; they knew that they were the main targets of the sailors' anger.

What the thousands of black slaves in the city thought as they realized that the two rival groups of free people were about to come to blows is impossible to know. The African ancestry they shared with the free people of color was not enough to guarantee the slaves' sympathy for

[20] Proclamation, June 20, 1793, in AN D XXV 5, d. 51.
[21] AN, D XXV 42, d. 409.
[22] Perkins, "Narrative," 337.

them: Many free colored families owned slaves themselves, and free colored militia units had done much of the fighting against the slave insurrection. Up until June 20, 1793, political leaders of the free colored group had concentrated on winning privileges for themselves and made no effort to bring about the abolition of slavery. As we have seen, the city's slave population had taken no part in the confrontations between the men of color and the whites in August and December 1792, and there had been no real indication that they were ready to revolt on their own behalf. Some had even been pressed into service during the military campaign against the insurgents in January 1793. Whether or not they sympathized with the slave insurrection, the slaves in Cap Français led very different lives from those of the slaves on the island's plantations. Many lived in their master's houses. Close contacts between masters and slaves hardly guaranteed close emotional bonds, but their behavior during the crisis shows that some blacks had indeed come to feel a certain concern, if not for their owners, at least for their owners' wives and children. Other urban slaves had their own living quarters and even some property of their own, which they risked losing if the city was destroyed. Some blacks may have welcomed the prospect of seeing Cap Français plunged into disorder if it meant the end of white rule, but there were undoubtedly others who worried about their own safety and that of the people – black, white, and mixed-race – with whom their lives were bound up.

At 3 P.M., the moment the whole city's population had braced themselves for arrived. As the boom of the *Jupiter*'s signal gun echoed across the harbor and the blue flag was hoisted up the ship's mast, boats from all points of the harbor made for the shore, converging on the quays at the north end of the harbor. By 4 P.M., at least 600 men – some estimates were as high as 2,000 – had landed. It immediately became clear that General Galbaud had made no plan of what to do once he got ashore. His supporters expected him to read his proclamation, to give their actions some kind of public justification, but he did not do so;[23] perhaps he feared that a pledge of loyalty to the Republic would offend white colonists with royalist sympathies. His failure to appeal explicitly to the city's population was significant: several city residents subsequently testified that, in the absence of an official call to arms, they felt justified in remaining in their own homes.[24] Since he encountered no opposition,

[23] Deposition of Poulain, AN D XXV 80, d. 784.
[24] Depositions of Mathieu Amat and Louis Joseph Presou, in AN, D XXV 81, d. 796.

Galbaud might have sent the boats back and had them bring a second wave of men, doubling the size of his force, but instead he let the undisciplined sailors start up the streets leading to the Government House immediately, with just a few soldiers accompanying them. "A spontaneous movement inspired by the general anger made it impossible to establish any order; everyone went off pell-mell and with no leadership," the general's aide-de-camp, André Conscience, recalled.[25]

Galbaud's forces were only lightly armed; above all, they had brought only a couple of small pieces of artillery with them. Galbaud's brother César went to try to talk his way into the arsenal, a walled enclosure just a block inland from the harbor, where he hoped to obtain some larger guns. When the officer on duty and the armed men of color there blocked his way, the younger Galbaud turned around and attached himself to one group of sailors heading up the streets toward the Government House; General Galbaud himself followed another group along a parallel street. "The general marched gaily, singing the hymn of the Marseillais, and his sense of himself was deliciously fed by the compliments that the enemies of the commissioners paid him as he passed," the newspaper editor, Saint-Maurice, recalled.[26] As a journalist, Saint-Maurice must have realized that he was covering the story of his life. The account he produced, as he followed Galbaud for the first day and a half of the crisis and then, with his unfailing ability to land on the winning side, managed to join the commissioners' camp when he realized that Galbaud's enterprise was doomed, is one of the most vivid descriptions of these events. It was fated, however, to remain unpublished, preserved only in the form of manuscript copies attached to two surviving collections of his *Moniteur général*.[27] (See Figure 6.1.)

The first few blocks inland from the harbor were familiar to the sailors: this was the "lower town," the district of the merchants' warehouses and of the *marché aux blancs*, the "whites' market," where

---

[25] André Conscience, "Rapport des derniers événements du Cap, fait à l'ambassadeur de France auprès des provinces unies d'Amérique, par le citoyen Conscience, officieur au 8e Regt d'inf.ie et aide-de-camp du Général Galbaud," Library of Congress, Genet papers, reel 7.

[26] " Historic narrative of the unhappy event that reduced to ashes the city of Cap français, capital of the North Province, colony of St. Domingue," in Popkin, *Facing Racial Revolution*, 188. Galbaud's singing of the Marseillaise was also recalled by Poulain, a crewman from the *Mouche*. AN, D XXV 80, d. 784.

[27] Slightly varying versions of the report are bound following the final printed number of the paper in the collections of the Bibliothèque nationale de France (call number Lc12.28) and the University of Wisconsin library.

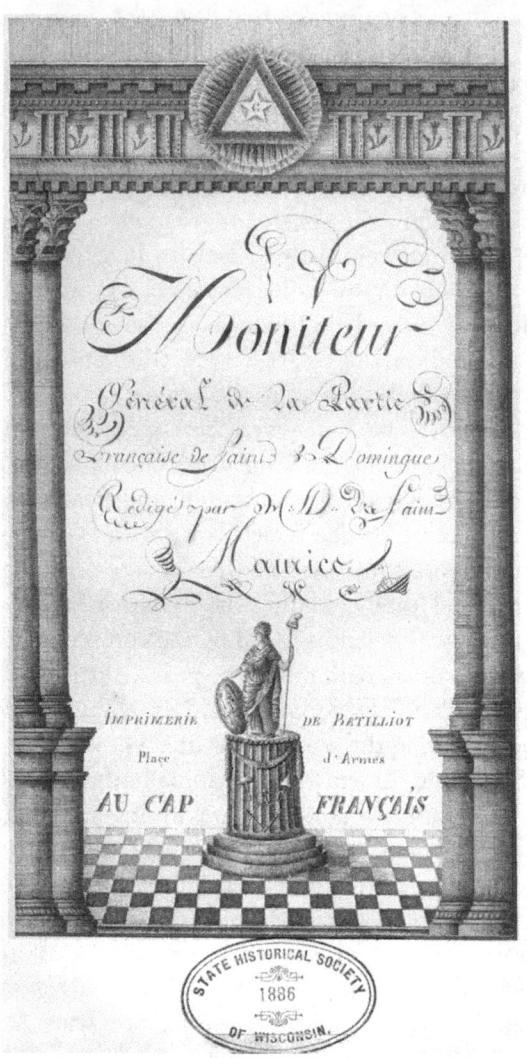

FIGURE 6.1. Title Page of the *Moniteur Général*.

An elaborate cover page prepared for a collection of one of the copies of the journalist H. D. de Saint-Maurice's *Moniteur général de la partie française de Saint-Domingue* and his manuscript account of the events of June 20, 1793 in Cap Français. Saint-Maurice lamented the destruction of the city, but he clearly recognized General Galbaud's incompetence and the courage of the free men of color and the freed slaves who fought on the side of the civil commissioners Sonthonax and Polverel. The symbols at the top of the page suggest that Saint-Maurice was, like many of the whites in Saint-Domingue, a Freemason; the figure at the bottom of the page holds symbols of the French Revolution, including a pike topped by a liberty cap.

Source: By courtesy of the Department of Special Collections, Memorial Library, University of Wisconsin-Madison.

the seamen came to buy and sell on their own account while their ships were in port. As they neared the Place Montarcher, a small open square in the center of the city, however, gunshots began coming from the windows on the upper stories of the buildings. "Shots came from the middle of the street, from the windows, from the attics, there never was a crueler civil war, and one that presented so much horror," a witness recalled.[28] Some of the snipers were on Galbaud's side: the printer Lefebvre, trying to get back to his own house, saw shots being fired at an unarmed man of color.[29] But the sailors in the streets could not tell where the gunfire was coming from or who it was aimed at, and some of them were hit.[30] They had assumed that the white population would rally to their side, and they were totally unprepared for this kind of urban warfare against invisible opponents. Their momentum carried them forward, but they were already becoming confused and uncertain. Galbaud was too far back in the column to exercise any control over them.

As the sailors headed inland, some of the city's white citizens prepared to join them. One was the young author of a remarkable memoir, *My Odyssey*, that is perhaps the liveliest eyewitness account of the Saint-Domingue uprising. "Still weak from an illness which was hardly terminated, I was, besides, on that day, overburdened from the effects of a very strong medicine," he wrote. "However, I got up and took my weapons. My family tried in vain to dissuade me; deaf to their prayers, insensible to their tears, I tore myself from the arms of those who were most dear to me in this world and I went to join the brave volunteers, already fighting in the Montarcher Square."[31] Galbaud had counted on stronger support in the city, however; he would later complain bitterly that only 150 volunteers had joined the fighting.[32] Most of the city's residents, fearful for their own safety, closed their doors and waited anxiously to see how events were going to turn out. A few tried to think of some way to ward off the disaster they saw approaching. Mahé de Corméré, a white city official hostile to the commissioners but distrustful of Galbaud's intentions, urged the rest of the municipal officers to march down to the waterfront in a body and "reconcile the spirits," but

---

[28] Deposition of Sautet, in AN, D XXV 81, d. 798.
[29] Declaration of Lefebvre, D XXV 14, d. 130.
[30] Conscience, "Rapport," Genet papers, reel 7.
[31] *My Odyssey*, in Popkin, *Facing Racial Revolution*, 209.
[32] Deposition of Artau, 3 Sept. 1793, in AN, D XXV 5, d. 53.

"they preferred to stay in their building, to wait for events, and to do what the victors dictated."[33]

On the other side of the Place Montarcher, the commissioners and their supporters prepared to defend themselves. Armed free men of color – initially a mere fifty men, according to Sonthonax and Polverel's subsequent account[34] – took up positions behind the iron grilles surrounding the formal garden in front of the large and imposing Government House. Unlike the sailors, these free colored militiamen were experienced fighters, veterans of the struggle against the slave insurrection and the campaign the commissioners had waged against their white opponents in the West and South Provinces. The commissioners had won the loyalty of the men of color by their uncompromising enforcement of the decree of April 4, 1792, which gave equal rights to all free people in the colonies. The men of color also knew that the sailors' anger was directed primarily against them, because of the many incidents between members of the two groups in the days leading up to June 20, 1793. As the newspaper editor Saint-Maurice wrote, "There was nothing to consider for them: they had no other choice than victory or death."[35]

While the men of color prepared to defend the Government House, Sonthonax and Polverel ordered fifty loyal white soldiers under Captain Boerner of the 92nd regiment, one of the units sent from France, to the Place d'Armes, an open square about halfway between the waterfront and the Government House. Before they could reach their position, they came under fire from the windows of the surrounding houses. Boerner's colleague, Captain Coeur, was killed, and Boerner himself, badly wounded, had to crawl into an open doorway and hide himself.[36] Sonthonax and Polverel had also ordered a unit of white militiamen to take up a blocking position at the corner of the Rue Notre Dame and the Rue Espagnole, across from the Government House. Fearing that these

---

[33] Mahé de Corméré, "Précis des faits relatifs à la malheureuse colonie de Ste. Domingue," AN D XXV 14, d. 127. This is an excerpt of a longer document about the troubles in Saint-Domingue, found in AN F 3 193; part of Mahé de Corméré's account (but not the section dealing with June 20, 1793) was also published as Guillaume François Mahy de Corméré, *Histoire de la révolution de la partie française de St. Domingue. Développement exact des causes et principes de cette révolution. Manoeuvres, intrigues employés pour son exécution* (Baltimore, MD: Samuel and John Adams, 1794).
[34] Sonthonax and Polverel, report to National Convention, July 10, 1793, in AN, D XXV 5, d. 52.
[35] "Historic narrative," in Popkin, *Facing Racial Revolution*, 188.
[36] Deposition of Boerner, September 9, 1793, AN D XXV 5, d. 53.

PLACE ET FONTAINE MONTARCHER,
DEVANT LE GOUVERNEMENT,
au Cap-Francois, Isle S.ᵗ Domingue.

FIGURE 6.2. The Place Montarcher and the Government House.

In their first attack on June 20, 1793, the sailors and white volunteers from the city nearly overran the Government House and captured the civil commissioners Sonthonax and Polverel. Armed free men of color commanded by the future National Convention deputy J.-B. Belley fought back from behind the iron grilles in front of the building, seen in this period engraving, and forced the attackers to retreat to the arsenal near the waterfront.

Source: The Library Company of Philadelphia.

troops might prove unreliable, the commissioners then told their commander, Milhet, to bring them inside the Government House enclosure. When the white soldiers refused to change their position, Sonthonax and Polverel realized that they were planning to make common cause with the insurgents.[37] "Charrier, the officer in charge of the position, arrives, asking which side the volunteers are on? 'Against the commissioners, long live Galbaud!' Immediately the volunteers charge toward the Government House, go along the grilles and fire at the men of color," one of them recorded.[38] (See Figure 6.2.)

[37] Anonymous account A, Moreau de Saint-Méry papers, CAOM F 3 198.
[38] Anonymous account B, Moreau de Saint-Méry papers, CAOM F 3 198.

The white volunteers' impetuous attack nearly determined the outcome of the entire battle. Led by their commander, the young chevalier
de Beaumont, they drove the men of color back, occupied one of the
pavilions in the garden,[39] and reached the main door of the Government
House. Beaumont himself "was about to cross the threshold, when a
ball, fired from inside, shattered his knee, and forced him to stop when
he was about to achieve a decisive victory by seizing the commissioners," his friend Antoine Dalmas wrote.[40] "He fell at the moment when
new troops came out of the arsenal and attacked us from the rear. In the
momentary disorder, occasioned by this unexpected attack, the absence
of the Chevalier de B. was not observed, and he remained at the mercy
of the Mulattoes, who let him perish without help or consolation,"
according to the author of *My Odyssey*. The troops who had attacked
the volunteers from the rear were the leaderless sailors coming from the
harbor. "They greeted us with a volley of balls and oaths, and it was
only after having charged them and broken their line that we made them
understand that we were fighting on the same side. These sailors were
the cause of almost all of our defeats, because of their excesses and their
lack of discipline."[41] In the confusion, the commissioners' defenders, led
by Jean-Baptiste "Mars" Belley, a free black officer who would later
become the first black man to sit as a deputy in the French national legislature, counterattacked and drove the whites out of the park in front of
the Government House.[42]

The failure of the volunteers' assault had momentous consequences.
If Beaumont and his men had broken into the Government House and
captured or killed Sonthonax and Polverel, there would have been no
one to issue an emancipation proclamation in Saint-Domingue, and
the chain of historical events that the commissioners were about to set
in motion would never have taken place. The two republican officials
were not yet out of danger, however. The sailors and the white volunteers backed away from the Government House to sort themselves out.
Galbaud finally reached the scene, and a decision was taken to launch a
more organized attack, aimed at capturing the *casernes*, the large barracks behind the Government House, where the commissioners and their

---

[39] Declaration of Garnier, in AN, D XXV 82, d. 799.
[40] Dalmas, *Révolution de Saint-Domingue*, 195.
[41] *My Odyssey*, in Popkin, *Facing Racial Revolution*, 210–11.
[42] *Relation détaillée des événemens malheureux qui se sont passés au Cap depuis
l'arrivée du ci-devant général Galbaud, jusqu'au moment où il a fait brûler cette ville
et a pris la fuite* (Paris: Imprimerie nationale, An II [1794]), 41.

defenders had taken refuge. Galbaud divided his men into three columns, but he was unable to keep them coordinated. His own group remained stuck in front of the Government House, and a second assault column was held up trying to get around the building's north side. Galbaud's troops again came under fire from the houses along the streets. "As we advanced toward the upper town, every building became the setting for an ambush, every window a hostile gunport," the author of *My Odyssey* complained. "At every step we lost a comrade; we didn't dare fire into the houses which, although held by the enemy, still held the women, the children and the sick of our party … Our merchant's clerk, who was marching ahead of me, fell back, leaning on my chest. I thought that a moment of panic had made him jump back, and I gave him a gentle shove: he fell to the pavement."[43]

Only the third column, led by Galbaud's brother César and the volunteers' commander Milhet, reached its objective. Once they were in position to attack the *casernes*, however, they fell to arguing among themselves about how to cross the large open square, the Champ de Mars, in front of the buildings. "Milhet was trying to reestablish order," one of his men wrote, "when a shot fired at him from one of the windows of the Rouannet house at the corner of the rue de Bourbon and the Champ de Mars blew out his brains. This loss caused a complete rout."[44] As the third column retreated toward the harbor, César Galbaud stopped and tried to set up the small mortar they had brought with them. While he was occupied getting the gun into firing position, a unit of men of color surrounded him. The sailors fled in disorder, leaving Galbaud behind to be taken prisoner.[45] Worry about his brother's fate would weigh heavily on General Galbaud throughout the rest of the crisis.

Two hours after their landing, the general and his supporters stumbled back toward the harbor; they had lost 50 men, whereas the commissioners' defenders had suffered about 100 casualties.[46] Having failed in their goal of capturing the commissioners, some of the sailors started to think of themselves. If they could not achieve the collective goal of rescuing the colony from Sonthonax and Polverel, they could at least come away with some of the town's wealth. In their minds, the fact

---

[43] *My Odyssey*, in Popkin, *Facing Racial Revolution*, 211.
[44] Anonymous account B, Moreau de Saint-Méry papers, CAOM F 3 198.
[45] César Galbaud described his capture in a letter to his brother, written from Cap Français, August 28 and 30, 1793, in *Débats entre les accusateurs et les accusés*, 8: 126–8.
[46] Letter by Perussel, Baltimore, MD, August 4, 1793, AN D XXV 14, d. 130bis.

that they had been fired on from some of the houses and that the city's residents had failed to rally to their side probably made them consider the inhabitants' property as fair game. They began breaking into houses and shops and plundering. Witnesses on all sides agree on the sailors' involvement in the looting; some also claim that the men of color began doing the same thing in the streets closer to the Government House. It is more likely that some of the city's slaves, realizing that white authority was falling apart, began to help themselves to some of their masters' goods.

While the sailors were searching for loot, Galbaud finally turned his attention to the arsenal. He now faced the prospect of having to spend the night on shore before he could mount a second attack on an enemy who would be better prepared. He certainly realized by now that he would need heavy artillery to bombard the Government House, and he could hardly leave the arsenal's 150-man garrison, composed largely of men of color, holding a strategic position so close to the harbor. The arsenal's defenders, for their part, had been curiously passive during the afternoon's fighting. If they had opened fire on Galbaud's support-ers as they came ashore, they could have disrupted the entire landing. The arsenal, however, was directly exposed to the menacing guns of the warships in the harbor, and its commander was afraid that if he began hostilities, the building would be reduced to rubble. Immediately after the landing, César Galbaud had presented himself and tried to per-suade lieutenant colonel Debray, the arsenal's commander, to recognize General Galbaud's authority or at least let him take some of the guns. When Debray refused, the younger Galbaud went away, but some of the naval officers who had come ashore stayed and continued to argue with him. Debray felt overwhelmed by the situation. "I ask you to consider how perplexed I was. I had no orders; I saw that if I opened fire on the men who wanted to take over the arsenal and if the warships that were broadside to us reduced the city to ashes, I would be condemned for having acted without orders, and I would be personally responsible for anything that happened," he wrote in a report justifying his actions after the destruction of the city.[47]

Galbaud, when he returned to the arsenal after the failure of the attack on the Government House, continued to display hesitancy out of character with his reputation as a republican war hero. The

---

[47] Deposition of lieutenant colonel Debray, June 25, 1793, on board the *Trois Amis de Nantes*, AN D XXV 80, d. 784.

journalist Saint-Maurice could hardly believe how reluctant he was to tackle the arsenal:

One citizen justly reproached him and showed him clearly how easy it would be to take it, since he had a superiority of three or four times in numbers. Who could have imagined this General's answer! "I presented myself there two or three times," he said, "but they wouldn't surrender." "General, if you would put yourself at the head of fifty willing men, I swear that you will get control of it easily." The general did not dare refuse, he marches, the doors open and he takes possession of this important position without firing a shot. Proud, no doubt, of this conquest, Galbaud walks around in the arsenal without thinking of making sure of the citizens of color who had been guarding it and who, taking advantage of his blindness, escape one by one. A citizen points this out to him and shows him the necessity of arresting these men, whose escape is going to increase the number of enemies. "I can't be everywhere," Galbaud replies, "nevertheless, you are right: Go give the order to the sentinels not to let any man of color leave." "But," the citizen says to him, "I don't have any authority to give orders to the sentinels…" "Ah, you're right," says Galbaud, and finally he gives the order to someone who could carry it out. Of the two hundred men who were guarding the arsenal, thirty are taken prisoner and sent on board the *Jupiter*.[48]

In reality, as other accounts indicate, Galbaud and his supporters succeeded in gaining control of the arsenal because of confusion among its defenders, rather than because of any belated show of determination on the general's part. According to Debray, the naval officers who had been pressuring him all afternoon finally proposed a compromise: the arsenal would be guarded by a joint force made up of equal numbers of men from the two camps. "At that instant, cries of '*Vive la République*' were heard from both sides, everyone wanted to embrace each other, and the two forces merged together; I had no power to stop this enthusiasm, particularly since there were at least twenty sailors for each soldier," Debray wrote. A key role in these events was played by Captain Daniel Vandongen of the *Concorde*, who took it on himself, as he saw it, to try to prevent bloodshed. "I throw myself between the two parties, luck is with me and I re-establish peace, everyone embraces and the general cry was 'Long live the Republic, long live our union forever!'" he wrote in his own deposition, an account substantiated by one of his men.[49]

It was at this point that Galbaud, retreating after the unsuccessful assault on the Government House, appeared at the arsenal. Annecy, one

---

[48] "Historic narrative," in Popkin, *Facing Racial Revolution*, 190.
[49] Vandongen, "Rapport," in SHM, BB 4 24; deposition of Bujon in AN, D XXV 81, d. 798.

of the free colored soldiers, reported that the general himself gave the men of his unit fraternal embraces and led the sailors in a cheer of "Long live the nation! Long live equality!" The hollowness of Galbaud's promises to the men of color was quickly exposed, as Debray related: "A few minutes later, he had the free companies [of men of color] sent on board the ships, after having disarmed them."[50] "This behavior outraged us," Vandongen's companion testified: he and the captain thought that they had achieved a reconciliation between the two parties.[51] Annecy and some of the other men of color escaped into the nearby suburb of the Petit Carénage, where they fought a two-hour battle against a group of white militiamen before escaping into the hills.[52] Well aware of the sailors' fury against them, the men of color still in the arsenal knew they were in danger. One of them, corporal Charles Hilarion, even decided he would be better off pretending to be a slave. He stripped off his uniform and shoes and hid himself among the black workers in the arsenal, who had taken no part in the contest for control there.[53] Although he now found himself in possession of the arsenal, Galbaud ignored advice to secure other important positions. "I myself told him that the brigands had just seized the ferry crossing, the most vital point for keeping the brigands from the countryside from entering," a civilian named Delage later testified. "He didn't send any troops; he told me to wait until the next day, when it was too late."[54]

Not yet aware of what had taken place at the arsenal, Sonthonax and Polverel hoped that the failure of the attack on the Government House would make the sailors rethink their engagement on Galbaud's behalf. They sent several groups of their supporters to spread their printed proclamation offering the sailors amnesty if they turned the general over to the commissioners. Polverel's own son, who had accompanied his father to Saint-Domingue, volunteered for this mission. Mounted on horseback and accompanied by four soldiers, a court official, and a civilian gendarme, he approached the arsenal, where a group of Galbaud's men gathered around them. Instead of listening to the proclamation, however, "they seized us, took our weapons, shoved us off our horses, and sent us onto different ships as prisoners," young Polverel reported.[55]

---

[50] Deposition of Annecy, AN, CC 9 A 8; deposition of Debray, in AN, D XXV 80, d. 784.
[51] Deposition of Bujon, in AN, D XXV 81, d. 798.
[52] Deposition of Debray, AN, D XXV 80, d. 784; deposition of Annecy, AN, CC 9 A 8.
[53] Deposition of Charles Hilarion, July 14, 1793, AN D XXV 48, d. 461.
[54] "Récit" of Cit. Delage, n.d., AN, D XXV 80, d. 787.
[55] François Polverel, *Coup d'oeil*, 50.

A similar fate befell a patrol led by lieutenant-colonel Leblanc, from the 16th dragoon regiment, which, as always, had stayed loyal to the commissioners and played a critical role in breaking up the assault on the *casernes* earlier in the day.[56] Sonthonax and Polverel now realized that Galbaud's force would not simply fall apart because of the failure of its first attack. And just as Galbaud was preoccupied by the fate of his brother, the commissioner Polverel now had to worry about his son: the two would not see each other again until they were reunited in France more than a year later.

Despite their initial setback, the commissioners' enemies still had the advantage of numbers, and the warships were still in the harbor, ready to open fire. Galbaud had, in fact, actually given several orders for them to do so, but both the officers on shore who were told to transmit these commands to the ships and the naval officers who had stayed behind on the vessels refused to carry them out. The journalist Saint-Maurice claimed to have witnessed a naval officer, "coming for the third time to ask the general whether he was still determined to carry out the terrible order he had given to open fire on the town" after he had secured the arsenal. "'I have thought of everything,' Galbaud replies, 'and when I've gone as far as giving an order, it must be executed.' This officer allowed himself to point out the awful consequences of such an order. 'Obey,' was the only answer he was given. He leaves to go see that this bloody command is carried out: the fuses are lit, a hundred mouths of bronze are ready to pour death and destruction on the unhappy city of Le Cap, but the officers of the merchant marine and some of the naval officers oppose it, humanity carries the day, and the order is left unexecuted."[57] Even the gunners on the *Jupiter*, despite their support for Galbaud, were shocked at the order and argued with hotheads from the other ships who tried to get them to execute it.[58]

The city and the commissioners were spared the fury of the naval guns, but the sailors' refusal to abandon Galbaud meant that the fight was not over. If Sonthonax and Polverel were to maintain the French Republic's sovereignty over its most important colonial port, they needed to recruit more defenders. They knew they could expect no help from the city's whites, even though they had provided less support to Galbaud than might have

[56] "Récit de ce que a vu le citoyen Delage," AN D XXV 80, d. 782; deposition of Sarrazin, D XXV 80, d. 784.
[57] "Historic narrative," in Popkin, *Facing Racial Revolution*, 188; see also the depositions of Sarrazin and Poulain in AN D XXV 80, d. 784.
[58] Interrogation of François Raimbault, 24 mess. II, in AN, D XXV 56, d. 557.

been expected. The men of color had been faithful to their French benefactors, but there were too few of them to defeat Galbaud's supporters,
especially now that the general had gotten his hands on the arsenal's heavy
cannon. That left only the black slaves. Putting weapons in the hands of
slaves obviously meant risking the destruction of the system on which the
foundations of French colonial rule had been built. Nevertheless, from
an early stage in the Saint-Domingue insurrection, rival factions in some
parts of the island had recruited slaves to fight for them.[59] Both the white
and the free colored plantation owners in the West Province had used slave
soldiers in their struggles with each other, and Sonthonax and Polverel
had enrolled some of these already armed slaves in their own forces during
their campaign in that region during the spring of 1793, as had their free
colored ally André Rigaud. These slaves, of course, fought under white or
free colored commanders and were carefully supervised to make sure that
they did not turn their guns on those who employed them. Slaves who
fought for their masters could expect some form of compensation, possibly even a grant of freedom for themselves, but this was quite different
from a general proclamation of emancipation.

Even before the outbreak of violence in Cap Français on June 20,
1793, the commissioners' enemies had accused them of a plan to arm the
slaves and turn them against the island's white population, and also of
planning to abolish slavery in the colony. It is clear that Sonthonax and
Polverel were indeed thinking about employing armed blacks to fight
for France. Knowing that the Spanish in neighboring Santo Domingo
were trying to recruit the organized black insurgent bands to fight on
their side, the French had little choice. Even General Galbaud had imagined leading a black army on an invasion of the Spanish colony and
rewarding them with grants of conquered land there, an arrangement
that would make it possible to leave the white-owned plantations on the
French side of the border intact.[60] Sonthonax and Polverel apparently
sent emissaries to propose some kind of agreement to the black leaders;
Jean-François forwarded a letter from one of these intermediaries to his
Spanish interlocutors, both to prove that he was not hiding anything
from them and, presumably, to get them to improve their own offer to
the blacks.[61] A letter from the insurgent leader Pierrot, one of the men
who would join the fight in Cap Français on the commissioners' side on

---

[59] David Geggus, "Slave, Soldier, Rebel: The Strange Career of Jean Kina," in Geggus,
    Haitian Revolutionary Studies, 138.
[60] Deposition of Armand, in AN, D XXV, d. 51.
[61] Letter signed "Frere," June 17, 1793, in Monte y Tejada, *Historia*, 4: 43–4.

June 21, 1793, shows that rumors of even more radical measures had reached the blacks in the weeks before the showdown there. Writing to an unidentified "citizen general," probably Galbaud himself, Pierrot said that "one of our brothers has come and announced to us that you had told him to tell us that it is your intention to grant us our freedom (*la liberté générale*) and ask us to defend the colony and the French nation." Pierrot was eager to hear more about this supposed offer, because "Spain and the English propose to give us freedom and have even furnished us with everything. We know that you have been told that we have gotten arms from the Spanish and it is true."[62]

Nevertheless, despite the white colonists' violent accusations, Sonthonax and Polverel had neither decided to make any proclamation of general emancipation prior to the events of June 20, 1793, nor even to recruit slaves as soldiers for their forces. Even as the crisis in Cap Français unfolded, they hesitated to take such drastic steps. The details of what they did on June 20–21, 1793 are important, because they reveal the true significance of the two men's decisions and the extent to which their actions, which set in motion the process that would lead to the legal emancipation of the slaves in the colony and then throughout the French empire, were conditioned by the very specific circumstances in which they found themselves. Determining exactly what happened is difficult, however. Various eyewitness accounts of these events disagree in many particulars, and we are at a special disadvantage in reconstructing the role of the black population because none of them left testimonies of what they saw or did. In general, accounts by white colonists hostile to Sonthonax and Polverel – the most numerous sources – tend to claim that the commissioners appealed to the slaves early on; some sources allege that blacks were being armed and incited to attack the whites even before the sailors landed on June 20, 1793. This was certainly not the case, and indeed, none of the detailed descriptions of the troubles in the city on June 19 or of the sailors' assaults on the Government House and the *casernes* on the afternoon of the June 20, 1793 mentions encounters with blacks, as opposed to clashes with the men of color. If the first attack on the Government House had succeeded – as it very nearly did – the fate of the commissioners would have been sealed before the city's slaves had any chance to act to affect their own destinies.

In making their decision to recruit slave soldiers, the commissioners did not act alone. Their actions were coordinated with their free colored

[62] Pierrot, in Port Français, June 4, 1793, to "citoyen général," AN AA 54, d. 1509.

supporters, and indeed several sources suggest that members of this group may have acted on their own initiative to summon support from the slaves, even before Sonthonax and Polverel had taken their decision. Faced with the prospect of being overrun by the sailors, the free men of color clearly saw no alternative but to abandon their effort to maintain their own racial privileges. When the commissioners did decide to appeal to the slaves, they had to consider three distinct groups. The first were the several hundred imprisoned insurgents in the city's jails. Captured, for the most part, during the military offensive in January, these men were experienced fighters. A decision to call on them, however, meant abandoning any hope of an understanding with the whites in the colony. These were, after all, rebel slaves who had been captured "with weapons in hand;" according to the French revolutionary government's decrees, they should have been executed without further ado, and the whites in Cap Français had been clamoring for their deaths for months before the uprising. The commissioners' decision not to kill them had been a sign of their hope to reach an agreement with the insurgent forces. At some point between the landing of the sailors and the capture of the arsenal, Sonthonax and Polverel made up their minds: one of their few white loyalists, the *seneschal* Vergniaud, freed these prisoners in exchange for their promise to help defend the commissioners. By late afternoon, former black prisoners were defending the barrier of La Providence on the northern edge of the city.[63] Adding them to the commissioners' forces approximately equalized the number of fighting men on the two sides, but they do not seem to have been deployed as a distinct unit; after mentioning their release from prison, none of the surviving documents says anything specific about their role in events.

The second group of blacks the commissioners now appealed to were the civilian slaves in the city itself. Before the start of the insurrection in 1791, they numbered about 10,000, although the population had probably fallen somewhat by June 1793. It is difficult to know when Sonthonax and Polverel launched their appeal to the city's slaves. The numerous accounts of Galbaud's first assault on the commissioners make no mention of slaves rallying to their defense; all the combat these documents describe took place between whites and free men of color. One white witness claims that he had heard emancipation being announced earlier in the day, before the sailors' landing. "Along the way, as I cross the town, I encounter no one except groups of mulattos and blacks who force the

[63] Deposition of Jean Nicolas Martin Isnard, in AN, D XXV 81, d. 796.

non-libres [slaves] to go with them, and who cry out to them, *zotes tous libres ça commissaires là io qui bas zotes libres, tout blanc ça legal à nous, tout pays-ce ça quine à nous.* ("You are all free; the commissioners say you are all free, all whites are now equal to us, this whole country belongs to us.") They led them to the arsenal or to the Government House, armed them from head to toe, and thus increased their party ...," this man wrote.[64] Antoine Dalmas, one of the white volunteers who had joined Galbaud's side, and André Conscience, the general's aide-de-camp, both testified, however, that the commissioners only made this decision in the evening, once it became clear that Galbaud would be attacking again the next day.[65] This timing is confirmed in the report furnished by Captain Jones of the *Eagle*, one of the American ships in the harbor: "At dark, after the firing had ceased, a drum was heard, the usual preliminary to publishing proclamations, and it was reported that the commissioners had published pardon and freedom to the revolted negroes."[66] The newspaper editor Saint-Maurice, whose account is the longest and most detailed we have, also puts this development after the end of the day's fighting, while assigning the main responsibility to the men of color: "Toward evening, the men of color, proud of their victory, and fearing a better-planned attack the next day, sought to increase their numbers and took advantage of the absence of the masters to win over the slaves who had long been disposed that way."[67]

The printed version of the commissioners' emancipation offer is dated June 21, 1793, and it is unlikely that they had a chance to circulate it on the evening of the previous day.[68] This proclamation, which Dalmas called "the decisive blow," was addressed originally only to the blacks in the city; in the dark, the commissioners had no way to contact the armed bands of insurgents in the surrounding hills. Even though the proclamation was drawn up in the heat of a crisis, Sonthonax and Polverel still proceeded with lawyer-like caution; the document they produced could not have been more carefully worded if they had been acting at their leisure. This caution reflected their understanding of their mission and the concerns that even the most radical French abolitionists had when they

---

[64] Anon., *Extrait d'une letter, sur les malheurs de Saint-Domingue en general, et principalement sur l'incendie de la ville du Cap Français*, 13–14.

[65] Dalmas, *Révolution de Saint-Domingue*, 197; Conscience, "Rapport," Genet papers, reel 7.

[66] *Gazette of the United States* (Philadelphia), July 10, 1793.

[67] "Historic narrative," in Popkin, *Facing Racial Revolution*, 191.

[68] Proclamation in AN D XXV 5, d. 51.

contemplated the impact of a sudden and uncontrolled emancipation of the slaves. The commissioners were acutely aware that they had been sent to preserve French control of Saint-Domingue, not to do away with slavery. The most expansive instructions they had received, the National Convention's decree of March 5, 1793, had authorized them to make changes to the regulations governing plantation work gangs, but this was still a far cry from abolishing slavery altogether.

The offer of freedom they extended on June 21, 1793 was therefore limited to "black warriors who will fight for the Republic, under the civil commissioners' orders, both against the Spanish and against other enemies, whether interior or exterior." The proclamation made no mention of "the rights of man" and did not specify whether the freedom it offered included the full rights of French citizenship. Slaves who wished to take advantage of this offer were to put themselves under military discipline and commit themselves to serve not just for the duration of the crisis in Cap Français, but until all fighting in the colony had ended. The reference to the Spanish and "other enemies" made it clear that the new soldiers could find themselves being deployed against other blacks, such as the insurgent armies led by Jean-François, Biassou, and Toussaint, all of whom were siding with the Spanish. In other words, the newly freed slaves in Cap Français risked finding themselves ordered to fight against the former slaves who had risen up against slavery in August 1791.

The proclamation of June 21, 1793 also addressed the situation of a third group of slaves: those outside the city. The commissioners promised "to improve the condition of other slaves, by preventing them from being mistreated as in the past," but it did not offer freedom for those slaves who remained on the plantations. At most, Sonthonax and Polverel spoke of "gradually extending freedom to those blacks who will have given the strongest evidence of their good conduct and their devotion to work." With their control of the colony hanging by a thread, the commissioners still stuck to the gradualist program of their friend Julien Raimond. Nevertheless, by promising freedom to any slave who offered to fight for them, rather than offering it only to a specified group of blacks, the commissioners' proclamation put the initiative in the slaves' hands: all those who chose to become soldiers could now claim their liberty, and the offer was not specifically limited to the slaves of Cap Français. Nor did it exclude the slaves who had joined the insurrection and fought against the French and the colonists. As the struggle for the city intensified, Sonthonax and Polverel would find themselves recruiting a far wider body of black supporters.

Limited though it was, the proclamation of June 21, 1793 marked a turning point in the struggle over slavery. Never before in the long history of the institution in the Americas had officials of a European government taken such a drastic step. The British general Lord Dunmore's famous offer of freedom to slaves who would join his forces and fight against the American colonists in 1775 had occurred in an entirely different context. "Dunmore's intention was neither to overthrow the [slave] system nor to make war on it," Sylvia Frey has written. There was no autonomous slave insurrection in the American colonies, and no prospect of a complete collapse of the system. A slave owner himself, Dunmore acted out of military expediency, creating a force in which blacks would be firmly under the control of white officers. In any event, most of the black soldiers he recruited were soon wiped out in battle or by disease.[69] From the start of the insurrection in August 1791 until that moment, the official policy of the French revolutionary government, faithfully executed by Sonthonax and Polverel despite their personal feelings about slavery, had been to fight the insurgents and to insist on the maintenance of slavery as the basis of the colony's economy. Now, for the first time, official representatives of the French revolutionary government offered freedom, not just to a handful of insurgent leaders, but to any male slaves willing to fight on their behalf. Having opened the door to mass emancipation, Sonthonax and Polverel would soon find themselves compelled to let ever-increasing numbers of slaves pass through it; within four months, they would have decreed the complete abolition of slavery in the colony.

It is, of course, paradoxical that Sonthonax and Polverel found themselves taking this radical step even though the black slaves had hardly taken any part in the organized episodes of combat in Cap Français on June 20, 1793. In reality, however, the slaves' actions had already had a strong influence on the outcome of events. Galbaud, as we have seen, was surprised and disappointed that so few of the city's white residents – no more than 150, he complained – joined his side. There were many reasons for the whites' reluctance. After the earlier episodes of conflict on August 13–14, 1792 and December 2–6, 1792, they certainly knew better than the sailors how skilled the free men of color were at fighting. Some of them distrusted Galbaud because of his outspoken declarations

[69] Sylvia R. Frey, *Water from the Rock: Black Resistance in a Revolutionary Age* (Princeton, NJ: Princeton University Press, 1991), 63; Simon Schama, *Rough Crossings: Britain, the Slaves and the American Revolution* (New York: HarperCollins, 2006), 70–87.

of loyalty to the Republic and because of the hesitancy he had shown about confronting the commissioners. Another important consideration for the white men, however, was that taking up their weapons and going out into the streets meant leaving their families and their property at the mercy of their slaves. An American ship's captain mentioned "women and others, who had locked themselves in their dwelling houses" when the fighting broke out.[70] One white citizen, interrogated by the commissioners after the events, admitted that he had spent the critical hours of June 20, 1793 in his second-floor office, in which he had seven hunting rifles and two pairs of pistols, but, he claimed, he never tried to use them, since he was being watched by "my four negroes."[71] His situation could not have been unique. Even though there is hardly any evidence of domestic slaves turning against their masters during the first day of fighting, their mere presence throughout the town effectively paralyzed white resistance.

As the night came on, however, some blacks began to descend into the streets and to take a more active role in events. Whether or not they realized that they were on the threshold of obtaining their freedom, they certainly saw that law and order in the city had broken down. Like the sailors, some blacks decided to take advantage of this opportunity. The two hostile camps – Galbaud's forces at the arsenal and the commissioners in the Government House – both sent out armed patrols to maintain order, but they both concentrated on the streets closest to their positions. The part of the town around the Place de Clugny, site of the "marché aux noirs," was unsupervised. According to Saint-Maurice, "The night was troubled: from every direction one heard gunshots and cries. No white dared show himself; each one, frozen with fear, kept himself carefully, not to say shamefully, hidden. The slaves, under cover of the darkness, the disorder, and the paralysis of their masters, fell on the town along with the citizens of color, pillaged a part of it, and committed several massacres. The stores on the place Clugny and some of the richest ones on the place d'Armes were completely emptied and devastated during this horrible night."[72]

All night long, gunfire could be heard throughout the city. Whites found themselves isolated in their own quarters, at the mercy of blacks who no longer felt compelled to obey them, and the rumors the whites

---

[70] Captain Joseph White, in *Virginia Chronicle*, July 13, 1793.
[71] Deposition of Duliepvre, July 15, 1793, AN D XXV 19, d. 186.
[72] "Historic narrative," in Popkin, *Facing Racial Revolution*, 191.

heard only magnified the sense of danger. "The city was given over to brigandage and pillage by the mulattos and the blacks. At eight p.m., five or six blacks and a black woman belonging to one Michel, a former lemonade-shop owner, had already filled a large room in the house where I was with liquor and different valuables they had pillaged ... The night of the 20th to the 21st was almost as stormy as the day. We passed it in the cruelest torments. At every moment, we heard blacks banging on our doors with their musket butts, threatening to set fire to the house if we didn't open, and saying angrily, 'there are white fuckers in there, we should kill them all. The colony's got to be either all white or all black,'" one witness later recalled.[73] The American merchant Samuel Perkins remembered that "the fears of the whites led them to dread every one who appeared, and as they could not distinguish between the whites and the blacks in the dark, it was only a cry of 'Who's there?' and a shot followed the sound before the question could be answered. Thus in the general panic whites destroyed whites and blacks destroyed blacks through the night."[74] A black woman protected the wounded white gendarme Caire from a band of blacks who broke into the house where he had sought shelter, but he heard them telling her that she should take her master's best linen for herself, since the city was going to be destroyed.[75]

As dawn approached on June 21, the outcome of the struggle between Galbaud and the commissioners remained in doubt. The fate of slavery in the city, however, had been determined: No matter who won the battle on the coming day, the slaves had already shaken off their bonds and begun to act for themselves. Whether anyone could have restored order in Cap Français in time to prevent the city's destruction is hard to say. Perhaps if Galbaud and the sailors had slipped away instead of continuing their attack, Sonthonax and Polverel and their free colored allies could have limited the looting and disorder and prevented the outbreak of the fires that were soon to consume the town, but they could hardly have forced the blacks back into slavery. Given his supporters' hostility to the blacks and the free people of color, it is unlikely that a victorious Galbaud could have imposed his authority over them except at the price of brutal massacres. By upsetting the fragile equilibrium that had enabled Cap Français to survive despite the slave uprising in the rest of

---

[73] Anon., *Extrait d'une lettre, sur les malheurs de Saint-Domingue en general, et principalement sur l'incendie de la ville du Cap Français*, 15–16.

[74] Perkins, "Narrative," 341.

[75] Deposition of Caire, AN D XXV 48, d. 461.

the North Province, General Galbaud, plantation owner and republican war hero, and the white sailors who had no stake in the institution of slavery at all had earned the unlikely honor of making the end of slavery in the colony of Saint-Domingue inevitable. Whether the commissioners Sonthonax and Polverel would live long enough to implement their policy of controlled emancipation, and whether the French National Convention in Paris would endorse their actions, depended on the outcome of the fighting that was about to resume in Cap Français.

7

Freedom and Fire

The sky was overcast on the morning of June 21, 1793, as the population of Cap Français braced itself for another day of fighting.[1] Throughout the city, residents from all three racial groups cautiously opened windows and doors to seek information about what had happened during the night and assess their prospects for the coming day. The city's slaves had already claimed their freedom, but the fate of Le Cap still hung in the balance. At the waterfront, sailors who had gone back to their ships during the night landed again, joining those who had stayed at the arsenal. The sailors who had remained on shore could not have had much sleep. Some had patrolled the streets, others had continued the pillaging that had begun the previous day, and many had taken advantage of the wine handed out at the arsenal to drink themselves into a stupor.[2] In the Government House, Sonthonax and Polverel must have spent an equally sleepless night. Their appeal to the city's slaves had brought them some additional defenders, but it had also unleashed a wave of disorder throughout the city. Before they could hope to bring things under control, however, they had to face a renewed assault from General Galbaud and his supporters.

Stung by his failure on Thursday afternoon, Galbaud tried to organize his forces better on Friday morning. He ordered the sounding of the general alarm, in response to which all citizens were supposed to report for duty, but only fifty volunteers appeared. They were added to the sailors – Sonthonax and Polverel thought there were about twice as

[1] For the weather, see "Journal du vaisseau l'*America*," in AN, D XXV 54, d. 523.
[2] Account of Poulain, in AN, D XXV 80, d. 784.

many of them as there had been the day before, perhaps 1,200 in all –
and other combatants. While the commissioners had been freeing the
slaves, Galbaud's supporters had engaged in an act of liberation of their
own, releasing some jailed British sailors from a ship called the *Hyena*,
captured as a prize shortly before the crisis. They "put themselves under
the command of a British officer, and fought bravely," according to an
American ship captain.[3] Galbaud divided his attacking force into three
columns of about 250 men each. The first was to go to the Champ de
Mars, opposite the *casernes* where the troops loyal to the commissioners
were housed. The second, equipped with a heavy 24-pounder cannon
from the arsenal, headed straight for the Government House, while the
third was ordered to swing south, through the Place de Clugny, thus
completely encircling the commissioners' redoubt.[4] Unfortunately for
the assailants, the wheels of the central column's heavy gun broke almost
immediately, delaying its advance and causing that force to lose contact
with the other columns. Once the central column starting moving again,
it came under fire from snipers hidden in the houses and in the church,
which men of color had occupied during the night.[5] "Several people were
wounded and taken to the arsenal," the newspaper editor Saint-Maurice
wrote. "The sight of them, which intimidated the less determined among
those at that post, began to discourage the bolder ones." Galbaud had
made no arrangements to care for the injured. "Unfortunately there was
no surgeon to aid them, no bandages, no instruments to perform operations. The brave men who had been misguided enough to trust in the
experience and intelligence of Galbaud suffered from the pain of their
wounds and the pain of seeing themselves sacrificed because of the general's incompetence and self-regard."[6]

By 8 A.M., the heavy gun had finally been set up in the Place d'Armes,
where it began bombarding the Government House. The commissioners
had set up their own smaller artillery piece in front of the building, but
it quickly became useless when its axle broke. The attackers managed
to fire twenty-three rounds before their gun, too, became disabled; their
shots shattered the Government House's façade and knocked plaster
loose from the walls inside.[7] Meanwhile, another detachment of sailors

---

[3] Captain Jones, in *Gazette of the United States* (Philadelphia), July 10, 1793.
[4] Account A, CAOM, F 3 198.
[5] Declaration of Cordeil, July 8, 1793, in LC, Genet papers, reel 5.
[6] "Historic narrative," in Popkin, *Facing Racial Revolution*, 192.
[7] Account A, CAOM, Moreau de Saint-Méry papers, F 3 198; "Historic narrative," in
Popkin, *Facing Racial Revolution*, 192; letter of Captain Fanning in *London Times*,
August 22, 1793.

dragged a smaller cannon up to the top of one of the *mornes*, or hills, above the Government House, creating a new threat for its defenders. As on the previous day, the fighting in the streets and squares in the center of the city was fierce. Saint-Maurice's news report captured the texture of what had truly become a struggle for freedom:

The citizens of color, emboldened by their enemies' lack of success, were sure of victory; they were wonderfully aided by the blacks they had armed and whose activities kept Galbaud's party from getting as close to the Government House as they had the day before. These new men [the blacks], proud to be called citizens, showed a dedication that one would not have expected from men without leaders, fighting without organization, without discipline. These were no longer men bent beneath the yoke of contempt and servitude; inspired by hatred and vengeance, these men had thrown off their masks. No more truce between the master and the slave in revolt! Those whose glance had made them tremble, those whom they had always believed to be a race superior to theirs, were nothing more in their eyes except tyrants: the spell was broken. The whites, one must confess, were at a great disadvantage in the fighting: they had to face enemies hidden in their houses, and whose blows were hard behind their walls.[8]

Despite the courage of their defenders, the commissioners' situation was rapidly becoming untenable. Although Sonthonax and Polverel had sworn to hold their position to the death, their free colored supporters urged them not to risk being killed or captured in the crumbling Government House. "Your commissioners gave in to the prayers of the citizens of color, and made their retreat," Dufay would tell the Convention in February 1794.[9] The sailors, wary after their defeat the day before, were reluctant to approach too closely, preferring to hang back and let the 24-pounder batter their foes, so the commissioners still had a chance to escape. In an attempt to ensure that at least one of them made it to safety, they split up: Polverel took the main road out of town to the south, even though it was exposed to the fire of the gun on the *morne*, while Sonthonax used a path up the hill that led to Fort Belair, one of the city's fortifications. By late morning, both had succeeded in reaching the village of Haut du Cap, a few miles south of the city.[10] The whites who entered the Government House after the commissioners' departure were able to measure the loyalty of the free men of color who had defended them: thirty-one of them lay dead.[11]

---

[8] "Historic narrative," in Popkin, *Facing Racial Revolution*, 194–5.
[9] *Réimpression de l'ancien Moniteur*, 18 pluviôse II (February 6, 1794).
[10] "Historic narrative," in Popkin, *Facing Racial Revolution*, 193.
[11] Account A, CAOM, F 3 198.

By letting Sonthonax and Polverel get away to Haut du Cap, Galbaud missed his second chance to change the course of the struggle over slavery in Saint-Domingue. "It was natural to think that the left-hand column [of Galbaud's forces] would block their passage and trap them between itself and the center column, in such a way that the mulattoes would have been defeated and the commissioners captured or killed," a frustrated white volunteer wrote.[12] To do so, however, the white troops would have had to push into the *Petite Guinée*, a part of the town inhabited primarily by free people of color and slaves, and they were afraid to do so. Although they had had to abandon the seat of government, the commissioners managed to salvage some of the essential instruments of sovereignty, including printing equipment that would enable them to issue proclamations. They were accompanied not only by the free men of color but by General Laveaux and a few other loyal whites, as well as by their prized prisoner, César Galbaud, who complained that he was forced to march "between two rows of black soldiers who poked me in the back with their bayonets."[13] Regardless of what happened in the city, Sonthonax and Polverel were determined to keep functioning as the government of Saint-Domingue.

As the commissioners installed themselves on the Bréda plantation at Haut du Cap – the birthplace of Toussaint Louverture – events in the city took a turn they had not anticipated. However careless he had been in letting Sonthonax and Polverel escape from the city, Galbaud was now on the verge of success. "If Galbaud had stood out 5 minutes longer, it is thought he must have gained a victory," one American ship captain wrote.[14] His forces no longer faced any organized opposition; even if they could not bring the southern, heavily black neighborhoods of the city under their control, they should have been able to set up a defense perimeter around the northern parts of it, including the Government House. Instead, however, as multiple eyewitness accounts make clear, Galbaud and his followers succumbed to the fear of black savagery that was the other side of the whites' assumption of their own superiority. Whether it was the general himself or some of the white sailors in the column nearest the *Petite Guinée* who were first seized by panic, a cry broke out: "We are lost! The mulattoes are coming to attack us!"[15] Even though none of the armed black insurgents who would shortly enroll

[12] Account A, CAOM, F 3 198.
[13] César Galbaud, in AN, D XXV 48, d. 465.
[14] Captain Jones (*Eagle*), in *Gazette of the United States* (Philadelphia), July 10, 1793.
[15] Deposition of Poulain, AN D XXV 48, d. 784.

themselves to fight on Sonthonax's and Polverel's side had yet entered the city, "everyone yelled that thousands of blacks were coming from Haut-du-Cap and that they were going to exterminate all of us."[16] The wave of fear swept through the other two columns as well, and Galbaud's entire force broke into a disorderly retreat to the arsenal. "From all sides came cries of 'To the ships! To the ships!' and fear had seized all the citizens. Continual fire from the upper windows of the buildings, armed blacks who we recognized, everything increased the terror and the unfortunate city was immediately abandoned and left to be looted," the colonial administrator Cordeil wrote. "Everyone was seized with fear for his father, his mother, his wife, his children, his friends who were sick or wounded; disorder and confusion took over," another witness remembered.[17]

The general himself was swept along by the crowd; one witness even claimed that it was he who first broke and ran.[18] Long after the event, Galbaud's supporters tried to claim that the general had been forced to take flight by some of his aides, who feared that the whites would be left leaderless if he was captured. One account even quoted a heroic speech Galbaud supposedly made once he reached the arsenal: "Citizens! let the friends of France, the true republicans, stay with me; they should die defending their country. Let the others disappear; I must die or triumph."[19] Most evidence tells a different story, however. The resounding words quoted by this particular pro-Galbaud witness bear a suspicious resemblance to those that the newspaper editor Saint-Maurice says Galbaud should have uttered, but never did.[20] Rather than rallying his forces, Galbaud actually headed straight to the waterfront, looking for a boat to take him to safety. One witness testified that he had seen "Galbaud run up with his whole troop, probably vigorously pursued, because they all threw themselves into the ship's boats and skiffs and Galbaud himself jumped into the water, crying '*Sauve, ...*' His splash in the water must have kept him from saying '*qui peut*,' or at least I didn't hear it."[21] Whether Galbaud threw himself

---

[16] Account A, CAOM, F 3 198.
[17] Deposition of Cordeil, July 8, 1793, in LC, Genet papers, reel 5; "Précis historique de l'événement du Cap," AN D XXV 14, d. 130.
[18] "Historic narrative," in Popkin, *Facing Racial Revolution*, 195.
[19] "Précis historique de l'événement du Cap," AN D XXV 14, d. 130. In testimony in Paris in 1795, one witness even named the two men who supposedly grabbed Galbaud and put him involuntarily on a boat. *Débats entre les accusateurs et les accusés, dans l'affaire des colonies* (Paris: Imprimerie nationale, An III (1795)), 8: 19.
[20] "Historic narrative," in Popkin, *Facing Racial Revolution*, 196.
[21] Deposition of Artau, September 3, 1793, AN D XXV 5, d. 53.

into the water or was pushed, he made an unforgettable sight, especially because, before he plunged into the harbor, he had stopped long enough to safeguard his most valuable possession. "Imagine everyone's surprise at seeing Galbaud in water up to his neck, holding his watch in his mouth to keep it dry!" one of the several people who had observed the general's concern for his timepiece recalled.[22]

The newspaper editor Saint-Maurice, who blamed Galbaud for the disaster that destroyed his city, gives an account of the dripping-wet general's conduct once he was safely back on board the *Jupiter* that deserves to be quoted at length:

On his arrival on board the *Jupiter*, Galbaud, soaked to the skin, sat down next to his wife in the stateroom, while waiting for someone to take some dry clothes out of his chest. His wife rubbed his hands and squeezed them while caressing him in a tender fashion. Ah, my dear one, she said, in a trembling voice, he is so useful to the Republic that we must take good care of him. An instant later, Galbaud, touched by his wife's tenderness, went into his cabin to change. Someone thought they heard him crying. "You are crying, general," someone said to him. "Oh, no," he replied, sobbing. "In any case, it would be from rage." After this touching scene, a frugal meal was served, to which Galbaud did the greatest honor. "It is really too bad," he said, "that I was pushed back. Thinking that I had won, I was already preparing to seize the *mornes* [the mountainous heights around Le Cap] in order to put a quick end to this war." [Rear admiral] Cambis listened to him from below and concealed a smile at the thought of a setback whose responsibility he didn't need to share. After the meal, Galbaud, wearing a small white vest and yellow slippers, wanted to show himself to the sailors to reassure them about his condition.[23] What a costume for a leader! "Tell me, am I all right like this?" he asked the rear admiral, putting his leg forward. "Can I show myself this way to your crew?" "Perfectly," the latter replied, "you must be worn out, you should take things easy." Mrs. Galbaud devoured her dear husband with her eyes, she couldn't contain her joy, and the poor man had no idea how pitiful he appeared to everyone. Pardon me this digression, it is completely true and really shows the character of the man who many hailed as the savior of Le Cap.[24]

While Galbaud was having his touching reunion with his wife on the *Jupiter*, events were moving rapidly in Cap Français. At the arsenal, with

---

[22] Deposition of Poulain, AN D XXV 48,d. 784. The watch is also mentioned in "Historic narrative" and Account A, Moreau de Saint-Méry papers, CAOM F 3 198.

[23] Antoine Dalmas's account also says that Galbaud was seen "seated in front of a desk, wearing a nightcap and slippers, with a pen in his hand... This was neither the right costume, nor the right place for a general whose army was engaged in a bloody and terrible combat." Dalmas, *Histoire de la révolution*, 201.

[24] "Historic narrative," in Popkin, *Facing Racial Revolution*, 196–7.

the general gone, "there was no leader and no one in charge. A crowd gone mad and subject to every kind of impulse came up with the craziest ideas and exaggerated both real and imaginary dangers," according to an account collected by Moreau de Saint-Méry.[25] Sailors, soldiers, and civilians became desperate to get on board the vessels in the harbor. "Everyone, their eyes unfocused, their mouths open and terror painted on their faces, thought they already saw an army of mulattoes, furious and covered with blood, about to fall on them with sabers in their hands. Everyone threw himself in the water without thinking, without knowing whether the nearest ships would be swamped by the crowd. Everyone threw away rifles, knapsacks, uniforms, hats, anything that might hamper them. The seashore, witness to a dishonorable flight, was covered with things left behind by cowards who threw themselves into the water trying to reach some distant rowboats," Saint-Maurice testified. "We all left the house as we stood, without a second shirt to our backs, and even without carrying off our watches, which were left in our bedrooms," the American merchant Samuel Perkins recalled.[26] (See Figure 7.1.)

Galbaud's flight was so precipitous that the center of the city was literally abandoned. The author of *My Odyssey* and some other white volunteers, after observing the commissioners' evacuation in the morning, had spent the day fighting bands of blacks on the slopes of the hills above the city. When they re-entered the town, "we were stupefied with astonishment. The streets were deserted, the houses closed. No noise, no movement, nothing to announce the proximity of an army victorious or defeated."[27] Those whites who did not simply give way to panic realized that they were on their own, as the blacks and people of color discovered that the city now belonged to them. The result was not, however, as many whites had expected, a racial massacre. Although Louis Dufay undoubtedly exaggerated when he claimed, in his address to the Convention on 4 February 1794, that "the citizens of 4 April and their auxiliaries [the freed blacks] devoted themselves exclusively to saving a large number of whites of every age and sex," while Galbaud and the sailors deliberately destroyed the town, there is nevertheless substantial evidence that many of the whites who survived owed their lives to the efforts of people of other races.[28] Moreau de Saint-Méry noted down the Creole "cries of the

[25] Account A, CAOM, F 3 198.
[26] Perkins, "Narrative," 342.
[27] "Mon Odyssée," in Popkin, *Facing Racial Revolution*, 213.
[28] *Compte rendu sur la situation actuelle de Saint-Domingue. Par Dufey [sic], député de la partie du nord. 16 plu. II* (Paris: Imprimerie nationale, An II), 6.

INCENDIE DU CAP FRANÇAIS,
le 20 21 22 et 23 Juin 1793, ou 2 3 4 et 5 Messidor An 1er de la République .

FIGURE 7.1. Refugees from Le Cap.
Separate groups of blacks (on the left) and whites (in the center) strike dramatic poses as flames ravage the city of Cap Français in the background. Although this engraving, whose depiction of the city is only approximate, was probably made in France, it is one of the rare acknowledgments that blacks, including the city's slaves, lost their homes and had to flee the fire along with the white population.
Source: Bibliothèque nationale de France.

Negroes who saved whites during the destruction of Le Cap": "Citognin! Na pas tiré! c'est gnon bon Citognin!" (Citizen! Don't shoot! It's a good citizen!"), words that emphasized both the speakers' good intentions and their consciousness of their new status as free men.[29]

The author of *My Odyssey* and his family were among those aided by members of other racial groups. On the first day of fighting, he became separated from his unit of volunteers. "I hid in the home of a colored girl, who took pity on my youth and my condition," he recalled. After feeding him, "she disguised me as a woman, and with her help I found a way to get to the arsenal." Weeks later, when he was finally reunited

[29] CAOM, F 3 198 (Moreau de Saint-Méry papers).

with his family in the United States, he learned that they owed their survival to the intervention of a black leader whose men invaded their house as it was burning. "He recognized my mother at first sight, whose former slave he had been," the author wrote. "'What! it is you, my mistress,' he said. 'Be reassured. My soldiers will henceforth respect you and I will save you from the fury of the others ...'" He had his men save what they could of the family's possessions, including the author's manuscripts, and escort them to the commissioners' camp at Haut du Cap.[30]

The individual and family dramas recounted by survivors shed a revealing light on the complicated relationships that led members of different racial groups to help each other even as the city they had shared on such unequal terms fell apart around them. Jean Nicolas Martin Isnard, a merchant, had been one of the guests at the commissioners' banquet on June 19, 1793. On the following morning, he and his family had gone to dine with a relative whose house was outside the defense perimeter surrounding the town. Hearing the sounds of the fighting in the afternoon, Isnard tried to return to his home but found the way barred by the freed black prisoners who were now manning the gate. That evening, however, "the negress Penelope, whom I had emancipated along with her children in exchange for the services she had performed for me," joined him, and he was able to send her into the city on the morning of June 21, 1793 to check on his house. She returned to tell him that all his property had been looted, with the exception of his dirty laundry. By the evening of June 22, as fires raged through the city, Isnard realized that he would never see his house again. He tried to take his family to the commissioners' camp at Haut-du-Cap, escorted by "five blacks among whom was the man named Pierre, who lived with the negress Penelope." They were stopped at a barrier on the road by a larger group of blacks on horseback, but when their escorts testified that they were "good citizens," the black cavalrymen lifted the group's children – three of Isnard's and four of Penelope's – onto their horses and guided the whole group to safety. Isnard concluded his account by naming a number of blacks and people of color, of both sexes, who had assisted his family during the month they spent before they found a ship to take them to the United States, including one man who had told him, "I will always recognize you for my master." When they finally left, Penelope was not allowed to accompany them, but

[30] "Mon Odyssée," in Popkin, *Facing Racial Revolution*, 211–12, 216.

she entrusted Isnard and his wife with her youngest daughter.[31] It may well be that Penelope's children were also Isnard's, and it is probable that Penelope had helped raise the family's white children. In any case, however, the relationships between the different members of the Isnard household were powerful enough so that all of them worked together to secure their mutual safety. According to Isnard, Penelope would have abandoned Pierre and taken all of her children to the United States if she had been able to.

Not all the cases in which whites were aided by members of other racial groups involved relationships as intimate as that described by Isnard. Another merchant named Seguin and his family had barricaded themselves behind locked doors in their house in the *Petite Guinée* neighborhood when the fighting began on June 20. When a group of about eighty blacks began to smash down their door, however, Seguin decided to risk coming out of hiding and to try to convince them to spare his family and property. Like many white survivors, he owed his life to the intervention of a man of color, one Bien-Aimé Noel, who persuaded the blacks to leave the building and then escorted Seguin's wife and children to the harbor. Seguin stayed behind, hoping to save his valuables; when Noel returned and saw the mounting danger, he finally convinced Seguin that he, too, needed to flee. Noel was evidently more level-headed than Seguin; the merchant was ready to leave without even thinking to take any money, until his protector reminded him that he would need it. Seguin was most distressed, however, because he had to leave behind his account books; he delivered his testimony to the French consul in Baltimore as soon as he arrived there, trying to provide himself with some legal protection against his creditors.[32] The nature of Noel's relationship with Seguin is unclear, but he was clearly motivated by basic humanity in intervening to save Seguin's family. In reminding Seguin to take his cash with him, Noel passed up the chance to appropriate it for himself. His ability to dissuade the blacks who had tried to loot the house indicates that the free population of color still had some moral authority over the former slaves, even as the colonial racial hierarchy was collapsing.

While Seguin and his family managed to reach the harbor and get on a ship, many whites found themselves, like the Isnards, cut off from the waterfront. Another white survivor recalled how he and his family

---

[31] Account of Isnard, in AN, D XXV 81, d. 796.
[32] Deposition of Seguin, Baltimore, MD, July 16, 1793, AN D XXV 80, d. 785.

"hurriedly packed our things with our most precious possessions, we gave them to our servants to carry, we took our children in our arms, and we fled." Whereas Seguin had been menaced by blacks and protected by a man of color, this family had the opposite experience. Although the family's slaves had been prepared to help them escape, "as soon as we were outside ... we were surrounded by mulattoes, who took our bags, forced our blacks to go with them to the Government House, and wanted to force us to come, too." The whites in the party managed to escape, although the author was hit by a musket ball and suffered a machete wound before he reached safety in the hills outside the city. "But what a painful spectacle presented itself to our eyes! In every direction, the only thing we saw was large groups of men, women, and children crowding around the gates of the town, emerging in disorder, fleeing their assassins while pleading for mercy; others, more fortunate, fell under their blows," he wrote. "I will never forget the tears of compassion I shed as I saw pious children carrying on their shoulders, in imitation of Aeneas, their fathers or their mothers, bent under the weight of their years."[33]

Free people of color and blacks clearly helped many whites escape the disaster engulfing the city, but humanitarian instincts did not always prevail. The wave of violence that swept the city claimed victims of all races, but only the whites were able to leave testimonies about their losses. Jean Baptiste Auguste Paris reported that on the evening of June 20, he had been part of a patrol that tried to disperse a group of men of color who were looting the warehouse of a Jewish merchant named Chabes near the Place Clugny. When they entered the building, "we found several citizens ... killed by saber blows in front of their doors, and a number of women and children, including a pregnant woman almost ready to give birth whose belly had been slit open, so that her intestines were between her legs, along with the fruit of her womb."[34] Ten days after the burning of Le Cap, another survivor wrote to his brother in Bordeaux to beg him to rescue their two younger siblings: "Our father and mother were slaughtered by the Negroes, I received two saber cuts, one on the head and one on the right arm ... When you receive this letter I may no longer be alive."[35]

---

[33] Anon., *Extrait d'une lettre, sur les malheurs de Saint-Domingue*, in Popkin, *Facing Racial Revolution*, 221.

[34] Deposition of Jean Baptiste Auguste Paris, in AN, D XXV 81, d. 796.

[35] Duvallon d'Etang to brother, July 2, 1793, in Musée d'Aquitaine (original in Archives municipales de Bordeaux).

As the whites in the city tried to save themselves, Sonthonax and Polverel began trying to save something of their authority over the colony. Not realizing that Galbaud's movement had already disintegrated by midday on June 21, their first concern was to prepare themselves for a possible attack from the town. Etienne Laveaux, their military commander, set up a gun covering the road, and some white colonists later accused him of "threatening to shoot them down for the slightest complaint, the slightest groan forced from them by their suffering."[36] After the events of the previous day and a half, it was understandable that the commissioners distrusted the city's whites, but they quickly realized that they were facing a crowd of helpless civilians and began taking measures to care for them. The commissioners managed to have their free colored allies bring flour and biscuit from the town. "Rations were distributed to the unfortunates; a sort of administration starts to be organized at Haut du Cap," Saint-Maurice reported.[37] For the most part, however, the refugees were forced to camp in the open, exposed to the elements, while Sonthonax and Polverel focused on more pressing matters.

With the city apparently lost to Galbaud's forces, the commissioners and their free colored allies had nowhere to look for support except to the black population. Seven months earlier, at the time of the crisis of December 2, 1792, bands of armed black insurgents had approached the town, hoping that they might have their long-awaited opportunity to storm it; now, they began to do so again. Five unidentified "citizens" who were at Haut du Cap before Sonthonax and Polverel arrived on the morning of June 21 testified that they had seen "a considerable descent of brigands from the *mornes.*" Once the commissioners and their supporters had reached the village, the blacks "approached the camp ... urged to advance by men of color who kept running in their direction."[38] On June 21, the black insurgents who reached Haut du Cap seem to have been groups who were already in the area, and the commissioners seemingly made no effort to organize them or direct them. Observers on the ships saw a regular stream of blacks coming into the city, where they joined the already liberated town population in pillaging and fighting with the remaining whites. The black insurgents in the area were not the only ones who heard the sounds of gunfire coming from the city. At a camp

---

[36] Dufresne, "Considérations," 195; see also Account A, in CAOM, F 3 198.
[37] "Historic narrative," in Popkin, *Facing Racial Revolution*, 199.
[38] Document in AN D XXV 48, d. 461.

twenty miles from the city, the plantation-owner François Carteaux had heard cannon shots that "made us think that fighting had broken out, but who was involved in it, and what it was about, we did not know," he wrote. "Full of thoughts, whites, mulattoes, and blacks mixed together in our position; each color silently held itself on guard against the others, preparing to sell its life dearly."[39]

During the afternoon of June 21, those observers watching the city from afar noted a new phenomenon: fire was breaking out in the city. Several reports specify that the conflagration began in a bakery located on the rue du Conseil, at the northern edge of the town.[40] In the aftermath of the city's destruction, partisans of Galbaud and supporters of the commissioners accused each other of arson. César Galbaud claimed to have heard Louis Dufay giving orders for the destruction of the city as the commissioners' party was preparing to abandon the Government House: "Start fires everywhere, burn all the houses, let them be roasted like pigs."[41] A white political prisoner from Port-au-Prince who had been on shore on June 21 claimed that he had heard many people say that their black servants had told them "that they had orders from the commissioners who had taken refuge at Haut du Cap to burn and loot the city."[42] Sonthonax and Polverel were equally emphatic in blaming Galbaud and his supporters. "As soon as we had left [the town], the sailors started to burn the neighborhood of the men of 4 April," they wrote to the minister Genet in Philadelphia. "Galbaud himself urged them to loot."[43] In his report to the Convention in February 1794, Dufay, himself accused of starting the fires, turned the accusation around, claiming that Galbaud's "satellites spread the fire with torches in their hands."[44] An American observer claimed that the first flames broke out on streets controlled by the sailors, "a proof that the Party of the Commissaries did not set fire to the town, as is reported."[45]

---

[39] François Carteaux, *Histoire des désastres de Saint-Domingue* (Bordeaux: Pellier-Lawalle, An X [1802]), cited in Popkin, *Facing Racial Revolution*, 229.

[40] Declaration of Garnier, in AN, D XXV 82, d. 799

[41] César Galbaud, in AN, D XXV 48, d. 465.

[42] Testimony of Jean Baptiste Augustin Deprat, Brest, 17 bru. II, in AN, D XXV 80, d. 788.

[43] Sonthonax and Polverel to Genet, July 8, 1793, in AN, D XXV 5, d. 46.

[44] *Relation détaillée des événemens malheureux qui se sont passés au Cap depuis l'arrivée du ci-devant général Galbaud, jusqu'au moment où il a fait brûler cette ville et a pris la fuite* (Paris: Imprimerie nationale, An II), 51.

[45] Prior, account in *Maryland Journal and Baltimore Advertiser*, August 13, 1793 (copy in AN, D XXV 38, d. 381).

In reality, it is highly unlikely that anyone consciously planned the destruction of Cap Français. However furious they may have been at what they regarded as the treachery of the city's whites, Sonthonax and Polverel could hardly have wanted to take responsibility for the loss of the most valuable city in the colony; furthermore, many of their free colored supporters stood to lose everything they owned if the city burned down. The sailors and the blacks who had begun entering the city from the hills had less of a stake in the city's survival, but no detailed account of events in the city depicts any deliberate effort on the part of either group to start the fires. The fact that reliable reports, such as the recollections of a white volunteer preserved in Moreau de Saint-Méry's papers and the log of the *America*, put the start of the fires in the afternoon or the evening of June 21, hours after the commissioners' escape to Haut du Cap and Galbaud's inglorious retreat to the harbor, suggests that they were the accidental result of the looting and disorder in the city. High winds helped them spread. On June 21, 1793, the fires affected only small parts of the city. In the absence of any functioning authority, however, no one could organize an effort to prevent the flames from getting out of control.[46]

However the fires may have started, the realization that much of the city was likely to be burned gave new impetus to the looting. As with the responsibility for the fires themselves, many survivors tried to blame this behavior exclusively on their enemies, but there is little doubt that partisans of both sides participated in what had now become a race against time to grab anything that could be carried away before it was destroyed. In their letter to Genet, Sonthonax and Polverel wrote that "the slaves armed themselves ... and pillaged, the disorder was universal, brigands of all colors fought over the booty, shot each other without regard for color, [and] some of them, full of strong liquor, fell in the midst of the flames, or were buried in the ruins."[47] From the other side of the conflict, Moreau de Saint-Méry's informant described much the same scene: "The Negroes, as if invited by the flames, soon appeared in all the roads leading to the town, where they arrived like a flood. Looting preceded the ravages of the destructive element and, in the lower town, the sailors themselves did what the colored brigands did in the upper part. The disorder was at its peak, it was universal."[48]

---

[46] Account A, in CAOM, F 3 198; "Journal du vaisseau l'*America*," in AN, D XXV 54, d. 523; account of Poulain, in AN, D XXV 80, d. 784.

[47] Sonthonax and Polverel to Genet, July 8, 1793, in AN, D XXV 11, d. 109 (rough draft of letter also found in AN, D XXV 5, d. 46).

[48] Account A, in CAOM, F 3 198.

The spread of the flames and the looting made those trapped in the city ever more desperate to reach the ships in the harbor. Captain Boerner, wounded on the first day of fighting, had been too weak from loss of blood to leave the bed on which his comrades had abandoned him. When he realized, however, that the house he was in was about to catch fire, "he threw himself, despite having had a ball through his body, on the floor next to his bed ... and ran, wrapped in a sheet, not having any other clothing, to the balcony to call for help." Two sailors took him prisoner and brought him to the *Jupiter*, where some men from his unit who had fought on Galbaud's side recognized him and freed him.[49] The American ship captain, Samuel Perkins, and his colleagues had left their possessions under the protection of their slaves when they fled to their vessel, even though their leader had told them "that he had been promised his liberty if he would join the rebels." When their black servants found themselves unable to keep plunderers out of the building, Perkins saw them in the harbor "wading off towards the ships;" he and a couple of sailors ended up rescuing the blacks who had tried to help them.[50]

Perkins's servants were not the only nonwhites who sought safety at the harbor. On the June 22, 1793, the officer keeping the log of the *Convention nationale*, one of the smaller warships, noted that "the townspeople are getting on the ships with their possessions and their slaves."[51] When ships from the convoy finally reached New York in early August, the French consulate recorded several family groups that included members of different races. Monsieur Baupaid, a merchant from Le Cap, landed with a tri-racial entourage consisting of his wife, their two-year-old son, the child's black nurse and the nurse's two five-year-old children, listed as "mulattoes;" they may have been his children. The same ship brought another white woman with a slave, as well as Marie Nouel Robert, a free black woman. The *Anarchisis*, originally from Nantes, reached New York with eighteen refugees from Le Cap, of whom four were black slave women accompanying their white mistresses; one had brought her own black child. The *Saint-Honoré* put nine refugee families ashore in Norfolk, of which five included black domestics.[52]

Female slaves who cared for their masters' children were probably the largest group who joined the exodus to the United States; they may

[49] Deposition of Boerner, in AN, D XXV 5, d. 53.
[50] Perkins, "Narrative," 342.
[51] Summary of log of *Convention nationale*, in AN, D XXV 54, d. 523, entry for June 22, 1793.
[52] "Rapatriement des réfugiés," in CADN, New York, 63.

have been genuinely reluctant to abandon their young white charges, and fearful of being left homeless as the city went up in flames. Unlike black men, they could not take advantage of the commissioners' offer of freedom in exchange for military service. A white man who had fled the city during the fighting reported that he had "encountered two female citizens and two black women who were all in tears, begging me to save their lives." He rowed them to a ship in the harbor.[53] Some male slaves also escaped on the ships. The captain of a ship called the *Félix* reported that he had carried "Nicolas, a Negro belonging to M. Jarrassay," who had come on board without his owner.[54] In addition to slaves, some free people of color also sailed with the convoy. Few men from this group are recorded; a number of accounts mention sailors forcing them to leave the ships before the convoy set sail. The situation was different for free women. An account published in a Philadelphia newspaper edited by an exiled Saint-Domingue journalist reported that "all the whites, the free women of color and a number of black slaves from Le Cap tried to escape," although the journalist also noted that "when the ships finally sailed, most of the women of color and the blacks who had taken refuge on them were cruelly sent back to shore."[55] A letter from the French consul in Charleston, Michel-Ange Mangourit, gleefully reporting to Genet that a South Carolina law banishing all individuals of African or part-African descent who had arrived in the state from the French colonies was forcing many of the white men from Saint-Domingue to say goodbye to their mistresses is evidence that a number of the latter had succeeded in joining their partners on the convoy.[56]

Even as the refugees were swarming onto the ships, Galbaud, on the *Jupiter*, still had not fully grasped the extent of the disaster his initiative had set off. The ship itself was a virtual battlefront: Admiral Cambis had to plead with angry sailors to keep them from killing the men of color who had been brought on board as prisoners.[57] Galbaud wrote out an order for the arrest of Sonthonax and Polverel if they tried to escape from the North Province, explaining that "the flight of Polverel and Sonthonax could cause movements among the brigands and the

---

[53] Dupuch to Sonthonax, September 5, 1793, in AN, D XXV 23, d. 236.
[54] "Rapatriement des refugiés," in CADN, New York 63.
[55] *Radoteur*, July 12, 1793.
[56] Mangourit to Genet, October 20, 1793, in CADN, Philadelphia 13 (correspondence from Charleston).
[57] "Déclaration de François Lapierre," in AN, D XXV 5, d. 53, translated in Popkin, *Facing Racial Revolution*, 224.

regenerated citizens [the men of color]."[58] He tried to persuade Cambis to transport him to some other part of the colony, "so that I can take charge of my government post."[59] When Cambis demurred, Galbaud summoned the captains of the other ships in the harbor to a meeting, at which he complained that the whites in the city were "cowards" who had not provided him with enough support, and that the warships had not provided the assistance he had counted on. Nevertheless, he had still not abandoned hope. "'Give me enough men, and tomorrow we'll make a third attempt which I am sure will succeed,'" he told the group, according to an eyewitness. "'The idea is impossible,' the merchant captains unanimously exclaimed, showing him the list of missing sailors, 'we have already lost a lot of men, and if a third attempt is equally unsuccessful, we won't have enough to get our ships back to France.'"[60]

Finally brought face to face with the failure of his project by the captains' refusal to back him, Galbaud was forced to start thinking about what he could do to limit the damage. The council agreed to send men ashore to set up a defensive perimeter around the arsenal and to save as many of the city's residents and as many supplies as they could; even Cambis set aside his quarrel with Galbaud for the moment to support this effort.[61] White residents of the city "saw flight as their only hope, everyone begged the men of color and even the slaves to escort them, everyone escaped however he could, and already almost all of the houses of Le Cap were left to the slaves," Saint-Maurice recalled. Refugees who were able to reach the waterfront were picked up by small boats and taken to ships in the harbor. Those trapped in the barracks had no food. They managed to send a delegation to Galbaud, begging for rations, but the general received them coldly, saying that he found it "strange that men who left him to his fate dare ask him for bread." Madame Galbaud, as always in the middle of things, persuaded him to change his mind, but the general was soon distracted by other matters and forgot his promise, leaving the refugees with empty stomachs in addition to their other miseries.[62] Unwilling to spare much thought for the civilian refugees, Galbaud did make an effort to rescue his brother, whom he proposed to trade for Polverel's son. Polverel rejected Galbaud's proposition and even

---

[58] AN, D XXV 48, d. 463.
[59] "Historic narrative," in Popkin, *Facing Racial Revolution*, 198.
[60] Account of Pierre-François Lachèze, July 7, 1793, in AN, D XXV 19, d. 186; deposition of Artau, in AN, D XXV 5, d. 53.
[61] Declaration of Cambis, in AN, D XXV 51, d. 489.
[62] "Historic narrative," in Popkin, *Facing Racial Revolution*, 197–8.

an offer made by the leaders of the free men of color to send one of their group as a hostage in the son's place. "I cannot consent to an exchange, because the delegates of the Republic cannot negotiate with Galbaud as they would with an enemy," Polverel wrote to Castaing and his colleagues. "They can only regard him as a rebel ... Any exchange made would be a crime against the sovereignty of the nation and a dishonorable act on my part."[63] Writing to a friend a few weeks afterward, when he still had no idea of his son's fate, Polverel said that Galbaud "had the audacity to propose to me to exchange him for his brother César Galbaud who was captured in arms at the head of a column of rebels. I don't need to tell you how I replied to him. You can imagine what I said. It is possible that I will never see my son again, it's the final sacrifice that remains for me to make."[64]

"All night and all morning, frequent fusillades at the arsenal and surrounding posts," Admiral Cambis noted in his ship's log on June 22. "Embarkation of women, children, and the slaves who stayed with them. Many citizens took refuge on the ships, instead of reinforcing the posts." Galbaud had been put back aboard the *Normande*, the ship on which he had been held before the start of the fighting, but he was still sending orders to the sailors. Among other things, he directed them to spike the guns of the city's forts to make sure they did not fire on the ships if they tried to depart. Meanwhile, Cambis tried to get the sailors to return to shore to help defend the arsenal, but, he noted, they showed more interest in getting their share of the goods in the state warehouse, which was now thrown open for looting, than in aiding the defense effort. Later in the day, he noted that "one began to see arriving in the city armed troops that were known to be those of Biassou and Jean-François, principal chiefs of the insurrection."[65] Cambis was correct that it was only now, two days after the start of the crisis, that organized bands of armed insurgents had entered the city, but these were not the men of Biassou and Jean-François. They were instead insurgents under the command of two local leaders, Pierrot and Macaya, who had responded to the commissioners' call for support in exchange for freedom.

In their report to the Convention, Sonthonax and Polverel, striving to convince the deputies that the destruction of Cap Français was outweighed by the new alliance with the blacks, claimed that these

[63] Polverel, letter of June 23, 1793, copy in AN, D XXV 12, d. 116.
[64] Polverel to Vernet, July 16, 1793, in AN, D XXV 5, d. 46.
[65] Cambis, log of *Jupiter*, in AN, D XXV 54, d. 521; Galbaud, order to spike guns, June 22, 1793, in AN, D XXV 48, d. 462; André Conscience, in AN, D XXV 14, d. 130.

former insurgents "begged on their knees to be allowed to fight for the French republic."[66] The journalist Saint-Maurice, who seems to have abandoned General Galbaud after the debacle on the morning of the June 21 and made his way to Haut du Cap, left what is probably a somewhat more accurate account of the encounter that resulted in the first alliance between the organized insurgents and the French republican authorities:

> Two troops of black rebels who had heard about the civil commissioners' proclamations appeared to put themselves under their orders. They advance, they are recognized, they enter the enclosure of Camp Breda in fairly good order and assemble in ranks across from the house occupied the civil commissioners. Their two leaders, Pierrot and Macaya, insist on their loyalty to the Republic and come to offer their arms and their soldiers. The civil commissioners give them their emancipation documents and tell them to await their orders. Then all the regular troops and free men in the general camp are assembled and put in battle formation at the head of the newly arrived slaves, and they are told that they are going to seize the arsenal. The cry of "Vive la République!" is heard all over. The commissioner Sonthonax makes all the leaders and then the entire troop take the oath to obey all the decrees of the National Convention, the orders of its delegates, and never to use their weapons except for the defense of the sole and indivisible Republic.

Sonthonax then gave a speech denouncing Galbaud but urging the motley army to treat the sailors as "'misled men'" and even "'to spare them, to welcome them into your midst,'"[67] and the column set off for Le Cap. The commissioners failed to comprehend the situation in the city: they optimistically assured a white officer that the arsenal would be retaken in two hours.[68] Rather than carrying out an organized attack on Galbaud's forces at the arsenal, however, this new republican army seems to have dissolved into the general chaos spreading across the city. A day after sending the black troops into the city, Sonthonax and Polverel had to order three of their free colored officers "to use all means in their power to drive the sailors out of the city of Le Cap, to stop the looting, and to make the Negroes return to their duty."[69]

Although they were not able to restore order in the city, much less win over the rebellious sailors, the rallying of these insurgent units to

[66] "Extrait de la lettre des commissaires civils, le 10 juillet 1793," in AN, D XXV 5, d. 52.
[67] "Historic narrative," in Popkin, *Facing Racial Revolution*, 200–1.
[68] Order to Bezos, June 22, 1793, in AN, D XXV 42, d. 409.
[69] Order of June 23, 1793, in AN, D XXV 7, file for June 6–26, 1793.

the commissioners was the first step toward the creation of a common front between the blacks of Saint-Domingue and the French Republic. Their apparent success in recruiting the principal representatives of the insurrection in their immediate vicinity raised Sonthonax's and Polverel's hopes that their proclamation of June 21, 1793 would bring the rest of the black movement to their side. After having made their agreement with Pierrot and Macaya on June 22, the commissioners issued orders to the commanders of the various armed posts guarding the roads to Le Cap not to take any action against the insurgent bands unless they were attacked. For the white forces that had been defending the approaches to the town and that had received no news about the crisis there, this change of policy was bewildering. Lieutenant Raison of the 18th infantry regiment spent the night of June 22 leading his men in a desperate firefight with a much larger black band; when he reported the action to Laveaux the next day, he was told "that I was supposed to treat those men as my brothers, and give them, in accordance with my means, the things they needed."[70] The commissioners also offered their long-time enemy Biassou a safe conduct to come to meet with them. Two free colored emissaries were authorized to "travel through this part of the North and, on our authority, order all the free men and even, if necessary, all other individuals who want to become free to join the regular troops."[71] The commissioners soon discovered, however, that convincing the former slaves of the good intentions of a French government that had opposed the insurrection for so long was going to be more difficult than they anticipated.

While the commissioners were taking the first steps to fuse the black insurgency with the French cause, the flames were devouring the city. "The nature of the merchandise in many of the French and American warehouses was such that it burned vividly, with occasional explosions, caused by the large quantities of brandy, rum, and other spirits left in them. Great quantities of oil, tar, and pitch contributed to feed and brighten the flame, so that all objects at a distance were distinctly visible," Samuel Perkins recalled. By nightfall, the separate fires that had started the previous day had grown into a single conflagration engulfing the entire town. Horrible though it was, "the sight of a great city in flames ... is sublime, and we sat watching the flames until daylight announced that something must be done for our own preservation and support."[72] On the evening of June 22, 1793, Cambis, who had temporarily regained

[70] Testimony of Lieutenant Raison, in AN, D XXV 80, d. 786.
[71] Orders in AN, D XXV 7, file for June 6–26, 1793.
[72] Perkins, "Narrative," 349.

VUE DE L'INCENDIE DE LA VILLE DU CAP FRANÇAIS,

FIGURE 7.2. View of the burning city.

"The sight of a great city in flames... is sublime," the American merchant Samuel Perkins wrote in his account of the events of June 20, 1793. He noted that the stores of sugar and coffee in the warehouses near the harbor fueled huge columns of fire, clearly seen in this contemporary engraving. In the foreground, small boats carry refugees to the ships in the harbor.

Source: © Musée d'Aquitaine, Bordeaux – Photo JM Arnaud.

authority over the *Jupiter*, convoked the other naval commanders for a meeting. Although they were still under formal orders from Sonthonax and Polverel not to leave Saint-Domingue, the commanders decided that they had no choice but to take matters into their own hands. The pleas of the merchant captains, who feared that the blacks on shore would try to set fire to the ships, the situation of the large number of refugees now on board the vessels, and the evident impossibility of saving the city seemed to justify their decision to escape. All the ships in the harbor were given orders to be ready to sail on the following day. Even the sailors of the *America*, who had refused to join in the attack on the commissioners, cooperated in helping to arrange ballast on the other warships.[73] (See Figure 7.2.)

[73] "Conseil de guerre extraordinairement convoqué. Séance du 22 Juin au soir," in AN, D XXV 19, d. 186; "Journal du vaisseau l'*America*, in AN, D XXV 54, d. 523.

The naval commanders justified their decision to set sail in part on the grounds that they were no longer able to communicate with the commissioners. Matters became more complicated on the morning of June 23, when the captains reconvened and learned that a package of orders from Sonthonax and Polverel had been delivered to the *Jupiter*. Among other things, the commissioners demanded that Cambis have Galbaud imprisoned on the *America*. The admiral attempted to carry out the order, but rebellious sailors brought Galbaud back to the *Jupiter* instead. After a lengthy debate, the captains sent two of their number, Daniel Vandongen and Augustin Truguet, to meet with the commissioners and make the case for the necessity of authorizing the ships to leave.[74] Sonthonax and Polverel reiterated their refusal to order the convoy's departure unless Galbaud and the two admirals, Cambis and Sercey, were first turned over to them, along with Polverel's son. According to Vandongen, "they were sure that [the convoy] had been betrayed to our enemies" and that the departure plan was a ruse to surrender it to the British. By the time the two captains returned to the *Jupiter*, however, the merchant fleet had acted on its own; Vandongen found "the whole convoy under sail and most of them beyond the outlet to the harbor."[75]

While Vandongen and Truguet had been carrying out their mission, Galbaud had succeeded in regaining control of the *Jupiter*. The crew remained loyal to him, and Admiral Cambis again found himself confined to his cabin. From below deck, Lapierre, a free man of color held as a prisoner on the ship, heard the sailors' "cries of 'Yes,' 'No,' 'Vive Galbaud,' 'Good patriot,' 'Long live Galbaud and the French Republic, etc.' He gathered from the words of the sailors that they were angry with Cambis ... they said 'He's scum, and it won't be long before we cut his throat; he's the agent of the fucking commissioners.'"[76] Cambis managed to let Admiral Sercey, on board the *Eole*, know that he was unable to exercise his command because of Galbaud's interference. Sercey convened yet another council of ships' captains and, with their approval, finally gave orders for the warships to accompany the merchant vessels.[77] On Galbaud's orders, all the remaining gunpowder from the arsenal was put on two captured British ships, which were then sunk in the harbor.

[74] Report of conseil de guerre, on board *Jupiter*, 7 a.m., June 23, 1793, in AN, AA 55, d. 1512.
[75] Vandongen, "Rapport," November 1, 1793, in SHM, BB 4 24.
[76] Cambis, "Journal du bord," in AN, D XXV 54, d. 521; deposition of Lapierre, cited in Popkin, *Facing Racial Revolution*, 226.
[77] Sercey, report of September 1, 1793, in AN, CC 9 A 8.

Because of the sailors' hostility to them, some of the free colored prisoners on the *Jupiter* and the *Eole* were killed, but most were either transferred to the *America* or put ashore.[78]

The departure of the ships made it clear to those whites remaining on shore that the colonial order was over forever. The journalist Saint-Maurice, who stayed behind, vividly imagined the feelings of the thousands of refugees on the departing ships: "Everyone wants to stop the vessel that flees with too much speed, everyone wants to touch for one last time, to at least moisten with his tears, the soil on which he was born, the soil that made him rich, this beloved and sacred soil that he tears himself away from so painfully. The man weeps for his missing wife, the wife cries out for the husband from whom she was separated, fathers and mothers seek their children ...The whistling of the wind, the prolonged and lugubrious calls through the megaphones, the sailors' cries, the sharp creaking of the masts, the hastiness of the departure add to the horror of this tableau."[79]

By the end of the day on June 24, 1793, the harbor, which for months had been crowded with ships waiting for the departure of the convoy, was virtually empty. Surveying the scene, the captain of the *America* counted only the *Jupiter*, the frigate *Fine*, which had been officially condemned as unseaworthy, the *Concorde* and the British prize ship the *Hyena*, along with some small merchant ships whose crews had abandoned them in favor of larger, safer vessels.[80] A final act of the drama in the harbor was played out on the *Jupiter*, the focus of so much agitation during the crisis and now crowded with hundreds of refugees in addition to its crew. All day long on June 24, the ship remained paralyzed by a confrontation pitting Galbaud against Cambis and his naval officers who refused to organize its departure unless the general relinquished his claim to command them. The sailors recognized that Galbaud was not competent to command the ship once it put to sea, but they were determined to keep the general safe and escort him back to France. Their stance was dictated not so much by loyalty as by their desire to make sure that the general would be on hand to take responsibility for the rebellion against the commissioners when they returned to France and faced the inevitable inquiry into the disaster of June 20, 1793. At midnight on June 24, 1793, apparently while Galbaud was sleeping, Cambis

[78] "Journal du vaisseau l'*America*," in AN, D XXV 54, d. 523, entry for 23–24 June 23–24, 1793; deposition of Lapierre, in AN, D XXV 5, d. 53.

[79] "Historic narrative," in Popkin, *Facing Racial Revolution*, 202.

[80] "Journal du vaisseau l'*America*," in AN, D XXV 54, d. 523.

summoned an assembly of the ship's crew. In exchange for his promise
to leave Galbaud under their protection, Cambis won the men's agreement to obey his orders. Transferring command of the naval forces in
Saint-Domingue to Truguet, the captain of the damaged *Fine*, Cambis
was finally able to follow the other ships of the convoy.[81] He could hardly
have imagined how much longer his duel with Galbaud for the crew's
loyalty was to last.

Before leaving, Cambis noted in his log that the fire in the city was
beginning to gutter out, since nearly all the houses had been consumed.
Contemporary maps indicate that some 85 percent of the buildings in Le
Cap had been burned; the only neighborhood that escaped unscathed
was the small suburb of the Petite Carénage, along the seashore north
of the arsenal.[82] The blacks who had taken over the city on the June 21
and 22, 1793 had either fallen victim to the conflagration or taken refuge
outside its boundaries. With the fleet gone and the flames giving way to
smoldering embers, Sonthonax and Polverel began to organize a cleanup
of the ruins. Already on June 23, they had issued an order authorizing
the seizure of any abandoned supplies of food found in the city.[83] By June
25, some semblance of regular administration began to reappear in the
city, with the commissioners issuing orders to the *commandant de la
place* to prevent further looting.[84] An edict calling on the remaining citizens to help patrol the city, issued on the June 26, was actually printed
on a press set up in the Carénage. Its lengthy denunciation of "the traitors, the conspirators, the counter-revolutionaries" whom it blamed for
the destruction of the city indicated the return of one form of normal-
ity: The commissioners had resumed expressing themselves in standard
revolutionary rhetoric.[85] (See Figure 7.3.)

The most painful task confronting the commissioners and the survivors was counting the dead. A white colonist remembered that "the
streets, recognizable between the ruins that were still smoldering, were
filled with bodies of all colors ... Orders were given to clear away these
horrible objects, which threatened to cause a plague. While the mulattoes
and blacks, gorged with loot, continued to enrich themselves, digging in
the smoking ruins, the unfortunate whites who had survived when their
houses burned, their fortunes destroyed, mistreated, dishonored, were

[81] Cambis, log of *Jupiter*, in AN, D XXV 54, d. 521.
[82] Map in Dufresne, "Considérations," opposite p. 198.
[83] AN, D XXV 7.
[84] Order to Galineau de Gascq, June 25, 1793, in AN, D XXV 42, d. 409.
[85] Edict of June 26, 1793, in CAOM, F 3 198 (Moreau de Saint-Méry papers).

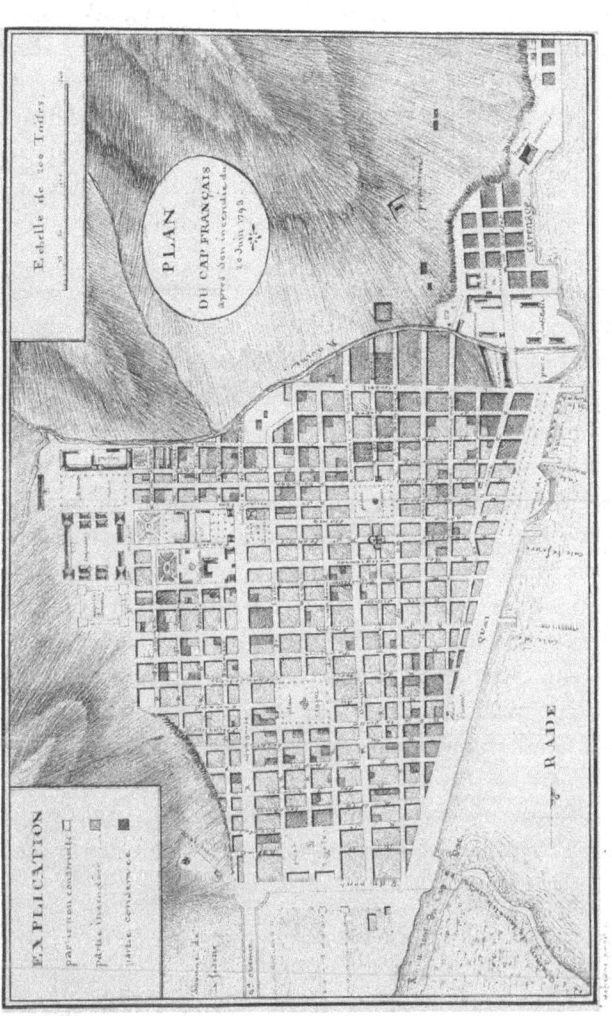

FIGURE 7.3. Cap Français after the fire.

A map from 1795 shows the extent of destruction caused by the fires that consumed Cap Français during the events of June 1793. Public buildings around the Government House and the area near the Arsenal were spared, but most of the rest of the city was reduced to ashes. Detailed maps from 1797 show that more than half of the buildings had been restored within a few years, but the city was set on fire again in 1802, when the French expeditionary force sent by Napoleon occupied the island. The city, now known as Cap Haïtien, retains its grid-like street plan, but the last vestiges of the buildings from the colonial era were demolished by a devastating earthquake in 1842.

Source: Bibliothèque nationale de France.

conscripted to carry away the stinking corpses. Villains, white like them, who had made themselves the vile ministers of the will of Polverel and Sonthonax, added to their suffering by insulting and outraging them."[86] In view of the circumstances, casualty figures were at best rough estimates. A note in Moreau de Saint-Méry's papers reported that "corpses of all parties and all colors infected the streets of Le Cap and made them insupportable. Using the remnants of wood from the burned houses, three great pyres were lit at the place d'Armes, the place Montarcher and the place Clugny and the bodies were thrown on them. Those found near the waterfront were thrown in the sea."[87] On a return visit to Le Cap in early August 1793, the American ship captain Perkins saw "bones ... lying in long rows across the squares in great masses" where the bodies had been burned.[88]

Estimates of the number of dead ranged from the figure of 1,200 cited by General Laveaux in a letter to his wife to totals of more than 10,000 mentioned by colonists hostile to Sonthonax and Polverel. In August 1793, the commissioners themselves wrote of "more than 3000" deaths.[89] A white volunteer who had fought on Galbaud's side gave figures of 1,500 to 1,800 white casualties and 6,000 blacks.[90] Most of the white population probably survived, but a number died, including, according to several accounts, invalids trapped in the city hospitals. Even harder to evaluate than the number of casualties was the loss of property. One survivor estimated it at between 120 and 140 million livres, a figure amounting to more than half of Saint-Domingue's annual exports before the Revolution, but this author added that others put the cost of the disaster as high as 300 million livres.[91] The losses in lives and property certainly exceeded those in any of the outbreaks of violence in Paris during the Revolution.

Regardless of what figure one accepts for the losses of life following the journée of June 20, 1793, there is little doubt that the majority of the

---

[86] Laplace, *Histoire des desastres de Saint-Domingue*, 302.
[87] CAOM, F 3 198 (Moreau de Saint-Méry papers).
[88] Perkins, "Narrative," 363.
[89] Laveaux to wife, August 1, 1793, in AN, D XXV 80, d. 786; colonists' estimate in AN, D XXV 76, register of Page and Brulley, entry for August 24, 1793; commissioners' estimate in AN, D XXV 5, d. 52, manuscript of article for no. 1 of *Affiches américaines*, August 11, 1793.
[90] Letter headed "Du bord de la Gentille dans la Baye de Chesapeake devant Hampton à la Nouvelle Angleterre le 9. juillet 1793," in CAOM, F 3 198 (Moreau de Saint-Méry papers).
[91] Letter of Perussel, August 4, 1793, in AN, D XXV 14, d. 130bis.

dead were blacks, killed either in the fighting in the city, in the clashes among looters described in many accounts, or in the ruins of buildings destroyed by the fire. Whereas the white casualties were mourned by relatives and friends spread throughout the Atlantic world, the blacks who died in Cap Français left no traces behind; no document seems to have preserved any of their names. For most white survivors, even those who acknowledged that they owed their own lives to black rescuers, the blacks were a mass of "assassins" and looters who deserved the fate they suffered. Some whites certainly were killed by blacks; as the city dissolved into chaos, with the armed men on Galbaud's side firing indiscriminately at every dark face they saw, it was inevitable that their targets would respond in kind. If they had stopped to think about the matter, blacks who participated in the looting might have said that they were simply imitating the white sailors, with the added justification that the wealth they were taking was the product of black labor. Doubtless, few of the fighters and looters on either side bothered to reflect on their motives; as the eyewitness accounts indicate, much of their behavior was fueled by the torrent of alcohol that they consumed during the fighting.

Sonthonax and Polverel, even though they acknowledged the role of blacks in the violence that destroyed the city, also insisted that the former slaves joined the melée to fight for their freedom. The truth, as we have seen, was more complicated. The crisis of June 20, 1793 was not simply an extension into the city of the slave uprising that had begun in August 1791, and there is little evidence that the city's own black slaves participated in the fighting on June 20 and the morning of June 21, although the black insurgents released from the prison joined the commissioners' forces. Fear of their slaves probably helped deter many whites from joining Galbaud's forces in the streets, and some blacks participated in the looting that began on the night of June 20, but most seem to have reacted as they had during the earlier confrontations between the whites and the free men of color on August 13–14, 1792 and December 2, 1792; that is, they waited to see how the conflict between the various groups of free people would end. Furthermore, there is no indication that the blacks who lived in the city were simply waiting for the opportunity to destroy it. A high proportion of the city's slaves were women, and some of them, at least, had meaningful emotional ties with whites, as their willingness to join their owners in fleeing to the ships showed. Many of Le Cap's slaves must have lost their own homes and the savings or *pécule* that they had been accumulating to buy their own freedom when the city was destroyed. If they helped themselves to their masters' property on

June 20 and 21, they no doubt did so in the hope of enjoying some of the comforts of their masters' urban lives, not with the thought that the city and the life it represented were about to disappear.

To the black insurgents who began to enter Le Cap on June 21, taking advantage of the power vacuum created by the flight of the commissioners and the panic of Galbaud's forces, the city meant something very different. Unlike the urban slaves, they were all men, and furthermore men who had already freed themselves from slavery. As events after June 21, 1793 were to prove, many of them saw no advantage to accepting legal emancipation on the restricted terms offered by the French. To these blacks, Cap Français was the visible symbol of the slaveholders' power, the bastion where the plantation owners had taken refuge, the fortified redoubt from which Laveaux's troops had ventured out to inflict painful defeats on them a few months earlier. If the city had fallen to them intact, they would not have known what to do with it: as their behavior throughout the Haitian Revolution consistently demonstrated, for most former plantation slaves, freedom meant either becoming soldiers or acquiring land of their own to cultivate. The city was profoundly alien to them, and they had little reason to care about its fate. The opportunity to plunder was undoubtedly welcome to them, and arson was one of the weapons they had regularly deployed to terrorize their enemies in the countryside; they may well have resorted to it in the city as well. It is not hard to imagine that some of the black casualties during the destruction of Le Cap were the result of clashes between insurgents from the countryside and black urban residents trying to protect their city.

It would thus be anachronistic to label all the blacks who died during the fighting and destruction of Cap Français as freedom fighters. Other motives – self-preservation and opportunism for the city's slaves, revenge and a desire to inflict a final defeat on the whites for the insurgents – also figured prominently, and the blacks certainly did not act as a unified group. The destruction of Le Cap nevertheless proved to be a turning point in the struggle for freedom in Saint-Domingue. Overnight, most of the white ruling class in the North Province disappeared, along with the soldiers and sailors who had represented the metropole's power in the colony. The free people of color, the "citizens of 4 April," remained, but their influence was greatly reduced. As soldiers, they were now outnumbered by the emancipated blacks, and many of them had lost their property in Le Cap. If they were to maintain any authority in the colony, the French republican commissioners were left with no alternative but to recruit supporters among the former slaves, and freedom was now the only thing they had to offer the blacks. The decree they had issued on June 21, 1793, before they realized how drastic the outcome of the crisis would be, still reflected their trepidation about taking such a radical step. The decree had furthermore failed in its immediate purpose of enabling the commissioners to save Cap Français. As they contemplated the city's smoking ruins and the piles of the dead, Sonthonax and Polverel still did not understand how far in the direction of abolition they were going to have to go to give themselves a chance to salvage French authority in Saint-Domingue.

8

The Road to General Emancipation

By nightfall on June 25, 1793, the city of Cap Français was little more than a field of blackened stone walls and smoldering rubble. The *Jupiter* had finally departed, taking with it General Galbaud, Admiral Cambis, the last of the mutinous sailors and soldiers who had attacked the city, and some 750 refugees; when they arrived in the United States, the American republic would become, together with Saint-Domingue itself and revolutionary France, one of the three arenas in which the events in Le Cap would set off struggles over the issue of slavery. While the survivors and the news of the events of June 20, 1793 began to make their way toward North America and Europe, however, the civil commissioners Sonthonax and Polverel had to deal with the consequences of the emancipation process they had begun during the five days of violence they had so narrowly survived. With Galbaud gone, they were once again the sole representatives of the French government in the colony. They could still count on the support of the free men of color, the "citizens of 4 April" with whom they had forged an alliance in the months before the crisis, but the newly freed "citizens of 20 June" now outnumbered the men of color among the commissioners' forces, compelling Sonthonax and Polverel to take their demands into account.

As they adjusted to this new situation, the commissioners still had to face the other problems that had confronted them before June 20, 1793. With the navy and many of the French troops now gone and Cap Français rendered defenseless by Galbaud's spiking of its forts' guns, the danger of invasion from Spanish Santo Domingo and British Jamaica and the loss of France's prized colony loomed larger than ever. Foreign invasion was only one of the threats facing the commissioners after the Galbaud crisis. Rebellious whites in the South Province were still resisting their authority: as they began restoring order in Cap Français, Sonthonax and Polverel learned that the army of free colored troops commanded by Pierre Pinchinat and André Rigaud that had been sent to reduce the colonists' stronghold of Jérémie had been driven back with heavy losses. "You would have shed a torrent of tears if you had witnessed the misfortune that has befallen my brothers," Rigaud wrote to the commissioners on June 21, 1793, unaware that they were facing far worse problems of their own.[1] Together with the disaster at Cap Français, this setback challenged the notion that the alliance Sonthonax and Polverel had forged with the free men of color was bound to be successful. The most recent news from France, dating to the middle of April, added to the commissioners' concerns. They knew they could not count on any fresh supplies, troops, or money from a metropole overwhelmed by its own crises; they also realized that their patrons, Brissot and his faction, were losing support in the National Convention, and that the white Saint-Domingue colonists whom Sonthonax had deported to Paris were gaining influence there.

Grim as the situation looked, there were some reasons for hope. Outside of the area around Jérémie, Sonthonax and Polverel no longer faced organized opposition from the white colonists, several thousand of whom had now left on the convoy. They had been promised help by the newly arrived French minister to the United States, Edmond Genet, who had been chosen, like them, by Brissot and charged, among other things, with obtaining funds and supplies for the French Antilles. Most importantly, the commissioners were now free to try to win over the colony's black population. Until June 20, 1793, despite their personal abolitionist sentiments, Sonthonax and Polverel had remained committed to upholding the institution of slavery and to bringing the insurrection to a conclusion that would see the slaves returned to their "duty" on the plantations. The terms of their mandate, the need to prevent a complete revolt among the island's whites, the reluctance of the free men of color to support emancipation, and the absence of encouragement from the Convention had served to limit their initiatives to promises to reform the institution of slavery, exemplified by their pacification of the revolt in Cul-de-Sac in April and their proclamation of May 5, 1793 reinstating Louis XIV's Code noir. The crisis they had faced on June 20, 1793 had driven both the commissioners and, equally importantly,

---

[1] Rigaud to Sonthonax and Polverel, June 21, 1793, in AN, D XXV 5, d. 51.

their supporters among the free men of color in Le Cap, to go beyond these limits. Several thousand armed blacks were now officially free men and French citizens. Nevertheless, the commissioners' appeal of June 21, 1793 was only a first step toward the abolition of slavery. It offered freedom only to former slaves who agreed to serve in the army, and it explicitly foresaw the continuation of slavery for the rest of the population, albeit with unspecified improvements in their condition.

Over the next four months, Sonthonax and Polverel would extend the scope of emancipation so that, by the end of October, all the slaves in the French-controlled portions of Saint-Domingue were legally free.[2] The best-known moment in this process, Sonthonax's decree of August 29, 1793 ending slavery in the North Province, was just one of a series of measures extending freedom to former slaves in certain categories, in certain parts of the colony, and under certain conditions. The incremental manner in which the decree of June 21, 1793 was broadened into a general proclamation of emancipation demonstrates that these measures were not a simple consequence of the commissioners' determination to apply the principles enshrined in the Declaration of the Rights of Man. Even after the crisis of June 20, 1793, Sonthonax and Polverel hesitated to take such a huge step. They were cautious about explaining to the Convention the extent of the emergency decision they had taken to ward off Galbaud's attack, particularly because the immediate result of their appeal to the blacks had been the destruction of the colony's richest city. True to the gradualist approach to abolition that they shared with Brissot and Raimond, they still tried to imagine procedures that would enable them to maintain control over the population, restore plantation production, and safeguard the colony's value to France.

Sonthonax and Polverel were driven toward general emancipation not so much by the logic of their principles as by the circumstances in which they found themselves, and above all by pressure from a black population that was now in a position to demand a better bargain than before the June crisis. Even as they gradually yielded to this pressure, however, Sonthonax and Polverel kept a wary eye on developments elsewhere in the Atlantic world. In the United States, the white refugees from Cap Français reconstituted the hostile milieu the commissioners had faced since their arrival in Saint-Domingue. From Baltimore and Philadelphia, the colonists were able to communicate with France more easily than the

---

[2] Robert [Louis] Stein, "The Abolition of Slavery in the North, West, and South of Saint Domingue," *The Americas* 41 (1985), 54.

commissioners; for months, the National Convention listened to their pleas and threatened to disavow everything Sonthonax and Polverel had done. The Convention's decree of February 4, 1794 upholding the abolition of slavery in Saint-Domingue and calling for emancipation in the other French colonies was not simply the inevitable consequence of the two men's initiatives, but rather the outcome of hard-fought political struggles, not only in the Caribbean, but in the port cities of the United States and in metropolitan France.

The first theater in which the battle over emancipation was fought was in Saint-Domingue itself, and the first opponents the commissioners had to face were, ironically, the black insurgents who had already asserted their own freedom by joining the insurrection. Although they had had no direct contact with the participants in the insurrection in the North Province until their meeting with Pierrot and Macaya at Haut-du-Cap on June 22, 1793, Sonthonax and Polverel had been confident of their ability to win over the slave population if they ever chose to do so. Sonthonax's boast to Admiral Cambis on June 19, 1793 that he could "create 400,000 soldiers with one whistle" was testimony to his belief that the slaves were simply waiting for a signal to join the French cause, and that in spite of the efforts its forces had made after August 1791 to defeat the insurrection, the black population would recognize that France truly was the country of liberty.[3]

Sonthonax's optimism reflected a profound misunderstanding of the insurgency. In February 1793, after interrogating whites found in the areas captured from the insurgents during Laveaux's offensive, he himself had reported to the Convention that the blacks had their own program, one that was clearly at odds with French republican ideas. The ease with which he and Polverel had pacified the slave revolt in the West Province, an area where the plantations had remained largely intact, may have misled the commissioners into thinking that they could achieve the same result in the north, where the black population had been creating its own society for a year and a half and where the French campaign of January 1793 had left painful memories. Rather than acknowledging that the participants in the black insurrection might have their own reasons for rejecting French revolutionary dogmas, however, Sonthonax chose to explain the blacks' behavior as evidence that they had been misled by counterrevolutionary conspirators: these "simple men" did not understand their own interests.[4]

---

[3] Cambis, letter to Sonthonax and Polverel, June 20, 1793, in AN, D XXV 51, d. 489.
[4] Sonthonax to Convention, February 18, 1793, in AN, D XXV 5, d. 48.

While the January campaign had left the commissioners' forces in control of many of the insurgents' former strongholds, the spread of the European war to the Caribbean in the spring of 1793 offered the black forces a new opportunity. From the start of the uprising in 1791, the Spanish in Santo Domingo had discreetly encouraged the insurgents. A French journalist noted that the Spanish had refused to aid the embattled French whites on the grounds that revolutionary France was a country "that no longer had a king or religion," indicating that they shared some of the values upheld by the slaves.[5] The Spanish had only limited forces in the island, but once the war started in 1793, they were willing to recruit the blacks as allies and to appoint their leaders as officers in the Spanish army. In return, Jean-François assured the Spaniards that he was ready to fight to "defend the right of his Majesty, that we will spill the last drop of our blood to support this good prince who has suffered all the obstacles and martyrdom in the world, from a troop of his barbarous people who failed to respect the crown and the throne of his Majesty in dethroning the king and imprisoning him to make whatever laws they wished."[6]

These approaches from the Spanish gave the black leaders hopes of recovering from their losses in January 1793 and, even more importantly, of persuading one or the other of the competing colonial powers to recognize their freedom. In particular, in the course of the summer of 1793, the most capable and articulate of the black generals would adopt the name under which he would become famous – Toussaint Louverture – and would make it increasingly clear that he was fighting for "liberty and equality," the fundamental rights that Sonthonax and Polverel claimed to be bringing to Saint-Domingue. For some ten months after the destruction of Cap Français and the first French offer of freedom, however, Toussaint would also make it clear that he considered the prospects for emancipation under the Spanish more attractive and more realistic than the offers emanating from the French; even Sonthonax's proclamation of general emancipation on August 29, 1793 failed to win him over. Without the support of at least some substantial fraction of the black insurgents, Sonthonax and Polverel had little prospect of successfully implementing their emancipation policy.

The black insurgents' efforts to play the French and Spanish off against each other had begun even before the crisis of June 20, 1793. As

---

[5] *Gazette universelle*, November 25, 1791.
[6] Jean-François to Don Bienithe Tabert, n.d., in AN, D XXV 20, d. 198.

we have seen, at the beginning of June, Pierrot, one of the insurgent leaders who joined Sonthonax and Polverel on June 22, 1793, wrote a letter apparently addressed to General Galbaud, who was at that moment the highest French authority in the North Province, telling him that "one of our brothers ... has told us that you had ordered him to communicate to us that it is your intention to give us general liberty and that you want us to be the defenders of the colony and the French nation. I ask you, general, to give us written assurance so that we can respond to your request. I warn you that Spain and the English propose to give us general liberty and even that we are furnished with everything. We know that you have been told that we have received arms from the Spanish and this is true, but up to this moment we hope for your assurance."[7] There is no indication that Galbaud ever considered such a drastic step, but Pierrot clearly thought that there was a possibility of obtaining important concessions by challenging the French to match the offers being made by their enemies.

The outbreak of fighting in Cap Français on June 20, 1793 opened new possibilities for the insurgent leaders and set off a wideranging debate among them. Once Pierrot and Macaya had accepted their offer of emancipation for their soldiers in exchange for joining the struggle against Galbaud and the sailors, Sonthonax and Polverel tried to broaden this tactical alliance with the insurgents closest to Le Cap into an agreement with the insurrection's top leaders. The first replies to the messages they tried to send to Toussaint, Biassou and Jean-François were discouraging: on June 25, 1793, Toussaint, camped at Bassin Cayman, told Nully, the commander of the chain of French posts known as the cordon de l'Ouest that had successfully kept the insurgents from invading the West Province, that he and his men were fighting "to gain the protection and under the orders of his Catholic Majesty [the king of Spain]; in consequence they will never negotiate with the civil commissioners, whose authority they do not recognize, they can add that having fought up to now alongside their brothers to uphold the right of the king, they will all shed the last drop of their blood to defend the Bourbons to whom they have promised unswerving loyalty to the death."[8] Toussaint nevertheless agreed to a truce with the French forces facing him, and even added the signatures of some thirty of his officers to his letter, indicating that

---

[7] Pierrot to "Citoyen général," in AN, AA 54, d. 1509. A note on the letter, presumably from Galbaud, indicates that the letter was passed to him by his free colored aide-de-camp.

[8] Copy of letter from Toussaint and Moyse, June 25, 1793, in AN, D XXV 20, d. 200.

he had communicated the news of the commissioners' offer to them.[9] Meanwhile, Jean-François saw the destruction of Le Cap as an opportunity to gain the upper hand over the weakened French. On June 27, 1793, the black leader wrote to Candy, a free colored military leader who had initially supported the August 1791 uprising before going over to the French camp, to tell him, "I have 60 whites from Le Cap who arrived on the 26th of this month, telling me about the disaster that happened at Le Cap ... Come here with two of your men; you are awaited with open arms to do like me and join the crown of Spain."[10]

While the commissioners were waiting to hear from the main insurgent leaders, they were discovering that the blacks who had agreed to fight on their side had their own notions about future policy. The royalist municipal official Mahé de Corméré, who had followed Sonthonax and Polverel to Haut du Cap during the fighting, claimed to have witnessed an interview between the two men and Macaya on June 26, 1793. The black leader allowed Sonthonax's mistress to adorn him with a large tricolor ribbon, but he had little interest in adopting the commissioners' political ideas or in putting himself under their authority. "I don't know your 'Public," he told them, "but long live the King; furthermore, you know that I have generals who are my superiors. I respect them, they are Jean-François and Biassou. You say that you commissioners of the 'Public are the fathers of the blacks, but the Spanish love us like a good mother. I think that fathers and mothers should be good friends, and if you like, I'll arrange all that with Jean-François and Biassou." Macaya, a man with a talent for vivid language, would soon return to his alliance with the Spanish; when the commissioners tried again to win him over, he reportedly told them, "I am the subject of three kings: of the King of Congo, master of all the blacks; of the King of France who represents my father; of the King of Spain who represents my mother. These three Kings are the descendants of those who, led by a star, came to adore God made man," thus reaffirming his combination of royalist and religious convictions.[11]

---

[9] Letter signed by Toussaint, Moyse, and other officers, June 26, 1793, with postscript dated June 27, in AN, D XXV 20, d. 199.

[10] Jean-François to Candy, from camp of Serca, June 27, 1793, in AN, D XXV 12, d. 117.

[11] Mahé de Corméré, in AN, D XXV 14, d. 127, pp. 64n-66n ; Pamphile de Lacroix, *La Révolution de Haïti* (orig. title *Mémoires pour servir à l'histoire de la Révolution de Saint-Domingue*), ed. Pierre Pluchon (Paris: Karthala, 1995, 167, trans. in Dubois and Garrigus, eds., *Slave Revolution*, 128.

Although Jean-François's initial reaction to the news of the crisis at Le Cap had been to try to win over the commissioners' supporters, he and Biassou did meet with envoys from Sonthonax and Polverel on June 28, 1793 and considered coming over to the French side, although not without conditions. "We were quite charmed by your proclamation," the black generals wrote in a joint letter. "We had declared a truce between our men and also held an assembly in the presence of your deputies to prepare nine thousand men to appear before you in triumph." They had stopped these preparations, however, when they received word from Bassin Cayman that the French forces were attacking their positions. Bassin Cayman was the location of Toussaint's camp, and it was his troops who had been involved in this incident; Biassou and Jean-François wrote that they had authorized Toussaint to defend himself. Deliberately or not, Toussaint thus played a key role in keeping the two sides apart.[12] On the same day that Jean-François and Biassou wrote their letter, Toussaint also arrested four emissaries sent by Sonthonax and Polverel and turned them over to the Spanish commander of the border town of San Rafael.[13] Jean-François and Biassou were not as hostile to the commissioners. They claimed to be excited to hear that "you were for us as well as all of those of color ["toutes la couleur"] and asserted that they were "ready to change against the Spanish knowing that we are French and we always will be." Before committing themselves, however, they demanded proof that Sonthonax and Polverel had ordered the end of hostilities against their forces. "After your reply you will see us return with your two deputies, triumphing," they concluded.[14]

This was as close as the black insurgent leaders came to joining the commissioners; within a few days, they had definitively sealed their alliance with the Spanish. On July 2, 1793, Jean-François wrote to Pierrot, denouncing his collaboration with the French: "How is it that for two years and ten months [sic] you have fought for the right of our good king, and today when you have learned that the crown of Spain supports us, you let yourself be carried away by the voice of these Messieurs Commissioners ... The best thing would be to try to seize these civil commissioners and send them so we can turn them over to the Spanish."[15]

---

[12] Letter of Biassou and Jean-François, "Aux gouvernement de la mine," June 28, 1793, in AN, D XXV 12, d. 118.

[13] Cabrera to Casasola, June 29, 1793, in Monte y Tejada, *Historia*, 4: 52.

[14] Letter of Biassou and Jean-François, "Aux gouvernement de la mine," June 28, 1793, in AN, D XXV 12, d. 118.

[15] Jean-François to Pierrot, July 2, 1793, in AN, D XXV 12, d. 118.

The black leaders' decision to side with the Spaniards was at least partly the result of an extensive campaign of flattery and seduction. The priest of the Spanish border town of Laxavon, Father Josef Vasquez, played a key role in courting the black generals. "I put all my confidence in you," Father Vasquez wrote to Jean-François on July 2, thanking him for forwarding his copies of his correspondence with Candy and Toussaint. The Spanish commander Cassasola joined in the letter-writing campaign the next day, assuring Jean-François of his belief that the black general "was incapable of doing anything against the interests of the King of Spain," and Vasquez wrote again, offering sympathy for a toothache from which Jean-François had been suffering and adding, "I hope in God who will help you, since your main object is the good cause and the re-establishment of order."[16]

Having sealed their alliance with the Spanish, Jean-François and Biassou now became their allies' agents in trying to win over the supporters of the commissioners. On July 6, 1793, the two generals, whose forces had laid siege to the key position at La Tannerie, wrote to its defenders, saying "We exhort you in the name of the apostolic and Roman Catholic church and we would sacrifice ourselves to see you under the protection of the King of Spain like all the other white men who are well regarded and receive a thousand favors ... In addition, the King of Spain offers to compensate all whites for their slaves and their land. They will not lose their fortunes." A letter to the commissioners, written on the same day, reiterated the generals' loyalty to the French and Spanish monarchies and rejected any possibility of an arrangement with the representatives of the Republic. "We cannot possibly recognize civil commissioners until you have found a king and followed this law. We could make arrangements that would be equally advantageous to white citizens and people of any color," they concluded.[17] Two days later, Jean-François assured Father Vasquez that he had been in contact with Pierrot and that the latter was ready to revert to the Spanish side.[18]

Not only did the commissioners fail to win over the main leaders of the insurrection, but they were barely able to hold the loyalty of the

[16] Letters of Father Vasquez, July 2 and 3, 1793, and Cassasola, July 3, 1793, in AN, D XXV 12, d. 117.

[17] Jean-François and Biassou, letters of July 6, 1793, in AN, D XXV 12, d. 118. The Spanish had offered support and compensation to French whites who came over to them even before the crisis of June 20, 1793. Cassasola's proclamation of June 7, 1793 to this effect was published in the Philadelphia émigré journal, the *Radoteur*, on July 9 1793.

[18] Jean-François to Vasquez, July 8, 1793, in AN, D XXV 12, d. 118.

one black commander who had joined them at the moment of the crisis of June 20, 1793. On July 9, Pierrot wrote to tell them that the only way to maintain the loyalty of their newly recruited black troops was to reach an agreement with Jean-François that included provisions for "general liberty." Time was of the essence, Pierrot warned, because "we were on the point of finishing with you."[19] The commissioners replied by telling Pierrot that he was in danger of putting his men back under the banner of "the kings, and consequently that of slavery ... Who sold you to the whites, it is the kings, who is it who sells black boys and girls to the Spanish? It is Jean-François and Biassou." Only the French, the commissioners insisted, would grant the blacks "general liberty; it is definitely our intention and that of the French nation to see that you get it, but everything has to be earned in this world, and you will only have it when you imitate the blacks of Le Cap, when you bear arms for the Republic."[20] At the same time, they warned other military commanders not to trust Pierrot or his men.[21]

As many of the black leaders' letters indicate, the religious and monarchist values of the Spanish made them more congenial allies than the French and their unfamiliar Republic. Other considerations also militated in favor of the Spanish alliance. The Spanish were prepared to let the black generals operate on their own, whereas the French wanted to integrate them into their own command structure, and Jean-François and Biassou were eager to regain control of the positions at La Tannerie and Dondon, which they had lost in January. Furthermore, the outcome of the crisis of June 20, 1793 and the news from Europe transmitted by the Spanish convinced the black leaders, not unreasonably, that the French revolutionary government had slim chances of survival. Throughout the spring of 1793, the reports arriving in the Americas told of one setback after another for the republican cause: the royalist uprising in the Vendée, Dumouriez's treason, the renewed Austrian invasion from Belgium, violent dissensions in the Convention and in the French provinces. Toussaint, who retook La Tannerie on July 5, 1793, had a captured French sergeant write to his comrades in Dondon telling them that further resistance was pointless: "Paris is burned ... the Spanish have taken seven or eight towns from the French."[22] "Le Cap is lost

---

[19] Pierrot to "commissioner," July 9, 1793, in AN, AA 55, d. 1512.
[20] Commissioners to Pierrot, July 13, 1793, in AN D XXV 43, d. 415.
[21] Commissioners to Dubuisson, July 13, 1793, in AN, D XXV 42, d. 409.
[22] Etienne Brandicourt to Sonthonax and Polverel, July 7, 1793, in AN, D XXV 20, d. 202.

to the nation forever as well as the rest of the colonies," Jean-François wrote to the defenders of Dondon on July 9, 1793.[23] Compared to all these other considerations, the French commissioners' narrowly framed emancipation offer did not impress the black leaders.

By the end of the first week of July, Sonthonax and Polverel were forced to recognize that they had lost their bid for the support of the main insurgent leaders. Biassou and Jean-François would remain loyal to the Spanish to the end; when Spain made peace with the French in 1795, Biassou became the commander of a black militia unit in the Spanish colony of Florida, and Jean-François crossed the Atlantic to settle in Cadiz.[24] In May 1794, Toussaint Louverture would finally abandon the Spanish and rally to the French cause, but only after Sonthonax and Polverel in Saint-Domingue and the revolutionary government in France had overcome the worst of the crises facing them and after the French National Convention had passed its own emancipation decree.[25] In July 1793, having failed to persuade the insurgent leaders, the commissioners had to appeal directly to the former slaves to abandon the chiefs who had led their movement since 1791. They had little other choice: every day after Galbaud's attack seemed to bring more bad news from the rest of the colony. From the South Province, the commissioners' former secretary Delpech, whom they had appointed as an emergency replacement for the defector Ailhaud, wrote of the "terrible state of distress we are in," a plea followed a few days later by the news of Rigaud's defeat by the whites of Jérémie. Shortly thereafter, Nully, the commander of the vital cordon de l'Ouest, became the first of a series of high-ranking white officers to abandon his post. Lieutenant-colonel Paul, who stepped in to replace him, reported that his men would not obey his orders and that the blacks employed for noncombat tasks were deserting, seduced by "those who have sworn to serve the Spanish, the king of France and religion." From the harbor came news that the sailors on the *America*, the only major warship left in the colony, were pressuring their captain to take them back to France. On June 29, 1793, François Pageot, the commander in Fort Dauphin, wrote, "My hand trembles as I set down the sad news of the capture of Ouanaminthe by the Spanish and the brigands."

[23] Jean-François, letter of July 9, 1793, in AN, D XXV 12, d. 118.
[24] David Geggus, "The Slave Leaders in Exile: Spain's Resettlement of its Black Auxiliary Troops," in Geggus, *Haitian Revolutionary Studies*, 185, 197–200.
[25] David Geggus, "The 'Volte-Face' of Toussaint Louverture," in Geggus, *Haitian Revolutionary Studies*, 119–36.

Left without supplies, the starving garrison had surrendered without a fight.[26]

On July 2, 1793, a week after the departure of the fleet, Sonthonax and Polverel published a proclamation summarizing a situation that seemed desperate in every respect. In addition to Galbaud and his followers, whose revolt had led to the destruction of Le Cap, they denounced a long series of traitors, including the whites in the South, who had, among other things, "armed hordes of slaves" to fight on their side, and the army officers who had abandoned their commands of the cordon de l'Ouest and Ouanaminthe to the Spanish. Sonthonax and Polverel invoked familiar Jacobin rhetoric to denounce their foes, insisting that "the conspirators are almost all the Europeans transplanted to Saint-Domingue, some sunk under their debts despite their air of opulence, the others eager for pillage, because they own nothing. They are the majority of the leaders of the military units from France, who only preferred Saint-Domingue to Coblentz because they thought they could serve the counterrrevolution better there." But they refused to despair. Freed from the necessity of respecting the sensibilities of the white population, Sonthonax and Polverel referred openly to the rights of man and announced their alliance with the free men of color and the Africans. "The citizens of April 4 1792, those of June 20 1793, and those who we will eventually raise to the dignity of free men, will not forget that of all the European powers, the French Republic is the only one that knows how to respect the rights of man, and that they cannot preserve the civil and political rights that they have received from her except by rallying around her delegates, by fighting for her and driving back the enemy, by uniting all parts of the island under the tricolor flag."[27]

Although the wording of their proclamation held out the promise of eventual emancipation for the whole of the slave population, Sonthonax and Polverel were still far from ready to proclaim general emancipation. The last instructions they had received from the Convention, the law of March 5, 1793, had authorized them to take all necessary steps for the defense of the colony; arming slaves to fight Galbaud certainly fell under that heading. The law had also authorized them to make changes

---

[26] Delpech to Sonthonax and Polverel, June 16, 1793, in AN, D XXV 12, d. 113; Sonthonax and Polverel to Nully, in AN, D XXV 42, June 24, 1793; Paul to Sonthonax and Polverel, June 27 and 29, 1793, in AN, D XXV 20, d. 199; Sonthonax and Polverel to crew of *America*, June 26, 1793, in AN, D XXV 42; Pageot to Sonthonax and Polverel, June 29, 1793, in AN, D XXV 20, d. 198.

[27] Proclamation of July 2, 1793, in AN, D XXV 5, d. 52.

in the regulations governing slave labor, but whether this extended to abolishing slavery altogether was hardly clear. Furthermore, the commissioners, true to the gradualist assumptions to which they had always adhered, were worried about the prospect of complete anarchy if all restrictions on the black population disappeared. They also had to take into consideration possible reactions to their policy in the United States, such as those mentioned by two republican officials in Port-au-Prince who, apparently acting on their own, wrote to the French minister Genet on June 29, 1793 urging him to denounce any rumors that Galbaud and his supporters might spread that "the general enfranchisement of the slaves has been decreed." They feared that "this calumny [might] prevent that aid and subsistence which we should expect from the United States, and cause all kind of shipments to this Island to cease."[28] In their decree, Sonthonax and Polverel were therefore determined to show that they were still in control of the black population. Although they repeated their offer to free slaves who enrolled in their army, they now set a deadline of July 8, 1793 for blacks wanting to take advantage of it, and they ended with a stiff warning that ex-slaves found carrying arms on their own would be "considered to be in revolt, and will be arrested and punished accordingly." Blacks found roaming at large, even if unarmed, were also threatened with punishment. The vocabulary of the slave system lived on in the proclamation: its Creole version warned slaves that they could only circulate with a pass, or "billet," and the versions in both languages used the word "marron" or "runaway" to denounce vagabonds.[29]

As they struggled to win over the black insurgents, Sonthonax and Polverel also had to reconstruct some kind of government in Le Cap. Mahé de Corméré, still concealing his seething hostility to the commissioners in order to survive in their camp at Haut du Cap, noted that they had constituted a small council of their white and free colored loyalists. The members included Laveaux and Galineau de Gascq, the military commander of the city, Vergniaud, Gignoux, whom Mahé identified as a "toothpuller," Boucher, the white head of the Interim Commission, and the free men of color who had been members of that institution, Michel, Castaing, and Boisrond, together with Dufay and

[28] Letter from Wante and Desfourneaux, June 29, 1793, in *Philadelphia General Advertiser*, July 30, 1793.
[29] Printed versions of proclamation of July 2, 1793 in French and Creole, in CAOM, F 3 198 (Moreau de Saint-Méry papers).

Castaing's two white brothers-in-law, Garnot and Robquin.[30] The abbé de la Haye, who had been held in prison since January on suspicion of complicity with the black insurgents, had been released and made a member of the council; probably Sonthonax and Polverel hoped that his firsthand acquaintance with Biassou would facilitate negotiations with him.[31] The composition of the group signaled the continuation of the commissioners' dependence on Castaing's circle and on the small group of their white supporters. There were no representatives of the newly freed "citizens of 20 June."

Castaing, who had lost his own house in the fire, remained loyal to the commissioners,[32] but other free men of color were not necessarily pleased to find themselves heavily outnumbered by black fighters. A report published in a Philadelphia émigré newspaper mentioned "the discouragement and distrust of the men of color, irritated by the armed blacks whose number had increased." According to this account, the commissioners had surrounded themselves with "African guards," while a number of the men of color had held an assembly at which threats to the commissioners had been voiced.[33] The commissioners themselves complained about the reluctance of the free men of color to accept their emancipation policy. "You have aristocrats of the skin, just like the whites; aristocrats who are even more inconsequent, even more ungrateful than the whites, because they only [show contempt] for their children and don't keep them perpetually in chains, whereas you declare yourself the enemies of your fathers, it is your fathers who you want to keep forever in slavery," they wrote to one of them.[34]

On July 4, 1793, the commissioners were finally able to return to Cap Français and install themselves in the Petit Carénage section that had escaped the fire. By July 11, 1793, they had resuscitated one of Cap Français's newspapers, the *Affiches américaines*, and used it lay out their plans. An article in the paper outlined their dilemma: "One cannot hide from oneself the effect that the enchanting word of *liberty* has had in all heads in Saint-Domingue. The more one might try to oppose strong dikes to this impetuous current, the more one would prolong the days of

---

[30] Robquin and Garnot were married to Castaing's sisters Françoise and Marthe. (Noel, "Le Sang Noir des Castaing," 174.) Later in the year, Sonthonax had Dufay and Garnot sent to Paris as deputies to the National Convention.

[31] Mahé de Corméré, in AN, D XXV 14, d. 127, p. 63n.

[32] Commissioners to La Salle, June 27, 1793, in AN, D XXV 43, d. 415.

[33] *Radoteur*, July 26, 1793.

[34] Commissioners to Duvigneau, July 18, 1793, in AN, D XXV 43, d. 415.

murder, fire and pillage. On the other hand, however, a sudden universal liberty would make the African people into a people of brigands, without restraint, without laws, without government, and left to the fury of its passions." The offer that had been made of liberty to any slave who would join the army "will cause a general revolution among all the Africans: all will want to serve the Republic to become free; all will want their wives and their children to be free like them; and among a people who naturally love combat, there will soon be no more cultivators. That is the difficulty we must avoid." The solution proposed in the article, probably composed by the commissioners themselves, was eminently gradualist. The slaves would first be given one free day a week to work on their private plots, and then another day during which they could hire themselves out to earn money, "and when it will be clear that the blacks are not misusing this concession, one can give them another day, and so on up to the whole of the week." Even in the chaotic conditions following the destruction of Cap Français, the dream of a controlled reform of slavery that would not affect the plantation owners or the economy remained alive.[35]

By the time this article appeared in print, the blacks in Cap Français had already succeeded in obtaining one of the concessions it mentioned: on July 11, 1793, the commissioners decided that, in order to keep the loyalty of their troops, they had no choice but to promise freedom to the families of the newly emancipated soldiers. "It was necessary to also free their wives and children," the commissioners wrote to the Convention, "and to make this just measure profitable for morals and public decency, we have ordered that the warriors who want to emancipate their wives must marry them according to the forms established by the decree of the National Assembly."[36] As historian Elizabeth Colwill has noted, the decree made freedom for women dependent on their association with a liberated man, and it imposed a European model of family structure on the new citizens.[37] Whether the black soldiers appreciated the moralizing terms of the Creole version of the decree, which informed them that "anyone who takes one woman today and leaves her for another tomorrow is not good," is unknown.[38] Not the least of the commissioners'

---

[35] *Affiches américaines*, July 11, 1793. This, the only copy of the paper published in Le Cap after June 20, 1793, appeared in a small single-column format, much reduced from the paper's previous size.

[36] Sonthonax and Polverel to Convention, July 30, 1793, in AN, D XXV 5, d. 52.

[37] Colwill, "'Fêtes de l'Hymen, Fêtes de la Liberté,'" in Geggus and Fiering, eds., *World of the Haitian Revolution*, 132–3.

[38] Proclamation of July 11, 1793, Creole version, in CAOM, F 3 198 (Moreau de Saint-Méry papers).

preoccupations was the question of how to present the situation of the colony to the French government. Although they had received no direct news from France for more than three months, they knew that the exiled white colonists had been mounting a campaign against them; among the long list of those they denounced to the Convention in their first report on the destruction of Le Cap were Pierre-François Page and Augustin-Jean Brulley, the chief colonial lobbyists in Paris.[39] They had to anticipate that accounts of the events of June 20, 1793 from Galbaud and the colonists on the convoy would arrive in France before their own letters; aware that their predecessor, Governor Blanchelande, had been turned over to the Revolutionary Tribunal for much lesser offenses, they could easily imagine their fate if they were held responsible for the disaster that had befallen the colony's most important city. Even before they wrote to the Convention, the two men drafted letters denouncing Galbaud to the French minister Genet and to some of the French consuls who were presumably going to be the first to encounter the refugees.

The commissioners had already been in correspondence with Genet before the crisis, and although the three men had never met, they knew that he was also one of Brissot's protégés. Genet, who had been the French representative in Saint Petersburg since 1789, had not returned to Paris until September 1792, three months after the civil commissioners' departure for Saint-Domingue.[40] "Lieutenant of Dumouriez in the Army of the North, [Galbaud] professed here the principles of his patron, his friend, and it is his intrigues, his maneuvers, his unbelievable audacity that brought about the catastrophe that almost annihilated the capital of Saint-Domingue," Sonthonax and Polverel told Genet. Their letter stressed the courage and loyalty of the free men of color; rather than mentioning their offer to free the blacks in return for support, the letter spoke of the slaves "arming themselves." Having thrown as much blame as possible on Galbaud and depicted themselves as innocent victims of a conspiracy, they ended their letter with a plea for more supplies.[41] A similar letter went to Mangourit, the French consul in Charleston, South Carolina, warning him against the stories the refugees were likely to spread.[42]

---

[39] Sonthonax and Polverel to Convention, July 10, 1793, in AN, D XXV 52, d. 52.
[40] Claude Moisy, *Le Citoyen Genet. La Révolution français à l'assaut de l'Amérique* (Paris: Privat, 2007), 107.
[41] Commissioners to Genet, July 8, 1793, draft with corrections in Sonthonax's handwriting, in AN, D XXV 11, d. 109.
[42] Sonthonax and Polverel to Mangourit, July 8 or 9, 1793, in AN, D XXV 5, d. 52.

Having rehearsed their lines several times, Sonthonax and Polverel were now ready to write to the National Convention. Their strategy was to emphasize the scale of the "great catastrophe" Galbaud had unleashed, and to contrast it with the positive results their own policies had achieved in the rest of the colony up to the moment of the crisis. "The West Province had been pacified: the leaders and known agents of the royalists and the aristocrats of the skin had been put under arrest on the ships of the convoy," they wrote, and they insisted on their success in getting the "25,000 insurgent blacks in the parish of Croix-des-Bouquets" to return to work. Meanwhile, Galbaud had landed in Le Cap and spread disorder by revealing how much value the French revolutionary paper currency had lost. Although they accused Galbaud of behaving like a dictator and ignoring their authority, the commissioners admitted that they had had little direct evidence of his intentions. To strengthen the case against him, they cited "the continual declamations against the Republic" of César Galbaud, denounced in the depositions of their henchmen Dufay, Robquin, and Vergniaud, which were attached to their report. After explaining how they put the general on board a ship in the harbor, they accused him of having "resuscitated the old quarrels between the sailors and the citizens of color" and described how he had organized the landing on June 20, 1793. Their description of the fighting stressed the "more than human courage" of the free men of color, while making no mention whatever of their decree of June 21 attempting to recruit supporters among the slaves. Instead, they claimed that upon their arrival at Haut du Cap, "we found various troops of insurgent slaves who had more than a month earlier given up the royal colors and put on those of the Republic" and who "asked to serve the nation against the kings while promising to obey all the orders of the civil commissioners." Having thus passed over the role of the blacks in the city itself and created the impression that the insurgent slaves had offered to defend the French on their own initiative, the commissioners added, "We promised them liberty in the name of the Republic."

In addition to greatly exaggerating the republican enthusiasm of the insurgent slaves, Sonthonax and Polverel chose to minimize the role of the sailors. "Incited to murder, to pillage by the relatives and friends of émigrés, by these naval officers who only preferred Saint-Domingue to Coblentz because, while eating the state's bread, they were confident of betraying it more easily, the sailors never lost sight of the Republic," they wrote. "They continually cried, 'Long live the nation,' they did not sully themselves with the signs and symbols of royalism." In reality, the situation had been just the reverse: the ordinary sailors and the more junior officers had stoked the conflict, while the senior officers had tried to head it off. As we have seen, however, Sonthonax and Polverel had consistently refused to accept the fact that the seagoing *sans-culottes* had turned against them; by accusing the officers, they also played to the Jacobins' tendency to blame all the Republic's troubles on conspiratorial aristocrats. "Spare the sailors," they concluded; "the people, always just in its views, always pure in its intentions, is the victim of its leaders; it is on them that the national justice should fall." They felt freer to denounce the white volunteers from the town, whom they accused of having "deployed flags with fleurs-de-lys and worn white neckties," a claim for which the surviving documents provide no support at all. Returning to Galbaud, they claimed that he had encouraged the island's whites to see him as "the restorer of the privilege of color and the protector of eternal slavery," whereas their own promises of "a better future, the certainty of gradually obtaining freedom," a considerable exaggeration of what they had actually offered, had persuaded most of the rebellious slaves in the south to return to work.

"That is, Citizen Representatives," Sonthonax and Polverel concluded, "the disastrous position in which Galbaud has left us in the North Province. Without a navy, without money, without any means of procuring it, with supplies only for one month, we do not yet despair of the salvation of the country. We go even further, we do not ask you for any soldiers; we do not ask for ships or sailors; we will save the property of Saint-Domingue for France with the natives of the country and with the Africans." They had, they claimed, "two thousand well armed blacks just in the town of Le Cap, we are forming them into battalions and legions, under the name of *liberty and equality*." They concluded by predicting that that they would be the targets of "all the absurdities that all the slavers of Saint-Domingue are going to spread against us." Their answer, they said, would be that "it is true we have all the confidence of those who had been freed, and that the slaves regard us as their liberators. It is entirely true that if it is a crime in the Convention's eyes to have scrupulously followed its principles, to have constantly protected the oppressed against the oppressors, we are guilty of this honorable crime." If the Convention was unhappy with them, it had only to recall them: "Neither ships nor troops will be needed to make us obey its decisions; a simple decree will bring us to its bar, where we will appear without fear or remorse." In a postscript, they attempted to justify one of their most controversial decisions in the wake of the June 20, 1793 crisis: they had instructed the military commanders of the other ports in the colony to use force if necessary to prevent any of the warships coming from Le Cap from entering their harbors. The measure was clearly meant at preventing Galbaud from landing anywhere else in Saint-Domingue, but they correctly anticipated that their enemies would blame them for authorizing attacks on the Republic's own military forces.

The double process of integrating the newly enfranchised blacks into the French republican community and justifying their actions to the Convention continued with the celebration of Bastille Day that Sonthonax and Polverel carefully stage-managed on July 14, 1793. The ceremony they held amid the ruins of Cap Français, attended, according to Mahé de Corméré, by 100 whites, 200 free people of color, and 6,000 blacks,[43] linked them to the metropole – where, two days later, the Convention was to vote for the recall and arrest of the two commissioners – and, ironically, to the white refugees who had just arrived in the United States and who proceeded with equal determination to make a public show of observing the holiday.[44] In Le Cap, Polverel spoke to the soldiers and the crowd assembled in front of an "altar of the *patrie*" decorated with a liberty tree topped with a red liberty cap that had been erected on the Champ de Mars, rebaptized as the "Place de la Fédération." He emphasized the common interests of the French soldiers, "who were beaten with blows to make them march," the "cultivators" of the metropole, who "fertilized the earth with their sweat, and did not share in its fruits," "the Africans" taken from their country and condemned to "an eternal slavery," and "the descendants of Africans," the free people of color, who, in spite of their legal status, "were considered unworthy of enjoying the rights of man." All had been victims of "the kings who trafficked in the lives and the freedom of men of all countries and all colors." The assembly took an oath to "fight to the death against all kings" and to be loyal to the Republic and sang the "Marseillaise." In his report to the Convention, Sonthonax noted proudly that "no priest sullied the ceremony with his presence."[45]

Later in the day, Sonthonax harangued the new citizens about the obligations they owed in return for the gift of liberty, "which took you from nothingness to existence ... You will prove that you deserved this,

---

[43] Mahé de Corméré, "Précis," in AN, D XXV 14, d. 127, p. 82.

[44] *Philadelphia General Advertiser*, July 29, 1793 (letter from Norfolk, VA, July 20, 1793).

[45] Procès-verbal of celebration of July 14, 1793, in AN, D XXV 19, d. 186; Sonthonax to Convention, July 30, 1793, in AN, D XXV 5, d. 52.

if you faithfully execute the orders of the civil commissioners, especially if you force this crowd of vagabonds and idlers, who do not want to cultivate the land or defend those who do, to work. In France, the people are free and they work; remember that liberty does not consist in being idle; without work, there is neither leisure nor happiness."[46] Polverel echoed this concern about the former slaves' willingness to work in a private letter two days later: "Who can calculate where our calamities will end, if more than 400,000 slaves who have nothing and who detest work, all become free at once, and if they become free through insurrection and by right of conquest?"[47]

As they labored to maintain their authority over the black population around Le Cap and to justify themselves to the Convention, the two commissioners also struggled to avoid a collapse of the French position in the rest of the colony. Whites who had fled into the hills during the fighting on June 20, 1793 had started to trickle back into the city; distrustful of their sentiments and not wanting to be responsible for supporting them, Sonthonax and Polverel let them leave on any ships they could find, in exchange for paying an exit tax that the refugees bitterly resented.[48] By early July, Sonthonax and Polverel had probably received Genet's letter of June 25, 1793, informing them that the American government was not going to advance any more money to support the French war effort.[49] In Saint-Domingue, the remaining troops needed constant encouragement and their commanders had to be exhorted to remain loyal. Sonthonax and Polverel were particularly exasperated when some of the free men of color threatened to desert the cause. "You, a child 4 April, you and all your brothers, are you going to abandon the republic whose essence is equality, and outside of which there is no equality?" they wrote to the commander of Ennery on July 17, 1793. "Are you going to leave us as the only ones defending the colony and the republic?"[50] The discipline of the new black troops was a constant concern. They were put to work cleaning up the ruins of Le Cap, but the commander there was reminded to "be sure that those who you employ for this work are not the first to loot and steal, as has been happening up to now."[51] On July 22, 1793,

[46] Procès-verbal of celebration of July 14, 1793, in AN, D XXV 19, d. 186.
[47] Polverel to Vernet, July 16, 1793, in AN, D XXV 5, d. 46.
[48] *Extrait d'une lettre, sur les malheurs de Saint-Domingue,* cited in Popkin, *Facing Racial Revolution,* 222.
[49] Genet to commissioners, June 25, 1793, in AN, D XXV 6, d. 58.
[50] Commissioners to Duvigneau, July 17, 1793, in AN, D XXV 42.
[51] Commissioners to commandant of Cap Français, July 21, 1793, in AN, D XXV 42.

Masse, the *ordonnateur*, or financial administrator, who had arrived with Galbaud in May and had been allowed to continue in his post by the commissioners, abruptly resigned.[52] A day later, the crew of the *America*, the only ship of the line that had not participated in the landing on June 20, 1793, mutinied, complaining that the blacks and people of color in Le Cap would not let them come ashore when they were in the harbor and that they were not being given adequate rations; the captain had to consent to leave the island. Within days, another warship, the *Inconstante*, followed the *America*'s example. The commissioners wrote its captain a furious letter, ending defiantly by promising that "we will manage to defend and save the colony without you," but were unable to prevent its departure.[53]

In the face of these setbacks, Sonthonax and Polverel somehow managed to keep going, but they were certainly under great strain. On July 30, 1793, they wrote to the Convention again, justifying their decree of July 11, 1793 freeing the black soldiers' families and complaining about the "hordes of slaves who, led by priests and émigrés, fight under the white standard [the royalist flag]." The blacks, the commissioners reported, were "as fanatical as the population of the Loire inférieure," the Vendean peasant rebels in France. Nevertheless, the commissioners vowed, they would not abandon their mission. "We will live on yams and bananas, if we run out of supplies. Our enterprise is too glorious for us to let obstacles deter us." However, they announced, it was time for the Convention to face up to the situation:

Citizen representatives, you now have a great question to decide, that of the condition of unfree persons in the colony. The time for indecision, for unsatisfactory measures, for hypocritical moderation is over. The prejudices that blinded the slaves are gone, and the Convention is too just and too completely the friend of humanity to do anything other than to proclaim the great principles. The Declaration of Rights no longer permits it to allow one man to be the property of another: the slavers and the kings should be treated the same. Either they cease to tyrannize, they abandon their prey, or they must disappear from the surface of the earth.[54]

Even as they called on the Convention to take a clear position on the issue of slavery, the commissioners were careful to respect its authority: they

[52] Masse to Sonthonax and Polverel, July 22, 1793, in AN, D XXV 23, d. 234.
[53] "Journal du Vaisseau l'*America*," July 23, 1793, in AN, D XXV 54, d. 523; commissioners to Riouff, captain of the *Inconstante*, July 28, 1793, in AN, D XXV 42.
[54] Sonthonax and Polverel to Convention, in AN, D XXV 5, d. 52.

excused themselves for the partial measures they had taken and made it clear that they left it up to the legislators to take the crucial step of abolishing slavery in principle. Clearly, however, they could not hold out much longer without doing something to satisfy the black population.

At the end of July, the commissioners decided that Polverel needed to return to the West Province, leaving Sonthonax alone in the North. A semblance of normal life was returning to the portion of Cap Français that had survived the fire. A French army officer in the city wrote that "the town is fairly calm and as tranquil as one could hope after the events to which it has fallen prey. The Americans continue to bring flour and other supplies ... They are paid either in coffee, sugar and so on that were found in warehouses that were not completely looted and burned and also with the gold, the copper and the lead from the ruins of the fire."[55] Samuel Perkins, the American merchant who had witnessed the burning of the city, returned there in early August to try to obtain some compensation for his property. He found commerce and government functioning, after a fashion, although "the quarter where business was now done was confined to a small space about the King's Wharf [near the arsenal] and the public stores, all the upper part of the town having been destroyed." As he landed, Perkins "observed a black man dressed in a suit of white dimity, wearing a white cocked hat bound with gold-lace on his head, having a gold-headed cane in his hand, and a large gold watch-chain hanging from his fob," who immediately came up and greeted him. The friendly black was the former slave of another merchant who had been killed: "Having by the new order of things become a citizen, [he] had thought it would well become the dignity of his new character to wear his master's Sunday suit and carry his gold-headed cane." Although he was pleased to see his master's old friend, the black man took pains to ensure that Perkins understood how much things had changed, advising him "to salute all the blacks I had occasion to speak to with the title of *Citoyen*, as all were now free and equal."

Perkins later found another white friend, "lately a gentleman of large fortune, now without hat or shoes, in a coarse checked shirt and trousers, doing the labor which but a few weeks before was the business of his slaves." When Perkins commented that his friend was "'working like a slave,'" his friend "cautioned me not to use the word *slave* on any occasion, as it might cost me my life."[56] Hostile to the blacks, Perkins

---

[55] Letter of Berger, July 24, 1793, in AN, D XXV 80, d. 786.
[56] Perkins, "Narrative," 363, 358–9.

nevertheless recognized that the basic functions of urban life were being restored. He found a boarding house to dine in and saw clerks working desperately to sort out the masses of commercial and government records that had survived the fire. Obviously, however, the remaining black population had helped themselves to whatever property they had been able to find, despite Sonthonax and Polverel's proclamation threatening that looters would be shot,[57] and former slaves had taken over many of the positions formerly filled by whites. The process was not an easy one, however. Charles Wante, the administrator appointed to replace the defecting Masse as *ordonnateur*, complained that the black workers on whom public services were dependent had become completely unreliable. "The operation of the bakery is about to break down and the supplies for those receiving rations are uncertain ... because the blacks who are employed there, although they were told they would only get their freedom after a year, are planning to quit ... The operation of the hospitals suffers because one can no longer get any work out of the blacks or even the black women ... Operations at the warehouses are barely functioning ... the blacks, although paid regularly, only work when they want to," he reported to Sonthonax.[58]

Surrounded by the newly emancipated blacks in the city, Sonthonax realized that further steps were needed to deal with their more numerous brethren in the countryside. Sonthonax's biographer Robert Stein suggests that the absence of his more cautious colleague freed Sonthonax to take the radical step toward general emancipation that he had dreamed of,[59] but the evidence can equally well be interpreted to suggest that he found himself with little choice. His right-hand man, General Laveaux, fell gravely ill and became seriously depressed in early August, and Sonthonax had to make frantic efforts to restore his morale. Laveaux was unhappy at finding himself left with an army composed overwhelmingly of recently freed slaves. "Don't criticize the citizens of 20 June," Sonthonax begged him. "All they need are leaders, and when you have commanded them, they didn't abandon you."[60] While the new troops were less than reliable, the civilian population was also restless. An informer in Cap Français claimed to have overheard a group of blacks saying that "they didn't need any ruler and that they could perfectly well

[57] Proclamation of July 18, 1793, in CAOM, F 3 198.
[58] Wante to Sonthonax, August 27, 1793, in AN, D XXV 23, d. 235.
[59] Stein, *Sonthonax*, 87.
[60] Sonthonax to Laveaux, August 10, 1793, in AN, D XXV 42.

govern themselves;" one of them had supposedly added that if some-one would pay him 50 portugaises, he would kill Sonthonax and deliver his head.[61]

In letters to Polverel, who was initially alarmed by reports that Sonthonax was planning to free the entire slave population, the lat-ter sketched the difficult situation that had led him to act. In Polverel's district, the West Province, "the slaves are not armed, they are accus-tomed to working, the charms of laziness, the attractions of brigandage are, luckily, unknown to them," Sonthonax wrote, but "the urgency of circumstances, the impossibility of waiting, in the midst of the disor-der and anarchy in which we live in the North, ... forced me to be in advance of you and to proclaim ... truths that are in your heart and in line with your intentions."[62] In another letter, Sonthonax gave his colleague a fuller picture of the circumstances facing him. The black soldiers on whom he was now dependent refused to discipline the agri-cultural work force, and those slaves who had resisted the temptation to leave their plantations "complained loudly and justifiably, no doubt, at seeing themselves condemned to slavery as the price of their virtues, while the others had conquered their freedom through crime and brig-andage." The black insurgents continued to win supporters by claiming that the French monarchy would grant them freedom, and "the black soldiers are reluctant to fight against their brothers." "In such difficult circumstances," Sonthonax concluded, "I thought that there was every-thing to be gained by being completely just, and in turning to the profit of humanity the great catastrophe of Le Cap."[63]

The moment for action came on August 25, 1793, when the occasion of a "festival of liberty" allowed a group of 600 black soldiers to present Sonthonax with a petition demanding general liberty.[64] Whether he had in fact encouraged this demonstration or whether he decided that he could not afford to resist it, Sonthonax seized the opportunity to announce his decision. The petitioners, he said, had asked "that the chains with which the Africans, these unfortunates taken from their birthplace and trans-planted to a foreign country to serve the cupidity of the Europeans, be broken. It was commendable of them to set an example that will mark an epoch in our annals, and which will surely be followed throughout the

---

[61] Pouzols to Sonthonax, August 21 1793, in AN, D XXV 14, d. 130bis.
[62] Sonthonax to Polverel, September 3, 1793, in AN, D XXV 5, d. 53.
[63] Sonthonax to Polverel, September 10, 1793, in AN, D XXV 5, d. 53.
[64] Sonthonax to Polverel, September 10, 1793, in AN, D XXV 5, d. 53.

islands of America." He would, he promised, proceed promptly to draft an edict of general emancipation; the Convention's decree of March 5, 1793, he insisted, gave him the authority to do so.[65]

Even as he spoke these fateful words, however, Sonthonax continued to worry about their consequences. He refused to simply announce to the crowd that all the slaves were free. "The law that I will proclaim needs to be carefully thought out," he insisted. "It must protect the rights of your masters and your own rights. The sudden passage to liberty has to be planned in such a way that it will not rupture the bonds on which all societies are based, so that agriculture will not suffer, so that the earth will yield enough produce to nourish the warriors employed in fighting the enemies of the Republic."[66]

The news that Sonthonax was preparing an emancipation decree sparked at least one remarkable reaction from a white resident of Cap Français, who sent him a letter urging him to use the opportunity to create a communist society. Richebourg, the colonist who wrote this proposal, said he had a plan, "which is not at all complicated and which comes from my heart," to establish not only universal liberty but also "the community of goods among all the individuals of the North Province, a province completely under your authority and for which you have the right to do everything that seems just and wise to you."[67] Richebourg failed to convince Sonthonax, who remained committed to defending the right of property, but he deserves credit for having proposed the idea of communism three years earlier than the French radical Gracchus Babeuf, whose "Manifesto of the Equals" is usually considered the first expression of such ideas.

Whereas Richebourg wanted Sonthonax to join the abolition of private property to the abolition of slavery, the commissioner's colleague Polverel blamed him for not turning the slaves into property owners. In the West Province, Polverel had been wrestling on his own with the problem of winning over black support. On August 26, 1793, he wrote to Sonthonax to report that he had broken up a conspiracy organized by a local supporter of Jean-François and Biassou that aimed to turn

---

[65] Sonthonax, speech of August 25, 1793, in AN, D XXV 5, d. 52.
[66] Sonthonax, speech of August 25, 1793, in AN, D XXV 5, d. 52.
[67] Richebourg to Sonthonax, August 26, 1793, in AN, D XXV 13, loose document. Richebourg's letter is published in Florence Gauthier, "En guise de conclusion: ouverture à de nouvelles recherches. Richebourg: comment abolir l'esclavage à Saint-Domingue? 1793," in Florence Gauthier, ed., *Périssent les colonies plutôt qu'un principe!* (Paris: Société d'études robespierristes, 2002), 105–7.

the colony over to the Spanish and to proclaim the "universal liberty of the slaves." In response, Polverel had tried to come up with a plan to "increase the number of free men and property-owners, without affecting the property of those who have neither betrayed the republic, nor abandoned the defense of the colony, and without harming the continuation or the progress of agriculture."[68] The first report of Sonthonax's more sweeping initiative in the North alarmed Polverel; he wrote on September 3, 1793, asking whether his colleague had been forced to yield to threats from the armed black soldiers. "You know that I detest slavery as much as you do," Polverel insisted. "I want to see liberty and equality be from now on the bases of the prosperity of Saint-Domingue. But what liberty, that of brigands! What equality, that where there is no law other than that of the stronger! What prosperity can one hope for without work? And what work can you hope for from liberated Africans, if you haven't started by making them understand the necessity by giving them properties, and introducing them to pleasures that were unknown to them up to now?"[69]

The eight-page document Sonthonax published on August 29, 1793 had none of the simplicity of Richebourg's proposal, or of the succinct abolition decree the National Convention would pass six months later, and it also did not fully address Polverel's concerns. Sonthonax's decree combined the grant of emancipation with an elaborate exercise in self-justification, addressed equally to the black population and to the National Convention, and with thirty-eight detailed articles regulating all the details of post-emancipation society. "Men are born and remain free and equal in rights; citizens, this is France's gospel," Sonthonax began. Rather than expounding on the consequences of this statement, however, he then devoted several paragraphs to explaining why he had been obliged to defend slavery for so long: an immediate attempt to end it would have driven the whites into revolt while unleashing bloody vengeance on the part of the slaves, and in any event, the commissioners had not had the authority to take such a step. Now, as a result of the flight

[68] Polverel to Sonthonax, August 26, 1793, in AN, D XXV 12, d. 114.

[69] Polverel to Sonthonax, September 3, 1793, in AN, D XXV 12, d. 119. The idea that the slaves needed to be inculcated with the desire to own property and taught to become market-oriented consumers was not original with Polverel: Julien Raimond had made similar points in one of his pamphlets. Julien Raymond, *Réflexions sur les véritables causes des troubles et des désastres de nos colonies, notamment sur ceux de Saint-Domingue; avec les moyens à employer pour préserver cette colonie d'une ruine totale; adressés à la Convention nationale; par Julien Raymond, colon de Saint-Domingue* (Paris, n.p., 1793), 20.

of most of the whites, their prejudices could be ignored, and, Sonthonax claimed, the Convention's decree of March 5, 1793 authorized him to abolish slavery. Before doing so, however, he paused to remind the blacks to be grateful to his allies, the free men of color. "These are men to whom you owe your freedom, the first to show you what it is to have the courage to fight for natural and human rights," he insisted, conveniently overlooking the fact that many of them were also slave owners.[70] (See Figure 8.1.)

After explaining the contradictions in his own behavior and giving credit both to the free men of color and to the Convention, Sonthonax exhorted the blacks to live up to their new responsibilities: "Your detractors and your tyrants maintain that an African who is set free will never work again. Prove them wrong. Work twice as hard to win the prize that awaits you."[71] The detailed clauses that followed – probably reflecting the counsels of Sonthonax's plantation-owning advisors such as Dufay and Castaing, since the commissioner himself had no firsthand experience in the matter – specified that ex-slaves were to be paid for their work and promised to create a system of government-appointed justices of the peace and inspectors to see that they were not abused. Whipping was specifically prohibited, but, unless they were serving in the army, the freed slaves were to remain on their plantations and continue working for their old masters. Domestic servants caring for the sick, the elderly, or for children could not leave their positions; women were promised pregnancy and maternity leave, but their pay was set at only two-thirds of the men's level. The justices of the peace would decide whether blacks could change plantations, and any black, male or female, who had not found a job within fifteen days of the issuance of the proclamation would be arrested. This final provision did not apply to male owners of property, but, of course, by definition, newly freed slaves did not fall into that category. A few days earlier, on the other side of the Atlantic, the National Convention had decreed the *levée en masse*, which also made the entire population liable either to military service or useful labor. Sonthonax's decree reflected the same assumption that the law had the right to direct the efforts of all for the general good, but, in Saint-Domingue, this meant

---

[70] Decree of August 29. 1793, cited in Dubois and Garrigus, *Slave Revolution*, 122; for the original text, see the printed copy in AN, D XXV 13. Marcel Dorigny has recently published what appears to be a draft of the proclamation, with some variants compared to the printed version: Dorigny, dir., *Sonthonax*, 196–205.

[71] Dubois and Garrigus, *Slave Revolution*, 122–3.

sous la direction de Marcel Dorigny

Léger-Félicité

Sonthonax

Publication : Société Française d'Histoire d'Outre-Mer
15 rue Catulienne - 93200 St-Denis
www.sfhom.com

et de l'Association pour l'étude de la Colonisation Française
17 rue de la Sorbonne - 75005 Paris

Paris 2005

FIGURE 8.1. Sonthonax the Liberator.

The only known portrait of Léger-Félicité Sonthonax, the younger of the two civil commissioners, reproduced on the cover of a book devoted to his career, shows him holding a scroll containing the emancipation proclamation he issued in Saint-Domingue on 29 August 1793. Sometimes attributed to Jacques-Louis David, this painting was probably made in Paris, perhaps as Sonthonax was preparing to return to the colony in 1796 as a member of the Third Civil Commission. No portrait of his colleague Etienne Polverel has been found.

Source: Musée du Pantheon National, Port-au-Prince; book cover reproduced with permission of Marcel Dorigny.

compelling the majority of the black population to continue performing the tasks they had done as slaves; in addition, the French population had, in theory, chosen their government, whereas the blacks had never been consulted about Sonthonax's appointment.

Sonthonax's hopes of winning black acceptance of his plans for the restoration of the plantations were soon disappointed. The Spanish authorities, who continued to follow events on the other side of the border closely, doubted that "the last proclamation of Sonthonax will produce the effect that he hopes, if the slaves and free people of color take time and ponder their interest and the regulation that assigns their place of residence to them ..." Even if the commissioner managed to implement his plan, the Spanish anticipated that it would result in "a new civil war between the workers and landowners who ... will want to take advantage of all of the benefits, intriguing against and mistreating the cultivators."[72] In districts where the blacks had continued to work on the plantations, the effect of Sonthonax's proclamation was often to encourage the newly freed slaves to seize their freedom and sometimes their masters' property as well; the system of regulated labor that Sonthonax had intended to set up never functioned. "The blacks who had behaved well in accordance with the rules have ended up doing like the others," one discouraged colonist wrote after reaching the United States. "The proclamation of general liberty turned their heads, and their only thought was to take everything from the plantation, and to go pillaging all around."[73] In other cases, slaves organized to prevent other blacks from raiding the food supplies on their own plantations, even if this meant rejecting Sonthonax's emancipation offer. "The conduct of the Negroes I've mentioned won the admiration of the whites," a colonist wrote about one such incident.[74]

The black leaders who had rejected the French commissioners' advances in June 1793 were no more receptive to Sonthonax's new policy. As Sonthonax moved toward granting general emancipation, Toussaint Louverture stepped up his denunciations of the commissioner, drafting a series of letters denouncing the French and reiterating his loyalty to the Spanish. The most frequently cited of these documents, sometimes labeled the "proclamation of Turel" because it was sent from Toussaint's headquarters there on the same date as Sonthonax's proclamation,

[72] J. Garcia to J. del Sasso, September 9, 1793, in Monte y Tejada, *Historia*, 4: 93.
[73] Unsigned letter from Philadelphia, March 15, 1794, in AN, D XXV 81, d. 790.
[74] Lacoste to Duplaa, November 22, 1793, in AN, D XXV 80, d. 786.

includes the famous lines, "I am Toussaint Louverture. My name is perhaps known to you. I have undertaken to avenge you. I want liberty and equality to reign throughout St. Domingue,"[75] which are often interpreted as a message addressed to the black population at large espousing the principles of the French Revolution. In reality, this passage occurs in a lengthy letter addressed to a few specific individuals, in an effort to persuade them not to trust the French, "deceivers who only want to bring you down," and to get them to come over to Toussaint's side in the ongoing fighting in the colony. In view of a passage lamenting the fate of Ogé and a postscript at the end stressing how humanely Toussaint had treated the whites who had surrendered to him, allowing them to either leave the country or to remain in possession of their properties, it seems likely that it was addressed to free colored landowners rather than to the former slaves.[76] Sonthonax, who saw the letter shortly after it was written, certainly did not interpret it as a sign that Toussaint had adopted republican ideas; instead, he directed one of his allies to refute it.[77]

In contrast to the enigmatic Turel letter, two other Toussaint letters from the end of August 1793 express an emphatic rejection of the French and their policies. When Chanlatte, one of the free colored officers in the commissioners' forces, tried to convince Toussaint to join the French, the black general responded indignantly, "It is not possible that you are fighting for liberty or the right [sic] of man, after all the cruelties that you commit every day." He reaffirmed his loyalty to the French monarchy, even though he wrote that "we know perfectly well that there is no more king because you republican traitors murdered him on a shameful scaffold," and he concluded with a scathing indictment of Sonthonax and Polverel: "As far as the commissioners are concerned, don't speak to me about them, their schemes are known to me and from the time of their arrival in the colony, we have followed their dishonest measures and they have put forth their so-called good intentions; [it is] too late, it was at the time when they were having us pursued and subjecting those of us they captured to the greatest cruelties, it was at the time, I say, that they should have made us the offer that they want us to believe in now in

---

[75] Cited in George F. Tyson, ed., *Toussaint L'Ouverture* (New York: Prentice Hall, 1973), 28.

[76] Letter of Toussaint Louverture to "Frères et amis," in AN, AA 53, d. 1490. I would like to thank David Geggus for providing me with a photocopy of this famous document, which was not in carton AA 53 when I consulted it at the Archives nationales in 2007.

[77] Sonthonax to Bramante Lazzary, August 30, 1793, in AN, D XXV 42.

order to fool us."[78] Toussaint's arguments were so persuasive that when the envoys Chanlatte had sent to deliver his letter returned to their camp, they set off a mutiny among their comrades.[79]

Equally unequivocal was a long letter that Toussaint signed on the same day and explicitly designated, unlike the Turel letter, as a public statement of his principles, or, as he put it, a document "to expose my sentiments, my plans, and demonstrate to these republican tyrants, that the spirits cannot be favorable to them." Toussaint began, "Perfidious republicans! You try to convince us that justice and the Republic assure us liberty, in the midst of a free people among whom reigns a perfect equality. Did the Republic need to shed so much innocent blood to establish itself?" Sounding like the white colonists denouncing the insurgents, Toussaint demanded to know, "how far are you going to extend your tyrannical powers after having ordered your infamous supporters to lay waste to our lands, burn our houses, slaughter our women, our children, our parents?" The commissioners, Toussaint charged, were lying about the state of affairs in Europe: rather than being defeated, the Spanish forces had occupied Languedoc and Gascony. The French had committed a great crime by executing their king: "what proof of criminality could you bring against his sacred person, in order to put him to death like the worst of villains? Did your powers extend to that point?" Louis XVI had been "the unshakable pillar of the church, which you have trampled under foot, impious as you are." The blacks owed loyalty to the Spanish, who had given them the means to defend themselves "when you had us pursued like ferocious beasts." "You try to make us believe that Liberty is a benefit that we will enjoy if we submit ourselves to order," Toussaint concluded, "but as long as God gives us the force and the means, we will acquire another Liberty, different from that which you tyrants pretend to impose on us."[80]

Despite the strong language of this declaration and of his letter to Chanlatte, Toussaint was not entirely indifferent to the new perspectives that Sonthonax's move toward general emancipation opened up. On August 30, 1793, just three days after he signed his declaration of

---

[78] "Toussaint Louverture, general of the king's army, to Monsieur Chanlatte the younger, criminal, traitor and liar," August 27, 1793, in AN, CC 9 A 8.

[79] Dufresne, "Expedition de Chanlatte contre Toussaint L'ouverture à La Marmelade en Septre 1793," in CAOM, F 3 198 (Moreau de Saint-Méry papers).

[80] Letter signed "Toussaint L'Ouverture, Général des armées du Roy, approuvé par tous nos Chefs et tous nos soldats royalistes," August 27, 1793 (dated at beginning "8 Aug. 1793"), in AN, AA 55, d. 1511.

sentiments, he wrote to some unnamed "brothers and friends" – a standard salutation among the French republicans – telling them that "your letter makes me think" and suggesting a meeting; he may well have been reacting to Sonthonax's proclamation of August 29, 1793.[81] As the Turel letter shows, he was capable of using phrases such as "liberty and equality" for his own purposes. Even if Toussaint privately entertained the possibility of switching to the French side, as he would do in the spring of 1794, throughout the summer of 1793 he remained loyal to the Spanish. The restrictions imposed on the former slaves by Sonthonax's decree were not an obstacle to his *ralliement*: when he came to power, he would establish virtually identical regulations.[82] Even after more than 200 years, Toussaint Louverture's motives remain an enigma. He was certainly concerned about committing himself to the French at a time when their chances of winning the war in Europe remained doubtful, and he was also concerned about his position in the ongoing rivalry with Jean-François and Biassou, which was in a heated phase at the end of August 1793.[83] What is certain is that his letters caused Sonthonax real concern; he directed a black spokesman, Bramante Lazzary, to write several letters of his own refuting Toussaint, setting out arguments for Lazzary to use.[84]

Limited as it was in many respects, and unsuccessful as it was in persuading the leaders of the insurrection in the North Province to change sides, Sonthonax's decree of August 29, 1793 was nevertheless a milestone in the revolutionary era's debates about slavery. In contrast to the decrees of June 21 and July 11, 1793, Sonthonax's edict broke out of the framework that had linked emancipation to military service. Unlike the earlier decrees, it explicitly cited the Declaration of the Rights of Man and insisted that there could be no difference between the rights of citizens in the colonies and those of the metropole. Polverel eventually allowed himself to be persuaded, although, obliged by circumstances in the West Province to pay more attention to the concerns of plantation owners, most of whom in that region were free men of color, he first made efforts to try to persuade them to free their slaves voluntarily.[85] Polverel also worried about the consequences of freeing urban slaves and

---

[81] Toussaint Louverture, letter of August 30, 1793, in AN, AA 55, d. 1511.
[82] Fick, *Making of Haiti*, 207–8.
[83] Matias de Armona to del Sasso, September 15, 1793, in Monte y Tejada, *Historia*, 4: 96–7.
[84] Sonthonax to Lazzary, AN, D XXV 42, letter of August 30, 1793.
[85] Stein, "Abolition of Slavery," 51.

domestic servants who might find themselves unemployed and without resources.[86] Nevertheless, he recognized that, in the wake of Sonthonax's action, general emancipation could not be avoided. When their third colleague, Delpech, expressed doubts that the powers granted to them by the Convention extended so far, it was Polverel who took the lead in firmly rebuking him. At the end of September, when Delpech unexpectedly died, Polverel wrote to Sonthonax, "I am sorry, because he was a decent man and a good citizen, but he died a month too late."[87] Forced to take responsibility for the South Province as well as the West, Polverel announced the extension of his own earlier edicts there, and then, on October 31, 1793, he promulgated the Declaration of the Rights of Man in both provinces, officially completing the process of abolishing slavery throughout the colony.[88]

Although Polverel's various decrees show a greater awareness of the practical problems involved in implementing emancipation, Sonthonax's decree of August 29, 1793 was decisive in one vital respect: it was Sonthonax's version of general emancipation that was communicated to France, resulting in the National Convention's decree of February 4, 1794. On September 9, 1793, he dispatched fifty printed copies of his proclamation to Paris, along with a letter outlining the desperation of his circumstances. "The only course of action to take in such difficult circumstances was to give a great example of justice," he wrote. "I have achieved this goal by proclaiming the rights of man in the North Province. I expect great results from this measure, and in any event, whatever future events may bring, I will have the consolation of having turned to the advantage of humanity a catastrophe of which I was not the cause."[89] In order to deliver this message to France, Sonthonax arranged the election of six men – two blacks, two free men of color, and two whites – to represent the North Province in the National Convention. According to a hostile white colonist, the names of the future deputies were known several days before the electoral assembly, which met on September 23–24, 1793.[90] They included the free black officer, J.-B. Belley, who had commanded the defenders of the Government House, and Louis Dufay, who had done much to provoke the quarrel between the commissioners and

---

[86] Polverel, declaration of September 10, 1791, in AN, D XXV 39, n. 397.
[87] Polverel to Delpech, September 19, 1793, and Polverel to Sonthonax, September 30, 1793, both in AN, D XXV 12, d. 114.
[88] Stein, "Abolition," 54 ; declaration of October 31, 1793, in AN, D XXV 39, n. 397.
[89] Sonthonax to Convention, September 9, 1793, in AN, D XXV 5, d. 53.
[90] Laplace, *Histoire des desastres de Saint-Domingue*, 363.

Galbaud; Dufay's white colleague, Garnot, was one of the free colored leader Castaing's brothers-in-law.[91] After a perilous stop in the United States, Belley, Dufay, and a free man of color named Jean-Baptiste Mills would become the first members of the delegation to reach France, and the justification of Sonthonax's decree of August 29, 1793 presented by Dufay would lead directly to the Convention's own abolition decree; Polverel's measures were not even mentioned in the debate.[92]

While Sonthonax's and Polverel's emancipation proclamations set the process of legal emancipation in motion, they were not enough to halt the deterioration of the French military situation in the colony. The month of September brought further disasters: British forces landed in the white colonists' stronghold of Jérémie in the south and at Môle Saint Nicolas, the naval bastion at the northwest corner of the island, where the garrison welcomed them. The much-feared alliance between the white colonists and France's most powerful enemy was now a fact: by the beginning of October, Sonthonax had obtained a copy of the agreement made in February 1793 between representatives of the white colonists and the British government, in which the latter promised to protect the slaveholders' rights pending the restoration of a monarchy in France.[93] The commissioners' supporters were in despair at the rapid deterioration of the situation. Pouzols, the administrator of the government warehouse in Le Cap, wrote that "I consider it impossible for us to hold out much longer against the woes that surround us ... famine threatens us, and we have no weapon to oppose this evil."[94] Of the 6,966 men originally sent with the units remaining under his command in the North Province in early September, Laveaux reported to Sonthonax, 3,939 had died. The survivors lacked almost everything: in the wake of the destruction of Le Cap, they were no longer receiving any food other than daily ration of a pound and a half of bread. In the fire, "many soldiers lost their whole kit, others a part of it, today most of them are barefoot and stay in their quarters, not being able to go out because they lack shoes." Until June 20, 1793, Galbaud had managed to pay the common soldiers some of their wages, but the officers had received nothing since early May.[95] Laveaux himself was no better off than his men; as he wrote to his wife, "I lost

[91] Stein, *Sonthonax*, 95 ; AN, D 1 § 39, d. 283.
[92] *Compte rendu sur la situation actuelle de Saint-Domingue. Par Dufey [sic], député de la partie du nord.* 16 plu. II (Paris: Imprimerie nationale, An II).
[93] Sonthonax to National Convention, October 2, 1793, in AN, D XXV 5, d. 53.
[94] Pouzols to Sonthonax, September 15, 1793, in AN, D XXV 5, d. 53.
[95] Laveaux to Sonthonax, September 10, 1793, in AN, D XXV 19, d. 188.

almost everything I had to the fire and the looting; all that remained was ten shirts, some trousers and two handkerchiefs."[96]

Laveaux was willing to continue the struggle, even in the face of all these difficulties, but for most of the remaining white civil and military officials, the succession of disasters was too much to cope with. Some French officers, realizing that they had little future in an army composed overwhelmingly of blacks, took advantage of Sonthonax's offer to let them resign their posts.[97] Wante, appointed as *ordonnateur* in Le Cap after the resignation of Masse in July, was overwhelmed by the challenges facing him. By early September, he concluded that the administration needed at least 4,100,000 livres to cover back wages to its employees and bills due for vital supplies. Sonthonax's proclamation of general emancipation might have been well intentioned, Wante wrote, but the breakdown in order that had followed it had made his own job impossible. "Surrounded by brigands who burn the plain, ravage the hills, who take the last of the means on which I based my hopes, I have to tell you frankly and without disguise, but with profound bitterness, that after 1 October I cannot be responsible for things, and that nothing will make me stay in office beyond that date."[98] Wante at least gave Sonthonax a few weeks' notice of his departure; General Lasalle, who had been appointed to replace Galbaud as overall commander of the armed forces after June 20, 1793 and who had initially written Sonthonax a fawning letter praising his decree of general emancipation, wrote to Laveaux at the beginning of October, denouncing "Sonthonax's dishonesty in granting freedom to all the slaves, in spite of the oath he took when he arrived … to protect and respect people's property." Lasalle then deserted his post and fled to the United States, leaving behind a denunciation of the commissioners' "almost dictatorial powers."[99]

Privately, Sonthonax was aware of an even more serious calamity: the British had begun to circulate the news that he and Polverel had been officially recalled by the French National Convention. In the absence of any official communication from France, Sonthonax was suspicious of a report coming from an enemy source and decided to keep on with his mission. "Could we believe, after all, that we were being treated as

---

[96] Laveaux to wife, August 1, 1793, in AN, D XXV 80, d. 786.
[97] Letter of Berger, July 24, 1793, in AN, D XXV 80, d. 786.
[98] Wante to Sonthonax, September 11 and 13, 1793, in AN, D XXV 23, d. 236.
[99] Lasalle, letter to Laveaux, September 29, 1793, in AN, CC 9 A 8, and proclamation of October 8, 1793, in AN, D XXV 19, d. 187; for Lasalle's earlier praise of Sonthonax's proclamation, see his letter to Sonthonax, August 30, 1793, in the same dossier.

public enemies, we who, blindly devoted to the principles of the National Convention, had braved every danger to establish them in America, we whose death had been ordered, with a reward, by Galbaud, the friend and envoy of Dumouriez?" he wrote to the Convention after his return to France in July 1794.[100] The news had already begun to circulate among the French exiles in the United States in early September, however, and by early November, Polverel had received an émigré newspaper containing details of the measure. In Saint-Marc, the local newspaper published the decree on November 16, 1793, together with an announcement that three of the parishes in that region, dominated by conservative free colored planters, had decided to reject the commissioners' authority.[101] The Convention's action, taken a month before reports of the Cap Français disaster reached Paris, raised a serious question about whether the French government would uphold any of the decrees the commissioners had issued, and above all the measures against slavery that they had taken. Polverel was as undeterred as his colleague. In the letter in which he told Sonthonax that he had received a copy of the recall decree, he also included the text of his own general emancipation decree of October 31, 1793, saying "at least you will see from it that I am not below the level of your principles," and he showed that he still had a sense of humor by composing a pamphlet with the ironic title *Critical Examination of the Prophecies of Jérémie, and of the Gospel according to Saint-Marc, on the Two Antichrists Polverel and Sonthonax*, in which he refuted the attacks coming from the whites in the South Province and the free men of color of Saint-Marc.[102] Both he and Sonthonax understood, however, that the Convention's action gave their enemies in Saint-Domingue a powerful new weapon against them.

Under these circumstances, and with the Spanish and British occupying most of the North Province, Sonthonax had little hope of actually implementing his carefully crafted emancipation plan; all he could try to do was defend a few remaining strongholds. At the beginning of October, he abandoned Cap Français for the small city of Port-de-Paix,

---

[100] Sonthonax to National Convention, 10 thermidor II (July 28, 1794), in AN, D XXV 13, document *hors chemise*.

[101] Polverel to Sonthonax, November 4, 1793, in AN, D XXV 12, d. 116; *Courier de S.-Marc*, November 16, 1793, in AN, D XXV 113, d. 893. For Sonthonax's account of the events leading up to the revolt of the free colored landowners in Saint-Marc, see his letter to Polverel, December 9, 1793, in AN, D XXV 44.

[102] *Examen critique des prophéties de Jérémie, et de l'évangile selon Saint-Marc. Sur les deux anthéchrists, Polverel et Sonthonax* (Aux Cayes, Dec. 1793), in AN, D XXV 113, d. 896.

from which he hoped to launch an expedition against the British-occupied fortress at Môle Saint-Nicolas.[103] Left behind to command the few remaining French troops in Le Cap, the normally resolute General Laveaux nearly succumbed to panic, warning Sonthonax that the blacks and free men of color were plotting to oust him from his post as soon as the commissioner had gone and to massacre the remaining white troops. He feared the "hatred that the Africans have in their hearts for the whites," even those who had espoused their cause.[104] Laveaux's fears were not irrational: in March 1796, the free colored commander Jean-Louis Villatte would in fact arrest him and try to seize power in the North Province.[105] Although Sonthonax tried to steady Laveaux's nerves, he was well aware that his departure might mean the loss of the city to the black insurgents. As he confessed to Polverel shortly after his departure, he had not succeeded in implanting any real loyalty to French principles in the black population. "The idea of a king is simple. It can be understood by the most stupid of Africans; even the most sophisticated of them cannot conceive of the idea of a republic ... The Convention's principles are so foreign to them that several times in Le Cap they proposed to make me king *in the name of the Republic* to end the war with Biassou. One cannot therefore be surprised if the brigands do not desert to come over to us and if our soldiers on the contrary leave in large numbers to join the rebels," he wrote.[106]

The months following Sonthonax's departure from Cap Français were difficult ones for the embattled commissioners and their small number of supporters. Arriving in Saint-Marc on the west coast in early November, Sonthonax had to combat the claim, asserted by General Lasalle when he defected, that the Convention had never given him the power to abolish slavery. "I declare that I will defend to the death the rights and the civil independence of those of mixed blood, of the Africans and the descendants of Africans," he insisted, "and, even if I should be ground in a mortar, I will never lower myself to renounce my proclamation of 29 August [1793]."[107] By the middle of the month, Sonthonax had reached Port-au-Prince, now renamed Port-Républicain, where he issued instructions to the reassembled Interim Commission: "A new order of things is going to be born, the African people will regain its rank among the

[103] Sonthonax to Polverel, October 27, 1793, in AN, D XXV 44, d. 420.
[104] Laveaux to Sonthonax, October 4, 1793, in AN, CC 9 A 8.
[105] Dubois, *Avengers*, 200–1; Ardouin, *Etudes*, 3: 28–33.
[106] Sonthonax to Polverel, October 27, 1793, in AN, D XXV 44, d. 420.
[107] Sonthonax, proclamation of November 5, 1793, in AN, AA 55, d. 1512.

nations of the world, and soon the sun of the Antilles will shine only on free men; it is the Interim Commission's duty to contribute as much as possible in reconciling the masters with freedom and in inculcating in the hearts of the former slaves a love of work and a respect for the laws ...."[108] At the same time, however, Laveaux was having to abandon more and more territory in the north, and Sonthonax instructed him to adopt scorched-earth tactics, burning crops and houses as he retreated. Cut off from Le Cap and from Sonthonax, Laveaux and his men had no bread and were reduced to eating the same yams and fruits that formed the blacks' diet. The general shared his men's meager rations and rallied them with patriotic rhetoric. "At a moment as critical as the one we find ourselves in," he told them, "a true citizen has to know how to accept privation. For myself, I declare that, no matter how bad our situation may become, I will never surrender to the enemies of the Republic."[109] Somehow, Laveaux managed to keep his army intact.

From his own location in the South, where conditions were less desperate, Polverel wrote to Sonthonax in exasperation, demanding to know "how are you going to get the cultivators back to work, when you can only offer them heaps of ashes, and three or four years of labor and expenses without revenue, and if you don't get them back to work, how are you going to keep them from engaging in brigandage, once they have begun or returned to that habit?"[110] A furious Sonthonax shot back, "Perish the plantations a thousand times rather than see them cultivated again by slaves!"[111] Polverel faced his own difficulties: among other things, the black military leader Jean Kina, who had been one of the heroes of the attack on the black insurgents at Platons that Polverel had supervised a year earlier, was now fighting on the side of the British and their white allies and writing letters telling the "unhappy slaves" that "[the commissioners] are fooling you with the promise of freedom when it is only an illusion; it is by fulfilling your duties to your masters that you will become free."[112] Although Polverel was confident that his own plan to motivate the former slaves by giving them shares in their plantations' profits would succeed, in fact the blacks resisted it, preferring to

[108] Sonthonax, "Au nom de la République française. Commission intermédiaire," (Port-Républicain: J.-B. Michel, 1793), in AN, D XXV 64, d. 640.

[109] Guadet, "Rapport fait au comité des colonies," in AN, D XVI 3.

[110] Polverel to Sonthonax, December 1, 1793, in AN, D XXV 12, d. 116.

[111] Sonthonax to Polverel, December 9, 1793, in AN, D XXV 44, d. 420.

[112] Jean Kina, letter of January 18, 1794, in AN, D XXV 20, d. 203. On Kina's role in the fighting in January 1793, see Crensac to Sonthonax and Polverel, January 19, 1793, in AN, D XXV 20, d. 206.

have more time to work for their own benefit even if it brought them less income.[113] Undaunted by the blacks' indifference, Polverel devoted himself to drawing up an even longer set of plantation regulations, which he finally issued at the end of February 1794. Perhaps the maniacal attention to detail in this document was his way of coping with the frustration of his situation.[114]

Unlike Polverel, who had established his headquarters in a quiet sector of the South Province, Sonthonax remained in a precarious position in Port-Républicain, threatened by the British. The absence of instructions and support from France exasperated him, as did a letter from General Laveaux asking whether the rumor of a decree recalling the two commissioners was accurate.[115] In early January 1794, a British squadron appeared in the harbor, and its commander urged him to surrender, an offer Sonthonax indignantly rejected.[116] In early March, he wrote to Polverel, from whom he had had no word for several months, complaining that "France ... is deaf to the cries of a people worthy of it [the black population]; occupied with its glory in Europe, it has written off its colonies, and we, victims of this neglect, are exposed to dishonor, for lack of means to support our enterprises." The behavior of the *anciens libres*, his former allies, also angered him. In his letter, he ticked off a long list of positions surrendered to the enemy by free colored commanders.[117] In mid-March, a fight between white and free colored military units in Port-Républicain led to a massacre of the remaining white population in the city and the flight of the sailors who had protected the city from the British. In early April, Sonthonax sent the still-silent Polverel a desperate plea for aid, reminding him how he had come from Cap Français to the West Province to rescue his colleague in March 1793.[118] This letter finally spurred Polverel to action; by the beginning of May, after more than eight months, the two men had joined forces again in Port-Républicain.[119]

In the short run, the reunion of the two commissioners failed to resolve the problems they were facing. Sonthonax and Polverel had fallen far short of raising the "400,000 soldiers with one whistle" they had

---

[113] Fick, *Making of Haiti*, 168–70.
[114] "Réglement de police sur la culture et les cultivateurs," in AN, D XXV 39, n. 397.
[115] Sonthonax to Genet, November 12, 1793, and to Polverel, December 23, 1793, in AN, D XXV 44, d. 420.
[116] Sonthonax to Polverel, January 12, 1794, in AN, D XXV 44, d. 420.
[117] Sonthonax to Polverel, March 5, 1794, in AN, D XXV 44, d. 420.
[118] Sonthonax to Polverel, March 21 and April 7, 1794, in AN, D XXV, d. 420.
[119] Polverel, register of correspondence in AN, D XXV 39, d. 397.

boasted that they could produce, and neither of their emancipation plans generated the disciplined plantation workforce they had sought to create. Nevertheless, their stubborn persistence in the face of one setback after another throughout the end of 1793 and in the early months of 1794 did have one vital result: they kept at least a part of Saint-Domingue under French sovereignty long enough for circumstances to change. "One cannot deny that the extraordinary courage of the civil commissioners has preserved the island of Saint-Domingue for the Republic," the French diplomatic officials in the United States wrote to Paris in May 1794.[120]

The courage and determination displayed by Sonthonax and Polverel owed as much or more to their devotion to the French Republic as it did to their determination to free the slaves. As patriotic Frenchmen, they were committed to maintaining French control over Saint-Domingue, and as loyal Jacobins, they hesitated a long time before asserting their authority to make the sweeping legal changes that emancipation required but that the Convention had not approved. The two men unquestionably shared common European prejudices about the backwardness of the blacks, as the patronizing tone of their proclamations often revealed. Sonthonax and Polverel had arrived in the colony imbued with the French abolitionists' conviction that the abolition of slavery needed to be carried out in a carefully controlled fashion, and they retained that belief even as they found themselves driven to take steps the metropolitan reformers had never imagined. All the same, their actions vindicate the seriousness of the French antislavery movement they represented. Finding themselves in a situation in which gradualist plans for emancipation proved unworkable, forced to fight against seemingly overwhelming odds, disavowed by the Convention and often at odds with each other, they might easily have decided that their mission was impossible. It was thanks to their determination that when the National Convention finally reversed itself and voted to abolish slavery, there was still a French foothold in Saint-Domingue where the law could be proclaimed and a French government and army with which Toussaint Louverture could ally himself.

The survival of the commissioners owed much to their personal courage, but their enemies also proved less dangerous than they had at first appeared. The Spanish themselves had been conscious that their policy of trying to appeal simultaneously to both the blacks and to their former

---

[120] Report of 15 prair. II, in Frederick J. Turner, ed., *Seventh Report of the Historical Manuscripts Commission. Correspondence of the French Ministers to the United States, 1791–1797* (Washington, DC: Government Printing Office, 1904), 366.

white owners risked alienating both groups.[121] The rival black generals Jean-François, Biassou, and Toussaint Louverture proved incapable of working together to wage an effective campaign, and the mass of the black population eventually realized that the Spanish had no intention of granting them freedom. The British troops sent ashore in the south and at Môle suffered as much from disease as the French had; by April 1794, there were only 900 red-coated soldiers fit for service, supported by several thousand French colonists. Initially, the British and Spanish had some success in winning support among the free population of color, many of whose members resented the increased status of the newly freed blacks, but it soon became clear that neither of the foreign occupiers was prepared to guarantee true equality between that group and the whites. Left in command of Le Cap when Laveaux moved his headquarters to Port-au-Paix, the free colored general Villatte, who had participated in the fight against Galbaud in June 1793, successfully fended off the black insurgents and the Spanish.[122]

Finally, at the end of April or the beginning of May – the details are not entirely clear – Toussaint Louverture, who had played a major role in scuttling the commissioners' hopes of winning black support after the June 20, 1793 crisis, decided to throw in his lot with the French and put himself under the command of the same General Laveaux whose attack had so enraged him in January 1793.[123] Although it is unclear whether Toussaint had learned of the French Convention's emancipation decree before he switched to the French side, his action nevertheless changed the balance of power in the colony and gave the republicans a chance to implement their policy. At the beginning of June 1794, Sonthonax and Polverel received a copy of the letter in which Toussaint had informed Laveaux of his change of heart and explained how he had been "misled by the enemies of the Republic and of the human race."[124] The commissioners responded with great relief. "You cannot imagine with what joy we have received such happy news … Since the brave Toussaint Louverture … has finally seen his mistake, we have the hope of seeing all the Africans in the North imitate his generous repentance, and coming

---

[121] Joaquin Garcia, letter of July 13, 1793, in Monte y Tejada, *Historia*, 4: 62–3.
[122] Geggus, "'Volte-Face,'" in *Haitian Revolutionary Studies*, 130–4.
[123] Geggus, "'Volte-Face,'" in *Haitian Revolutionary Studies*, 121–3.
[124] Toussaint Louverture, letter of May 18, 1794, in Gérard Laurent, *Toussaint Louverture à travers sa correspondance (1794–1798)* (Madrid: Industrias Graficas España, 1953), 103.

to defend their freedom by fighting for France. As long as that freedom had not been proclaimed, you could be excused and in fact even praised for shedding the blood of your tyrants in order to conquer it; we ourselves regretted having to give orders to march against you and we were forced to obey those which we had received," they wrote.[125]

Even as Toussaint Louverture's about-face was vindicating the commissioners' efforts, however, their mission was coming to an abrupt end; they did not have the time to meet the black general whose resistance had frustrated them for so long but whose efforts would ultimately guarantee the success of their policy of emancipation.[126] On June 4, 1794, the British drove Sonthonax and Polverel out of Port-Républicain and forced them to flee south to Jacmel.[127] There, on June 8, 1794, the *Espérance*, the first ship from France to reach Saint-Domingue since the events of June 20, 1793, arrived. Its captain had been sent to deliver two official documents: the text of the National Convention's decree of 16 pluviôse II (February 4, 1794) emancipating the slaves in the French colonies, and the decree of July 16, 1793, ordering the arrest of the two men whose actions had led to the abolition decree, which the Committee of Public Safety had explicitly refused to cancel even after the vote for emancipation.[128] Fearing that the commissioners, used to acting independently for so long, might try to resist, Captain Chambon conspired with the town's military commander to lure them on board his ship for a banquet. After the meal, according to an account by a white colonist who claimed to have talked to witnesses, "the captain had them enter the council cabin with General Beauvais, where he showed them the order to return to France to give an account of their conduct. It was then that the ferocious Sonthonax showed himself as cowardly as he was cruel; an aide-de-camp of General Beauvais told me that when they were shown this order, he cried like a baby. Polverel, in contrast, showed his character and seemed resigned. He said these words to his colleague: 'What, my friend! You who braved the dangers in the North Province ..., you lack courage, and you fear what you should desire. We have nothing on our consciences to

---

[125] Sonthonax and Polverel to Toussaint Louverture, June 1794, in AN, D XXV 23, d. 232.
[126] Sonthonax would meet Toussaint Louverture when he returned to Saint-Domingue as a member of the Third Civil Commission in 1796–97, but the two men would become bitter enemies. Stein, *Sonthonax*, 158–71.
[127] Stein, *Sonthonax*, 102.
[128] Stein, *Sonthonax*, 111.

reproach ourselves for, we can appear before the nation without having anything to fear, we wanted the good of the colony, but they do not want to give us the time we need.'"[129]

Denied even the chance to go ashore and collect their papers, which were put under seal and sent to France along with the commissioners, Sonthonax and Polverel had just time to notify General Laveaux that he was now in charge of the colony, and that the Convention had endorsed the abolition of slavery. Uncertain of the course events would take, Sonthonax closed by urging his loyal ally to "hold out until you have burned your last cartridge and then follow the course that prudence will dictate."[130] The commissioners arrived in the port of Rochefort just as Robespierre was being overthrown in Paris: the two experiments in revolutionary government that had developed so dramatically on the two sides of the ocean came to an end simultaneously. Rather than being hailed for bringing liberty to the slaves, Sonthonax and Polverel were treated as suspects and immediately dispatched to the capital. In the confusion following thermidor, their return attracted little attention. They were released from prison a week after Robespierre's execution but ordered to await the results of a parliamentary inquiry into the responsibility for the "disasters" that had occurred in Saint-Domingue during their mission. It would be six months before a commission was set up to take testimony on the subject and another six months before it reached its verdict. In the meantime, Sonthonax and Polverel had time to learn the strange story of how the news of the destruction of Cap Français and the granting of freedom to the colony's slaves had reached the wider world, and how emancipation had become official French policy, even though its strongest supporters in the Americas had been disavowed by the Convention.

---

[129] Anon., "Manuscrit d'un Voyage de France à Saint-Domingue, à la Havanne et aux Unis états [sic] d'Amérique. Contenant le séjour de la personne, qui écrit, avec une Description générale, de toutes les cultures de St. Domingue. Un rapport des Evénemens, de la révolution de ce pays, qui ont eu lieu, depuis 1789, jusqu'en 1804. Diverses observations politiques, & autres détails, divisés en deux parties." (1816) John Carter Brown Library, Codex Fr. 20, 2:50.

[130] Sonthonax to Laveaux, June 8, 1794, in AN, CC 9 A 8.

9

Saint-Domingue in the United States

Throughout the long months when Sonthonax, Polverel, Laveaux, and their supporters were fighting to keep Saint-Domingue under French control, another struggle over the future of the colony took place in the United States. In Baltimore, Philadelphia, Charleston, and New York, the white refugees who fled the island after the journée of June 20, 1793 reconstituted the factions that had confronted each other in Cap Français and Port-au-Prince. They formed clubs, issued manifestoes, and denounced each other in the press. The rebellious sailors who had played such a large role in the events of June 20 continued to agitate, and General Galbaud, having defied the authority of the civil commissioners with such tragic results, now played the leading role in a clash with another French official, the diplomat Edmond Genet, in a drama punctuated by moments of farce. The quarreling colonists from Saint-Domingue confronted the young American republic with its first foreign refugee crisis. In a pattern that would repeat itself many times afterward, the citizens of the United States and their leaders reacted with an outpouring of sympathy mixed with fears that the new arrivals were bringing subversive foreign ideas with them. In particular, there was fear about the impact that emancipated "French Negroes" might have on slavery in the United States. The refugees' lurid tales of violence tempered the enthusiasm for abolition that had led most of the northern states to pass laws for the gradual extinction of slavery in the 1780s.[1]

---

[1] On the impact of the Saint-Domingue refugees in the United States, see Frances Sergeant Childs, *French Refugee Life in the United States, 1790–1800* (Baltimore: Johns Hopkins University Press, 1940), Gordon S. Brown *Toussaint's Clause: The Founding Fathers and*

The Saint-Domingue refugees also strongly influenced reactions to the Cap Français disaster in France. For the overwhelming majority of the refugees, the journée of June 20, 1793 was the final proof that talk of rights for people of African descent was a recipe for catastrophe. Unable to reach France during the summer and fall of 1793, the refugees flooded the metropole with letters denouncing the blacks and the civil commissioners Sonthonax and Polverel, the "monsters" who had "opened up a mine of crimes and atrocities unknown among humans up to now," as one of them wrote.[2] The much-maligned minister Genet was one of the few whites who embraced the idea of emancipation. Infuriating the white colonists, he became the first French official outside of Saint-Domingue to endorse the measures Sonthonax and Polverel had taken. Genet's intervention was decisive in expediting the arrival in France of the "tri-color" delegation of deputies to the Convention chosen in Saint-Domingue in September 1793. Without Genet's assistance, they might never have made it across the Atlantic, where their arrival turned the tide against the white colonists' lobby and led the French assembly to pass its historic decree of 16 pluviôse An II abolishing slavery. The acute phase of the Saint-Domingue refugee crisis in the United States was short-lived: by the spring of 1794, many of the survivors of the journée of June 20, 1793 were on their way to France, and the others were slowly integrating into American life. Nevertheless, the episode was crucial in determining what the consequences of that event would be. The refugee crisis also demonstrated how closely connected events in the Caribbean, in North America and in Europe were in the age of the "Atlantic revolutions."

The refugees who scrambled aboard the ships in the Cap Français harbor between June 21–23, 1793, many of them with only the clothes they were wearing, had no idea what future awaited them. Their only concern was to escape the fighting in the city and the fires that were

---

the *Haitian Revolution* (Jackson, Miss.: University Press of Mississippi, 2005), Gary B. Nash, "Reverberations of Haiti in the American North," *Pennsylvania History* 65 (1998), 44–73, Ashli White, *Encountering Revolution: Haiti and the Making of the Early Republic* (Baltimore, MD: Johns Hopkins University Press, 2010); James Alexander Dun, "Dangerous Intelligence: Slavery, Race, and St. Domingue in the early American Republic," Ph. D. diss., Princeton, 2004, Winston G. Babb, "French Refugees from Saint-Domingue to the Southern United States, 1791–1810" Ph. D. diss., University of Virginia, 1955, John Davies, "Class, Culture, and Color: Black Saint-Dominguan Refugees and African-American Communities in the Early Republic," Ph. D. diss., University of Delaware, 2008, and Rachel Hope Cleves, *The Reign of Terror in America* (Cambridge: Cambridge University Press, 2009).

[2] Tarin to "ma chère mère," September 12, 1793, in AN, D XXV 80, d. 785.

destroying it. In the confusion, families were separated, members of the same army unit found themselves dispersed, and sailors wound up on unfamiliar ships. Most of the hundred or more small merchant ships in the harbor took only a few refugees: according to a document in Moreau de Saint-Méry's papers, many of them sailed with only a handful of passengers, and none carried more than forty-five. The warships saved larger numbers: The frigate *Concorde* had 52, the *Eole* 250, and the *Jupiter*, the last ship to leave the harbor, was packed with 750.[3] Most of the refugees who succeeded in staying on the ships were white; numerous testimonies state that the sailors forced men of color who had come on board to return to shore before the convoy sailed.[4] Nevertheless, as we have seen, a significant number of mixed-race and black women and children also left with the ships.

The total number of refugees is difficult to estimate. The initial contingent who sailed on the convoy that departed on June 24, 1793 probably amounted to 3,000 to 5,000 people, but hundreds of other whites who had been unable to reach the harbor during the crisis or who lived in other parts of the colony managed to leave Saint-Domingue in the months that followed. In September 1793, the *ordonnateur* Wante organized a small convoy that brought an additional 1,200 people, many of them soldiers unfit for duty, to the United States.[5] Although whites had been leaving Saint-Domingue for the United States, France, and safe havens in the Caribbean since the start of the slave insurrection in August 1791, the wave that left the colony after June 20, 1793 certainly outnumbered all the previous departures, and the dramatic circumstances under which they arrived gave them a much larger impact than that of the previous refugees. Neither the refugees nor the ships they sailed on had had any time to prepare for the voyage. Food and water were in short supply on many of the vessels. On the merchant ships, some captains did everything they could to accommodate their unexpected guests, but, as the French vice-consul in Norfolk noted after the fleet arrived, others "mistreated or ransomed them."[6] The experience of the young author of *My Odyssey* was typical. He found himself on the French merchant

---

[3] Note in CAOM, F 3 198 (Moreau de Saint-Méry papers).

[4] *Radoteur*, July 12, 1793.

[5] Charles Etienne Pierre Wante, *Mémoire relatif à l'administration de la partie française de St. Domingue* (Baltimore : Samuel and John Adams, 1793), 11 ; Mangourit to Genet, November 17, 1793, in CADN, Philadelphia 13 ; Sonthonax to Polverel, October 27, 1793, in AN, D XXV 44, d. 420.

[6] Acting Norfolk vice-consul Mallet to Genet, July 15, 1793, in CADN, Philadelphia 15 (correspondence from Norfolk).

ship *Rosalie*, "exhausted with fatigue and in need of food. My clothing, which I had not been able to change for three days, was covered with blood, sweat and dirt, and was almost entirely in tatters." The ship's captain lent him a shirt and trousers, but "Nature had given that good man dimensions and proportions very different from my own," the author recalled, and "the clothes he lent me made my appearance so ludicrous that they even caused some of my companions in misfortune to smile. This borrowed outfit, the only one I had then in the world, had to serve me for the entire voyage ... As soon as the ladies had gone to bed, I went each night on the prow and did the work of a laundryman, and enveloped myself in a sail until the breeze had dried my clothes. Sometimes, armed with a needle, I stopped the too rapid progress of much wear. I carefully guarded my hat and shoes, so that they would honor me at my debarkation." Although his life had been saved, "I was completely ruined, without home, without money, without clothes; I was going to a country of which I knew not the language, the customs, nor habits, and where I had not one person whom I could approach for assistance. I was ignorant of the fate of my family; in vain did I question for news of them among the passengers of our convoy; everyone, as I did, believed them among the number of victims."[7]

Traumatic as his situation was, the author of *My Odyssey* was still better off than many other refugees. Six months after his arrival in Baltimore, a man named Robin wrote that after the fighting, "I was carried to Baltimore without being aware of it; throughout the crossing, I was in a state of imbecility that I could hardly believe when I was told of it." Like the author of *My Odyssey*, Robin "landed on this continent with only the rags that covered my skeleton, and without a coin in my pocket."[8] On board the overcrowded *Jupiter*, with its hundreds of refugees, conditions were in complete disorder at the start of the voyage. "The passengers not knowing or not being able or willing to maintain order, most of the crew more interested in exchanging items they pillaged or saved than in helping to maneuver the ship," Admiral Cambis wrote in his log two days after leaving Le Cap. He managed to improve the situation somewhat over the next few days. "All the passengers now have some place to lie down," he wrote on June 28. "The service they are supposed to perform has been determined; the women and children are no longer exposed on the deck. The distributions of water and food

[7] *My Odyssey*, cited in Popkin, *Facing Racial Revolution*, 216.
[8] Robin, letter of March 12, 1794, in AN, D XXV 81, d. 789.

are regular. The crew is regaining its coherence, but there are still many irregularities due to the disorder of the property saved from the burning of Le Cap ... there are accusations of theft, they gamble, they sell, they trade, and it all results in a very bad spirit of discipline."[9]

Fortunately for the refugees, the convoy enjoyed good weather and favorable winds. At 10 a.m. on July 5, 1793, the *Jupiter* arrived off Cape Henry, Virginia, near the port of Norfolk. Cambis tried to organize an orderly debarkation, but he rapidly lost control not only of the civilian passengers but also of the soldiers and the crew, all of them eager to go ashore as soon as possible. He was left with those who were too ill to get themselves off the ship; it took nearly a week to make arrangements for them.[10] While the French warships left most of their civilian passengers in Norfolk – by July 16, 844 refugees were receiving rations there[11] – most of the merchant ships sailed further into Chesapeake Bay and docked in Baltimore. By July 9, 1793, the French consul there, J. F. Moissonnier, was trying to aid over 1,300 refugees, "men, women, children, old people, wounded and most of them escaped from the sword and the flame, naked, lacking everything, asking me for bread, clothes, shelter. I am overwhelmed by the number," he told the French minister Genet in Philadelphia.[12]

The arrival of these refugees on their shores was not a complete surprise to the residents of the United States. The rich French colony was one of the main destinations for Yankee traders: between August 1789 and the end of 1793, ships coming from Saint-Domingue constituted at least 18 percent and sometimes as much as 25 percent of the total arriving in Philadelphia, the largest port in the United States, and hundreds of Philadelphia merchants did regular business with the French colony. From the start of the troubles in Saint-Domingue, the American press carried extensive reports on events there, including the reaction to the French National Assembly's decree of May 15, 1791 granting rights to a small number of free people of color, and the outbreak of the slave insurrection in the North Province in August 1791.[13] The sudden and violent collapse of the white dominated colonial order in Cap Français

---

[9] Cambis, log of *Jupiter*, entries for June 26 and 28, 1793, in AN, D XXV 54, d. 521.
[10] Cambis, log of *Jupiter*, entries for July 6–10 and 13, 1793, in AN, D XXV 54, d. 521.
[11] Account memorandum, 4 vent. II, in CADN, Philadelphia 15 (correspondence from Norfolk).
[12] Moissonnier, letter to Genet, July 9, 1793, in CADN, Philadelphia 10 (correspondence from Baltimore). A copy of this letter is in AN, D XXV 11.
[13] Dun, "Dangerous Intelligence," 28–30, 69, 121–6.

seemed to confirm both abolitionists' predictions that the cruelty of slavery would drive its victims to revolt and the fears of anti-abolitionists
that a slave rebellion would result in widespread destruction. Regardless
of their attitudes toward slavery, however, Americans' first impulse was
to help the refugees landing on their shores.

The stories of horror that the refugees and the American ship captains
immediately transmitted to the local newspapers inspired an outpouring of sympathy. "The man who would withhold his assistance, under
these circumstances, we hope, does not reside in America," the *Virginia
Chronicle* editorialized.[14] In Norfolk, a large building was turned into a
common shelter, while a Frenchman established in the town worked to
place as many of the refugees as possible with local families.[15] By July 11,
citizens of Baltimore had contributed more than $10,000 to a relief fund.
A committee was set up to allocate the aid, a French doctor offered free
medical care for refugees, and a local theater organized a benefit performance to raise funds for them.[16] A letter from Baltimore reported that
by mid-July, 1,000 white refugees and 500 blacks – a category that no
doubt included individuals of mixed race as well as former slaves – had
reached the city. Four hundred individuals were being housed by private
families, and the city was providing aid to 600 who had no money of
their own.[17] Within a few weeks, the refugees had begun to fan out from
their original landing places. On July 21, 1793 Michel-Ange Mangourit,
the French consul in Charleston, South Carolina, told Genet that he had
registered 66 of them. "Their arrival has stimulated the charity of the
inhabitants of Charleston to the highest degree," Mangourit wrote.[18]

Philadelphia, the largest city in the country, anticipated a bigger
influx. Even before any significant number of refugees had arrived, a
relief committee was established, with designated fund collectors in
each of the city's wards. By July 22, 1793, the committee had recruited
more than fifty members and set up thirteen subcommittees to deal with
issues such as housing, food, and employment for the new arrivals.[19]
The Philadelphia committee divided the six to seven hundred refugees it

[14] *Virginia Chronicle and Norfolk and Plymouth General Advertiser*, July 13, 1793.
[15] Mallet to Genet, in CADN, Philadelphia 15 (correspondence from Norfolk).
[16] Moissonnier to Genet, July 11, 1793, in CADN 10 (correspondence from Baltimore);
   Baltimore Evening Post, July 18, 1793.
[17] Letter from Baltimore, July 16, 1793, in *Philadelphia General Advertiser*, July 20,
   1793.
[18] Mangourit to Genet, July 21, 1793, in CADN 13 (correspondence from Charleston).
[19] *Philadelphia General Advertiser*, 16, July 22, 1793.

anticipated aiding – a figure that turned out to be an underestimate, since 1,273 Saint-Dominguans actually debarked in the city between early July and the end of the year[20] – into categories, depending on whether they expected to go on to France, return to Saint-Domingue, look for employment in the city, buy land and establish themselves as farmers, or whether they fell into the class of "widows whose husbands were massacred, and such as are in an helpless condition." By the first week of August, the committee had collected more than $11,000 and estimated that it would need more than $14,000 before it completed its work.[21] In New York City, a similar committee established by the local chamber of commerce raised more than $10,000.[22]

Even as they cooperated with the Americans to arrange humanitarian assistance for the refugees, the French representatives in the United States – the minister Genet and the French consuls in Norfolk, Baltimore, Philadelphia, New York, and Charleston – also tried to puzzle out the political background to the crisis that had forced the colonists to flee Cap Français and decide what implications it had for national policy. From the start of his mission in the United States, Genet had understood that part of his job involved providing support for the French colonies in the Caribbean. Arriving in the United States shortly after the outbreak of the war between France and Britain, Genet tried to arrange supplies for the colonies; he was also supposed to provide them with funds drawn against the American debt to France for its aid during the War of Independence. Genet wrote to Sonthonax and Polverel during the first days of his mission, and they wrote back in early May 1793, promising to stay in close touch with him and urging him to persuade the press in the United States to give favorable publicity to their measures.[23] Whereas the two commissioners did not know Genet personally, they may have been acquainted with Mangourit, the consul in Charleston, who had been a patriotic journalist in France at the start of the Revolution. In March 1793, Sonthonax wrote a long letter to Mangourit, telling him that "you will see from the scum that Saint-Domingue ejects on your shores that we are driving out the enemies of our two divinities that are really one [liberty and equality] and that our so-called patriots in this country want to separate."[24] Not all the consuls could be counted on to

[20] Nash, "Reverberations," 49.
[21] *Philadelphia General Advertiser*, 7, August 9, 1793.
[22] *New York Diary, or Loudon's Register*, August 10, 1793.
[23] Sonthonax and Polverel to Genet, May 8, 1793, in AN, D XXV 6, d. 59.
[24] Sonthonax to Mangourit, March 26, 1793, in CADN, Philadelphia 13 (Charleston).

endorse Sonthonax's and Polverel's views – Alexandre Hauterive, the French representative in New York City, was not won over to their racial policy until the very end of 1793 – but most of them were Girondin sympathizers predisposed to regard the white colonists from Saint-Domingue with suspicion.

The overwhelming majority of the Cap Français refugees arrived in the United States telling a story that put the entire responsibility for the disaster of June 20, 1793 on the two civil commissioners, Sonthonax and Polverel. The American ships' captains, the source of most of the initial stories published in the press, gave varying accounts, but on the whole, they emphasized the violence perpetrated by the "mulattoes" and blacks in the city, who reportedly "spared neither men, women, nor children."[25] Nevertheless, the Baltimore consul Moissonnier immediately decided that "the perfidious Galbaud" was "the author of all these woes." Even though he had not talked to any of the naval officers, Moissonnier was sure that they, too, had helped incite the violence. "The commissioners, seeing no other way to block the traitor's project, called to their aid the Negroes of the countryside. Twenty-five thousand came to their aid, they were armed and promised their liberty if they would fight for their cause, and in their rage there was no way to hold them back. They slaughtered everyone, burned everything without exception and those who arrive here only saved themselves by their flight and their willingness to abandon their property to save their wretched lives," Moissonnier told Genet on July 9, two days after he had talked to the first refugees.[26] Even before he had received Moissonnier's letter, Genet had embraced the same position. "All the facts that I have been able to assemble up to now bear witness in favor of the purity of your principles and your firmness," he wrote to Sonthonax and Polverel on July 12, 1793, long before he could have received their letter of July 8, 1793.[27]

Genet's rapid decision to embrace the civil commissioners' position owed something to his personal distaste for the institution of slavery and his rejection of racial prejudices. On the tour of the United States he had made in the spring of 1793, from South Carolina to Pennsylvania, he had concluded that the slave states were falling behind their northern neighbors economically because the system accustomed the whites to idleness. "They fear being put on the same level as their slaves if they

[25] *Virginia Chronicle*, July 13, 1793, letter from Baltimore, July 6.
[26] Moissonnier to Genet, July 9, 1793, in CADN, Philadelphia 10 (correspondence from Baltimore).
[27] Genet to Sonthonax and Polverel, July 12, 1793, in AN, D XXV 6, d.58.

do the same work," he commented.[28] In his first letter to Sonthonax and Polverel after receiving the news of the destruction of Le Cap, he assured the two men that he shared their "respect for the rights of men, whatever their color."[29] A month later, he told them that the Philadelphia Quakers supported their policy of abolition. "They do regret that it is not carried out as in Pennsylvania without spilling blood, but they understand the difference in circumstances and, satisfied by the result, they accept the means used."[30] Nevertheless, in spite of all the other ways in which he offended the Americans he encountered, Genet was careful not to make any public remarks against slavery. He had found some of his most enthusiastic supporters among the southern slave-holding supporters of Thomas Jefferson's Democratic-Republican party, and Jefferson himself was initially his strongest ally. Prior to the arrival of the Saint-Domingue refugees, Genet's main concern was to turn the United States into a base for attacks on British shipping and, if possible, to organize invasions of the British and Spanish territories on the continent; he could hardly afford to alienate a substantial part of American opinion by coming out in support of abolition, particularly since the French revolutionary government had not yet taken any steps against slavery in its own colonies. In November 1793, Genet published an open letter complaining about critics who "denounce us as conspirators against property, which is secured by the laws," a phrase clearly referring to slavery in the United States.[31] By throwing his support to Sonthonax and Polverel against their enemies among the refugee colonists, however, Genet was able to contribute to the campaign against slavery without having to mention the issue openly.

At the moment when he was confronted with the Saint-Domingue refugees, Genet's mission was already at a critical point. Encouraged by the enthusiastic welcome he received from American republicans, Genet had refused to accept the United States government's policy of neutrality in the war between France and Britain and tried to appeal over the head of president Washington to the Congress and the American people for support. He had armed privateers in defiance of the American government's orders. His attempt to ignore Washington's authority provoked a strong rebuke from the secretary of state Thomas Jefferson, who told him that

---

[28] Genet, report on America, in LC, Genet papers, reel 7.
[29] Genet to Sonthonax and Polverel, July 12, 1793, in AN, D XXV 6, d. 58.
[30] Genet to Sonthonax and Polverel, August 21, 1793, in AN, D XXV 11, d. 110.
[31] Genet, open letter to the French consuls, in *New York Daily Advertiser*, November 27, 1793.

"the Executive is the sole organ of our communications with foreign governments; that the Agents of those governments are not authorized to judge what cases are to be decided by this or that department." By the last week of July, Washington and his cabinet were beginning preparations to demand that the French government recall the troublesome minister.[32] The debate about Genet divided the American public. As the refugees from Le Cap were arriving in mid-July 1793, a number of newspapers were publishing the "Principles, Articles, and Regulations Agreed Upon by the members of the Democratic Society in Philadelphia" at the end of May, a document asserting that "the Rights of Man, the genuine object of Society, and the legitimate principles of government have been clearly developed by the successive Revolutions of America, and France" and calling for a close alliance between the two countries. Other newspaper articles, however, warned readers to "keep a watchful eye on the true interests of the United States, and upon those naturalized Citizens who seem to prefer their own or a foreign interest to that of their new country."[33] Genet, as yet unaware of the Washington administration's decision to demand his recall, continued to try to stir up public support, but from mid-July onward, more and more of his time and energy was consumed by the Saint-Domingue refugee crisis.

Even as they recognized the scope of the disaster in Cap Français, Moissonnier, the enterprising Baltimore consul, and Genet initially thought that it might turn out to be a blessing in disguise. Genet had been struggling to outfit a few lightly armed privateers in American ports; now he suddenly seemed to have at his disposal the most powerful naval force in the western hemisphere. Furthermore, he knew that just as Sonthonax and Polverel had been assembling a sizable merchant convoy in Saint-Domingue when the journée of June 20, 1793 took place, the British had been preparing a similar group of ships in Jamaica, "the largest and richest fleet of merchantmen ever dispatched from this island," as a letter from the British colony reported when the ships set sail on June 22, 1793.[34] Moissonnier was apparently the first to imagine the possibility of using the warships from Saint-Domingue to intercept the Jamaica convoy. On July 16, 1793, he communicated his brilliant idea to Genet: "There are 200 sail and not one will escape. Furthermore, it

[32] Jefferson to Genet, July 16, 1793, in John Catanzariti, ed., *The Papers of Thomas Jefferson*, v. 26 (Princeton, NJ: Princeton University Press, 1995), 513; Jefferson notes, July 23, 1793, in ibid., 524.
[33] *Baltimore Evening Post*, July 18, 1793, July 20, 1793.
[34] Letter from Kingston, Jamaica, June 23, 1793, in *New York Diary*, August 1, 1793.

would be a useful way to occupy the sailors who, accustomed to disorder, are difficult to manage when they are in port."[35] Moissonnier claimed to have persuaded Admiral Sercey to support the venture. "All America is watching us at this moment, our friends are impatiently waiting for this vigorous stroke, our enemies tremble and try to ascertain our plans," he insisted.[36] Moissonnier's brainstorm had some basis in fact: the Jamaica convoy, which passed off the coast of the United States in the weeks following the Le Cap convoy's arrival in American waters, was guarded only by a single fifty-gun ship of the line and three armed sloops, a force much inferior to the Saint-Domingue squadron.[37] Genet was certainly attracted to the idea of using the fleet for some purpose, but he soon realized that the ships were in no condition to undertake operations on the high seas, both because they were badly in need of repairs and because their crews were in a virtual state of anarchy.[38] Moissonnier's dream of winning the war against the British in one afternoon faded as he and Genet realized that they would be fortunate if they managed to prevent General Galbaud and the rebellious sailors from taking control of the squadron.

While Moissonnier and Genet were reconciling themselves to the reality of the Saint-Domingue crisis, the refugees, the sailors, and General Galbaud, their basic humanitarian needs taken care of thanks to American generosity, were beginning to think about their political futures. Although they all found themselves for the moment in the United States, their eyes were on France. In April 1793, the Revolutionary Tribunal had ordered the execution of Governor Blanchelande for what seemed, in comparison to the loss of Cap Français, relatively minor offenses. Who would the leaders of the embattled metropolitan republic hold responsible for the disaster that had just engulfed the country's most valued colony, and what punishment would they impose? The question was certainly on General Galbaud's mind. Held in custody on the *Jupiter* by the agreement that Cambis had reached with the ship's sailors, he wrote to Genet on July 8, 1793, insisting on his patriotism and demanding that the minister give him the opportunity to present his side of

---

[35] Moissonnier to Genet, July 16, 1793, in LC, Genet papers, reel 5.
[36] Moissonnier to Genet, July 20, 1793, in CADN, Philadelphia 10 (correspondence from Baltimore).
[37] *London Times*, August 21, 22, 1793. According to the *Times*, Moissonnier overestimated the size of the convoy, which in fact contained only 140 merchant vessels, carrying goods the newspaper valued at 3 million pounds. (*London Times*, September 6, 1793).
[38] Genet to minister of foreign affairs, July 28, 1793, in LC, Genet papers, reel 5.

the story.[39] He was well prepared to do so: he had begun working out his line of argument even before the crisis of June 20, 1793, and throughout the months that followed, he continued to draft memoranda justifying himself, often in close collaboration with his wife. In one of the more curious versions of his defense, written in Madame Galbaud's handwriting and alternating between the third person and his own voice, he even made a virtue out of the fact that the first assault on the commissioners on June 20 had been completely disorganized: the fact that he had not appointed commanders for the sailors, or made any serious effort to win over the white residents or the troops, proved that "there was no shadow of conspiracy in my conduct."[40]

On July 12, 1793 – the same day when Genet wrote to Sonthonax and Polverel promising them his support – Galbaud's appeal was resoundingly echoed in a letter to the National Convention from the crews of the ships: "Treason, perfidy, brigandage, assassins, fires, uprising of the freedmen against their benefactors and their fathers, and, due to these same freedmen, revolt of the slaves who mixed their cruelty with that of their instigators ... We denounce to you the authors of these crimes, it is your duty to look into them and to punish with severity those who, in ... ruining, slaughtering, tormenting in every manner the white population, have finally succeeded in procuring for the negroes in revolt an independence that will soon result, after having destroyed the wealth of the nation, in bringing about their own destruction," the sailors' manifesto read. After denouncing Sonthonax's and Polverel's attack on Port-au-Prince, the sailors charged them with the destruction of Le Cap: "We have left it absolutely looted, devastated, all the riches that it contained carried away or left to the flames that consumed it for four days. And all these horrors, who ordered them? Polverel and Sonthonax. General Galbaud wanted to join us in opposing the commission of all these crimes, Galbaud was betrayed ... We demand justice and vengeance."[41] The sailors thus endorsed the most uncompromising version of the white colonists' version of events and allied themselves with General Galbaud.

---

[39] Galbaud to Genet, July 8, 1793, in LC, Genet papers, reel 5.
[40] Notes for Galbaud's defense, n.d., in AN, D XXV 48, d. 465. On the last page of this document, Galbaud himself copied out the words "A tous les coeurs bien nés que la patrie est chert [sic]" ("to all well-born hearts, how the fatherland is dear") a dozen times.
[41] "Les hommes de mer et canonniers employés sur les v.aux de la république et sur les navires de commerce» to National Convention, July 12, 1793, in AN, D XXV 80, d. 785.

By the same token, they put themselves in conflict with Genet, the French Republic's official representative in the United States.

Galbaud, the sailors, and the civilian colonists were united in insisting that they were true French patriots, whereas Sonthonax and Polverel were conspirators bent on sabotaging their country's vital interests. Just as the holiday of July 14 had given Sonthonax and Polverel a chance to symbolically integrate the newly emancipated blacks in Saint-Domingue into the French national community, the celebration offered their enemies among the Saint-Domingue refugees an opportunity to reaffirm their patriotism. The occasion was especially important because American supporters of the French cause were eager to join in the celebrations, giving the refugees the chance to impress on their hosts the notion that they were oppressed champions of liberty. In Baltimore, the sailors decorated the ships with tricolor flags, and the naval vessels fired salutes. Moissonnier was less pleased when eighty sailors, armed with heavy sticks decorated with tricolor ribbons, paraded through the streets of the city; he feared they were looking for a fight. In Charleston, Americans and French refugees held joint festivities.[42] In Norfolk, Admiral Cambis allowed American Francophiles to come on board the *Jupiter* for the holiday; he had to break up a dispute that ensued when some of the sailors noticed that one of the visitors was carrying letters from the British colony of Jamaica.[43]

In addition to demonstrating their patriotism, many of the refugee colonists imagined that they could somehow reconquer Saint-Domingue and reclaim their lost properties. In late July, Moissonnier complained to the city magistrates in Baltimore about a tumultuous assembly the refugees had held in the city to discuss their plans. "The disorder reached the point where there were fisticuffs," he reported. "Seduced by a few agitators who managed to save their wealth, [they] were ready to renew almost before your eyes the massacres of which they have been the victims and which their intrigues in a friendly country show that they deserved," he continued, before urging the city government to ban any such gatherings that did not have his approval.[44] Genet had already decided that he needed to prevent the colonists from returning to the island, where

[42] *Philadelphia General Advertiser*, July 22, 1793 (Baltimore, July 16); Moissonnier to Genet, July 16, 1793, in LC, Genet correspondence, reel 5; Mangourit to Genet, July 21, 1793, in CADN, Philadelphia 13 (correspondence from Charleston).
[43] Cambis to Genet, July 15, 1793, in AN, D XXV 51, d. 489.
[44] Moissonnier to Baltimore city magistrates, July 29, 1793, in CADN, Philadelphia 10 (correspondence from Baltimore).

he realized they would try to undermine Sonthonax and Polverel; he specifically ordered Moissonnier to prevent any of them from chartering ships to go to Jérémie, where they could join the white forces opposing the commissioners.[45] Having abandoned hope of using the warships to capture the British convoy from Jamaica, Genet's next impulse was to send the ships and the refugees back to France immediately. By late July, however, admirals Cambis and Sercey had convinced the French minister that the warships were in such bad condition and the crews so insubordinate that it would be unsafe to rely on them as an escort for the merchant convoy, which, in spite of everything, was still carrying a substantial cargo of colonial products whose loss could not be risked. The merchant captains, eager as they were to return to France, also reported that their ships needed refitting before they could sail.[46] Hoping to break up the collusion between the civilian refugees on shore and the sailors on the warships, Genet ordered the naval vessels to leave the Chesapeake area for New York City.[47]

As he grappled with the many dimensions of the crisis facing him, one of Genet's top priorities was dealing with General Galbaud. Having decided that the general's revolt against the civil commissioners in Saint-Domingue was unjustified, Genet felt himself compelled to see that Galbaud was held responsible for his actions; otherwise, the authority of the Republic would be severely compromised and he himself might be accused of colluding with a traitor. The difficulty was that Galbaud was on board the *Jupiter*, a heavily armed warship whose crew was unwilling to let him go. Even after he abandoned Moissonnier's dream of using the navy vessels to attack the Jamaica convoy, Genet was still full of plans for their deployment; he was as reluctant to let the *Jupiter* return to France as he was to leave Galbaud unpunished. Galbaud, on the other hand, was fearful of being sent to France alone, without supporters to back up his version of the events of June 20, 1793. The warship crews, for their part, had made it clear even before those events that they were desperate to return to France; their frustration at being stuck in the colony had been one of the main reasons for their hostility to Sonthonax and Polverel. In addition, however, the sailors were determined to keep

---

[45] Genet to Sonthonax and Polverel, July 26, 1793, in AN, D XXV 6, d. 58; Genet to Moissonnier, July 30, 1793, in CADN, Baltimore 8.

[46] Memorandum from "The Captains of the commercial vessels assembled extraordinarily at the Consulary House under the sanction and presidency of Citizen Hauterive Consul of the French Republic," n. d., in LC, Genet papers, reel 5.

[47] Genet to minister of foreign affairs, July 28, 1793, in LC, Genet papers, reel 5.

General Galbaud in their midst as an alibi for their actions in Cap Français. Cambis tried unsuccessfully to convince the sailors to obey orders, but they "think they are the people and that as a result it is their will that decides," he noted in his logbook.[48] On July 21, 1793, a council of sailors from the warships drafted a letter to Genet stating their position: "Citizen Galbaud led us in the fight: we all followed him. We flew in his wake, and we expected to be able to follow him to France, without any difficulties other than those of the voyage ... Our interests dictate that we watch over him more than anyone else."[49] Genet's representative in Norfolk tried to convince the sailors that their fears were unfounded and their resistance to the minister's instructions unjustified, but they ignored him.[50] To reinforce their position, the *Jupiter* sailors refused to release Polverel's son and lieutenant-colonel Le Blanc of the 16th dragoons, both of whom had been taken prisoner by Galbaud's forces on June 20, 1793 and both of whom had appealed to Genet for help when the ship reached the United States.[51]

At the beginning of August, admirals Cambis and Sercey did manage to move the naval vessels to New York harbor, where, as a local newspaper reported, "the citizens, to the number of several thousands, collected on the battery, to welcome them."[52] The minister Genet arrived from Philadelphia shortly afterward; throughout the most critical period of his dealings with the American government, he was constantly preoccupied with the problem of Galbaud and the warships.[53] From the *Jupiter*, Galbaud complained to Genet about the health problems that he and his family were suffering as a result of their confinement and about the fact that he had not received his salary since the events of June. "Consider, Citizen, that most of my things and those of my family were stolen at Le Cap, [and] that I have with me my wife, three children, a tutor, a

---

[48] Logbook of *Jupiter*, entry for July 20, 1793, in AN, D XXV 54, d. 521.
[49] Committee of sailors to Genet, July 21, 1793, in LC, Genet papers, reel 5. The committee meeting was held on the *Jupiter*, but the letter was also signed by sailors from six other ships.
[50] Cassan to crew of *Jupiter*, July 23, 1793, in AN, D XXV 6, d. 60.
[51] Polverel fils and Le Blanc, letters of July 9, 1793, in LC, Genet papers, reel 5.
[52] *New York Diary*, August 3, 1793.
[53] On Genet's mission, see Harry Ammon, *The Genet Mission* (New York: W. W. Norton, 1973), John Catanzariti, "The Recall of Edmond Charles Genet," in Catanzariti, ed., *The Papers of Thomas Jefferson*, v. 26 (Princeton, NJ: Princeton University Press, 1995), 685–92, Stanley Elkins and Eric McKitrick, *The Age of Federalism* (New York: Oxford University Press, 1993), 330–73, and William R. Casto, *Foreign Affairs and the Constitution in the Age of Fighting Sail* (Columbia, SC: University of South Carolina Press, 2006).

secretary, two aides-de-camp, two chambermaids and a cook," Galbaud protested, adding that "the sad lesson about the human heart that I am experiencing at this moment will make me abandon without regret a life that one can hardly share except with sensitive souls."[54] On August 10, 1793, the first anniversary of the overthrow of the French monarchy, the sailors staged another patriotic celebration. "To evince to the world the pleasure they felt on the return of this day, all the French ships riding at anchor in our harbour were beautifully decorated, with the flags of different unions, which exhibited a delightful variety; and at 12 o'clock, the Admiral's ship fired a salute, which was immediately followed by all the others," the *New York Daily Gazette* wrote. Prevented from taking part in the public ceremony, Galbaud sent letters to the New York papers insisting on his republican sentiments.[55] He was nevertheless resigned to the idea of being sent back to France without the sailors; on the day of the republican festival, he wrote to Thomas Millet, one of the leaders of the colonists' campaign against Sonthonax and Polverel, asking Millet to accompany him on his trip, so that he would be "surrounded by real patriots ... capable of shedding light on the events of Saint-Domingue and above all on the innumerable crimes of the commissioners."[56] (See Figure 9.1.)

Although Galbaud was willing to return to France with a small coterie of supporters, the sailors remained adamantly opposed to his departure. Genet worried that the behavior of the sailors and the soldiers on the ships was undermining his campaign to win American support. "The sailors and soldiers did not recognize any authority, did not obey any order. They went all over the town and caused scandals whose effect, among a calm and peaceful people, could only be very detrimental to the French cause and furnish new ammunition to the enemies of liberty and of our new laws," he wrote in a subsequent report.[57] On August 16, 1793, Genet, despite the dubious nature of his claim to authority over military forces, convened a council of the naval commanders to announce his decision to send Galbaud back to France on one of the smaller warships while retaining the rest of the squadron for operations in the western hemisphere. The troublesome crew of the *Jupiter* were to be disarmed and allowed to leave the ship; they would be replaced by sailors from

---

[54] Galbaud to Genet, August 8, 1793, in LC, Genet papers, reel 5.
[55] *New York Daily Gazette*, August 12, 1793; *New York Diary*, August 12, 1793.
[56] Galbaud to Thomas Millet, August 10, 1793, in AN, D XXV 48, d. 460.
[57] Genet, "Rapport sur la réorganisation de l'escadre venue de St. Domingue," in LC, Genet papers, reel 6.

FIGURE 9.1. The *Jupiter* in New York Harbor.

A French warship, believed to be the *Jupiter*, the 74-gun flagship of the Saint-Domingue squadron, lies at anchor off lower Manhattan in this drawing from 1793–94. The *Jupiter*'s crew supported General Galbaud and, in August 1793, they mutinied to prevent the French minister Edmond Genet from sending him back to France. One of the small boats that allowed communication between the warships and the shore can be seen tied up to the warship's starboard side.

Source: Collection of The New York Historical Society (Negative no. 81520d).

one of the other vessels.[58] On board the *Jupiter*, the restive sailors and soldiers held a meeting, with Madame Galbaud in attendance, and then sent a delegation led by a certain Bonne, a soldier who emerged as the leader of the movement, to meet with Admiral Cambis. "This delegation spoke of plots, of treason, of traitors, et cetera, and [spoke] with little respect about the minister," a naval officer reported.[59] Using the same procedure they had followed in organizing the movement of June 20, 1793 in Cap Français, the sailors from the *Jupiter* sent delegates to the other warships, urging them to refuse orders to sail for any destination other than France. And, as they had on that day, the sailors imprisoned

[58] Genet to ministre des affaires étrangères, August 15, 1793, and proces-verbal de conseil de guerre, in LC, Genet papers, reel 6.

[59] Voisin, "Rapport de la garde du 16 aout 1793," in LC, Genet papers, reel 6.

Admiral Cambis in his cabin, with a guard at the door.[60] According to Polverel's son, still held prisoner on the *Jupiter*, the soldiers guarding him threatened to kill him and other supporters of the commissioners.[61]

Confronted with this disobedience, Genet convened a second council meeting on August 18, which reaffirmed the decisions taken two days earlier.[62] In reply, the *Jupiter* sailors wrote a letter accusing him of "trying to force us to leave without your approval" or of wanting "to keep us here, so that we will see some event take place, organized for some political reason, of which we will inevitably be the victims."[63] For more than a week, the warship lay off lower Manhattan while Genet tried to regain control of it through a combination of threats to cut off the sailors' food supplies and promises that they would not be punished if they submitted to his authority.[64] On board the ship, Cambis, by now something of an old hand at waiting out mutinies, concluded that many of the crew were looking for a way out of the impasse they found themselves in. He noted, however, that the latest reports from Europe, concerning the expulsion of the Girondin deputies from the Convention and the federalist uprisings that had followed, were confusing the situation and giving the mutineers "courage that they would not have had if there had not been an expectation of some disorder in France."[65] Nevertheless, individual sailors began slipping off the vessel to submit themselves to Genet's authority, even though Madame Galbaud reproached these turncoats for violating the oath they had sworn to defend her husband. "She was very familiar with the sailors; I heard that she even took their arms," one witness later testified.[66]

Still unable to dislodge the general from his floating redoubt, Genet tried a different tack. Admiral Cambis having alerted him to the fact that Galbaud was receiving messages from the colonists on shore, Genet directed a raid on the lodgings of the Saint-Domingue journalist Tanguy-Laboissière and seized his papers. According to Genet, they provided evidence of "the infernal conspiracy threatening the Republic's squadron." In fact, Tanguy's papers consisted mostly of letters and newspaper articles written months earlier in Cap Français and fanciful plans for creating

---

[60] Cambis, logbook of *Jupiter*, in AN, D XXV 54, entry for August 17, 1793.

[61] Polverel fils to Polverel and Sonthonax, September 21, 1793, in AN, AA 55, d. 1511.

[62] Proces-verbal of conseil de guerre, August 18, 1793, in LC, Genet papers, reel 6.

[63] *Jupiter* crew to Genet, August 19, 1793, in LC, Genet papers, reel 6.

[64] See the report, "Comité permanent. 24 Aug. au soir," in AN, D XXV 6, d. 59.

[65] Cambis, logbook of *Jupiter*, entry for August 22, 1793, in AN, D XXV 54, d. 521.

[66] Genet, "Suite de rapport de mon voyage a New York," in LC, Genet papers, reel 6; testimony of François Raimbault, 24 mess. II, in AN, D XXV 56, d. 557.

an army of colonists to return to Saint-Domingue, but the fear of being formally accused of counterrevolutionary conspiracy led more of the sailors to abandon Galbaud. "The publication of this project detached from Galbaud those [sailors] who really wanted to go back to France," Polverel's son wrote to his father.[67] On August 28, the sailors finally released Cambis from confinement and allowed Captain Jean-Baptiste François Bompard, who had gained a hero's reputation earlier in the month when his ship, the *Embuscade*, bested the *Boston*, a British frigate, in a prearranged duel, to take command of the ship;[68] Galbaud's family was sent ashore.

Realizing that he was no longer safe on the *Jupiter*, Galbaud made another of the impulsive moves that had characterized his conduct in the New World. On the night of August 29, 1793, he and his devoted aide-de-camp, André Conscience, succeeded in commandeering the *Jupiter*'s longboat. The duty officer sounded the alarm, and a boat from the *Eole* chased them back to the *Jupiter*, where Conscience harangued the crew, telling them that if they did not stand by the general, he would be delivered into "the bloody hands of the civil commissioners." He succeeded in winning the support of enough of the sailors so that Galbaud was able to set off again. Accompanied by Conscience, the mutiny leader, Bonne, and several other supporters, he finally reached the shore.[69] Galbaud's escape set the stage for a farcical police pursuit. Informed of Galbaud's evasion on August 30, 1793, Genet promptly demanded arrest warrants for him, Conscience, and Bonne from the local authorities. Learning that Galbaud's party had hired two coaches and started up the road along the Hudson river, Genet dispatched two French gendarmes, Arnaud Préty and a colleague named Vesprès, to follow them. The two policemen kept up the pursuit all night and finally reached the Westchester County inn where the Galbaud party was sleeping at 2 A.M. in the morning. Suitably bribed, the innkeeper led them to the upstairs room in which Galbaud was sleeping, and the general initially indicated that he would surrender peacefully; the gendarmes retreated to let him put on his clothes.[70]

An hour later, Madame Galbaud emerged from the general's room and informed the gendarmes that her husband "had changed his mind, and ... was determined to defend himself to the death." The

---

[67] Genet, "Suite de rapport" and "Pieces inventoriées appartenant aux papiers trouvés chez Tangui," in LC, Genet papers, reel 6; papers of Tanguy-Laboissière, in AN, D XXV 73, d. 734; Polverel fils, letter of September 21, 1793, in AN, AA 55, d. 1511.

[68] On the *Embuscade*'s duel with the British frigate *Boston*, see Casto, *Foreign Affairs*, 122–38.

[69] Lelay, "Rapport de l'officier de Garde," August 29, 1793, in LC, Genet papers, reel 6.

[70] Report of Arnaud Préty and Vesprès, August 30, 1793, in LC, Genet papers, reel 6.

French gendarmes sent an American constable who spoke French to investigate: he retreated down the stairs and announced that Galbaud's companion Bonne was blocking the door, holding his unsheathed saber in his hand. The French gendarmes, "after careful reflection," were finally preparing to go after their quarry when "the American citizens pointed out to us, that we could not do any such thing, seeing that our papers were only dated the first of September and were only enforceable on the following day": the magistrate's clerk in New York City had forgotten that August had thirty-one days! Undaunted, the two French gendarmes requested assistance from the local authorities and prepared to wait until midnight, when their arrest warrants would finally be valid. Over the course of August 31, 1793, the inn filled up with people, and the French gendarmes realized that Galbaud's partisans, led by Madame Galbaud, were winning the sympathy of the local citizenry. Once night fell, "the citizen Galbaud and his adherents escaped in the crowd, with clothes they had been lent, and in the darkness we could not recognize them," as Préty later reported. Unaware of the general's evasion, he and Vesprès remained in the inn, distracted by Madame Galbaud, who "was speaking English a mile a minute." Préty explained to Genet that "the lady tried to touch my heart with her tears and her pretty ways of persuasion ... she poses her body in the most advantageous postures. I await your orders to tell me what to do." Préty may have been more susceptible to Madame Galbaud's influence than he admitted: he was a former colonist from Jérémie who had distinguished himself by his hostility to the free men of color before changing sides and joining Sonthonax's party. He remained at the inn for another week, enjoying Madame Galbaud's company and telling Genet not to worry, since "we have Galbaud surrounded."[71] Meanwhile, the general, Conscience, and Bonne had made their escape and were on their way to Canada.

Galbaud's decision to take refuge in territory belonging to a country at war with France was another example of his penchant for hasty and ill-considered decisions: it allowed Genet to depict him as a traitor to the republican cause. To Galbaud's surprise, the British showed him no sympathy: when he reached the border settlement of Saint John's, he was arrested and sent to Quebec City. At the end of October, he, Bonne and Conscience escaped and crossed back into the United States. Galbaud

---

[71] Report of Arnaud Préty and Vesprès, August 30, 1793, and letters to Genet, September 1 and 6, 1793, in LC, Genet papers, reel 6. On Préty's background, see Ardouin, *Etudes sur l'histoire d'Haïti*, 3:51.

wanted to remain close to the Canadian border, in case he had to flee again, but he was increasingly miserable. From his refuge, he wrote to a correspondent in New York City in early December, complaining that he had received no word of the fate of his family and that he was running out of money. His last resource was the prized possession he had taken such pains to safeguard when he jumped into the water in Le Cap on June 21: "I have a gold watch; maybe you could find me some sympathetic person who would lend me seven or eight guineas on it," he wrote.[72]

While the conflict with Galbaud and the sailors was Genet's most pressing problem, the French consuls were more preoccupied with the ongoing issue of providing relief for the refugees and with the political difficulties posed by their campaign against Sonthonax and Polverel. From Charleston, Mangourit wrote to tell Genet that other Dominguans had expelled a soldier from the 16th dragoons, the military unit most loyal to the commissioners, from the hotel where they had been staying, and that they had taken over the republican club Genet had founded in April. "You can imagine how all these Frenchmen in general poison the spirits of the Charlestonians," Mangourit wrote. "Some depict their fellow citizens as killers or brigands; others say that everything is well in France, but that everything is wrong in Saint-Domingue ... they go into ecstasy about the heroism of *citoyenne* Galbaud and the story of her motions on the *Jupiter*: They wish the squadron was in Jérémie." According to Mangourit, a certain Edward Penman, who had founded a Benevolent Society to aid the refugees, was acting as a British agent and recruiting support by loaning them money and inviting them to dinners.[73] In Baltimore, Moissonnier claimed that some of the French sailors had "sworn to exterminate me" because of his support for the commissioners in Saint-Domingue.[74] In Philadelphia, the *Radoteur*, a French-language newspaper written by the Saint-Domingue journalist Gaterau, who had arrived in the United States some time before the events of June 20, 1793, circulated the most bloodcurdling accounts of the events in Le Cap and laid the blame for them on the commissioners, whose names Gaterau disfigured as "Satanas and Pulvereux." Tanguy-Laboissière

[72] Galbaud to "Citoyens législateurs," December 30, 1793,in AN, D XXV 48, d. 462, and letter to Sailly, December 1793, in AN, D XXV 48, d. 460.
[73] Mangourit to Genet, August 16, 1793 and September 18, 1793, in CADN, Philadelphia 13 (correspondence from Charleston).
[74] Moissonnier to Genet, August 6, 1793, in CADN, Philadelphia 10 (correspondence from Baltimore).

resumed publishing his *Journal des Révolutions de la partie française de Saint-Domingue* and put out an appeal from "the Père Duchêne" to the French sailors, urging them to take their ships back to Saint-Domingue to "counter ... the projects of these two criminals who ruin our country, by turning the colony upside down, to take the money they have stolen, and to distribute it to the conquerors, and to the unfortunates who have lost everything, and to take away from the damned negroes the republican bonnets which they don't know how to wear, and which don't go, great God, with the appearance of their faces ... Course for the south, a thousand bombs! course for the south, and the Père Duchêne, in spite of his swollen legs and his fat butt, claims the honor of unfurling the topsail."[75]

In response to this agitation, Genet and Moissonnier, the consul in Baltimore, adopted a deliberate policy of trying to prevent the most militant opponents of Sonthonax and Polverel from either returning to Saint-Domingue or from reaching France, where their accusations would strengthen the campaign against the commissioners and their policies. "Do not think ... of favoring the return of the Saint-Domingue refugees to the colony and try on the contrary to prevent the various expeditions that these gentlemen are said to want to launch for Jérémie," Genet wrote to the Baltimore consul on July 30, 1793. Moissonnier needed little urging; over the next several months, he diligently compiled a long "list of inhabitants of Saint-Domingue who conspire against the French Republic in the United States of America."[76] By early October, the refugees in the major seacoast cities had organized themselves and chosen deputies to carry their accusations against Sonthonax, Polverel, and Genet to France. The news of Sonthonax's general emancipation proclamation added to the urgency of their efforts.[77] At the same time, however, dissension broke out in their ranks. The journalist Tanguy-Laboissière came out in opposition to the National Convention, and a number of the refugees openly supported the British and Spanish invasions of the colony, while others continued to assert their patriotism

---

[75] *Supplement au no. 1, tome II, du Journal des révolutions de la partie française de Saint-Domingue. Le Pere Duchesne aux Bons Enfans des vaisseaux le Jupiter, l'Eole, & à tous les Français qui pechent à la ligne dans la rivière du Nord, & mangent des pommes aux coins des rues. Salut.* in AN, D XXV 115.

[76] Genet to Moissonnier, July 30, 1793, in CADN, Baltimore 8; Moissonnier, list, in AN, D XXV 6, d. 59, and in CADN, Philadelphia 10 (correspondence from Baltimore).

[77] Baudru to Larchevesque-Thibaud, September 27, 1793, in AN, D XXV 80, d. 785.

and their devotion to republican principles.[78] Citing the evidence of their counterrevolutionary sentiments, Genet refused to allocate funds for the refugees' deputies' voyage or to give them the passports they demanded. At the beginning of November 1793, he told them that he considered their assembly illegal, since it was composed exclusively of whites and since its members had defended the rebellious slaveowners in Jérémie.[79] The infuriated colonists replied with an eight-page denunciation of him. After they had fought for the cause of the Revolution for four years, they complained, "your beloved commissioners have deprived us of our liberty and, together with the mulattoes, stripped us of everything we still had." Genet had given aid to "mulattoes and negroes, free or unfree ... who are [the commissioners'] accomplices, while you have inhumanly refused to grant subsistence to us who have been robbed, looted, and burned out by these criminals, or by the people of their caste." Genet had pursued General Galbaud, "this brave man, so persistently that he was obliged to flee to save his life," whereas he had secured the freedom of Polverel's son and Leblanc, the commander of the 16th dragoons, "worthy satellites of the tyrants," and protected "the mulatto Castaing," accused of having killed 600 whites.[80]

Even as they attempted to confront Genet, the refugees had other pressing problems to deal with. Those who reached the United States in the months following the destruction of Le Cap were often as destitute as those who had come with convoy. Many had been robbed by privateers. One of Stephen Girard's friends was victimized during a voyage in early September 1793. "The vessel was searched repeatedly and the sailors who were sent on board as a prize crew carried on their investigations most rigorously and almost demolished the 'Polly' in their examination of cabins, storerooms and hold; pirates could not have carried things more to excess. The value of the passengers' property amounts to about one hundred thousand pounds, and the loss of my belongings deprives me of every resource," he wrote.[81] By the end of August 1793,

[78] *Journal des Révolutions de la partie française de Saint-Domingue*, October 23, 1793, with Tanguy-Laboissière's denunciation of the Convention and other refugees' protests against his position; dossiers of Eustache, in AN, D XXV 77, and Senac in AN, D XXV 78, d.766.

[79] Genet to Barrault Narcay, November 1, 1793, in AN, D XXV 6, d. 60.

[80] Dumontellier, Parran, Simonot, Forestier, and Barrault Narcay to Genet, November 30, 1793, in AN, D XXV 6, d. 58. Polverel and Leblanc had been freed from the *Jupiter* in early September. François Polverel, letter of September 21, 1793, in AN, AA 55, d. 1511.

[81] Aubert to Stephen Girard, September 5, 1793, in APS, Girard papers, roll 11.

the devastating epidemic of yellow fever in Philadelphia was adding to the misery of those in that city. The disease may well have been brought by the refugees themselves, although Jean Devèze, a doctor from Saint-Domingue who had come with the refugees, insisted that there had been no cases of sickness among them before their arrival.[82] "One sees nothing but coffins in the street. They blame the origin of this malady on the French and yet one hardly sees any sick among them! They do not want to treat it the way we do, fear seizes them from the other side, and soon it is all over! In 36 hours they have been deported to the house of the Eternal Father. I'm afraid that if this continues, Philadelphia will soon belong to the French," one refugee wrote.[83] Devèze and some of the other doctors from Saint-Domingue, more familiar with such illnesses than their North American colleagues, threw themselves into the struggle to save the victims, but many of their countrymen who had survived one urban catastrophe in the Caribbean succumbed to another one on the continent. In addition, as one of Genet's assistants explained to Moissonnier, it became impossible to obtain passports for refugees given permission to return to France because Jefferson, the American secretary of state, had left town to escape the plague.[84]

Even the refugees who survived the epidemic had their worries. A collection of letters confiscated by the revolutionary authorities in France in the spring of 1794 gives a vivid picture of their situations in the fall of 1793 and the first months of the following year. "Most of the colonists are reduced to misery, even though the generous and hospitable nation that has taken us in gives assistance to the women, the children, the elderly and the infirm," a colonist named Ferrié wrote to a correspondent in Bordeaux. Adjustment to American life was not easy. "This country is not what people in France imagine," a certain Bolliue wrote to his sister. "The people are not helpful, very uncouth, and show no gratitude for

[82] The standard account of the yellow fever epidemic remains John Harvey Powell, *Bring Out Your Dead: The Great Plague of Yellow Fever in Philadelphia in 1793* (Philadelphia: University of Pennsylvania Press, 1949). Powell concludes that "the presence of yellow fever victims from the sugar islands, whom *aegypti* could feed on before biting native Philadelphians, was a primary social cause of the epidemic" (293). For Devèze's testimony, see Jean Devèze, *Enquiry Into, and Observations upon the Causes and Effects of the Epidemic Disease, which raged in Philadelphia, from the month of August till towards the middle of December, 1793* (Philadelphia: Parent, 1794), 14. According to Powell, Devèze's greatest contribution to the fight against the epidemic was his opposition to the highly toxic regime the American doctor Benjamin Rush wanted to administer to the sick (159–64).
[83] Clausson to Millet, September 18, 1793, in AN, D XXV 69, d. 696.
[84] Bournonville to Moissonnier, September 11, 1793, in CADN, Baltimore 8.

the services that the French have done them."[85] Finding gainful employment was difficult. "The positions here are very scarce, since almost all the colonists and creoles have gone all over the continent and there is not enough work for everyone," another colonist wrote.[86] Those who had arrived with money or skills could sometimes find economic opportunities: one man invested in a brewery, while Batilliot, the former owner of the *Moniteur général*'s prosperous printing shop, settled for work as a journeyman printer.[87] A wealthier refugee reported that he had been able to buy a farm in western Pennsylvania, and that his brother had returned to Saint-Domingue, hoping to bring back some of their slaves: "Land is not expensive here, but labor is, and if we could bring over three or four of our Negroes, it would help us a lot."[88]

Like all refugees, the Dominguans clutched eagerly at every scrap of news coming from the homeland they had left and from the metropole that many of them had not seen for years. Letters were highly valued; Robin, a doctor who had ended up in Philadelphia, complained when he had to depend on "the newspapers ... which I have never read with confidence."[89] Many of the colonists welcomed reports that the British and the Spanish had occupied parts of Saint-Domingue. The news "makes us hope that we will be able to go gather the debris of our fortunes. Three quarters of the negroes demand their masters with all their heart and say that they were fooled by the cannibals of commissioners," one Guyton wrote to a Bordeaux correspondent.[90] "When I get back to the Cape, which I trust will be in May, I'll send you news about your mulatress," another optimistic colonist wrote to a friend in France.[91] Other refugees were less hopeful. A certain Lambert gathered from talking to American ships' captains that the British and Spanish were only interested in plundering the territories they had occupied. "They are even said to be cooperating with the criminal civil commissioners," he wrote.[92] Reports from France inspired equally conflicting reactions. "We thank you for the news that you send us; it causes great concern.

---

[85] Bolliue to sister, January 10, 1794, in AN, D XXV 81, d. 790.
[86] Letter of February 3, 1794, unsigned, addressed to abbé Champion, in AN, D XXV 81, d. 790.
[87] Letter of De Sannay, March 18, 1794, from Baltimore; letter of Robin, March 12, 1794, both in AN, D XXV 81, d. 790.
[88] Letter to Carles, March 18, 1794, in AN, D XXV 81, d. 790.
[89] Letter of Robin, March 12, 1794, in AN, D XXV 81, d. 790.
[90] Letter of Guyton, January 12, 1794, in AN, D XXV 81, d. 790.
[91] Bertrand to Devincent, March 18, 1794, in AN, D XXV 81, d. 790.
[92] Lambert to Riviere, March 4, 1794, in AN, D XXV 81, d. 790.

We see that many members of the National Convention who betrayed it have been guillotined, no doubt some other conspirators will be discovered and then order and tranquility will return," two colonists wrote to a friend in Paris.[93] After recounting his own sufferings in America, another writer added a nervous p.s., saying that there was a rumor that "you, Charrier, Carinau and Roustant have all been guillotined. Relieve me of this cruel worry."[94] But for other refugees, France remained a beacon of hope. Madame Isnard, who had given birth just after making it to safety in the United States, wrote to her relatives to say that her son "wants to live so he can go to Provence and tell his uncles about the misfortunes that his father and mother suffered."[95] Those who wanted to return to France in the fall of 1793 faced numerous obstacles. Genet did not want to help them, and the threat of British privateers discouraged American shippers from carrying them. One French captain who offered refugees passage on his ship assured them that it was well equipped to handle human cargo since he normally used it to carry slaves from Africa![96]

Although as many as a third of the refugees who fled Le Cap in June 1793 may have been people of color, documentation about their fate in the United States is scanty. The French consuls rarely mentioned them, and none of their letters were preserved in the archives. In the southern states, their presence inspired fear. A letter from Portsmouth, Virginia, admitted that "the household family negroes are trusty and well disposed," but the author had heard that "many others ... belong to the insurrection in Hispaniola." The local militia was called out to maintain security.[97] Even in states like Pennsylvania, where a law foreseeing the gradual abolition of slavery had been passed, Saint-Domingue slaves who arrived with their masters were not immediately freed. The Philadelphia merchant Stephen Girard assured a refugee friend that "it is ... quite easy to forward them from here to any southern state on this continent, where they are sold just as in St. Domingo."[98] Most of the more than 400 blacks who arrived in Philadelphia in 1793 were relatively young and so were subjected to the provision of the Pennsylvania law that allowed their masters to retain them as indentured servants until they reached the age of twenty-eight. Knowing no English and

---

[93] Bertrand and Boulineau to Reynouard, March 11, 1794, in AN, D XXV 81, d. 790.
[94] Dumon to Félix Lagarde, March 7, 1794, in AN, D XXV 81, d. 790.
[95] Letter of Madame Isnard, March 3, 1794, in AN, D XXV 81, d. 790.
[96] François Artur of Saint-Malo to Genet, August 25, 1793, in CADN, Philadelphia 15.
[97] Letter of August 21, 1793, cited in Babb, "French Refugees," 60.
[98] S. Girard to Labattut, August 28, 1793, in APS, Girard papers, roll 122.

having no contacts among the local population, many of them wound up working for their former owners.⁹⁹ The knowledge that the law in Pennsylvania guaranteed them certain rights and, even more, the news of the emancipation decrees issued in Saint-Domingue, did encourage some blacks to express their desire for freedom. One white refugee, put in charge of several blacks brought to Baltimore by a friend, wrote that "of all your negroes, only Perroquet behaves himself. The others have been impossible since they learned of the general liberty proclaimed in Saint Domingue by the commissioner-executioners ... I swear to you ... that your negroes are a worry and a burden for me and that the little money they produce is not enough to clothe them."¹⁰⁰ In New York, a refugee complained to the French consul that a slave who had been a domestic servant in Saint-Domingue was insisting that he could not be ordered to do field labor in the United States.¹⁰¹ The chaotic conditions under which the exodus from Saint-Domingue had taken place produced great confusion about the black arrivals' status. Sometimes this benefited former slaves, but in other cases, it worked against them. In Baltimore, an angry refugee denounced Moissonnier for allowing another white to sell eighteen slaves from Saint-Domingue who were not even his legal property.¹⁰²

Conditions were not easy either for the free people of color who had joined the exodus from Saint-Domingue in June 1793 or for those who fled later in the year, fearing the consequences that the decree of general emancipation would have for them. White refugees who blamed the free colored population for inspiring the slave insurrection gave them a frosty welcome.¹⁰³ Many of them were women who had accompanied their white male partners. When Madame Rouvray, the wife of one of the Saint-Domingue military officers who had been forced out of the island in October 1792, caught up with her husband in New York in the summer of 1793, she was furious to find him living with "a quadroon and her bastard, for whom he lays out money that is more than we can afford in our position." Her erring husband was not the only offender. "They all have their mulatress," Madame Rouvray complained, "whom they brought along or who has come to find them."¹⁰⁴ In the United States,

⁹⁹ Nash, "Reverberations," 54–5.
¹⁰⁰ Letter of Lalanne, December 20, 1793, from Baltimore, in AN, D XXV 81, d. 790.
¹⁰¹ Rey de la Rousse to New York Consulate, July 26,1793, in CADN, New York 64.
¹⁰² Duverger de Sermet to Moissonnier, December 5, 1793, in CADN, Baltimore 8.
¹⁰³ Letter of Lacoste, from Baltimore, October 15, 1793, in AN, D XXV 80, d. 786.
¹⁰⁴ Letter of Madame Rouvray to her daughter, August 13, 1793, in M. E. McIntosh and B. C. Weber, eds., *Une Correspondance familiale au temps des troubles de*

tolerance for the racially mixed households that some of the refugees had arrived with was more limited than in Saint-Domingue. Years later, a Philadelphia resident remembered how the local population was shocked by the sight of "Mestizo Ladies, with complexions of the palest marble, jet black hair, and eyes of the gazelle, and of the most exquisite symmetry ... escorted along the pavement, by white French gentlemen."[105] In October 1793, as the consul Mangourit reported to Genet, the South Carolina legislature passed a resolution ordering all free people of color and blacks from the French colony to leave the state within ten days. The consul took a certain pleasure in recounting the effect this had on the white male refugees in Charleston: "Living for the most part in concubinage with mulatresses or free negresses, the proclamation ... was a thunderbolt for them. They thought that if they took responsibility for these loose women, they could keep them, but [the enforcement of the law] was inexorable. They had to let the objects of their caresses depart, or go with them."[106]

Although the French diplomatic officials recognized that most of the refugees were violently hostile to the policy Genet had adopted, they had no alternative but to continue trying to organize practical assistance for them. "Winter is coming, we cannot let a crowd of unfortunates who demand bread and clothes from us die of cold," a consular official wrote to Sonthonax and Polverel.[107] Even as he continued to try to deal with all the different aspects of the crisis caused by the Saint-Domingue refugees, however, Genet realized that his own position was in terrible jeopardy. By late September 1793, he learned that the American government, including Jefferson, whom he had considered an ally, had officially requested his recall. By this time, he had also received a stern letter from the French ministry of foreign affairs, written even before the Americans had made their complaint, denouncing his irresponsible conduct.[108] Genet spent the first days of October churning out a long series of reports justifying himself and explaining to the French ministry the many dimensions

Saint-Domingue. Lettres du Marquis et de la Marquise de Rouvray à leur fille. Saint-Domingue – Etats-Unis (1791–1796) (Paris : Société de l'histoire des colonies françaises, 1959), 101–2.

[105] Cited in Davies, "Class, Culture, and Color," 65.

[106] Mangourit to Genet, in CADN, Philadelphia 13 (correspondence from Charleston), October 20, 1793.

[107] Bournonville, secretary of the Philadelphia legation, to Sonthonax and Polverel, September 20, 1793, in AN, D XXV 6, d. 58.

[108] Ammon, *Genet Affair*, 128; Paul Mantoux, "Le Comité de Salut public et la mission de Genet aux Etats-Unis," *Revue d'histoire moderne et contemporaine* 13 (1909), 6–8.

of the Saint-Domingue crisis. His efforts were in vain: on October 11, 1793, three days after receiving the official American complaint, the Committee of Public Safety decided not only to recall him but to have him returned to France under arrest, along with several other French diplomatic officials accused of complicity in his "criminal conduct." The order, part of the same purge of Brissot's protegés that had resulted in the Convention's vote to recall Sonthonax and Polverel in July, was signed by six members of the Committee, including Robespierre and Saint-Just.[109]

Genet would not learn of this decision for several more months, but he had more than enough bad news to cope with on his own side of the Atlantic. After the resolution of the crisis on board the *Jupiter* at the end of August, the minister had finally succeeded in getting the sailors on the warships to agree to demonstrate their patriotism by undertaking an operation against the British. On October 4, 1793, Genet ordered Admiral Sercey to head into the North Atlantic and recapture the French islands of Saint-Pierre and Miquelon, which the British had seized; after he had accomplished that task, he was to raid the Canadian port of Halifax.[110] Once the ships put to sea, however, the crews, led by the celebrated Captain Bompard, staged yet another mutiny and forced the admiral to give orders to sail back to France. "We are sorry that your labors and those of your worthy assistant Hauterive have met with so little success," an informant on the ships wrote to Genet.[111] By early November, the sailors and soldiers from the warships would be back in France, adding to the number of denunciations against Sonthonax and Polverel for their conduct on June 20, 1793.[112]

Even before Genet learned of the defection of the naval squadron and the collapse of the naval scheme in which he had invested so much effort, news of another disaster in Saint-Domingue had reached him. On October 26, he wrote to inform the French government that the British had landed in Saint-Domingue, with the complicity of the white colonists: "The long conspiracy some of whose threads I informed you about in an earlier dispatch has broken out. Our colonies have their own Vendée revolt. Three officers who escaped from Môle St. Nicolas have just told me that that place and Jérémie have given themselves to the

[109] Mantoux, "Comité de Salut public," 18–19.
[110] Genet to Sercey, October 4, 1793, in LC, Genet papers, reel 6.
[111] "Défection de l'escadre," October 16, 1793, in LC, Genet papers, reel 6.
[112] See the file of depositions from soldiers and sailors from the *Jupiter* in AN, D XXV 80, d. 788.

English ... The arrival of despotism was celebrated and the symbol of our liberty trampled upon." Echoing Sonthonax's and Polverel's defiant response, Genet assured the minister of foreign affairs that the French cause was not lost. "Do not alarm yourself too much about this momentary conquest by our enemies. The volcano of Saint Domingue will soon throw them out along with the traitors who summoned them; nature demands it, all the blacks are free and all of them know they will be put back in chains if the Republic goes under."[113]

Although he already knew that the United States had requested his recall and that he had lost the confidence of the French government, Genet used the opening provided by the news from Saint-Domingue to gain a little leverage with Jefferson. He reminded his interlocutor how much of American commerce depended on Saint-Domingue, and complained bitterly that "it is in this land of liberty that all the projects, all the counterrevolutionary plans that have just been carried out were made." The Saint-Domingue refugees, he warned, were "now plotting, not only against their own country, but against your own independence and your security;" in particular, those in the slave states were irresponsibly spreading the news of the abolition of slavery in Saint-Domingue, thereby "furnishing your southern planters the matter of the continual alarms they experience. France, your friend, will no doubt be pained to learn that such men are not only tolerated, but that they hold public assemblies in Charleston, in Baltimore, in Philadelphia, in New York, and that they freely circulate newspapers full of invectives against France and against its representatives." The least the United States could do, Genet concluded, was to expel these men to the British and Spanish colonies.[114] Jefferson replied that he could not restrict the white colonists' freedom of speech, but he urged local authorities to take measures to protect the French consuls from the refugees' menaces.[115] In the meantime, however, Jefferson himself helped spread the rumor that Sonthonax's close ally, the free colored leader Castaing, was planning to incite a slave insurrection in the south.[116]

Although Genet was unable to get the American government to aid him in his campaign against the French refugees who were determined

---

[113] Genet to minister of foreign affairs, October 26, 1793, in LC, Genet papers, reel 6.
[114] Genet to Jefferson, October 30, 1793, in AN, D XXV 6, d. 58, and LC, Genet papers, reel 6.
[115] Jefferson, letters of November 30, 1793 to Genet and to local authorities, French translations in AN, D XXV 6, ds. 60 and 59.
[116] Letter of December 23, 1793, in Catanzriti, ed., *Papers of Jefferson*, 27: 614.

to overturn Sonthonax's and Polverel's policy of slave emancipation, American merchants, more interested in profits than in politics, did provide vital assistance to the embattled commissioners. Despite the swarms of British and Spanish privateers in the Caribbean, who repeatedly boarded neutral ships looking for French citizens and their property, American vessels continued to carry supplies to Saint-Domingue and to bring back colonial products from regions that had not been devastated by the fighting there. An article published at the beginning of August 1793 reminded readers that "the American public are more interested in the fate of St. Domingo, than they appear to be aware of. One-half of the foreign trade of the French part of this island, which is the richest and most productive portion, and the other French islands, was with the United States, carried on in 1392 vessels, of the burthen of 105,995 tons; and producing, by estimation, an annual balance of one million, one hundred, and sixty-two thousand, four hundred dollars, in favour of the United States."[117] A merchant who made the voyage in October 1793 wrote to a correspondent in Philadelphia that "Cape Français is as quiet as could be desired. The Americans sell their cargoes to the citizens peaceably. If you send me a vessel you may be sure that I shall make as much out of it as possible for your profit."[118] The destruction of the North Province and the activities of the privateers had driven the price of these goods to a level where the potential profits offset the risks of the voyage; in addition, as a French colonist who escaped on one of the ships later wrote, "these good Americans ... had charitably quadrupled the ordinary price of these trips;" after overcharging their desperate passengers, the traders often added to their sufferings by making lengthy detours along the Saint-Domingue coast to pick up sugar and coffee.[119] In spite of all the difficulties besetting him, the *ordonnateur* Wante reported to Sonthonax in early September 1793 that he had somehow managed to pay out 1,500,000 livres for merchandise imported to the island, an indication of the volume of trade still going on despite the events of June 20, 1793.[120] The commissioners were able to generate some income because they had sequestered the plantations of colonists who had fled; the produce of those properties became government revenue.

[117] *Maryland Journal and Baltimore Advertiser*, August 13, 1793, copy in AN, D XXV 38, d. 381.
[118] H. J. Sulanze to Stephen Girard, October 30, 1793, in APS, Girard papers, roll 11.
[119] Laplace, *Histoire des desastres de Saint-Domingue*, 304.
[120] Wante to Sonthonax, September 13, 1793, in AN, D XXV 23, d. 236.

Genet could not claim much credit for the continuation of American trade with Saint-Domingue, but in November 1793, he used his position to make a crucial contribution to the triumph of the abolitionist cause in France. The protection that he gave to the tri-racial delegation of deputies to the National Convention elected under Sonthonax's supervision in Cap Français in late September 1793 was his only policy success, aside from the ardent courtship of New York governor George Clinton's daughter Cornelia that he undertook in the midst of all his other preoccupations.[121] On November 8, 1793, a ship carrying the deputies arrived in Philadelphia. As soon as word of their arrival spread among the white refugees, trouble broke out. Most of the deputies, including the the whites Dufay and Garnot and the black J.-B. Belley, as well as the members of the party accompanying them, had been intimately involved in the events of June 20, 1793 on the commissioners' side. "As I write this, I have learned that what I feared has happened," an official in the Philadelphia consulate wrote to Genet. "The citizens Dufay and Garnot, deputies, have been insulted and struck. The deputies of color are in danger of being massacred. I'm going to ask for police protection."[122] The mayor of Philadelphia issued a public proclamation denouncing the violence against the deputies' entourage, one of whom had been "attacked ... with swords, sticks and fists" and thrown in the water.[123] The Saint-Domingue deputies promptly left Philadelphia for New York, where the consul Hauterive noted their presence on November 10. Hauterive, who had come to despise Genet, was initially as hostile to Sonthonax's allies as any of the refugees. Trying to imagine what a society dominated by black ex-slaves might look like, he speculated that in the end, they would "turn their senseless fury against their own kind and exterminate themselves, leaving no one to mourn so much debris of the unhappy human race." He claimed that one of the black deputies had actually abandoned his mission when he encountered his former master: "he forgot that he was the representative of his color to the National Convention and, trampling underfoot his assignment and his privileges, he said, 'Me find my master. Me happy!' and he put himself back in the chains of slavery."[124]

[121] See "Entretien d'hier au soir," a fictionalized version of his marriage proposal, dated 13th day, 5th month of An II (Feb. 1794), in LC, Genet papers, reel 7.
[122] Beauvarlet to Genet, November 8, 1793, in AN, D XXV 6, d. 60.
[123] Proclamation of Matthew Clarkson, November 8, 1793, in *New York Daily Advertiser*, November 13, 1793.
[124] Hauterive, journal, entries for November 10, 11, 12, 1793, ms. in New York Historical Society (NYHS) collection. No confirmation of the story about the deputy who voluntarily returned to slavery is known.

Genet's reaction to the arrival of the Saint-Domingue delegation was entirely different. In a diary entry on November 16, 1793, the scandalized Hauterive denounced Genet for permitting the scene he had witnessed at the minister's house:

The three colors of Saint-Domingue: men, women, servants ... an addition to the tide of *métis* in the form of Madame Robquin, mulatress belonging to the philanthropic couch of citizen Robquin, soldier, commander of the unit of which the citizen Belley, a black of distinction, wears the epaulettes, so many good things all brought together at once in the same house, at the same table ... the rays of the minister breaking forth on so many foreshadowings of the coming triumph of the inferior colors ... while Saint-Domingue is perhaps at this moment the tomb of an entire generation, while two races fight to exterminate each other, while in America your close connections with a party that almost all of America abhors, mean that your conduct is spied out, and they will call the reception you give to men it fears a crime, adding a horde of enemies to those who your thoughtlessness has already earned you ...[125]

The refugee colonists were equally furious. In a long letter denouncing Genet's various offenses, they did not fail to mention his association with "Dufay and others as criminal as himself," and in particular "three negroes whom the ferocious Sonthonax only freed, without having the power to do so, only elevated in rank, only named or had named deputies to the Convention because they had distinguished themselves from their comrades by the quantity of crimes they had committed and by their atrocities."[126]

Genet's public reception for the Saint-Domingue deputies was indeed an epoch-making event, both for France and for the United States. He was the first representative of the French Republic outside of Saint-Domingue to endorse the validity of the measures Sonthonax and Polverel had taken, and the first to recognize the official status of the deputies of African descent sent from the colony. Hauterive was entirely accurate in seeing Genet's gesture as a defiance of racial norms in the United States as well as in Saint-Domingue: slavery was still legal in New York City – a law providing for its gradual abolition would not be passed until 1799[127] – and the notion of a black man or even a man of mixed race holding political office remained unthinkable there. Furthermore, Genet's determination to stand by the Saint-Domingue deputies had

[125] Hauterive, journal, entry for November 16, 1793, ms. in NYHS.
[126] Colonists' denunciation, November 30, 1793, in AN, D XXV 6, d. 58.
[127] Patrick Rael, "The Long Death of Slavery," in Ira Berlin and Leslie M. Harris, eds., *Slavery in New York* (New York: The New Press, 2005), 125–9.

some real effect. The most unexpected convert to the new order was consul Hauterive. Ten days after his denunciation of Genet's conduct, he confided his change of heart to his diary:

I saw a deputation of color arrive, at first I judged them unjustly, in consider-ing things more closely, it is a reunion of men infinitely kinder, more sociable, less impassioned, more thoughtful than any of those who have accused them of frenzy, of stupidity, of obstination. Dufay is a well-educated man, with good manners, and who shows none of the penchants for extermination that have been imputed over and over again for so many months to the party whose organ he is going to be at the National Convention. Garnot is less attractive, but given that his mind is less cultivated and his manners more common, he would be more inclined to get carried away ... These two blacks have the air of good fellows, the most humane character expresses itself in the dusky tone of their faces, all they have gotten from the revolution is the confidence provided by the certainty that their color does not degrade them. They have with them women who appear lovable and decent. It is a long way from that to cannibal women, to cannibal principles, to cannibal sentiments. I find it hard to believe that any of these men killed whites for revenge, and there are few sailors who have passed through here of whom I would say as much.[128]

Hauterive was not the only person favorably influenced by contact with the Saint-Domingue deputies. Louis Dufay, the white representa-tive who would deliver the speech that would convince the National Convention to vote to abolish slavery three months later, told Sonthonax and Polverel, "we were listened to: people saw that our language was that of truth. They read an account I had written up on board, of the events in Saint-Domingue, and everyone's eyes were finally opened. They begin to see that the colonists tried to mislead all the inhabitants of the continent."[129] Basing himself on the reports Dufay and his colleagues had given him, Genet wrote a long memorandum to the French minister of foreign affairs laying out the case for Sonthonax's and Polverel's poli-cies. "Whatever may happen there is no disguising that St. Domingo has determinately fixed its system. And I believe that the Republic may draw all the advantages of its commerce from the People that it found in the old colony system," Genet wrote. "We shall have a colony which will more and more attach itself to us, children who will love us like Fathers, and soldiers able to a create a new France in the midst of the Mexican archipelago."[130]

[128] Hauterive, journal, entry for November 27, 1793, ms. in NYHS.
[129] Dufay to Sonthonax and Polverel, December 4, 1793, in AN, D XXV 6, d. 54.
[130] Genet to minister of foreign affairs, n.d. but late November 1793, English translation in LC, Genet papers, reel 7.

Although he knew that the Convention had voted to recall Sonthonax and Polverel, Genet boldly supported them. "These two men alone lead on this great Child who still trembles at wooden [idols] and who the Convulsionists strike with a sort of stupefaction," he claimed. He admitted that the emancipation of the slaves in Saint-Domingue was causing some concern in the United States, particularly in the south, but he was confident that the Americans would eventually accept the situation. "If the Revolution is so established as that it cannot be overturned, and if it is indisputable that the new Citizens will for ever remain attached to us, what other thing remains for them to do but to consolidate themselves and not to alienate the Natives of an Island so essential to their commerce in openly favouring the old Tyrants of these Natives and the sworn enemy of the French people?"[131] On December 10, even as he continued to refuse to help the representatives of the white refugees to return to France, Genet gave urgent orders for one of the French government's fast messenger boats to take the three Saint-Domingue deputies, Dufay, Mills, and Belley, to France as quickly as possible. "During their stay in the United States, they have given me indubitable proofs of their civic principles, and I have no doubt that, entrusted with the confidence of the only defenders that the colony of Saint-Domingue has against the enemies of the Republic at this moment that you will take the same interest in them that they have inspired in me," Genet wrote to the naval official responsible for the voyage. The ship's captain was told to take care to put them ashore in a French port where they would not risk encountering a hostile reception.[132]

Sending the deputies from Saint-Domingue on their way to France was Genet's main contribution to the success of the emancipation policy Sonthonax and Polverel had adopted during the crisis of June 20, 1793. As he awaited further news about his own replacement, however, Genet found himself confronted with one final challenge growing out of the events in the Caribbean colony. On December 23, 1793, General Galbaud suddenly resurfaced in New York City. Consul Hauterive, who had a certain flair for drama, outdid himself in his report to Genet about the visit he had received from Galbaud and his supporters, including, as always, Madame Galbaud: "The burning gazes of this arrogant band were fixed on me ... I rang and ordered the guard to come up and make

[131] Genet to minister of foreign affairs, n.d. but late November 1793, English translation in LC, Genet papers, reel 7.

[132] Genet, letters to the *ordonnateur* in New York, December 10, 1793, and to Captain Fuel of the *Impatient*, December 11, 1793, in LC, Genet papers, reel 7.

them leave. Immediately [André Conscience] pulled a pistol out of his pocket, displayed it and pointed it successively at all the people with me. I smiled mockingly and recommended to all those who followed my orders to show their contempt and their moderation. This word shocked Galbaud, who told me he didn't take any orders from me. I replied that if he hadn't come to hear my orders, he could leave … A flood of curses coming from all their throats repeatedly interrupted my conversation with the so-called governor of the Leeward Isles who told me that he was *maréchal du camp*, governor and a hundred other extravagances that ended with an order for me to state my intentions toward him in writing … The ex-general of the Leeward Isles left, menacing me with Tanguy's newspaper, 'me, my Genet and our assassins.'"[133]

While Hauterive was writing to Genet about Galbaud's eruption in his office, Galbaud was writing to the local newspapers and authorities to make his own case. In a letter published in the *New York Daily Advertiser*, the general explained that he refused to allow himself to be sent back to France on a ship designated by the French minister because "although innocent I might become dejected on account of the incredible persecutions which I have suffered, and intimidated at the thought of sinking beneath the load of ridiculous accusations, and perhaps at the moment of my disembarking I may fall a victim to the dagger, guided by the hand of a subaltern agent of the infernal cabal which persecutes me, and approved of by a people irritated against the man who is branded with the odious appellation of a traitor."[134] Unable to convince the American authorities to let them arrest Galbaud, Genet and Hauterive finally agreed that the general could pay his own way back to France on an American ship.[135]

By this time, the United States government had cut off relations with Genet, even though his official replacement, Joseph Fauchet, did not arrive in the country until February 20, 1794. At the same time, the political unity among the white Saint-Domingue refugees was disintegrating, as some of them openly proclaimed their royalist sympathies. The journalist Tanguy-Laboissière's denunciations of the republic threatened to undermine the colonists' claim to be loyal French patriots; on January 27, 1794, sixty-one of them presented the Philadelphia consulate with an address denouncing those Dominguans who had supported the British landing in

---

[133] Hauterive to Genet, December 23, 1793, in AN, D XXV 6, d. 60.
[134] *New York Daily Advertiser*, December 30, 1793.
[135] Contract for Galbaud family's return voyage to France, February 1, 1794, in AN, D XXV 81, d. 791.

the island.[136] Genet's replacement assured the Saint-Domingue refugees, many of them increasingly unhappy in their American asylum – "the life that we lead is pretty hard, shut in around a stove," one of them wrote to a relative in France during the worst of the winter[137] – that any of them who wished to could return to the metropole. Although the new French representatives who replaced Genet recognized that the majority of the refugees were anything but loyal republicans, they decided that they could not attempt to discriminate among them.[138] In April 1794, the so-called Vanstabel convoy, made up of over 100 ships under the command of a naval officer sent from France, set out, carrying a large number of refugees, the remains of the colonial cargoes from Saint-Domingue, and 100,000 barrels of American flour to augment French supplies.[139] The convoy's arrival in France would provide much-needed relief for the French economy, but its passengers were too late to influence the debates there about the abolition of slavery.

By early 1794, the political phase of the crisis caused by the sudden arrival of the refugees from Cap Français was essentially at an end. The Saint-Dominguans who settled in the United States would continue to influence their new country's life in various ways – introducing their fellow citizens to French dance styles, for example – but they largely ceased to be perceived as a potential problem. The most politically engaged refugees either left to pursue the campaign against Sonthonax and Polverel in Paris or else found their way back to Saint-Domingue, like the young author of *My Odyssey*, who joined first the Spanish and then the British in order to fight against the emancipated blacks.[140] The American government and public continued to follow events in Saint-Domingue closely, but they were no longer so concerned that those events would have a direct impact on the United States. The "Genet affair" was also over. Replaced by a new French minister, Genet, summoned

---

[136] Address to Convention, 8 plu. II (January 27, 1794), in AN, D XXV 6, d. 59.

[137] Franjon to brother, January 10, 1794, in AN, D XXV 81, d. 790.

[138] French diplomatic delegation to Minister of Foreign Affairs, 25 ger. II, in Frederick J. Turner, ed. *Seventh Report of the Historical Manuscripts Commission. Correspondence of the French Ministers to the United States, 1791–1797* (Washington, DC: Government Printing Office, 1904), 325.

[139] Letter of Trémis, 28 prairial II, in AN, D XXV 81, d. 797. This dossier also contains numerous lists of refugees who went to France on the Vanstabel convoy. On the arrangements for the colonists' return, see the letter of the French diplomatic mission in the United States, 25 ger. II, in Turner, ed., *Seventh Report of the Historical Manuscripts Commission*, 325.

[140] For the adventures of the author of *My Odyssey*, see "A Colonist among the Spanish and the British," in Popkin, *Facing Racial Revolution*, 252–69.

to return to France to answer the charges brought against him for his conduct, chose to remain in the United States rather than risk the fate of his patron Brissot. He married Cornelia Clinton and bought himself a farm on Long Island. The French warships whose crews had caused so much unrest in the United States were refitted, and some of them went on to serve in a number of subsequent campaigns. Between mid-1793 and early 1794, however, the eastern seaboard of the United States had been the site of a crucial interlude in the political struggles that culminated with the passage of the National Convention's abolition decree of 16 pluviôse An II. By continuing to trade with the French-held parts of Saint-Domingue even after the destruction of Cap Français and the emancipation of the slaves, Americans helped Sonthonax and Polverel hold out long enough for Toussaint Louverture to make up his mind to join their side. And by expediting the voyage of the Saint-Domingue deputies to France, while delaying the return of Galbaud and the white refugees, the minister Genet made it possible for Brissot's policies to triumph, even though Brissot himself was dead.

10

The Decree of 16 Pluviôse An II

On January 23, 1794, Louis Dufay, Jean-Baptiste Mills and Jean-Baptiste Belley, the members of the "tricolor" delegation of Saint-Domingue deputies to the National Convention elected under Sonthonax's supervision in September 1793, finally arrived in Paris. They were the first official emissaries dispatched by the civil commissioners Sonthonax and Polverel to reach the metropole since the journée of June 20, 1793 in Cap Français. Dufay and Belley had played major roles in that event: Dufay's reports had excited the commissioners' suspicions of General Galbaud, and Belley had commanded the free men of color who defended the Government House against Galbaud's first assault. If Dufay, Mills, and Belley had expected to be welcomed in Paris as the representatives of a colony where the principles of the French Revolution had finally been fulfilled, however, they were in for a shock. A few days after their arrival, four policemen entered the apartment where they were staying. Acting on a warrant from the Committee of General Security, which, together with the Committee of Public Safety, constituted the center of France's all-powerful revolutionary government, the policemen interrogated all three men and took Dufay and Mills off to prison.[1] Before they could present their story of the events of June 20, 1793 to the Convention, the Saint-Domingue deputies had to overcome the opposition of the white Saint-Domingue colonists'

---

[1] Interrogations of Dufay and Mills, 10 plu. II, in AN, F 7 4685, d. Dufay, and Dufay and Mills, letter of 12 plu. II, in AN, D XXV 57, d. 563. Belley, the black member of the delegation, was apparently not arrested because the white colonists who had denounced the men had given the police a different name for the black member of the delegation.

lobby and of the leading revolutionary politicians who had come to endorse the colonists' views.

Having narrowly escaped from the Saint-Domingue colonists' wrath in the United States, Dufay, Mills, and Belley already knew that there was strong opposition to the emancipation policy Sonthonax and Polverel had adopted. What they had not fully appreciated before their arrival in Paris was how thoroughly the colonists' campaign against the two civil commissioners had succeeded in shaping the French government's policies. While Sonthonax and Polverel had been crushing white colonial opposition in Saint-Domingue and building their alliance with the free men of color, their political allies in Paris, especially Brissot and Julien Raimond, had been losing their influence and, in Brissot's case, his life. On July 16, 1793, six months before the Saint-Domingue deputies reached France, the National Convention had voted to recall Sonthonax and Polverel and put them on trial, a decision that it reaffirmed in September 1793. Influenced by the colonial lobby, the French revolutionaries had interpreted the journée of June 20, 1793 as evidence of a counterrevolutionary conspiracy, carried out, not by General Galbaud and the white colonists, but by the "Brissotin" civil commissioners. Like Toussaint Louverture's "volte-face" in Saint-Domingue three months later, the Convention's historic decree of 16 pluviôse An II marked the sudden reversal of a policy that had identified Sonthonax and Polverel as enemies rather than recognizing them as key proponents of the extension of the rights of man to the black inhabitants of France's colonies.

To understand the situation that confronted Dufay, Mills, and Belley when they arrived in France, it is necessary to go back to the first half of 1792, when Sonthonax and Polverel were chosen for their mission to Saint-Domingue. As we have seen, the law of April 4, 1792, which created the Second Civil Commission, represented a major defeat for the lobbying efforts of the white Saint-Domingue colonists. The colonial lobby had succeeded in writing into the first French revolutionary constitution of 1791 an explicit guarantee of what would have been called, in the constitutional tradition of the United States, "states' rights" with respect to slavery and racial discrimination. The law of April 4, 1792 said nothing about slavery, but it emphatically asserted the metropolitan government's power to legislate about the "status of persons" in the colonies, and the white colonists regarded it as a mortal threat to their interests. Its passage, coming just seven months after the colonial lobby's success of September 24, 1791, when the Constituent Assembly had repealed its decree of May 15, 1791 granting rights to free men of color whose parents had been free, was a crushing setback for the Club Massiac, the center of the colonial lobby. "Not only the members of the National Assembly, but also the galleries were excited to the point where it would have been dangerous for anyone who expressed a contrary opinion," the Paris representatives of the Saint-Domingue colonists wrote to their correspondents.[2] When the French monarchy was overthrown on August 10, 1792, the Club Massiac was closed down and its papers seized.[3]

Just at the moment when the colonial lobby appeared completely defeated, however, a new set of advocates for the white slaveholders of Saint-Domingue arrived in Paris. Almost at the same time when the French government was selecting Sonthonax, Polverel, and Ailhaud to impose its policies in the colony, the Colonial Assembly in Cap Français was nominating commissioners of its own to make the case for slavery in the metropole. The two groups of men might have hailed each other's ships as they crossed the Atlantic in opposite directions in July 1792. Ironically, one of the three lobbyists sent from Saint-Domingue would abandon his position soon after arriving, just as Ailhaud quit his post in the colony, but the remaining commissioners – two plantation owners named Pierre-François Page and Augustin-Jean Brulley – would, like Sonthonax and Polverel, doggedly pursue their mission until they, like Sonthonax and Polverel, were finally arrested on orders of the Committee of Public Safety.[4] The struggle over the issues of race and slavery in Saint-Domingue in 1793 and early 1794 was, in many ways, a long-distance duel between the two Frenchmen sent to Saint-Domingue and the two Dominguan colonists sent to Paris, and from mid-1793 until 16 pluviôse An II, it was Page and Brulley, not Sonthonax and Polverel, who had the ear of the French Republic's leaders.

Page, Brulley, and their third colleague were named by the Colonial Assembly for the specific purpose of seeking metropolitan approval for a resolution that that body had passed on May 15, 1792, declaring

---

[2] AN, D XXV 76, entry for March 26, 1792.
[3] Debien, *Club Massiac*, 376.
[4] Blanche Maurel. *Saint-Domingue et la Révolution française. Les représentants des colons en France de 1789 à 1795* (Paris: Presses Universitaires de France, 1943), 35. For their nominations, see *Moniteur général de la partie française de Saint-Domingue*, June 2, 1792 (Assemblée coloniale, session of June 1, 1792). Page represented the colony's South Province, Brulley the West. They were originally accompanied by a third man, Lux, representing the North Province, but he quickly disappeared once he reached Paris. Both Page and Brulley owned plantations in several parts of the colony. Brulley was a member of the Société des Philadelphes, the scientific society founded in Cap Français in 1784.

that "the colony of Saint-Domingue cannot exist without slavery" and that "the slave is the master's property; no authority can restrict this property."[5] The news of the law of April 4, 1792 and of the impending arrival of the Second Civil Commission reached Cap Français just as the Colonial Assembly was choosing its own commissioners. Since the reaffirmation of slavery was not in contradiction with the law of April 4, 1792, the three men duly sailed for France; Brulley even took along one of his black domestics.[6] Recognizing that the Legislative Assembly, dominated by Brissot and other radical members of the Jacobin movement, was thoroughly hostile to them, they initially looked to the king and his ministers for support, as their first letters home indicated.[7] Page and Brulley quickly realized, however, that their only hope of success was to identify themselves with the now-dominant radical revolutionaries. Just as Sonthonax and Polverel, chosen as civil commissioners to Saint-Domingue because of their known antislavery sentiments, found themselves obliged to swear to defend that institution once they reached the colony, the colonial commissioners decided that they needed to make a show of their loyalty to the new republican regime in France.

On the day after the journée of August 10, 1792 that overthrew the monarchy in France, Page drafted a letter to Larchevesque-Thibaud, who was then preparing to welcome the members of the Civil Commission in Saint-Domingue, laying out this new strategy. He denounced the now-defunct Club Massiac – with which Larchevesque-Thibaud himself had once been associated[8] – as "an assemblage of big landowners who didn't know Saint-Domingue well enough" and lamented that "this society displayed principles that have discredited Saint-Domingue in the eyes of the philanthropic and democratic people." Since the club members had presented themselves as counterrevolutionaries, "this opinion extends to all of us, and, with the pleasure of humiliating us [being] joined to the great principles of humanity, of liberty, of equality, you will soon see the arrival of some decree destructive of our country." The great mistake of the Club Massiac, Page continued, was that it had never openly denounced the real cause of the troubles in the colony,

---

[5] Text in *Journal politique de St. Domingue*, May 30, 1792.

[6] Passport for Brulley and family, April 23, 1793, in AN, D XXV 71, d. 712.

[7] Page to Larchevesque-Thibaud, July 17, 1792, and Brulley to Delaire and Chaudrue, July 30, 1792, both in AN, CC 9 A 8.

[8] On February 15, 1791, Larchevesque-Thibaud had written a letter to the Club, saying that he was too sick to attend their meeting but that "I won't hesitate to sign everything these gentlemen may have decided as if I had been present." AN, AA 54, d. 1509.

namely "the counterrevolutionary aristocracy." By this he meant the officials of the royal administration in the colony and the commanders of the troops there.[9] Page thus endorsed in advance the policy that Larchevesque-Thibaud and the other white "patriots" in Cap Français adopted when Sonthonax and Polverel first arrived: an alliance with the pro-revolutionary commissioners from France to oust the remaining royally appointed officials in the colony, the policy that culminated in the journée of October 19, 1792 in Cap Français.

The rhetoric of the revolutionaries who had overthrown the monarchy and the constitution of 1791 on August 10, 1792 suggested that the new French government would be thoroughly hostile to the idea of slavery. A proclamation issued by the newly installed provisional government announced that the sole bases of the new regime would be the principles of "liberty and equality." The new authorities, however, were also ardent patriots charged with defeating a foreign invasion; they had no intention of adding to their problems by creating a crisis in the colonies. On August 25, 1792, the new navy minister, Gaspard Monge, considered a supporter of the provisional government's leader, Georges Danton, reassured the Saint-Domingue colonists' representatives in Paris that "the National Assembly did not intend to extend to the unfree blacks the decree on liberty and equality." Three days later, the colonists met with Danton himself and came away convinced that he "took the liveliest interest in the misfortunes of Saint-Domingue."[10] Nevertheless, the political situation in Paris hardly seemed favorable to the white colonists' interests. Brissot and his allies, who had dominated the debates about the colonies in the Legislative Assembly, were re-elected to the National Convention, which began its sessions on September 20, 1792, as were a number of former deputies from the Constituent Assembly who had been members of the Société des amis des noirs, notably the abbé Grégoire and Robespierre. Although the colonies were theoretically supposed to have deputies in the Convention, no attempt was made to organize elections in Saint-Domingue, and, in contrast to the first two revolutionary assemblies, there were no identified spokesmen for slaveholders' interests in the new legislature.

By the time the National Convention convened, it was already clear that Brissot and Robespierre, who had fought on the same side in the

9 Page to Larchevesque-Thibaud, August 11, 1792, in AN, D XXV 68, d. 685.
10 AN, D XXV 76, entries of August 20, 25, 28, 1792. On Monge's political orientation, see François Pairault, *Gaspard Monge. Le fondateur de Polytechnique* (Paris: Taillandier, 2000), 68, 77.

struggles against the colonial lobby in 1790 and 1791, were now the leaders of opposing factions. Although the Convention voted unanimously on September 22, 1792 to proclaim France a republic, its members divided violently on almost every other issue, and particularly on the question of how to deal with the deposed king. Entirely absorbed by domestic controversies and the war, the Convention devoted only passing attention to the colonies. Furthermore, throughout the fall of 1792, there was a surprising degree of consensus about events in Saint-Domingue. Everyone – the Brissot group, the supporters of Robespierre, and the white colonists – welcomed the dismissal of Governor Blanchelande, and there was similar unanimity in reaction to the news of the journée of October 19, 1792 in Cap Français, which reached Paris in December.[11] Because it took close to two months for ships to cross the Atlantic, the Saint-Domingue lobbyists did not learn of the rupture between their white allies in the colony and the civil commissioners until the beginning of 1793.

Page and Brulley soon settled into a routine that they would follow until their arrest in March 1794. Their activities can be followed day by day and sometimes almost hour by hour in the voluminous register of minutes kept in nearly illegible handwriting by their faithful secretary, Legrand, which is now in the Archives nationales in Paris.[12] Nearly every one of their meetings began with their discussion of requests submitted by one or more colonists for official certificates entitling them to receive the payments the revolutionary government doled out to refugees who had lost the revenues from their properties in Saint-Domingue. This function legitimated the "Commission of Saint-Domingue" in the eyes of the revolutionary bureaucracy, which needed some way to determine

[11] *Moniteur universel*, December 19, 1792 (letter from Le Cap, October 21, 1792).
[12] Sections of Page and Brulley's register are found in several cartons on the Archives nationales, making it possible to reconstruct the lobbyists' activities for the period from August 16, 1792, shortly after the overthrow of the monarchy, until February 25, 1793, and again from June 19, 1793 to the moment of their arrest on March 15, 1794. AN, D XXV 76 contains one register that actually begins with the minutes of Page and Brulley's predecessors, from June 7, 1792 onward, and ends with their meeting of November 2, 1792. AN, D XXV 63, d. 639 contains a register beginning on December 10, 1792 and ending on January 20, 1793, which is continued in a register now found in AN, D XXV 64, d. 640, covering the dates from January 21, 1793 to February 25, 1793. The earlier parts of their register – the documents in cartons 63 and 64 – were sent back to Saint-Domingue, to enable the colonists there to verify that the commissioners were defending their interests. The longest section of the register, in carton 76, which runs from June 19, 1793 until the arrest of Page, Brulley, and their secretary Legrand on 15 vent. An II (March 5, 1794), does not appear to have been sent to Saint-Domingue.

who was entitled to relief; it also gave Page and Brulley a certain power over their fellow colonists who needed certificates from the two men to obtain aid. "Residence certificates and all other official papers the colonists needed in Paris needed to be signed and issued by these two persons, who had no special authority to do it," the journalist Milscent, their sharpest opponent, complained.[13] Once they had disposed of this chore, Page and Brulley would turn to their main concern: figuring out how to influence government policy and public opinion. One of the paradoxes of their mission was that although the defense of slavery was their major priority, they decided that it would be a mistake to defend the institution openly, as members of the Club Massiac had done in the first years of the Revolution. As they explained in a letter to the Commission intermédiaire in Saint-Domingue in January 1793, the political situation in France was not ripe for an effort to get the Convention to explicitly approve the principle of slavery; their first goal had to be to counter the unfavorable image of the white colonists prevalent among the revolutionaries. Instead of trying to convince metropolitan opinion that black slaves were well treated and happy, they concentrated instead on the sufferings of the whites caused by the insurrection and the violations of their rights by metropolitan officials.[14]

While the lobbyists for the white colonists were adapting themselves to the new political situation created by the proclamation of the Republic, their adversaries were falling into disarray. The Société des amis des noirs had long since ceased to meet; even though many of its former members now occupied leading positions in the Convention, they no longer formed a cohesive group. Brissot's newspaper, the *Patriote français*, continued to cover colonial news, but Brissot himself no longer had much time for the subject. Other leading participants in the debates of 1789 to 1791, such as Condorcet and Grégoire, also fell silent on these issues. Condorcet did include a prohibition on slavery in the declaration of rights of the draft constitution he put forward in February 1793, but the curious wording of his proposition – "Every man can sell his labor, his services, his time, but he cannot sell himself; his person is not an alienable property" – showed how remote his thinking was from the reality of colonial life.[15] The blacks in Saint-Domingue had not sold themselves into slavery.

---

[13] *Créole patriote*, September 25, 1793.
[14] AN, D XXV 63, d. 639, entry for January 6, 1793.
[15] [Condorcet], *Projet des principes et des motifs du plan présenté à la Convention nationale,; par le comité de Constitution* (Paris: Imprimerie nationale, 1793), pt. 2, 4.

As the French scholar Jean-Daniel Piquet has shown, there were individuals among the more radical Montagnard opponents of the Girondins who spoke out against slavery during the first half of 1793. In April 1793, the Convention deputy Joseph Lequinio put out a work entitled *Les préjugés détruits* ("Prejudices demolished") in which he devoted a chapter to the issue of slavery. He defended the right of slaves to rise up against their oppressors and dismissed the idea that the European demand for sugar and coffee justified the exploitation of those who produced them. Lequinio was prepared to accept a gradual process of emancipation, but insisted that it needed to be started immediately. On April 24, 1793, Robespierre denounced the slave trade in a speech to the Convention in the course of a critique of Condorcet's proposed declaration of rights. His own proposed declaration, however, was equally abstract and did not specifically mention slavery.[16] While some of the Montagnards clearly identified slavery as a violation of human rights, the movement as a whole never took a coherent position on the issue, or on the more specific question of policy in Saint-Domingue. Furthermore, as part of their campaign against the Girondins, the Montagnards were willing to ally themselves with the Saint-Domingue slave owners. In September 1791, the Jacobin club had expelled all members who had voted with the colonists in favor of repealing the law of May 15, 1791 on the rights of free men of color, but on February 24, 1793, when Page and Brulley applied for membership, the future Committee of Public Safety member Collot d'Herbois spoke in their favor and they were duly admitted.[17]

The only prominent participant in the earlier revolutionary debates about the racial order in the colonies who continued to raise these issues on a regular basis in the first half of 1793 was Julien Raimond, the semi-official spokesman for the free men of color in Saint-Domingue. Until his arrest in September 1793, Raimond was the main opponent of the white colonial lobbyists. It was Raimond, drawing on his extensive network of correspondents in Saint-Domingue, who furnished most of the letters from the colony printed in the *Patriote français* in late 1792 and early 1793, and the two pamphlets he published in February 1793 were the most extensive discussions of these issues from the reformers' point of view to appear before the final defeat of the Brissot party on 31 May

---

[16] Piquet, *Emancipation des noirs*, 226–33, 261; Robespierre, *Oeuvres* 9: 460.
[17] AN, D XXV 64, d. 640, entry for February 24, 1793. On Collot's endorsement, see Garran-Coulon, *Rapport*, 4: 481.

31–June 2, 1793. Nevertheless, Raimond was an abolitionist only in the most limited sense. In the longer of his two pamphlets, *Réflexions sur les véritables causes des troubles et des désastres de nos colonies*, Raimond outlined a policy by which, he claimed, the Convention "would reconcile ... its principles of justice with the commercial interests of the metropole, and those of the colonists who have properties in the colonies." In exchange for the elimination of the worst abuses of slavery, he called on the blacks in Saint-Domingue to lay down their arms. "Return immediately to order, misled men, and wait, in respectful silence, for the laws which will regenerate you," he told them. The proposal he laid out would have required slaves to purchase their freedom individually from their masters. Raimond was as insistent as any white author on the need for the blacks to undergo a civilizing process before they could be trusted with their freedom. Among other things, they needed to learn the behaviorial habits of European society, which he called "the customs of the class of free and well-disciplined men; these customs require various kinds of consumption. You will realize, then, that in order to be put on the same level as the free population, you will have to work, after receiving your freedom, in order to procure for yourselves all the luxuries and conveniences that distinguish the free man from the slave."[18] Raimond's main concern remained, as it always had been, to secure the rights of the free population of color. His second pamphlet, *Lettre au citoyen D***, député à la Convention nationale*, was a justification of the alliance Sonthonax had made with them in Saint-Domingue.[19]

With Raimond willing to make only the most gradualist proposals for eliminating slavery, and the colonial lobbyists determined to avoid even mentioning the subject, the violent confrontation between the two parties took the form of an argument about Sonthonax's and Polverel's treatment of the whites in Saint-Domingue, rather than about the freedom of the blacks. The colonists had never trusted Sonthonax and Polverel, but their campaign of denunciation against the two men really took off with

---

[18] Julien Raymond [sic], *Réflexions sur les véritables causes des troubles et des désastres de nos colonies, notamment sur ceux de Saint-Domingue; avec les moyens à employer pour préserver cette colonie d'une ruine totale; adressés à la Convention nationale; par Julien Raymond, colon de Saint-Domingue* (Paris, n.p., 1793, "l'an second de la République"), 19, 28. The pamphlet can be dated by a reference at the end to articles that appeared in *Patriote français* of 10 February 10, 1793.

[19] Julien Raimond, *Lettre au citoyen D***, député à la Convention nationale, par Julien Raymond, colon de Saint-Domingue, sur l'état des divers partis de cette colonie, et sur le caractère des déportés* (Paris: 1793, "l'an second de la République"). The text is dated February 24, 1793.

the arrival of the white "patriots" deported from Cap Français after the journée of December 2, 1792. One of the unintended consequences of Sonthonax's hardline policy toward the white agitators in Le Cap was that he provided the lobbyists Page and Brulley with valuable reinforcements: the more suspects he sent to France, the larger the number of militants bent on destroying him became. While Sonthonax's metropolitan allies, such as Brissot, were increasingly distracted by other problems, the exiled *colons* had nothing else to do except pursue their campaign of vengeance.

The first group of arrestees reached Paris just before the execution of the king on January 21, 1793; while the rest of the capital's population lined the streets to observe that event, Page and Brulley spent the day meeting with members of the Convention's colonial committee to denounce the mistreatment of their friends.[20] A month later, the four colonists were allowed to address the Convention personally and complain that "in violation of the laws, without any formalities, each of us was taken from his domicile on the night of last 6 December, at 3 a.m. in the morning."[21] The legislators were sufficiently impressed to grant the men provisional freedom. At this early date, however, Raimond's influence was still at least as powerful as that of the Saint-Domingue lobbyists. He met with the colonial committee several times in late January and early February, lobbying for a Convention decree that would officially sanction Sonthonax's initiative in creating "free companies" composed exclusively of men of color.[22] The result was a measure voted by the Convention on March 5, 1793, in response to a long report presented by the deputy Simon Camboulas, which faithfully reproduced the arguments of Sonthonax and Raimond to the effect that the free men of color were "the real friends of France ... the men on whom you can count to carry out your laws, and to preserve the most valuable of colonies." In addition to authorizing the free companies, the decree gave the civil commissioners the power to "make whatever provisional alterations they judge necessary to the police regulations and the discipline of the slave gangs (*"atteliers"*) for the maintenance of domestic peace in the colonies." In view of Raimond's generally acknowledged influence in the drafting of the decree, it is hardly likely that this clause was intended to

[20] Page and Brulley, register, entry for January 21, 1793, in AN, D XXV 64, d. 640.
[21] "Discours prononcé à la barre de la Convention nationale, par les Citoyens Verneuil, Gervais, Baillo jeune et Fournier," in AN, D XXV 80, d. 784.
[22] Minutes of Colonial Committee, January 25, 1793, February 4, 1793, February 8, 1793, in AN, D* XVI 3-4-5.

open the way to the abolition of slavery, but when they decided to proclaim general emancipation, Sonthonax and Polverel would cite it as the
basis of their authority.[23]

The decree of March 5, 1793 proved to be Raimond's last victory. Its
endorsement of the alliance between the civil commissioners and the free
men of color enraged the white colonists. On March 19, their protest
campaign, organized by Page and Brulley, led the Convention to suspend
the March 5, 1793 decree and to order a debate between Raimond and
the whites from Saint-Domingue.[24] The Convention's change of heart
had no impact on events in Saint-Domingue: the news of the repeal of
the decree of March 5, 1793 never reached Sonthonax and Polverel. But
it marked a reversal in the Convention's attitude toward colonial policy.
Two sessions of angry public discussion between Raimond and the colonists took place on March 26 and 27, 1793, after which the Convention,
overwhelmed with urgent domestic crises – the revolt in the Vendée,
Dumouriez's treason, and the growing atmosphere of violence in the
French provinces – adjourned the sessions until mid-May. By that time,
the *sans-culotte* campaign against the Girondins was nearing its climax,
and Page and Brulley now received a much more favorable hearing than
they had initially. At the outset of the hearings, Page wrote, the deputies
had been "prejudiced against the commissioners of Saint-Domingue in
particular, and against the white colonists in general, because of intriguers who had an interest in preventing a discussion that would expose
them," but as the debates proceeded, the mood had changed.[25]

The struggle between Raimond and the colonial lobbyists received
little publicity in the press. In April 1793, however, the colonists won
a major public victory, one which set a lethal precedent, not only for
the treatment of their issues but for revolutionary politics in general.
Responding primarily to demands from the Jacobin left, the Convention
had voted to establish a Revolutionary Tribunal, which went into

[23] *Moniteur universel*, March 7, 1793 (Convention, March 5, 1793). On Raimond's role
in drawing up the decree, see Larchevesque-Thibaud's denunciation of him, 1 plu. II,
in AN, D XXV 73, d. 729.

[24] Page and Brulley to minister of the navy, March 19, 1793, in AN, D XXV 56, d. 557.
That the Convention did in fact repeal the decree of March 5, 1793 is confirmed in
Garran-Coulon, *Rapport*, 4: 23, 4: 468.

[25] *Développement des causes des troubles et désastres des colonies françaises, présenté
à la Convention nationale, par les Commissaires de Saint-Domingue, sur la demande
des comités de Marine et des Colonies, réunis, après en avoir donné communication
aux Colons résidens à Paris, & convoqués, à cet effet, le 11 juin 1793, l'an 2e de la
République* (N. p., n. p.), 95.

operation at the beginning of April 1793. The first few cases it heard were inconsequential, but on April 11, 1793, the court took up the accusations against General Blanchelande, the last royal governor of Saint-Domingue. The main witnesses against him were white colonists from Saint-Domingue, led by Page and Brulley. Page announced that "he knew that Blanchelande had gone all over the colony to destroy the local institutions and popular societies, corrupt public opinion and reestablish the Old Regime," and Brulley added that "he had incited the blacks on several occasions and had them armed," a charge repeated by the future republican commissioner to Guadeloupe, Victor Hugues.[26] The hapless Blanchelande, guilty at most of indecisiveness and incompetence, was convicted and executed on April 15, 1793.[27] His trial set a precedent for the judicial murder of high-ranking public officials, opening the door for the show trials that would claim so many lives during the Terror. Blanchelande's condemnation was not the fault of the colonial lobby alone. He was an easy target because everyone, including Brissot as well as the anti-Brissot Jacobins, was convinced of his guilt. Nevertheless, it was the colonists who insistently pushed for his trial and provided all the testimony against him. The success of their campaign against Blanchelande established a dangerous precedent: it was now clear that anyone convicted of having sabotaged the colonies would pay with his life.

The Montagnard-organized popular uprising of May 31–June 2, 1793, which resulted in the ouster of the leading Girondin deputies from the Convention, was primarily the outcome of metropolitan political disputes, but it ended up greatly strengthening the colonial lobby's position. In its official address to the national club network justifying the journée, the Paris Jacobins included among the crimes of the defeated "faction" their "having embroiled us in war with the whole of Europe, having covered France with sufferings, the colonies with ruins."[28] That the ouster of the Girondins would set back the struggle against slavery was not immediately clear, because the first consequence of journée was an important abolitionist demonstration. On June 3, 1793, just one day after the expulsion of the Girondins from the Convention, a delegation of men from the "batallion of the colonies," a unit of free men of color who

---

[26] AN, D XXV 47, d. 444bis.
[27] *Bulletin du Tribunal criminel révolutionnaire*, no. 10.
[28] Address of the Jacobin Club, June 7, 1793, in François Aulard, *La Société des Jacobins. Recueil des documents pour l'histoire du Club des Jacobins de Paris*, 6 vs. (Paris: Jouaust, 1889–97), 5: 240.

had volunteered for military service in accordance with one of the provisions of the law of March 5, 1793, visited the Jacobin club. Originally, the plan had been to send this unit, commanded by the celebrated musician and officer Joseph de Saint-Georges, to Saint-Domingue, although the Convention had changed its mind in mid-May, after Page and Brulley had accused one of the volunteers of having said that "to have peace in Saint-Domingue, we need to exterminate and expel all the whites," and ordered that it not be employed in the colonies.[29] The group that appeared at the Jacobins on June 3 was led by a free man of color, Julien Labuissonnière, who had published a petition calling for the emancipation of the slaves in mid-May 1793.[30] They were accompanied by Pierre Chaumette, an official of the Paris Commune and a prominent supporter of abolition, and one Jeanne Odo, "a *citoyenne* of color, 114 years old," whose presence excited great enthusiasm.[31]

The members of the group at the Jacobins were free people of color, and Odo herself was "une femme mulâtre," as one newspaper account indicated,[32] but in the confused discussion that followed their appearance, some Jacobins referred to "blacks" and one referred to "drying the tears of the Africans," whereas the resolution finally adopted said nothing about slavery. It referred specifically to "men of color" and in fact decreed that they would not be given any special consideration if they applied for club membership.[33] The only speaker who used the word

[29] Page and Brulley to Committee of Public Safety, May 5, 1793, in AN, D XXV 5, d. 50. On the chevalier de Saint-Georges, the mixed-race son of a planter from Guadeloupe, see Gabriel Banat, *The Chevalier de Saint-Georges: Virtuoso of the Sword and the Bow* (Hillsdale, NY: Pendragon Press, 2006), 371–85; on his family origins, see Luc Nemeth, "Un état-civil chargé d'enjeux: Saint-George, 1745–1799," *Annales historiques de la révolution française* no. 339 (2005), 79–97. The idea of creating a volunteer unit composed of free men of color had been advanced by Raimond in September 1792. For the Convention's decision not to send the unit to the colonies, see *Journal de Perlet*, May 17, 1793 (Convention, May 16, 1793).

[30] *Adresse à la convention nationale, à tous les clubs et sociétés patriotiques, pour les Nègres détenus en esclavage dans les Colonies françaises de l'Amérique, sous le régime de la République* (Paris: Galletti, 1793, reprinted in *La Révolution française et l'abolition de l'esclavage* (Paris: EDHIS, 1968)), t. 5.

[31] *Journal des Débats de la société des Amis de la Constitution séante aux Jacobins à Paris*, June 6–7, 1793 (meeting of the Jacobin club, June 3, 1793).

[32] *Le Batave*, June 5, 1793, cited in Piquet, *Emancipation des noirs*, 257.

[33] "La société arrête que les hommes de couleur seront présenté à la société dans les formes ordinaires" ("The club declares that the men of color will be presented to the club [for consideration for membership] according to the regular procedures.") *Journal des Débats de la société des Amis de la Constitution séante aux Jacobins à Paris*, June 6–7, 1793 (meeting of the Jacobin club, June 3, 1793).

"slave" did so in the context of a demand that Brissot "be made a slave in front of the Africans." Robespierre entered the debate to remind the club that "many patriots have been swallowed up in the colonies, and that is one more of Brissot's crimes."[34] On June 4, 1793, the men of color who had appeared at the Jacobins went to the National Convention and presented a petition whose content has not been preserved; a day later, the head of their delegation complained publicly that the legislators had refused to let him read the text, which, he claimed, called for the outright abolition of slavery.[35] While the appearance of the free men of color at the Jacobins on June 3, 1793 and at the Convention on June 4, 1793 does prove that some members of that group were willing to go well beyond Raimond's cautious position on slavery and that some members of the Jacobins were willing to support them, the Convention's refusal to even listen to them shows that the legislators were still unwilling to move from vague expressions of sympathy for the sufferings of black slaves to legislation that would actually alter their situation. A few days after the black delegation's public appearances, its leader, Labuissonnière, was arrested; he seems to have had the unfortunate habit of stealing valuables from his friends, including Raimond and the journalist Milscent.[36] His imprisonment brought the brief public campaign for immediate abolition to a halt; there would be no further public discussion of the issue in Paris until the following February.

At the end of the hearings between Raimond and the white colonists, just prior to the journée of May 31 – June 2, 1793, both parties had been told to submit memoranda presenting their positions. Raimond's response repeated the customary accusations against the white "counterrervolutionaries" and "independentists" and concluded, like his earlier works, by insisting that the slave rebellion had been incited by the whites and could easily be ended by announcing an amnesty and a plan that would allow hardworking blacks to earn their freedom. Although he opposed the recall of Sonthonax, he suggested that additional civil commissioners could be sent to make sure that the policies followed in Saint-Domingue were in accordance with the wishes of the French government.[37] Page and Brulley presented the Convention with the longest

[34] *Journal des Débats de la société des Amis de la Constitution séante aux Jacobins à Paris,* June 6–7, 1793 (meeting of the Jacobin club, June 3, 1793).

[35] Piquet, *Emancipation des noirs,* 258–60.

[36] Yves Bénot, "Un anti-esclavagiste kleptomane? En marge de l'affaire Milscent," *Dix-huitième siécle* 22 (1990), 295–300.

[37] Julien Raimond, *Mémoire sur les causes des troubles et des désastres de la Colonie de Saint-Domingue, présenté aux comités de Marine et des Colonies, dans les premiers*

of all their works of propaganda, subsequently published as a pamphlet entitled *Développement des causes des troubles et désastres des colonies françaises*, in which they, too, summarized all their arguments. The troubles in the colonies, Page and Brulley claimed, were the result of a monstrous conspiracy organized by French aristocrats, the British government, Brissot, and Raimond, all of them bent on "using the ashes of the colonies to bring feudalism back to life." They demanded punishment for all those involved, including Brissot, "this social monster," Raimond, "paid for spreading hatred and discord among us," Roume and Saint-Léger, members of the First Civil Commission sent to Saint-Domingue in 1791–92, and Sonthonax and Polverel. At the moment when they compiled this pamphlet, Page and Brulley did not know of the commissioners' decree of May 5, 1793, reinstating the Code noir's provisions in favor of the slaves, but this was irrelevant to their argument, which was based on accusations that the two men had committed a long list of crimes against the whites in the colony, not on anything they had done for the slaves. [38]

Like Raimond, Page and Brulley claimed to accept the principle of emancipation, and they also agreed with him that the slaves needed to be prepared for it. They contended, however, that only the colonists themselves understood what this would entail. In the meantime, the colonists' own rights needed to be respected. As Page had told the Colonial Committee during the debates with Raimond, the Convention "has declared that man is born free; it cannot legalize his slavery, without putting itself in opposition to its own principles. But, if the Convention has recognized the rights of man, it cannot ignore the rights of the people, and since no one owes obedience to a law that he has not made, or which had been freely consented to by him or his representatives, and since the colonies, aside from Cayenne, are not represented in the National Convention, as a result of the actions of the agents of the Republic, who have prevented the colonists from holding primary assemblies to name their deputies, the National Convention cannot impose any law on them, without at the same time legitimating the resistance that they might oppose, if the law was disastrous for them." In June 1789, Condorcet had answered similar arguments by writing that "any man who violates one of the natural rights of humanity, immediately loses the right to invoke this principle in his own

---

jours de juin dernier, par les Citoyens de couleur; d'après l'invitation que leur en avoit été faite par les comités (Paris: Cercle social, 1793), 65–6.
[38] *Développement des causes*, 67, 72, 38, 139–64.

favor."³⁹ By June 1793, however, Condorcet, like his Girondin colleagues, was in flight from the wrath of the victorious Montagnards,
and there was no one to refute the colonists' sophistries.

Page and Brulley did not limit themselves to printed propaganda. The
Montagnard deputy and member of the Committee of Public Safety,
Louis Saint-Just, had been charged with presenting a report on the mis-
deeds of the Girondins; between mid-June and mid-July, the two lobbyists had at least five meetings with him.⁴⁰ On July 12 and 13, 1793, they
met with Jeanbon Saint-André, the member of the Committee of Public
Safety with special responsibility for naval and colonial affairs, who was
also at that moment president of the National Convention, to discuss a
proposal to recall Sonthonax and Polverel from Saint-Domingue. On
July 15, Jeanbon Saint-André transmitted to the Convention an address
from them, restating in the strongest possible terms their denunciations
of the two commissioners. "Polverel and Sonthonax have alienated all
the citizens; some slavishly bow their heads under the feet of the two
dictators so as not to fall under the ax of their executioners," they wrote.
"Others flee into the mountains, in the midst of forests uninhabited until
now; others, less unfortunate, take themselves to foreign soil. Some who
have been unjustly deported languish here in complete poverty. Here
Polverel and Sonthonax arm the slaves to dominate Saint-Domingue and
oppress the citizens. There the citizens arm their own slaves to defend
themselves. Soon, all the armed slaves, set in opposition to each other,
will turn this colony into a vast field of carnage and the traitors who
have incited them will go enjoy at a distance the fruit of so many crimes
and the leavings of the fortune of this beautiful colony." The explanation
for all these crimes was simple: "Sonthonax and Polverel, creatures of
Brissot, this disorganizer of the colonies, were sent to Saint Domingue
by [Jean-Marie] Roland and Clavière, at the time of the first ministry," formed when the Girondins made their agreement with the king
in 1792.⁴¹

On July 16, 1793, the lobbying efforts of Page and Brulley succeeded. Their address was read to the Convention. When a motion was
made to refer it to the Committee of Public Safety for consideration,
the Montagnard deputy, Jean-Jacques Bréard, a member of the colonial

---

³⁹ [Condorcet], *Sur l'admission des députés des planteurs de Saint-Domingue, dans
l'Assemblée nationale* (Paris: EDHIS, 1968 (orig. June 1789)), 163.
⁴⁰ Page and Brulley, register, in AN, D XXV 76, entries for June 19 and 23, July 5, 9, and
12, 1793.
⁴¹ Page and Brulley, register, in AN, D XXV 76, entries for July 12, 13, 15, 1793.

committee, objected, saying that the Convention should make a decision immediately, and that it should not only recall Sonthonax and Polverel, but indict them as well. Nicolas Billaud-Varennes, a leading radical who would be added to the Committee of Public Safety in September 1793, supported Bréard and insisted that "these commissioners are the agents of Brissot, of Clavière, etc." The Convention, preoccupied with the assassination of Marat three days earlier, hastily approved the motion.[42] Page and Brulley were not satisfied with words: in the weeks that followed, they besieged Saint-Just and the Committee of Public Safety with demands that the recall decree be sent to Saint-Domingue as quickly as possible and with suggestions of trustworthy men who could be appointed to carry it out. They also drew up several lists of measures to be taken by the officials sent to replace Sonthonax and Polverel in the colony: the dissolution of all the armed groups of free men of color, a complete purge of the administration, and, somewhat unexpectedly, the arming of "non-libres" for defense purposes.[43]

Realizing what a blow the news of the dismissal of Sonthonax and Polverel would be for the free men of color in the colony, Julien Raimond wrote to his correspondents to warn them against doing anything rash in response, as the supporters of the Girondins had in France. "It is not up to you to judge them," he said; "only the Convention has that right. ... Be careful, *frères et amis*, not to fall into the criminal errors of some of the departments who soon either recognized their mistakes or were punished for them."[44] Jean Dalbarade, the navy minister, ordered the dispatch of a ship and the nomination of a commissioner to carry out the decree, and as of late August, the only thing holding up the fulfillment of the Convention's decree was bad weather that had retarded the ship's departure.[45] The recall decree of July 16, 1793 was, of course, a response to the white colonists' claims that Sonthonax and Polverel had abused their authority, not a sign that the Convention endorsed slavery. At the moment of its passage, the most that Page and Brulley had said about that subject was that the commissioners had interfered with the rights of slave owners and armed some slaves; on July 16, 1793, no one in France knew about the journée of June 20, 1793 or its consequences.

[42] *Moniteur universel*, July 17, 1793 (Convention, July 16, 1793).
[43] Letters of Page and Brulley, August 11 and 28, 1793, in AN, D XXV 54, d. 523.
[44] Julien Raimond, *Correspondance de Julien Raimond, avec ses frères, de Saint-Domingue, et les pièces qui lui ont été adressés par eux* (Paris: Cercle social, An 2), 123, letter of August 1, 1792.
[45] Dalbarade to Convention, September 5, 1793, in AN, D XXV 56, d. 557.

Less than two weeks after voting to recall the commissioners, the Convention also voted, on July 27, 1793, to abolish the longstanding subsidies granted to French slave traders.[46] Page and Brulley, entirely focused on the situation in Saint-Domingue, did not even mention the matter in their voluminous register.

When the first news of the *journée* of June 20, 1793 in Cap Français reached France in late August 1793, Page and Brulley had thus already won their political battle against Sonthonax and Polverel. Had General Galbaud allowed himself to be sent back to France, instead of launching his disastrous attack on the commissioners, he would have found that the Convention had already voted to remove them, and it is not impossible that he would have gotten his wish and been sent back to carry out the measures against them personally. The first news of the crisis of June 20, 1793 reached Paris on August 23, 1793. On the following day, a number of colonists visited the Saint-Domingue commissioners' office to discuss the situation. "According to these reports, nothing was spared: men, women, children, old people, all have been massacred by the ferocious executors of the vengeances of Sonthonax and Polverel," Page and Brulley noted in their register. They hastened to inform Saint-Just, who flatly refused to believe the news; the following day, the minister of the navy also dismissed the reports.[47] Over the next few days, however, more letters from refugees in the United States arrived in Paris. From Page's and Brulley's point of view, the disaster simply underlined the villainy of Sonthonax and Polverel. Their most urgent concern was to make sure that the story was given the proper interpretation in Paris. On August 31, they organized a protest against the newspaper of the abolitionist journalist Claude Milscent, who had cast doubt on the reports about the disaster of Le Cap and written that "the denunciations of the colonists against the national commissioners are those of nobles opposing sans-culottes. What importance should one give to them?"[48] In the short run, their demand for the closing of Milscent's newspaper was

---

[46] *Moniteur universel*, July 29, 1793 (Convention, July 27). Grégoire, who had remained silent in the debates about the commissioners, proposed the measure as an amendment to a broader law regarding economic subsidies. No one seems to have objected to the abolition of the slave trade subsidies, although the British blockade had rendered the matter moot for the time being. Contrary to the assertions in some scholarship on the French Revolution and slavery, the decree of July 27 did not prohibit French slave trading; it only ended government subsidies to the traders.

[47] AN, D XXV 76, August 24 and 25, 1793.

[48] *Créole patriote*, August 29, 1793; AN, D XXV 76, 31 August 31 and September 1, 1793.

unsuccessful, but he would eventually be sent to the guillotine, largely as a result of their efforts.[49]

They had better luck with their visit to Jeanbon Saint-André. On September 3, 1793, after a meeting with them, he delivered the bad news to the Convention. As one newspaper summarized his speech: "The city of Le Cap has been burned; the national commissioners Polverel and Sonthonax have usurped a dictatorial authority in the island, and their criminal ambition is the cause of these latest misfortunes." Jeanbon Saint-André insisted on the need for quick action. "The whole Republic has suffered considerable losses; it needs to think of ways to remedy these calamities, if there is still time ... I demand this for the sake of commerce itself, for the huge quantity of workers who it provides with work to support themselves and their families." At his urging, the Convention gave the navy minister twenty-four hours to explain what he had done to carry out the recall decree of July 16, 1793, and the colonial committee was charged to present its long-awaited report on the situation in Saint-Domingue as soon as possible.[50] The entire revolutionary government was now publicly committed to the version of the events of June 20, 1793 advanced by the Saint-Domingue lobbyists.

The news did not create as great a public sensation as might have been expected. The Convention was more preoccupied with the British occupation of Toulon, which had cost France its Mediterranean war fleet, and with the ongoing siege of the rebellious city of Lyon. On September 5, 1793, two days after Jeanbon Saint-André's speech, a massive crowd of *sans-culottes* surrounded the Convention, demanding that "terror be made the order of the day." Overwhelmed with these domestic crises, the deputies barely paid any attention to colonial matters again until Sonthonax's delegation arrived in February 1794. Among the general public, Page and Brulley were perhaps victims of their own success: they had sounded the alarm about the disastrous state of the colony so often that no one could distinguish the new catastrophe from earlier events. Only a few newspapers, notably the *Nouvelles politiques*, the successor to a banned newspaper that had been closely tied to the Club Massiac, published significant stories about the destruction of Cap Français.[51] The journalist Milscent, the most persistent opponent of the pro-slavery

---

[49] AN, D XXV 56, ds. 554, 556.
[50] *Nouvelles politiques*, September 4, 1793 (Convention, September 3); *Moniteur universel*, September 4, 1793 (Convention, September 3).
[51] *Nouvelles politiques*, August 31, 1793, September 4, 1793, September 11, 1793, September 23, 1793, September 27, 1793.

colonists, allowed himself to be misled by his ideological views: since the reports from Saint-Domingue seemed so favorable to his enemies' cause, he decided they must be false. He helped persuade the Jacobin club to refuse even to listen to the reading of a letter about the Le Cap disaster at one of its meetings.[52]

Although there was little public discussion of the events of June 20, 1793 in France, numerous private individuals received letters from family members or acquaintances who had fled to the United States. A dossier of correspondence intercepted by the French authorities in the spring of 1794 gives some idea of how extensive the contacts between the colonies and the metropole were. The thirty-nine letters in the collection are addressed to individuals in fifteen different French cities, including not only major centers with longstanding links to Saint-Domingue such as Bordeaux, Paris, and Nantes, but also small towns such as Pontarlier, Castres, Roanne, Grasse, and Xaintray.[53] Celestin Guittard de Floriban, an elderly pensioner in Paris who followed colonial news closely because he had loaned money to a plantation owner, was one of the recipients of such letters; his diary allows us to see how one private individual reacted to the news. He did not mention the burning of Le Cap in his diary until early October 1793, more than a month after the first reports had appeared in the press; even then, he devoted more space to the events in Port-au-Prince in April than to the crisis of June.[54] By mid-September, the first eyewitnesses to the events in Cap Français had reached France, bringing more detailed accounts that contradicted the version of the story that the Saint-Domingue commissioners were spreading. Page and Brulley met with several of these survivors, including Captain Duclos-Guyot, the commander of the *America*, the warship whose crew had not participated in the attack on June 20, 1793, but they simply dismissed any testimony that did not support their conviction that Sonthonax and Polverel were solely responsible for the disaster. In some cases, they tried to have inconvenient witnesses arrested.[55]

---

[52] *Créole patriote*, August 29, 1793; September 24, 1793 (Jacobins, September 23).

[53] Archives nationales, D XXV 81, d. 790.

[54] Célestin Guittard de Floriban, *Journal de Célestin Guittard de Floriban, bourgeois de Paris sous la Révolution*, ed. Raymond Aubert (Paris: Editions France-Empire, 1974), entry for October 7, 1793, 283–4. Guittard's correspondent, a colonist named Clausson, was one of those arrested after the Port-au-Prince affair.

[55] AN, D XXV 76, September 14, 1793, October 12, 1793, November 18, 1793 (request for arrest of Admiral Cambis, the naval commander in Le Cap on June 20, 1793). Duclos-Guyot had reached France on September 2, 1793. Letter from Rochefort to ministry of the navy, September 2, 1793, in AN, D XXV 54, d. 523.

Having persuaded the Committee of Public Safety and the Convention to endorse their version of events, the Saint-Domingue lobbyists set out to wreak vengeance on anyone who contradicted them. On September 11, 1793, they arranged another confrontation with their archenemy, Julien Raimond, in front of the members of the Convention's colonial committee. Page told the legislators that "Citizen Raimond has always showed himself an enemy of the colony, by the vigor with which he has always defended its enemies, particularly Polverel and Sonthonax, who have always been in violation of the law and recently distinguished themselves by burning down Le Cap."[56] Although this particular confrontation ended badly for Page and Brulley when Raimond demonstrated to the committee that the two men had falsified quotations they had extracted from his writings,[57] the Saint-Domingue commissioners kept up the attack. On September 16, 1793, they had the first of what would be nineteen meetings with the deputy André Amar, a key member of the Committee of General Security. Amar was responsible for drawing up the indictment of Brissot and his associates. Page and Brulley were more than happy to assist him; he would become their firmest ally inside the revolutionary government. On September 26, 1793, after their embarrassing defeat by Raimond in front of the colonial committee, Page and Brulley took their complaints about him to their new friend; Amar had Raimond arrested a day later.[58] He remained in prison and unable to intervene in debates about the colonies for the next fourteen months.[59]

While Raimond was imprisoned, the white colonial agitators deported by Sonthonax were vindicated. On October 2, 1793, the colonial committee issued a report clearing them of all charges. The report stigmatized the commissioner as "this new Sylla" and proposed the payment of compensation to the colonists he had deported.[60] The issuance of this report emboldened Larchevesque-Thibaud, one of those directly concerned, to write a letter to the Committee of Public Safety explicitly defending slavery, something the colonial lobbyists had been careful not to do up till then. He claimed that the planters themselves would gladly

---

[56] AN, D* 16 3–4, entry for September 11, 1793.
[57] Ibid., entry for September 23, 1793.
[58] Page and Brulley, register, entries for September 25 and 26, 1793, in AN, D XXV 76.
[59] Raimond, letters of September 29, 1793 and 28th day of 1st month of An II, in AN, D XXV 78, d. 765.
[60] [Pourçain] Martel. *Rapport Général sur les déportés des Colonies Françoises, par le Citoyen Martel, membre du comité de Marine* (Paris: Imprimerie nationale, s.d. [October 2, 1793]), 16, 34.

end the slavery system if any other way of exploiting their property was possible. "It is only the complete and recognized impossibility of using any other method to cultivate our lands that could make us maintain such a regime, which, in itself, is so unappealing, above all for free men," he wrote. But the revolutionary government should decide whether it wanted to encourage the whites in Saint-Domingue to continue risking their lives trying to bring the slaves back under control. Of course, Larchevesque-Thibaud added, if the Convention decreed the emancipation of the slaves, "you will simply have made of Saint-Domingue a second Vendée, where these rebels, strengthened by the aid the Spanish have long been giving them, will spit on these kindnesses and will only want to recognize the phantom king for whom they fight."[61]

Whereas the defenders of slavery now felt safe in making their case to the revolutionary government, the arrest of Raimond, the impending trial of Brissot, and the colonists' success in pinning the blame for the troubles in Saint-Domingue on the abolitionists forced the latter to tread cautiously. On October 6, Brulley recorded in the Saint-Domingue commission's register that the abbé Grégoire, whose consistent opposition to slavery and racial inequality had made him one of the most hated revolutionary figures among the colonists, had sought him out, ostensibly to discuss the improvement of agriculture in the colonies. According to Brulley, Grégoire had expressed "the pain that he feels about the disasters in Saint-Domingue; he excuses himself for what he wrote during the Constituent Assembly, admits that he was misled, and promises to make up for his unintentional faults by writing about the colonies in accordance with the more accurate information that has been given to him."[62] Although Brulley certainly has to be regarded as a hostile witness, his story is not implausible; Grégoire, facing danger because of his status as a priest as the revolutionaries' de-Christianization campaign heated up, may well have wanted to try to ward off an assault from the colonists. In any event, he had never advocated the kind of abrupt abolition of slavery that had just taken place in Saint-Domingue.

A few weeks after Brulley's putative meeting with Grégoire, the Saint-Domingue colonists had the satisfaction of seeing Brissot and his Girondin colleagues sentenced to death. The indictment against the Girondins incorporated the colonists' accusation that "Pitt wanted to destroy our

[61] Larchevesque-Thibaud to Committee of Public Safety, October 4, 1793, in AN, D XXV 80, d. 786.
[62] Page and Brulley, register, entry for October 6, 1793, in AN, D XXV 76.

colonies; they [the Girondins] destroyed our colonies. Brissot, Pétion, Guadet, Gensonné, Vergniaud, Ducos, Fonfrède, directed the operations concerning our colonies, and our colonies are in the most terrible situation. The guilty commissioners who have overturned them from top to bottom, Sonthonax and Polverel, are both their creation and their accomplices."[63] To the disappointment of the colonial lobbyists, however, little attention was given to the colonial issue at the Girondins' trial, and they were never allowed to speak.[64] Chaumette, who had organized the demonstration in favor of abolition at the Jacobin club in early June, did testify, but not on behalf of emancipation: he claimed that Sonthonax and Polverel had "erected a throne on the bleeding skulls of the inhabitants of the colony, and you can judge the merits of those who named them for that mission."[65] Page and Brulley were allowed to speak against Antoine Barnave, who had headed the Constituent Assembly's colonial committee in 1790–91, and noted with satisfaction the judgment condemning him.[66] No attention was paid to Barnave's protest that if Brissot was guilty of destroying the colonies, he could not also be convicted on the same charge, since they had always advocated diametrically opposing policies.[67] Under the circumstances, it is understandable that the imprisoned Raimond told his interrogators that he had had only minimal contacts with Brissot and that he made no mention of his close connection with Sonthonax.[68] Meanwhile, as additional survivors of the events of June 20, 1793 arrived in Brest, they were interrogated by Joseph Brudieu, an ally of Page and Brulley, who demanded to know whether they could provide testimony to the "commissioners having committed arbitrary and vexatory acts." Those who answered negatively were given to understand that they risked being accused of aristocratic sympathies.[69]

By the end of October 1793, Sonthonax and Polverel had proclaimed the emancipation of the slaves in all parts of Saint-Domingue. In France, however, the revolutionary government multiplied its denunciations of them, even though the ship bearing the agent named to arrest Sonthonax and Polverel remained stuck in the Brest harbor. On November 15, 1793,

---

[63] *Bulletin du Tribunal révolutionnaire*, no. 40 (n.d.)

[64] AN, D XXV 76, 9 bru. II (October 30, 1793).

[65] *Bulletin du Tribunal criminel révolutionnaire*, no. 41.

[66] AN, D XXV 76, 6, 7, 8 fri. II.

[67] Gérard Walter, ed., *Actes du Tribunal révolutionnaire* (Paris: Mercure de France, 1968), 310.

[68] Interrogation of Raimond, 4 fri. II, in AN, D XXV 56, d. 547.

[69] AN, D XXV 80, d. 788. Brudieu was a political deportee from Port-au-Prince. See AN, D* XVI 5, entry for February 1, 1793.

the Committee of Public Safety issued its instructions to the four-member diplomatic commission being sent to the United States to replace Genet. The new representatives were told to "take care to collect all the facts that can shed light on the conduct of Sonthonax and Polverel and the unfortunate events that they caused" and to "take all necessary measures, together with the government of the United States, to arrest these two commissioners and transfer them to France."[70] Two days later, Page and Brulley had the unexpected experience of hearing Robespierre himself publicly endorse their position. Despite their contacts with other members of the Committee of Public Safety, the two men seem to have scrupulously avoided Robespierre, regarded as the colonial slaveholders' most dangerous enemy ever since he had uttered the famous words, "Let the colonies perish rather than a principle!" during the debate about the legitimacy of slavery in May 1791. On November 17, 1793, however, Page and Brulley were in the audience at the Convention when the Incorruptible presented an overview of the revolutionary government's foreign policy, in which he announced that "the same faction which wanted to reduce the poor in France to the status of helots, and force the people to submit to the aristocracy of wealth, wanted to emancipate and arm all the blacks over night to destroy our colonies."[71] Page's and Brulley's satisfaction was heightened by the fact that Robespierre delivered this line in the course of a denunciation of the French minister to the United States, Edmond Genet, who had added himself to Page and Brulley's list of enemies by endorsing Sonthonax and Polverel's version of the events of June 20, 1793 rather than that of the white colonists.[72]

At the beginning of December 1793, the indefatigable Saint-Domingue lobbyists received a report about the pending arrival in France of representatives sent by Sonthonax. On December 1, 1793, Page and Brulley asked the municipality of Paris to be on the lookout for six men, whose names they listed.[73] The report was both premature and inaccurate: of the six names listed, only two – Dufay and Réchin – had actually been

[70] Instructions for French representatives, 25 bru. II, in Turner, ed., *Seventh Report of the Historical Manuscripts Commission*), 290.
[71] Robespierre, speech of 27 brumaire II (November 17, 1793), in Robespierre, *Oeuvres*, 10: 173–4. For the commissioners' pleased reaction to the speech, see AN, D XXV 76, 27 bru. II.
[72] AN D XXV 76, November 19, 1793 (nominating a replacement for Genet).
[73] Page and Brulley, register, entry for December 1, 1793, in AN, D XXV 76. Page and Brulley's information was not entirely inaccurate: a man named Réchin had, in fact, been chosen as one of the Saint-Domingue deputies, but he had withdrawn from the post before leaving the colony. Letter of Laforest aîné, 19 mess. II, in AN, D 1 § 39.

elected as Convention deputies, and it does not appear that any members of the group had actually made it to France. Page and Brulley were clearly preparing to go after any emissaries from the commissioners when they did arrive, however. They continued to propose plans for the reoccupation of the colony, assuring the Committee of Public Safety that if their recommendations were followed, "two months would suffice to bring order back to Saint-Domingue and annihilate the revolt." Their allies within the revolutionary government were numerous. On December 26, 1793, one of them, Pierre Adet, recommended that the Committee of Public Safety send Verneuil, the agitator who had set off the violent riot against Sonthonax in Cap Français on December 2, 1792, to the United States to "bring words of consolation to the Saint-Domingue colonists who are refugees there."[74]

By the end of December, however, Page and Brulley were facing the first threat to their solid support from the revolutionary committees: news had finally reached Paris of both the treaty between the colonists and the British, signed the previous February, and of the surrender of Jérémie and Môle. An anonymous report on the situation, prepared for the Committee of Public Safety, proposed a radical shift in policy, going even beyond what Sonthonax and Polverel had done. Writing soon after the young Napoleon Bonaparte's success in recapturing France's Mediterranean naval base, the report's author predicted that Saint-Domingue could be turned into "another Toulon" for the British, a trap that would draw in and destroy their forces. All that was necessary was to "send [the blacks] arms and munitions, confirm the rights granted to the mulattoes and the Negroes, and give them the right to choose for themselves the new government that they want to have, under French protection ... Then the genius of liberty will spur these new republicans to prodigious feats ... Proud Albion and old Spain will pay for their sins."[75] Although the unknown author of this report was poorly informed about realities in the colony – at the moment when he wrote, the majority of the blacks were fighting on the side of the Spanish, and not even Sonthonax and Polverel had dreamed of simply letting the black population create its own government – the notion that the proclamation of emancipation in Saint-Domingue would be a powerful weapon against France's enemies would help win passage of the abolition decree of 16 pluviôse.

---

[74] Adet to Committee of Public Safety, 5 niv. II, in AN, AF II 302.
[75] Anonymous report to Committee of Public Safety and Navy Committee, 7 niv. II (December 28, 1793), in AN, D XXV 6, d. 54.

To fend off such dangerous suggestions, Page and Brulley took the risk of defending their fellow colonists' appeal to the British. "Despair led our brothers in the Grande Anse and Môle to commit a great crime; [they were] abandoned by the Republic, torn apart by Sonthonax and Polverel, forced to choose between death or subjection to the king of England," they wrote to the Committee of Public Safety on December 26, 1793.[76] For the moment, the members of the Committee, who had sent Brissot and his colleagues to their deaths on charges of a purely imaginary conspiracy with the British, accepted this justification of very real collusion with the enemy, and Page and Brulley were able to continue their lobbying activities. A delegation of colonists was allowed to address the Convention on December 31, 1793, and members of the Committee of Public Safety continued to meet with Page and Brulley on a regular basis. In early January, they persuaded the War Ministry to circulate a long list of men they denounced as counterrevolutionaries to the government committees, with a request for their arrests.[77] On January 2, 1794, Page and Brulley explained to Committee of Public Safety member Robert Lindet why the emancipation of the slaves was impossible: if they were freed, they would turn on each other in a general massacre. They also continued their campaign to have Raimond tried by the Revolutionary Tribunal; Amar and the prosecutor Antoine Fouquier-Tinville, another of their regular interlocutors, assured them that they would soon be satisfied.[78] White colonists throughout the country remained confident that they had the backing of the revolutionary government. On 10 pluviôse, one day after the arrival in Paris of the tri-color deputation from Saint-Domingue, one of Page's and Brulley's friends in Bordeaux wrote them, "the National Convention is about to decree the re-establishment of order in Saint-Domingue, and you will be compensated for all the efforts you have made to explain the state of our unhappy colony, and the remedy that needs to be applied."[79]

It was, therefore, only the arrival of the Saint-Domingue deputies – an event that would not have taken place had it not been for the crisis of June 20, 1793 and Genet's intervention in the United States – that provoked the sudden reversal of the revolutionary government's policy

---

[76] Page and Brulley, register, December 26, 1793, in AN, D XXV 76.

[77] Page and Brulley, letter to War Ministry, 16 niv. II, and War Ministry circular, 23 niv., in SHAT, Xi 71, d. "An II."

[78] Page and Brulley, register, entries for December 31, 1793, January 10 and 12, 1794, in AN, D XXV 76.

[79] Honoré Guérin to Brulley, 10 plu. II, from Bordeaux, in AN, D XXV 71, d. 713.

and the passage of the abolition decree on 16 pluviôse An II (February 4, 1794). As Genet had foreseen when he instructed the captain of the ship carrying the deputies to France to choose his port of debarkation carefully, the men had to run a gauntlet set up by the white colonists to reach Paris safely. According to Polverel's son, the white colonists had even tried to get the sailors on the ship bringing them from America to assassinate them en route.[80] In France, Page and Brulley had a network of supporters in the coastal cities ready to intercept the deputies. Victor Hugues, an ally of Page and Brulley's who was soon to leave on his mission to Guadeloupe, narrowly missed a chance to have them arrested in port of Lorient, where they came ashore.[81] The three men reached the capital on 4 pluviôse; by the following day, Page and Brulley had learned of their presence and gone to demand that Amar have them arrested. It took all day on 6 pluviôse before the Committee of General Security was ready to issue the arrest warrants, which were not actually executed until the night of 9 pluviôse. In the meantime, the Saint-Domingue deputies had succeeded in contacting the Committee of Public Safety. Robert Lindet told Page and Brulley that Dufay and his colleagues had convinced them that Sonthonax and Polverel had only erred because of "exaggerated principles of liberty, poorly applied, and not at all ... with views of royalism or counterrevolution."[82] The two colonial lobbyists fully realized the danger that this challenge to their version of events presented. On 9 pluviôse, Fouquier-Tinville warned them that the Committee of Public Safety had intervened to prevent the indictment of Raimond, even though Amar was still pushing to have the Committee of General Security deliver an accusation against him. This was another ominous sign from Page and Brulley's point of view.

Events now moved rapidly. On 12 pluviôse, the two arrested Saint-Domingue deputies wrote to the Convention, announcing that they had important information about the colonies and explaining that they were victims of a plot to prevent that body from consecrating "the principle of equality, of the fraternity of colors."[83] On 13 pluviôse, the two men were released from prison on orders from the Committee of General

---

[80] François Polverel, "Supplément au Coup d'oeil sur St. Domingue par François Polverel ci-devant secrétaire de la commission civile délégué aux isles sous le vent," 19 fri. III, in AN, D XXV 13, d. 127.

[81] Piquet, *Emancipation des noirs*, 322; Dastugne, letters to Brulley, from Nantes, 5 and 8 plu. II, in AN, D XXV 71, d. 713.

[82] Page and Brulley, register, 6 and 7 pluviôse II, in AN, D XXV 76.

[83] Dufay and Mills to Convention, 12 plu. II, in AN, D XXV 57, d. 563.

Security, which apparently yielded to pressure from the Committee of Public Safety. When Page and Brulley managed to meet with a member of the latter committee, Bertrand Barère, on 14 pluviôse, he told them in no uncertain terms that his colleagues were not happy about the lobbyists' efforts to have the newly arrived deputies arrested, and added that "it is well known that the whites are aristocrats in that colony and that the men of color and the negroes are patriots." He added that the committee had now seen the letters that Page and Brulley had written in July 1792, affirming their royalist sentiments. The two lobbyists turned to their ally Amar, who agreed with them that "if [the Saint-Domingue deputies] were admitted to the Convention, they would have general liberty decreed, which would lose all the colonies once and for all."[84] Page and Brulley continued their frantic efforts on 15 pluviôse, but while they were meeting with various allies, Dufay, Mills, and Belley succeeded in presenting themselves to the Convention and were admitted as official representatives of the colony's North Province. Several deputies spoke on their behalf, including Camboulas, who had overseen the passage of the decree of March 5, 1793 endorsing Sonthonax's and Polverel's policies, and Danton, who denounced the "aristocratic colonists." The deputy J.-F. Delacroix, an ally of Danton's, exclaimed, "For a long time, the assembly wished to have in its midst some men of color, who were oppressed for so many years. Today it has two; I ask that their entry be marked with a fraternal accolade," and Belley and Mills were accordingly embraced by the assembly's president.[85] Page and Brulley had been outmaneuvered. (See Figure 10.1.)

Historiographical legend long made it seem as though the Convention reacted to the appearance of the tri-color deputation from Saint-Domingue on 15 pluviôse An II by passing its decree against slavery in a burst of unanimous enthusiasm on the following day. The French scholar Yves Bénot's careful reconstruction of the actual proceedings has shown that matters were not so simple.[86] One significant fact is that none of the eleven members of the Committee of Public Safety was even present for the debate. Three were away on mission, one was sick, and the remaining seven, including Robespierre, were closeted with two individuals many of them knew well, namely Page and Brulley, who had

[84] Page and Brulley, register, 14 pluviôse II, in AN, D XXV 76.
[85] *Archives parlementaires*, 15 plu. II, 84:58–9; *Moniteur universel*, 17 plu. II (Convention, 15 plu. II).
[86] Yves Bénot, "Comment la Convention a-t-elle voté l'abolition de l'esclavage en l'an II?" *Annales historiques de la Révolution française*, nos. 293–4 (1993), 349–61.

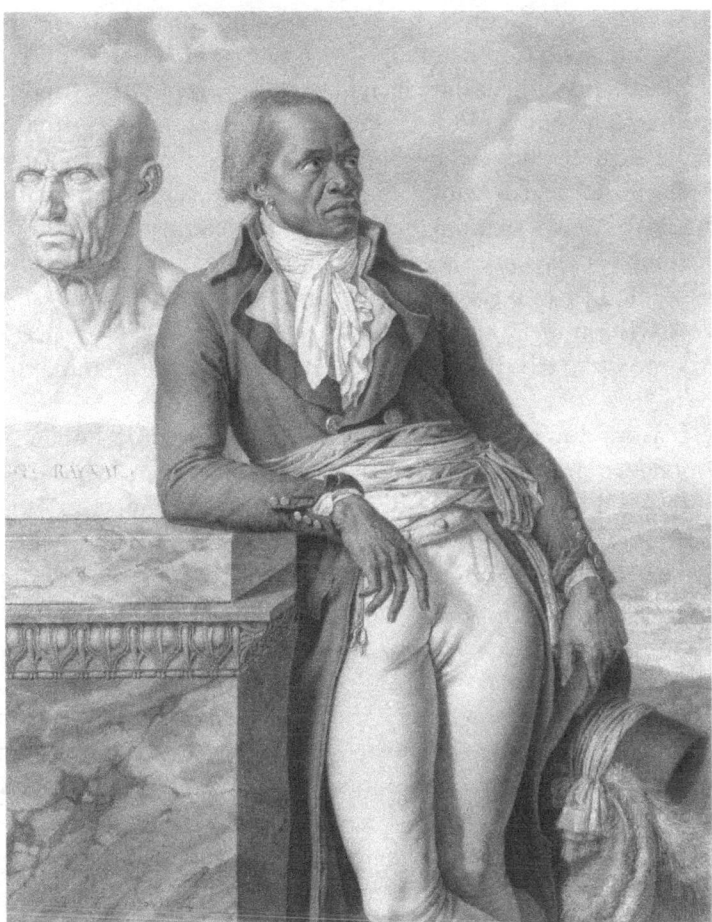

FIGURE 10.1. Deputy Jean-Baptiste Belley.

The seating of Jean-Baptiste Belley, a free black man, in the National Convention on 15 pluviôse An II (February 3, 1794) was one of the epoch-making consequences of the events of June 20, 1793 in Cap Français. Belley commanded the free men of color who defended the commissioners Sonthonax and Polverel during the fighting in the city. At the end of the twentieth century, the French artist Anne-Louis Girodet's full-length portrait of Belley in his deputy's uniform, made in 1798 and for which this pencil drawing may be a preliminary sketch, became one of the iconic images of the revolutionary era.

Source: Chicago Art Institute.

demanded a meeting to present their charges that the deputies' election could not be valid. The lobbyists complained that "a former marquis [Dufay], an Englishman [Mills] and an African Bambara [Belley] have been presented to you as deputies of Saint-Domingue ... These men have

been denounced as guilty of general and specific crimes that are attested
to by eyewitnesses." According to Page and Brulley's notes, Barère was
more sympathetic to them than he had been two days earlier, and Lindet
suggested that action could be taken when the remaining three Saint-
Domingue deputies named by Sonthonax arrived in Paris. Page and
Brulley protested that it would then be too late, since they had heard
that Dufay "proposes to immediately deliver a report whose result could
be damaging for the entire regime of the colonies." The committee, in
the classic manner of busy men of government, told the lobbyists to go
prepare a written memorandum. As the two men left its offices, other
colonists ran up to tell them that the Convention had just voted to abolish slavery.[87]

The reasons for the behavior of the Committee of Public Safety
on 16 pluviôse are unclear. At this stage in the reign of Terror, the
Convention did not take major decisions without its approval, and the
sudden reversal of a policy that had been repeatedly affirmed by both
the legislators and the Committee was hardly an inconsequential action.
The Committee of Public Safety had clearly intervened to persuade the
Committee of General Security to release the Saint-Domingue deputies
from prison three days earlier, and its members were unquestionably
aware of the enthusiastic welcome the three men had received from the
Convention on 15 pluviôse. It is worth noting, however, that two of the
speakers who had most vocally supported the admission of the Saint-
Domingue deputies were Danton and Delacroix, leading members of the
"Indulgent" faction whose public criticism of the Committees' policy
of terror had shaken the revolutionary government's authority for the
previous six weeks. Outside of the Convention, the strongest supporter
of abolition was Chaumette, the *procureur* of the Paris Commune, a
member of the Hébertist group that the Committee of Public Safety
considered as the radical counterpart to the moderate Dantonists. For
the Committee to openly oppose the abolition of slavery risked putting
its members in the awkward position of seeming to defend an institution that obviously contradicted the principles of liberty and equality,
while allowing the two enemy factions to take credit for demanding its
elimination.

Faced with this dilemma, Robespierre and his colleagues apparently
decided to let the Convention proceed on its own, without providing the
legislators any guidance. Perhaps they had concluded that the issue was

---

[87] Page and Brulley, register, 16 pluviôse II, in AN, D XXV 76.

moot, since, as Dufay was about to explain to the Convention, the slaves in Saint-Domingue had already been granted freedom, and there was no practical way to reverse that decision. Nevertheless, the Committee of Public Safety's enthusiasm for the emancipation decree was clearly limited. It would be nearly two months before they finally promulgated the decree officially. Even though clear evidence of Page and Brulley's royalist sentiments was now in front of them, in the form of the letters the two men had written in July 1792, the committee also took no action against them for nearly a month, and they continued to meet with Barère to try to undo the effects of the vote of 16 pluviôse. If the Convention's vote to outlaw slavery appeared to be a decision taken in a moment of enthusiasm, the Committee of Public Safety's reaction seemed like that of a group reluctantly acquiescing to a result for which they did not want to take responsibility.

Whatever the reasons for the Committee of Public Safety's decision not to intervene in the Convention's debate, their inaction provided the white Saint-Domingue deputy Louis Dufay a historic opportunity. While the presence of his colleagues, Mills and Belley, gave the moment its symbolic weight, Dufay was the only one of the three with the oratorical skills and political experience to present the argument for emancipation to the deputies. Even after the warm welcome the Convention had given the men the day before, Dufay's task was not easy. As a plantation owner himself, he was hardly the ideal person to make a moral argument against slavery. It had taken the French Revolution, he confessed, to make him realize that the practice needed to be ended, and that "a friend of liberty and equality had to also be a friend of humanity."[88] Addressing the same legislators who had voted, six months earlier, to have the civil commissioners Sonthonax and Polverel arrested for abusing their powers, he had to convince them to reverse themselves and uphold the most radical action these two supposed criminals had taken. Less than three months earlier, on 27 brumaire II, the same deputies had applauded when Robespierre denounced the abolitionists for destroying the colonies; now Dufay asked them to repudiate the Incorruptible's argument. With nationalist and patriotic sentiments running high, he had to convince the legislators not only that the abolition of slavery was morally necessary, but that it was in France's interest, despite the fact that it seemed to have led to the destruction of the colony's major city and to foreign occupation of key parts of its territory.

---

[88] Dufay, speech of 16 pluviôse II, in *Réimpression de l'ancien Moniteur*, 20: 394.

Dufay had prepared carefully for this moment. As we have seen, he arrived in the United States in November already armed with, if not a fully written-out speech, at least a list of what would today be called "talking points" to justify Sonthonax's and Polverel's actions. Upon landing in the United States, one of his first concerns had been to inform himself about recent political events in France and to assess their consequences for his mission. In a long letter to Sonthonax, written from New York on December 4, 1793, Dufay had sketched out the picture he had managed to put together, and in particular his understanding of the situation created by the defeat of Brissot's faction. He recognized the significance of the creation of the Committee of Public Safety, although he wrongly deduced that Danton was now the leading figure in the government, with Robespierre "in second place"; he correctly concluded that there was now greater unity in the leadership, and that "the country is coming together with a common desire to save itself." He underlined the obvious fact that the civil commissioners were in trouble because of their association with the Girondins: "You were known to be their friends, and it is natural enough that there should have been attempts to include you in their disgrace." Although Dufay did not underestimate the significance of the decree against Sonthonax and Polverel voted on July 16 and reaffirmed on September 3, 1793, he convinced himself that the political forces behind this measure were probably not all-powerful. He suspected that the July decree had been an attempt to pacify the merchant interests in the port cities that had supported the uprisings against the Convention after the ouster of the Girondins: "It's a bone that they were given to chew on, [the Convention] feigned to sacrifice for the moment two men whom it nevertheless undoubtedly did not want to lose," a speculation that, he said, seemed plausible given that nothing had yet been done to implement the recall decree.[89] Although Dufay misunderstood a number of aspects of the rapidly changing revolutionary political scene, he saw that he would have to function in a situation in which the commissioners' Girondin patrons had been demonized. Nevertheless, he was convinced that the political forces opposing emancipation were not unbeatable.

The long and detailed speech he delivered to the Convention on 16 pluviôse II, which he had certainly written out in advance and which was immediately published in the *Moniteur universel*, reflected his

---

[89] Dufay, letter to Sonthonax and Polverel, December 4, 1793, in AN, D XXV 6, d. 54, and D XXV 16, d. 158.

careful preparation.[90] Dufay decided not to evoke the principled arguments against the institution of slavery: the speech that provoked the most radical abolition decree the world would see until Abraham Lincoln's Emancipation Proclamation of 1862 barely mentioned the subject. Despite his close ties to Sonthonax and Polverel, Dufay also decided not to mention their names, referring only to "your commissioners" or "your delegates." This precaution enabled him to urge the legislators to approve what the two men had done, without raising the question of whether the Convention had erred when it condemned them in July 1793. Instead, Dufay, following the strategy already worked out by Sonthonax and Polverel in their report to the Convention after the journée of June 20, 1793, accorded the leading role in his speech to General Galbaud, "the second-in-command and friend of the perfidious Dumouriez." In the course of an indictment relying on the same conspiratorial logic used by the white colonists and the Montagnards themselves, Dufay also associated Galbaud with "the gold of the Spanish Bourbons and the English," "the [colonial] whites, plantation-owners like himself," "the counterrevolutionaries who had arrived from France and Coblentz," the naval officers, "impure holdovers from the Old Regime," and the "merchants of your principal commercial cities": in short, the entire cast of malefactors who peopled the revolutionaries' paranoid imagination.

The first half of Dufay's speech was largely devoted to a narrative of the events of June 20, 1793; he had also prepared a longer chronological account that was later published separately.[91] "Galbaud, agent of the vengeances of his caste," was accused of having provoked the catastrophe as part of a conscious plot to "slaughter" the free men of color. He had "corrupted, seduced, misled the crews of the warships and the merchant vessels, and made them into blind instruments of his rage and his ambition." Dufay gave all the credit for resisting Galbaud to "the citizens of color ... the people, the true sans-culottes in the colonies," who "immediately rallied around your commissioners." Forestalling any possible criticism of Sonthonax and Polverel for fleeing the city on June

---

[90] The text of Dufay's speech can be found in vol. 84 of the *Archives parlementaires*, 1er sér. (Paris: CNRS, 1962), in the original edition of the *Moniteur universel* of 18 plu. II (Convention, 16 plu.), in the *Réimpression de l'Ancien Moniteur*, 20: 389–95, and in *Compte rendu sur la situation actuelle de Saint-Domingue. Par Dufey [sic], député de la partie du nord. 16 plu. II* (Paris: Imprimerie nationale, An II).

[91] *Relation détaillée des événemens malheureux qui se sont passés au Cap depuis l'arrivée du ci-devant général Galbaud, jusqu'au moment où il a fait brûler cette ville et a pris la fuite* (Paris: Imprimerie nationale, An II).

21, Dufay insisted that it was the men of color who had begged them to move to safety. Without even mentioning the commissioners' proclamation of June 21, 1793, he described the blacks as having spontaneously come forward to join the struggle against Galbaud: "'We are negroes, French,' they said; 'we are going to fight for France, but as a reward, we ask for freedom.' They even added, 'the Rights of Man.'" The commissioners, Dufay indicated, had no choice but to accept this offer: "We were in confusion; the blacks understood their strength; they might even have turned it against us if we had offended them."

Dufay had to explain not only why Sonthonax and Polverel had offered freedom to the blacks who offered to fight for them on June 21, 1793, an action that could be justified as a military necessity, but why, having won the battle, they then took it upon themselves, without authorization from the Convention, to emancipate the rest of the slave population. "You will be convinced, I trust," he told his listeners, "that it is the force of events that then led to the great measure of liberty in the North Province, as the only means of saving the white population and even the citizens of 4 April." The black insurgents had been fighting for their freedom for two years, and "one could never hope to make them return to their duty," he insisted, going on to explain why it had been necessary to grant legal freedom not only to the fighting men but also to their women and children. Again, rather than emphasizing the initiative of the commissioners, he stressed the role of the free men of color, "the first to sacrifice their slaves," and he pointed dramatically to his colleagues, Mills and Belley, claiming that "they were the first to give the example." In any event, the commissioners really had no choice, since the Spanish and the British were also offering the insurgents freedom, along with money and officers' titles. "Was it not a wise and enlightened policy to create new citizens for the republic who would oppose our enemies?" Dufay asked.

Having established that "the measure taken by the civil commissioners was not spontaneous, that they were constrained to adopt it to save the sovereignty of the nation," and that it was really Galbaud who bore the responsibility for creating the situation that compelled them to act, Dufay went on to argue that Sonthonax's decree of August 29, 1793 would not harm either the national interest or that of the property owners in the colony and the merchants who dealt with them. (Since he officially represented only the North Province, he did not discuss the measures Polverel had taken in the West.) "The proclamation, in declaring [the slaves] free, assigned them to remain at their respective plantations," he noted, "and subjected them to severe discipline as well as daily work, in return for a set salary; they are more or less attached to the estate [*attachés à la glèbe*]." The newly freed slaves were now eager to earn money, and they would be good customers for French commerce. "You will see that your colony of Saint-Domingue, cultivated by free hands, will be more flourishing ... that this new colony will produce more for the metropole than before, that your political influence is assured in Saint-Domingue and that soon it will dominate the entire archipelago of the Gulf of Mexico," Dufay promised the deputies.

To be sure, Dufay went on, some people in France feared that the blacks were uncivilized and uncontrollable. In the account of events in Le Cap in June 1793 that he published a few weeks after his speech, he incautiously described the blacks who had joined the commissioners' forces as "these still savage peoples, of whom many even came from hordes of cannibals [*anthropophages*]," words that the pro-slavery colonists would later seize on to discredit him and Sonthonax.[92] On 16 pluviôse, however, Dufay was more careful in his language, emphasizing that these supposedly ferocious men had, until recently, been members of work teams that "allowed themselves to be ordered around by a single white man, and went along with all his whims." If there had been a certain amount of disorder following emancipation, it amounted to no more than "a few movements of effervescence" that would quickly pass. "They are naturally sweet, charitable, hospitable, very devoted to their parents," Dufay assured the deputies. "They love justice and have the greatest respect for their elders." Although in fact most of the black insurgents were still fighting for the Spanish, Dufay claimed that they had become French patriots. "The story of all that you have done for liberty enlightened, warmed, inflamed their hearts; the story of your victories raised their souls, and inspired in them sentiments of patriotism that had previously been unknown to them." All that was left was for the French legislators to accept the opportunity that the population of Saint-Domingue offered them: "You can ... earn a consoling memory for yourselves in honoring humanity and in carrying out the great act of justice it expects from you. Create a new world for the second time, or at least let it be remade thanks to you; be its benefactors; your names will be blessed like those of tutelary deities. You will be another Providence for this country," Dufay concluded.

---

[92] *Relation détaillée des événemens malheureux*, 55. For the colonists' use of Dufay's reference to "cannibals," see *Débats entre les accusateurs et les accusés*, 8: 22.

Since the expulsion of the Girondins at the beginning of June 1793, Convention debates were no longer epic jousts between orators representing contrasting viewpoints, but differences among the deputies still manifested themselves in the form of parliamentary maneuvers. After Dufay's speech, one deputy tried to sidetrack the debate by moving to refer the question to the Committee of Public Safety.[93] In response, René Levasseur, an obscure Montagnard, moved instead that the Convention, "not ceding to a movement of enthusiasm, but to the principles of justice, faithful to the Declaration of the Rights of Man, decree as of this moment that slavery is abolished throughout the territory of the Republic ... I want all men to be free, without distinction of color." Delacroix, who had called for the admission of the deputies the day before, added that "in carrying out this act of justice, you will give a great example to the colored slaves in the British and Spanish colonies." He then called on the president of the assembly to cut off any further debate: "Do not allow the Convention to dishonor itself with a longer discussion." According to the *Moniteur*'s account, "the Assembly rises in acclamation. The president pronounces the abolition of slavery, amidst applause and a thousand repetitions of the cries, 'Long live the Republic! Long live the Convention! Long live the Mountain!' The two deputies of color are at the tribune, they embrace each other. (Applause.) [De]lacroix takes them to the president, who gives them the fraternal embrace. They are then embraced in turn by all the deputies."[94]

One particularly enthusiastic legislator moved that the navy minister be ordered to send messenger ships to all the colonies immediately announcing the news. Danton stepped in to keep things under control. "The Convention has done its duty," he said. "But after having given the gift of liberty, we need to be, so to speak, its moderators. Let us refer to the committees of Public Safety and of the colonies, to come up with means to make this decree useful for humanity, without any danger for it." He added his famous prediction that, thanks to the decree, "as of today, England is dead;" the slaves in its colonies would now demand their own freedom.[95] It is ironic that this, one of the great tribune's last significant interventions in the Convention's debates, was aimed at upholding the authority of the same Committee of Public Safety that would order him arrested just a few weeks later. There was another

---

[93] Bénot, "Comment la Convention," 354.
[94] *Moniteur universel*, 17 plu. II (Convention, 16 plu.).
[95] *Moniteur universel*, 17 plu. II (Convention, 16 plu.).

parliamentary squabble when some deputies objected to the use of the word "slavery" in a Convention decree; the abbé Grégoire, recognizing that the word's absence might leave room for doubt about what the legislature really intended, insisted strongly that it be retained.[96] The deputies finally approved the phrasing proposed by Delacroix: "The National Convention declares negro slavery abolished in all the colonies; in consequence, it decrees that all men, regardless of color, who are domiciled in the colonies, are French citizens, and enjoy all the rights guaranteed by the constitution."[97] On the next day, several deputies tried again to modify the wording of the decree or give the Committee of Public Safety more latitude to redact it, but in the end, the Convention stuck with the text it had voted on 16 pluviôse.[98]

The decree the Convention passed was quite different from what any of the major proponents of abolition in revolutionary France had actually advocated. Even the most daring critics of slavery had always acknowledged that it could not be phased out overnight without grave dangers. Dufay's speech did not make a principled case against slavery: he limited himself to asking the Convention to validate an action that, he argued, Sonthonax had been forced to take, and he specifically defended the system of virtual forced labor that Sonthonax had imposed, asserting that it would provide the guarantees that supporters of gradual emancipation had always insisted on. It was the Convention that decided to issue a decree framed in general terms, with no provisions to keep the plantations functioning, and to apply it to the entire French empire. Almost all of the French reformers had also explicitly endorsed the creation of a system in which the free population of color would have played a dominant role. Dufay's speech singled them out for praise, but the Convention's decree ended any hope the "citizens of 4 April" might have had for special recognition.

The decree of 16 pluviôse was equally remote from the most urgent concerns of the insurgent blacks in Saint-Domingue. As their behavior after the issuance of Sonthonax's and Polverel's decrees showed, the former slaves were more interested in liberating themselves from the constraints of plantation labor and in acquiring access to land than in abstract legal freedom coupled with an obligation to continue working in the sugar fields. No one in Paris considered how the Convention's

---

[96] Bénot, "Comment la Convention," 353.
[97] *Moniteur universel*, 17 plu. II (Convention, 16 plu. II).
[98] Bénot, "Comment la Convention," 356–7.

decree granting the freed slaves full constitutional rights could be rec-
onciled with the numerous restrictions on their behavior incorporated
in Sonthonax's document. Despite the wide gap between the political
realities that had led to the emancipation decrees in Saint-Domingue and
the more ideological approach reflected in the Convention's measure,
the two were intimately related. The Convention would not have taken
up the issue without the impetus provided by the arrival of the Saint-
Domingue deputies, but both the de facto freedom the slaves had claimed
for themselves and the measures Sonthonax and Polverel had taken after
the journée of June 20, 1793 would have remained local improvisa-
tions of uncertain significance if the Convention had not declared them
to be consequences of the French constitution's basic principles. Even
though there was no conscious cooperation between the different parties
involved in the process, on 16 pluviôse, their actions all came together
to produce a result whose consequences were greater than what any of
them could have achieved in isolation.

The absence of any explicit debate about the decree of 16 pluviôse
makes it difficult to assess the motives of the Convention deputies who
voted for it. No doubt some of them simply accepted Dufay's argument
that there was no alternative, and others may have shared Danton's
hope that, if nothing else, the decree would encourage unrest in the
British colonies. The memoirs of the deputy Levasseur, who played a
key role in the debate, offer a suggestive insight into the motives of a
man who described himself as an "obscure Montagnard." Writing under
the Restoration, when the memory of the Terror was still anathema,
Levasseur admitted that the Convention had made many mistakes. Men
like himself, who had "devoted our life to the Republic ... could not see
without shuddering the temporary results of our energetic measures and
of the resistance they had excited," he claimed. For him, the memory
of the passage of the abolition decree was a ray of light in an otherwise
somber tableau. "I never recall this session without an emotion that is
both sweet and consoling," he wrote in his memoir. But the issue had
also been a personal one for him. As an idealistic youth, he claimed, he
had been "disinherited by one of my uncles, a rich colonist, because I
had blamed the infamous slave trade in his presence. In the session that
I have just described," he continued, "I reaped the reward for my devotion to the cause of humanity."[99] While Levasseur found it consoling to

[99] R[ené] Levasseur, *Mémoires de R. Levasseur (de la Sarthe) ex-Conventionnel*, ed.
Michel Vovelle (Paris: Messidor/Editions sociales, 1989 (orig. 1829–31)), 422, 426.

be able to vote for the elimination of slavery at a time when he was having to endorse so many decisions that troubled him, the abbé Grégoire, the most prominent opponent of slavery in the Convention, looked back on the vote of 16 pluviôse with certain misgivings. In his memoirs, he recalled how he and the other members of the Société des amis des noirs had agreed that "with regard to the slaves, it was necessary not to emancipate them suddenly, but to lead them gradually to the advantages of the social state ... . You can understand that the sudden emancipation pronounced by the decree of 16 pluviôse An II, which Levasseur had provoked, seemed disastrous to us: it was the political equivalent of a volcano."[100] Once the decree had been voted, however, Grégoire, unlike many of the other deputies, consistently opposed any attempt to roll back the decision.

Clear and simple as it was, the decree passed by the Convention on 16 pluviôse An II still left some important questions in suspense. One of the most obvious concerned the status of the earlier decree of July 16, 1793 ordering the recall and arrest of Sonthonax and Polverel. Deputy François Bourdon de l'Oise raised the issue after the passage of the abolition decree, but the Convention hesitated to reverse its own earlier decision and instead referred the matter to the Committee of Public Safety.[101] The incongruity of a situation in which the French government endorsed the freeing of the slaves but disavowed the men who had carried it out was striking, as the members of the French diplomatic mission in the United States pointed out. After receiving news of the decree of 16 pluviôse, they wrote to Paris, "One cannot fail to recognize that the decree of accusation against [Sonthonax and Polverel], and then the failure to execute it, have caused the greatest misfortunes ... This state of indecision, in spite of the firmness of the commissioners, has shaken the whole system."[102] More than two months after the passage of the emancipation decree, as it was finally preparing to dispatch an official to promulgate that measure in Saint-Domingue, the Committee of Public Safety decided that the recall decree would stand; as we have seen, Sonthonax and Polverel were subjected to the indignity of being treated as suspects even as they saw their most important action officially endorsed. Sonthonax's biographer, Robert Stein, notes that Robespierre signed the

[100] Henri Grégoire, *Mémoires*, ed. Hippolyte Carnot, intro. Jean-Michel Leniaud (Paris: Editions de Santé, 1989), 81.
[101] *Nouvelles politiques*, 18 plu. II (Convention, 16 plu.); Stein, *Sonthonax*, 111.
[102] Letter of 15 prair. II, in Turner, ed., *Seventh Report of the Historical Manuscripts Commission*, 366.

official paper approving this decision, but not the document containing the committee's endorsement of the abolition decree. As the Committee was discussing this matter, it was also debating the charges to be brought against the Dantonists, who were about to be put on trial. In notes that he passed to his colleague Saint-Just on the subject, Robespierre wrote, "Danton once said to me, 'It is too bad that we cannot propose to give our colonies to the Americans; it would be a way to seal an alliance with them.' Subsequently, Danton and Lacroix have had a decree passed whose likely result was the loss of our colonies." Saint-Just did not allude to the matter in the official indictment, but Robespierre was clearly convinced that, like the Brissotins, the Dantonists had seized on abolition as a way of concealing their counterrevolutionary intentions.[103]

On 17 pluviôse II, the day after the passage of the emancipation decree, Robespierre delivered to the Convention one of his most celebrated speeches, his discourse on the moral bases of the revolutionary government and the necessity of a policy of terror to support republican virtue. He praised the French for being the first people to "summon all men to equality and liberty, and to their full rights as citizens," but he made no mention of the epoch-making decree passed the day before. The two uses of the word "slavery" in his speech of 17 pluviôse were entirely abstract and had nothing to do with the colonies, and he never mentioned the subject again in the remaining months before his overthrow.[104] After the conclusion of Robespierre's speech, the deputy Roger Ducos tried to link the previous day's decree against colonial slavery with the general principle of universal human freedom by proposing that French citizens be forbidden from recognizing the legitimacy of slavery anywhere in the world. His proposal was referred to the Committee of Public Safety and buried.[105] The revolutionary government's continuing unease with the issue of abolition was reflected in the official version of Dufay's detailed account of the events leading up to the journée of June 20, 1793, which was prefaced with a long diatribe reiterating the accusations against Brissot for destroying the colony, and a reminder that he had been responsible for the choice of the civil commissioners.[106]

---

[103] Stein, *Sonthonax*, 111–12; Albert Mathiez, *Études sur Robespierre (1758-1794)*, ed. Georges Lefebvre (Paris: Éditions sociales, 1958), 146.

[104] Robespierre, speech of 17 plu. II, in *Archives parlementaires*, 84: 331.

[105] *Moniteur universel*, 19 plu. II (Convention, 17 plu. II).

[106] *Rélation détaillée des événemens malheureux*. The pamphlet was compiled by the Saint-Domingue deputies and issued in the name of the Comité d'instruction publique.

In addition to the question of the recall of the civil commissioners, the Committee of Public Safety had to make a number of other decisions about the implementation of the abolition decree. Amar encouraged Page and Brulley to hope that the intent of the decree could be sabotaged, telling them that it was "unheard of, that the Convention had done what Brissot and his faction never dared to do; that it was to go back on what it had decided, to contradict everything that had been done, to protest against the indictment of the Girondins and against justice, that it was astounding that Danton had lent himself to such a thing." He added that "all was not lost; that the Committee of Public Safety, which disapproved of counterrevolutionary measures, would surely make an intelligent decision that would preserve the French colonies, which would otherwise inevitably be lost."[107] Members of the Convention's Colonial Committee also hoped that the decree could be shaped so as to "assure its execution for the greater interest of the Republic and of the white men, without departing from the constitutional principle," and they appointed Benoît Gouly, a slave owner from the Indian Ocean colonies, as one of their representatives to the Committee of Public Safety.[108] That committee, however, had decided not to water down the decree. On 27 pluviôse, Page and Brulley had a lengthy meeting with Barère, who had been tasked with preparing the Committee of Public Safety's report on the question. When he made it clear to them that the committee had decided to implement the emancipation decree, Page and Brulley insisted that this could only be done by leaving the details to the colonists themselves, to which Barère replied that "it is as if one had proposed to let the seigneurs in France decide how to abolish their feudal rights." He was sure that the problems of carrying out the measure could be solved by sending "some good sans-culottes who will get along well with the negroes." Returning to their office after this discouraging conversation, Page and Brulley drafted a letter to the Saint-Domingue refugees in the United States, vowing to keep up their efforts and promising that, sooner or later, their opponents would suffer the same fate as Governor Blanchelande, Brissot, and Barnave, "who have paid with their heads for the harm they did to our country."[109]

In contrast to the situation before the arrival of the deputies from Saint-Domingue, however, the white colonists now faced a counterlobby

---

[107] Page and Brulley, register, 18 plu. II, in AN, D XXV 76.
[108] AN, D*16 3-4-5, entry for 17 plu. II.
[109] AN, D XXV 76, 27 plu. II (February 15, 1794).

that actively opposed their efforts. Dufay, Mills, and Belley went to work to turn the tables on Page and Brulley, denouncing their activities and demanding their arrest. In a letter written on 6 ventôse II, the Saint-Domingue deputies urged the police to seize Page's and Brulley's registers and called for the imprisonment of not just the two lobbyists but of all the white colonists, or at least all those who had played any role in the various colonial assemblies or served as officers in colonial military units.[110] On 15 ventôse, Page, Brulley, and their secretary Legrand had just begun their daily meeting when the police descended on them; their register breaks off dramatically in the middle of a sentence.[111] Four days later, the Convention adopted the broader measure the Saint-Domingue deputies had called for, ordering the arrest of all colonists who had been members of any of the various assemblies created in the colonies since 1789. One deputy, obviously aware of Page and Brulley's activities, noted that "every day the colonists in Paris and their emissaries repeat to the Committee of Public Safety that [the emancipation decree] is unwise, that its execution is impossible; not having succeeded by these means, they denounce all the agents designated to take it to the colonies, in order to prevent their departure, and to thereby gain time to turn minds against your just and humane law."[112] The result was a roundup of almost all politically active white colonists in Paris; they would remain in prison until after the fall of Robespierre, although it appears that none of them were ever put on trial. Arrest and imprisonment did not entirely halt the lobbying efforts of the colonists. The imprisoned colonist Deraggis sent the Committee of General Security a long denunciation of Dufay, and Page and Brulley seized on the execution of Danton, who had spoken for the emancipation decree of 16 pluviôse II, as evidence that the abolition of slavery had been promoted by a traitor and should therefore be nullified.[113] Nevertheless, the colonial lobby's political influence was greatly diminished.

In the political culture of the Revolution, the passage of a major law called for public manifestations of support and an effort to articulate the meaning of the Convention's actions for the broader public. Dufay's

[110] Dufay, Mills and Belley, letter of 6 vent. II, in Florence Gauthier, "Inédits de Belley, Mills et Dufay, députés de Saint-Domingue, de Roume et du comité de Salut public, concernant le démantèlement du réseau du lobby esclavagiste en France février-mars 1794," *Annales historiques de la Révolution française*, no. 4 (1995), 607–11.
[111] Page and Brulley, register, 15 vent. II, in AN, D XXV 76.
[112] *Moniteur universel*, 21 vent. II (Convention, 19 vent.).
[113] Deraggis to CSG, 9 ger. II, in AN, F 4685, d. Dufay; Page and Brulley to Couthon, 16 prair. II, in AN, D XXV 81, d. 794.

speech, calculated to persuade the legislators, was less suitable for the purpose of stirring public enthusiasm; as Aimé Césaire wrote in 1960, it "lacked grandeur."[114] The task of publicizing and celebrating the decree of 16 pluviôse was taken in hand by the group of free people of color who had spoken in favor of abolishing slavery at the Paris Commune in early June and by their political patron, the Commune official Pierre Chaumette; the Saint-Domingue deputies also joined in the effort. Chaumette himself had his limitations as an advocate of universal human rights: while the Convention was decreeing the abolition of slavery on 16 pluviôse, the Commune had been denying a request from the Jews of Paris for permission to bake matzah for Passover, and just before one of his speeches celebrating the abolition of slavery, Chaumette had restated his emphatic opposition to political rights for women, telling a mother who had taught her daughter to recite patriotic verse that a girl should be trained to knit stockings instead.[115] It was also ironic that Chaumette, who had declined the invitation to go to Saint-Domingue in 1792 because he did not trust Sonthonax's abolitionist intentions and who had testified against Brissot at the Girondins' trial, became the most emphatic defender of what Brissot's protégé had done. Nevertheless, it was Chaumette, more than anyone else, who managed to put the significance of the Convention's actions into words and organize appropriate ceremonies in honor of the event.

On the evening after the vote, the three deputies from Saint-Domingue were fêted at the Jacobin club.[116] Two days later, the focus shifted to the Commune. "This decree is not the work of men," Chaumette told the Commune on 18 pluviôse, "it is more the work of the Eternal ... who wants all men henceforth to be nothing but a family of brothers. ... Here begin the annals of patriarchal *moeurs* and the universality of the Republic."[117] On 20 pluviôse, Chaumette and the men of color appeared at the Convention, praising the deputies for their action and urging them to break up the white colonists' network. The delegation carried a tri-color flag they had first displayed in June, with figures of a white,

---

[114] AiméCésaire, *Toussaint Louverture. La Révolution française et le problème colonial,* éd. revue (Paris: Présence Africaine, 1961), 198.

[115] *Journal de la Montagne,* 18 plu. II (Commune, 16 plu.); 23 plu. (Commune, 21 plu.) Among the objections raised to the Jews' request was the claim that it would amount to official recognition of a religious sect, and that equality dictated that all citizens should eat the same bread. The representative of the Jewish community was told to come back with a redrafted request omitting all mention of the specific purposes for which the matzah was to be used.

[116] *Moniteur universel,* 22 plu. II (Jacobins, 16 plu.).

[117] *Journal de la Montagne,* 20 plu. II (Commune, 18 plu.).

a black, and a man of color superimposed on its blue, white, and red stripes; just as the original tri-color flag had combined the colors of the king and the people, symbolizing the unity of the French nation, this banner communicated the message that the three racial groups were now equally united.[118] The next day, the three Saint-Domingue deputies appeared at the Commune, where Chaumette welcomed them with a speech that supplied the emotion that had been missing in Dufay's address. He took the opportunity to remind the audience that he and his allies had tried to get the Convention to end slavery seven months earlier, but "at that time, the Convention was not itself;" it needed all its energy to "deliver the French people from the tyranny of the federalists." Addressing the blacks in the colonies, he cried out, "Oh you, unhappy mothers, obliged to curse your fecundity, take courage: your children will be citizens ... you will bring them up to enjoy freedom, and to bless their liberators." Finally, he announced the holding of a great public ceremony at Notre Dame cathedral, recently rebaptized as the temple of Reason, on the following décadi.[119] In the meantime, the round of celebrations continued. A deputation of men of color addressed the Jacobins on 23 pluviôse and the Commune on 26 pluviôse, with a speaker assuring the members that "among the blacks, there are customs that are very interesting and republican," and the group appeared at the Convention again on 30 pluviôse.[120]

On that same day, Chaumette presided over the ceremony he had organized at Notre Dame. Whereas Dufay's address to the Convention two weeks earlier had presented the abolition of slavery as a pragmatic response to the crisis of June 20, 1793 in Saint-Domingue, Chaumette elevated it to an event of world-historical significance. His speech was replete with references to classical antiquity and the philosophes, but it made no mention of Sonthonax and Polverel, and its only allusion to events in Saint-Domingue was a vague but bloodcurdling evocation of the "great whirlwinds of fire and smoke" marking "the scene of the most horrible of all wars." Chaumette's central argument was that the emancipation decree would reverse the centuries of decadence that had followed man's emergence from the state of nature. As a result of primitive man's deviation from the purity of his original customs, "brazenness and injustice replaced patriarchal decisions, force took the place of reason,

---

[118] *Moniteur universel*, 21 plu. (Convention, 20 plu.).
[119] *Journal de la Montagne*, 25 plu. II (Commune, 21 plu.).
[120] *Journal de la Montagne*, 26 plu. II, 28 plu. II, 1 vent. II.

greed, the overwhelming lust for pleasures gave birth to *mine* and *thine*; laws were required to settle differences ... Arbitrariness having made its appearance, force necessarily became the supreme law." Now, thanks to the recognition of "this truth, that slavery is the worst of evils, and its abolition the greatest of all goods, both for states and for individuals: for states, in preserving them from those violent agitations that hasten their fall, for individuals, in preserving them from the contagion of all the vices that that are born of slavery, which kills men," a new era of human history would begin.[121] Despite his connections to the pro-slavery colonists, the elderly diarist Guittard found the ceremony impressive. He described the march of "all the sections, the revolutionary committees of the sections, the clubs sent deputations with their banners, along with women and drummers, the members of the city assembly, a deputation from the National Assembly accompanied by veterans and grenadiers of the Convention, the musicians from the opera and a procession of Negroes and Negresses who live in Paris along with their three deputies who came from Saint-Domingue to obtain this decree. ... Speeches were given, odes and appropriate songs sung. There was a big crowd. I was there and I had a good view."[122] Similar festivals were held in almost twenty other French cities and towns, sometimes at the behest of local Montagnard leaders, but sometimes as the result of an apparently spontaneous initiative.[123] In some cases, the enthusiasm manifested at these gatherings was forced, as in the case of the large celebration held in the port city of Le Havre, well known as a stronghold of support for the colonial lobby,[124] but the popularity of the engravings of black men and, especially, attractive young women, shown wearing French revolutionary symbols such as the liberty cap or the level of equality, is a sign that the emancipation decree touched a genuine chord with part of the French public. (See Figure 10.2.)

---

[121] *Discours prononcé par le citoyen Chaumette, au nom de la Commune de Paris, le décadi 30 pluviôse, l'an II de la République française, une et indivisible, à la fête célébrée à Paris, en réjouissance de l'abolition de l'Esclavage* (Paris: Imprimerie nationale, [1794]), 17, 2, 10 (reprinted in *Révolution française et l'abolition de l'esclavage*, t. 5).

[122] Guittard, *Journal*, entry for February 18, 1794, 320–1.

[123] Jean-Claude Halpern, "Les Fêtes révolutionnaires et l'abolition de l'esclavage en l'An II," in Marcel Dorigny, ed., *Les abolitions de l'esclavage, de L. F. Sonthonax à V. Schoelcher* (Paris: Editions UNESCO, 1995), 187–98.

[124] Lucie Maquerlot, "Rouen et Le Havre face à la traite et à l'esclavage: le mouvement de l'opinion (1783–1794)," in Marcel Dorigny, dir. *Esclavage, résistances et abolitions* (Paris: Editions du CTHS, 1999), 184–6.

FIGURE 10.2. Celebrating the abolition of slavery.

Four engravings produced in Paris to commemorate the emancipation decree of
16 pluviôse An II show blacks wearing symbols of the French Revolution. The
number of engravings produced on this theme suggests that there was genuine
enthusiasm for the measure. The two images at the top show figures with recog-
nizably Negroid figures and a caption in Creole, "Moi libre aussi" ("I am free,
too"), emphasizing the distinct non-European identity of the freed slaves. The
two images at the bottom show women with more European features; their cap-
tions appeal to French viewers to consider themselves as brothers and sisters of
the newly freed blacks.

Source: Bibliothèque nationale de France.

The National Convention's decree of 16 pluviôse An II was by no means the end of the struggle against slavery, even within the context of the French empire. Historians of a cynical cast have argued that, in reality, it liberated very few slaves: the blacks in the French-controlled parts of Saint-Domingue were already free thanks to their own efforts and those of Sonthonax and Polverel, but neither those in the British- and Spanish-occupied parts of the colony, nor the slave populations of Guadeloupe and Martinique, both occupied by the British at the moment when the decree was passed, benefitted from it. Nor did the decree free the slaves in the French Indian Ocean colonies: Benoît Gouly, a Jacobin Convention deputy from the Mascareignes, succeeded in getting the application of the decree there suspended.[125] Only the small number of slaves in the colony of Cayenne (today's French Guiana) received their freedom as a direct consequence of the Convention's action. Despite the imprisonment of most of its leaders after the law of 19 ventôse An II, the colonial lobby in France remained active. Its allies succeeded in keeping Julien Raimond in prison until some months after the fall of Robespierre, and they claimed the life of the journalist Milscent, guillotined in May 1794.[126] The question of whether the radical emancipation policy enacted on 16 pluviôse would survive the revolutionary conjuncture that gave birth to it was a serious one; after thermidor, the opponents of abolition would lobby vociferously for its abandonment and would finally achieve success under Napoleon, whose decree of 30 floréal An X (May 20, 1802) made slavery legal again in French territory.[127]

Despite the ambivalence of many French revolutionaries about what the Convention had done on 16 pluviôse and the continuation of pro-slavery agitation, Pierre Chaumette was right to see the decree as an epoch-making event. The black insurgents in Saint-Domingue had stood up against their own enslavement; Sonthonax and Polverel had justified emancipation as a response to an emergency situation. Without these initiatives in Saint-Domingue, the revolutionary government in France might well have continued to duck the issue of slavery because of the threat it seemed to pose to the nation's economy and its strategic interests in the conflict with Britain. It was the deputies of the French

---

[125] Claude Wanquet, *La France et la première abolition de l'esclavage 1794–1802* (Paris: Karthala, 1998), 133.

[126] AN, D XXV 56, d. 554.

[127] On the reimposition of slavery under Napoleon, see Yves Bénot and Marcel Dorigny, eds., *Rétablissement de l'esclavage dans les colonies françaises. Aux origines de Haïti* (Paris: Maisonneuve et Larose, 2004).

National Convention who took the occasion of Louis Dufay's defense of Sonthonax's actions to elevate the abolition of slavery to a matter of principle and to make it clear that if the words of the Declaration of the Rights of Man – "all men are born and remain free and equal in rights" – meant anything, they required the abolition of the institution, regardless of any practical difficulties that might be involved. Legally limited to French territory, the decree of 16 pluviôse nevertheless implicitly condemned slavery wherever it existed. An institution that had been accepted as normal since the dawn of human history was, in one stroke, declared to be illegitimate in principle. Similarly, by granting full citizenship rights to former black slaves, the Convention asserted the equality of the races, a principle that even the American states that adopted emancipation laws in the 1780s had hesitated to endorse.

Even though the achievement of 16 pluviôse An II proved to be a fragile one, the principles enunciated in the Convention's decree have become the standards by which our contemporary world claims to be guided. However, since it now seems obvious to us that the principles of liberty and equality proclaimed in 1789 necessarily entailed the abolition of slavery, it is difficult to understand the fact that the French revolutionaries themselves managed to avoid drawing that conclusion for four and a half years after the drafting of the Declaration of the Rights of Man. The vital role that the events of June 20, 1793 in Cap Français – events that grew out of conflicts between actors, none of whom consciously intended to bring about the total abolition of slavery at that moment – played in provoking the decree of 16 pluviôse An II are a reminder of how easily the men of the French Revolution might have avoided taking that step, and how different the history of the western world's struggle against slavery might have been if General Galbaud had not decided to join the sailors in their fateful assault on the civil commissioners and the free men of color in Le Cap.

Like many milestones in the human struggle for freedom, the French Revolution's renunciation of slavery came at a high cost in human lives. Thousands of blacks, French soldiers, and colonists died in the fighting in Saint-Domingue between August 1791 and the summer of 1793, and even more would die in the brutal war unleashed by Napoleon's attempt to reimpose white rule there in 1802–03. This was the tragic but unavoidable price to be paid for ending the harshest and most exploitative system of plantation slavery to which the New World had given birth. Ironically, however, the decisive blow to slavery in Saint-Domingue came, not in the colony's sugarcane fields, but in the streets of Cap Français. The destruction of the city was not instigated by the city's slaves nor by its free population of color, but by outsiders, above all General Galbaud, the sailors of the French navy, and the black insurgents who rallied to the republican cause. Urban slavery was an unjust system, and the whites of the city had worked hard to maintain a discriminatory system that kept free people of color in a subordinate position. Nevertheless, their behavior before and during the crisis of June 1793 strongly suggests that the city's blacks and free people of color were at least ambivalent about the destruction of the urban milieu that had offered them opportunities to shape some aspects of their own lives and to participate in the transatlantic civilization of the late eighteenth century. The banquet hosted by Sonthonax and Polverel in Cap Français on June 19, 1793, in which free men and women of all colors, some of them emancipated only the day before, joined together to sing the *Marseillaise*, was a symbolic representation of the kind of society that had been evolving in the city even before the outbreak of the Revolution. The celebration on June 19 also embodied the hopes of the French antislavery reformers for a controlled and peaceful reform of slavery that would permit the assimilation of the colonial population into a prosperous transatlantic empire. The events of June 20, 1793 opened the door to the rapid abolition of slavery in Saint-Domingue and to the Convention's decree of February 4, 1794, but they terminated the experiment in cultural synthesis that had been taking place in "the Paris of the Antilles."

II

Conclusion

By the spring of 1794, the shock waves set off by the events of June 20, 1793 in Cap Français had transformed the situation on both sides of the Atlantic. The black population of Saint-Domingue was now legally free, and the French revolutionaries had fulfilled the promise of the Declaration of the Rights of Man and Citizen by recognizing that freedom. The abolition of slavery resulting from the events of June 20, 1793 had taken forms that neither the black insurgents in Saint-Domingue nor the French abolitionists had anticipated. Even after Sonthonax and Polverel issued their appeal to the slaves, most of the blacks continued to find it easier to imagine gaining their goals through the action of a benevolent monarch than from membership in an abstract entity calling itself a republic. For their part, the French opponents of slavery, including Sonthonax and Polverel, had consistently expected abolition to result from a carefully guided process of gradual reform that would preserve the sugar islands' plantation economy and respect the financial interests of the white colonists. They had also expected to create a reformed society in which the free population of color would have a dominant position. The peculiar political circumstances prevailing in Paris at the moment when the Saint-Domingue deputies dispatched by Sonthonax arrived, however, produced a very different result: an emancipation decree shaped by abstract notions of liberty, passed with no concern for the practical consequences of its implementation, and, ironically, with no support from the revolutionary leader – Robespierre – who had, three years earlier, exclaimed that it would be better to let the colonies perish than to violate the principle of natural rights. The decree of 16 pluviôse II said nothing about the situation of the "citizens of 4 April," whom the metropolitan revolutionaries quite wrongly imagined as selfless advocates of universal freedom for all people of African descent. The fact that revolutionary France took such a strong position against slavery in 1794 was entirely due to the unique situation created by the journée of June 20, 1793 in Cap Français.

The events of 1793 and 1794 did not usher in a new age based on simple natural laws and "patriarchal *moeurs*," as Pierre Chaumette had promised, but for the next eight years, until the Napoleonic law of 30 floréal An X (May 10, 1802) reversing the decree of 16 pluviôse An II, the French empire offered the world the first example of a society in which slavery had been abolished and men of all races enjoyed equal rights. From 1794 to 1799, black and mixed-race deputies from Saint-Domingue sat in France's national legislatures, participating fully in their debates.[1] In 1796, Etienne Laveaux made Toussaint Louverture deputy governor of Saint-Domingue, and by the fall of 1797, Toussaint had made himself the de facto ruler of France's most important colony. Under his aegis, former slaves rose to important positions in the army and government, and a new propertied elite made up of black and mixed-race military officers largely replaced the whites who had dominated colonial society. Until 1793, the notions that African slavery in the New World could be ended, not at some far-off date in the future, but immediately, and that people of African descent might enjoy full legal rights, on the same footing with whites, in a transatlantic polity, seemed mere hypotheses; for a few years in the 1790s, they became concrete realities.

The remarkable achievements of 1793 and 1794 in Saint-Domingue and in France proved to be more fragile than they appeared. In contrast to England, where abolition, although supported by a mass movement, came about only after decades of debate and repeated defeats, the mechanisms of revolutionary government elaborated independently in Saint-Domingue and in metropolitan France made it possible to silence opposition and make sweeping changes with great rapidity, but the measures enacted under these conditions often lacked a firm base of support. Somewhat surprisingly, the conservative thermidorian Convention that overthrew Robespierre and the Committee of Public Safety in the summer of 1794 and promptly repudiated so many radical initiatives taken during the Year Two did uphold the abolition of slavery and the equality

---

[1] Bernard Gainot, "La députation de Saint-Domingue au corps législatif du Directoire," in Dorigny, dir., *Sonthonax*, 95–110.

of the races, as did its successor regime, the government of the Directory
(1795–99). The promise that France's colonies and the metropole would
share a common set of laws was never entirely fulfilled – despite a law
to that effect passed on 12 nivôse An VI (January 1, 1798), French civil
and political institutions were never fully implanted in Saint-Domingue,
and no serious effort was made to end slavery in the Mascareigne
islands – but the principles adopted in 1794 remained official policy. In
Saint-Domingue itself, Toussaint Louverture tried to encourage white
plantation owners to return and resume management of their properties,
thereby recreating a multiracial society, but he maintained Sonthonax's
strict regulations on the former slaves, which generated resentment from
blacks who felt that the freedom they had been promised had turned
out to be largely a fiction. How the situation in Saint-Domingue might
have evolved if the French republican regime had survived and if the
Caribbean had not continued to be a theater of war between France
and Britain is impossible to know, but it is at least possible that a black-
dominated society of free citizens with continuing ties to France would
have established itself on a lasting basis.

Napoleon's seizure of power after the coup d'état of 18 brumaire An
VIII (November 9, 1799) radically altered conditions on both sides of
the French Atlantic. The new constitution of the Year VIII repudiated
the promise that the colonies would be governed by the same laws as
the metropole, and the omission from the document of a declaration
of rights meant that slavery could no longer be opposed by reference to
basic constitutional principles.[2] As long as France was still at war with
Britain, Napoleon was unable to intervene directly in the Caribbean,
but he clearly meant to reassert direct French control as soon as circumstances permitted. Toussaint Louverture responded to the looming
menace of French intervention by ordering the drafting of a constitutional document for the colony itself, which declared that "there can be
no slaves in this territory" and established Toussaint as governor "for
the rest of his glorious life."[3] Together with his decision to occupy the
Spanish territory of Santo Domingo in the east of the island, the enact-
ment of this constitution convinced Napoleon that Toussaint meant to
set up an independent government. As negotiations for a peace settlement with the British neared completion in late 1801, Napoleon prepared

---

[2] Yves Bénot, *La Démence coloniale sous Napoléon* (Paris: La Découverte, 1991), 21.
[3] "Constitution of the French Colony of Saint-Domingue," in Dubois and Garrigus, *Slave
Revolution in the Caribbean*, 167–70.

a massive expeditionary force under the command of his brother-in-law, General Charles-Victor-Emmanuel Leclerc, to bring the colony back under control.

The arrival of the Leclerc expedition in February 1802 opened the final and most violent phase of what we now label the Haitian Revolution. Although the French did not openly announce their intention to restore slavery, they massacred blacks who resisted them and made no secret of their determination to re-establish white rule. The result was a desperate struggle that was much bloodier than any earlier phase of the Haitian Revolution. Henri Christophe, a participant in the fighting in Le Cap in June 1793, set fire to the city again in 1802 to prevent the French from occupying it. Although Leclerc enjoyed some initial successes and managed to capture and deport Toussaint Louverture himself in June 1802, he was unable to subdue resistance in the countryside, and his army soon began to suffer debilitating losses from yellow fever. By October 1802, Leclerc was dead, and command of the French forces passed to the same General Rochambeau who had helped Sonthonax establish his authority in the fall of 1792. Rochambeau, who had expressed support for the idea of the abolition of slavery at that time, now waged an increasingly brutal campaign, terrorizing not only the blacks but also the men of color and even the colonial whites who, in his view, were insufficiently supportive of his efforts. In response, many black and free colored soldiers and officers who had initially submitted to the French rejoined the fight against them. Once the war with Britain resumed in March 1803, Napoleon realized that the French effort in the Caribbean was doomed. He cut his losses by quickly negotiating the sale of the vast Louisiana Territory to the United States, thereby keeping it out of British or Spanish hands, and Rochambeau was left to his fate; he finally evacuated Cap Français in November 1803, and he and his men were taken prisoner by the British.

On January 1, 1804, Jean-Jacques Dessalines, who had emerged as the leader of the resistance forces after Toussaint Louverture's arrest, proclaimed the independence of the Republic of Haiti. The constitution he promulgated in 1805 proclaimed that "slavery is abolished forever" and that "because all distinctions of color among children of the same family must necessarily stop, Haitians will henceforth only be known generically as Blacks."[4] The principles of liberty and equality first articulated in the struggles in France and in Saint-Domingue in the early 1790s thus

---

[4] Dubois and Garrigus, *Slave Revolution in the Caribbean*, 191–96.

became part of the heritage of the new nation, although the constitution
of 1805 also specified that "no white man, regardless of his nationality,
may set foot in this territory as a master or landowner," and the instal-
lation of Dessalines's regime in 1804 was accompanied by systematic
massacres of most of the remaining whites in the island.⁵ Meanwhile, in
France, the ideals of racial equality and freedom were repudiated altogether. A Napoleonic decree of 13 messidor An X (July 2, 1802) forbade
the entry of blacks and people of color in France, and those who were
already living there suffered increasing legal discrimination. A spate of
overtly racist literature, claiming that blacks were inherently inferior,
accompanied these legal measures; the violence in Saint-Domingue was
frequently cited as evidence of their savage nature. Slavery was reintro-
duced in the colony of Guadeloupe and in Cayenne, where it had been
abolished in the 1790s, and it was maintained in Martinique, which had
been under British occupation from 1793 to 1802 and thus had never
been affected by the law of 16 pluviôse.⁶ Not until the second French
abolition decree of April 27, 1848 would the slaves in these French colonies gain their freedom.⁷

The developments in Saint-Domingue and in France during the
Napoleonic era were very different from what the participants in the
events of 1793 and 1794 had hoped to achieve. Instead of a transatlantic republican empire based on racial equality, Saint-Domingue became
an independent black nation, and France turned into an authoritarian
state that had abandoned both the principle of liberty and any commitment to racial equality. After 1804, France ceased to be at the center
of the western world's debates about slavery. Its remaining colonies
were small and their economic importance could not compare to that
of pre-revolutionary Saint-Domingue. Plantation-based sugar production expanded to new areas, such as Cuba and Brazil, often with the
help of former Saint-Domingue slave owners who brought their experience with them. While great public debates about abolition took place

⁵ On the Dessalines massacres, see Philippe R. Girard, "Caribbean genocide: racial war in Haiti, 1802–4," *Patterns of Prejudice* 39 (2005), 138–61; Ardouin, *Etudes sur l'histoire d'Haiti* 6: 10–17; Peter S. Chazotte, *Historical Sketches of the Revolution and the Foreign and Civil Wars in the Island of St. Domingo* (New York: Wm. Applegate, 1840), excerpted in Popkin, *Facing Racial Revolution*, 345–62.
⁶ On Napoleonic policy, see Bénot, *Démence*, and Bénot and Dorigny, eds., *Rétablissement de l'esclavage dans les colonies françaises.*
⁷ Nelly Schmidt, "The Drafting of the 1848 Decrees: Immediate Application and Long-Term Consequences," in Dorigny, ed., *Abolitions of Slavery*, 305–13.

in Britain, which banned the slave trade in 1807 and began to phase out slavery in its Caribbean colonies in 1833, and in the United States, where the issue increasingly dominated national life and finally resulted in the Civil War of 1861–65, the subject attracted little public attention in France during the first half of the nineteenth century.[8] By this time, French concerns had shifted from the "old colonies" linked to slavery and the plantation system to the new overseas venture in Algeria that was begun in 1830. A second abolition decree, this one providing compensation for slave owners, was passed with little debate in April 1848, thanks to the efforts of the reformer Victor Schoelcher. Unlike the 1794 decree, this measure did not guarantee the nonwhite populations of the colonies complete citizen rights; Guadeloupe, Martinique, and Réunion would not be fully integrated into the French political system until 1946.

As slavery became less important in French life after 1804, memory of the events in Saint-Domingue shrank until all that was recalled about the episode was the violence of the initial slave uprising and perhaps the name of Toussaint Louverture. Neither the abolition decree of 1794 nor the complicated series of events leading up to it were mentioned in most accounts of the Revolution. C. L. R. James's impassioned *The Black Jacobins*, originally published in 1938, drew some attention to the subject in the English-speaking world, but not in France. In 1960, as the movement of decolonization swept through the territories of France's vast "second empire" in Asia and Africa, the great Martiniquais writer and politician, Aimé Césaire, underlined the intimate connection between the events of the 1790s and those of the mid-twentieth century, but his essay had little impact on French memory.[9] The celebration of the bicentennial of the French Revolution in 1989 brought renewed attention to France's claim to be "the country of the rights of man" and more frequent mentions of the pioneering French abolition edict, even though the one important historical work devoted to the subject that appeared in conjunction with the bicentennial – Yves Bénot's *La Révolution française et la fin des colonies*, originally published in 1987 – demonstrated convincingly how reluctant the revolutionary legislators had been to tackle the problem of slavery.

---

[8] On the French abolitionist movement in the nineteenth century, see Lawrence C. Jennings, *French Anti-Slavery: The Movement for the Abolition of Slavery in France, 1802–1848* (Cambridge: Cambridge University Press, 2000).

[9] Aimé Césaire, *Toussaint Louverture. La Révolution française et le problème colonial.* (Paris: Présence Africaine, 1961).

Since the mid-1990s, the situation has changed radically. The issue of slavery, long omitted from discussions of the French Revolution, is now recognized as a central aspect of that movement, and the events of the Haitian Revolution have become the subject of intense historical investigation. In 1998, the United Nations urged all countries to celebrate August 23, the date of the outbreak of the 1791 slave insurrection in Saint-Domingue, as an international holiday commemorating the struggle against slavery. No longer "silenced," as the Haitian-American scholar Michel-Rolph Trouillot eloquently put it in a seminal essay,[10] the Haitian Revolution and the French revolutionary abolitionist movement have instead been made to bear the weight of present-day concerns. There has been a tendency to elevate the protagonists in these struggles to an almost superhuman status, to isolate opposition to slavery from the other issues of the time, and to attribute to some of the participants in these debates the views of twenty-first-century defenders of human rights, while condemning other historical figures for their failure to measure up to this anachronistic standard. For understandable and entirely justified reasons, historians have been urged to give full credit to the role of Saint-Domingue's black population in challenging slavery, but this has sometimes resulted in a reductionist account of these events. The events of the 1790s are often read through the lens of a binary opposition between whites and blacks, a way of looking at race and slavery that comes easily to historians from the United States but that profoundly distorts the nature of Saint-Dominguan society, whose tri-racial system created a radically different set of conflicts and possible alliances.

As this detailed examination of the events in Saint-Domingue and France in 1793 and 1794 has shown, the first total abolitions of slavery were not simply the result of struggles between heroic slaves and idealistic abolitionists on the one hand and vicious exploiters and counter-revolutionaries on the other. Indeed, it is misleading even to speak of an abolitionist movement in revolutionary France or in Saint-Domingue, on the model of those that existed in Britain or the northern United States, during those years. The abolition decrees of 1793 and 1794 were not the result of a campaign by "a small group of thoughtful, committed citizens" out to "change the world," as Adam Hochschild has described the

---

[10] "An Unthinkable History: the Haitian Revolution as a Non-Event," in Michel-Rolph Trouillot, *Silencing the Past: Power and the Production of History* (Boston, MA: Beacon Books, 1995), 70–107.

British abolitionists, nor were they the outcome of mass mobilization.[11] Instead, they resulted from the unplanned and uncoordinated actions of individuals who were often motivated less by dedication to principles than by the pressure of unforeseen circumstances, particularly those created by the unanticipated crisis of June 20, 1793 in Cap Français. Some of those who played major roles in the sequence of events that unfolded after that crisis, such as Sonthonax, Toussaint Louverture, and Pierre Chaumette, had perhaps hoped that they would see the moment when slavery would disappear, although they did not expect it to be imminent. Others, like the free men of color who helped rouse the slaves of Cap Français on June 20, the French diplomat Edmond Genet, and Louis Dufay, had shown no concern about the issue beforehand or had even been actively implicated in maintaining the slavery system. Furthermore, the abolition of slavery clearly meant very different things to the different people who helped bring it about. To the black population of Saint-Domingue, freedom meant, above all, the right to decide how to live their own lives, on a very concrete and practical level. For Sonthonax and Polverel, it meant a system of rules under which the former slaves would be "regenerated" as hardworking republican citizens living in monogamous family units and contributing to the military might and economic prosperity of France. And for the republican legislators in France, the abolition of slavery was a grand gesture to vindicate the revolutionary movement and, perhaps, inaugurate a new era in human history. Yet it was in Saint-Domingue and in France, not in Britain or the United States with their more coherent antislavery movements, that the centuries-old institution of African slavery was first totally abolished and people of all races were made citizens of a single polity. Recognition of this fact should make us more cautious about assuming that major historical changes must grow out of conscious human intentions, and that the Anglo-American model of political mobilization best explains the eventual success of abolition.

Like most human beings in every historical era, the participants in these events were complicated people who often thought and acted in contradictory ways. It was possible for black slaves to be conscious of their oppression and at the same time to fear some of the consequences of trying to overthrow the system, or to decide that other matters, such as

[11] Adam Hochschild, *Bury the Chains*, 7. The phrase was originally coined by Mirabeau to describe the instigators of the French Revolution.

living in accordance with the dictates of religion, were more important. It was possible for free men of color to seek rights for themselves without necessarily advocating freedom for the slaves, and for free women of color to identify themselves more with white men than with those of their own color. And it was possible for white advocates of the rights of man to balance the obvious injustice of slavery with the equally obvious – to them – necessity of defending the national interests of the only country that had proclaimed those rights. Furthermore, all the participants in the great dramas of 1793 and 1794 acted in the face of unexpected and constantly changing circumstances. When Maximilien Robespierre found himself faced, as he convinced himself, with the evidence of a monstrous British-royalist-Brissotin conspiracy, he put aside his principled opposition to slavery in order to, as he saw it, save his country. The plantation owner Louis Dufay had to make an equally difficult decision when he found himself obliged to persuade the National Convention to abolish the institution on which his fortune had depended. And Toussaint Louverture, a free black man and, to all appearances, a devout Catholic and instinctive monarchist, must have wrestled with himself as he decided to take a leadership role in the slave insurrection, to oppose the French forces, to spurn their offers of emancipation, and then to switch his allegiance and put himself under the command of a white general who had inflicted a humiliating defeat on him.

To see the very specific history of the events of 1793 and 1794 as the outcome of the actions of people confronted with difficult dilemmas is to understand that even remarkable achievements, such as the abolition of slavery, are brought about, not by heroes set above the rest of humanity, but by ordinary men and women: people who are ambivalent, who make mistakes, and who often act out of narrow personal motives as well as great idealistic ones. To be sure, even if we recognize the human limitations of all the actors in this story, we are hardly obliged to put them on the same moral plane. Toussaint Louverture, Sonthonax, Polverel, and Pierre Pinchinat, as well as the many anonymous men and women who saved others' lives during the catastrophe of Le Cap, were capable of seeing broader issues in moments of crisis. At the other extreme, one might put individuals such as the racist agitator Verneuil, who nearly brought about the destruction of the city on December 2, 1792, or the ineffable Madame Galbaud, unable to see beyond her own prejudices and the interests of her husband's career. Occasionally in this story, we do encounter genuine evil, particularly in the personages of the colonial lobbyists Page and Brulley, who strove cold-bloodedly to send anyone who challenged the slavery system to the guillotine. The damage they caused, however, pales before that brought about by the actions of General Galbaud, and yet it is hard to put him in the same moral category as men like Page and Brulley. The general's story reminds us that weakness and bad judgment can often cause more destruction than outright malignity. Yet without Galbaud and his disastrous miscalculation on the morning of June 20, 1793, there would have been no emancipation decree of June 21 and very likely no abolition law of 16 pluviôse. History does indeed move in mysterious ways.

Crises like that of June 20, 1793 in Cap Français are one of the ways in which the direction of historical development is determined. In addition to illuminating the circumstances under which slavery was abolished in the French empire, this study of the events of June 20, 1793 provides an opportunity to consider what it means to call a historical event a "turning point." The history of the Haitian uprising does not begin in June 1793: that distinction clearly belongs to the revolt of August 22–23, 1791 and the organizational meeting or meetings that preceded it. That event could be labelled the turning point in the struggle against slavery, but it seems more appropriately described as the origin or beginning of the sequence of events that eventually culminated in the independence of Haiti, even though it is unlikely that any of those who took up arms in August 1791 imagined such an outcome. As a result of that uprising, a conflict developed, but, as of June 20, 1793, its outcome was still impossible to predict. If the insurgency had by then truly reached the point where its success was only a matter of time, the journée of June 20, 1793 would not deserve the status of a turning point, but this was not the case. At that moment, the black combatants still had no recognized leader and no articulated program. It was still unclear whether the insurgency could actually defeat the whites, and it was equally unclear what an insurgent victory at that point would have meant. Some of the black generals were actually selling other blacks to the Spanish as slaves, for example; none of them had announced a determination to abolish slavery, and the possibility of turning Saint-Domingue into an independent, black-dominated nation was also beyond the realm of imaginable outcomes. In France, too, the abolition of slavery still seemed a utopian aspiration, and the permanent loss of the colony a barely conceivable nightmare.

The journée of June 20, 1793 was a turning point because it decisively eliminated certain plausible historical outcomes, most notably the continuation of white colonial rule, and moved others from the realm of remote possibilities to realities. The elimination of the white colonists as a significant factor and the massive breach in the institution of slavery that the journée opened led in less than four months to the abolition of slavery throughout the French-controlled parts of the island. Three months later, the National Convention endorsed this result and extended abolition to the rest of the French empire. The new possibility of an alliance between the black insurgency and the French republican cause created by the journée providing the "opening," the "ouverture," by which Toussaint Louverture would convert himself from Spanish-backed warlord to recognized ruler of the colony. The journée of June 20, 1793 was also true turning point because its outcome was not foreordained. At the microhistorical level, the contest between General Galbaud and the republican commissioners could easily have failed to take place, if Galbaud had stuck to his intention of returning to France, or could have had a completely different outcome, as a detailed reconstruction of events of June 20–21, 1793 shows. If either of these things had happened, some of the major consequences that followed from the actual outcome of the journée would not have materialized: no emancipation proclamation, no overnight elimination of the white colonists, and no French abolition decree. Beyond that, we enter the realm of hypothetical speculation. Would Toussaint Louverture have found another route to power? Would the colonial whites have managed to turn the entire colony over to the British and the Spanish, and would those occupying powers have managed to maintain the institution of slavery, as the British did in the occupied French colony of Martinique? It is surely implausible to argue that, without the journée of June 20, 1793, slavery would never have been abolished, but it is clear that the road to abolition would have been a very different one.

From the example of June 20, 1793, then, we can derive a definition of the concept of turning point that is relevant not only to the study of the Haitian Revolution but to historical analysis more generally. To truly deserve the status of a turning point, an event must (a) decisively alter the direction in which things in some already existing conflict or process of development had previously been moving; (b) it must also significantly change the range of historical possibilities that were previously present, ruling out some of them and making others plausible in a way that they had not been beforehand; and (c) there must have been a realistic possibility that if the details of the event had gone differently, the large-scale consequences of the event would also have been different in significant ways. Like the storming of the Bastille, the journée of June 20, 1793 was such an event. The usefulness of analyzing it in these terms shows how much of a contribution the study of the Haitian Revolution can make, not only to our understanding of the "age of revolutions" and of the struggle against slavery, but to our understanding of how human agency and contingency combine to shape the past.

Fate dealt very differently with the individuals who played the key roles in the dramatic events of June 20, 1793 and their aftermath. Toussaint Louverture, who had so eloquently denounced the hypocrisy of the French revolutionaries after the journée of June 20, 1793 and insisted that he fought for "another liberty," was a sufficiently flexible politician to change his mind when circumstances changed. After allying himself with the French in 1794 and assuring the success of Sonthonax and Polverel's efforts, he rose to become the ruler of Saint-Domingue before falling victim to Napoleon's invasion in 1802. He died in prison in France in 1803, but his memory has lived on as an inspiration for freedom movements throughout the non-European world. Etienne Polverel died only a few months after his return to France, in the middle of the six months of hearings ordered by the thermidorian Convention to determine the responsibility for the "disasters" of Saint-Domingue. These hearings brought Polverel and Sonthonax face to face, for the first time, with their enemies Page and Brulley, supported by many of the colonists the civil commissioners had deported from Saint-Domingue in 1793. After a long battle, Sonthonax was vindicated by that inquiry. He continued the fight for freedom for the former slaves, first in Saint-Domingue as a member of the Third Civil Commission in 1796–97 and then in France during the last years of the Directory. Under Napoleon, he was excluded from political life; he died in obscurity in his home town in southeastern France in 1813.[12] Etienne Laveaux, who had made an essential contribution to the survival of Sonthonax and Polverel, took over the government of Saint-Domingue when they were recalled and had his remaining troops swear an oath "to die at our posts rather than surrender."[13] He forged a strong personal relationship with Toussaint Louverture, and together they warded off the British and Spanish invasions of the colony. As his ambitions increased, Toussaint eventually eased Laveaux out of the colony by appointing him as a deputy to the Directorial legislature. In 1799, just before Napoleon's coup d'état, Laveaux volunteered for a mission in Guadeloupe, hoping to help consolidate the rights of the

---

[12] See Stein, *Sonthonax*, and the contributions in Dorigny, dir., *Sonthonax*.
[13] Laveaux, letter of June 28, 1794, in CAOM, F 3 198 (Moreau de Saint-Méry papers).

blacks there, only to be arrested and expelled by his own colleagues who were confident that Napoleon would reverse the Directory's racial policy. They charged Laveaux with having "sought and obtained, at the price of miserable adulations, the title of *Papa of the blacks.*"[14]

Louis Dufay, whose lengthy speech persuaded the National Convention to pass its emancipation decree, remained in France after his term as deputy ended in 1798. In 1796, he wrote to Toussaint Louverture, asking the black general to help him find a new manager for his plantation; he also offered to adopt the black leader's children and see that they received a proper French education.[15] His black colleague, Jean-Baptiste Belley, served for four years, first in the thermidorian Convention and then in the Directory's Council of 500, and spoke on several occasions to defend the abolition of slavery. He is remembered today above all because of the artist Anne-Louis Girodet's striking full-length 1798 portrait showing him in his deputy's uniform, which has now become one of the iconic images of the revolutionary period. Under Napoleon, however, he was treated with suspicion; he died in prison in France in 1805[16]. Dufay's close associate, Charles Guillaume Castaing, the leader of Le Cap's free men of color, came to France with the members of the "tricolor" deputation and also stayed there. After the death of his first wife in 1797, he married into the Beauharnais family, thus becoming an in-law of Napoleon's wife Josephine. His descendants eventually managed to disguise the family's Antillean ancestry.[17] Edmond Genet, who enabled Dufay, Belley, and Castaing to reach France at the beginning of 1794, never returned to his native country. By 1831, having outlived his beloved Cornelia and remarried, the former revolutionary diplomat was living near Albany, New York, where he was visited by a young Frenchman eager to understand the workings of American democracy. Whether he told Alexis de Tocqueville anything about his role in making the abolition of slavery in France possible is unknown.[18]

[14] Letter of 9 vent. VIII, in SHAT, 7 YD 137, d. 2.
[15] Dufay, letters to Toussaint Louverture, in Schomberg Center for Research in Black Culture, New York Public Library, Toussaint Louverture correspondence. I would like to thank Claire Payton for furnishing me with photocopies of these documents.
[16] On Girodet's portrait and Belley's fate, see Darcy Grimaldo Grigsby, *Extremities: Painting Empire in Post-Revolutionary France* (New Haven, CT: Yale University Press, 2002), 9–63.
[17] Noel, "Le sang noir des Castaing."
[18] George C. Genet, *Washington, Jefferson, and "Citizen" Genet, 1793* (New York: n.p., 1899), 51.

Brissot, the founder of the *Société des amis des noirs* and the driving force behind the French abolitionist movement in the early years of the Revolution, was executed in October 1793, a victim of the murderous politics of the Reign of Terror. Julien Raimond, the free man of color who had played such a crucial role in revolutionary debates about race and colonial policy, survived the strenuous attempts of the white colonists to send him to the guillotine. Released from prison after thermidor, he returned to Saint-Domingue in 1796 as a member of the Third Civil Commission, accepted Toussaint Louverture's dominant position, and enriched himself by acquiring plantations abandoned by their white owners. He died in 1801, before the arrival of the Leclerc expedition.[19] Of the Convention deputies who played the key roles in passing the decree of 16 pluviôse II, one, Levasseur, was fortunate enough to fade into obscurity. His colleague Delacroix and the far more famous Danton, who made a crucial intervention in the debate, were not so lucky. Robespierre's speech on 17 pluviôse II foreshadowed the Committee of Public Safety's coming attack on the Indulgent group of which Danton was the leader; on April 5, 1794, Danton and Delacroix went to the guillotine. Eight days later, Pierre Chaumette, the organizer of the Notre Dame celebration of abolition, followed him; he was convicted because of his association with Hébert, the "Père Duchêne." The accusations against Danton and Chaumette made no reference to their role in promoting the abolition decree, but their common fate demonstrated the dangers faced by everyone who occupied the limelight during the Terror. Robespierre, an eloquent opponent of slavery in the first years of the Revolution, outlived Danton and Chaumette by less than four months. After his death, the advocates of slavery would claim that, thanks to Sonthonax and Polverel, the "system of Robespierre reigns in Saint-Domingue."[20] Finding himself associated with two "creatures of Brissot" was an indignity that the Incorruptible would have bitterly resented. Of the two men who had worked harder than anyone else to convince the Committee of Public Safety that the abolition of slavery was a "Brissotin" plot, one – Page – changed his views: consulted in 1800 by the new Napoleonic administration, he recommended against any attempt to undo the emancipation edicts of 1793 and 1794. His colleague Brulley, however, remained a steadfast proponent of slavery until his death during the Restoration.[21]

[19] Garrigus, "Raimond."
[20] *Journal historique et politique de la marine et des colonies*, 5 vend. V.
[21] Bénot, *Démence*, 51–3, 290.

Nothing better illustrates the strange workings of revolutionary politics and the ironies of history, however, than the fate of General Galbaud and his family. After his long struggle with Genet for an opportunity to return to France, the man who had caused the destruction of the richest city in the French colonies finally reached Paris in the spring of 1794. He was promptly incarcerated in the Abbaye prison. His wife and children were thoroughly interrogated by revolutionary officials in France; even his eight-year-old son Jean was solemnly asked what he knew about the "origin, the causes and the course of the evils that afflicted the colony," a question to which he responded "that he had always stayed with his mama, that he was too young to pay attention to what was going on ..., that he saw the fire in the city of Le Cap, and that after three days, the convoy sailed."[22] The campaign against the white colonists had been launched a few weeks earlier, and, since many of them had taken up Galbaud's defense, he ought logically to have been considered a leading suspect. The letter Galbaud himself wrote from prison on 4 floréal An II demanding an immediate trial was one more reckless act in a career repeatedly marked by such decisions. Fortunately for Galbaud, no one paid any attention to him. After thermidor, his aide-de-camp André Conscience published a response to Dufay's denunciation of him, and the general demanded his freedom again, complaining that Sonthonax and Polverel, now also back in Paris, would "succeed in consummating their colonicidal crimes" if he was not allowed to expose them.[23] As always, Madame Galbaud threw herself into action, soliciting testimonials on her husband's behalf and drafting letters and memoranda justifying his actions. After eight months in prison, Galbaud was finally given a conditional release but ordered to remain in Paris. Although his name came up repeatedly during the lengthy hearings about Sonthonax and Polverel in 1795, Galbaud's request to testify on his own behalf was rejected, ostensibly because he was under suspicion of being an émigré.[24] The commission thus spent six months investigating the reasons for the destruction of Saint-Domingue while the man most directly responsible for that result was working in a government office: unable to rejoin the army,

---

[22] Interrogation of Galbaud family, 30 mess. II, in AN, D XXV 56, document hors chemise.

[23] André Conscience, *André Conscience à la Convention nationale, sur les derniers événemens de Saint-Domingue* (N.p.: n.p., July 1794); Galbaud, letters to Committee of Public Safety, 4 flor. II and 21 ther. II, in AN, D XXV 48, d. 465.

[24] Galbaud to colonial commission, 29 mess. III, in AN, D XXV 48, d. 465.

Galbaud had found employment in the bureaus of the post-thermidor-
ian Committee of Public Safety.

The transition from the thermidorian Convention to the Directory
was accompanied by an amnesty for all remaining political suspects.
Galbaud found himself in bureaucratic limbo: he was no longer in
danger of being punished, but he also could not get himself cleared
so that he could be reinstated in the army. He continued petitioning
throughout the Directory, without success. Galbaud's luck changed
when another former artillery officer took over the French government.
Within a month of Napoleon's coup, he was back in the army, assigned
to join the French forces in Egypt that Bonaparte had left behind when
he returned to France. As always, Madame Galbaud accompanied her
husband. The man who had done more damage to France's colonial
empire in one day than any other person in history gave his life trying to acquire a new possession for his country: he died of the plague
in Cairo in 1801. In 1810, citing the patriotism of her three sons who
had all followed their father into the army, Madame Galbaud wrote to
Napoleon, requesting an increase in her pension.[25] Galbaud's younger
brother César remained in prison in Cap Français for at least a year
and a half after the events of June 20, 1793, where he occupied himself
writing several long memoranda insisting on the legitimacy of slavery.
Eventually he returned to France and rejoined the army, receiving a
promotion in 1805.[26]

While the individuals whose lives had been irrevocably altered by its
destruction in June 1793 pursued their personal destinies, the city of
Cap Français struggled to emerge from its ashes. In 1797, officials of the
Third Civil Commission compiled two elegant six-colored maps whose
varied hues, showing the progress of reconstruction, unfortunately cannot be reproduced here. These maps indicate that, by May 1797, about
half of the buildings destroyed in the fire had been rebuilt; most of the
reconstruction had been undertaken before the commission arrived in
December 1796 (see Figure 11.1). "There are not even enough tenants to
occupy them," one observer wrote in 1798. "It is something compared to
July 1793, but not much compared to '92." To encourage reconstruction,
the authorities promised that anyone who rebuilt a house would have the
use of it for three years, after which the former owner of the property

---

[25] SHAT, 4 Yd. 3912, dossier Galbaud; H. Duchêne-Marullez, "François-Thomas
Galbaud-Dufort," *Dictionnaire de biographie française.*
[26] AN, D XXV 48, ds. 463 and 465; SHAT, 4 Yd. 3912.

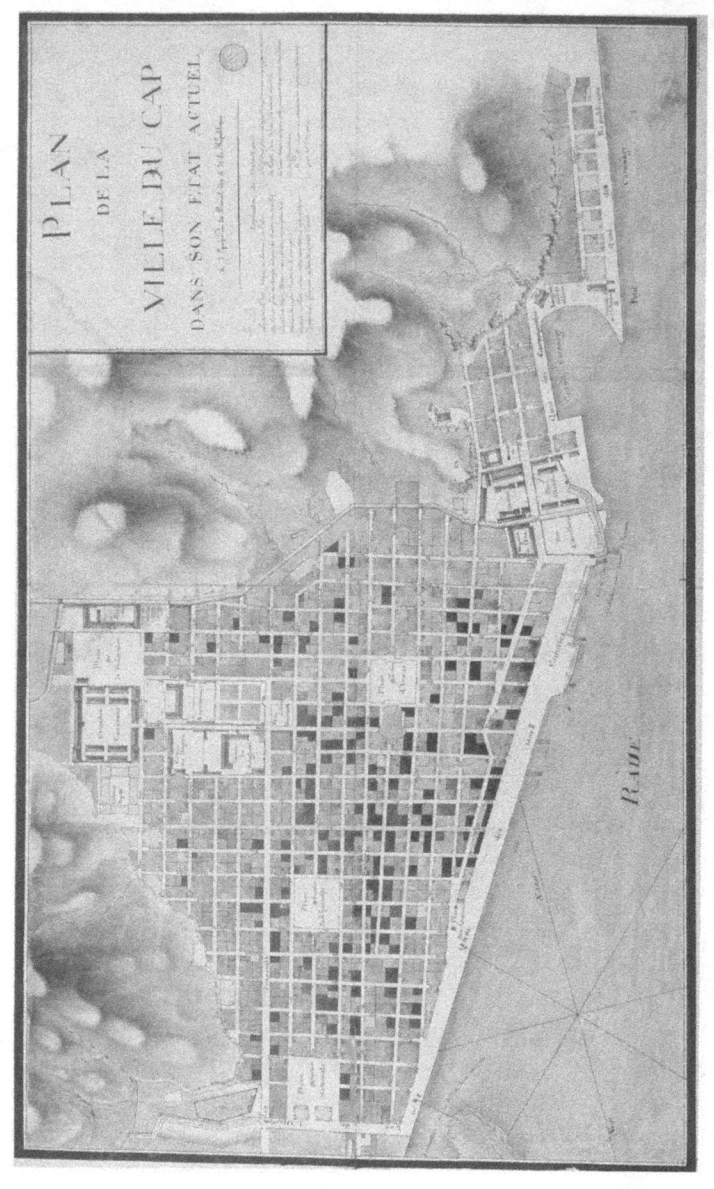

FIGURE 11.1. Map of Cap Français in its present state (May 1797).

Drawn up during the Third Civil Commission's mission to Saint-Domingue in 1797, this elegant six-color map shows the progress that had been made in reconstructing the city after the fire of June 1793. Streets and public squares were given appropriate French revolutionary names, such as "Quai des Sans-Culottes."

Source: Bibliothèque nationale de France, section "Cartes et estampes."

could buy it; otherwise, it would become state property.[27] Whether or not the black population had thoroughly absorbed the principles of French republicanism, they now lived in a city whose street names proclaimed its values: Cap Français now had its rues de la Liberté and de l'Egalité and its quais des Sans-Culottes and des Républicains.[28] With Port-au-Prince occupied by the British until 1798, Le Cap regained its function as the colony's capital, and American merchant ships continued to visit its port, encouraged by Toussaint Louverture, who ignored the fact that France was virtually at war with the United States from 1796 to 1800.[29] For a few years, Cap Français offered the world the spectacle of a European-style city inhabited and run by black citizens.

Le Cap's rapid recovery came to a sudden halt with the arrival of the Leclerc expedition in February 1802. Toussaint Louverture's lieutenant, Henri Christophe, warned Leclerc that if the French tried to take it by force, "You will enter the town of Le Cap only once it has been reduced to ashes, and even on these ashes I will fight you."[30] When Leclerc ignored his threat, Christophe personally took the lead in starting fires that once again consumed the city. The French reoccupied the site and, despite the renewed devastation, within a few months, Cap Français began to revert to its colonial past. Large numbers of whites flooded in, from France and from the United States. The returnees "found the town a heap of ruins," the novelist Leonora Sansay, who lived there in 1802–03, later wrote in her novel, *Secret History, or, The Horrors of Saint-Domingue*. "A more terrible picture of desolation cannot be imagined." Nevertheless, the thick masonry walls of the buildings made it possible to start reconstruction again fairly quickly. "The people live in tents, or make a kind of shelter, by laying a few boards across the half-consumed beams; for the buildings being here of hewn stone, with walls three feet thick, only the roofs and floors have been destroyed," Sansay explained.[31] Sansay's novel, based on her own experience, described the

---

27 Letter of Pierre Paul Morange, July 3, 1798, cited in Christian Goguet, *L'Architecture de la ville historique du Cap Haïtien* (Cap Haïtien: Projet I.S.P.A.N., 1989), 36. This publication is a report on the state of the city's architectural heritage, as of 1989, prepared under the sponsorship of UNESCO.

28 "Plan de l'état actuel de la ville du Cap, servant à indiquer les progrès de ses reconstructions" and "Plan de la ville du Cap dans son état actuel," dated 20 prair. An V, in Bibliothèque nationale, département des cartes et plans, SH 18 pf 149, d.4, nos. 23 and 23/1.

29 Brown, *Toussaint's Clause*, 137.

30 Dubois, *Avengers*, 264.

31 Leonora Sansay ["Mary Hassal"], *Secret History, or, The Horrors of St. Domingo*, Michael J. Drexler, ed. (Peterborough, ON: Broadview Books, 2007), 61.

revival of social life, as the military garrison entertained itself with balls and elaborate dinners. The economy also began to revert to its colonial pattern. A French merchant, J.-J. Borie, wrote to Bordeaux to announce that "I have definitively rented ... a large and beautiful house, in one of the most commercial sections of Le Cap. Excellent warehouses put me in a position to receive whatever consignments my several friends may send me."[32] Once again, however, as in 1791–93, the city found itself under siege, with black insurgents camped in the surrounding hills. In a letter, Sansay wrote that "there is no means of going a mile in any direction beyond it without I chose to make a sortie on the brigands. ..."[33] Sansay was among the fortunate whites who were able to escape before the city fell to Dessalines in November 1803. The French colonists who remained fell victim to the implacable black general's determination to demonstrate once and for all that white rule was ended. One of the few survivors left an account as chilling as any of the testimonies about the violence of June 20, 1793: "A cordon of sentinels surrounded the town. Armed barges cruised the harbor to make sure that no white could reach the American ships there. Free to do as they pleased, sure of their victims, these monsters, thirsty for human blood and armed with daggers and sabers, went from house to house to take the life of the unfortunate whites."[34]

After his victory, Dessalines established the capital of the new Haitian state in Port-au-Prince. In the aftermath of Dessalines's assassination in 1806, the country was split in two. Renamed Cap Haïtien, the former Cap Français became the capital of Henri Christophe's kingdom in northern Haiti, while Port-au-Prince remained the seat of government for the southern republic headed by the mixed-race leader Alexandre Pétion. Christophe's defeat in 1820 allowed his enemies to reunite the country and made Port-au-Prince its definitive seat of government. In 1842, Cap Haïtien was struck by a disaster even more devastating than the fires of 1793 and 1802: an earthquake destroyed the city's buildings so thoroughly that the entire population was evacuated for a year.

---

[32] Borie to Domecq, 29 vent. XI, in Borie family papers, Historical Society of Pennsylvania, ms. coll. 1602.

[33] Leonora Sansay, letter to Aaron Burr, May 6, 1803, cited in Popkin, *Facing Racial Revolution*, 318–9.

[34] Antoine Frinquier, "Relation des évènemens arrivés à Cap Français depuis l'évacuation de l'armée de Général Rochambeau jusqu'au 20 mai 1804, jour après le massacre général des Blancs de cette colonie," in SHAT, 1 M 597. I would like to thank Julia Gaffield for permission to cite from her transcription of this document.

The stone walls that had stood up to the conflagrations during the revolutionary years collapsed; none of the buildings in present-day Cap Haïtien date back to that period.[35] The city was slowly rebuilt in the years that followed. During the American occupation of 1915–34, the streets, which had reverted to their prerevolutionary names after 1804, were relabeled with numbers and letters of the alphabet, an arbitrary scheme that hardly fit with the "raffish charm" and the "air of gracious civility" that struck a late twentieth-century travel writer, despite the city's increasingly dilapidated condition.[36]

In November 2008, I had the opportunity to visit Cap Haïtien, or O'Kap as it is called in Creole, and to walk the streets where the extraordinary events of June 1793 took place. The Morne du Cap still towers over the city. Although the buildings from the colonial era are no longer standing, the edifices constructed on their foundations often resemble those depicted in Moreau de Saint-Méry's engravings. The pre-revolutionary street names are still visible on some of the buildings, and the graceful public squares laid out in the 1700s still attract strollers in the afternoon. The Place Clugny, home of the pre-revolutionary *marché des noirs*, is still a bustling street market. One of the city's *lycées* occupies the site of the Government House, where Jean-Baptiste Belley and the free men of color defended the commissioners Sonthonax and Polverel on June 20, 1793. The Hôpital Saint-Julien, O'Kap's main hospital, stands on the site of the *casernes*, or army barracks, in front of which the confrontation of December 2, 1792 took place. Along the harbor, now largely deserted, the waterline has been somewhat altered by landfill projects, and a long jetty that did not exist in 1793 extends out into the water. Armed with the 1795 map reproduced in this book, my colleagues Elizabeth Colwill, Aletha Stahl, and I located the spot where General Galbaud made his plunge into the sea on June 21, 1793; it is perhaps appropriate that it is now a trash dump.

Despite the rundown condition of Cap Haïtien, the city's inhabitants today are free people, as the black insurgents of 1793 and the French commissioners hoped they would be. Present-day Haiti's social and economic problems are all too evident in the city's streets, but so, too, is the hope for a better future represented by the groups of schoolchildren, in their neatly pressed uniforms, who crowd the sidewalks in the mornings.

---

[35] Goguet, *Architecture*, 41.
[36] Ian Thomson, *Bonjour Blanc: A Journey Through Haiti* (London: Vintage, 2004 (orig. 1992)), 340–1.

That hope first blossomed amid the ruins of the city in 1793. The journalist H. D. de Saint-Maurice, the editor of the *Moniteur général de
la partie française de Saint-Domingue*, sensed it, even as he lamented
the destruction of the city whose life he had chronicled for two intense
years. In the long manuscript account of the events of June 20, 1793
that is now bound with the copy of that newspaper in the Bibliothèque
nationale de France, Saint-Maurice addressed himself to the whites who
had fled the city, urging them to accept the fact that, whether they liked
it or not, "this black individual is free, because neither the nation nor
the Supreme Being created slaves. He is your equal, because he is a man.
He is a citizen, because he serves the country." Saint-Maurice hoped
that the former residents of the city would return, and that they would
"practice the love of equality." If the whites would "open [their] soul to
[the blacks], embrace them, show them that [they] no longer act like masters, like tyrants," the races could live together for their mutual benefit.[37]
Saint-Maurice was one of the few colonial whites who understood that
the destruction of their world was a result of the injustice of slavery.
History dashed Saint-Maurice's dreams for a racially integrated society
in Le Cap, but we can still hope for a world in which the people of Haiti
and those of the rest of the world will be able to live together peacefully
and share the benefits of that freedom to which the conflicts in Saint-
Domingue more than 200 years ago made a crucial contribution.

[37] Saint-Maurice, "Récit historique du malheureux événement," cited in Popkin, *Facing
Racial Revolution*, 206–7.

Bibliography

A. Archival Sources

Archives nationales (Paris)

AA 53, 54, 55, 61
AF II 302
CC 9 A 8[1]
D I § 39
D XVI 3
D* XVI 4, 5
D XXV 1, 4, 5, 6, 7, 11, 12, 13, 14, 15, 16, 19, 20, 23, 25, 38, 39, 40, 41, 42, 43,
    46, 47, 48, 49, 51, 53, 54, 55, 56, 57, 58, 63, 64, 68, 69, 70, 71, 73, 76, 77,
    78, 80, 81, 82, 83, 84, 110, 112, 113, 115
F 7 4685
107 AP 28 (Gallifet papers)
446 AP 13 (Brissot papers)

Centre des Archives d'Outre-Mer (Aix)[2]

F 3 141, 193, 197–198 (Moreau de Saint-Méry papers)

Centre des Archives Diplomatiques de Nantes

Baltimore 8
Philadelphia 10, 13, 15
New York 63, 64

---

[1] This archival series can also be consulted at the Centre des Archives d'Outre-Mer.
[2] This archival series can also be consulted on microfilm at the Archives nationales in Paris.

Service Historique de l'Armée de la Terre (Vincennes)

1 M 597
4 Yd. 3912 (Galbaud)
7 Yd. 137 (Laveaux)
Xi 71

Service Historique de la Marine (Vincennes)

BB 4 24

Library of Congress

Genet papers, microfilm reels 5, 6, 7
"Journal historique du Comité colonial de St. Domingue" (1788), ms. MMC
    2671.

Bibliothèque nationale de France

Ms. N.a.f. 6846 (Sonthonax papers)
Dufresne, Guillaume Thomas, "Considérations politiques sur la Révolution des
    colonies françaises mais particulièrement sur celle de Saint Domingue,"
    (1805), ms. n.a.f. 4372.

Newberry Library (Chicago)

Rochambeau papers (Ms. Ruggles 410)

Historic New Orleans Collection

Puech Parham family papers (Ms. 85–117-L, "Mon Odyssée")

John Carter Brown Library (Providence, Rhode Island)

"Manuscrit d'un voyage de France à Saint-Domingue, à la Havanne et aux Unis
    états [sic] d'Amérique," Codex fr. 20.

New-York Historical Society

Journal of Alexandre-Maurice Hauterive

American Philosophical Society

Stephen Girard papers[3]

---

[3] References to the Stephen Girard papers are based on notes generously shared with me by
    Ashli White. Translations from the Girard correspondence are from transcripts prepared
    by the American Philosophical Society staff.

B. Printed Primary Sources

1. Newspapers
a. Published in Saint-Domingue
Affiches américaines (Port-au-Prince and Cap Français)
Ami de l'égalité (Port-au-Prince)
Courrier politique et littéraire (Cap Français)
Journal des Révolutions de la Partie Française de Saint-Domingue (Cap Français)
Journal politique de Saint-Domingue (Cap Français)
Moniteur générale de la partie française de Saint-Domingue (Cap Français)
b. Published in France (in Paris unless otherwise noted)
Annales patriotiques et littéraires
Bulletin du tribunal criminel révolutionnaire
Créole patriote
Feuille villageoise
Gazette universelle
Indicateur politique, mercantile et littéraire, par le Citoyen Petit (Rouen)
Journal de la Montagne
Journal de Perlet
Journal des Débats de la société des Amis de la Constitution séante aux Jacobins à Paris
Journal historique et politique de la marine et des colonies
Moniteur universel
Nouvelles politiques
Patriote françois
Révolutions de Paris
c. Published in the United States
Baltimore Evening Post
Federal Gazette (Philadelphia)
Gazette of the United States (Philadelphia)
New York Daily Advertiser
New York Daily Gazette
New York Diary, or Loudon's Register
Philadelphia General Advertiser
Radoteur (Philadelphia)
Virginia Chronicle and Norfolk and Plymouth General Advertiser

2. Books and Pamphlets

Anon., *Adresse des Négocians de la ville du Port-au-Prince, aux citoyens commissaires Nationaux-Civils, à bord de l'Amérique en rade du Port-au-Prince* (Port-au-Prince: F. Chaidron & Cie, April 8, 1793).
Concordat passé entre les citoyens du Port-au-Prince & les citoyens de couleur de la même partie de Saint-Domingue (N. p., September 11, 1791).
Débats qui ont eu lieu entre les accusateurs & les accusés, dans l'affaire des Colonies, imprimés en exécution de la loi du 4 pluviôse, 9 vs. (Paris: Imprimerie nationale, 1795).

Extrait d'une lettre, sur les malheurs de Saint-Domingue en général, et principalement sur l'incendie de la ville du Cap Français (Paris: Pain, An II [1793]).

Extrait des minutes de la municipalité du Cap, (Cap Français, April 29, 1792).

Extrait du procès-verbal de l'Assemblée des citoyens-libres et propriétaires de couleur des Isles et Colonies Françoises, constituée sous le titre de Colons américains (N. p., 1789).

Extrait du registre des délibérations de la Chambre du Commerce de la ville de Bordeaux, et adresses du Directoire du département de la Gironde à l'Assemblée nationale; de la Société des Amis de la Constitution; du Club du café national de la ville de Bordeaux, à l'Assemblée nationale: relatifs au décret rendu par Elle le 14 Mai 1791, au sujet des colonies (Paris, Imprimerie nationale, May 24, 1791).

Lettres des diverses sociétés des Amis de la Constitution, qui réclament les droits de citoyen actif en faveur des hommes de couleur des colonies (Paris: Imprimerie du *Patriote françois*, 1791).

My Odyssey, trans. Althéa de Puech Parham (Baton Rouge, LA: Louisiana State University Press, 1959).

Nouvelles arrivées de Saint-Domingue, depuis celles officielles venues par l'ambassadeur d'Angleterre (Paris: Didot, 1791).

Procès-verbaux de l'Assemblée générale de la partie française de Saint Domingue (Cap Français: Dufour de Rians, 1791).

Rélation détaillée des événemens malheureux qui se sont passés au Cap depuis l'arrivée du ci-devant général Galbaud, jusqu'au moment où il a fait brûler cette ville et a pris la fuite (Paris: Imprimerie nationale, An II).

Relation du séjour de M. de Blanchelande, lieutenant pour le roi au gouvernement général de Saint-Domingue, au Port-au-Prince. Par un Créole (Port-au-Prince: Chaidron, 1792).

Brissot, Jacques-Pierre, *Discours sur un projet de décret relatif à la révolte des Noirs, prononcé à l'Assemblée nationale, le 30 octobre 1791, par J. P. Brissot, député* (Paris: Imprimerie nationale, 1791).

Discours de J. P. Brissot, député, sur les causes des troubles de Saint-Domingue, prononcé à la séance du premier décembre 1791(Paris: Imprimerie nationale, 1791).

Cambefort, Joseph-Paul-Augustin, *Mémoire justificatif de Joseph-Paul-Augustin Cambefort, Colonel du Régiment du Cap; Commun à Anne-Louis Tousard, Lieutenant-Colonel, à tous les officiers, sous-officiers & soldats du même regiment, déportés de Saint-Domingue, par ordre des commissaires civils, délégués par le Pouvoir-Exécutif aux Isles Françaises de l'Amérique-sous-le-vent* (Paris: Frères Chaigneau, January 31, 1793).

Carteaux, François, *Histoire des désastres de Saint-Domingue* (Bordeaux: Pellier-Lawalle, An X [1802]).

Chaumette, Pierre [Anaxagoras], *Discours prononcé par le citoyen Chaumette, au nom de la Commune de Paris, le décadi 30 pluviôse, l'an II de la République française, une et indivisible, à la fête célébrée à Paris, en réjouissance de l'abolition de l'Esclavage* (Paris: Imprimerie nationale, 1794).

Conscience, André, *André Conscience à la Convention nationale, sur les derniers événemens de Saint-Domingue* (N.p.: n.p., July 1794).

Corméré, Guillaume François Mahy de, *Histoire de la révolution de la partie française de St. Domingue. Développement exact des causes et principes de cette révolution. Manoeuvres, intrigues employés pour son exécution* (Baltimore, MD: Samuel and John Adams, 1794).

Dalmas, Antoine, *Histoire de la Révolution de Saint-Domingue, depuis le commencement des troubles, jusqu'à la prise de Jérémie et du Mole St. Nicolas par les Anglais*, 2 vs. (Paris: Mame, 1814).

Dufay, Louis, *Compte rendu sur la situation actuelle de Saint-Domingue. Par Dufey [sic], député de la partie du nord. 16 plu. II* (Paris: Imprimerie nationale, An II [1794]).

J. B. Dusaulx, *L'Oeuvre de sept jours* (Paris, 1790).

Garran-Coulon, J.-P., *Rapport sur les troubles de Saint-Domingue, fait au nom de la Commission des Colonies, des Comités de Salut Public, de Législation, et de Marine, réunis*, 4 vs. (Paris: Imprimerie nationale, An V [1797–98]).

Grégoire, Henri, *Mémoires*, ed. Hippolyte Carnot, intro. Jean-Michel Leniaud (Paris: Editions de Santé, 1989).

Gros, *Historick Recital, of the Different Occurrences in the Camps of Grand-Reviere [sic], Dondon, Sainte-Suzanne and others* (Baltimore, MD: Samuel and John Adams, 1793).

Guittard de Floriban, Célestin, *Journal de Célestin Guittard de Floriban, bourgeois de Paris sous la Révolution*, ed. Raymond Aubert (Paris: Editions France-Empire, 1974).

Labuissonnière, Julien, *Adresse à la convention nationale, à tous les clubs et sociétés patriotiques, pour les Nègres détenus en esclavage dans les Colonies françaises de l'Amérique, sous le régime de la République* (Paris: Galletti, 1793, reprinted in *La Révolution française et l'abolition de l'esclavage*, t. 5 (Paris: EDHIS, 1968)).

La Croix, Pamphile de, *La Révolution de Haïti* (orig. title *Mémoires pour servir à l'histoire de la Révolution de Saint-Domingue*), ed. Pierre Pluchon (Paris: Karthala, 1995 [orig. 1819]).

Laplace, François, *Histoire des désastres de Saint-Domingue* (Paris: Garnéry, 1795).

La Salle, A. N., *Papiers du général A. N. de La Salle (Saint-Domingue, 1792–1793)* ed. Corre (Quimper: Cotonnec, 1897).

Levasseur, René A., *Mémoires de R. Levasseur (de la Sarthe) ex-Conventionnel*, ed. Michel Vovelle (Paris: Messidor/Editions sociales, 1989 [orig. 1829–31]).

Milscent, Claude, *Sur les Troubles de Saint-Domingue* (Paris: Imprimerie du Patriote français, 1791).

Moreau de Saint-Méry, Méderic Louis Elie, *Description topographique, physique, civile, politique et historique de la partie française de l'isle Saint-Domingue*, nouv. ed. by Blanche Maurel and Etienne Taillemite, 3 vs. (Paris: Société de l'histoire des colonies françaises, 1958).

Page, François, and Augustin Brulley, *Développement des causes des troubles et désastres des colonies françaises, présenté à la Convention nationale, par les*

Commissaires de Saint-Domingue, sur la demande des comités de Marine et des Colonies, réunis, après en avoir donné communication aux Colons résidens à Paris, & convoqués, à cet effet, le 11 juin 1793, l'an 2e de la République (Paris: n. p., 1793).

Perkins, Samuel G., "Sketches of St. Domingo from January, 1785, to December, 1794. Written by a Resident Merchant at the Request of a Friend, December, 1835," *Proceedings of the Massachusetts Historical Society*, 2nd ser., 2 (1886), 305–90.

Polverel, Etienne, *Examen critique des prophéties de Jérémie, et de l'évangile selon Saint-Marc. Sur les deux anthéchrists, Polverel et Sonthonax* (Aux Cayes, December 1793).

Polverel François, *Coup d'oeil impartial sur Saint-Domingue, ou Notions sur les événements qui ont eu lieu dans cette isle, depuis le commencement de la Révolution, jusqu'à la proclamation de la liberté générale* (Paris: Marchands de nouveautés, An III [1795]).

Ponce, *Recueil des vues des lieux principaux de la colonie française de Saint-Domingue, gravées par les soins de M. Ponce* (Paris: Moreau de Saint-Méry, 1791).

Pons, de, *La Question politique des affranchis et descendans des affranchis* (Cap Français: Batilliot, 1792).

Raimond, Julien, *Lettre au citoyen D***, député à la Convention nationale, par Julien Raymond, colon de Saint-Domingue, sur l'état des divers partis de cette colonie, et sur le caractère des déportés* (Paris: n.p., An II [1793]).

Lettres de J. Raimond, à ses frères les hommes de couleur. Et comparaison des originaux de sa correspondance, avec les extraits perfides qu'en ont fait MM. Page et Brulley, dans un libelle intitulé: Développement des causes, des troubles, et des désastres des Colonies françaises (Paris: Cercle social, an 2 de la république française, 1793).

Mémoire sur les causes des troubles et des désastres de la Colonie de Saint-Domingue, présenté aux comités de Marine et des Colonies, dans les premiers jours de juin dernier, par les Citoyens de couleur; d'après l'invitation que leur en avoit été faite par les comités (Paris: Cercle social, 1793).

Réflexions sur les véritables causes des troubles et des désastres de nos colonies, notamment sur ceux de Saint-Domingue; avec les moyens à employer pour préserver cette colonie d'une ruine totale; adressés à la Convention nationale; par Julien Raymond, colon de Saint-Domingue (Paris, n.p., An II [1793]).

Sansay, Leonora ["Mary Hassal"], *Secret History, or, The Horrors of St. Domingo*, Michael J. Drexler, ed. (Peterborough, ON: Broadview Books, 2007 [orig. 1808]).

Tanguy-Laboissière, Claude-Corentin, *Adresse de Tanguy-Laboissière à la Commission Nationale-Civile de Saint-Domingue* (Cap Français: n. p., 1793).

Vèze, Jean de, *Enquiry Into, and Observations upon the Causes and Effects of the Epidemic Disease, which raged in Philadelphia, from the month of August till towards the middle of December, 1793* (Philadelphia: Parent, 1794).

Wante, Charles Etienne Pierre, *Mémoire relatif à l'administration de la partie française de St. Domingue* (Baltimore, MD: Samuel and John Adams, 1793).

C. Secondary Sources

Accilien, Cécile, Jessica Adams and Elmide Méléance, eds., *Revolutionary Freedoms: A History of Survival, Strength and Imagination in Haiti* (Coconut Creek, FL: Caribbean Studies Press, 2006).

Ammon, Harry, *The Genet Mission* (New York: W. W. Norton, 1973).

Antoine, Régis, "Aventures d'un jeune négrier français d'après un manuscrit inédit du XVIIIe siècle," *Notes africaines* no. 142 (April 1974), 51–6

Ardouin, [Alexis] Beaubrun, *Etudes sur l'histoire d'Haiti, suivies de la vie du général J.-M. Borgella* (Port-au-Prince: Dr. François Dalencour, 1958 [orig. 1853]).

Babb, Winston C., "French Refugees from Saint-Domingue to the Southern United States, 1791–1810," Ph. D. diss., University of Virginia, 1955.

Banat, Gabriel, *The Chevalier de Saint-Georges: Virtuoso of the Sword and the Bow* (Hillsdale, NY: Pendragon Press, 2006).

Bégaud, Stéphane, Marc Belissa and Joseph Visser, *Aux Origines d'une alliance improbable. Le réseau consulaire français aux Etats-Unis (1776–1815)* (Paris: Ministère des Affaires étrangères, 2005).

Bell, Madison Smartt, *All Souls' Rising* (New York: Penguin, 1995).

Toussaint Louverture: A Biography (New York: Pantheon, 2007).

Bénot, Yves, "La chaîne des insurrections des esclaves dans les Caraïbes de 1789 à 1791," in Dorigny, Marcel, dir., *Les abolitions de l'esclavage. De L. F. Sonthonax à V. Schoelcher* (Paris: Editions UNESCO, 1995). 179–86.

"Comment la Convention a-t-elle voté l'abolition de l'esclavage en l'an II?" *Annales Historiques de la Révolution Française*, nos. 293–4 (1993), 349–61.

La Démence coloniale sous Napoléon (Paris: La Découverte, 1991).

Bénot, Yves, and Marcel Dorigny, eds., *Rétablissement de l'esclavage dans les colonies françaises. Aux origines de Haïti* (Paris: Maisonneuve et Larose, 2004).

Bénot, Yves, *La Révolution française et la fin des colonies* (Paris: La Découverte, 1987).

"Un anti-esclavagiste kleptomane? En marge de l'affaire Milscent," *Dix-huitième siècle* 22 (1990), 295–300.

Benzaken, Jean-Charles, "Documents inédits sur la famille Castaing de Saint-Domingue," *Bulletin de la Société Archéologique de Tarn-et-Garonne* 129 (2004), 81–6.

"Who was the author of *l'Histoire des désastres de Saint-Domingue*, published in Paris in the Year III?" *French History* (2009), 262–7.

Blackburn, Robin, *The Overthrow of Colonial Slavery, 1776–1848* (London: Verso, 1988).

Bongie, Chris, "Introduction," in Jean-Baptiste Picquenard, *Adonis suivi de Zoflora et de documents inédits*, Chris Bongie, ed. (Paris: L'Harmattan, 2006), ix-xiii.

Bradby, H. D., *The Life of Barnave*, 2 vs. (Oxford: Clarendon Press, 1915).

Branson, Susan, and Leslie Patrick, "Etrangers dans un Pays Etrange: Saint-Domingan Refugees of Color in Philadelphia," in David P. Geggus, ed.,

The Impact of the Haitian Revolution in the Atlantic World (Columbia, SC: University of South Carolina Press, 2001), 193–208.

Brière, Jean-François, *Haïti et la France 1804–1848. Le rêve brisé* (Paris: Karthala, 2008).

Brown, Gordon S., *Toussaint's Clause: The Founding Fathers and the Haitian Revolution* (Jackson, MS: University Press of Mississippi, 2005).

Bruley, Georges, *Les Antilles pendant la Révolution française, d'après la correspondance inédite de César-Dominique Duny, consul de France à Curaçao, né à Tours le 22 juillet 1758* (Paris: Editions Caraibéennes, 1989 (orig. 1890)).

Cabon, Alphonse, *Notes sur l'histoire religieuse d'Haïti. De la Révolution au Concordat (1789–1860)* (Port-au-Prince: Petit Séminaire Collège Saint-Martial, 1933).

Camara, Evelyne, Isabelle Dion and Jacques Dion, *Esclaves. Regards de Blancs 1672–1913* (Marseille: Archives nationales d'outre-mer, 2008).

Casto, William R., *Foreign Affairs and the Constitution in the Age of Fighting Sail* (Columbia, SC: University of South Carolina Press, 2006).

Catanzariti, John, "The Recall of Edmond Charles Genet," in Catanzariti, ed., *The Papers of Thomas Jefferson*, v. 26 (Princeton, NJ: Princeton University Press, 1995), 26: 685–92.

Cauna, Jacques, "Polverel ou la révolution tranquille," in Michel Hector, ed., *La Révolution française et Haïti: Filiations, Ruptures, Nouvelles Dimensions*, 2 vs. (Port-au-Prince: Société Haïtienne d'histoire et de géographie et Editions Henri Deschamps, 1995), 1: 384–99.

Césaire, Aimé, *Toussaint Louverture. La Révolution française et le problème colonial*, éd. revue (Paris: Présence Africaine, 1961).

Childs, Frances Sergeant, *French Refugee Life in the United States, 1790–1800* (Baltimore, MD: Johns Hopkins University Press, 1940).

"The Hauterive Journal," *New-York Historical Society Quarterly* 33 (1949), 69–86.

Colwill, Elizabeth, "'Fêtes de l'Hymen, Fêtes de la liberté': Marriage, Manhood, and Emancipation in Revolutionary Saint Domingue," in David Geggus and Norman Fiering, eds., *The World of the Haitian Revolution* (Bloomington, IN: Indiana University Press, 2009), 125–55.

Cormack, William S., *Revolution and Political Conflict in the French Navy 1789–1794* (Cambridge: Cambridge University Press, 1995).

Davies, John, "Class, Culture, and Color: Black Saint-Dominguan Refugees and African-American Communities in the Early Republic," Ph. D. diss., University of Delaware, 2008.

Debbasch, Yvan, *Couleur et liberté. Le jeu du critère ethnique dans un ordre juridique esclavagiste. T. 1: L'affranchi dans les possessions françaises de la Caraïbe (1635–1833)* (Paris: Dalloz, 1967).

"Le Marronnage. Essai sur la désertion de l'esclave antillais," *Année sociologique*, 3e ser. (1961), 1–112, (1962), 117–95.

Debien, Gabriel, *Les Colons de Saint-Domingue et la Révolution. Essai sur le Club Massiac (août 1789-août 1792)* (Paris: Armand Colin, 1951).

Les Esclaves aux Antilles Françaises (XVIIe-XVIIIe siècles) (Basse-Terre and Fort-de-France: Sociétés d'histoire de la Guadeloupe et de la Martinique, 1974).

Gens de couleur libres et colons de Saint-Domingue devant la Constituante (1789-mars 1790) (Montréal: Revue d'histoire de l'Amérique française, 1951).

Une Plantation de Saint-Domingue. La Sucrerie Galbaud du Fort (Cairo: Institut français du Caire, 1941).

Dorigny, Marcel, dir., *Les abolitions de l'esclavage. De L. F. Sonthonax à V. Schoelcher* (Paris: Editions UNESCO, 1995).

dir., *Esclavage, résistances et abolitions* (Paris: Editions du CTHS, 1999).

dir., *Léger-Félicité Sonthonax. La première abolition de l'esclavage. La Révolution française et la Révolution de Saint-Domingue* (Paris: Association pour l'étude de la colonisation française, 2005 [orig. 1987]).

Dorigny, Marcel, and Bernard Gainot, eds., *La Société des Amis des Noirs 1788-1799. Contribution à l'histoire de l'abolition de l'esclavage* (Paris: Editions UNESCO, 1998).

Drescher, Seymour, *Abolition: A History of Slavery and Antislavery* (Cambridge and New York: Cambridge University Press, 2009).

Drescher, Seymour, and Pieter C. Emmer, eds., *Who Abolished Slavery? Slave Revolts and Abolitionism. A Debate with João Pedro Marques* (New York: Berghahn, 2010).

Dubois, Laurent, *Avengers of the New World: The Story of the Haitian Revolution* (Cambridge, MA: Harvard University Press, 2004).

A Colony of Citizens: Revolution and Slave Emancipation in the French Caribbean, 1787-1804 (Chapel Hill, NC: University of North Carolina Press, 2004).

Dubois, Laurent, and John D. Garrigus, *Slave Revolution in the Caribbean 1789-1804* (New York: Bedford/St. Martin's, 2006).

Duchet, Michèle, *Anthropologie et histoire au siècle des Lumières* (Paris: Albin Michel, 1995 [orig. 1971]).

Dun, James Alexander, "Dangerous Intelligence: Slavery, Race, and St. Domingue in the early American Republic," Ph. D. diss., Princeton, 2004.

Ehrard, Jean, *Lumières et esclavage. L'esclavage colonial et l'opinion publique en France au XVIIIe siècle* (Brussels: André Versaille, 2008).

Elicona, Anthony Louis, *Un colonial sous la Révolution en France et en Amérique: Moreau de Saint-Méry* (Paris: Jouve, 1934).

Elkins, Stanley, and Eric McKitrick, *The Age of Federalism* (New York: Oxford University Press, 1993).

Fick, Carolyn E., *The Making of Haiti: The Saint Domingue Revolution from Below* (Knoxville, TN: University of Tennessee Press, 1991).

Frey, Sylvia R., *Water from the Rock: Black Resistance in a Revolutionary Age* (Princeton, NJ: Princeton University Press, 1991).

Gainot, Bernard, "La constitutionalisation de la liberté générale sous le Directoire (1795-1800)," in Dorigny, dir., *Les Abolitions de l'esclavage*, 213-30. (English translation: "The Constitutionalization of General Freedom under the Directory," in Dorigny, ed., *The Abolitions of Slavery*, 180-96)

"La députation de Saint-Domingue au corps législatif du Directoire," in Dorigny, dir., *Sonthonax*, 95-110.

Garrigus, John D., *Before Haiti: Race and Citizenship in French Saint-Domingue* (New York: Palgrave MacMillan, 2006).

"Opportunist or Patriot? Julien Raimond (1744–1801) and the Haitian Revolution," *Slavery and Abolition* 28 (2007), 1–21.

Gauthier, Florence, *L'Aristocratie de l'épiderme: Le combat de la Société des Citoyens de Couleur 1789–1791* (Paris: CNRS Editions, 2007).

"En guise de conclusion: ouverture à de nouvelles recherches. Richebourg: comment abolir l'esclavage à Saint-Domingue? 1793," in Florence Gauthier, ed., *Périssent les colonies plutôt qu'un principe!* (Paris: Société d'études robespierristes, 2002), 105–7.

"Inédits d Dufay, Santerre, et Léonard Leblois, au sujet de l'arrivée de la députation de Saint-Domingue à Paris, janvier-février 1794," *Annales historiques de la Révolution française* nos. 293–4 (1993), 514–18.

"Le rôle de la députation de Saint-Domingue dans l'abolition de l'esclavage," in Dorigny, dir., *Les Abolitions de l'Esclavage*, 199–211. (English translation: "The Role of the Saint-Domingue Deputation in the Abolition of Slavery," in Dorigny, ed., *The Abolitions of Slavery*, 167–79)

Triomphe et mort du droit naturel en Révolution 1789-1795-1802 (Paris: Presses Universitaires de Paris, 1992).

"Y a-t-il une politique des colonies en l'an II?" *Annales historiques de la Révolution française*, no. 300 (1995), 223–31.

Gautier, Arlette, *Les soeurs de solitude. La condition féminine dans l'esclavage aux Antilles du XVIIe au XIXe siècle* (Paris: Editions caribbéennes, 1985).

Geggus, David, "The Arming of Slaves in the Haitian Revolution," in Christopher Leslie Brown and Philip D. Morgan, eds., *Arming Slaves: From Classical Times to the Modern Age* (New Haven, CT: Yale University Press, 2006), 209–32.

Haitian Revolutionary Studies (Bloomington, IN: Indiana University Press, 2002).

"The Major Port Towns of Saint Domingue in the Later Eighteenth Century," in Franklin W. Knight and Peggy K. Liss, eds., *Atlantic Port Cities: Economy, Culture, and Society in the Atlantic World, 1650–1850* (Knoxville, TN: University of Tennessee Press, 1991).

"Print Culture and the Haitian Revolution: The Written and the Spoken Word," in *Liberty! Egalité! ¡Independencia!: Print Culture, Enlightenment, and Revolution in the Americas, 1776–1838* (American Antiquarian Society, 2007), 79–96.

Slavery, War, and Revolution: The British Occupation of Saint-Domingue 1791–1798 (Oxford: Clarendon Press, 1982).

Geggus, David, and Norman Fiering, eds., *The World of the Haitian Revolution* (Bloomington, IN: Indiana University Press, 2009).

Ghachem, Malick, "Sovereignty and Slavery in the Age of Revolution: Haitian Variations on a Metropolitan Theme," Ph. D. diss., Stanford University, 2001.

Girard, Philippe R., "Caribbean Genocide: Racial War in Haiti, 1802–4," *Patterns of Prejudice* 39 (2005), 138–61.

Goguet, Christian, *L'Architecture de la ville historique du Cap Haïtien* (Cap Haïtien: Projet I.S.P.A.N., 1989).

Grigsby, Darcy Grimaldo *Extremities: Painting Empire in Post-Revolutionary France* (New Haven, CT: Yale University Press, 2002).

Halpern, Jean-Claude, "Les Fêtes révolutionnaires et l'abolition de l'esclavage en l'An II," in Marcel Dorigny, ed., *Les abolitions de l'esclavage, de L. F. Sonthonax à V. Schoelcher* (Paris: Editions UNESCO, 1995), 187–98. (English translation: "The Revolutionary Festivals and the Abolition of Slavery in Year II," in Dorigny, ed., *The Abolitions of Slavery*, 155–66)

Hochschild, Adam, *Bury the Chains: Prophets and Rebels in the Fight to Free an Empire's Slaves* (Boston, MA: Mariner Books, 2005).

Hurbon, Laennec, "Le clergé catholique et l'insurrection de Saint-Domingue," in Laënnec Hurbon, dir., *L'Insurrection des esclaves de Saint-Domingue (22–23 août 1791). Actes de la table ronde internationale de Port-au-Prince (8 au 10 décembre 1997)* (Paris: Karthala, 2000), 29–39.

James, C. L. R., *The Black Jacobins* (New York: Vintage Books, 1963 [orig. 1938]).

Jennings, Lawrence C., *French Anti-Slavery: The Movement for the Abolition of Slavery in France, 1802–1848* (Cambridge: Cambridge University Press, 2000).

Jordan, Winthrop D., *White Over Black: American Attitudes Toward the Negro, 1550–1812* (Baltimore, MD: Pelican Books, 1969 [orig. 1968]).

King, Stewart R., *Blue Coat or Powdered Wig: Free People of Color in Pre-Revolutionary Saint Domingue* (Athens, GA: University of Georgia Press, 2001).

Knight, Franklin W., and Peggy K. Liss, eds., *Atlantic Port Cities: Economy, Culture, and Society in the Atlantic World, 1650–1850* (Knoxville, TN: University of Tennessee Press, 1991).

Laurent, Gérard, *Le Commissaire Sonthonax à Saint-Domingue. I: Le Lutteur* (Port-au-Prince: La Phalange, 1965).

Toussaint Louverture à travers sa correspondance (1794–1798) (Madrid: Industrias Graficas España, 1953).

Mantoux, Paul, "Le Comité de Salut public et la mission de Genet aux Etats-Unis," *Revue d'histoire moderne et contemporaine* 13 (1909), 5–35.

Marques, João Pedro, "Slave Revolts and the Abolition of Slavery: An Overinterpretation," trans. Richard Wall, in Seymour Drescher and Pieter C. Emmer, eds., *Who Abolished Slavery? Slave Revolts and Abolitionism A Debate with João Pedro Marques* (New York: Berghahn, 2010), 1–89.

Maurel, Blanche, *Saint-Domingue et la Révolution française. Les représentants des colons en France de 1789 à 1795* (Paris: Presses Universitaires de France, 1943).

McClellan, James E., *Colonialism and Science: Saint-Domingue in the Old Regime* (Baltimore, MD: Johns Hopkins University Press, 1992).

McMaster, John Bach, *The Life and Times of Stephen Girard, Mariner and Merchant*, 2 vs. (Philadelphia: J. P. Lippincott, 1918).

Meadows, R. Darrell, "The Planters of Saint-Domingue, 1750–1804: Migration and Exile in the French Revolutionary Atlantic," unpub. ms. (2008).

Melish, Joanne Pope, *Disowning Slavery: Gradual Emancipation and 'Race' in New England, 1780–1860* (Ithaca, NY: Cornell University Press, 1998).

Mintz, Sidney, and Michel-Rolph Trouillot, "The Social History of Haitian Vodou," in Donald J. Cosentino, ed., *Sacred Arts of Haitian Vodou* (Los Angeles: UCLA Fowler Museum of Cultural History, 1995).

Moisy, Claude, *Le Citoyen Genet. La Révolution français à l'assaut de l'Amérique* (Paris: Privat, 2007).

Moitt, Bernard, *Women and Slavery in the French Antilles, 1635–1848* (Bloomington, IN: Indiana University Press, 2001).

Monte y Tejada, Antonio de, *Historia de Santo Domingo*, 4 vs. (Santo Domingo: Imprenta de Garcia Hermanos, 1890–1892).

Nash, Gary B., "Reverberations of Haiti in the American North: Black Saint Dominguans in Philadelphia," *Pennsylvania History* 65 (1998), 44–73.

Navarre, Marcel, "La Révolte de l'escadre française de Saint-Domingue, le 20 juin 1793. Ses causes et ses conséquences." Typed manuscript (incomplete) in Service historique de la marine, Vincennes, France.

Nemeth, Luc, "Un état-civil chargé d'enjeux: Saint-George, 1745–1799," *Annales historiques de la révolution française* no. 339 (2005), 79–97.

Nesbitt, Nick, ed., *Jean-Bertrand Aristide Presents Toussaint L'Ouverture. The Haitian Revolution* (London: Verso, 2008).

Nesbitt, Nick, *Universal Emancipation: The Haitian Revolution and the Radical Enlightenment* (Charlottesville, VA: University of Virginia Press, 2008).

Noel, Eric, "Le sang noir des Castaing, ou l'insolite ascension d'une famille des isles (milieu XVIIIe – fin XIXe siècles)," *Bulletin du Centre d'histoire des espaces atlantiques* 7 (1995), 171–82.

Pairault, François, *Gaspard Monge. Le fondateur de Polytechnique* (Paris: Taillandier, 2000).

Pérotin-Dumon, Anne, *La ville aux îles, la ville dans l'île. Basse-Terre et Pointe-à-Pitre, Guadeloupe, 1650–1820* (Paris: Karthala, 2000).

Piquet, Jean-Daniel, *L'Emancipation des Noirs dans la Révolution française* (Paris: Karthala, 2002).

Piquionne, Nathalie, "Lettre de Jean-François, Biassou et Belair, juillet 1792," *Chemins critiques*, 3 (1997), 206–10.

Pierre Pluchon, *Toussaint Louverture* (Paris: Fayard, 1989).

Pluchon, Pierre, *Vaudou, sorciers, empoisonneurs. De Saint-Domingue à Haïti* (Paris: Karthala, 1987).

Popkin, Jeremy D., *Facing Racial Revolution: Eyewitness Accounts of the Haitian Revolution* (Chicago: University of Chicago Press, 2007).

   "The French Revolution's Other Island," in David Geggus and Norman Fiering, eds., *The World of the Haitian Revolution* (Bloomington, IN: Indiana University Press, 2009), 199–222.

   "Saint-Domingue, Slavery and the Origins of the French Revolution," in Thomas Kaiser and Dale Van Kley, eds., *From Deficit to Deluge* (Stanford, CA: Stanford University Press, forthcoming).

Powell, John Harvey, *Bring Out Your Dead: The Great Plague of Yellow Fever in Philadelphia in 1793* (Philadelphia: University of Pennsylvania Press, 1949).

Rael, Patrick, "The Long Death of Slavery," in Ira Berlin and Leslie M. Harris, eds., *Slavery in New York* (New York: The New Press, 2005), 111–46.

Régent, Frédéric, *La France et ses esclaves. De la colonisation aux abolitions* (Paris: Grasset, 2007).

Rogers, Dominique, "Les Libres de couleur dans les capitales de Saint-Domingue: Fortune, Mentalités et intégration à la fin de l'ancien régime (1776–1789)," Thèse de doctorat, Université de Bordeaux III, 1999.

Sannon, Pauléus, *Histoire de Toussaint-Louverture*, 3 vs. (Port-au-Prince: N. p., 1920–23).

Schama, Simon, *Rough Crossings: Britain, the Slaves and the American Revolution* (New York: HarperCollins, 2006).

Stein, Robert Louis, "The Abolition of Slavery in the North, West, and South of Saint Domingue," *The Americas* 41 (1985), 47–55.

Léger Félicité Sonthonax: The Lost Sentinel of the Republic (Rutherford, NJ: Fairleigh Dickinson University Press, 1985).

Taffin, Dominique, ed., *Moreau de Saint-Méry ou les ambiguïtés d'un créole des Lumières* (Martinique: Société des amis des archives et de la recherche sur le patrimoine culturel des Antilles, 2006).

Tarrade, Jean, "L'esclavage est-il réformable? Les projets des administrateurs coloniaux à la fin de l'ancien régime," in Marcel Dorigny, dir., *Les abolitions de l'esclavage. De L. F. Sonthonax à V. Schoelcher* (Paris: Editions UNESCO, 1995), 133–41. (English Translation: "Is Slavery Reformable? Proposals of Colonial Administrators at the End of the Ancien Regime," in Dorigny, ed., *Abolitions of Slavery*, 101–110.)

Thomson, Ian, *Bonjour Blanc: A Journey Through Haiti* (London: Vintage, 2004 [orig. 1992]).

Thornton, John, "'I am the Subject of the King of Kongo': African Ideology and the Haitian Revolution," *Journal of World History* 4 (1993), 181–214.

Trouillot, Michel-Rolph, *Silencing the Past: Power and the Production of History* (Boston, MA: Beacon Books, 1995).

Turner, Frederick J., ed., *Seventh Report of the Historical Manuscripts Commission. Correspondence of the French Ministers to the United States, 1791–1797* (Washington, DC: Government Printing Office, 1904).

Tyson, George F., *Toussaint L'Ouverture* (New York: Prentice Hall, 1973).

Wanquet, Claude, *La France et la première abolition de l'esclavage 1794–1802* (Paris: Karthala, 1998).

White, Ashli, "'A Flood of Impure Lava': Saint-Dominguan Refugees in the United States, 1791–1820.," Ph. D. diss., Columbia University, 2003.

Encountering Revolution: Haiti and the Making of the Early Republic (Baltimore, MD: Johns Hopkins University Press, 2010).

Index

CPSIA information can be obtained
at www.ICGtesting.com
Printed in the USA
LVHW011514051021
699597LV00001B/42

9 780521 731942